THE TONY WINNERS

Books and Plays by Stanley Richards

BOOKS:

THE TONY WINNERS
AMERICA ON STAGE: TEN GREAT PLAYS OF AMERICAN HISTORY
BEST PLAYS OF THE SIXTIES
GREAT MUSICALS OF THE AMERICAN THEATRE: VOLUME ONE
GREAT MUSICALS OF THE AMERICAN THEATRE: VOLUME TWO
BEST MYSTERY AND SUSPENSE PLAYS OF THE MODERN THEATRE
10 CLASSIC MYSTERY AND SUSPENSE PLAYS OF THE MODERN THEATRE
MODERN SHORT COMEDIES FROM BROADWAY AND LONDON
BEST SHORT PLAYS OF THE WORLD THEATRE: 1968–1973
BEST SHORT PLAYS OF THE WORLD THEATRE: 1958–1967
THE BEST SHORT PLAYS 1976
THE BEST SHORT PLAYS 1975
THE BEST SHORT PLAYS 1974
THE BEST SHORT PLAYS 1973
THE BEST SHORT PLAYS 1972
THE BEST SHORT PLAYS 1971
THE BEST SHORT PLAYS 1970
THE BEST SHORT PLAYS 1969
THE BEST SHORT PLAYS 1968
CANADA ON STAGE

PLAYS:

THROUGH A GLASS, DARKLY
AUGUST HEAT
SUN DECK
TUNNEL OF LOVE
JOURNEY TO BAHIA
O DISTANT LAND
MOOD PIECE
MR. BELL'S CREATION
THE PROUD AGE
ONCE TO EVERY BOY
HALF-HOUR, PLEASE
KNOW YOUR NEIGHBOR
GIN AND BITTERNESS
THE HILLS OF BATAAN
DISTRICT OF COLUMBIA

THE
TONY
WINNERS

A Collection of Ten Exceptional Plays,
Winners of the Tony Award
for the Most Distinguished Play of the Year

———◆———

Edited with Prefaces and an Introductory Note by

STANLEY RICHARDS

DOUBLEDAY & COMPANY, INC.
GARDEN CITY, NEW YORK
1977

Library of Congress Cataloging in Publication Data
Main entry under title:
The Tony winners.
CONTENTS: Heggen, T. and Logan, J. Mister
Roberts.—Williams, T. The rose tattoo.—Hartog, J.
de. The fourposter.—Patrick, J. The teahouse
of the August moon. [etc.]
1. American drama—20th century. 2. English drama—
20th century. I. Richards, Stanley, 1918—
PS634.T59   812′.5′408

ISBN: 0-385-11380-3
Library of Congress Catalog Card Number 76–23792

for
JIM MENICK
and
LIZ PEREIRA

CONTENTS

AN INTRODUCTORY NOTE   9

MISTER ROBERTS   *Thomas Heggen and Joshua Logan*   13

THE ROSE TATTOO   *Tennessee Williams*   111

THE FOURPOSTER   *Jan de Hartog*   215

THE TEAHOUSE OF THE AUGUST MOON   *John Patrick*   279

THE DIARY OF ANNE FRANK   *Frances Goodrich and Albert Hackett*   377

LUTHER   *John Osborne*   477

THE SUBJECT WAS ROSES   *Frank D. Gilroy*   565

BRENDAN BEHAN'S BORSTAL BOY   *Frank McMahon*   645

STICKS AND BONES   *David Rabe*   737

THE RIVER NIGER   *Joseph A. Walker*   835

AN INTRODUCTORY NOTE

The annual presentation of the Tony Awards is to the theatre what the Academy Awards are to Hollywood. Originating in 1947 by the American Theatre Wing (whose genesis goes back to World War I when a group of dedicated theatre people formed an organization to aid war relief), the Tonys are small silver medallions (initiated in 1949) with the traditional masks of comedy and tragedy on one side and the profile of Antoinette Perry on the other, in whose honor the awards are named. Miss Perry was a distinguished actress, director and producer who served as Chairman of the Board and Secretary of the Wing during World War II.

Although the American Theatre Wing founded the awards, the League of New York Theatres and Producers administers them. And contrary to popular belief—in the media and among theatrical professionals as well—the awards are not for the "best" in any category but rather for "distinguished achievement" in the theatre.

From 1947 through 1965, the Tony Award presentations were held in the festive atmosphere of dinner-and-dance in various Manhattan hotel ballrooms. The ceremonies were televised for the first time in 1956 over a local network.

Now grown to a notable and eagerly anticipated event in the theatre, in 1967 the American Theatre Wing authorized the League of New York Theatres to present the Tony Awards and the ceremonies were transferred from hotel ballrooms to Broadway theatres, a considerably more suitable setting for so significant a theatrical occasion. Produced annually by Alexander H. Cohen as a nationwide television show, it has since become one of the home screen's outstanding spring specials. The 1976 presentations, for example, were seen by an estimated twenty-five million viewers.

Unlike the Academy Awards presentations, there is a strong stress on entertainment values, including full-scale production numbers from major musicals, both past and present, rather than merely a parade of presenters and award winners.

The Tonys are voted by members of the League of New York Theaters and Producers, the governing bodies of The Dramatists Guild, Actors Equity Association, the American Theatre Wing, the Society of Stage Directors and Choreographers, the United Scenic Artists Union, and members of the first and second night press. Thus, all branches of theatre craftsmen are represented in the voting.

Nominations—a minimum of three and a maximum of six—in eighteen official categories are made by a committee of from five to ten people appointed by the president of the League with the approval of the Tony Administration Committee.

Voters' ballots are mailed directly to an independent accounting firm where they are counted and tabulated and the names of the winners are not made public until the presentation of the Awards.

Rather than assembling a collection of consecutive Tony Award plays, it was decided by this editor to provide a sampling of ten winners through three decades, beginning with the first, *Mister Roberts* (1948), to one of the most recent, *The River Niger* (1974).

As the reader will note in the individual prefaces, a number of these plays also garnered other major awards and honors and each reflects, dramatically, the high standards and "distinguished achievements" as originally established by the American Theatre Wing.

STANLEY RICHARDS
New York, N.Y.

THE TONY WINNERS

MISTER ROBERTS

Thomas Heggen and Joshua Logan

(Based on the Novel by Thomas Heggen)

Thomas Heggen and Joshua Logan

The first play ever to be named a Tony Award winner, *Mister Roberts* also was destined to become one of the greatest successes in the history of the American theatre.

The Broadway opening night on February 18, 1948 was nothing short of explosive. As one first-nighter later recalled: "The audience wouldn't go home until Henry Fonda, who portrayed the title role, made a curtain speech. Said he: 'This is all Tom Heggen and Josh Logan wrote for us. If you want we can start all over again.' I hung around for awhile, hoping they would."

The critics, to a man, were equally effusive in their praise for both play and production. Howard Barnes of the New York *Herald Tribune* joyously transmitted the news to his readers: "A superior novel has been fashioned into a magnificent play in *Mister Roberts*. The new production at the Alvin Theatre has heart, humor, profound meaning and an almost intolerable emotional tension. In its lusty and stirring testament to the men who fought without glory in the back areas of the Pacific, it has no peers among war dramas. Thomas Heggen and Joshua Logan have adapted the former's book with tremendous resourcefulness and artistry. Henry Fonda and a perfect company play it to the hilt on a series of dramatic planes. And Jo Mielziner has given it backgrounds which are supremely complementary to the action. Here, indeed, is a memorable stage work . . . a tumultuous and moving drama that no one who witnesses it will soon forget."

Superlatives were heaped upon superlatives.

"Here's a sharp, vehement and enormously entertaining play that immediately takes its place as the finest that the second world war has produced. And it belongs, definitely, in the glorious category of *What Price Glory?* (1924). The authors have packed it with a vast amount of emotion and have crammed it with gusty, jolting, stinging humor. It is positively magnificent!"

"*Mister Roberts* is a synthesis of perfection. Every art that contributes to the mosaic of the theatre has contributed to making this play one of the best of our generation."

"A salty, rowdy, hilarious play! . . . It's immensely funny. Its characters are people—lusty, recognizable, greatly likeable people. *Mister Roberts* is unquestionably the season's smash comedy hit and one of the finest American plays to come to Broadway in many a season."

Mister Roberts won the 1948 Tony Award; other individual Tony citations also were presented to the authors, Mr. Fonda, and producer Leland Hayward.

The play ran for 1,157 performances in New York, and touring companies entertained the nation for a period of several years.

A film version of *Mister Roberts* was released in 1955. Its leading players were Henry Fonda, James Cagney, William Powell, and Jack Lemmon. Directed by John Ford, it was nominated for an Academy Award for the year's best motion picture and brought Mr. Lemmon an "Oscar" for his performance as Ensign Pulver.

Thomas Heggen was born on December 23, 1919, in Fort Dodge, Iowa. He received a Bachelor of Arts degree in 1941 from the University of Minnesota, where he wrote for the school paper and was considered one of the most promising writers the university had ever developed.

Like *Mister Roberts*, the hero of his book, Mr. Heggen was deeply conscious of his role in the world in which he lived and enlisted in the Navy shortly after Pearl Harbor. Most of his years in the Navy were spent at sea: one year in the Atlantic, the rest in the Pacific. He served on a variety of ships—a tanker, a cargo ship, an assault transport, and a battleship, and was a lieutenant upon his discharge. He participated in the Guam, Iwo Jima, and Okinawa campaigns.

Returning to civilian life, he joined the editorial staff of the *Reader's Digest* and it was during this period that he wrote *Mister Roberts* which was published in book form in 1946.

Thomas Heggen died in 1949, at the age of twenty-nine.

Joshua Logan was born on October 5, 1908, in Texarkana, Texas. He was educated at Princeton University and also studied with Konstantin Stanislavsky at the Moscow Art Theatre.

As director, author, producer, or a combination of all three, Mr. Logan has given the theatre some of its brightest moments.

Among the plays and musicals he has been associated with are: *On Borrowed Time, I Married an Angel, Knickerbocker Holiday* (1938); *Stars in Your Eyes, Morning's at Seven* (1939); *Two for the*

Show, Higher and Higher, Charley's Aunt (1940); *By Jupiter, This Is the Army* (1942); *Annie Get Your Gun, Happy Birthday* (1946); *John Loves Mary* (1947); *Mister Roberts* (1948); *South Pacific* (1949); *The Wisteria Trees* (1950); *Wish You Were Here* (1952); *Picnic, Kind Sir* (1953); *Fanny* (1954); *Middle of the Night* (1956); *The World of Suzie Wong, Blue Denim* (1958); *All American,* and *Mr. President* (1962).

He has also directed many films, including: *Bus Stop; Picnic; Sayonara; South Pacific; Tall Story; Fanny; Ensign Pulver; Paint Your Wagon;* and *Camelot.*

In 1976, Mr. Logan published his memoirs: *JOSH: My Up and Down, In and Out Life.*

Mister Roberts was first presented by Leland Hayward on February 18, 1948, at the Alvin Theatre, New York. The cast was as follows:

CHIEF JOHNSON	*Rusty Lane*
LIEUTENANT (jg) ROBERTS	*Henry Fonda*
DOC	*Robert Keith*
DOWDY	*Joe Marr*
THE CAPTAIN	*William Harrigan*
INSIGNA	*Harvey Lembeck*
MANNION	*Ralph Meeker*
LINDSTROM	*Karl Lukas*
STEFANOWSKI	*Steven Hill*
WILEY	*Robert Baines*
SCHLEMMER	*Lee Krieger*
REBER	*John Campbell*
ENSIGN PULVER	*David Wayne*
DOLAN	*Casey Walters*
GERHART	*Fred Barton*
PAYNE	*James Sherwood*
LIEUTENANT ANN GIRARD	*Jocelyn Brando*
SHORE PATROLMAN	*John Jordan*
MILITARY POLICEMAN	*Marshall Jamison*
SHORE PATROL OFFICER	*Murray Hamilton*
SEAMEN, FIREMEN AND OTHERS:	*Tiger Andrews, Joe Bernard, Ellis Eringer, Mikel Kane, Bob Keith, Jr., Walter Mullen, John (Red) Kullers, Jack Pierce, Len Smith, Jr., Sanders (Sandy) Turner.*

Directed by Joshua Logan
Settings and Lighting by Jo Mielziner

SCENE: *Aboard the U.S. Navy Cargo Ship, AK 601, oper-*
ating in the back areas of the Pacific.

TIME: *A few weeks before V-E Day until a few weeks be-*
fore V-J Day.

ACT ONE

The curtain rises on the main set, which is the amidships section of a navy cargo ship. The section of the ship shown is the house, and the deck immediately forward of the house. Dominating center stage is a covered hatch. The house extends on an angle to the audience from downstage left to upstage right. At each side is a passageway leading to the after part of the ship. Over the passageways on each side are twenty-millimeter gun tubs; ladders lead up to each tub. In each passageway and hardly visible to the audience is a steep ladder leading up to a bridge. Downstage right is a double bitt. At the left end of the hatch cover is an opening. This is the entrance to the companionway which leads to the crew's compartment below. The lower parts of two kingposts are shown against the house. A life raft is also visible. A solid metal rail runs from stage right and disappears behind the house. Upstage center is the door to the CAPTAIN's cabin. The pilothouse with its many portholes is indicated on the bridge above. On the flying bridge are the usual nautical furnishings: a searchlight and two ventilators. Over the door is a loudspeaker. There is a porthole to the left of the door and two portholes to the right. These last two look into the CAPTAIN's cabin.

The only object which differentiates this ship from any other navy cargo ship is a small scrawny palm tree, potted in a five-gallon can, standing to the right of the CAPTAIN's cabin door. On the container, painted in large white letters, is the legend: "PROP.T OF CAPTAIN, KEEP AWAY."

At rise, the lighting indicates that it is shortly after dawn. The stage is empty and there is no indication of life other than the sound of snoring from below.

CHIEF JOHNSON, *a bulging man about forty, enters through passageway upstage left. He wears dungaree shirt and pants and a chief petty officer's cap. He is obviously chewing tobacco, and he starts down the hatchway, notices the palm tree, crosses to the* CAPTAIN's *door cautiously, peering into the porthole to see that he is not being watched, then deliberately spits into the palm tree container. He wipes his mouth smugly and shuffles over to the hatch. There he stops, takes out his watch and looks at it, then disappears down the hatchway. A shrill whistle is heard.*

JOHNSON: [*Offstage—in a loud singsong voice which is obviously just carrying out a ritual*] Reveille . . . Hit the deck . . . Greet the new day . . . [*The whistle is heard again*] Reveille . . .

INSIGNA: [*Offstage*] Okay, Chief, you done your duty—now get your big fat can out of here!

[JOHNSON *reappears at the head of hatchway calling back*]

JOHNSON: Just thought you'd like to know about reveille. And you're going to miss chow again.

STEFANOWSKI: [*Offstage*] Thanks, Chief. Now go back to bed and stop bothering us.

[*His duty done,* JOHNSON, *still chewing, shuffles across the stage and disappears. There is a brief moment of silence, then the snoring is resumed below*]

[*After a moment,* ROBERTS *enters from the passageway at right. He wears khaki shirt and trousers and an officer's cap. On each side of his collar he wears the silver bar indicating the rank of Lieutenant (junior grade). He carries a rumpled piece of writing paper in his left hand, on which there is a great deal of writing and large black marks indicating that much has been scratched out. He walks slowly to the bitt, concentrating, then stands a moment looking out right. He suddenly gets an idea and goes to hatch cover, sitting and writing on the paper.* DOC *enters from the left passageway.* DOC *is between thirty-five and forty and he wears khakis and an officer's fore-and-aft cap; he wears medical insignia and the bars of Lieutenant (senior grade) on his collar. A stethoscope sticks out of his hip pocket. He is wiping the sweat off his neck with his handkerchief as he crosses above hatch cover. He stops as he sees* ROBERTS]

DOC: That you, Doug?

ROBERTS: [*Wearily, looking up*] Hello, Doc. What are you doing up?

DOC: I heard you were working cargo today so I thought I'd get ready. On days when there's any work to be done I can always count on a big turnout at sick call.

ROBERTS: [*Smiles*] Oh, yeah.

DOC: I attract some very rare diseases on cargo days. That day they knew you were going to load five ships I was greeted by six more cases of beriberi—double beriberi this time. So help me, I'm going down to the ship's library and throw that old copy of *Moby Dick* overboard!

[*He sits on hatch cover*]

ROBERTS: What are you giving them these days for double beriberi?

DOC: Aspirin—what else? [*He looks at* ROBERTS] Is there something wrong, Doug?

ROBERTS: [*Preoccupied*] No.

DOC: [*Lying back on the hatch*] We missed you when you went on watch last night. I gave young Ensign Pulver another drink of alcohol and orange juice and it inspired him to relate further sexual feats of his. Some of them bordered on the supernatural!

ROBERTS: I don't doubt it. Did he tell you how he conquered a forty-five-year-old virgin by the simple tactic of being the first man in her life to ask her a direct question?

DOC: No. Last night he was more concerned with quantity. It seems that on a certain cold and wintry night in November, 1939—a night when most of us mortal men would have settled for a cup of cocoa—he rendered pregnant three girls in Washington,

D.C., caught the 11:45 train, and an hour later performed the same service for a young lady in Baltimore.

ROBERTS: [Laughing] Oh, my God!

DOC: I'm not sure what to do with young Pulver. I'm thinking of reporting his record to the American Medical Association.

ROBERTS: Why don't you just get him a job as a fountain in Radio City?

DOC: Don't be too hard on him, Doug. He thinks you are approximately God. . . . Say, there *is* something wrong, isn't there?

ROBERTS: I've been up all night, Doc.

DOC: What is it? What's the matter?

ROBERTS: I saw something last night when I was on watch that just about knocked me out.

DOC: [Alarmed] What happened?

ROBERTS: [With emotion] I was up on the bridge. I was just standing there looking out to sea. I couldn't bear to look at that island any more. All of a sudden I noticed something. Little black specks crawling over the horizon. I looked through the glasses and it was a formation of our ships that stretched for miles! Carriers and battleships and cans—a whole task force, Doc!

DOC: Why didn't you break me out? I've never seen a battleship!

ROBERTS: They came on and they passed within half a mile of that reef! Carriers so big they blacked out half the sky! And battlewagons sliding along—dead quiet! I could see the men on the bridges. And this is what knocked me out, Doc. Somehow—I thought I was on those bridges—I thought I was riding west across the Pacific. I watched them until they were out of sight, Doc—and I was right there on those bridges all the time.

DOC: I know how that must have hurt, Doug.

ROBERTS: And then I looked down from our bridge and saw our Captain's palm tree! [Points at palm tree, then bitterly] Our trophy for superior achievement! The Admiral John J. Finchley award for delivering more toothpaste and toilet paper than any other Navy cargo ship in the safe area of the Pacific. [*Taking letter from pocket and handing it to* DOC] Read this, Doc—see how it sounds.

DOC: What is it?

ROBERTS: My application for transfer. I've been rewriting it ever since I got off watch last night.

DOC: O God, not another one!

ROBERTS: This one's different—I'm trying something new, Doc—a stronger wording. Read it carefully.

>   [DOC *looks for a moment skeptically, then noticing the intensity in his face decides to read the letter*]

DOC: [*Reading*]
"From: Lieutenant (jg) Douglas Roberts
To: Bureau of Naval Personnel
16 April 1945
Subject: Change of Duty. Request for . . ."
[*He looks up*]
Boy, this is sheer poetry.

ROBERTS: [*Rises nervously*] Go on, Doc.

DOC: [*Reads on*]
"For two years and four months I have served aboard this vessel as Cargo Officer. I feel that my continued service aboard can only reduce my own usefulness to the Navy and increase disharmony aboard this ship."

>   [*He looks at* ROBERTS *and rises.* ROBERTS *looks back defiantly*]

ROBERTS: How about *that!*

DOC: [*Whistles softly, then continues*]
"It is therefore urgently requested that I be ordered to combat duty, preferably aboard a destroyer."

ROBERTS: [*Tensely, going to* DOC] What do you say, Doc? I've got a chance, haven't I?

DOC: Listen, Doug, you've been sending in a letter every week for God knows how long . . .

ROBERTS: Not like this . . .

DOC: . . . and every week the Captain has screamed like a stuck pig, disapproved your letters and forwarded them that way . . .

ROBERTS: That's just my point, Doc. He *does* forward them. They go through the chain of command all the way up to the Bureau . . . Just because the Captain doesn't . . .

DOC: Doug, the Captain of a Navy ship is the most absolute monarch left in this world!

ROBERTS: I know that.

DOC: If he endorsed your letter "approved" you'd get your orders in a minute . . .

ROBERTS: Naturally, but I . . . [*Turns away from* DOC]

DOC: . . . but "disapproved," you haven't got a prayer. You're stuck on this old bucket, Doug. Face it!

ROBERTS: [*Turns quickly back*] Well, grant me this much, Doc. That one day I'll find the perfect wording and one human guy way up on top will read those words and say, "Here's a poor son-of-a-bitch screaming for help. Let's put him on a fighting ship!"

DOC: [*Quietly*] Sure . . .

ROBERTS: [*After a moment*] I'm not kidding myself, am I, Doc? I've got a chance, haven't I?

DOC: Yes, Doug, you've got a chance. It's about the same chance as putting your letter in a bottle and dropping it in the ocean . . .

ROBERTS: [*Snatching letter from* DOC] But it's still a chance, goddammit! It's still a chance!

[ROBERTS *stands looking out to sea.* DOC *watches him for a moment then speaks gently*]

DOC: I wish you hadn't seen that task force, Doug. [*Pauses*] Well, I've got to go down to my hypochondriacs.

[*He goes off slowly through passageway*]

[ROBERTS *is still staring out as* DOWDY *enters from the hatchway. He is a hard-bitten man between thirty-five and forty and is wearing dungarees and no hat. He stands by hatchway with a cup of coffee in his hand]*

DOWDY: Morning, Mister Roberts.

ROBERTS: Good morning, Dowdy.

DOWDY: Jeez, it's even hotter up here than down in that messhall! [*He looks off*] Look at that cruddy island . . . smell it! It's so hot it *already* smells like a hog pen. Think we'll go out of here today, sir?

[ROBERTS *take* DOWDY's *cup as he speaks and drinks from it, then hands it back*]

ROBERTS: I don't know, Dowdy. There's one LCT coming alongside for supplies . . . [*Goes to hatchway, looks down*] Are they getting up?

DOWDY: [*Also looking down hatch*] Yeah, they're starting to stumble around down there—the poor punch-drunk bastards. Mister Roberts, when are you going to the Captain again and ask him to give this crew a liberty? These guys ain't been off the ship for over a year except on duty.

ROBERTS: Dowdy, the last time I asked him was last night.

DOWDY: What'd he say?

ROBERTS: He said "No."

DOWDY: We gotta get these guys ashore! They're going Asiatic! [*Pause*] Will you see him anyhow, Mister Roberts—just once more?

ROBERTS: You know I will, Dowdy. [*Hands* DOWDY *the letter*] In the meantime, have Dolan type that up for me.

[*He starts off right*]

DOWDY: [*Descending hatchway*] Oh, your letter. Yes, sir!

ROBERTS: [*Calling over his shoulder*] Then will you bring a couple of men back aft?

[*He exits through passageway*]

DOWDY: Okay, Mister Roberts. [*He disappears down hatchway. He is heard below*] All right, you guys in there. Finish your coffee and get up on deck. Stefanowski, Insigna, off your tails . . .

[*After a moment the center door opens and the* CAPTAIN *appears wearing pajamas and bathrobe and his officer's cap. He is carrying water in an engine-room oil can. He waters the palm tree carefully, looks at it for a moment tenderly and goes back into his cabin. After a moment,* DOWDY's *voice is heard from the companionway and he .appears followed by members of the crew*]

DOWDY: All right, let's go! Bring me those glasses, Schlemmer. [SCHLEMMER *exits by ladder to the bridge. Other men appear from the hatchway. They are* INSIGNA, STEFANOWSKI, MANNION, WILEY, REBER *and* LINDSTROM—*all yawning, buttoning pants, tucking in shirts and, in general, being comatose. The men do not appear to like one another very much at this hour—least of all* INSIGNA *and* MANNION] All right, I got a little recreation for you guys. Stefanowski, you take these guys and get this little rust patch here. [*He hands* STEFANOWSKI *an armful of scrapers and wire brushes, indicating a spot on the deck.* STEFANOWSKI *looks at instruments dully, then distributes them to the men standing near him.* SCHLEMMER *returns from the bridge, carrying four pairs of binoculars and a spy glass. He drops them next to* INSIGNA *who is sitting on the hatch*] Insigna, I got a real special job for you. You stay right here and clean these glasses.

INSIGNA: Ah, let me work up forward, Dowdy. I don't want to be around this crud, Mannion.

MANNION: Yeah, Dowdy. Take Insigna with you!

DOWDY: Shut up, I'm tired of you two bellyaching! [*Nodding to others to follow him*] All right, let's go, Reber . . . Schlemmer.

[DOWDY, REBER *and* SCHLEMMER *leave through passageway right. The others sit in sodden silence.* LINDSTROM *wanders slowly over to* INSIGNA. *He picks up spy glass and examines it. He holds the large end toward him and looks into it*]

LINDSTROM: Hey, look! I can see myself!

STEFANOWSKI: Terrifying, ain't it?

[INSIGNA *takes the spy glass from him and starts polishing it.* LINDSTROM *removes his shoe and feels inside it, then puts it back on*]

MANNION: [*After a pause*] Hey, what time is it in San Francisco?

INSIGNA: [*Scornfully*] When?

MANNION: Anybody ask you? [*Turns to* WILEY] What time would it be there?

WILEY: I don't know. I guess about midnight last night.

STEFANOWSKI: [*Studying scraper in his hand*] I wonder if you could get sent back to the States if you cut off a finger.

[*Nobody answers*]

INSIGNA: [*Looking offstage*] Hey, they got a new building on that island. Fancy—two stories . . .

[*Nobody shows any curiosity*]

MANNION: You know, I had a girl in San Francisco wore flowers in her hair—instead of hats. Never wore a hat . . .

[*Another sodden pause*]

INSIGNA: [*Holding spy glass*] Hey, Stefanowski! Which end of this you look through?

STEFANOWSKI: It's optional, Sam. Depends on what size eyeball you've got.

[INSIGNA *idly looks through spy glass at something out right. Another pause*]

INSIGNA: Hey, the Japs must've took over this island—there's a red and white flag on that new building.

MANNION: Japs! We never been within five thousand miles of a Jap! Japs! You hear that, Wiley?

WILEY: Yeah, smart, ain't he?

MANNION: Japs! That's a hospital flag!

INSIGNA: Anybody ask you guys? [*Nudging* LINDSTROM *and point-*

ing to the other group] The goldbrick twins! *[Looks through spy glass]* Hey, they got a fancy hospital . . . big windows and . . .

[Suddenly rises, gasping at what he sees]

STEFANOWSKI: What's the matter, Sam?

INSIGNA: Oh, my God! She's bare-assed!

STEFANOWSKI: *She!*

INSIGNA: Taking a shower . . . in that bathroom . . . that nurse . . . upstairs window!

[Instantly the others rush to hatch cover, grab binoculars and stand looking out right]

WILEY: She's a blonde—see!

LINDSTROM: I never seen such a beautiful girl!

MANNION: She's sure taking a long time in that shower!

WILEY: Yeah, honey, come on over here by the window!

INSIGNA: Don't do it, honey! You take your time!

STEFANOWSKI: There's another one over by the washbasin—taking a shampoo.

INSIGNA: *[Indignantly]* Yeah. But why the hell don't she take her bathrobe off! That's a stupid goddamn way to take a shampoo!

[For a moment the men watch in silent vigilance]

STEFANOWSKI: Ah-hah!

WILEY: She's coming out of the shower!

MANNION: She's coming over to the window! *[A pause]* Kee-ri-mi-ny!

[For a moment the men stand transfixed, their faces radiant. They emit rapturous sighs. That is all]

LINDSTROM: Aw, she's turning around the other way!

MANNION: What's that red mark she's got . . . there?

INSIGNA: *[Authoritatively]* That's a birthmark!

MANNION: [*Scornfully*] Birthmark!

INSIGNA: What do you think it is, wise guy?

MANNION: Why, that's paint! She's sat in some red paint!

INSIGNA: Sat in some red paint! I'm tellin' you, that's a birthmark!

MANNION: Did you ever see a birthmark down there?

INSIGNA: [*Lowers his spy glass, turns to* MANNION] Why, you stupid jerk! I had an uncle once had a birthmark right down . . .

WILEY: Aww!

[INSIGNA *and* MANNION *return quickly to their glasses*]

STEFANOWSKI: [*Groaning*] She's put her bathrobe on!

MANNION: Hey, she's got the same color bathrobe as that stupid bag taking the shampoo!

[*The four men notice something and exclaim in unison*]

INSIGNA: Bag, hell! Look at her now with her head out of the water . . .

LINDSTROM: She's just as beautiful as the other one . . .

STEFANOWSKI: They look exactly alike with those bathrobes on. Maybe they're twins.

MANNION: That's my gal on the right—the one with the red birthmark.

INSIGNA: You stupid crud, the one with the birthmark's on the left!

MANNION: The hell she is . . .

[MANNION *and* INSIGNA *again lower their glasses*]

INSIGNA: The hell she ain't . . .

WILEY: Awwww!

[MANNION *and* INSIGNA *quickly drop their argument and look*]

STEFANOWSKI: They're both leaving the bathroom together . . .

[*The men are dejected again*]

LINDSTROM: Hey, there ain't no one in there now!

STEFANOWSKI: [*Lowering his glasses*] Did you figure that out all by yourself? [*He looks through his glasses again*]

MANNION: [*After a pause*] Come on girls, let's go!

WILEY: Yeah. Who's next to take a nice zippy shower?

INSIGNA: [*After a pause*] They must think we got nothing better to do than stand here!

LINDSTROM: These glasses are getting heavy!

STEFANOWSKI: Yeah. We're wasting manpower. Let's take turns, okay? [*The others agree*] All right, Mannion, you take it first.

[MANNION *nods, crosses and sits on bitt, keeping watch with his binoculars. The others pick up their scrapers and wire brushes*]

INSIGNA: [*Watching* MANNION] I don't trust that crud.

LINDSTROM: Gee, I wish we was allowed to get over to that island. We could get a closer look.

STEFANOWSKI: No, Lindstrom. They'd see us and pull the shades down.

LINDSTROM: No, they wouldn't. We could cover ourselves with leaves and make out like we was bushes—and sneak up on them— like them Japs we seen in that movie . . .

[*He starts to sneak around front of hatch, holding his wire brush before his face.* STEFANOWSKI *hears a noise from the* CAPTAIN's *cabin and quickly warns the others*]

STEFANOWSKI: Flash Red! [*The men immediately begin working in earnest as the* CAPTAIN, *now in khaki, enters. He stands for a moment, looking at them, and then wanders over to the group scraping the rust patch to inspect their work. Then, satisfied that they are actually working, he starts toward passageway. He sees* MANNION, *siting on the bitt, looking through his glasses and smiling. The* CAPTAIN *goes over and stands beside him, looking off in the same direction.* STEFANOWSKI *tries frantically to signal a warning to* MANNION *by beating out code with his scraper.* MANNION *suddenly sees the* CAPTAIN *and quickly lowers his glasses and pre-*

tends to clean them, alternately wiping the lenses and holding them up to his eyes to see that they are clean. The CAPTAIN *watches him suspiciously for a moment, then he exits by the ladder to the bridge.* STEFANOWSKI *rises and looks up ladder to make certain the* CAPTAIN *has gone*] Flash White! [*He turns and looks at* MANNION] Hey, Mannion. Anyone in there yet?

MANNION: [*Watching something happily through glasses*] No, not yet!

INSIGNA: [*Picks up spy glass and looks, and rises quickly*] Why, you dirty, miserable cheat!

[*Instantly all the men are at the glasses*]

LINDSTROM: There's one in there again!

STEFANOWSKI: The hell with her—she's already got her clothes on!

INSIGNA: And there she goes! [*Slowly lowers his glass, turning to* MANNION *threateningly*] Why, you lousy, cheating crud!

MANNION: [*Idly swinging his glasses*] That ain't all. I seen three!

STEFANOWSKI: You lowdown Peeping Tom!

LINDSTROM: [*Hurt*] Mannion, that's a real dirty trick.

INSIGNA: What's the big idea?

MANNION: Who wants to know?

INSIGNA: I want to know! And you're damn well going to tell me!

MANNION: You loudmouthed little bastard! Why don't you make me?

INSIGNA: You're damn right I will. Right now!

[*He swings on* MANNION *as* LINDSTROM *steps clumsily between them*]

LINDSTROM: Hey, fellows! Fellows!

INSIGNA: No wonder you ain't got a friend on this ship . . . except this crud, Wiley.

[*He jerks his head in direction of* WILEY *who stands behind him on a hatch cover.* WILEY *takes him by shoulder and whirls him around*]

WILEY: What'd you say?

STEFANOWSKI: [*Shoving* WILEY] You heard him!

[MANNION *jumps on hatch cover to protect* WILEY *from* STEFANOWSKI. INSIGNA *rushes at* MANNION *and for a moment they are all in a clinch.* LINDSTROM *plows up on the hatch and breaks them apart. The men have suddenly formed into two camps*—MANNION *and* WILEY *on one side,* INSIGNA *and* STEFANOWSKI *facing them,* LINDSTROM *is just an accessory, but stands prepared to intervene if necessary*]

MANNION: [*To* WILEY] Look at them two! Everybody on the ship hates their guts! The two moochingest, no-good loudmouths on the ship!

[STEFANOWSKI *starts for* MANNION *but* INSIGNA *pulls him back and steps menacingly toward* MANNION]

INSIGNA: Why, you slimy, lying son-of-a-bitch!

[*Suddenly* MANNION *hits* INSIGNA, *knocking him down. He jumps on* INSIGNA *who catches* MANNION *in the chest with his feet and hurls him back.* WILEY *and* STEFANOWSKI *start fighting with* LINDSTROM, *attempting to break them apart.* MANNION *rushes back at* INSIGNA. INSIGNA *sidesteps* MANNION'S *lunge and knocks him to the deck.* INSIGNA *falls on him. They wrestle to their feet and stand slugging. At this point* ROBERTS *and* DOWDY *run on from passageway.* ROBERTS *flings* INSIGNA *and* MANNION *apart.* DOWDY *separates the others*]

ROBERTS: Break it up! Break it up, I tell you!

[INSIGNA *and* MANNION *rush at each other.* ROBERTS *and* DOWDY *stop them*]

DOWDY: Goddamn you guys, break it up!

ROBERTS: All right! What's going on?

INSIGNA: [*Pointing at* MANNION] This son-of-a-bitch here . . .

ROBERTS: Did you hear me?

MANNION: [*To* INSIGNA] Shut your mouth!

DOWDY: Shut up, both of you!

INSIGNA: Slimy son-of-a-bitch!

[*Picks up scraper and lunges at* MANNION *again.* ROBERTS *throws him back*]

ROBERTS: I said to cut it out! Did you hear me? [*Wheels on* MANNION] That goes for you, too! [*Includes entire group*] I'm going to give it to the first one who opens his mouth! [*The men stand subdued, breathing hard from the fight*] Now get to work! All of you! [*They begin to move sullenly off right*] Mannion, you and the rest get to work beside number two! And, Insigna, take those glasses way up to the bow and work on them! Stefanowski, keep those two apart.

STEFANOWSKI: Yes, sir.

[*The men exit.* ROBERTS *and* DOWDY *look after them*]

DOWDY: [*Tightly*] You seen that, Mister Roberts. Well, last night down in the compartment I stopped three of them fights—worse than that. They've got to have a liberty, Mister Roberts.

ROBERTS: They sure do. Dowdy, call a boat for me, will you? I'm going ashore.

DOWDY: What are you going to do?

ROBERTS: I just got a new angle.

DOWDY: Are you going over the Captain's head?

ROBERTS: No, I'm going around his end—I hope. Get the lead out, Dowdy.

[*He exits left as* DOWDY *goes off right and the lights fade out*]

During the darkness, voices can be heard over the squawk box saying:
Now hear this . . . now hear this. Sweepers, man your brooms. Clean sweep-down fore and aft. Sweep-down all ladders and all passageways. Do *not* throw trash over the fantail.

Now, all men on report will see the master-at-arms for assignment to extra duty.

Now hear this . . . now hear this. Because in violation of

the Captain's orders, a man has appeared on deck without a shirt on, there will be no movies again tonight—by order of the Captain.

SCENE TWO

The lights dim up revealing the stateroom of PULVER *and* ROBERTS. *Two lockers are shown, one marked "Ensign F. T. Pulver," the other marked "Lt. [jg] D. A. Roberts." There is a double bunk along the bulkhead right. A desk with its end against the bulkhead left has a chair at either side. There is a porthole in the bulkhead above it. Up center, right of* PULVER'S *locker is a washbasin over which is a shelf and a medicine chest. The door is up center.*
An officer is discovered with his head inside ROBERT'S *locker, throwing skivvy shirts over his shoulder as he searches for something.* DOLAN, *a young, garrulous, brash yeoman, second class, enters. He is carrying a file folder.*

DOLAN: Here's your letter, Mister Roberts. [*He goes to the desk, taking fountain pen from his pocket*] I typed it up. Just sign your old John Henry here and I'll take it in to the Captain . . . then hold your ears. [*No answer*] Mister Roberts! [PULVER'S *head appears from the locker*] Oh, it's only you, Mister Pulver. What are you doing in Mister Roberts' locker?

PULVER: [*Hoarsely*] Dolan, look in here, will you? I know there's a shoe box in there, but I can't find it.

[DOLAN *looks in the locker*]

DOLAN: There ain't no shoe box in there, Mister Pulver.

PULVER: They've stolen it! There's nothing they'll stop at now. They've broken right into the sanctity of a man's own locker.

[*He sits in chair at desk*]

DOLAN: [*Disinterested*] Ain't Mister Roberts back from the island yet?

PULVER: No.

DOLAN: Well, as soon as he gets back, will you ask him to sign this baby?

PULVER: What is it?

DOLAN: What is it! It's the best damn letter Mister Roberts writ yet. It's going to blow the Old Man right through the overhead. And them big shots at the Bureau are going to drop their drawers, too. This letter is liable to get him transferred.

PULVER: Yeah, lemme see it.

DOLAN: [*Handing letter to* PULVER] Get a load of that last paragraph. Right here.

PULVER: [*Reading with apprehension*] ". . . increase disharmony aboard this ship . . ."

DOLAN: [*Interrupting gleefully*] Won't that frost the Old Man's knockers? I can't wait to jab this baby in the Old Man's face. Mister Pulver, you know how he gets sick to his stomach when he gets extra mad at Mister Roberts—well, when I deliver this letter I'm going to take along a waste basket! Let me know when Mister Roberts gets back.

> [DOLAN *exits.* PULVER *continues reading the letter with great dismay. He hears* ROBERTS *and* DOC *talking in the passageway, offstage, and quickly goes to his bunk and hides the letter under a blanket. He goes to the locker and is replacing skivvy shirts as* ROBERTS *and* DOC *enter*]

ROBERTS: . . . so after the fight I figured I had to do something and do it quick!

DOC: What did you do over on the island, Doug?

ROBERTS: [*Sitting in chair and searching through desk drawer*] Hey, Frank, has Dolan been in here yet with my letter?

PULVER: [*Innocently*] I don't know, Doug boy. I just came in here myself.

DOC: You don't know anybody on the island, do you, Doug?

ROBERTS: Yes. The Port Director—the guy who decides where to send this ship next. He confided to me that he used to drink a quart of whiskey every day of his life. So this morning when I broke up that fight it came to me that he might just possibly sell his soul for a quart of Scotch.

PULVER: [*Rises*] Doug, you didn't give that shoe box to the Port Director!

ROBERTS: I did. "Compliments of the Captain."

DOC: You've had a quart of Scotch in a shoe box?

ROBERTS: Johnny Walker! I was going to break it out the day I got off this ship—Resurrection Day!

PULVER: Oh, my God! It's really gone!

[*He sinks to the bunk*]

DOC: Well, did the Port Director say he'd send us to a Liberty Port?

ROBERTS: Hell, no. He took the Scotch and said, "Don't bother me, Roberts. I'm busy." The rummy!

PULVER: How could you do it!

DOC: Well, where there's a rummy, there's hope. Maybe when he gets working on that Scotch he'll mellow a little.

PULVER: You gave that bottle to a goddamn *man*!

ROBERTS: Man! Will you name me another sex within a thousand miles . . . [PULVER, *dejected goes up to porthole*] What the hell's eating you anyhow, Frank?

[DOC *crosses to bunk. He sees two fancy pillows on bottom bunk, picks up one and tosses it to* ROBERTS. *He picks up the other*]

DOC: Well, look here. Somebody seems to be expecting company!

ROBERTS: Good Lord!

DOC: [*Reads lettering on pillowcase*] "Toujours l'amour . . . Souvenir of San Diego . . . Oh, you kid!"

ROBERTS: [*Reading from his pillowcase*] "Tonight or never . . . Compliments of Allis-Chalmers, Farm Equipment . . . We plow

deep while others sleep." [*He looks at* DOC, *then rises*] Doc—
that new hospital over there hasn't got nurses, has it?

DOC: Nurses! It didn't have yesterday!

PULVER: [*Turning from porthole*] It has today!

DOC: But how did you find out they were there?

PULVER: [*Trying to recall*] Now let me think . . . it just came to
me all of a sudden. This morning it was so hot I was just lying on
my bunk—thinking . . . There wasn't a breath of air. And then,
all of a sudden, a funny thing happened. A little breeze came up
and I took a big deep breath and said to myself, "Pulver boy,
there's women on that island."

ROBERTS: Doc, a thing like this could make a bird dog self-conscious as hell.

PULVER: [*Warming up*] They just flew in last night. There's
eighteen of them—all brunettes except for two beautiful blondes
—twin sisters! I'm working on one of those. I asked her out to the
ship for lunch and she said she was kind of tired. So then I got
kind of desperate and turned on the old personality—and I said,
"Ain't there anything in the world that'll make you come out to
the ship with me?" And she said, "Yes, there is, one thing and one
thing only—" [*Crosses to* ROBERTS, *looks at him accusingly*] "A
good stiff drink of Scotch!"

[*He sinks into the chair*]

ROBERTS: [*After a pause*] I'm sorry, Frank. I'm really sorry. Your
first assignment in a year.

[*He pats* PULVER *on the shoulder*]

PULVER: I figured I'd bring her in here . . . I fixed it up real cozy
. . . [*Fondling pillow on desk*] . . . and then I was going to
throw a couple of fast slugs of Scotch into her and . . . but, hell,
without the Scotch, she wouldn't . . . she just wouldn't, that's all.

ROBERTS: [*After a pause*] Doc, let's make some Scotch!

DOC: Huh?

ROBERTS: As naval officers we're supposed to be resourceful. Frank here's got a great opportunity and I've let him down. Let's fix him up!

DOC: Right! [*He goes to desk.* ROBERTS *begins removing bottles from medicine chest*] Frank, where's the rest of that alcohol we were drinking last night?

PULVER: [*Pulling a large vinegar bottle half filled with colorless liquid from the waste basket and handing it to* DOC] Hell, that ain't even the right color.

DOC: [*Taking the bottle*] Quiet! [*Thinks deeply*] Color . . . [*With sudden decision*] Coca-Cola! Have you got any?

ROBERTS: I haven't seen a Coke in four months—no, by God, it's five months!

PULVER: Oh, what the hell! [*He rises, crosses to bunk, reaches under mattress of top bunk and produces a bottle of Coca-Cola. The others watch him.* DOC *snatches the bottle.* PULVER *says apologetically*] I forgot I had it.

[DOC *opens the bottle and is about to pour the Coca-Cola into the vinegar bottle when he suddenly stops*]

DOC: Oh—what shade would you like? Cutty Sark . . . Haig and Haig . . . Vat 69 . . .

PULVER: [*Interested*] I told her Johnny Walker.

DOC: Johnny Walker it is!

[*He pours some of the Coca-Cola into the bottle*]

ROBERTS: [*Looking at color of the mixture*] Johnny Walker Red Label!

DOC: Red Label!

PULVER: It may look like it—but it won't taste like it!

ROBERTS: Doc, what does Scotch taste like?

DOC: Well, it's a little like . . . uh . . . it tastes like . . .

ROBERTS: Do you know what it's always tasted a little like to me? Iodine.

DOC: [*Shrugs as if to say "Of course" and rises. He takes dropper from small bottle of iodine and flicks a drop in the bottle*] One drop of iodine—for taste.

[*Shakes the bottle and pours some in glass*]

PULVER: Lemme taste her, Doc!

DOC: [*Stops him with a gesture*] No. This calls for a medical opinion.

[*Takes a ceremonial taste while the others wait for his verdict*]

PULVER: How about it?

DOC: We're on the right track! [*Sets glass down. Rubs hands professionally*] Now we need a little something extra—for age! What've you got there, Doug?

ROBERTS: [*Reading labels of bottles on desk*] Bromo-Seltzer . . . Wildroot Wave Set . . . Eno Fruit Salts . . . Kreml Hair Tonic . . .

DOC: Kreml! It has a coal-tar base! And it'll age the hell out of it! [*Pours a bit of Kreml into mixture. Shakes bottle solemnly*] One drop Kreml for age. [*Sets bottle on desk, looks at wrist watch for a fraction of a second*] That's it!

[*Pours drink into glass.* PULVER *reaches for it.* ROBERTS *pushes his arm aside and tastes it*]

ROBERTS: By God, it does taste a little like Scotch!

[PULVER *again reaches for glass.* DOC *pushes his arm aside and takes a drink*]

DOC: By God, it does!

[PULVER *finally gets glass and takes a quick sip*]

PULVER: It's delicious. That dumb little blonde won't know the difference.

DOC: [*Hands the bottle to* PULVER] Here you are, Frank. Doug and I have made the Scotch. The *nurse* is your department.

[PULVER *takes the bottle and hides it under the mattress, then replaces the pillows*]

PULVER: [*Singing softly*] Won't know the difference . . . won't know the difference. [DOC *starts to drink from Coca-Cola bottle as* PULVER *comes over and snatches it from his hand*] Thanks, Doc. [*Puts cap on the bottle and hides it under the mattress. Turns and faces the others*] Thanks, Doug. Jeez, you guys are wonderful to me.

ROBERTS: [*Putting bottles back in medicine chest*] Don't mention it, Frank. I think you almost deserve it.

PULVER: You do—really? Or are you just giving me the old needle again? What do you really think of me, Doug—honestly?

ROBERTS: [*Turning slowly to face* PULVER] Frank, I like you. No one can get around the fact that you're a hell of a likable guy.

PULVER: [*Beaming*] Yeah—yeah . . .

ROBERTS: But . . .

PULVER: But what?

ROBERTS: But I also think you are the most hapless . . . lazy . . . disorganized . . . and, in general, the most lecherous person I've ever known in my life.

PULVER: I am not.

ROBERTS: Not what?

PULVER: I'm not disorganized—for one thing.

ROBERTS: Have you ever in your life finished anything you started to do? You sleep sixteen hours a day. You pretend you want me to improve your mind and you've never even finished a book I've given you to read!

PULVER: I finished *God's Little Acre*, Doug boy!

ROBERTS: I didn't give you that! [*To* DOC] He's been reading *God's Little Acre* for over a year! [*Takes dog-eared book from* PULVER's *bunk*] He's underlined every erotic passage, and added exclamation points—and after a certain pornographic climax, he's inserted the words "well written." [*To* PULVER] You're the Laundry and Morale Officer and I doubt if you've ever seen the laundry.

PULVER: I was down there only last week.

ROBERTS: And you're scared of the Captain.

PULVER: I'm not scared of the Captain.

ROBERTS: Then why do you hide in the passageway every time you see him coming? I doubt if he even knows you're on board. You're scared of him.

PULVER: I am not. I'm scared of myself—I'm scared of what I might do to him.

ROBERTS: [*Laughing*] What you might do to him! Doc, he lies in his sack all day long and bores me silly with great moronic plots against the Captain and he's never carried out one.

PULVER: I haven't, huh.

ROBERTS: No, Frank, you haven't. What happened to your idea of plugging up the line of the Captain's sanitary system? "I'll make it overflow," you said. "I'll make a backwash that'll lift him off the throne and knock him clean across the room."

PULVER: I'm workin' on that. I thought about it for half an hour—yesterday.

ROBERTS: Half an hour! There's only one thing you've thought about for half an hour in your life! And what about those marbles that you were going to put in the Captain's overhead—so they'd roll around at night and keep him awake?

PULVER: Now you've gone too far. Now you've asked for it. [*Goes to bunk and produces small tin box from under mattress. Crosses to* ROBERTS *and shakes it in his face. Opens it*] What does that look like? Five marbles! I'm collecting marbles all the time. I've got one right here in my pocket! [*Takes marble from pocket, holds it close to* ROBERTS' *nose, then drops it in box. Closes box*] Six marbles! [*Puts box back under mattress, turns defiantly to* ROBERTS] I'm looking for marbles all day long!

ROBERTS: Frank, you asked me what I thought of you. Well, I'll tell you! The day you finish one thing you've started out to do, the day you actually put those marbles in the Captain's overhead, and then have the guts to knock on his door and say, "Captain, I put those marbles there," that's the day I'll have some respect for you —that's the day I'll look up to you as a man. Okay?

PULVER: [Belligerently] Okay!

[ROBERTS goes to the radio and turns it up. While he is listening, DOC and PULVER exchange worried looks]

RADIO VOICE: . . . intersecting thirty miles north of Hanover. At the same time, General George S. Patton's Third Army continues to roll unchecked into Southern Germany. The abrupt German collapse brought forth the remark from a high London official that the end of the war in Europe is only weeks away—maybe days . . .

[ROBERTS turns off radio]

ROBERTS: Where the hell's Dolan with that letter! [Starts toward the door] I'm going to find him.

PULVER: Hey, Doug, wait! Listen! [ROBERTS pauses at the door] I wouldn't send in that letter if I were you!

ROBERTS: What do you mean—that letter!

PULVER: [Hastily] I mean any of those letters you been writin'. What are you so nervous about anyway?

ROBERTS: Nervous!

PULVER: I mean about getting off this ship. Hell, this ain't such a bad life. Look, Doug—we're a threesome, aren't we—you and Doc and me? Share and share alike! Now look, I'm not going to keep those nurses all to myself. Soon as I get my little nursie organized today, I'm going to start working on her twin sister—for you.

ROBERTS: All right, Frank.

PULVER: And then I'm going to scare up something for you too, Doc. And in the meantime you've got a lot of work to do, Doug boy—improvin' my mind and watching my grammar. And speaking of grammar, you better watch your grammar. You're going to get in trouble, saying things like "disharmony aboard this ship!"

[ROBERTS *looks at* PULVER *quickly.* PULVER *catches himself*] I mean just in case you ever said anything like "disharmony aboard this ship" . . . or . . . uh . . . "harmony aboard this ship" or . . .

ROBERTS: Where's that letter?

PULVER: I don't know, Doug boy . . . [As ROBERTS *steps toward him, he quickly produces the letter from the blanket*] Here it is, Doug.

ROBERTS: [*Snatching the letter*] What's the big idea!

[ROBERTS *goes to desk, reading and preparing to sign the letter.* PULVER *follows him*]

PULVER: I just wanted to talk to you before you signed it. You can't send it in that way—it's too strong! Don't sign that letter, Doug, please don't! They'll transfer you and you'll get your ass shot off. You're just running a race with death, isn't he, Doc? It's stupid to keep asking for it like that. The Doc says so, too. Tell him what you said to me last night, Doc—about how stupid he is.

ROBERTS: [*Coldly, to* DOC] Yes, Doc, maybe you'd like to tell me to my face.

DOC: [*Belligerently*] Yes, I would. Last night I asked you why you wanted to fight this war. And you said: anyone who doesn't fight it is only half-alive. Well, I thought that over and I've decided that's just a crock, Doug—just a crock.

ROBERTS: I take it back, Doc. After seeing my task force last night I don't even feel half-alive.

DOC: You are stupid! And I can prove it! You quit medical school to get into this thing when you could be saving lives today. Why? Do you even know yourself?

ROBERTS: Has it ever occurred to you that the guys who fight this war might also be saving lives . . . yours and mine, for instance! Not just putting men together again, but *keeping* them together! Right now I'd rather practice that kind of medicine—Doctor!

DOC: [*Rising*] Well, right now, that's exactly what you're doing.

ROBERTS: What, for God's sake!

DOC: Whether you like it or not, this sorry old bucket does a neces- sary job. And you're the guy who keeps her lumbering along. You keep this crew working cargo, and more than that—you keep them *alive*. It might just be that right here, on this bucket, you're deeper and more truly in this war than you ever would be any- where else.

ROBERTS: Oh, Jesus, Doc. In a minute, you'll start quoting Emer- son.

DOC: *That* is a lousy thing to say!

ROBERTS: We've got nothing to do with the war. Maybe that's why we're on this ship—because we're not good enough to fight. [*Then quietly with emotion*] Maybe there's some omniscient son-of-a-bitch who goes down the line of all the servicemen and picks out the ones to send into combat, the ones whose glands secrete enough adrenalin, or whose great-great-grandfathers weren't afraid of the dark or something. The rest of us are packed off to ships like this where we can't do any harm.

DOC: What is it you want to be—a hero or something?

ROBERTS: [*Shocked*] Hero! My God, Doc! You haven't heard a word I said! Look, Doc, the war's way out there! I'm here. I don't want to be here—I want to be out there. I'm sick and tired of being a lousy spectator. I just happen to believe in this thing. I've got to feel I'm *good* enough to be in it—to *participate!*

DOC: Good enough! Doug, you're good enough! You just don't have the opportunity. That's mostly what physical heroism is—op- portunity. It's a reflex. I think seventy-five out of a hundred young males have that reflex. If you put any one of them—say, even Frank Thurlowe Pulver, here—in a B-29 over Japan, do you know what you'd have?

ROBERTS: No, by God, I don't.

DOC: You'd have Pulver, the Congressional Medal of Honor win- ner! You'd have Pulver, who, singlehanded, shot down twenty- three attacking Zeroes, then with his bare hands held together the severed wing struts of his plane, and with his bare feet successfully landed the mortally wounded plane on his home field. [PULVER *thinks this over*] Hell, it's a reflex. It's like the knee jerk. Strike the patella tendon of any human being and you produce the knee jerk. Look.

[*He illustrates on* PULVER. *There is no knee jerk. He strikes again—still no reaction*]

PULVER: What's the matter, Doc?

DOC: Nothing. But stay out of B-29s, will you, Frank?

ROBERTS: You've made your point very vividly, Doc. But I still want to get into this thing. I've got to get into it! And I'm going to keep on sending in these letters until I do.

DOC: I know you are, Doug.

ROBERTS: [*Signs the letter. Then to* DOC] I haven't got much time. I found that out over on the island. That task force I saw last night is on its way to start our last big push in the Pacific. And it went by me, Doc. I've got to catch it.

[*He exits*]

PULVER: [*After a pause*] Doc, what are you going to give Doug on his birthday?

DOC: I hadn't thought of giving him anything.

PULVER: You know what? I'm gonna show him he's got old Pulver figured out all wrong. [*Pulls small cardboard roll from under mattress*] Doc, what does that look like?

DOC: Just what it is—the cardboard center of a roll of toilet paper.

PULVER: I suppose it doesn't look like a firecracker.

DOC: Not a bit like a firecracker.

PULVER: [*Taking a piece of string from the bunk*] I suppose that doesn't look like a fuse.

DOC: [*Rising and starting off*] No, that looks like a piece of string.

[*He walks slowly out of the room.* PULVER *goes on*]

PULVER: Well, you just wait till old Pulver gets through with it! I'm going to get me some of that black powder from the gunner's mate. No, by God, this isn't going to be any peanut firecracker—

I'm going to pack this old thing full of that stuff they use to blow up bridges, that fulminate of mercury stuff. And then on the night of Doug's birthday, I'm going to throw it under the Old Man's bunk. Bam—bam—bam! [*Knocks on* ROBERTS' *locker, opens it*] Captain, it is I, Ensign Pulver. I just threw that firecracker under your goddamn bunk.

[*He salutes as the lights fade out*]

[*In the darkness we hear the sound of a winch and shouted orders*]

LCT OFFICER: On the AK—where do you want us?

AK VOICE: Starboard side, up for'd—alongside number two!

LCT OFFICER: Shall we use our fenders or yours?

AK VOICE: No, we'll use ours! Stand off till we finish with the barge!

SCENE THREE

The curtain rises and the lights dim up on the deck. ROBERTS *stands on the hatch cover.* SCHLEMMER, GERHART *and another* SEAMAN *are sitting on the hatch cover. They are tired and hot. A cargo net, filled with crates, is disappearing off right. Offstage we hear the shouts of men working cargo. Two officers walk across the stage. Everyone's shirt is wet with perspiration.*

ROBERTS: [*Calling through megaphone*] Okay—take it away—that's all for the barge. On the LCT—I'll give you a bow line.

LCT OFFICER: [*Offstage*] Okay, Lieutenant.

ROBERTS: [*To crew*] Get a line over!

DOWDY: [*Offstage*] Yes, sir.

REBER: [*Off right*] Heads up on the LCT!

ROBERTS: That's good. Make it fast.

[PAYNE, *wearing the belt of a messenger, enters from companionway as* DOWDY *enters from right*]

PAYNE: Mister Roberts, the Captain says not to give this LCT any fresh fruit. He says he's going to keep what's left for his own mess.

ROBERTS: Okay, okay . . .

PAYNE: Hold your hat, Mister Roberts. I just saw Dolan go in there with your letter.

[*He grins and exits as* ROBERTS *smiles at* DOWDY]

DOWDY: Here's the list of what the LCT guy wants.

ROBERTS: [*Reading rapidly*] One ton dry stores . . . quarter-ton frozen food . . . one gross dungarees . . . twenty cartons toothpaste . . . two gross skivvy shirts . . . Okay, we can give him all that.

DOWDY: Can these guys take their shirts off while we're working?

ROBERTS: Dowdy, you know the Captain has a standing order . . .

DOWDY: Mister Roberts, Corcoran just passed out from the heat.

ROBERTS: [*Looks at men, who wait for his decision*] Hell, yes, take 'em off [DOWDY *exits.* SCHLEMMER, REBER *and* SEAMAN *remove shirts saying, "Thanks, Mister Roberts" and exit right.* ROBERTS *calls through megaphone*] LCT, want to swap movies? We've got a new one.

LCT: [*Offstage*] What's that?

ROBERTS: *Charlie Chan at the Opera.*

LCT: [*Offstage*] No, thanks, we've seen that three times!

ROBERTS: What you got?

LCT: [*Offstage*] Hoot Gibson in *Riders of the Range.*

ROBERTS: Sorry I brought the subject up.

DOWDY: [*Entering from right*] All set, Mister Roberts.

LCT: [*Offstage*] Lieutenant, one thing I didn't put on my list because I wanted to ask you—you couldn't spare us any fresh fruit, could you?

ROBERTS: You all out?

LCT: [*Offstage*] We haven't seen any for two months.

ROBERTS: [*To* DOWDY] Dowdy, give 'em a couple of crates of oranges.

DOWDY: Yes, sir.

ROBERTS: Compliments of the Captain.

DOWDY: Aye-aye sir.

[*He exits*]

ROBERTS: [*To* LCT] Here comes your first sling-load! [*There is the grinding sound of a winch. With hand-signals* ROBERTS *directs placing of the sling-load. Then he shouts*] Watch that line!

DOWDY: [*Offstage*] Slack off, you dumb bastards! Slack off!

[PAYNE *enters.* ROBERTS *turns to him sharply*]

ROBERTS: What!

PAYNE: The Captain wants to see you, Mister Roberts.

DOWDY: [*Offstage*] Goddammit, there it goes! You've parted the line!

ROBERTS: Get a fender over! Quick! [*To* PAYNE] You go tell the Captain I'm busy! [PAYNE *exits.* ROBERTS *calls offstage*] Get a line over—his bow's coming in!

REBER: [*Offstage*] Heads up!

GERHART: [*Offstage*] Where shall we secure?

DOWDY: [*Offstage*] Secure here!

ROBERTS: No. Take it around the bitt!

DOWDY: [*Offstage*] Around the bitt!

ROBERTS: That's too much! Give him some slack this time! [*Watches intently*] That's good. Okay, let's give him the rest of his cargo.

GERHART: [*Entering quickly and pointing toward companionway*] Flash Red!

[*He exits. The* CAPTAIN *enters, followed by* PAYNE *and* DOLAN]

CAPTAIN: All right, Mister! Let's have this out right here and now! What do you mean—telling me you're busy!

ROBERTS: We parted a line, Captain. You didn't want me to leave the deck with this ship coming in on us?

CAPTAIN: You're damn right I want you to leave the deck. When I tell you I want to see you, I mean, *now*, Mister! I mean jump! Do you understand?

[*At this point a group of men, attracted by the noise, crowd in. They are naked to the waist. They pretend they are working, but actually they are listening to the* CAPTAIN'S *fight with* ROBERTS]

ROBERTS: Yes, Captain. I'll remember that next time.

CAPTAIN: You're damn right you'll remember it! Don't *ever* tell me you're too busy to see me! Ever! [ROBERTS *doesn't answer. The* CAPTAIN *points to the letter he is carrying*] By God, you think you're pretty cute with this letter, don't you? You're trying to get me in bad with the Admiral, ain't you? Ain't you?

ROBERTS: No, I'm not, Captain.

CAPTAIN: Then what do you mean by writing "disharmony aboard this ship"?

ROBERTS: Because it's true, Captain.

[*The men grin at each other*]

CAPTAIN: Any disharmony on this ship is my own doing!

ROBERTS: That's true too, Captain.

CAPTAIN: Damn right it's true. And it ain't gonna be in any letter that leaves this ship. Any criticism of this ship stays on this ship. I got a reputation with the Admiral and I ain't gonna lose it on account of a letter written by some smart-alec college officer. Now you retype that letter and leave out that disharmony crap and I'll send it in. But this is the last one, understand?

ROBERTS: Captain, every man in the Navy has the right to send in a request for transfer . . . and no one can change the wording. That's in Navy regs.

CAPTAIN: [*After a pause*] How about that, Dolan?

DOLAN: That's what it says, sir.

CAPTAIN: This goddamn Navy! I never put up with crap like that in the merchant service. All right, I'll send this one in as it is— disapproved, like I always do. But there's one thing I don't have to do and that's send in a letter that ain't been written. And, Mister, I'm tellin' you here and now—you ain't gonna write any more. You bring one next week and you'll regret it the rest of your life. You got a job right here and, Mister, you ain't *never* going to leave this ship. Now get on with your work. [*He looks around and notices the men. He shouts*] Where are your shirts?

ROBERTS: Captain, I . . .

CAPTAIN: Shut up! *Answer me, where are your shirts?* [*They stare at him*] Get those shirts on in a goddamn quick hurry.

[*The men pick up their shirts, then pause, looking at* ROBERTS]

ROBERTS: Captain, it was so hot working cargo, I . . .

CAPTAIN: [*Shouting louder*] I told you to shut up! [*To the men*] I'm giving you an order: get those shirts on!

[*The men do not move*]

ROBERTS: [*Quietly*] I'm sorry. Put your shirts on.

[*The men put on their shirts. There is a pause while the* CAPTAIN *stares at the men. Then he speaks quietly*]

CAPTAIN: Who's the Captain of this ship? By God, that's the rankest piece of insubordination I've seen. You've been getting pretty smart playing grab-ass with Roberts here . . . but now you've gone too far. I'm givin' you a little promise—I ain't never gonna forget this. And in the meantime, every one of you men who disobeyed my standing order and appeared on deck without a shirt—every one—is on report, do you hear? On report!

ROBERTS: Captain, you're not putting these men on report.

CAPTAIN: What do you mean—I'm not!

ROBERTS: I'm responsible. I gave them permission.

CAPTAIN: You disobeyed my order?

ROBERTS: Yes, sir. It was too hot working cargo in the sun. One man passed out.

CAPTAIN: I don't give a damn if fifty men passed out. I gave an order and you disobeyed it.

LCT: [*Offstage*] Thanks a million for the oranges, Lieutenant.

CAPTAIN: [*To* ROBERTS] Did you give that LCT fresh fruit?

ROBERTS: Yes, sir. We've got plenty, Captain. They've been out for two months.

CAPTAIN: I've taken all the crap from you that I'm going to. You've just got yourself ten days in your room. Ten days, Mister! Ten days!

ROBERTS: Very well, Captain. Do you relieve me here?

CAPTAIN: You're damn right, I relieve you. You can go to your room for ten days! See how you like that!

LCT: [*Offstage*] We're waiting on you, Lieutenant. We gotta shove off.

[ROBERTS *gives the megaphone to the* CAPTAIN *and starts off. The* CAPTAIN *looks in direction of the* LCT *then calls to* ROBERTS]

CAPTAIN: Where do you think you're going?

ROBERTS: [*Pretending surprise*] To my room, Captain!

CAPTAIN: Get back to that cargo! I'll let you know when you have ten days in your room and you'll damn well know it! You're going to stay right here and do your job! [ROBERTS *crosses to the crew. The* CAPTAIN *slams the megaphone into* ROBERTS' *stomach.* PULVER *enters around the corner of the house, sees the* CAPTAIN *and starts to go back. The* CAPTAIN *sees* PULVER *and shouts*] Who's that? Who's that officer there?

PULVER: [*Turning*] Me, sir?

CAPTAIN: Yes, you. Come here, boy. [PULVER *approaches in great confusion and can think of nothing better to do than salute. This visibly startles the* CAPTAIN] Why, you're one of my officers!

PULVER: Yes, sir.

CAPTAIN: What's your name again?

PULVER: Ensign Pulver, sir.

[*He salutes again. The* CAPTAIN, *amazed, returns the salute, then says for the benefit of* ROBERTS *and the crew:*]

CAPTAIN: By God, I'm glad to see one on this ship knows how to salute. [*Then to* PULVER] Pulver . . . oh, yes . . . Pulver. How is it I never see you around?

PULVER: [*Terrified*] I've wondered about that myself, sir.

CAPTAIN: What's your job?

PULVER: [*Trembling*] Officer in charge of laundry and morale, sir.

CAPTAIN: How long you been aboard?

PULVER: Fourteen months, sir.

CAPTAIN: Fourteen months! You spend most of your time down in the laundry, eh?

PULVER: Most of the time, sir. Yes, sir.

[ROBERTS *turns his face to hide his laughter*]

CAPTAIN: Well, you do a good job, Pulver, and . . . you know I'd like to see more of you. Why don't you have lunch with me in my cabin today?

PULVER: Oh, I can't today.

CAPTAIN: Can't? Why not?

PULVER: I'm on my way over to the hospital on the island. I've got to pick up a piece . . . of medical equipment.

ROBERTS: [*Calling over*] Why, I'll take care of that, Frank.

CAPTAIN: That's right, Roberts. You finish here and you go over and fetch it.

ROBERTS: Yes, sir.

[*He nods and turns away, grinning*]

CAPTAIN: [*To* PULVER] Well, how about it?

PULVER: This is something I've got to take care of myself, sir. If you don't mind, sir.

CAPTAIN: Well, some other time then.

PULVER: Yes, sir. Thank you, sir.

CAPTAIN: Okay, Pulver.

[*The* CAPTAIN *baits another salute from* PULVER, *then exits.* PULVER *watches him go, then starts to sneak off*]

ROBERTS: [*Grinning and mimicking the* CAPTAIN] Oh, boy! [PULVER *stops uneasily.* ROBERTS *salutes him*] I want to see more of you, Pulver!

PULVER: [*Furiously*] That son-of-a-bitch! Pretending he doesn't know me!

[*He looks at watch and exits.* ROBERTS *turns laughing to the crew who are standing rather solemnly*]

DOWDY: [*Quietly*] Nice going, Mister Roberts.

SCHLEMMER: It was really beautiful the way you read the Old Man off!

GERHART: Are you going to send in that letter next week, Mister Roberts?

ROBERTS: Are we, Dolan?

DOLAN: You're damn right we are! And I'm the baby who's going to deliver it!

SCHLEMMER: He said he'd fix you good. What do you think he'll do?

REBER: You got a promotion coming up, haven't you?

SCHLEMMER: Yeah. Could he stop that or something?

DOLAN: Promotion! This is Mister Roberts. You think he gives a good hoot-in-hell about another lousy stripe?

ALL: Yeah.

GERHART: Hey, Mister Roberts, can I take the letter in next week?

DOLAN: [*Indignantly*] You can like hell. That's my job—isn't it, Mister Roberts?

GERHART: Can I, Mister Roberts?

ROBERTS: I'm afraid I've promised that job to Dolan.

DOLAN: [*Pushing* GERHART *away*] You heard him. [*To* ROBERTS] We gotta write a really hot one next week.

ROBERTS: Got any asbestos paper?

[*He starts off, the men follow happily as the lights fade out*]

SCENE FOUR

The lights come up immediately on the main set. REBER *and* GERHART *enter from right passageway. As they get around the corner of the house, they break into a run.* REBER *dashes off through left passageway.*

GERHART: [*Excitedly, descending hatchway*] Hey, Schlemmer!

[MISS GIRARD, *a young, attractive, blonde Army nurse, and* PULVER *enter from right passageway*]

PULVER: Well, here it is.

MISS GIRARD: This is a ship?

PULVER: Unh-hunh.

MISS GIRARD: My sister and I flew over some warships on our way out from the States and they looked so busy—men running around like mad.

PULVER: It's kinda busy sometimes up on deck.

MISS GIRARD: Oh, you mean you've seen a lot of action?

PULVER: Well, I sure as hell haven't had much in the last year . . . Oh, battle action! Yeah . . . Yeah . . .

MISS GIRARD: Then you must have a lot of B.F. on here.

PULVER: Hunh?

MISS GIRARD: You know—battle fatigue?

PULVER: Yeah, we have a lot of that.

MISS GIRARD: Isn't that too bad! But they brief us to expect a lot of that out here. [*Pause*] Say, you haven't felt any yourself, have you?

PULVER: I guess I had a little touch of it . . . just a scratch.

MISS GIRARD: You know what you should do then? You should sleep more.

PULVER: Yeah.

MISS GIRARD: What's your job on the ship?

PULVER: Me? I'm . . . Executive Officer . . .

MISS GIRARD: But I thought that Executive Officers had to be at least a . . .

PULVER: Say, you know what I was thinking? That we should have that little old drink of Scotcharoo right now—

MISS GIRARD: I think so, too. You know, I just love Scotch. I've just learned to drink it since I've joined the Army. But I'm already an absolute connoisseur.

PULVER: [*Dismayed*] Oh, you are?

MISS GIRARD: My twin sister has a nickname for me that's partly because I like a particular brand of Scotch . . . [*Giggles*] and partly because of a little personal thing about me that you wouldn't understand. Do you know what she calls me? "Red Label!" [*They both laugh*] What are you laughing at? You don't know what I'm talking about—and what's more you never will.

PULVER: What I was laughing about is—that's the kind I've got.

MISS GIRARD: Red Label! Oh, you're God's gift to a thirsty nursie! But where can we drink it? This is a Navy ship . . . isn't it?

PULVER: Oh, yeah, yeah, we'll have to be careful . . . We mustn't be seen . . . Lemme see, where shall we go . . . [*Considers*] I have it! We'll go back to my cabin. Nobody'd bother us there.

MISS GIRARD: Oh, you're what our outfit calls an operator. But you look harmless to me.

PULVER: Oh, I don't know about that.

MISS GIRARD: What's your first name—Harmless?

PULVER: Frank.

MISS GIRARD: Hello, Frank. Mine's Ann.

PULVER: Hello, Ann.

MISS GIRARD: All right. We'll have a little sip in your room.

PULVER: Right this way. [*They start off toward left passageway.* INSIGNA, MANNION, STEFANOWSKI, WILEY *and* LINDSTROM *enter from right, carrying the spy glass and binoculars.* STEFANOWSKI *trips on hatch cover.* MISS GIRARD *and* PULVER *turn*] Hello, Mannion . . . Insigna . . . Stefanowski . . .

MANNION: [*Hoarsely*] Hello, Mister Pulver . . .

PULVER: This is—Lieutenant Girard.

[*The men murmur a greeting*]

MISS GIRARD: What're you all doing with those glasses?

INSIGNA: We're . . . cleaning them.

[*Suddenly pulls out shirt tail and begins lamely polishing spy glass. The others follow his example. More men crowd onto the stage*]

PULVER: Well, don't work too hard . . . [*They turn to leave, but find themselves hemmed in by the men*] It's getting a little stuffy up here, I guess we better . . .

[ROBERTS *enters, very excited, carrying a piece of paper and a small book*]

ROBERTS: [*Entering*] Hey, Insigna . . . Mannion . . . get a load of this . . . Hey, Frank . . .

[*He stops short, seeing* MISS GIRARD]

PULVER: Hiya, Doug boy! This is Ann Girard—Doug Roberts.

ROBERTS: How do you do?

MISS GIRARD: [*Beaming*] How do you do? You're Frank's roommate. He's told me all about you.

ROBERTS: Really?

MISS GIRARD: What are you doing on this ship?

ROBERTS: Now there you've got me.

MISS GIRARD: No, I mean what's your job? Like Frank here is Executive Officer.

ROBERTS: Oh, I'm just the Laundry and Morale Officer.

MISS GIRARD: Why, that's wonderful—I've just been made Laundry and Morale Officer in our outfit!

PULVER: Oh, for Christ's sake!

[MANNION *and* INSIGNA *begin an argument in whispers*]

MISS GIRARD: Maybe we can get together and compare notes.

ROBERTS: I'd enjoy that very much.

PULVER: [*Attempting to usher* MISS GIRARD *off*] Look, Doug. Will you excuse us? We're going down to have a little drink.

MISS GIRARD: Frank, I don't think that's very nice. Aren't you going to ask Doug to join us?

PULVER: Hell, no—I mean—he doesn't like Scotch.

ROBERTS: That's right, Miss Girard. I stay true to alcohol and orange juice.

PULVER: Come on, Ann . . .

MISS GIRARD: Wait a minute! A lot of the girls at the hospital swear by alcohol and orange juice. We ought to all get together and have a party in our new dayroom.

INSIGNA: [*To* MANNION] I bet you fifty bucks . . .

[STEFANOWSKI *moves* INSIGNA *and* MANNION *away from* MISS GIRARD]

MISS GIRARD: Seems to be an argument.

PULVER: Yeah.

MISS GIRARD: Well, anyhow, we're fixing up a new dayroom. [*She looks offstage*] Look, you can see it! The hospital! And there's our new dormitory! That first window . . .

[PULVER *takes glasses from* WILEY *to look at island*]

INSIGNA: [*To* MANNION, *his voice rising*] All right, I got a *hundred* bucks says that's the one with the birthmark on her ass.

[*There is a terrible silence.* MISS GIRARD, *after a moment, takes the glasses from* PULVER *and looks at the island. After a moment she lowers the glasses and speaks to* PULVER]

MISS GIRARD: Frank, I won't be able to have lunch with you after all. Would you call the boat, please? [*To* ROBERTS] Good-bye, Doug. It was nice knowing you. You see, I promised the girls I'd help them hang some curtains and I think we'd better get started right away. Good-bye, everybody. [*To* MANNION] Oh, what's your name again?

INSIGNA: Mine?

MISS GIRARD: No. Yours.

MANNION: Mine? [MISS GIRARD *nods*] Mannion.

MISS GIRARD: Well, Mannion. I wouldn't take that bet if I were you because you'd lose a hundred bucks. [*To* PULVER] Come on, Harmless.

[*She exits, followed by a bewildered* PULVER. *The men watch her off.* STEFANOWSKI *throws his cap on the ground in anger*]

MANNION: [*To* INSIGNA] You loudmouthed little bastard! Now you've gone and done it!

ROBERTS: Shut up! Insigna, how did you . . .

INSIGNA: We seen her taking a bath.

LINDSTROM: Through these glasses, Mister Roberts! We could see everything!

STEFANOWSKI: [*Furious*] You heard what she said—she's going to hang some curtains.

MANNION: Yeah . . .

LINDSTROM: Gee, them nurses was pretty to look at.

[*He sighs. There is a little tragic moment*]

ROBERTS: She's got a ten-minute boat ride. You've still got ten minutes.

WILEY: It wouldn't be any fun when you know you're going to be rushed.

LINDSTROM: This was the first real good day this ship has ever had. But it's all over now.

ROBERTS: Well, maybe you've got time then to listen to a little piece of news . . . [*He reads from the paper in his hands*] "When in all respects ready for sea, on or about 1600 today, the AK 601 will proceed at ten knots via X-Ray, Yolk and Zebra to Elysium Island, arriving there in seven days and reporting to the Port Director for cargo assignment." [*Emphatically*] "During its stay in Elysium, the ship will make maximum use of the recreational facilities of this port."

[*The men look up in slow surprise and disbelief*]

STEFANOWSKI: But that means liberty!

LINDSTROM: That don't mean liberty, Mister Roberts?

ROBERTS: That's exactly what it means!

INSIGNA: [*Dazed*] Somebody must've been drunk to send us to a Liberty Port!

[ROBERTS *nods*]

LINDSTROM: Has the Old Man seen them orders?

ROBERTS: He saw them before I did.

[*Now the men are excited*]

WILEY: Elysium! Where's that?

MANNION: Yeah! Where's that, Mister Roberts?

[*The men crowd around* ROBERTS *as he sits on the hatch*]

ROBERTS: [*Reading from guide-book*] "Elysium is the largest of the Limbo Islands. It is often referred to as the 'Polynesian Paradise.' Vanilla, sugar, cocoa, coffee, copra, mother-of-pearl, phosphates and rum are the chief exports."

INSIGNA: Rum! Did you hear that?

[*He gooses* LINDSTROM]

LINDSTROM: Cut that out!

[DOLAN *gooses* INSIGNA]

INSIGNA: Cut that out!

MANNION: Shut up!

ROBERTS: "Elysium City, its capital, is a beautiful metropolis of palm-lined boulevards, handsome public buildings and colorful stucco homes. Since 1900, its population has remained remarkably constant at approximately 30,000."

INSIGNA: I'll fix that!

[*The men shout him down*]

ROBERTS: That's all there is here. If you want the real dope on Elysium, there's one man on this ship who's been there.

STEFANOWSKI: Who's that?

MANNION: Who?

ROBERTS: Dowdy!

[*The men run off wildly in every direction, shouting for* DOWDY. *The call is taken up all over the ship.* ROBERTS *listens to them happily, then notices a pair of binoculars. He looks toward the island for a moment, shrugs and is lifting the binoculars to his eyes as the lights fade out*]

SCENE FIVE

During the darkness we can hear the exciting strains of Polynesian music.

*The lights come up slowly through a porthole, casting a strong late-afternoon shaft of light onto motionless white figures. It is the enlisted men's compartment below decks. Except for a few not yet fully dressed, the men are all in white uniforms. The compartment is a crowded place with three-tiered bunks against the bulkheads. Most of the men are crowded around the porthole, downstage left. The men who cannot see are listening to the reports of INSIGNA, who is standing on a bench, looking out the porthole. The only man who is not galvanized with excitement is DOWDY, who sits calmly on a bench, downstage center, reading a magazine—*True Detective.

GERHART: [*To* INSIGNA] What do you see now, Sam?

INSIGNA: There's a lot of little boats up forward—up around the bow.

PAYNE: What kind of boats?

INSIGNA: They're little sort of canoes and they're all filled up with flowers and stuff. And there's women in them boats, paddling them . . .

PAYNE: Are they coming down this way?

INSIGNA: Naw. They're sticking around the bow.

STEFANOWSKI: Sam, where's that music coming from?

INSIGNA: There's a great big canoe up there and it's filled with fat bastards with flowers in their ears playing little old git-tars . . .

SCHLEMMER: Why the hell can't we go up on deck? That's what I'd like to know!

LINDSTROM: When are we going ashore! That's what I'd like to know!

[INSIGNA *suddenly laughs*]

PAYNE: What is it, Sam?

INSIGNA. I wish you could see this . . .

[CHIEF JOHNSON *enters, looking knowingly at the men, shakes his head and addresses* DOWDY]

JOHNSON: Same story in here, eh? Every porthole this side of the ship!

DOWDY: They're going to wear themselves down to a nub before they ever get over there . . .

LINDSTROM: [*Takes a coin from pocket and thrusts it at* INSIGNA] Hey, Sam, here's another penny. Make them kids down below dive for it.

INSIGNA: [*Impatiently*] All right! [*Throws coin out the port*] Heads up, you little bastards!

[*The men watch tensely*]

LINDSTROM: Did he get that one, too?

INSIGNA: Yeah . . .

[*The men relax somewhat*]

LINDSTROM: Them kids don't ever miss!

INSIGNA: Hey, Dowdy—where's that little park again? Where you said all the good-looking women hang out?

DOWDY: For the last time—you see that big hill over there to the right . . .

INSIGNA: Yeah.

DOWDY: You see a big church . . . with a street running off to the left of it.

INSIGNA: Yeah.

DOWDY: Well, you go up that street three blocks . . .

INSIGNA: Yeah, I'm there.

DOWDY: That's the park.

INSIGNA: Well, I'll be damned . . .

LINDSTROM: Hey, show me that park, Sam?

[*The other men gather around* INSIGNA, *asking to see the park*]

INSIGNA: [*The authority now*] All right, you bastards, line up. I'll show you where the women hang out.

[*The men form a line and each steps up to the porthole where* INSIGNA *points out the park*]

JOHNSON: [*To* DOWDY] Smell that shoe polish? These guys have gone nuts!

DOWDY: I went down the ship's store the other day to buy a bar of soap and, do you know, they had been sold out for a week! No soap, no Listerine, no lilac shaving lotion—hell, they even sold eighteen jars of Mum! Now these bastards are bootlegging it! They're gettin' ten bucks for a used jar of Mum!

[REBER, *wearing the messenger's belt, enters. The men greet him excitedly*]

STEFANOWSKI: What's the word on liberty, Reber? Is the Old Man still asleep?

MANNION: Yeah, what's the word?

REBER: I just peeked in on him. He's snoring like a baby.

GERHART: Jeez, how any guy can sleep at a time like this!

INSIGNA: I'll get him up! I'm going up there and tap on his door!

[*Picks up a heavy lead pipe*]

DOWDY: [*Grabbing* INSIGNA] Like hell you are! You're going to stay right here and pray. You're going to pray that he wakes up feeling good and decides he's kept you guys sweating long enough!

MANNION: That's telling the little crud!

[INSIGNA *and* MANNION *threaten each other*]

REBER: Hey, Lindstrom. I got good news for you. You can take them whites off.

LINDSTROM: I ain't got the duty *tonight*?

REBER: That's right. You and Mister Roberts got the duty tonight
—the twelve to four watch. The Exec just posted the list . . .

[*He is interrupted by the sound of static on the squawk box.
Instantly all men turn toward it eagerly*]

DOLAN: [*On squawk box*] Now hear this! Now hear this!

WILEY: Here we go! Here we go!

STEFANOWSKI: [*Imitating the squawk box*] Liberty . . . will commence . . . immediately!

GERHART: Quiet!

DOLAN: [*On squawk box*] Now hear this! The Captain's messenger will report to the Captain's cabin on the double!

REBER: My God! He's awake!

[*He runs out*]

PAYNE: Won't be long now!

WILEY: Get going, Mannion! Get into those whites! We're going
to be the first ones over the side!

MANNION: Hell, yes! Give me a hand!

[*Now there is a general frenzy of preparation—the men put
the last-minute touches to shoes, hair, uniforms*]

GERHART: [*Singing to the tune of "California, Here I Come"*]
Ee-liss-*ee*-um, here I come! . . .
Ta-ta-ta-ta-*ta*-da-tah . . .

SCHLEMMER: [*To* GERHART] Watch where you're going! You stepped
on my shine!

INSIGNA: Schlemmer . . . Stef . . . Gerhart . . . come here!
[*These men gather around him.* LINDSTROM *remains unhappily
alone*] Now listen! Stefanowski and me are going to work alone
for the first hour and a half! But if you pick up something first
. . . [*Produces small map from his pocket*] We'll be working up
and down this street here . . .

[*They study the map. Now the squawk box is clicked on
again. All the men stand rigid, listening*]

DOLAN: [*On squawk box*] Now hear this! Now hear this! The Captain is now going to make a personal announcement.

[*Sound of squawk box switch*]

CAPTAIN: [*On squawk box*] Goddammit, how does this thing work? [*Sound of squawk box switch again*] This is the Captain speaking. I just woke up from a little nap and I got a surprise. I found out there were men on this ship who were expecting liberty. [*At this point, the lights start dimming until the entire scene is blacked out. The speech continues throughout the darkness. Under the CAPTAIN's speech the strains of Polynesian music can be heard*] Now I don't know how such a rumor got around, but I'd like to clear it up right now. You see, it's like this. Because of cargo requirements and security conditions which has just come to my personal attention there will be no liberty as long as we're in this here port. And one other thing—as long as we're here, no man will wear white uniforms. Now I would like to repeat for the benefit of complete understanding and clearness, NO LIBERTY. That is all.

SCENE SIX

The lights come up on the CAPTAIN's cabin. Against the left bulkhead is a settee. A chair is placed center. Up center is the only door. The CAPTAIN is seated behind his desk, holding a watch in one hand and the microphone in the other, in an attitude of waiting. Just over the desk and against the right bulkhead is a ship's intercommunication board. There is a wall-safe in the right bulkhead. After a moment there is a knock on the door.

CAPTAIN: Come in, Mister Roberts. [*As ROBERTS enters, the CAPTAIN puts the microphone on the desk*] Thirty-eight seconds. Pretty good time! You see, I been expectin' you ever since I made my little announcement.

ROBERTS: Well, as long as you're expecting me, what about it— when does this crew get liberty?

CAPTAIN: Well, in the first place, just kinda hold your tongue. And in the second place, sit down.

ROBERTS: There's no time to sit down. When are you going to let this crew go ashore?

CAPTAIN: I'm not. This wasn't my idea—coming to a Liberty Port. One of my officers arranged it with a certain Port Director—gave him a bottle of Scotch whiskey—compliments of the Captain. And the Port Director was kind enough to send me a little thank-you note along with our orders. Sit down, Mister Roberts. [ROBERTS *sits*] Don't worry about it. I'm not going to make trouble about that wasted bottle of Scotch. I'll admit I was a little pre-voked about not being consulted. Then I got to thinking maybe we oughta come to this port anyway so's you and me could have a little talk.

ROBERTS: You can make all the trouble you want, Captain, but let's quit wasting time. Don't you hear that music? Don't you know it's tearing those guys apart? They're breakable, Captain! I promise you!

CAPTAIN: That's enough! I've had enough of your fancy educated talks. [*Rises, goes to* ROBERTS] Now you listen to me. I got two things I want to show you. [*He unlocks the wall-safe, opens it and takes out a commander's cap with gold braid "scrambled eggs" on the visor*] You see that? That's the cap of a full commander. I'm gonna wear that cap some day and you're going to help me. [*Replaces cap in safe, goes back to* ROBERTS] I guess there's no harm in telling you that you helped me get that palm tree by working cargo. Now don't let this go to your head, but when Admiral Finchley gave me that award, he said, "You got a good Cargo Officer, Morton; keep him at it, you're going places." So I went out and bought that hat. There's nothing gonna stand between me and that hat—certainly not you. Now last week you wrote a letter that said "disharmony aboard this ship." I told you there wasn't going to be any more letters. But what do I find on my desk this morning . . . [*Taking letter from desk*] Another one. It says "friction between myself and the Commanding Officer." That ain't gonna go in, Mister.

ROBERTS: How are you going to stop it, Captain?

CAPTAIN: I ain't, you are. [*Goes to his chair and sits*] Just how much do you want this crew to have a liberty anyhow? Enough to stop this "disharmony"? To stop this "friction"? [*Leans forward*] Enough to get out of the habit of writing letters ever? Because that's the only way this crew is ever gonna get ashore. [*Leans back*] Well, we've had our little talk. What do you say?

ROBERTS: [*After a moment*] How did you get in the Navy? How did you get on our side? You're what I joined to fight *against*. You ignorant, arrogant, ambitious . . . [*Rises*] *jackass!* Keeping a hundred and sixty-seven men in prison because you got a palm tree for the work *they* did. I don't know which I hate worse—you or that other malignant growth that stands outside your door!

CAPTAIN: Why, you goddamn . . .

ROBERTS: How did you ever get command of a ship? I realize that in wartime they have to scrape the bottom of the barrel, but where the hell did they ever scrape you up?

CAPTAIN: [*Shouting*] There's just one thing left for you, by God —a general court-martial.

ROBERTS: That suits me fine. Court-martial me!

CAPTAIN: By God, you've got it!

ROBERTS: I'm asking for it!

CAPTAIN: You don't have to ask for it, you've got it now!

ROBERTS: If I can't get transferred off here, I'll get court-martialed off! I'm fed up! But you'll need a witness. Send for your messenger. He's down below. I'll say it all again in front of him. [*Pauses*] Go on, call in Reber! [*The* CAPTAIN *doesn't move*] Go on, call him. [*Still the* CAPTAIN *doesn't move*] Do you want me to call him?

CAPTAIN: No. [*He walks upstage, then turns to* ROBERTS] I think you're a pretty smart boy. I may not talk very good, Mister, but I know how to take care of smart boys. Let me tell you something. Let me tell you a little secret. I hate your guts, you college son-of-a-bitch! You think you're better than I am! You think you're better because you've had everything handed to you! Let me tell you something, Mister—I've worked since I was ten years old, and all my life I've known you superior bastards. I knew you people when

I was a kid in Boston and I worked in eating-places and you ordered me around. . . . "Oh, bus-boy! My friend here seems to have thrown up on the table. Clean it up, please." I started going to sea as a steward and I worked for you then . . . "Steward, take my magazine out to the deck chair!" . . . "Steward, I don't like your looks. Please keep out of my way as much as possible!" Well, I took that crap! I took that for years from pimple-faced bastards who weren't good enough to wipe my nose! And now I don't have to take it any more! There's a war on, by God, and I'm the Captain and you can wipe my nose! The worst thing I can do to you is to keep you on this ship! And that's where you're going to stay! Now get out of here!

[*He goes to his chair and sits.* ROBERTS *moves slowly toward the door. He hears the music, goes to the porthole and listens. Then he turns to the* CAPTAIN]

ROBERTS: Can't you hear that music, Captain?

CAPTAIN: Yeah, I hear it.

[*Busies himself at desk, ignoring* ROBERTS]

ROBERTS: Don't you know those guys below can hear it, too? Oh, my God.

CAPTAIN: Get out of here.

[*After a moment,* ROBERTS *turns from the porthole and slumps against the* CAPTAIN's *locker. His face is strained*]

ROBERTS: What do you want for liberty, Captain?

CAPTAIN: I want plenty. You're through writin' letters—ever.

ROBERTS: Okay.

CAPTAIN: That's not all. You're through givin' me trouble. You're through talkin' back to me in front of the crew. You ain't ever gonna open your mouth—except in civil answer. [ROBERTS *doesn't answer*] Mister Roberts, you know that if you don't take my terms I'll let you go out that door and that's the end of any hope for liberty.

ROBERTS: Is that all, Captain?

CAPTAIN: No. Anyone know you're in here?

ROBERTS: No one.

CAPTAIN: Then you won't go blabbin' about this to anyone ever. It might not sound so good. And besides I don't want you to take credit for gettin' this crew ashore.

ROBERTS: Do you think I'm doing this for credit? Do you think I'd *let* anyone know about this?

CAPTAIN: I gotta be sure.

ROBERTS: You've got my word, that's all.

CAPTAIN: [*After a pause*] Your word. Yes, you college fellas make a big show about keeping your word.

ROBERTS: How about it, Captain. Is it a deal?

CAPTAIN: Yeah. [ROBERTS *picks up the microphone, turns on a switch and thrusts the microphone at the* CAPTAIN] Now hear this. This is the Captain speaking. I've got some further word on security conditions in this port and so it gives me great pleasure to tell you that liberty, for the starboard section . . .

ROBERTS: [*Covering the microphone with his hand*] For the entire crew, goddammit.

CAPTAIN: Correction: Liberty for the entire crew will commence immediately.

[ROBERTS *turns off the microphone. After a moment we hear the shouts of the crew.* ROBERTS *goes up to porthole. The* CAPTAIN *leans back on his chair. A song, "Roll Me Over," is started by someone and is soon taken up by the whole crew*]

ROBERTS: [*Looking out of the porthole. He is excited and happy*] Listen to those crazy bastards. Listen to them.

[*The crew continues to sing with increasing volume. Now the words can be distinguished:*

Roll me over in the clover,
Roll me over, lay me down
And do it again.]

CURTAIN

ACT TWO

SCENE ONE

The curtain rises on the main set. It is now 3:45 A.M. The night is pitch-black, but we can see because of a light over the head of the gangway, where a temporary desk has been rigged; a large ship's logbook lies open on this desk. A small table on which are hospital supplies is at left of the door.

At rise, ROBERTS, DOC, LINDSTROM, JOHNSON *and four* SEAMEN *are discovered onstage.* LINDSTROM, *in web belt, is writing in the log.* ROBERTS *is standing with a pile of yellow slips in his hand; he wears the side-arms of the Officer of the Deck.* JOHNSON *and a* SEAMAN *are standing near the hatchway, holding the inert body of another* SEAMAN, *who has court plaster on his face. Two more* SEAMEN *lie on the hatch cover where* DOC *is kneeling, bandaging one of them. As the curtain rises we hear the sound of a siren off right. Everyone turns and looks—that is, everyone who is conscious.*

LINDSTROM: Here's another batch, Mister Roberts—a whole paddy wagon full. And this one's an Army paddy wagon.

ROBERTS: We haven't filed this batch yet. [*To* DOC] Hurry up, Doc.

JOHNSON: [*To* DOC, *indicating body he is carrying*] Where do we put number twenty-three here, Doc? Sick bay or what?

DOC: Just put him to bed. His condition's only critical.

JOHNSON: [*Carrying* SEAMAN *off*] They just roll out of their bunks, Doc. Now I'm stacking 'em on the deck down there—I'm on the third layer already.

VOICE: [*Offstage*] Okay, Lieutenant! All set down here! You ready?

ROBERTS: [*Calling offstage—and giving hand signal*] Okay! [*To DOC*] Here they come, Doc! Heads up!

SHORE PATROLMAN'S VOICE: [*Offstage*] Lieutenant!

ROBERTS: Oh, not you again!

SHORE PATROLMAN'S VOICE: [*Offstage*] I got a bunch of real beauties for you this time.

ROBERTS: [*Calling offstage*] Can they walk?

SHORE PATROLMAN'S VOICE: [*Offstage*] Just barely!

ROBERTS: [*Calling*] Then send 'em up.

LINDSTROM: Man, oh, man, what a liberty! We got the record now, Mister Roberts! This makes the seventh batch since we went on watch!

[*The sound of a cargo winch and a voice offstage singing the Army Air Corps song are heard.* ROBERTS *is looking offstage*]

ROBERTS: [*Signaling*] Looks like a real haul this time. Schlemmer, look out!

LINDSTROM: Schlemmer, look out!

ROBERTS: Okay, Doc. [DOC *and* ROBERTS *lift the two bodies from the hatch cover and deposit them farther upstage. At this moment, the cargo net appears, loaded with bodies in once-white uniforms and leis. Riding on top of the net is* SCHLEMMER, *wearing a lei and singing "Off We Go into the Wild Blue Yonder"*] Let her in easy . . .

LINDSTROM: Let her in easy . . .

[*The net is lowered onto the hatch cover and* LINDSTROM *detaches it from the hook. All start untangling bodies*]

ROBERTS: Well, they're peaceful anyhow.

[*At this point a* SHORE PATROLMAN *enters from the gangway*]

SHORE PATROLMAN: [*Handing* ROBERTS *a sheaf of yellow slips*] For your collection. [*Points down gangway*] Take a look at them.

ROBERTS: [*Looks offstage*] My God, what did they do?

SHORE PATROLMAN: They done all right, Lieutenant. Six of them busted into a formal dance and took on a hundred and twenty-eight Army bastards. [*Calls off*] All right, let's go!

[STEFANOWSKI, REBER, WILEY, PAYNE *and* MANNION, *with his arm around* INSIGNA, *straggle on—a frightening sight—followed by a* MILITARY POLICEMAN. INSIGNA's *uniform is torn to shreds.* MANNION *is clad in a little diaper of crepe paper. All have bloody faces and uniforms. A few bear souvenirs—a Japanese lantern, leis, Army caps, a Shore Patrol band, etc. They throw perfunctory salutes to the colors, then murmur a greeting to* ROBERTS]

MILITARY POLICEMAN: Duty Officer?

ROBERTS: That's right.

MILITARY POLICEMAN: [*Salutes*] Colonel Middleton presents his compliments to the Captain and wishes him to know that these men made a shambles out of the Colonel's testimonial dinner-dance.

ROBERTS: Is this true, Insigna?

INSIGNA: That's right, Mister Roberts. A shambles. [*To* MANNION] Ain't that right, Killer?

MANNION: That's right, Mister Roberts.

ROBERTS: You men crashed a dance for Army personnel?

MANNION: Yes, sir! And they made us feel unwelcome! [*To* INSIGNA] Didn't they, Slugger?

ROBERTS: Oh, they started a fight, eh?

WILEY: No, sir! We started it!

STEFANOWSKI: We finished it, too! [*To* MILITARY POLICEMAN] Tell Mister Roberts how many of you Army bastards are in the hospital.

MANNION: Go on.

MILITARY POLICEMAN: Thirty-eight soldiers of the United States Army have been hospitalized. And the Colonel himself has a very bad bruise on his left shin!

PAYNE: *I* did that, Mister Roberts.

MILITARY POLICEMAN: And that isn't all, Lieutenant. There were young ladies present—fifty of them. Colonel Middleton had been lining them up for a month, from the finest families of Elysium. And he had personally guaranteed their safety this evening. Well, sir . . .

ROBERTS: Well?

MILITARY POLICEMAN: Two of those young ladies got somewhat mauled, one actually got a black eye, six of them got their clothes torn off and then went screaming off into the night and they haven't been heard from since. What are you going to do about it, Lieutenant?

ROBERTS: Well, I'm due to get relieved here in fifteen minutes—I'll be glad to lead a search party.

MILITARY POLICEMAN: No, sir. The Army's taking care of that end. The Colonel will want to know what punishment you're going to give these men.

ROBERTS: Tell the Colonel that I'm sure our Captain will think of something.

MILITARY POLICEMAN: But . . .

ROBERTS: That's all, Sergeant.

MILITARY POLICEMAN: [*Salutes*] Thank you, sir.

[*He goes off*]

SHORE PATROLMAN: Lieutenant, I been pretty sore at your guys up till now—we had to put on ten extra Shore Patrolmen on account of this ship. But if you knew Colonel "Chicken" Middleton—well, I'd be willing to do this every night. [*To the men*] So long, fellows!

[*The men call "So long."* SHORE PATROLMAN *exits, saluting* ROBERTS *and quarter-deck*]

ROBERTS: Well, what've you got to say for yourselves?

STEFANOWSKI: [*After a moment*] Okay if we go ashore again, Mister Roberts?

ROBERTS: [*To* LINDSTROM] Is this the first time for these guys?

LINDSTROM: [*Showing log*] Yes, sir, they got a clean record—they only been brought back once.

ROBERTS: [*To* DOC] What do you say, Doc?

[*The men turn eagerly to* DOC]

DOC: Anybody got a fractured skull?

MEN: No.

DOC: Okay, you pass the physical.

ROBERTS: Go down and take a shower first and get into some clothes.

[*The men rush to the hatchway*]

STEFANOWSKI: We still got time to get back to that dance!

[*As they descend hatchway,* INSIGNA *pulls crepe paper from around* MANNION *as he is halfway down the hatchway*]

ROBERTS: How you feeling, Doc?

DOC: These alcohol fumes are giving me a cheap drunk—otherwise pretty routine. When do you get relieved, Doug?

[*Takes box from table and gestures for men to remove table. They carry it off*]

ROBERTS: Soon as Carney gets back from the island. Any minute now.

DOC: What are you grinning like a skunk for?

ROBERTS: Nothing. I always grin like a skunk. What have you got in the box?

DOC: [*Descending hatchway—holding up small packet he has taken from the box*] Little favors from the Doc. I'm going to put one in each man's hand and when he wakes up he'll find pinned to his shirt full instructions for its use. I think it'll save me a lot of work later on.

[*His head disappears*]

LINDSTROM: I wish Gerhart would get back here and relieve me. I've got to get over to that island before it runs out of women.

[DOLAN *enters from gangway*]

DOLAN: Howdy, Mister Roberts! I'm drunk as a goat! [*Pulls a goat aboard*] Show him how drunk I am. Mister Roberts, when I first saw her she was eatin', and you know, she just eat her way into my heart. She was eatin' a little old palm tree and I thought to myself, our ship needs a mascot. [*He points out palm tree to goat*] There you are kid. Chow!

[ROBERTS *blocks his way*]

ROBERTS: Wait a minute . . . wait a minute. What's her name?

DOLAN: I don't know, sir.

ROBERTS: She's got a name plate.

DOLAN: Oh, so she has . . . her name is . . . [*Reads from tag on goat's collar*] . . . Property Of.

ROBERTS: What's her last name?

DOLAN: Her last name . . . [*Reads again*] Rear Admiral Wentworth.

[*Approaching siren is heard offstage*]

ROBERTS: Okay, Dolan, hit the sack. I'll take care of her.

DOLAN: Okay, Mister Roberts. [*Descends hatchway*] See that she gets a good square meal.

[*He points to the* CAPTAIN'S *palm tree and winks, then disappears.* GERHART *enters from gangway*]

LINDSTROM: Gerhart!

[*He frantically removes his web belt and shoves it at* GERHART]

GERHART: Okay, okay—you're relieved.

LINDSTROM: [*Tosses a fast salute to* ROBERTS *and says in one breath*] Requestpermissiontogoashore!

[*He hurries down gangway*]

[SHORE PATROLMAN *enters from gangway*]

SHORE PATROLMAN: Lieutenant, has one of your men turned up with a . . . [*Sees goat and takes leash*] Oh, thanks. [*To goat*] Come on, come on, your papa over there is worried about you.

[*Pulls goat down gangway*]

GERHART: Where's your relief, Mister Roberts?

ROBERTS: [*Sitting on hatch*] He'll be along any minute. How was your liberty, Gerhart?

[GERHART *grins. So does* ROBERTS. DOC *enters from hatchway*]

DOC: What are you looking so cocky about anyway?

ROBERTS: Am I looking cocky? Maybe it's because for the first time since I've been on this ship, I'm seeing a crew.

DOC: What do you think you've been living with all this time?

ROBERTS: Just a hundred and sixty-seven separate guys. There's a big difference, Doc. Now these guys are bound together. You saw Insigna and Mannion. Doc, I think these guys are strong enough now to take all the miserable, endless days ahead of us. I only hope I'm strong enough.

DOC: Doug, tomorrow you and I are going over there and take advantage of the groundwork that's been laid tonight. You and I are going to have ourselves a liberty.

[PULVER *enters slowly from the gangway and walks across the stage.* DOC *calls* ROBERTS' *attention to him*]

ROBERTS: Hello, Frank. How was your liberty?

[PULVER *half turns, shrugs and holds up seven fingers, then exits. A* SHORE PATROL OFFICER *enters from the gangway and calls offstage. He speaks with a Southern accent*]

SHORE PATROL OFFICER: That's your post and that's your post. You know what to do. [*He salutes the quarter-deck, then* ROBERTS] Officer of the Deck? [ROBERTS *nods. The* SHORE PATROL OFFICER *hesitates a moment*] I hope you don't mind but I've stationed two of my men at the foot of the gangway. I'm sorry but this ship is restricted for the rest of its stay in Elysium. Your Captain is to report to the Island Commander at seven o'clock this morning. I'd recommend that he's there on time. The Admiral's a pretty tough cookie when he's mad, and he's madder now than I've ever seen him.

ROBERTS: What in particular did this?

SHORE PATROL LIEUTENANT: A little while ago six men from your ship broke into the home of the French Consul and started throwing things through the plate-glass living-room window. We found some of the things on the lawn: a large world globe, a small love seat, a lot of books and a bust of Balzac—the French writer. We also found an Army private first class who was unconscious at the time. He claims they threw him, too.

ROBERTS: Through the window?

SHORE PATROL LIEUTENANT: That's right! It seems he took them there for a little joke. He didn't tell them it was the Consul's house; he said it was a—what we call in Alabama—a cat-house. [ROBERTS *and* DOC *nod*] Be sure that your Captain is there at seven o'clock sharp. If it makes you feel any better, Admiral Wentworth says this is the worst ship he's ever seen in his entire naval career. [*Laughs, then salutes*] Good night, Lieutenant.

ROBERTS: [*Returning salute*] Good night.

[*The* SHORE PATROL LIEUTENANT *exits down gangway—saluting the quarter-deck*]

GERHART: Well, there goes the liberty. That was sure a wham-bam-thank you, ma'am!

DOC: Good night.

[*He exits through left passageway*]

GERHART: But, by God, it was worth it. That liberty was worth anything!

ROBERTS: I think you're right, Gerhart.

GERHART: Hunh?

ROBERTS: I think you're right.

GERHART: Yeah.

[*He smiles.* ROBERTS *looks over the log.* GERHART *whistles softly to himself "Roll Me Over" as the lights slowly fade out*]

During the darkness we hear JOHNSON *shouting:*

JOHNSON: All right, fall in for muster. Form two ranks. And pipe down.

SCENE TWO

The lights come up, revealing the deck. Morning sunlight. A group of men, right and left, in orderly formation. They are talking.

JOHNSON: 'Ten-shun!

[*The command is relayed through the ship. The* CAPTAIN *enters from his cabin, followed by* ROBERTS. *The* CAPTAIN *steps up on the hatch cover.* ROBERTS *starts to fall in with the men*]

CAPTAIN: [*Calling to* ROBERTS *and pointing to a place beside himself on hatch cover*] Over here, Roberts. [ROBERTS *takes his place left of* CAPTAIN] We're being kicked out of this port. I had a feeling this liberty was a bad idea. That's why we'll never have one again. We're going to erase this blot from my record if we have to work twenty-four hours a day. We're going to move even more cargo than we've moved before. And if there ain't enough cargo work, Mister Roberts here is gonna find some. Isn't that right, Mister Roberts? [ROBERTS *doesn't answer*] Isn't that right, Mister Roberts?

ROBERTS: Yes, sir.

CAPTAIN: I'm appointing Mister Roberts here and now to see that you men toe the line. And I can't think of a more honorable man for the job. He's a man who keeps his word no matter what. [*Turns to* ROBERTS] Now, Roberts, if you do a good job—and if the Admiral begins to smile on us again—there might be something in it for you. What would you say if that little silver bar on your collar got a twin brother some day? [ROBERTS *is startled. The* CAPTAIN *calls offstage*] Officer of the Deck!

OFFSTAGE VOICE: Yes, sir!

CAPTAIN: [*To* ROBERTS] You wasn't expectin' that, was you? [*Calling offstage*] Get ready to sail!

OFFSTAGE VOICE: Aye-aye, sir!

CAPTAIN: You men are dismissed!

JOHNSON: Fall out!

[*The men fall out. Some exit. A little group forms downstage*]

CAPTAIN: Wait a minute! Wait a minute! Roberts, take these men here back aft to handle lines. And see that they work up a sweat. [ROBERTS *and men look at him*] Did you hear me, Roberts? I gave you an order!

ROBERTS: [*Carefully*] Yes, Captain. I heard you.

CAPTAIN: How do you answer when I give an order?

ROBERTS: [*After a pause*] Aye-aye, sir.

CAPTAIN: That's more like it . . . that's more like it!

[*He exits into his cabin*]

STEFANOWSKI: What'd he mean, Mister Roberts?

ROBERTS: I don't know. Just what he said, I guess.

GERHART: What'd you let him give you all that guff for?

DOLAN: [*Stepping up on hatch, carrying a file folder*] Because he's tired, that's why. He had the mid-watch last night. Your tail'd be dragging too if you had to handle all them customers.

ROBERTS: Come on. Let's get going . . .

DOLAN: Wait a minute, Mister Roberts. Something come for you in the mail this morning—a little love letter from the Bureau. [*Pulls out paper from file folder*] Get a load of this! [*Reads*] "To All Ships and Stations: Heightened war offensive has created urgent need aboard combat ships for experienced officers. [*He clicks his teeth and winks at* ROBERTS] All commanding officers are hereby directed to forward with their endorsements all applications for transfer from officers with twenty-four months' sea duty." [ROBERTS *grabs the directive and reads it.* DOLAN *looks at* ROBERTS *and smiles*] You got twenty-nine months—you're the only officer aboard that has. Mister Roberts, the Old Man is hanging on the ropes from the working-over the Admiral give him. All he needs to flatten him is one more little jab. And here it is. Your letter. I typed it up. [*He pulls out triplicate letter from file cover—then a fountain pen which he offers to* ROBERTS] Sign it and I'll take it in—

MANNION: Go on, sign it, Mister Roberts. He'll take off like a bird.

DOLAN: What're you waitin' for, Mister Roberts?

ROBERTS: [*Handing directive back to* DOLAN] I'll want to look it over first, Dolan. Come on, let's get going.

DOLAN: There's nothing to look over. This is the same letter we wrote yesterday—only quoting this new directive.

ROBERTS: Look, Dolan, I'm tired. And I told you I wanted—

DOLAN: You ain't too tired to sign your name!

ROBERTS: [*Sharply*] Take it easy, Dolan. I'm not going to sign it. So take it easy! [*Turns to exit right, finds himself blocked by crew*] Did you hear me? Let's get going!

    [*Exits*]

STEFANOWSKI: What the hell's come over him?

    [*They look at one another*]

INSIGNA: Aye-aye, sir—for Christ's sake!

MANNION: [*After a moment*] Come on. Let's get going.

DOLAN: [*Bitterly*] "Take it easy . . . take it easy!"

[*The men start to move off slowly as the lights fade out*]

During the darkness we hear a radio. There is considerable static.

AMERICAN BROADCASTER: Still, of course, we have no official word from the Headquarters of the Supreme Allied Command in Europe. I repeat, there is no official announcement yet. The report that the war in Europe has ended has come from only one correspondent. It has not been confirmed by other correspondents or by SHAEF headquarters. But here is one highly intriguing fact—that report has not been denied either in Washington or in SHAEF headquarters in Europe. IT HAS NOT BEEN DENIED. Right now in those places the newsmen are crowded, waiting to flash to the world the announcement of V-E Day.

SCENE THREE

The lights come up on ROBERTS' *and* PULVER'S *cabin.* DOC, *at the desk, and* PULVER, *up in his bunk, are listening to the radio.*

PULVER: Turn that damn thing off, Doc. Has Doug ever said anything to you about wanting a promotion?

DOC: Of course not. I doubt if he's even conscious of what rank he is.

PULVER: You can say that again!

DOC: I doubt if he's even conscious of what rank he is.

PULVER: That's what I said. He doesn't even think about a promotion. The only thing he thinks about is the war news—up in the radio shack two weeks now—all day long—listening with a headset, reading all the bulletins . . . Anyone who says he's bucking for another stripe is a dirty liar.

DOC: Who says he is, Frank?

PULVER: Insigna, Mannion and some of the other guys. I heard them talking outside the porthole. They were talking loud on purpose so I could hear them—they must've guessed I was lying here on my bunk. What's happened to Doug anyway, Doc?

DOC: How would I know! He's spoken about ten words to me in as many days. But I'm damn well going to find out.

PULVER: He won't talk, Doc. This morning I followed him all around the room while he was shaving. I begged him to talk to me. I says, "You're a fellow who needs a friend and here I am." And I says, "What's all this trouble you're having with the crew? You tell me and I'll fix it up like that." And then I give him some real good advice—I says, "Keep your chin up," and things like that. And then do you know what he did? He walked out of the room just as though I wasn't here.

[*There is a knock on the door*]

DOC: Come in.

[DOWDY *enters*]

DOWDY: Doc, Mister Pulver—could we see you officers a minute?

DOC: Sure. [GERHART *and* LINDSTROM *enter, closing the door*] What is it?

DOWDY: Tell them what happened, Gerhart.

GERHART: Well, sir, I sure don't like to say this but . . . Mister Roberts just put Dolan on report.

LINDSTROM: Me and Gerhart seen him.

PULVER: On report!

GERHART: Yes, sir. Tomorrow morning Dolan has to go up before the Captain—on account of Mister Roberts.

LINDSTROM: On account of Mister Roberts.

GERHART: And we was wondering if you officers could get him to take Dolan off report before . . . well, before—

DOC: Before what, Gerhart?

GERHART: Well, you see, the guys are all down in the compartment, talking about it. And they're saying some pretty rough things about Mister Roberts. Nobody just ever expected to see him put a man on report and . . .

LINDSTROM: He ain't gonna turn out to be like an officer, is he, Doc?

DOWDY: Lindstrom . . .

LINDSTROM: Oh, I didn't mean you, Doc . . . or even you, Mister Pulver!

DOC: That's all right, Lindstrom. What was this trouble with Dolan?

DOWDY: This letter business again!

GERHART: Yes, sir. Dolan was just kiddin' him about not sending in any more letters. And all of a sudden Mister Roberts turned just white and yelled, "Shut up, Dolan. Shut your goddamn mouth. I've had enough." And Dolan naturally got snotty back at him and Mister Roberts put him right on report.

LINDSTROM: Right on report.

[ROBERTS *enters*]

PULVER: Hello, Doug boy. Aren't you listening to the war news?

DOWDY: All right, Doctor. We'll get that medical store cleaned out tomorrow.

[DOWDY, GERHART *and* LINDSTROM *leave*]

PULVER: We thought you were up in the radio shack.

ROBERTS: [*To* PULVER] Don't you want to go down to the wardroom and have a cup of coffee?

PULVER: [*Jumping down from bunk*] Sure. I'll go with you.

ROBERTS: I don't want any. Why don't you go ahead?

PULVER: Nah. [*He sits back on bunk. There is another little pause*]

ROBERTS: Will you go on out anyway? I want to talk to Doc.

PULVER: [*Rising and crossing to door*] All right, I will. I'm going for a cup of coffee. [*Stops, turns and gets cup from top of locker*] No! I'm going up to the radio shack. You aren't the only one interested in the war news.

[*He exits*]

ROBERTS: [*With emotion*] Doc, transfer me, will you? [DOC *looks at him*] Transfer me to the hospital on this next island! You can do it. You don't need the Captain's approval! Just put me ashore for examination—say there's something wrong with my eyes or my feet or my head, for Christ's sake! You can trump up something!

DOC: What good would that do!

ROBERTS: Plenty! I could lie around that hospital for a couple of weeks. The ship would have sailed—I'd have missed it! I'd be off this ship. Will you do it, Doc?

DOC: Doug, why did you put Dolan on report just now?

ROBERTS: [*Angrily*] I gave him an order and he didn't carry it out fast enough to suit me. [*Glares at* DOC, *who just studies him.* ROBERTS *rises and paces right*] No, that's not true. It was the war. I just heard the news. The war was ending and I couldn't get to it and there was Dolan giving me guff about something—and all of a sudden I hated him. I hated all of them. I was sick of the sullen bastards staring at me as though I'd sold them down the river or something. If they think I'm bucking for a promotion—if they're stupid enough to think I'd walk ten feet across the room to get anything from that Captain, then I'm through with the whole damn ungrateful mob!

DOC: Does this crew owe you something?

ROBERTS: What the hell do you mean by that?

DOC: You talk as if they did.

[ROBERTS *rises and crosses to bunk*]

ROBERTS: [*Quietly*] That's exactly how I'm talking. I didn't realize it but that's exactly the way I've been feeling. Oh, Jesus, that shows you how far gone I am, Doc. I've been taking something out on them. I've been blaming them for something that . . .

DOC: What, Doug? Something what? You've made some sort of an agreement with the Captain, haven't you, Doug!

ROBERTS: [*Turns*] Agreement? I don't know what you mean. Will you transfer me, Doc?

DOC: Not a chance, Doug. I could never get away with it—you know that.

ROBERTS: Oh, my God!

PULVER: [*Offstage*] Doug! Doc! [*Entering*] Listen to the radio, you uninformed bastards! Turn it up!

[ROBERTS *reaches over and turns up the radio. The excited voice of an* ANNOUNCER *can be heard*]

ANNOUNCER: . . . this broadcast to bring you a special news flash! The war is over in Europe! THE WAR IS OVER IN EUROPE! [ROBERTS *grasps* DOC's *arm in excitement*] Germany has surrendered unconditionally to the Allied Armies. The surrender was signed in a schoolhouse in the city of Rheims . . .

[ROBERTS *stands staring.* DOC *turns off the radio. For a moment there is silence, then:*]

DOC: I would remind you that there's still a minor skirmish here in the Pacific.

ROBERTS: I'll miss that one, too. But to hell with me. This is the greatest day in the world. We're going to celebrate. How about it, Frank!

PULVER: Yeah, Doug. We've got to celebrate!

DOC: [*Starting to pull alcohol from waste basket*] What'll it be—alcohol and orange juice or orange juice and alcohol?

ROBERTS: No, that's not good enough.

PULVER: Hell, no, Doc!

[*He looks expectantly at* ROBERTS]

ROBERTS: We've got to think of something that'll lift this ship right out of the water and turn it around the other way.

[PULVER *suddenly rises to his feet*]

PULVER: [*Shouting*] Doug! Oh, my God, why didn't I think of this before. Doug! Doc! You're going to blow your tops when you hear the idea I got! Oh, Jesus, what a wonderful idea! It's the only thing to do. It's the only thing in the whole world to do! That's all! Doug, you said I never had any ideas. You said I never finished anything I started. Well, you're wrong—tonight you're wrong! I thought of something and I finished it. I was going to save it for your birthday, but I'm going to give it to you tonight, because we gotta celebrate . . .

ROBERTS: [*Waves his hands in* PULVER's *face for attention*] Wait a minute, Frank! What is it?

PULVER: A firecracker, by God. [*He reaches under his mattress and pulls out a large, wobbly firecracker which has been painted red*] We're gonna throw a firecracker under the Old Man's bunk. Bam-bam-bam! Wake up, you old son-of-a-bitch, IT'S V-E DAY!

ROBERTS: [*Rising*] Frank!

PULVER: Look at her, Doc. Ain't it a beauty? Ain't that the greatest hand-made, hand-painted, hand-packed firecracker you ever saw?

ROBERTS: [*Smiling and taking firecracker*] Yes, Frank. That's the most beautiful firecracker I ever saw in my life. But will it work?

PULVER: Sure it'll work. At least, I think so.

ROBERTS: Haven't you tested it? It's got to work, Frank, it's just got to work!

PULVER: I'll tell you what I'll do. I'll take it down to the laundry and test it—that's my laboratory, the laundry. I got all the fixings down there—powder, fuses, everything, all hid behind the soapflakes. And if this one works, I can make another one in two minutes.

ROBERTS: Okay, Frank. Take off. We'll wait for you here. [PULVER *starts off*] Be sure you got enough to make it loud. What'd you use for powder?

PULVER: Loud! This ain't a popgun. This is a firecracker. I used fulminate of mercury. I'll be right back.

[*He runs out*]

ROBERTS: Fulminate of mercury! That stuff's murder! Do you think he means it?

DOC: [*Taking alcohol bottle from waste basket*] Of course not. Where could he get fulminate of mercury?

ROBERTS: I don't know. He's pretty resourceful. Where did he get the clap last year?

DOC: How about a drink, Doug?

[*He pours alcohol and orange juice into two glasses*]

ROBERTS: Right! Doc, I been living with a genius. This makes it all worthwhile—the whole year and a half he spent in his bunk. How else could you celebrate V-E Day? A firecracker under the Old Man's bunk! The silly little son-of-a-bitch!

DOC: [*Handing* ROBERTS *a drink*] Here you are, Doug. [DOC *holds the drink up in a toast*] To better days!

ROBERTS: Okay. And to a great American, Frank Thurlowe Pulver . . . Soldier . . . Statesman . . . Scientist . . .

DOC: Friend of the Working Girl . . .

[*Suddenly there is a tremendous explosion.* DOC *and* ROBERTS *clutch at the desk*]

ROBERTS: Oh, my God!

DOC: He wasn't kidding! That's fulminate of mercury!

CAPTAIN: [*Offstage*] What was that?

[ROBERTS *and* DOC *rush to porthole, listening*]

JOHNSON: [*Offstage*] I don't know, Captain. I'll find out!

[*We hear the sounds of running feet*]

ROBERTS: Doc, we've got to go down and get him.

DOC: This may be pretty bad, Doug.

[*They turn to start for the door when suddenly a figure hurtles into the room and stops. For a moment it looks like a combination scarecrow and snowman but it is* PULVER—*his uniform tattered; his knees, arms and face blackened; he is*

*covered with soapsuds and his eyes are shining with excite-
ment.* ROBERTS *stares in amazement*]

PULVER: Jeez, that stuff's terrific!

DOC: Are you all right?

PULVER: I'm great! Gee, you should've been there!

ROBERTS: You aren't burned—or anything?

PULVER: Hell, no. But the laundry's kinda beat up. The mangle's
on the other side of the room now. And there's a new porthole on
the starboard side where the electric iron went through. And I
guess a steam-line must've busted or something—I was up to my
ass in lather. And soapflakes flyin' around—it was absolutely beautiful!

[*During these last lines,* DOC *has been making a brisk, professional examination*]

DOC: It's a miracle. He isn't even scratched!

PULVER: Come on down and see it, Doug. It's a Winter Wonderland!

CAPTAIN: [*Offstage*] Johnson!

ROBERTS: Quiet!

JOHNSON: [*Offstage*] Yes, sir.

CAPTAIN: [*Offstage*] What was it?

JOHNSON: [*Offstage*] The laundry, Captain. A steam-line must've
blew up.

PULVER: [*Explaining*] Steam-line came right out of the bulkhead.
[*He demonstrates*] Whish!

CAPTAIN: [*Offstage*] How much damage?

JOHNSON: [*Offstage*] We can't tell yet, Captain. We can't get in
there—the passageway is solid soapsuds.

PULVER: Solid soapsuds.

[*He pantomimes walking blindly through soapsuds*]

CAPTAIN: [*Offstage*] Tell those men to be more careful.

ROBERTS: [*Excitedly*] Frank, our celebration is just getting started. The night is young and our duty's clear.

PULVER: Yeah! What're we gonna do now, Doug?

ROBERTS: Get cleaned up and come with me.

PULVER: Where we goin' now, Doug?

ROBERTS: We're going down and get the rest of your stuff. You proved it'd work—you just hit the wrong target, that's all. We're going to make another firecracker, and put it where it really belongs.

PULVER: [*Who has slowly wilted during* ROBERTS' *speech*] The rest of my stuff was—in the laundry, Doug. It all went up. There isn't any more. I'm sorry, Doug. I'm awful sorry.

ROBERTS: [*Sinks into chair*] That's all right, Frank.

PULVER: Maybe I can scrounge some more tomorrow.

ROBERTS: Sure.

PULVER: You aren't sore at me, are you, Doug?

ROBERTS: What for?

PULVER: For spoilin' our celebration?

ROBERTS: Of course not.

PULVER: It was a good idea though, wasn't it, Doug?

ROBERTS: Frank, it was a great idea. I'm proud of you. It just didn't work, that's all.

[*He starts for the door*]

DOC: Where are you going, Doug?

ROBERTS: Out on deck.

PULVER: Wait'll I get cleaned up and I'll come with you.

ROBERTS: No, I'm going to turn in after that. [*To* PULVER] It's okay, Frank.

[*He exits*]

[PULVER *turns pleadingly to* DOC]

PULVER: He was happy there for a minute though, wasn't he, Doc? Did you see him laughing? He was happy as hell. [*Pause*] We gotta do something for that guy, Doc. He's in bad shape. What's the matter with him anyhow, Doc. Did you find out?

DOC: No, he couldn't tell me. But I know one thing he's feeling tonight and that's panic. Tonight he feels his war is dying before he can get to it.

[*He goes to radio and turns up volume*]

PULVER: I let him down. He wanted to celebrate and I let him down.

[*He drops his head*]

[ANNOUNCER'S VOICE *on radio comes up as the lights fade out*]

During the darkness and under the first part of Scene Four we hear the voice of a British broadcaster:

BRITISH BROADCASTER: . . . we hope that the King and the Queen will come out. The crowds are cheering—listen to them—and at any second now we hope to see Their Majesties. The color here is tremendous—everywhere rosettes, everywhere gay, red-white-and-blue hats. All the girls in their summer frocks on this lovely, mild, historic May evening. And although we celebrate with joyous heart the great victory, perhaps the greatest victory in the history of mankind, the underlying mood is a mood of thanksgiving. And now, I believe, they're coming. They haven't appeared but the crowd in the center are cheering madly. Handkerchiefs, flags, hands waving—HERE THEY COME! First, Her Majesty, the Queen, has come into view. Then the King in the uniform of an Admiral of the Fleet. The two Princesses standing on the balcony —listen to the crowd—

[*Sound of wild cheering*
This broadcast continues throughout the blackout and the next scene. Several times the station is changed, from a broadcast of the celebration in San Francisco to the speaker in New York and the band playing "The Stars and Stripes Forever" in Times Square]

SCENE FOUR

*The lights dim up on the main set. It is a few minutes later,
and bright moonlight. The ship is under way—this is indicated by the apparent movement of the stars, slowly up and
down. A group of men are sitting on the hatch cover in a late
bull session. They are* INSIGNA, MANNION, DOLAN *and* STE-
FANOWSKI. GERHART *stands over them; he has obviously just returned from some mission for the group.*

GERHART: I'm telling you, that's all it was. A steam pipe busted in
the laundry—they're cleaning it up now. It ain't worth going to
see.

[*The others make way for him and he sits down beside
them.* INSIGNA *cocks his head toward the sound of the radio*]

INSIGNA: What the hell's all that jabbering on the radio now?

MANNION: I don't know. Something about the King and Queen . . .

[*The men listen for a moment without curiosity; then, as the
radio fades, they settle back in indolent positions*]

INSIGNA: Well, anyhow, like I was telling you, this big sergeant in
Elysium was scared to fight me! Tell 'em how big he was, Killer.

MANNION: Six foot seven or eight . . .

STEFANOWSKI: That sergeant's grown eight inches since we left
Elysium . . . Did you see me when I swiped that Shore Patrol
band and went around arresting guys? That Shore Patrol Lieutenant said I was the best man he had. I arrested forty-three guys . . .

MANNION: [*Smiles at* DOLAN *who is looking depressed*] Come on,
Dolan, don't let him get you down.

INSIGNA: Yeah, come on, Dolan.

[ROBERTS *enters. He looks at the men, who have their backs
turned, hesitates, then goes slowly over to them*]

GERHART: [*Idly*] What was them croquette things we had for chow tonight?

[STEFANOWSKI *looks up and notices* ROBERTS. *Instantly he sits upright*]

STEFANOWSKI: Flash Red!

[*The men sit up. There is an embarrassed silence*]

ROBERTS: Good evening. [*The men smile politely.* ROBERTS *is very embarrassed*] Did you hear the news? The war's over in Europe.

MANNION: [*Smiling*] Yes, sir. We heard.

STEFANOWSKI: [*Helping out the conversation*] Sure. Maybe somebody'll get on the ball out here now . . .

[DOLAN *rises, starts down hatchway*]

ROBERTS: Dolan, I guess I kind of blew my top tonight. I'm sorry. I'm taking you off report.

DOLAN: Whatever you want, sir . . . [*He looks ostentatiously at his watch and yawns*] Well, I guess I'll hit the old sack . . .

[*He goes down hatchway*]

MANNION: Yeah, me too . . .

INSIGNA: Yeah . . .

GERHART: It's late as hell.

STEFANOWSKI: I didn't realize how late is was . . .

[*All the men get up, then go down the hatchway.* ROBERTS *stands looking after them. Now the radio is heard again.* ROBERTS *goes to hatchway and sits listening*]

SPEAKER: . . . Our boys have won this victory today. But the rest is up to you. You and you alone must recognize our enemies: the forces of ambition, cruelty, arrogance and stupidity. You must recognize them, you must destroy them, you must tear them out as you would a malignant growth! And cast them from the surface of the earth!

[*The end of the speech is followed by a band playing "The Stars and Stripes Forever."* ROBERTS' *face lights up and a new determination is in it. He repeats the words "malignant growth." The band music swells. He marches to the palm tree, salutes it, rubs his hands together and, as the music reaches a climax, he jerks the palm tree, earth and all, from the container and throws it over the side. Then, as the music continues, loud and climactic, he brushes his hands together, shrugs, and walks casually off left singing the tune to himself. For a moment the stage is empty. Then the lights go up in the* CAPTAIN'S *cabin. The door to the* CAPTAIN'S *cabin opens and the* CAPTAIN *appears. He is in pajamas and bathrobe, and in one hand he carries his watering can. He discovers the empty container. He looks at it, then plunges into his cabin. After a moment, the General Alarm is heard. It is a terrible clanging noise designed to rouse the dead. When the alarm stops, the* CAPTAIN'S *voice is heard, almost hysterical, over the squawk box]*

CAPTAIN: General Quarters! General Quarters! Every man to his battle station on the double!

[JOHNSON, *in helmet and life jacket, scurries from hatchway into the* CAPTAIN'S *cabin.* WILEY *enters from right passageway and climbs into the right gun tub. Now men appear from all directions in various degrees of dress. The stage is filled with men frantically running everywhere, all wearing helmets and life preservers]*

INSIGNA: [*Appearing from hatchway*] What happened? [*He runs up the ladder and into the left gun tub.* PAYNE *enters from left and starts to climb up to left gun tub*] Get the hell out of here, Payne. This ain't your gun—your gun's over there!

DOLAN: [*Also trying to climb the ladder with* PAYNE] Over there . . . over there . . .

[PAYNE *crosses to right gun tub*]

REBER: [*Entering from hatchway*] What the hell happened?

SCHLEMMER: Are *we* in an air raid?

PAYNE: Submarine . . . must be a submarine!

GERHART: Hey, Wiley, what happened?

DOWDY: [*Calling to someone on life raft*] Hey, get away from that life raft. He didn't say abandon ship!

[*During the confusion,* STEFANOWSKI, *bewildered, emerges from the hatchway and wanders over to right gun tub*]

STEFANOWSKI: Hey, Wiley, Wiley—you sure you're supposed to be up there?

WILEY: Yeah.

STEFANOWSKI: [*Crossing to left gun tub*] Hey, Sam. Are you supposed to be up there?

INSIGNA: Yeah, he was here last year!

STEFANOWSKI: Hey, Dowdy. Where the hell's my battle station?

DOWDY: I don't know where your battle station is! Look around!

[STEFANOWSKI *wanders aimlessly about.* WILEY, *in the gun tub right, is receiving reports of battle readiness from various parts of the ship:*]

WILEY: Twenty millimeters manned and ready. [*Pause*] Engine room manned and ready. [*Pause*] All battle stations manned and ready.

STEFANOWSKI: [*Sitting on corner of hatch*] Yeah, all but mine . . .

JOHNSON'S VOICE: [*In* CAPTAIN'S *cabin*] All battle stations manned and ready, Captain.

CAPTAIN'S VOICE: Give me that thing.

JOHNSON'S VOICE: [*"On mike"—that is, speaking directly into squawk box microphone. "Off mike" means speaking unintentionally into this live microphone*] Attention . . . Attention . . . The Captain wishes to . . .

CAPTAIN'S VOICE: [*Off mike*] Give me that thing! [*On mike*] All right, who did it? Who did it? You're going to stay here all night until someone confesses. You're going to stay at those battle stations until hell freezes over until I find out who did it. It's an insult to the honor of this ship, by God! The symbol of our cargo record has been destroyed and I'm going to find out who did it if it takes all night! [*Off mike*] Johnson, read me that muster list!

JOHNSON'S VOICE: [*Reading muster list off mike*] Abernathy . . .

MANNION: Symbol of our cargo record? What the hell's that?

[STEFANOWSKI *rises, sees empty container, kneels and ceremoniously bows to it*]

DOWDY: For God's sake, Stefanowski, find some battle station!

[STEFANOWSKI *points to empty container.* DOWDY *sees it and spreads the news to the men on left.* SCHLEMMER *sees it and tells the other men. Now from all parts of the ship men enter and jubilantly look at the empty container. Bits of soil fly into the air as the men group around the empty can*]

CAPTAIN'S VOICE: No, not Abernathy . . .

JOHNSON'S VOICE: Baker . . .

CAPTAIN'S VOICE: No . . .

JOHNSON'S VOICE: Bartholomew . . . Becker . . . Billings . . . Carney . . . Daniels . . . Dexter . . . Ellison . . . Everman . . . Jenkins . . . Kelly . . . Kevin . . . Martin . . . Olsen . . . O'Neill . . .

CAPTAIN'S VOICE: No, not O'Neill . . .

JOHNSON'S VOICE: Pulver . . .

CAPTAIN'S VOICE: No, not Pulver. He hasn't the guts . . .

JOHNSON'S VOICE: Roberts . . .

CAPTAIN'S VOICE: [*Roaring, off mike*] Roberts! He's the one! Get him up here!

JOHNSON'S VOICE: [*On mike*] Mister Roberts will report to the Captain's cabin on the double!

[*The men rush back to their battle stations*]

CAPTAIN'S VOICE: Get him up here, I tell you! Get him up here . . .

JOHNSON'S VOICE: [*On mike*] Mister Roberts will report to the Captain's cabin on the . . .

CAPTAIN: [*Off mike*] Give me that thing! [*On mike*] Roberts, you get up here in a goddamn quick hurry. Get up here! Roberts, I'm giving you an order—get the lead out of your pants.

[ROBERTS *appears from left passageway and, walking slowly, enters the* CAPTAIN'S *cabin*]

[*The men move onstage and* LINDSTROM *gets to a position on the ladder where he can look through the porthole of the* CAPTAIN'S *cabin*]

ROBERTS' VOICE: Did you want to see me, Captain?

CAPTAIN'S VOICE: You did it. You did it. Don't lie to me. Don't stand there and lie to me. Confess it!

ROBERTS' VOICE: Confess what, Captain? I don't know what you're talking about.

CAPTAIN'S VOICE: You know damn well what I'm talkin' about because you did it. You've double-crossed me—you've gone back on your word!

ROBERTS' VOICE: No, I haven't, Captain.

CAPTAIN: Yes, by God, you have. I kept my part of the bargain! I gave this crew liberty—I gave this crew liberty, by God, but you've gone back on *your* word.

[DOWDY *takes off his helmet and looks at the men*]

ROBERTS' VOICE: I don't see how you can say that, Captain. I haven't sent in any more letters.

[DOLAN, *on the gun tub ladder, catches* INSIGNA'S *eye*]

CAPTAIN'S VOICE: I'm not talking about your goddamn sons-a-bitchin' letters. I'm talkin' about what you did tonight.

ROBERTS' VOICE: Tonight? I don't understand you, Captain. What do you think I did?

CAPTAIN: Quit saying that, goddammit, quit saying that. You know damn well what you did! You stabbed me in the back! You stabbed me in the back . . . aaa . . . aa . . .

JOHNSON'S VOICE: Captain! Get over to the washbasin, Captain!

CAPTAIN'S VOICE: Aaaaaaa . . .

INSIGNA: What the hell happened?

DOLAN: Quiet!

JOHNSON: [*On mike*] Will the Doctor please report to the Captain's cabin on the double?

[DOC *appears from left, pushing his way through the crowd, followed by two* MEDICAL CORPSMEN *wearing Red Cross brassards and carrying first-aid kits and a stretcher.* DOC *walks slowly; he is idly attaching a brassard and smoking a cigarette. He wears his helmet sloppily*]

DOC: Gangway . . . gangway . . .

DOWDY: Hey, Doc, tell us what's going on.

DOC: Okay. Okay.

[*He enters the* CAPTAIN's *cabin followed by the* CORPSMEN *who leave stretcher leaning against the bulkhead. The door closes. There is a tense pause. The men gather around the cabin again.* LINDSTROM *is at the porthole*]

REBER: Hey, Lindstrom, where's the Old Man?

LINDSTROM: He's sittin' in the chair—leaning way forward.

PAYNE: What's the Doc doin'?

LINDSTROM: He's holdin' the waste basket.

REBER: What waste basket?

LINDSTROM: The one the Old Man's got his head in. And he needs it, too. [*Pause*] They're helpin' him over to the couch. [*Pause*] He's lying down there and they're takin' off his shoes. [*Pause*] Look out, here they come.

[*The men break quickly and rush back to their battle stations. The door opens and* ROBERTS, DOC *and the* CORPSMEN *come out*]

DOC: [*To* CORPSMEN] We won't need that stretcher. Sorry. [*Calls*] Dowdy! Come here.

[DOWDY *comes down to* DOC. *He avoids* ROBERTS' *eyes*]

ROBERTS: Dowdy, pass the word to the crew to secure from General Quarters.

DOC: And tell the men not to make any noise while they go to their bunks. The Captain's resting quietly now, and I think that's desirable.

ROBERTS: Pass the word, will you, Dowdy?

DOWDY: Yes, Mister Roberts.

[*He passes the word to the crew who slowly start to leave their battle stations. They are obviously stalling*]

DOC: [*To* ROBERTS] Got a cigarette? [ROBERTS *reaches in his pocket and offers* DOC *a cigarette. Then he lights* DOC's *cigarette.* DOC *notices the men stalling*] Well, guess I'd better get back inside. I'll be down to see you after I get through.

[*He enters cabin and stands there watching. The men move offstage, very slowly, saying "Good night, Mister Roberts," "Good night, sir." Suddenly* ROBERTS *notices that all the men are saying good night to him*]

DOLAN: [*Quietly*] Good night, Mister Roberts. [ROBERTS *does not hear him*] Good night, Mister Roberts.

ROBERTS: Good night, Dolan.

[DOLAN *smiles and exits down hatch.* ROBERTS *steps toward hatch, removes helmet, looks puzzled as the lights fade out*]

During the darkness, over the squawk box the following announcements are heard:

FIRST VOICE: Now hear this . . . Now hear this . . . C, E and S Divisions and all Pharmacist's Mates will air bedding today—positively!

SECOND VOICE: There is now available at the ship's store a small supply of peanut brittle. Ship's store will be open from 1300 to 1315.

THIRD VOICE: Now, Dolan, Yeoman Second Class, report to the radio shack immediately.

SCENE FIVE

The lights come up on the stateroom of ROBERTS *and* PULVER.
PULVER *is lying in the lower bunk.* DOC *is sitting at the desk
with a glass and a bottle of grain alcohol in front of him.*
ROBERTS *is tying up a sea bag. A small suitcase stands beside
it. His locker is open and empty.* WILEY *picks up the sea bag.*

WILEY: Okay, Mister Roberts, I'll take these down to the gangway.
The boat from the island should be out here any minute for you.
I'll let you know.

ROBERTS: Thanks, Wiley.

WILEY: [*Grinning*] That's okay, Mister Roberts. Never thought
you'd be taking this ride, did you?

[*He exits with the bags*]

ROBERTS: I'm going to be off this bucket before I even wake up.

DOC: They flying you all the way to the *Livingston?*

ROBERTS: I don't know. The radio dispatch just said I was transferred and travel by air if possible. I imagine it's all the way
through. They're landing planes at Okinawa now and that's where
my can is probably running around. [*Laughs a little*] Listen to
me, Doc—my can!

PULVER: [*Studying map by* ROBERTS' *bunk*] Okinawa! Jeez, you be
might-y careful, Doug.

ROBERTS: Okay, Frank. This is *too* much to take, Doc. I even got a
destroyer! The *Livingston!* That's one of the greatest cans out
there.

PULVER: I know a guy on the *Livingston.* He don't think it's so hot.

DOLAN: [*Entering. He has a file folder under his arm*] Here you
are, Mister Roberts. I typed up three copies of the radio dispatch.
I've got to keep a copy and here's two for you. You're now
officially detached from this here bucket. Let me be the first.

ROBERTS: Thanks, Dolan. [*They shake hands.* ROBERTS *takes papers, and looks at them*] Dolan, how about these orders? I haven't sent in a letter for a month!

DOLAN: [*Carefully*] You know how the Navy works, Mister Roberts.

ROBERTS: Yeah, I know, but it doesn't seem . . .

DOLAN: Listen, Mister Roberts, I can tell you exactly what happened. Those guys at the Bureau need men for combat duty awful bad and they started looking through all the old letters and they just come across one of yours.

ROBERTS: Maybe—but still you'd think . . .

DOLAN: Listen, Mister Roberts. We can't stand here beating our gums! You better get cracking! You seen what it said there, "Proceed immediately." And the Old Man says if you ain't off of here in an hour, by God, he's going to throw you off!

ROBERTS: Is that all he said?

DOLAN: That's all he said.

ROBERTS: [*Grinning at* DOC] After fighting this for two years you'd think he'd say more than that . . .

CAPTAIN'S VOICE: [*Offstage*] Be careful of that one. Put it down easy.

DOC: What's that?

DOLAN: A new enlarged botanical garden. That's why he can't even be bothered about you today, Mister Roberts. Soon as we anchored this morning he sent Olsen over with a special detail—they dug up two palm trees . . . He's busy as a mother skunk now and you know what he's done—he's already set a twenty-four-hour watch on these new babies with orders to shoot to kill. [*To* PULVER] That reminds me, Mister Pulver. The Captain wants to see you right away.

PULVER: Yeah? What about?

DOLAN: I don't know, sir. [*To* ROBERTS] I'll be back to say goodbye, Mister Roberts. Come on, Mister Pulver. [*He exits*]

PULVER: [*Following* DOLAN *out*] What the hell did I do with his laundry this week?

[ROBERTS *smiles as he starts putting on his black tie*]

DOC: You're a happy son-of-a-bitch, aren't you?

ROBERTS: Yep. You're happy about it too, aren't you, Doc?

DOC: I think it's the only thing for you. [*Casually*] What do you think of the crew now, Doug?

ROBERTS: We're all right now. I think they're nice guys—all of them.

DOC: Uuh-hunh. And how do you think they feel about you?

ROBERTS: I think they like me all right . . . till the next guy comes along.

DOC: You don't think you're necessary to them?

ROBERTS: [*Sitting on bunk*] Hell, no. No officer's necessary to the crew, Doc.

DOC: Are you going to leave this ship believing that?

ROBERTS: That's nothing against them. A crew's too busy looking after themselves to care about anyone else.

DOC: Well, take a good, deep breath, Buster. [*He drinks some alcohol*] What do you think got you your orders? Prayer and fasting? Sending in enough Wheatie box tops?

ROBERTS: My orders? Why, what Dolan said—one of my old letters turned up . . .

DOC: Bat crap! This crew got you transferred. They were so busy looking out for themselves that they took a chance of landing in prison for five years—any one of them. Since you couldn't send in a letter for transfer, they sent one in for you. Since they knew the Captain wouldn't sign it approved, they didn't bother him—they signed it for him.

ROBERTS: What do you mean? They forged the Captain's name?

DOC: That's right.

ROBERTS: [*Rising*] Doc! Who did? Which one of them?

DOC: That would be hard to say. You see, they had a mass meeting down in the compartment. They put guards at every door. They called it the Captain's-Name-Signing contest. And every man in this crew—a hundred and sixty-seven of them—signed the Captain's name on a blank sheet of paper. And then there were judges who compared these signatures with the Captain's and selected the one to go in. At the time there was some criticism of the decision on the grounds that the judges were drunk, but apparently, from the results, they chose well.

ROBERTS: How'd you find out about this, Doc?

DOC: Well, it was a great honor. I am the only officer aboard who does know. I was a contestant. I was also a judge. This double honor was accorded me because of my character, charm, good looks and because the medical department contributed four gallons of grain alcohol to the contest. [*Pauses*] It was quite a thing to see, Doug. A hundred and sixty-seven guys with only one idea in their heads—to do something for Mister Roberts.

ROBERTS: [*After a moment*] I wish you hadn't told me, Doc. It makes me look pretty silly after what I just said. But I didn't mean it, Doc. I was afraid to say what I really feel. I love those bastards, Doc. I think they're the greatest guys on this earth. All of a sudden I feel that there's something wrong—something terribly wrong—about leaving them. God, what can I say to them?

DOC: You won't say anything—you don't even know. When you're safely aboard your new ship I'm supposed to write and tell you about it. And at the bottom of the letter, I'm supposed to say, "Thanks for the liberty, Mister Roberts. Thanks for everything."

ROBERTS: Jesus!

[PULVER *enters, downcast*]

PULVER: I'm the new Cargo Officer. And that's not all—I got to have dinner with him tonight. He *likes* me!

[*There is a polite rap on the door*]

DOC: Come in. [*Enter* PAYNE, REBER, GERHART, SCHLEMMER, DOLAN *and* INSIGNA, *all carrying canteen cups except* INSIGNA *whose cup is in his belt. He carries a large, red fire extinguisher*] What's this?

INSIGNA: Fire and rescue squad. Heard you had a fire in here.

[*All are looking at* ROBERTS]

ROBERTS: No, but—since you're here—I—

INSIGNA: Hell, we got a false alarm then. Happens all the time. [*Sets extinguisher on desk*] In that case, we might as well drink this stuff. Give me your glass, Mister Roberts, and I'll put a head on it—yours too, Doc. I got one for you, Mister Pulver.

[*He fills their glasses from the fire extinguisher*]

ROBERTS: What's in that, a new batch of jungle juice?

INSIGNA: Yeah, in the handy, new, portable container. Everybody loaded?

[*All nod*]

DOLAN: Go ahead, Sam.

INSIGNA: [*To* ROBERTS] There's a story going around that you're leaving us. That right?

ROBERTS: [*Carefully*] That's right, Sam. And I . . .

INSIGNA: Well, we didn't want you to get away without having a little drink with us and we thought we ought to give you a little sort of going-away present. The fellows made it down in the machine shop. It ain't much but we hope you like it. [REBER *prompts him*] We all sincerely hope you like it. [*Calls offstage*] All right, you bastards, you can come in now.

[*Enter* LINDSTROM, MANNION, DOWDY *and* STEFANOWSKI. MANNION *is carrying a candy box. He walks over to* ROBERTS *shyly and hands him the box*]

ROBERTS: What is it?

SCHLEMMER: Open it.

[ROBERTS *opens the box. There is a deep silence*]

PULVER: What is it, Doug?

[ROBERTS *holds up the box. In it is a brass medal shaped like a palm tree attached to a piece of gaudy ribbon*]

LINDSTROM: It's a palm tree, see.

DOLAN: It was Dowdy's idea.

DOWDY: Mannion here made it. He cut it out of sheet brass down in the machine shop.

INSIGNA: Mannion drilled the words on it, too.

MANNION: Stefanowski thought up the words.

STEFANOWSKI: [*Shoving* LINDSTROM *forward*] Lindstrom gets credit for the ribbon from a box of candy that his sister-in-law sent him. Read the words, Mister Roberts.

ROBERTS: [*With difficulty*] "Order . . . order of . . ."

[*He hands the medal to* DOC]

DOC: [*Rises and reads solemnly*] "Order of the palm. To Lieutenant (jg) Douglas Roberts for action against the enemy, above and beyond the call of duty on the night of eight May 1945."

[*He passes the medal back to* ROBERTS]

ROBERTS: [*After a moment—smiling*] It's very nice but I'm afraid you've got the wrong guy.

[*The men turn to* DOWDY, *grinning*]

DOWDY: We know that, but we'd kinda like for you to have it anyway.

ROBERTS: All right, I'll keep it.

[*The men beam. There is an awkward pause*]

GERHART: Stefanowski thought up the words.

ROBERTS: They're fine words.

[WILEY *enters*]

WILEY: The boat's here, Mister Roberts. I put your gear in. They want to shove off right away.

ROBERTS: [*Rising*] Thanks. We haven't had our drink yet.

REBER: No, we ain't.

[*All get to their feet.* ROBERTS *picks up his glass, looks at the crew, and everyone drinks*]

ROBERTS: Good-bye, Doc.

DOC: Good-bye, Doug.

ROBERTS: And thanks, Doc.

DOC: Okay.

ROBERTS: Good-bye, Frank.

PULVER: Good-bye, Doug.

ROBERTS: Remember, I'm counting on you.

[PULVER *nods.* ROBERTS *turns to the crew and looks at them for a moment. Then he takes the medal from the box, pins it on his shirt, shows it to them, then gives a little gestured salute and exits as the lights fade out*]

During the darkness we hear voices making announcements over the squawk box:

FIRST VOICE: Now hear this . . . now hear this . . . Sweepers, man your brooms. Clean sweep-down fore and aft!

SECOND VOICE: Now hear this! All men put on report today will fall in on the quarter-deck—and form three ranks!

THIRD VOICE: Now hear this! All divisions will draw their mail at 1700—in the mess hall.

SCENE SIX

The lights come up showing the main set at sunset. DOC *is sitting on the hatch, reading a letter.* MANNION, *wearing sidearms, is pacing up and down in front of the* CAPTAIN'S *cabin. On each side of the door is a small palm tree in a five-gallon can—on one can is painted in large white letters, "Keep Away"; on the other, "This Means You." After a moment,* PULVER *enters from the left passageway, carrying a small packet of letters.*

PULVER: Hello, Mannion. Got your mail yet?

MANNION: No. I've got the palm tree watch.

PULVER: Oh. [*To* DOC] What's your news, Doc?

DOC: My wife got some new wallpaper for the living room.

[PULVER *sits on hatch cover*. DOWDY *enters wearing work gloves*]

DOWDY: Mister Pulver, we'll be finished with the cargo in a few minutes.

PULVER: How'd it go?

DOWDY: Not bad. I've got to admit you were right about Number Three hold. It worked easier out of there. Mister Pulver, I just found out what the Captain decided—he ain't going to show a movie again tonight.

PULVER: Why not?

DOWDY: He's still punishing us because he caught Reber without a shirt on two days ago. You've got to go in and see him.

PULVER: I did. I asked him to show a movie yesterday.

DOWDY: Mister Pulver, what the hell good does that do us today? You've got to keep needlin' that guy—I'm tellin' you.

PULVER: Don't worry. I'll take care of it in my own way.

DOWDY: [*Going off, but speaking loud enough to be heard*] Oh, God, no movie again tonight.

[DOWDY *exits*. PULVER *starts looking at his packet of mail*]

PULVER: [*Looking at first letter*] This is from my mother. All she ever says is stay away from Japan. [*He drops it on the hatch cover*] This is from Alabama. [*Puts it in his pocket and pats it. Looks at third letter*] Doc! This is from Doug!

DOC: Yeah? [PULVER *rips open the envelope*] What does he say?

PULVER: [*Reading*] "This will be short and sweet, as we're shoving off in about two minutes . . ." [*Pauses and remarks*] This is dated three weeks ago.

DOC: Does he say where he is?

PULVER: Yeah. He says: "My guess about the location of this ship was just exactly right." [*Looks up*] That means he's around Okinawa all right! [*Reads on and chuckles*] He's met Fornell. That's that friend of mine . . . a guy named Fornell I went to college with. Listen to this: "Fornell says that you and he used to load up your car with liquor in Omaha and then sell it at an indecent profit to the fraternity boys at Iowa City. How about that?" We did, too. [*Smiles happily*] "This part is for Doc." [DOC *gestures for him to read it*] "I've been aboard this destroyer for two weeks now and we've already been through four air attacks. I'm in the war at last, Doc. I've caught up with that task force that passed me by. I'm glad to be here. I had to be here, I guess. But I'm thinking now of you, Doc, and you, Frank, and Dolan and Dowdy and Insigna and everyone else on that bucket—all the guys everywhere who sail from Tedium to Apathy and back again— with an occasional side trip to Monotony. This is a tough crew on here, and they have a wonderful battle record. But I've discovered, Doc, that the most terrible enemy of this war is the boredom that eventually becomes a faith and, therefore, a sort of suicide—and I know now that the ones who refuse to surrender to it are the strongest of all.

"Right now, I'm looking at something that's hanging over my desk: a preposterous hunk of brass attached to the most bilious piece of ribbon I've ever seen. I'd rather have it than the Congressional Medal of Honor. It tells me what I'll always be proudest of—that at a time in the world when courage counted most, I lived among a hundred and sixty-seven brave men.

"So, Doc, and especially you, Frank, don't let those guys down. Of course, I know that by this time they must be very happy because the Captain's overhead is filled with marbles and . . ." [*He avoids* DOC's *eyes*] "Oh, hell, here comes the mail orderly. This has to go now. I'll finish it later. Meanwhile you bastards can write too, can't you?

"Doug."

DOC: Can I see that, Frank?

[PULVER *hands him the letter, looks at the front of his next letter and says quietly:*]

PULVER: Well, for God's sake, this is from Fornell!

DOC: [*Reading* ROBERTS' *letter to himself*] ". . . I'd rather have it than the Congressional Medal of Honor." I'm glad he found that out. [*He looks at* PULVER, *sensing something wrong*] What's the matter? [PULVER *does not answer*] What's the matter, Frank?

[PULVER *looks at him slowly as* DOWDY *enters*]

DOWDY: All done, Mister Pulver. We've secured the hatch cover. No word on the movie, I suppose.

DOC: [*Louder, with terror*] Frank, what is it?

PULVER: Mister Roberts is dead. [*Looks at letter*] This is from Fornell . . . They took a Jap suicide plane. It killed everyone in a twin-forty battery and then it went on through and killed Doug and another officer in the wardroom. [*Pause*] They were drinking coffee when it hit.

DOWDY: [*Quietly*] Mister Pulver, can I please give that letter to the crew?

DOC: No. [*Holding out* ROBERTS' *letter*] Give them this one. It's theirs. [DOWDY *removes gloves and takes the letter from* DOC *and goes off*] Coffee . . .

[PULVER *gets up restlessly.* DOC *stares straight ahead.* PULVER *straightens. He seems to grow. He walks casually over to* MANNION]

PULVER: [*In a friendly voice*] Go on down and get your mail. I'll stand by for you.

MANNION: [*Surprised*] You will? Okay, thanks, Mister Pulver.

[MANNION *disappears down hatch. As soon as he exits* PULVER *very calmly jerks the rooted palms, one by one, from their containers and throws them over the side.* DOC *looks up to see* PULVER *pull second tree.* DOC *ducks as tree goes past him. Then* PULVER *knocks loudly on the* CAPTAIN's *door*]

CAPTAIN: [*Offstage. His voice is very truculent*] Yeah. Who is it?

PULVER: Captain, this is Ensign Pulver. I just threw your palm trees overboard. Now what's all this crap about no movie tonight?

[*He throws the door open, banging it against the bulkhead, and is entering the* CAPTAIN's *cabin as the curtain falls*]

THE ROSE TATTOO

Tennessee Williams

Tennessee Williams

As Tennessee Williams admitted in various interviews of the period, *The Rose Tattoo* "was inspired by the vitality, warmth and unquenchable ebulliance of the Italian people" as he came to know them during an extensive stay in Italy. Perhaps because of this the play is not only more robust than most of his previous works, but is a comedy-drama in which laughter seasons violent emotions and concludes on an optimistic note.

The play opened on February 3, 1951, "to the thunderous acclaim of the first night audience." Most critics were equally enthusiastic. Brooks Atkinson reported in the New York *Times* that *The Rose Tattoo* was "original, imaginative and tender . . . The respect for character and the quality of the writing are Mr. Williams at the top of his form." In his coverage for the New York *Herald Tribune*, Otis L. Guernsey, Jr., declared: "It is a rare and warm experience, distinguished in form and striking in effect . . . and certainly the finest new American play of the season."

Whitney Bolton imparted to the readers of *The Morning Telegraph*: "If I had a bucket of paint and a brush I'd daub up every sidewalk within eight blocks of the Martin Beck Theatre and tell people to go see *The Rose Tattoo*, the new play by Tennessee Williams. Best I can do at the moment is to say it in print . . . Mr. Williams' new play concerns itself, as most of his work does, with the tragedies and exaltations of little people, with the glory that they can make for themselves and the disaster they can create for themselves. He writes with singular power, with vast, sweeping compassion for his people and a breadth of understanding rare in the literature of the theatre."

Other first-night jurors concurred that "Williams has written a drama that is brimful of feeling, packed with power, and enlivened by shrapnel bursts of homey humor . . . It is easily the lushest, most provocative, most original and the best play this season has uncovered."

In addition to the play's winning the 1951 Tony Award, the production garnered five additional citations: including one for its author; the two leading players, Maureen Stapleton and Eli Wallach; the producer, Cheryl Crawford; and scenic designer Boris Aronson. It also was chosen as one of the ten best plays of the 1950–51 season and ran for 306 performances.

In 1966, the play was revived at the New York City Center with Miss Stapleton repeating her role of Serafina Delle Rose and Harry Guardino as Alvaro. After a successful limited engagement at the municipal playhouse, the production was transferred to the Billy Rose Theatre for an extended run.

A film of *The Rose Tattoo* was released in 1955, with Anna Magnani and Burt Lancaster as co-stars. The role of Serafina won for Miss Magnani the 1955 Academy Award for Best Actress. According to Nathalie Fredrik's informative book, *Hollywood and the Academy Awards*: "Among her many admirers was Tennessee Williams, and he wrote a stage play for her, *The Rose Tattoo*. Magnani was a stage veteran in Italy . . . But she was hesitant to try Broadway, fearing her English wasn't up to the task.

"In 1955, she did agree to do the movie. Her English proved adequate and, as the Sicilian-born seamstress who shuts up in her own neurotic, grieving world when her husband dies, then emerges with a vengeance when she becomes enamored of a simple-minded truckdriver (Burt Lancaster), her portrayal was frenzied, yet believable. She was a screaming, object-throwing virago one moment, a deeply loving woman, the next, and she won both the Oscar and the New York Film Critics best actress citation for it."

The life and career of Tennessee Williams (born Thomas Lanier Williams in Columbus, Mississippi, on March 26, 1911) have been so thoroughly documented in countless periodicals and books, as well as in critical and biographical studies, that there seems little need for reiteration in the pages of this collection. Merely to list Mr. Williams' plays is sufficient for the evocation of many memorable moments in the theatre, for he has peopled the world's stages with characters so durably vibrant that their presences still stalk the corridors of a playgoer's memory.

Named by *Time* magazine as "the greatest living playwright in the Western World," Tennessee Williams, recipient of two Pulitzer prizes and four New York Drama Critics' Circle awards, remains, indisputably, a consummate master of theatre. His plays pulsate with the heart's blood of the drama: passion. When one re-examines Mr.

Williams' predominant works, one cannot but be awed by the dazzling skill of a remarkable dramatist whose major plays no longer tend to be merely plays but, somehow, through the process of creative genius, have transcended into haunting realities.

Tennessee Williams is, at his best, an electrifying dramatist because, in the main, he creates people who are the sort who breathe fire into scenes, explosively and woundingly. His dialogue reverberates with a lilting eloquence far from the drab, disjunctive patterns of everyday speech and, above all, he is a master of mood. At times, it is hot, oppressive, simmering with catastrophe as in *A Streetcar Named Desire* and *Cat on a Hot Tin Roof*; at other times, it is sad, autumnal, elegiac as in *The Glass Menagerie* and *The Night of the Iguana*, or brimming over with passion tempered by laughter as in *The Rose Tattoo*. To achieve it, he utilizes the full complement of theatrical instruments: setting, lighting, music, plus that most intangible of gifts, the genuis for making an audience forget that any other world exists except the one on stage.

As Mr. Williams often has stated, his special compassion is for "the people who are not meant to win—the lost, the odd, the strange, the difficult people—fragile people who lack talons for the jungle." The clarion call of many, if not most, of his plays is loneliness. Just as the captured iguana in *The Night of the Iguana* symbolizes the bondage to which the people who populate the play are chained, so do his characters in others of his dramas yearn to break loose, out of the cell of the lonely self, to touch and reach another person. "Hell is yourself," Mr. Williams has said. "When you ignore other people completely, that is hell." The revelation toward which all of his plays aspire is that "moment of self-transcendence, when a person puts himself aside to feel deeply for another person."

The author first won general recognition with the 1945 production of *The Glass Menagerie*, starring Laurette Taylor. Thereafter, he attained worldwide repute with a succession of impressive plays, notably: *A Streetcar Named Desire* (1947); *Summer and Smoke* (1948); *The Rose Tattoo* (1951); *Cat on a Hot Tin Roof* (1955); and *The Night of the Iguana* (1961). Among his other plays in nonchronological order: *Sweet Bird of Youth*; *Camino Real*; *Orpheus Descending*; *Period of Adjustment*; *The Milk Train Doesn't Stop Here Anymore*; *Kingdom of Earth* (known in its Broadway manifestation as *The Seven Descents of Myrtle*); *In the Bar of a Tokyo Hotel*; *Out Cry*; and *Small Craft Warnings*, in which he made his first (and, as he has indicated, his last) appearance as an actor. Two of his most recent plays *This Is (An Entertainment)* was tested in San Francisco in 1976, while *The Red Devil Battery Sign* foundered in Boston during its 1975 pre-Broadway tryout tour. Reportedly, the author presently is revising the drama for a new production.

Mr. Williams also has written a number of short plays, including: *27 Wagons Full of Cotton; This Property Is Condemned; I Rise in Flame, Cried the Phoenix; The Lady of Larkspur Lotion; The Last of My Solid Gold Watches; Moony's Kid Don't Cry; Suddenly Last Summer; Slapstick Tragedy (The Mutilated and The Gnädiges Fräulein); I Can't Imagine Tomorrow; The Frosted Glass Coffin;* and *A Perfect Analysis Given by a Parrot.* Additionally, he has published several volumes of short stories, a book of poetry and a novella, *The Roman Spring of Mrs. Stone.* In 1975, he published his *Memoirs* which remained on the best seller list for a number of months.

A firm disciplinarian where his work is concerned, the dramatist dedicates four hours of each day—"year in, year out"—to writing and about every two years completes a new play. Before settling down to the actual task of writing, however, he "marinates impressions, characters, experiences."

In 1969, Tennessee Williams received a Gold Medal for Drama from the prestigious National Institute of Arts and Letters and, more recently, he was given the National Theatre Conference Annual Award honoring his "countless contributions to the American theatre spanning the past three decades."

The *Rose Tattoo* was first presented by Cheryl Crawford on February 3, 1951, at the Martin Beck Theatre, New York. The cast was as follows:

SALVATORE	*Salvatore Mineo*
VIVI	*Judy Ratner*
BRUNO	*Salvatore Taormina*
ASSUNTA	*Ludmilla Toretzka*
ROSA DELLE ROSE	*Phyllis Love*
SERAFINA DELLE ROSE	*Maureen Stapleton*
ESTELLE HOHENGARTEN	*Sonia Sorel*
THE STREGA	*Daisy Belmore*
GIUSEPPINA	*Rossana San Marco*
PEPPINA	*Augusta Merighi*
VIOLETTA	*Vivian Nathan*
MARIELLA	*Penny Santon*
TERESA	*Nancy Franklin*
FATHER DE LEO	*Robert Carricart*
A DOCTOR	*Andrew Duggan*
MISS YORKE	*Dorrit Kelton*
FLORA	*Jane Hoffman*
BESSIE	*Florence Sundstrom*
JACK HUNTER	*Don Murray*
THE SALESMAN	*Eddie Hyans*
ALVARO MANGIACAVALLO	*Eli Wallach*
A MAN	*David Stewart*
ANOTHER MAN	*Martin Balsam*

Directed by Daniel Mann
Setting by Boris Aronson
Music by David Diamond
Production Associate: Bea Lawrence
Assistant to Producer: Paul Bigelow

ACT ONE

Scene 1: Evening.
Scene 2: Almost morning, the next day.
Scene 3: Noon of that day.
Scene 4: A late spring morning, three years later.
Scene 5: Immediately following.
Scene 6: Two hours later that day.

ACT TWO

Scene 1: Two hours later that day.

ACT THREE

Scene 1: Evening of the same day.
Scene 2: Just before dawn of the next day.
Scene 3: Morning.

ACT ONE

SCENE ONE

The locale of the play is a village populated mostly by Sicilians somewhere along the Gulf Coast between New Orleans and Mobile. The time is the present.

As the curtain rises we hear a Sicilian folk-singer with a guitar. He is singing. At each major division of the play this song is resumed and it is completed at the final curtain.

The first lighting is extremely romantic. We see a frame cottage, in a rather poor state of repair, with a palm tree leaning dreamily over one end of it and a flimsy little entrance porch, with spindling pillars, sagging steps and broken rails, at the other end. The setting seems almost tropical, for, in addition to the palm trees, there are tall canes with feathery fronds and a fairly thick growth of pampas grass. These are growing on the slope of an embankment along which runs a highway, which is not visible, but the cars passing on it can occasionally be heard. The house has a rear door which cannot be seen. The facing wall of the cottage is either a transparency that lifts for the interior scenes, or is cut away to reveal the interior.

The romantic first lighting is that of late dusk, the sky a delicate blue with an opalescent shimmer more like water than air. Delicate points of light appear and disappear like lights reflected in a twilight harbor. The curtain rises well above the low tin roof of the cottage.

We see an interior that is as colorful as a booth at a carnival. There are many religious articles and pictures of ruby and gilt, the brass cage of a gaudy parrot, a large bowl of goldfish, cutglass decanters and vases, rose-patterned wallpaper and a rose-colored carpet; everything is exclamatory in its brightness like the projection of a woman's heart passionately in love.

*There is a small shrine against the wall between the rooms,
consisting of a prie-dieu and a little statue of the Madonna in
a starry blue robe and gold crown. Before this burns always a
vigil light in its ruby glass cup. Our purpose is to show these
gaudy, childlike mysteries with sentiment and humor in equal
measure, without ridicule and with respect for the religious
yearnings they symbolize.*

An outdoor sign indicates that SERAFINA, *whose home the cottage is, does* "SEWING." *The interior furnishings give evidence
of this vocation. The most salient feature is a collection of
dressmaker's dummies. There are at least seven of these life-
size mannequins, in various shapes and attitudes. (They will
have to be made especially for the play as their purpose is not
realistic. They have pliable joints so that their positions can
be changed. Their arms terminate at the wrist. In all their attitudes there is an air of drama, somewhat like the poses of
declamatory actresses of the old school.) Principal among
them are a widow and a bride who face each other in violent
attitudes, as though having a shrill argument, in the parlor.
The widow's costume is complete from black-veiled hat to
black slippers. The bride's featureless head wears a chaplet of
orange blossoms from which is depended a flowing veil of
white marquisette, and her net gown is trimmed in white satin
—lustrous, immaculate.*

*Most of the dummies and sewing equipment are confined to
the dining room which is also* SERAFINA's *work room. In that
room there is a tall cupboard on top of which are several
dusty bottles of imported Sicilian Spumanti.*

*It is the hour that the Italians call "prima sera," the begin-
ning of dusk. Between the house and the palm tree burns the
female star with an almost emerald lustre.*

*The mothers of the neighborhood are beginning to call their
children home to supper, in voices near and distant, urgent
and tender, like the variable notes of wind and water. There
are three children:* BRUNO, SALVATORE, *and* VIVI, *ranged in
front of the house, one with a red paper kite, one with a
hoop, and the little girl with a doll dressed as a clown. They
are in attitudes of momentary repose, all looking up at something—a bird or a plane passing over—as the mother's voices
call them.*

BRUNO: The white flags are flying at the Coast Guard station.

SALVATORE: That means fair weather.

VIVI: I love fair weather.

GIUSEPPINA: Vivi! Vivi mangiare!

PEPPINA: Salvatore! Come home!

VIOLETTA: Bruno! Come home to supper!

[*The calls are repeated tenderly, musically.*
The interior of the house begins to be visible. SERAFINA
DELLE ROSE *is seen on the parlor sofa, waiting for her husband
Rosario's return. Between the curtains is a table set lovingly
for supper; there is wine in a silver ice-bucket and a great
bowl of roses.*
SERAFINA *looks like a plump little Italian opera singer in the
role of Madame Butterfly. Her black hair is done in a high
pompadour that glitters like wet coal. A rose is held in place
by glittering jet hairpins. Her voluptuous figure is sheathed in
pale rose silk. On her feet are dainty slippers with glittering
buckles and French heels. It is apparent from the way she sits,
with such plump dignity, that she is wearing a tight girdle.
She sits very erect, in an attitude of forced composure, her ankles daintily crossed and her plump little hands holding a yellow paper fan on which is painted a rose. Jewels gleam on her
fingers, her wrists and her ears and about her throat. Expect-
ancy shines in her eyes. For a few moments she seems to be
posing for a picture.*
ROSA DELLE ROSE *appears at the side of the house, near the
palm tree.* ROSA, *the daughter of the house, is a young girl of
twelve. She is pretty and vivacious, and has about her a particular intensity in every gesture*]

SERAFINA: Rosa, where are you?

ROSA: Here, Mama.

SERAFINA: What are you doing, cara?

ROSA: I've caught twelve lightning bugs.

[*The cracked voice of* ASSUNTA *is heard, approaching*]

SERAFINA: I hear Assunta! Assunta!

[ASSUNTA *appears and goes into the house,* ROSA *following her in.* ASSUNTA *is an old woman in a grey shawl, bearing a basket of herbs, for she is a* fattuchiere, *a woman who practises a simple sort of medicine. As she enters the children scatter*]

ASSUNTA: Vengo, vengo. Buona sera. Buona sera. There is something wild in the air, no wind but everything's moving.

SERAFINA: I don't see nothing moving and neither do you.

ASSUNTA: Nothing is moving so you can see it moving, but everything is moving, and I can hear the star-noises. Hear them? Hear the star-noises?

SERAFINA: Naw, them ain't the star-noises. They're termites, eating the house up. What are you peddling, old woman, in those little white bags?

ASSUNTA: Powder, wonderful powder. You drop a pinch of it in your husband's coffee.

SERAFINA: What is it good for?

ASSUNTA: What is a husband good for! I make it out of the dry blood of a goat.

SERAFINA: Davvero!

ASSUNTA: Wonderful stuff! But be sure you put it in his coffee at supper, not in his breakfast coffee.

SERAFINA: My husband don't need no powder!

ASSUNTA: Excuse me, Baronessa. Maybe he needs the opposite kind of a powder, I got that, too.

SERAFINA: Naw, naw, *no* kind of powder at all, old woman.

[*She lifts her head with a proud smile*]

[*Outside the sound of a truck is heard approaching up on the highway*]

ROSA: [*Joyfully*] Papa's truck!

[*They stand listening for a moment, but the truck goes by without stopping*]

SERAFINA: [*To* ASSUNTA] That wasn't him. It wasn't no 10-ton truck. It didn't rattle the shutters! Assunta, Assunta, undo a couple of hooks, the dress is tight on me!

ASSUNTA: Is it true what I told you?

SERAFINA: Yes, it is true, but nobody needed to tell me. Assunta, I'll tell you something which maybe you won't believe.

ASSUNTA: It is impossible to tell me anything that I don't believe.

SERAFINA: Va bene! Senti, Assunta!—I knew that I had conceived on the very night of conception!

[*There is a phrase of music as she says this*]

ASSUNTA: Ahhhh?

SERAFINA: Senti! That night I woke up with a burning pain on me, here, on my left breast! A pain like a needle, quick, quick, hot little stitches. I turned on the light, I uncovered my breast!—On it I saw the rose tattoo of my husband!

ASSUNTA: Rosario's tattoo?

SERAFINA: On me, on my breast, his tattoo! And when I saw it I knew that I had conceived . . .

[SERAFINA *throws her head back, smiling proudly, and opens her paper fan.* ASSUNTA *stares at her gravely, then rises and hands her basket to* SERAFINA]

ASSUNTA: Ecco! *You* sell the powders!

[*She starts toward the door*]

SERAFINA: You don't believe that I saw it?

ASSUNTA: [*Stopping*] Did Rosario see it?

SERAFINA: I screamed. But when he woke up, it was gone. It only lasted a moment. But I *did* see it, and I *did* know, when I seen it, that I had conceived, that in my body another rose was growing!

ASSUNTA: Did he believe that you saw it?

SERAFINA: No. He laughed.—He laughed and I cried . . .

ASSUNTA: And he took you into his arms, and you stopped crying!

SERAFINA: Si!

ASSUNTA: Serafina, for you everything has got to be different. A sign, a miracle, a wonder of some kind. You speak to Our Lady. You say that She answers your questions. She nods or shakes Her head at you. Look, Serafina, underneath Our Lady you have a candle. The wind through the shutters makes the candle flicker. The shadows move. Our Lady seems to be nodding!

SERAFINA: She gives me signs.

ASSUNTA: Only to you? Because you are more important? The wife of a barone? Serafina! In Sicily they called his uncle a baron, but in Sicily everybody's a baron that owns a piece of the land and a separate house for the goats!

SERAFINA: They said to his uncle "Voscenza!" and they kissed their hands to him!

[*She kisses the back of her hand repeatedly, with vehemence*]

ASSUNTA: His uncle in Sicily!—Si—But *here* what's he do? Drives a truck of bananas?

SERAFINA: [*Blurting out*] No! *Not* bananas!

ASSUNTA: Not bananas?

SERAFINA: Stai zitta! [*She makes a warning gesture*]—No—Vieni qui, Assunta!

[*She beckons her mysteriously. Assunta approaches*]

ASSUNTA: Cosa dici?

SERAFINA: On top of the truck is bananas! But underneath—something else!

ASSUNTA: Che altre cose?

SERAFINA: Whatever it is that the Brothers Romano want hauled out of the state, he hauls it for them, underneath the bananas! [*She nods her head importantly*] And money, he gets so much it spills from his pockets! Soon I don't have to make dresses!

ASSUNTA: [*Turning away*] Soon I think you will have to make a black veil!

SERAFINA: Tonight is the last time he does it! Tomorrow he quits hauling stuff for the Brothers Romano! He pays for the 10-ton truck and works for himself. We live with dignity in America, then! Own truck! Own house! And in the house will be everything electric! Stove—deep-freeze—*tutto!*—But tonight, stay with me . . . I can't swallow my heart!—Not till I hear the truck stop in front of the house and his key in the lock of the door!—When I call him, and him shouting back, "*Si, sono qui!*" In his hair, Assunta, he has—oil of roses. And when I wake up at night—the air, the dark room's—full of—roses . . . Each time is the first time with him. Time doesn't pass . . .

[ASSUNTA *picks up a small clock on the cupboard and holds it to her ear*]

ASSUNTA: Tick, tick, tick, tick.—You say the clock is a liar.

SERAFINA: No, the clock is a fool. I don't listen to it. My clock is my heart and my heart don't say tick-tick, it says love-love! And now I have two hearts in me, both of them saying love-love!

[*A truck is heard approaching, then passes.* SERAFINA *drops her fan.* ASSUNTA *opens a bottle of Spumanti with a loud pop.* SERAFINA *cries out*]

ASSUNTA: Stai tranquilla! Calmati! [*She pours her a glass of wine*] Drink this wine and before the glass is empty he'll be in your arms!

SERAFINA: I can't—swallow my heart!

ASSUNTA: A woman must not have a heart that is too big to swallow!

[*She crosses to the door*]

SERAFINA: Stay with me!

ASSUNTA: I have to visit a woman who drank rat poison because of a heart too big for her to swallow.

[ASSUNTA *leaves.* SERAFINA *returns indolently to the sofa. She lifts her hands to her great swelling breasts and murmurs aloud:*]

SERAFINA: Oh, it's so wonderful, having *two* lives in the body, not *one* but two! [*Her hands slide down to her belly, luxuriously*] I am heavy with life, I am big, big, big with life!

[*She picks up a bowl of roses and goes into the back room*]

[ESTELLE HOHENGARTEN *appears in front of the house. She is a thin blonde woman in a dress of Egyptian design, and her blonde hair has an unnatural gloss in the clear, greenish dusk.* ROSA *appears from behind the house, calling out:*]

ROSA: Twenty lightning bugs, Mama!

ESTELLE: Little girl? Little girl?

ROSA: [*Resentfully*] Are you talking to me?

[*There is a pause*]

ESTELLE: Come here. [*She looks* ROSA *over curiously*] You're a twig off the old rose-bush.—Is the lady that does the sewing in the house?

ROSA: Mama's at home.

ESTELLE: I'd like to see her.

ROSA: Mama?

SERAFINA: Dimi?

ROSA: There's a lady to see you.

SERAFINA: Oh. Tell her to wait in the parlor. [ESTELLE *enters and stares curiously about. She picks up a small framed picture on the cupboard. She is looking at it as* SERAFINA *enters with a bowl of roses.* SERAFINA *speaks sharply*] That is my husband's picture.

ESTELLE: Oh!—I thought it was Valentino.—With a mustache.

SERAFINA: [*Putting the bowl down on the table*] You want something?

ESTELLE: Yes. I heard you do sewing.

SERAFINA: Yes, I do sewing.

ESTELLE: How fast can you make a shirt for me?

SERAFINA: That all depends.

[*She takes the picture from* ESTELLE *and puts it back on the cupboard*]

ESTELLE: I got the piece of silk with me. I want it made into a shirt for a man I'm in love with. Tomorrow's the anniversary of the day we met . . .

[*She unwraps a piece of rose-colored silk which she holds up like a banner*]

SERAFINA: [*Involuntarily*] Che bella stoffa!—Oh, that would be wonderful stuff for a lady's blouse or for a pair of pyjamas!

ESTELLE: I want a man's shirt made with it.

SERAFINA: Silk this color for a shirt for a *man*?

ESTELLE: This man is wild like a Gypsy.

SERAFINA: A woman should not encourage a man to be wild.

ESTELLE: A man that's wild is hard for a woman to hold, huh? But if he was tame—would the woman want to hold him? Huh?

SERAFINA: I am a married woman in business. I don't know nothing about wild men and wild women and I don't have much time— so . . .

ESTELLE: I'll pay you twice what you ask me.

[*Outside there is the sound of the goat bleating and the jingle of its harness; then the crash of wood splintering*]

ROSA: [*Suddenly appearing at the door*] Mama, the black goat is loose!

[*She runs down the steps and stands watching the goat.* SERAFINA *crosses to the door*]

THE STREGA: [*In the distance*] Hyeh, Billy, hyeh, hyeh, Billy!

ESTELLE: I'll pay you three times the price that you ask me for it.

SERAFINA: [*Shouting*] Watch the goat! Don't let him get in our yard! [*To* ESTELLE]—If I ask you five dollars?

ESTELLE: I will pay you fifteen. Make it twenty; money is not the object. But it's got to be ready tomorrow.

SERAFINA: Tomorrow?

ESTELLE: Twenty-five dollars! [SERAFINA *nods slowly with a stunned look.* ESTELLE *smiles*] I've got the measurements with me.

SERAFINA: Pin the measurements and your name on the silk and the shirt will be ready tomorrow.

ESTELLE: My name is Estelle Hohengarten.

[*A little boy races excitedly into the yard*]

THE BOY: Rosa, Rosa, the black goat's in your yard!

ROSA: [*Calling*] Mama, the goat's in the yard!

SERAFINA: [*Furiously, forgetting her visitor*] Il becco della strega! —Scusi! [*She runs out onto the porch*] Catch him, catch him before he gets at the vines!

[ROSA *dances gleefully. The* STREGA *runs into the yard. She has a mop of wild grey hair and is holding her black skirts up from her bare hairy legs. The sound of the goat's bleating and the jingling of his harness is heard in the windy blue dusk.*
SERAFINA *descends the porch steps. The high-heeled slippers, the tight silk skirt and the dignity of a baronessa make the descent a little gingerly. Arrived in the yard, she directs the goat-chase imperiously with her yellow paper fan, pointing this way and that, exclaiming in Italian.*
She fans herself rapidly and crosses back of the house. The goat evidently makes a sudden charge. Screaming, SERAFINA *rushes back to the front of the house, all out of breath, the glittering pompadour beginning to tumble down over her forehead*]

SERAFINA: Rosa! You go in the house! Don't look at the Strega!

[*All alone in the parlor,* ESTELLE *takes the picture of Rosario. Impetuously, she thrusts it in her purse and runs from the house, just as* SERAFINA *returns to the front yard*]

ROSA: [*Refusing to move*] Why do you call her a witch?

[SERAFINA *seizes her daughter's arm and propels her into the* *house*]

SERAFINA: She has a white eye and every finger is crooked.

[*She pulls* ROSA's *arm*]

ROSA: She has a cataract, Mama, and her fingers are crooked because she has rheumatism!

SERAFINA: Malocchio—the evil eye—*that's* what she's got! And her fingers are crooked because she shook hands with the devil. Go in the house and wash your face with salt water and throw the salt water away! *Go in! Quick!* She's coming!

[*The boy utters a cry of triumph.*

SERAFINA *crosses abruptly to the porch. At the same moment the boys runs triumphantly around the house leading the captured goat by its bell harness. It is a middle-sized black goat with great yellow eyes. The* STREGA *runs behind with the broken rope. As the grotesque little procession runs before her— the* STREGA, *the goat and the children—*SERAFINA *cries out shrilly. She crouches over and covers her face. The* STREGA *looks back at her with a derisive cackle*]

SERAFINA: Malocchio! Malocchio!

[*Shielding her face with one hand,* SERAFINA *makes the sign of the horns with the other to ward off the evil eye. And the scene dims out*]

SCENE TWO

It is just before dawn the next day. FATHER DE LEO, *a priest, and several black-shawled women, including* ASSUNTA, *are standing outside the house. The interior of the house is very dim.*

GIUSEPPINA: There is a light in the house.

PEPPINA: I hear the sewing machine!

VIOLETTA: There's Serafina! She's working. She's holding up a piece of rose-colored silk.

ASSUNTA: She hears our voices.

VIOLETTA: She's dropped the silk to the floor and she's . . .

GIUSEPPINA: Holding her throat! I think she . . .

PEPPINA: Who's going to tell her?

VIOLETTA: Father De Leo will tell her.

FATHER DE LEO: I think a woman should tell her. I think Assunta must tell her that Rosario is dead.

ASSUNTA: It will not be necessary. She will know when she sees us.

[It grows lighter inside the house. SERAFINA is standing in a frozen attitude with her hand clutching her throat and her eyes staring fearfully toward the sound of voices]

ASSUNTA: I think she already knows what we have come to tell her!

FATHER DE LEO: Andiamo, Signore! We must go to the door.

[They climb the porch steps. ASSUNTA opens the door]

SERAFINA: [Gasping] Don't speak!

[She retreats from the group, stumbling blindly backwards among the dressmaker's dummies. With a gasp she turns and runs out the back door. In a few moments we see her staggering about outside near the palm tree. She comes down in front of the house, and stares blindly off into the distance]

SERAFINA: [Wildly] Don't speak!
[The voices of the women begin keening in the house. ASSUNTA comes out and approaches SERAFINA with her arms extended. SERAFINA slumps to her knees, whispering hoarsely: "Don't speak!" ASSUNTA envelopes her in the grey shawl of pity as the scene dims out]

SCENE THREE

It is noon of the same day. ASSUNTA *is removing a funeral wreath on the door of the house. A* DOCTOR *and* FATHER DE LEO *are on the porch.*

THE DOCTOR: She's lost the baby. [ASSUNTA *utters a low moan of pity and crosses herself*] Serafina's a very strong woman and that won't kill her. But she is trying not to breathe. She's got to be watched and not allowed out of the bed. [*He removes a hypodermic and a small package from his bag and hands them to* ASSUNTA]—This is morphia. In the arm with the needle if she screams or struggles to get up again.

ASSUNTA: Capisco!

FATHER DE LEO: One thing I want to make plain. The body of Rosario must not be burned.

THE DOCTOR: Have you seen the "body of Rosario?"

FATHER DE LEO: Yes, I have seen his body.

THE DOCTOR: Wouldn't you say it was burned?

FATHER DE LEO: Of course the body was burned. When he was shot at the wheel of the truck, it crashed and caught fire. But deliberate cremation is not the same thing. It's an abomination in the sight of God.

THE DOCTOR: Abominations are something I don't know about.

FATHER DE LEO: The Church has set down certain laws.

THE DOCTOR: But the instructions of a widow have to be carried out.

FATHER DE LEO: Don't you know why she wants the body cremated? So she can keep the ashes here in the house.

THE DOCTOR: Well, why not, if that's any comfort to her?

FATHER DE LEO: Pagan idolatry is what I call it!

THE DOCTOR: Father De Leo, you love your people but you don't understand them. They find God in each other. And when they lose each other, they lose God and they're lost. And it's hard to help them.—Who is that woman?

[ESTELLE HOHENGARTEN *has appeared before the house. She is black-veiled, and bearing a bouquet of roses*]

ESTELLE: I am Estelle Hohengarten.

[*Instantly there is a great hubbub in the house. The women mourners flock out to the porch, whispering and gesticulating excitedly*]

FATHER DE LEO: What have you come here for?

ESTELLE: To say good-bye to the body.

FATHER DE LEO: The casket is closed; the body cannot be seen. And you must never come here. The widow knows nothing about you. Nothing at all.

GIUSEPPINA: We know about you!

PEPPINA: Va via! Sporcacciona!

VIOLETTA: Puttana!

MARIELLA: Assassina!

TERESA: You sent him to the Romanos.

FATHER DE LEO: Shhh!

[*Suddenly the women swarm down the steps like a cloud of attacking birds, all crying out in Sicilian.* ESTELLE *crouches and bows her head defensively before their savage assault. The bouquet of roses is snatched from her black-gloved hands and she is flailed with them about the head and shoulders. The thorns catch her veil and tear it away from her head. She covers her white sobbing face with her hands*]

FATHER DE LEO: Ferme! Ferme! Signore, fermate vi nel nome di Dio! —Have a little respect!

[*The women fall back from* ESTELLE, *who huddles weeping on the walk*]

ESTELLE: See him, see him, just see him . . .

FATHER DE LEO: The body is crushed and burned. Nobody can see it.
Now go away and don't ever come here again, Estelle Hohengarten!

THE WOMEN: [*In both languages, wildly*] Va via, va via, go way.

[ROSA *comes around the house.* ESTELLE *turns and retreats.
One of the mourners spits and kicks at the tangled veil and
roses.* FATHER DE LEO *leaves. The others return inside, except*
ROSA.
*After a few moments the child goes over to the roses. She
picks them up and carefully untangles the veil from the
thorns.
She sits on the sagging steps and puts the black veil over her
head. Then for the first time she begins to weep, wildly, his-
trionically. The little boy appears and gazes at her, momentarily impressed by her performance. Then he picks up a
rubber ball and begins to bounce it.*
ROSA *is outraged. She jumps up, tears off the veil and runs to
the little boy, giving him a sound smack and snatching the
ball away from him*]

ROSA: Go home! My papa is dead!

[*The scene dims out, as the music is heard again*]

SCENE FOUR

*A June day, three years later. It is morning and the light is
bright. A group of local mothers are storming* SERAFINA'S
*house, indignant over her delay in delivering the graduation
dresses for their daughters. Most of the women are chattering
continually in Sicilian, racing about the house and banging
the doors and shutters. The scene moves swiftly and violently
until the moment when* ROSA *finally comes out in her graduation dress.*

GIUSEPPINA: Serafina! Serafina Delle Rose!

PEPPINA: Maybe if you call her "Baronessa" she will answer the door. [*With a mocking laugh*] Call her "Baronessa" and kiss your hand to her when she opens the door.

GIUSEPPINA: [*Tauntingly*] Baronessa!

[*She kisses her hand toward the door*]

VIOLETTA: When did she promise your dress?

PEPPINA: All week she say, "Domani—domani—domani." But yestiddy I told her . . .

VIOLETTA: Yeah?

PEPPINA: Oh yeah. I says to her, "Serafina, domani's the high school graduation. I got to try the dress on my daughter *today*." "Domani," she says, "Sicuro! sicuro! sicuro!" So I start to go away. Then I hear a voice call, "Signora! Signora!" So I turn around and I see Serafina's daughter at the window.

VIOLETTA: Rosa?

PEPPINA: Yeah, Rosa. An' you know how?

VIOLETTA: How?

PEPPINA: *Naked!* Nuda, nuda! [*She crosses herself and repeats a prayer*] In nominis padri et figlio et spiritus sancti. Aaahh!

VIOLETTA: What did she do?

PEPPINA: Do? She say, "Signora! Please, you call this numero and ask for Jack and tell Jack my clothes are lock up so I can't get out from the house." Then Serafina come and she grab-a the girl by the hair and she pull her way from the window and she slam the shutters right in my face!

GIUSEPPINA: Whatsa the matter the daughter?

VIOLETTA: Who is this boy? Where did she meet him?

PEPPINA: Boy! What boy? He's a sailor. [*At the word "sailor" the women say "Ahhh!"*] She met him at the high school dance and somebody tell Serafina. That's why she lock up the girl's clothes so she can't leave the house. She can't even go to the high school to take the examinations. Imagine!

VIOLETTA: Peppina, this time *you* go to the door, yeah?

PEPPINA: Oh yeah, I go. Now I'm getting nervous. [*The women all crowd to the door*] Sera-feee-na!

VIOLETTA: Louder, louder!

PEPPINA: Apri la porta! Come on, come on!

THE WOMEN: [*Together*] Yeah, apri la porta! . . . Come on, hurry up! . . . Open up!

GIUSEPPINA: I go get-a police.

VIOLETTA: Whatsa matta? You want more trouble?

GIUSEPPINA: Listen, I pay in advance five dollars and get no dress. Now what she wear, my daughter, to graduate in? A couple of towels and a rose in the hair?

[*There is a noise inside: a shout and running footsteps*]

THE WOMEN: Something is going on in the house! I hear someone! Don't I? Don't you?

[*A scream and running footsteps are heard. The front door opens and* SERAFINA *staggers out onto the porch. She is wearing a soiled pink slip and her hair is wild*]

SERAFINA: Aiuto! Aiuto!

[*She plunges back into the house*]

[MISS YORKE, *a spinsterish high school teacher, walks quickly up to the house. The Sicilian women, now all chattering at once like a cloud of birds, sweep about her as she approaches*]

MISS YORKE: You ladies know I don't understand Italian! So, please . . .

[*She goes directly into the house. There are more outcries inside. The* STREGA *comes and stands at the edge of the yard, cackling derisively*]

THE STREGA: [*Calling back to someone*] The Wops are at it again!—She got the daughter lock up naked in there all week. Ho, ho, ho! She lock up all week—naked—shouting out the window tell people to call a number and give message to Jack. Ho, ho, ho! I guess she's in trouble already, and only fifteen!—They ain't civilized, these Sicilians. In the old country they live in caves in the hills and the country's run by bandits. Ho, ho, ho! More of them coming over on the boats all the time.

[*The door is thrown open again and* SERAFINA *reappears on the porch. She is acting wildly, as if demented*]

SERAFINA: [*Gasping in a hoarse whisper*] She cut her wrist, my daughter, she cut her wrist! [*She runs out into the yard*] Aiiii-eeee! Aiutatemi, aiutatemi! Call the dottore! [ASSUNTA *rushes up to* SERAFINA *and supports her as she is about to fall to her knees in the yard*] Get the knife away from her! Get the knife, please! Get the knife away from—she cut her wrist with—Madonna! Madonna mia . . .

ASSUNTA: Smettila, smettila, Serafina.

MISS YORKE: [*Coming out of the back room*] Mrs. Delle Rose, your daughter has not cut her wrist. Now come back into the house.

SERAFINA: [*Panting*] Che dice, che dice? Che cosa? Che cosa dice?

MISS YORKE: Your daughter's all right. Come back into the house. And you ladies please go away!

ASSUNTA: Vieni, Serafina. Andiamo a casa.

[*She supports the heavy, sagging bulk of* SERAFINA *to the steps. As they climb the steps one of the Sicilian mothers advances from the whispering group*]

GIUSEPPINA: [*Boldly*] Serafina, we don't go away until we get our dresses.

PEPPINA: The graduation begins and the girls ain't dressed.

[SERAFINA's *reply to this ill-timed request is a long, animal howl of misery as she is supported into the house.* MISS YORKE]

*follows and firmly closes the door upon the women, who then
go around back of the house. The interior of the house is
lighted up*]

MISS YORKE: [*To* SERAFINA] No, no, no, she's not bleeding. Rosa?
Rosa, come here and show your mother that you are not bleeding
to death.

[ROSA *appears silently and sullenly between the curtains that
separate the two rooms. She has a small white handkerchief
tied around one wrist.* SERAFINA *points at the wrist and cries
out: "Aiieee!"*]

MISS YORKE: [*Severely*] Now *stop* that, Mrs. Delle Rose!

[SERAFINA *rushes to* ROSA, *who thrusts her roughly away*]

ROSA: Lasciami stare, Mama!—I'm so ashamed I could die. This is
the way she goes around all the time. She hasn't put on clothes
since my father was killed. For three years she sits at the sewing
machine and never puts a dress on or goes out of the house, and
now she has locked up my clothes so I can't go out. She wants me
to be like her, freak of the neighborhood, the way she is! Next
time, I won't cut my wrist but my throat! I don't want to live
locked up with a bottle of ashes!

[*She points to the shrine*]

ASSUNTA: Figlia, figlia, figlia, non devi parlare cosí!

MISS YORKE: Mrs. Delle Rose, please give me the key to the closet
so that your daughter can dress for the graduation!

SERAFINA: [*Surrendering the key*] Ecco la—chiave . . .

[ROSA *snatches the key and runs back through the curtains*]

MISS YORKE: Now why did you lock her clothes up, Mrs. Delle
Rose?

SERAFINA: The wrist is still bleeding!

MISS YORKE: No, the wrist is not bleeding. It's just a skin cut, a
scratch. But the child is exhausted from all this excitement and
hasn't eaten a thing in two or three days.

ROSA: [*Running into the dining room*] Four days! I only asked her one favor. Not to let me go out but to let Jack come to the house so she could meet him!—Then she locked my clothes up!

MISS YORKE: Your daughter missed her final examinations at the high school, but her grades have been so good that she will be allowed to graduate with her class and take the examinations later. —You understand me, Mrs. Delle Rose!

[ROSA *goes into the back of the house*]

SERAFINA: [*Standing at the curtains*] See the way she looks at me? I've got a wild thing in the house, and her wrist is still bleeding!

MISS YORKE: Let's not have any more outbursts of emotion!

SERAFINA: Outbursts of—you make me sick! Sick! Sick at my stomach you make me! Your school, you make all this trouble! You give-a this dance where she gets mixed up with a sailor.

MISS YORKE: You are talking about the Hunter girl's brother, a sailor named Jack, who attended the dance with his sister?

SERAFINA: "Attended with sister!"—Attended with *sister!*—My daughter, she's nobody's sister!

[ROSA *comes out of the back room. She is radiantly beautiful in her graduation gown*]

ROSA: Don't listen to her, don't pay any attention to her, Miss Yorke.—I'm ready to go to the high school.

SERAFINA: [*Stunned by her daughter's beauty, and speaking with a wheedling tone and gesture, as she crouches a little*] O tesoro, tesoro! Vieni qua, Rosa, cara!—Come here and kiss Mama one minute!—Don't go like that, now!

ROSA: Lasciami stare!

[*She rushes out on the porch.* SERAFINA *gazes after her with arms slowly drooping from their imploring gesture and jaw dropping open in a look of almost comic desolation*]

SERAFINA: Ho solo te, solo te—in questo mondo!

MISS YORKE: Now, now, Mrs. Delle Rose, no more excitement, please!

SERAFINA: [*Suddenly plunging after them in a burst of fury*] Senti, senti, per favore!

ROSA: Don't you dare come out on the street like that!—*Mama!*

[*She crouches and covers her face in shame, as* SERAFINA *heedlessly plunges out into the front yard in her shocking deshabille, making wild gestures*]

SERAFINA: You give this dance where she gets mixed up with a sailor. What do you think you want to do at this high school? [*In weeping despair,* ROSA *runs to the porch*] How high is this high school? Listen, how high is this high school? Look, look, look, I will show you! It's high as that horse's dirt out there in the street! [SERAFINA *points violently out in front of the house*] Si! 'Sta fetentissima scuola! Scuola maledetta!

[ROSA *cries out and rushes over to the palm tree, leaning against it, with tears of mortification*]

MISS YORKE: Mrs. Delle Rose, you are talking and behaving extremely badly. I don't understand how a woman that acts like you could have such a sweet and refined young girl for a daughter!— You don't deserve it!—Really . . .

[*She crosses to the palm tree*]

SERAFINA: Oh, you want me to talk refined to you, do you? Then do me one thing! Stop ruining the girls at the high school!

[*As* SERAFINA *paces about, she swings her hips in the exaggeratedly belligerent style of a parading matador*]

ASSUNTA: Piantala, Serafina! Andiamo a casa!

SERAFINA: No, no, I ain't through talking to this here teacher!

ASSUNTA: Serafina, look at yourself, you're not dressed!

SERAFINA: I'm dressed okay; I'm not naked!

[*She stares savagely at the teacher by the palm tree. The Sicilian mothers return to the front yard*]

ASSUNTA: Serafina, cara? Andiamo a casa, adesso!—Basta! Basta!

SERAFINA: Aspetta!

ROSA: I'm so ashamed I could die, I'm so ashamed. Oh, you don't know, Miss Yorke, the way that we live. She never puts on a dress; she stays all the time in that dirty old pink slip!—And talks to my father's ashes like he was living.

SERAFINA: Teacher! Teacher, senti! What do you think you want to do at this high school? Sentite! per favore! You give this a dance! What kind of a spring dance is it? Answer this question, please, for me! What kind of a spring dance is it? She meet this boy there who don't even go to no high school. What kind of a boy? Guardate! A *sailor that wears a gold earring!* That kind of a boy is the kind of boy she meets there!—That's why I lock her clothes up so she can't go back to the high school! [*Suddenly to* ASSUNTA] She cut her wrist! It's still bleeding!

[*She strikes her forehead three times with her fist*]

ROSA: Mama, you look disgusting! [*She rushes away*]

[MISS YORKE *rushes after her.* SERAFINA *shades her eyes with one hand to watch them departing down the street in the brilliant spring light*]

SERAFINA: Did you hear what my daughter said to me?—"You look —disgusting."—She calls me . . .

ASSUNTA: Now, Serafina, we must go in the house.

[*She leads her gently to the porch of the little house*]

SERAFINA: [*Proudly*] How pretty she look, my daughter, in the white dress, like a bride! [*To all*] Excuse me! Excuse me, please! Go away! Get out of my yard!

GIUSEPPINA: [*Taking the bull by the horns*] No, we ain't going to go without the dresses!

ASSUNTA: Give the ladies the dresses so the girls can get dressed for the graduation.

SERAFINA: That one there, she only paid for the goods. I charge for the work.

GIUSEPPINA: Ecco! I got the money!

THE WOMEN: We got the money!

SERAFINA: The names are pinned on the dresses. Go in and get them. [*She turns to* ASSUNTA] Did you hear what my daughter called me? She called me "disgusting!"

[SERAFINA *enters the house, slamming the door. After a moment the mothers come out, cradling the white voile dresses tenderly in their arms, murmuring "carino!" and "bellissimo!" As they disappear the inside light is brought up and we see* SERAFINA *standing before a glazed mirror, looking at herself and repeating the daughter's word*]

SERAFINA: Disgusting!

[*The music is briefly resumed to mark a division*]

SCENE FIVE

Immediately following. SERAFINA's *movements gather momentum. She snatches a long-neglected girdle out of a bureau drawer and holds it experimentally about her waist. She shakes her head doubtfully, drops the girdle and suddenly snatches the $8.98 hat off the millinery dummy and plants it on her head. She turns around distractedly, not remembering where the mirror is. She gasps with astonishment when she catches sight of herself, snatches the hat off and hastily restores it to the blank head of the dummy. She makes another confused revolution or two, then gasps with fresh inspiration and snatches a girlish frock off a dummy—an Alice blue gown with daisies crocheted on it. The dress sticks on the dummy.* SERAFINA *mutters savagely in Sicilian. She finally overcomes this difficulty but in her exasperation she knocks the dummy over. She throws off the robe and steps hopefully into the gown. But she discovers it won't fit over her hips. She seizes the girdle again; then hurls it angrily away. The parrot calls to her; she yells angrily back at the parrot: Zitto! In the distance the high school band starts playing.* SERAFINA*

*gets panicky that she will miss the graduation ceremonies,
and hammers her forehead with her fist, sobbing a little. She
wriggles despairingly out of the blue dress and runs out back
in her rayon slip just as* FLORA *and* BESSIE *appear outside the
house.* FLORA *and* BESSIE *are two female clowns of middle
years and juvenile temperament.* FLORA *is tall and angular;*
BESSIE *is rather stubby. They are dressed for a gala.* FLORA
runs up the steps and bangs at the cottage door.

BESSIE: I fail to understand why it's so important to pick up a
polka-dot blouse when it's likely to make us miss the twelve
o'clock train.

FLORA: Serafina! Serafina!

BESSIE: We only got fifteen minutes to get to the depot and I'll
get faint on the train if I don't have m' coffee . . .

FLORA: Git a coke on th' train, Bessie.

BESSIE: Git nothing on the train if we don't git the train!

[SERAFINA *runs back out of the bedroom, quite breathless, in
a purple silk dress. As she passes the millinery dummy she
snatches the hat off again and plants it back on her head*]

SERAFINA: Wrist watch! Wrist watch! Where'd I put th' wrist
watch?

[*She hears* FLORA *shouting and banging and rushes to the
door*]

BESSIE: Try the door if it ain't open.

FLORA: [*Pushing in*] Just tell me, is it ready or not?

SERAFINA: Oh! You. Don't bother me. I'm late for the graduation
of my daughter and now I can't find her graduation present.

FLORA: You got plenty of time.

SERAFINA: Don't you hear the band playing?

FLORA: They're just warming up. Now, Serafina, where is my
blouse?

SERAFINA: Blouse? Not ready! I had to make fourteen graduation dresses!

FLORA: A promise is a promise and an excuse is just an excuse!

SERAFINA: I got to get to the high school!

FLORA: I got to get to the depot in that blouse!

BESSIE: We're going to the American Legion parade in New Orleans.

FLORA: There, there, there, there it is! [*She grabs the blouse from the machine*] Get started, woman, stitch them bandanas together! If you don't do it, I'm a-gonna report you to the Chamber of Commerce and git your license revoked!

SERAFINA: [*Anxiously*] What license you talking about? I got no license!

FLORA: You hear that, Bessie? *She hasn't got no license!*

BESSIE: *She ain't even got a license?*

SERAFINA: [*Crossing quickly to the machine*] I—I'll stitch them together! But if you make me late to my daughter's graduation, I'll make you sorry some way . . .

[*She works with furious rapidity. A train whistle is heard*]

BESSIE: [*Wildly and striking at* FLORA *with her purse*] Train's pullin' out! Oh, God, you made us miss it!

FLORA: Bessie, you know there's another at 12:45!

BESSIE: It's the selfish—principle of it that makes me sick!

[*She walks rapidly up and down*]

FLORA: Set down, Bessie. Don't wear out your feet before we git to th' city . . .

BESSIE: Molly tole me the town was full of excitement. They're dropping paper sacks full of water out of hotel windows.

FLORA: Which hotel are they dropping paper sacks out of?

BESSIE: What a fool question! The Monteleone Hotel.

FLORA: That's an old-fashioned hotel.

BESSIE: It might be old-fashioned but you'd be surprised at some of the modern, up-to-date things that go on there.

FLORA: I heard, I heard that the Legionnaires caught a girl on Canal Street! They tore the clothes off her and sent her home in a taxi!

BESSIE: I double dog dare anybody to try that on me!

FLORA: You?! Huh! You never need any assistance gittin' undressed!

SERAFINA: [*Ominously*] You two ladies watch how you talk in there. This here is a Catholic house. You are sitting in the same room with Our Lady and with the blessed ashes of my husband!

FLORA: [*Acidly*] Well, ex-cuse *me!* [*She whispers maliciously to* BESSIE] It sure is a pleasant surprise to see you wearing a dress, Serafina, but the surprise would be twice as pleasant if it was more the right size. [*To* BESSIE, *loudly*] She used to have a sweet figure, a little bit plump but attractive, but setting there at that sewing machine for three years in a kimona and not stepping out of the house has naturally given her hips!

SERAFINA: If I didn't have hips I would be a very uncomfortable woman when I set down.

[*The parrot squawks.* SERAFINA *imitates its squawk*]

FLORA: Polly want a cracker?

SERAFINA: No. He don't want a cracker! What is she doing over there at that window?

BESSIE: Some Legionnaires are on the highway!

FLORA: A Legionnaire? No kidding?

[*She springs up and joins her girl friend at the window. They both laugh fatuously, bobbing their heads out the window*]

BESSIE: He's looking this way; yell something!

FLORA: [*Leaning out the window*] Mademoiselle from Armentieres, parley-voo!

BESSIE: [*Chiming in rapturously*] Mademoiselle from Armentieres, parley-voo!

A VOICE OUTSIDE: [*Gallantly returning the salute*] Mademoiselle from Armentieres, hadn't been kissed for forty years!

BOTH GIRLS: [*Together; very gaily*] Hinky-dinky parley-voooo!

[*They laugh and applaud at the window. The Legionnaires are heard laughing. A car horn is heard as the Legionnaires drive away.* SERAFINA *springs up and rushes over to the window, jerks them away from it and slams the shutters in their faces*]

SERAFINA: [*Furiously*] I told you wimmen that you was not in a honky-tonk! Now take your blouse and git out! Get out on the streets where you kind a wimmen belong.—This is the house of Rosario Delle Rose and those are his ashes in that marble urn and I won't have—unproper things going on here or dirty talk, neither!

FLORA: Who's talking dirty?

BESSIE: What a helluva nerve.

FLORA: I want you to listen!

SERAFINA: You are, you are, dirty talk, all the time men, men, men! You men-crazy things, you!

FLORA: Sour grapes—sour grapes is your trouble! You're wild with envy!

BESSIE: Isn't she green with jealousy? Huh!

SERAFINA: [*Suddenly and religiously*] When I think of men I think about my husband. My husband was a Sicilian. We had love together every night of the week, we never skipped one, from the night we was married till the night he was killed in his fruit truck on that road there! [*She catches her breath in a sob*] And maybe that is the reason I'm not man-crazy and don't like hearing the talk of women that are. But I am interested, now, in the happiness of my daughter who's graduating this morning out of high school. And now I'm going to be late, the band is playing! And I have lost her wrist watch!—her graduation present!

[*She whirls about distractedly*]

BESSIE: Flora, let's go!—The hell with that goddam blouse!

FLORA: Oh, no, just wait a minute! I don't accept insults from no one!

SERAFINA: Go on, go on to New Orleans, you two man-crazy things, you! And pick up a man on Canal Street but not in my house, at my window, in front of my dead husband's ashes! [*The high school band is playing a martial air in the distance.* SERAFINA's *chest is heaving violently; she touches her heart and momentarily seems to forget that she must go*] I am not at all interested, I am not interested in men getting fat and bald in soldier-boy play suits, tearing the clothes off girls on Canal Street and dropping paper sacks out of hotel windows. I'm just not interested in that sort of man-crazy business. I remember my husband with a body like a young boy and hair on his head as thick and black as mine is and skin on him smooth and sweet as a yellow rose petal.

FLORA: Oh, a *rose*, was he?

SERAFINA: Yes, yes, a rose, a rose!

FLORA: Yes, a rose of a Wop!—of a gangster!—shot smuggling dope under a load of bananas!

BESSIE: Flora, Flora, let's go!

SERAFINA: My folks was peasants, contadini, but he—he come from *land*-owners! *Signorile*, my husband!—At night I sit here and I'm satisfied to remember, because I had the best.—Not the third best and not the second best, but the *first* best, the *only* best!—So now I stay here and am satisfied now to remember . . .

BESSIE: Come on, come out! To the depot!

FLORA: Just wait, I wanta hear this, it's too good to miss!

SERAFINA: I count up the nights I held him all night in my arms, and I can tell you how many. Each night for twelve years. Four thousand—three hundred—and eighty. The number of nights I held him all night in my arms. Sometimes I didn't sleep, just held him all night in my arms. And I am satisfied with it. I grieve for him. Yes, my pillow at night's never dry—but I'm satisfied to remember. And I would feel cheap and degraded and not fit to live with my daughter or under the roof with the urn of his blessed ashes, those—ashes of a rose—if after that memory, after knowing that man, I went to some other, some middle-aged man, not young, not full of young passion, but getting a pot belly on him and losing his hair and smelling of sweat and liquor—and trying to fool myself that *that* was love-making! I *know* what love-making was. And I'm satisfied just to remember . . . [*She is panting as though she had run upstairs*] Go on, you do it, you go on the streets and let them drop their sacks of dirty water on you!—I'm satisfied to remember the love of a man that was mine—*only mine!* Never touched by the hand of *nobody! Nobody* but *me!*—Just me!

[*She gasps and runs out to the porch. The sun floods her figure. It seems to astonish her. She finds herself sobbing. She digs in her purse for her handkerchief*]

FLORA: [*Crossing to the open door*] Never touched by nobody?

SERAFINA: [*With fierce pride*] Never nobody but me!

FLORA: I know somebody that could a tale unfold! And not so far from here neither. Not no further than the Square Roof is, that place on Esplanade!

BESSIE: Estelle Hohengarten!

FLORA: Estelle Hohengarten!—the blackjack dealer from Texas!

BESSIE: Get into your blouse and let's go!

FLORA: Everybody's known it but Serafina. I'm just telling the facts that come out at the inquest while she was in bed with her eyes shut tight and the sheet pulled over her head like a female ostrich! Tie this damn thing on me! It was a romance, not just a fly-by-night thing, but a steady affair that went on for more than a year.

[SERAFINA *has been standing on the porch with the door open behind her. She is in the full glare of the sun. She appears to have been struck senseless by the words shouted inside. She turns slowly about. We see that her dress is unfastened down the back, the pink slip showing. She reaches out gropingly with one hand and finds the porch column which she clings to while the terrible words strike constantly deeper. The high school band continues as a merciless counterpoint*]

BESSIE: Leave her in ignorance. Ignorance is bliss.

FLORA: He had a rose tattoo on his chest, the stuck-up thing, and Estelle was so gone on him she went down to Bourbon Street and had one put on her. [SERAFINA *comes onto the porch and* FLORA *turns to her, viciously*] Yeah, a rose tattoo on her chest same as the Wop's!

SERAFINA: [*Very softly*] Liar . . .

[*She comes inside; the word seems to give her strength*]

BESSIE: [*Nervously*] Flora, let's go, let's go!

SERAFINA: [*In a terrible voice*] Liar!—Lie-arrrrr!

[*She slams the wooden door shut with a violence that shakes the walls*]

BESSIE: [*Shocked into terror*] Let's get outa here, Flora!

FLORA: Let her howl her head off. I don't care.

[SERAFINA *has snatched up a broom*]

BESSIE: What's she up to?

FLORA: I don't care what she's up to!

BESSIE: I'm a-scared of these Wops.

FLORA: I'm not afraid of nobody!

BESSIE: She's gonna hit you.

FLORA: She'd better not hit me!

[*But both of the clowns are in retreat to the door.* SERAFINA *suddenly rushes at them with the broom. She flails* FLORA *about the hips and shoulders.* BESSIE *gets out. But* FLORA *is trapped in a corner. A table is turned over.* BESSIE, *outside, screams for the police and cries:* "Murder! Murder!" *The high school band is playing* The Stars and Stripes Forever. FLORA *breaks wildly past the flailing broom and escapes out of the house. She also takes up the cry for help.* SERAFINA *follows them out. She is flailing the brilliant noon air with the broom. The two women run off, screaming*]

FLORA: [*Calling back*] I'm going to have her arrested! Police, police! I'm going to have you arrested!

SERAFINA: *Have* me arrested, *have* me, you dirt, you devil, you *liar!* Li-i-arrrr!

[*She comes back inside the house and leans on the work table for a moment, panting heavily. Then she rushes back to the door, slams it and bolts it. Then she rushes to the windows, slams the shutters and fastens them. The house is now dark except for the vigil light in the ruby glass cup before the Madonna, and the delicate beams admitted through the shutter slats*]

SERAFINA: [*In a crazed manner*] Have me—have me—arrested—dirty slut—bitch—liar! [*She moves about helplessly, not knowing what to do with her big, stricken body. Panting for breath, she repeats the word "liar" monotonously and helplessly as she thrashes about. It is necessary for her, vitally necessary for her, to believe that the woman's story is a malicious invention. But the words of it stick in her mind and she mumbles them aloud as she thrashes crazily around the small confines of the parlor.*] Woman —Estelle—[*The sound of band music is heard*] Band, band, already—started.—Going to miss—graduation. Oh! [*She retreats toward the Madonna*] Estelle, Estelle Hohengarten?—"A shirt for a man I'm in love with! This man—is—wild like a gypsy."—Oh, oh, Lady—The—rose-colored—silk. [*She starts toward the dining room, then draws back in terror*] No, no, no, no, no! I don't remember! It wasn't that name, I don't remember the name! [*The band music grows louder*] High school—graduation—late! I'll be—late for it.—Oh, Lady, give me a—*sign!* [*She cocks her head toward the statue in a fearful listening attitude*] Che? Che dice, Signora? Oh, Lady! Give me a sign!

[*The scene dims out*]

SCENE SIX

It is two hours later. The interior of the house is in complete darkness except for the vigil light. With the shutters closed, the interior is so dark that we do not know SERAFINA *is present. All that we see clearly is the starry blue robe of Our*

Lady above the flickering candle of the ruby glass cup. After a few moments we hear SERAFINA's *voice, very softly, in the weak, breathless tone of a person near death.*

SERAFINA: [*Very softly*] Oh, Lady, give me a sign . . .

[*Gay, laughing voices are heard outside the house.* ROSA *and* JACK *appear, bearing roses and gifts. They are shouting back to others in a car*]

JACK: Where do we go for the picnic?

A GIRL'S VOICE: [*From the highway*] We're going in three sail-boats to Diamond Key.

A MAN'S VOICE: Be at Municipal Pier in half an hour.

ROSA: Pick us up here! [*She races up the steps*] Oh, the door's locked! Mama's gone *out!* There's a key in that bird bath.

[JACK *opens the door. The parlor lights up faintly as they enter*]

JACK: It's dark in here.

ROSA: Yes, Mama's gone out!

JACK: How do you know she's out?

ROSA: The door was locked and all the shutters are closed! Put down those roses.

JACK: Where shall I . . .

ROSA: Somewhere, anywhere!—Come here! [*He approaches her rather diffidently*] I want to teach you a little Dago word. The word is "bacio."

JACK: What does this word mean?

ROSA: This and this and this! [*She rains kisses upon him till he forcibly removes her face from his*] Just think. A week ago Friday —I didn't know boys existed!—Did you know girls existed before the dance?

JACK: Yes, I knew they existed . . .

ROSA: [*Holding him*] Do you remember what you said to me on the dance floor? "Honey, you're dancing too close?"

JACK: Well, it was—hot in the Gym and the—floor was crowded.

ROSA: When my girl friend was teaching me how to dance, I asked her, "How do you know which way the boy's going to move?" And she said, "You've got to feel how he's going to move with your body!" I said, "How do you feel with your body?" And she said, "By pressing up close!"—That's why I pressed up close! I didn't realize that I was—Ha, ha! Now you're blushing! Don't go *away!*— And a few minutes later you said to me, "Gee, you're beautiful!" I said, "Excuse me," and ran to the ladies' room. Do you know why? To look at myself in the mirror! And I saw that I was! For the first time in my life I was beautiful! You'd made me beautiful when you *said* that I was!

JACK: [*Humbly*] You *are* beautiful, Rosa! So much, I . . .

ROSA: *You've* changed, *too*. You've stopped laughing and joking. Why have you gotten so old and serious, Jack?

JACK: Well, honey, you're sort of . . .

ROSA: What am I "sort of?"

JACK: [*Finding the exact word*] Wild! [*She laughs. He seizes the bandaged wrist*] I didn't know nothing like this was going to happen.

ROSA: Oh, that, that's nothing! I'll take the handkerchief off and you can forget it.

JACK: How could you do a thing like that over me? I'm—nothing!

ROSA: Everybody is nothing until you love them!

JACK: Give me that handkerchief. I want to show it to my shipmates. I'll say, "This is the blood of a beautiful girl who cut her wrist with a knife because she loved me!"

ROSA: Don't be so pleased with yourself. It's mostly Mercurochrome!

SERAFINA: [*Violently, from the dark room adjoining*] Stai zitta!— Cretina!

[ROSA *and* JACK *draw abruptly apart*]

JACK: [*Fearfully*] I knew somebody was here!

ROSA: [*Sweetly and delicately*] Mama? Are you in there, Mama?

SERAFINA: No, no, no, I'm not, I'm dead and buried!

ROSA: Yes, Mama's in there!

JACK: Well, I—better go—and wait outside for a—while . . .

ROSA: You stay right here!—Mama?—Jack is with me.—Are you dressed up nicely? [*There is no response*] Why's it so dark in here?—Jack, open the shutters!—I want to introduce you to my mother . . .

JACK: Hadn't I better go and . . .

ROSA: No. Open the shutters!

> [*The shutters are opened and* ROSA *draws apart the curtains between the two rooms. Sunlight floods the scene.* SERAFINA *is revealed slumped in a chair at her work table in the dining room near the Singer sewing machine. She is grotesquely surrounded by the dummies, as though she had been holding a silent conference with them. Her appearance, in slovenly deshabille, is both comic and shocking*]

ROSA: [*Terribly embarrassed*] Mama, Mama, you said you were dressed up pretty! Jack, stay out for a minute! What's happened, Mama?

> [JACK *remains in the parlor.* ROSA *pulls the curtains, snatches a robe and flings it over* SERAFINA. *She brushes* SERAFINA's *hair back from her sweat-gleaming face, rubs her face with a handkerchief and dusts it with powder.* SERAFINA *submits to this cosmetic enterprise with a dazed look*]

ROSA: [*Gesturing vertically*] Su, su, su, su, su, su, su, su, su!

> [SERAFINA *sits up slightly in her chair, but she is still looking stupefied.* ROSA *returns to the parlor and opens the curtains again*]

ROSA: Come in, Jack! Mama is ready to meet you!

> [ROSA *trembles with eagerness as* JACK *advances nervously from the parlor. But before he enters* SERAFINA *collapses again into her slumped position, with a low moan*]

ROSA: [*Violently*] Mama, Mama, su, Mama! [SERAFINA *sits half erect*] She didn't sleep good last night.—Mama, this is Jack Hunter!

JACK: Hello, Mrs. Delle Rose. It sure is a pleasure to meet you.

[*There is a pause.* SERAFINA *stares indifferently at the boy*]

ROSA: Mama, Mama, say something!

JACK: Maybe your Mama wants me to . . . [*He makes an awkward gesture toward the door*]

ROSA: No, no, Mama's just tired. Mama makes dresses; she made a whole lot of dresses for the graduation! How many, Mama, how many graduation dresses did you have to make?

SERAFINA: [*Dully*] Fa niente . . .

JACK: I was hoping to see you at the graduation, Mrs. Delle Rose.

ROSA: I guess that Mama was too worn out to go.

SERAFINA: Rosa, shut the front door, shut it and lock it. There was a—policeman . . . [*There is a pause*] What?—What?

JACK: My sister was graduating. My mother was there and my aunt was there, a whole bunch of cousins—I was hoping that you could —all—get together . . .

ROSA: Jack brought you some flowers.

JACK: I hope you are partial to roses as much as I am.

[*He hands her the bouquet. She takes them absently*]

ROSA: Mama, say something, say something simple like "Thanks."

SERAFINA: Thanks.

ROSA: Jack, tell Mama about the graduation; describe it to her.

JACK: My mother said it was just like fairyland.

ROSA: Tell her what the boys wore!

JACK: What did—what did they wear?

ROSA: Oh, you know what they wore. They wore blue coats and white pants and each one had a carnation! And there were three couples that did an old-fashioned dance, a minuet, Mother, to

Mendelssohn's *Spring Song!* Wasn't it lovely, Jack? But one girl slipped; she wasn't used to long dresses! She slipped and fell on her—ho, ho! Wasn't it funny, Jack, wasn't it, wasn't it, Jack?

JACK: [*Worriedly*] I think that your Mama . . .

ROSA: Oh, my prize, my prize, I have forgotten my prize!

JACK: Where is it?

ROSA: You set them down by the sewing sign when you looked for the key.

JACK: Aw, excuse me, I'll get them.

[*He goes through the parlor.* ROSA *runs to her mother and kneels by her chair*]

ROSA: [*In a terrified whisper*] Mama, something has happened! What has happened, Mama? Can't you tell me, Mama? Is it because of this morning? Look. I took the bandage off, it was only a scratch! So, Mama, forget it! Think it was just a bad dream that never happened!

[*She gives her several quick kisses on the forehead.* JACK *returns with two big books tied in white satin ribbon*]

JACK: Here they are.

ROSA: Look what I got, Mama.

SERAFINA: [*Dully*] What?

ROSA: The Digest of Knowledge!

JACK: Everything's in them, from Abracadabra to Zoo! My sister was jealous. She just got a diploma!

SERAFINA: [*Rousing a bit*] Diploma, where is it? Didn't you get no diploma?

ROSA: Si, si, Mama! Eccolo! Guarda, guarda!

[*She holds up the diploma tied in ribbon*]

SERAFINA: Va bene.—Put it in the drawer with your father's clothes.

JACK: Mrs. Delle Rose, you should be very, very proud of your daughter. She stood in front of the crowd and recited a poem.

ROSA: Yes, I did. Oh, I was so excited!

JACK: And Mrs. Delle Rose, your daughter, Rosa was so pretty
when she walked on the stage—that people went "Oooooooooo!"
—like that! Y'know what I mean? They all went—"Oooooooooo!"
Like a—like a—*wind* had—blown over! Because your daughter,
Rosa, was so—*lovely* looking! [*He has crouched over to* SERAFINA
*to deliver this description close to her face. Now he straightens up
and smiles proudly at* ROSA] How does it feel to be the mother of
the prettiest girl in the world?

ROSA: [*Suddenly bursting into pure delight*] Ha, ha, ha, ha, ha,
ha! [*She throws her head back in rapture*]

SERAFINA: [*Rousing*] Hush!

ROSA: Ha, ha, ha, ha, ha, ha, ha, ha, ha, ha!

[*She cannot control her ecstatic laughter. She presses her
hand to her mouth but the laughter still bubbles out*]

SERAFINA: [*Suddenly rising in anger*] Pazza, pazza, pazza! Fini-
scila! Basta, via! [ROSA *whirls around to hide her convulsions of
joy. To* JACK:] Put the prize books in the parlor and shut the
front door; there was a policeman come here because of—some
trouble . . .

[JACK *takes the books*]

ROSA: Mama, I've never seen you like this! What will Jack think,
Mama?

SERAFINA: Why do I care what Jack thinks?—You wild, wild crazy
thing, you—with the eyes of your—father . . .

JACK: [*Returning*] Yes, ma'am, Mrs. Delle Rose, you certainly
got a right to be very proud of your daughter.

SERAFINA: [*After a pause*] I am proud of the—memory of her—
father.—He was a baron . . . [ROSA *takes* JACK'S *arm*] And who
are *you*? What are you?—per piacere!

ROSA: Mama, I just introduced him; his name is Jack Hunter.

SERAFINA: Hunt-er?

JACK: Yes, ma'am, Hunter. Jack Hunter.

SERAFINA: What are you hunting?—Jack?

ROSA: Mama!

SERAFINA: What all of 'em are hunting? To have a good time, and the Devil cares who pays for it? I'm sick of men, I'm almost as sick of men as I am of wimmen.—Rosa, get out while I talk to this boy!

ROSA: I didn't bring Jack here to be insulted!

JACK: Go on, honey, and let your Mama talk to me. I think your Mama has just got a slight wrong—impression . . .

SERAFINA: [Ominously] Yes, I got an impression!

ROSA: I'll get dressed! Oh, Mama, don't spoil it for me!—the happiest day of my life!

[She goes into the back of the house]

JACK: [After an awkward pause] Mrs. Delle Rose . . .

SERAFINA: [Correcting his pronunciation] Delle Rose!

JACK: Mrs. Delle Rose, I'm sorry about all this. Believe me, Mrs. Delle Rose, the last thing I had in mind was getting mixed up in a family situation. I come home after three months to sea, I docked at New Orleans, and come here to see my folks. My sister was going to a high school dance. She took me with her, and there I met your daughter.

SERAFINA: What did you do?

JACK: At the high school dance? We danced! My sister had told me that Rosa had a very strict mother and wasn't allowed to go on dates with boys so when it was over, I said, "I'm sorry you're not allowed to go out." And she said, "Oh! What gave you the idea I wasn't!" So then I thought my sister had made a mistake and I made a date with her for the next night.

SERAFINA: What did you do the next night?

JACK: The next night we went to the movies.

SERAFINA: And what did you do—that night?

JACK: At the movies? We ate a bag of popcorn and watched the movie!

SERAFINA: She come home at midnight and said she had been with a girl-friend studying "civics."

JACK: Whatever story she told you, it ain't my fault!

SERAFINA: And the night after that?

JACK: Last Tuesday? We went roller skating!

SERAFINA: And afterwards?

JACK: After the skating? We went to a drug store and had an ice cream soda!

SERAFINA: Alone?

JACK: At the drug store? No. It was crowded. And the skating rink was full of people skating!

SERAFINA: You mean that you haven't been alone with my Rosa?

JACK: Alone or not alone, what's the point of that question? I still don't see the point of it.

SERAFINA: We are Sicilians. We don't leave the girls with the boys they're not engaged to!

JACK: Mrs. Delle Rose, this is the United States.

SERAFINA: But we are Sicilians, and we are not cold-blooded.—My girl is a *virgin*! She *is*—or she *was*—I would like to know—*which*!

JACK: Mrs. Delle Rose! I got to tell you something. You might not believe it. It is a hard thing to say. But I am—*also* a—*virgin* . . .

SERAFINA: *What? No.* I do not believe it.

JACK: Well, it's true, though. This is the first time—I . . .

SERAFINA: First time you *what*?

JACK: The first time I really wanted to . . .

SERAFINA: Wanted to what?

JACK: Make—love . . .

SERAFINA: You? A sailor?

JACK: [*Sighing deeply*] Yes, ma'am. I had opportunities to!—But I—always thought of my mother . . . I always asked myself, would she or would she not—think—this or that person was—decent!

SERAFINA: But with my daughter, my Rosa, your mother tells you *okay?*—go ahead, son!

JACK: Mrs. Delle Rose! [*With embarrassment*]—Mrs. Delle Rose, I . . .

SERAFINA: Two weeks ago I was slapping her hands for scratching mosquito bites. She rode a bicycle to school. Now all at once—I've got a wild thing in the house. She says she's in love. And you? Do you say *you're* in love?

JACK: [*Solemnly*] Yes, ma'am, I do, I'm in love!—very much . . .

SERAFINA: Bambini, tutti due, bambini!

[ROSA *comes out, dressed for the picnic*]

ROSA: I'm ready for Diamond Key!

SERAFINA: Go out on the porch. Diamond Key!

ROSA: [*With a sarcastic curtsy*] Yes, Mama!

SERAFINA: What are you? Catholic?

JACK: Me? Yes, ma'am, Catholic.

SERAFINA: You don't look Catholic to me!

ROSA: [*Shouting, from the door*] Oh, God, Mama, how do Catholics look? How do they look different from anyone else?

SERAFINA: Stay out till I call you! [ROSA *crosses to the bird bath and prays.* SERAFINA *turns to* JACK] Turn around, will you?

JACK: Do what, ma'am?

SERAFINA: I said, *turn around!* [JACK *awkwardly turns around*] Why do they make them Navy pants so tight?

ROSA: [*Listening in the yard*] Oh, my God . . .

JACK: [*Flushing*] That's a question you'll have to ask the Navy, Mrs. Delle Rose.

SERAFINA: And that gold earring, what's the gold earring for?

ROSA: [*Yelling from the door*] For crossing the equator, Mama; he crossed it three times. He was initiated into the court of Neptune and gets to wear a gold earring! He's a shellback!

[SERAFINA *springs up and crosses to slam the porch door.* ROSA *runs despairingly around the side of the house and leans, exhausted with closed eyes, against the trunk of a palm tree. The* STREGA *creeps into the yard, listening*]

SERAFINA: You see what I got. A wild thing in the house!

JACK: Mrs. Delle Rose, I guess that Sicilians are very emotional people . . .

SERAFINA: I want nobody to take advantage of that!

JACK: You got the wrong idea about me, Mrs. Delle Rose.

SERAFINA: I know what men want—not to eat popcorn with girls or to slide on ice! And boys are the same, only younger.—Come here. Come here!

[ROSA *hears her mother's passionate voice. She rushes from the palm tree to the back door and pounds on it with both fists*]

ROSA: Mama! Mama! Let me in the door, Jack!

JACK: Mrs. Delle Rose, your daughter is calling you.

SERAFINA: Let her call!—Come here. [*She crosses to the shrine of Our Lady*] Come here!

[*Despairing of the back door,* ROSA *rushes around to the front. A few moments later she pushes open the shutters of the window in the wall and climbs half in.* JACK *crosses apprehensively to* SERAFINA *before the Madonna*]

SERAFINA: You said you're Catholic, ain't you?

JACK: Yes, ma'am.

SERAFINA: Then kneel down in front of Our Lady!

JACK: Do—do what, did you say?

SERAFINA: I said to get down on your knees in front of Our Lady!

[ROSA *groans despairingly in the window.* JACK *kneels awkwardly upon the hassock*]

ROSA: Mama, Mama, *now* what?!

[SERAFINA *rushes to the window, pushes* ROSA *out and slams the shutters*]

SERAFINA: [*Returning to* JACK] Now say after me what I say!

JACK: Yes, ma'am.

[ROSA *pushes the shutters open again*]

SERAFINA: I promise the Holy Mother that I will respect the innocence of the daughter of . . .

ROSA: [*In anguish*] Ma-*maaa!*

SERAFINA: Get back out of that window!—Well? Are you gonna say
it?

JACK: Yes, ma'am. What was it, again?

SERAFINA: I promise the Holy Mother . . .

JACK: I promise the Holy Mother . . .

SERAFINA: As I hope to be saved by the Blessed Blood of Jesus . . .

JACK: As I hope to be saved by the . . .

SERAFINA: Blessed Blood of . . .

JACK: Jesus . . .

SERAFINA: That I will respect the innocence of the daughter, Rosa,
of Rosario Delle Rose.

JACK: That I will respect the innocence—of—Rosa . . .

SERAFINA: Cross yourself! [*He crosses himself*] Now get up, get
up, get up! I am satisfied now . . .

[ROSA *jumps through the window and rushes to* SERAFINA
with arms outflung and wild cries of joy]

SERAFINA: Let me go, let me breathe!

[*Outside the* STREGA *cackles derisively*]

ROSA: Oh, wonderful Mama, don't breathe! Oh, Jack! *Kiss* Mama!
Kiss Mama! Mama, please kiss Jack!

SERAFINA: Kiss? Me? No, no, no, no!—Kiss my *hand* . . .

[*She offers her hand, shyly, and* JACK *kisses it with a loud
smack.* ROSA *seizes the wine bottle*]

ROSA: Mama, get some wine glasses!

[SERAFINA *goes for the glasses, and* ROSA *suddenly turns to* JACK. *Out of her mother's sight, she passionately grabs hold of his hand and presses it, first to her throat, then to her lips and finally to her breast.* JACK *snatches her hand away as* SERAFINA *returns with the glasses. Voices are heard calling from the highway*]

VOICES OUTSIDE: Ro-osa!—Ro-osa!—Ro-osa!

[A *car horn is heard blowing*]

SERAFINA: Oh, I forgot the graduation present.

[*She crouches down before the bureau and removes a fancily wrapped package from its bottom drawer. The car horn is honking, and the voices are calling*]

ROSA: They're calling for us! *Coming!* Jack! [*She flies out the door, calling back to her mother*] G'bye, Mama!

JACK: [*Following* ROSA] Good-bye, Mrs. Delle Rose!

SERAFINA: [V*aguely*] It's a Bulova wrist watch with seventeen jewels in it . . . [*She realizes that she is alone*] Rosa! [*She goes to the door, still holding out the present. Outside the car motor roars, and the voices shout as the car goes off.* SERAFINA *stumbles outside, shielding her eyes with one hand, extending the gift with the other*] Rosa, Rosa, your present! Regalo, regalo—tesoro!

[*But the car has started off, with a medley of voices shouting farewells, which fade quickly out of hearing.* SERAFINA *turns about vaguely in the confusing sunlight and gropes for the door. There is a derisive cackle from the witch next door.* SERAFINA *absently opens the package and removes the little gold watch. She winds it and then holds it against her ear. She shakes it and holds it again to her ear. Then she holds it away from her and glares at it fiercely*]

SERAFINA: [*Pounding her chest three times*] Tick—tick—tick! [*She goes to the Madonna and faces it*] Speak to me, Lady! Oh, Lady, give me a sign!

[*The scene dims out*]

It is two hours later the same day.
SERAFINA *comes out onto the porch, barefooted, wearing a rayon slip. Great shadows have appeared beneath her eyes; her face and throat gleam with sweat. There are dark stains of wine on the rayon slip. It is difficult for her to stand, yet she cannot sit still. She makes a sick moaning sound in her throat almost continually.*
A hot wind rattles the cane-brake. VIVI, *the little girl, comes up to the porch to stare at* SERAFINA *as at a strange beast in a cage.* VIVI *is chewing a licorice stick which stains her mouth and her fingers. She stands chewing and staring.* SERAFINA *evades her stare. She wearily drags a broken grey wicker chair down off the porch, all the way out in front of the house, and sags heavily into it. It sits awry on a broken leg.*
VIVI *sneaks toward her.* SERAFINA *lurches about to face her angrily. The child giggles and scampers back to the porch.*

SERAFINA: [*Sinking back into the chair*] Oh, Lady, Lady, Lady, give me a sign . . .

[*She looks up at the white glare of the sky*]

[FATHER DE LEO *approaches the house.* SERAFINA *crouches low in the chair to escape his attention. He knocks at the door. Receiving no answer, he looks out into the yard, sees her, and approaches her chair. He comes close to address her with a gentle severity*]

FATHER DE LEO: Buon giorno, Serafina.

SERAFINA: [*Faintly, with a sort of disgust*] Giorno . . .

FATHER DE LEO: I'm surprised to see you sitting outdoors like this. What is that thing you're wearing?—I think it's an undergarment! —It's hanging off one shoulder, and your head, Serafina, looks as if

you had stuck it in a bucket of oil. Oh, I see now why the other ladies of the neighborhood aren't taking their afternoon naps! They
find it more entertaining to sit on the porches and watch the spec-
tacle you are putting on for them!—Are you listening to me?—I
must tell you that the change in your appearance and behavior
since Rosario's death is shocking—shocking! A woman can be
dignified in her grief but when it's carried too far it becomes a sort
of self-indulgence. Oh, I knew this was going to happen when you
broke the Church law and had your husband cremated!
[SERAFINA *lurches up from the chair and shuffles back to the
porch.* FATHER DE LEO *follows her*]—Set up a little idolatrous
shrine in your house and give worship to a bottle of ashes. [*She
sinks down upon the steps*]—Are you listening to me?

> [*Two women have appeared on the embankment and de-
> scend toward the house.* SERAFINA *lurches heavily up to meet
> them, like a weary bull turning to face another attack*]

SERAFINA: You ladies, what you want? I don't do sewing! Look, I
quit doing sewing. [*She pulls down the "*SEWING*" sign and hurls
it away*] Now you got places to go, you ladies, go places! Don't
hang around front of my house!

FATHER DE LEO: The ladies want to be friendly.

SERAFINA: Naw, they don't come to be friendly. They think they
know something that Serafina don't know; they think I got *these*
on my head! [*She holds her fingers like horns at either side of her
forehead*] Well, I ain't got them!

> [*She goes padding back out in front of the house.* FATHER DE
> LEO *follows*]

FATHER DE LEO: You called me this morning in distress over something.

SERAFINA: I called you this morning but now it is afternoon.

FATHER DE LEO: I had to christen the grandson of the Mayor.

SERAFINA: The Mayor's important people, not Serafina!

FATHER DE LEO: You don't come to confession.

SERAFINA: [*Starting back toward the porch*] No, I don't come, I
don't go, I—Ohhh!

[*She pulls up one foot and hops on the other*]

FATHER DE LEO: You stepped on something?

SERAFINA: [*Dropping down on the steps*] No, no, no, no, no, I don't step on—noth'n . . .

FATHER DE LEO: Come in the house. We'll wash it with antiseptic. [*She lurches up and limps back toward the house*] Walking barefooted you will get it infected.

SERAFINA: Fa niente . . .

[*At the top of the embankment a little boy runs out with a red kite and flourishes it in the air with rigid gestures, as though he were giving a distant signal.* SERAFINA *shades her eyes with a palm to watch the kite, and then, as though its motions conveyed a shocking message, she utters a startled soft cry and staggers back to the porch. She leans against a pillar, running her hand rapidly and repeatedly through her hair.* FATHER DE LEO *approaches her again, somewhat timidly*]

FATHER DE LEO: Serafina?

SERAFINA: Che, che, che cosa vuole?

FATHER DE LEO: I am thirsty. Will you go in the house and get me some water?

SERAFINA: Go in. Get you some water. The faucet is working.—I can't go in the house.

FATHER DE LEO: Why can't you go in the house?

SERAFINA: The house has a tin roof on it. I got to breathe.

FATHER DE LEO: You can breathe in the house.

SERAFINA: No, I can't breathe in the house. The house has a tin roof on it and I . . .

[*The* STREGA *has been creeping through the cane-brake pretending to search for a chicken*]

THE STREGA: Chick, chick, chick, chick, chick?

[*She crouches to peer under the house*]

SERAFINA: What's that? Is that the . . . ? Yes, the Strega! [*She picks up a flower pot containing a dead plant and crosses the yard*] Strega! Strega! [*The* STREGA *looks up, retreating a little*] Yes, you, I mean you! You ain't look for no chick! Getta hell out of my yard!

[*The* STREGA *retreats, viciously muttering, back into the cane-brake.* SERAFINA *makes the protective sign of the horns with her fingers. The goat bleats*]

FATHER DE LEO: You have no friends, Serafina.

SERAFINA: I don't want friends.

FATHER DE LEO: You are still a young woman. Eligible for—loving and—bearing again! I remember you dressed in pale blue silk at Mass one Easter morning, yes, like a lady wearing a—piece of the —weather! Oh, how proudly you walked, *too* proudly!—But now you crouch and shuffle about barefooted; you live like a convict, dressed in the rags of a convict. You have no companions; women you don't mix with. You . . .

SERAFINA: No, I don't mix with them women. [*Glaring at the women on the embankment*] The dummies I got in my house, I mix with them better because they don't make up no lies!—What kind of women are them? [*Mimicking fiercely*] "Eee, Papa, eeee, baby, eee, me, me!" At thirty years old they got no more use for the letto matrimoniale, no. The big bed goes to the basement! They get little beds from Sears Roebuck and sleep on their bellies!

FATHER DE LEO: Attenzione!

SERAFINA: They make the life without glory. Instead of the heart they got the deep-freeze in the house. The men, they don't feel no glory, not in the house with them women; they go to the bars, fight in them, get drunk, get fat, put horns on the women because the women don't give them the love which is glory.—I did, I give him the glory. To me the big bed was beautiful like a religion. Now I lie on it with dreams, with memories only! But it is still beautiful to me and I don't believe that the man in my heart gave me horns! [*The women whisper*] What, what are they saying? Does ev'rybody know something that I don't know?—No, all I want is a sign, a sign from Our Lady, to tell me the lie is a lie! And then I . . . [*The women laugh on the embankment.* SERAFINA *starts fiercely toward them. They scatter*] Squeak, squeak, squawk, squawk! Hens—like water thrown on them!

[*There is the sound of mocking laughter*]

FATHER DE LEO: People are laughing at you on all the porches.

SERAFINA: I'm laughing, too. Listen to me, I'm laughing! [*She breaks into loud, false laughter, first from the porch, then from the foot of the embankment, then crossing in front of the house*] Ha, ha, ha, ha, ha, ha, ha! Now ev'rybody is laughing. Ha, ha, ha, ha, ha, ha!

FATHER DE LEO: Zitta ora!—Think of your daughter.

SERAFINA: [*Understanding the word "daughter"*] You, *you* think of my daughter! Today you give out the diplomas, today at the high school you give out the prizes, diplomas! You give to my daughter a set of books call the Digest of Knowledge! What does she know? How to be cheap already?—Oh, yes, that is what to learn, how to be cheap and to cheat!—You know what they do at this high school? They ruin the girls there! They give the spring dance because the girls are man-crazy. And there at that dance my daughter goes with a sailor that has in his ear a gold ring! And pants so tight that a woman ought not to look at him! This morning, this morning she cuts with a knife her wrist if I don't let her go!—Now all of them gone to some island, they call it a picnic, all of them, gone in a—boat!

FATHER DE LEO: There *was* a school picnic, chaperoned by the teachers.

SERAFINA: Oh, lo so, lo so! The man-crazy old-maid teachers!— They all run wild on the island!

FATHER DE LEO: Serafina Delle Rose! [*He picks up the chair by the back and hauls it to the porch when she starts to resume her seat*] —I *command* you to go in the house.

SERAFINA: Go in the house? I will. I will go in the house if you will answer one question.—Will you answer one question?

FATHER DE LEO: I will if I know the answer.

SERAFINA: Aw, you know the answer!—You used to hear the confessions of my husband.

[*She turns to face the priest*]

FATHER DE LEO: Yes, I heard his confessions . . .

SERAFINA: [*With difficulty*] Did he ever speak to you of a woman?

[*A child cries out and races across in front of the house.* FATHER DE LEO *picks up his panama hat.* SERAFINA *paces slowly toward him. He starts away from the house*]

SERAFINA: [*Rushing after him*] Aspettate! Aspettate un momento!

FATHER DE LEO: [*Fearfully, not looking at her*] Che volete?

SERAFINA: Rispondetemi! [*She strikes her breast*] Did he speak of a woman to you?

FATHER DE LEO: You know better than to ask me such a question. I don't break the Church laws. The secrets of the confessional are sacred to me.

[*He walks away*]

SERAFINA: [*Pursuing and clutching his arm*] I got to know. You could tell me.

FATHER DE LEO: Let go of me, Serafina!

SERAFINA: Not till you tell me, Father. Father, you tell me, please tell me! Or I will go mad! [*In a fierce whisper*] I will go back in the house and smash the urn with the ashes—if you don't tell me! I will go mad with the doubt in my heart and I will smash the urn and scatter the ashes—of my husband's body!

FATHER DE LEO: What could I tell you? If you would not believe the known facts about him . . .

SERAFINA: Known facts, who knows the known facts?

[*The neighbor women have heard the argument and begin to crowd around, muttering in shocked whispers at* SERAFINA'S *lack of respect*]

FATHER DE LEO: [*Frightened*] Lasciatemi, lasciatemi stare!—Oh, Serafina, I am too old for this—please!—Everybody is . . .

SERAFINA: [*In a fierce, hissing whisper*] Nobody knew my rose of the world but me and now they can lie because the rose ain't living. They want the marble urn broken; they want me to smash it. They want the rose ashes scattered because I had too much glory. They don't want glory like *that* in nobody's heart. They want—mouse-squeaking!—known facts.—Who knows the known facts? You—padres—wear black because of the fact that the facts are known by nobody!

FATHER DE LEO: Oh, Serafina! There are people watching!

SERAFINA: Let them watch something. That will be a change for them.—It's been a long time I wanted to break out like this and now I . . .

FATHER DE LEO: I am too old a man; I am not strong enough. I am sixty-seven years old! Must I call for help, now?

SERAFINA: Yes, call! Call for help, but I won't let you go till you tell me!

FATHER DE LEO: You're not a respectable woman.

SERAFINA: No, I'm not a respectable; I'm a woman.

FATHER DE LEO: No, you are not a woman. You are an animal!

SERAFINA: Si, si, animale! Sono animale! Animale. Tell them all, shout it all to them, up and down the whole block! The widow Delle Rose is not respectable, she is not even a woman, she is an animal! She is attacking the priest! She will tear the black suit off him unless he tells her the whores in this town are lying to her!

[*The neighbor women have been drawing closer as the argument progresses, and now they come to* FATHER DE LEO's *rescue and assist him to get away from* SERAFINA, *who is on the point of attacking him bodily. He cries out, "Officer! Officer!" but the women drag* SERAFINA *from him and lead him away with comforting murmurs*]

SERAFINA: [*Striking her wrists together*] Yes, it's me, it's me!! Lock me up, lock me, lock me up! Or I will—*smash!*—the marble . . .

[*She throws her head far back and presses her fists to her eyes. Then she rushes crazily to the steps and falls across them*]

ASSUNTA: Serafina! Figlia! Figlia! Andiamo a casa!

SERAFINA: Leave me alone, old woman.

[*She returns slowly to the porch steps and sinks down on them, sitting like a tired man, her knees spread apart and her head cupped in her hands. The children steal back around the house. A little boy shoots a bean-shooter at her. She starts up with a cry. The children scatter, shrieking. She sinks back down on the steps, then leans back, staring up at the sky, her body rocking*]

SERAFINA: Oh, Lady, Lady, Lady, give me a sign!

[*As if in mocking answer, a novelty* SALESMAN *appears and approaches the porch. He is a fat man in a seersucker suit and a straw hat with a yellow, red and purple band. His face is beet-red and great moons of sweat have soaked through the armpits of his jacket. His shirt is lavender, and his tie, pale blue with great yellow polka dots, is a butterfly bow. His entrance is accompanied by a brief, satiric strain of music*]

THE SALESMAN: Good afternoon, lady. [*She looks up slowly. The salesman talks sweetly, as if reciting a prayer*] I got a little novelty here which I am offering to just a few lucky people at what we call an introductory price. Know what I mean? Not a regular price but a price which is less than what it costs to manufacture the article, a price we are making for the sake of introducing the product in the Gulf Coast territory. Lady, this thing here that I'm droppin' right in youah lap is bigger than television; it's going to revolutionize the domestic life of America.—Now I don't do house to house canvassing. I sell directly to merchants but when I stopped over there to have my car serviced, I seen you taking the air on the steps and I thought I would just drop over and . . .

[*There is the sound of a big truck stopping on the highway, and a man's voice,* ALVARO's, *is heard, shouting*]

ALVARO: Hey! Hey, you road hog!

THE SALESMAN: [*Taking a sample out of his bag*] Now, lady, this little article has a deceptive appearance. First of all, I want you to notice how *compact* it is. It takes up no more space than . . .

[ALVARO *comes down from the embankment. He is about twenty-five years old, dark and very goodlooking. He is one of*

*those Mediterranean types that resemble glossy young bulls.
He is short in stature, has a massively sculptural torso and
bluish-black curls. His face and manner are clownish; he has a
charming awkwardness. There is a startling, improvised air
about him; he frequently seems surprised at his own speeches
and actions, as though he had not at all anticipated them. At
the moment when we first hear his voice the sound of a tim-
pani begins, at first very pianissimo, but building up as he
approaches, till it reaches a vibrant climax with his appearance to* SERAFINA *beside the house*]

ALVARO: Hey.

THE SALESMAN: [*Without glancing at him*] Hay is for horses!—
Now, madam, you see what happens when I press this button?

[*The article explodes in* SERAFINA's *face. She slaps it away
with an angry cry. At the same time* ALVARO *advances, trembling with rage, to the porch steps. He is sweating and stam-
mering with pent-up fury at a world of frustrations which are
temporarily localized in the gross figure of this salesman*]

ALVARO: Hey, you! Come here! What the hell's the idea, back
there at that curve? You make me drive off the highway!

THE SALESMAN: [*To* SERAFINA] Excuse me for just one minute.
[*He wheels menacingly about to face* ALVARO] Is something giving you gas pains, Maccaroni?

ALVARO: My name is not Maccaroni.

THE SALESMAN: All right. Spaghetti.

ALVARO: [*Almost sobbing with passion*] I am not maccaroni. I
am not spaghetti. I am a human being that drives a truck of bananas. I drive a truck of bananas for the Southern Fruit Company
for a living, not to play cowboys and Indians on no highway with
no rotten road hog. You got a 4-lane highway between Pass Christian and here. I give you the sign to pass me. You tail me and give
me the horn. You yell "Wop" at me and "Dago." "Move over,
Wop, move over, Dago." Then at the goddamn curve, you go pass
me and make me drive off the highway and yell back "Son of a
bitch of a Dago!" I don't like that, no, no! And I am glad you stop
here. Take the cigar from your mouth, take out the cigar!

THE SALESMAN: Take it out for me, greaseball.

ALVARO: If I take it out I will push it down your throat. I got three dependents! If I fight, I get fired, but I will fight and get fired. Take out the cigar!

[*Spectators begin to gather at the edge of the scene.* SERAFINA *stares at the truck driver, her eyes like a somnambule's. All at once she utters a low cry and seems about to fall*]

ALVARO: Take out the cigar, take out, take out the cigar!

[*He snatches the cigar from the* SALESMAN'S *mouth and the* SALESMAN *brings his knee up violently into* ALVARO'S *groin. Bending double and retching with pain,* ALVARO *staggers over to the porch*]

THE SALESMAN: [*Shouting, as he goes off*] I got your license number, Maccaroni! I know your boss!

ALVARO: [*Howling*] Drop dead! [*He suddenly staggers up the steps*] Lady, lady, I got to go in the house!

[*As soon as he enters, he bursts into rending sobs, leaning against a wall and shaking convulsively. The spectators outside laugh as they scatter.* SERAFINA *slowly enters the house. The screen door rasps loudly on its rusty springs as she lets it swing gradually shut behind her, her eyes remaining fixed with a look of stupefied wonder upon the sobbing figure of the truck driver. We must understand her profound unconscious response to this sudden contact with distress as acute as her own. There is a long pause as the screen door makes its whining, catlike noise swinging shut by degrees*]

SERAFINA: Somebody's—in my house? [*Finally, in a hoarse, tremulous whisper*] What are you—doing in here? Why have you—come in my house?

ALVARO: Oh, lady—leave me alone!—Please—now!

SERAFINA: You—got no business—in here . . .

ALVARO: I got to cry after a fight. I'm sorry, lady. I . . .

[*The sobs still shake him. He leans on a dummy*]

SERAFINA: Don't lean on my dummy. Sit down if you can't stand up.—What is the matter with you?

ALVARO: I always cry after a fight. But I don't want people to see me. It's not like a man.

[*There is a long pause;* SERAFINA's *attitude seems to warm toward the man*]

SERAFINA: A man is not no different from no one else . . . [*All at once her face puckers up, and for the first time in the play* SERAFINA *begins to weep, at first soundlessly, then audibly. Soon she is sobbing as loudly as* ALVARO. *She speaks between sobs*] —I always cry—when somebody else is crying . . .

ALVARO: No, no, lady, *don't* cry! Why should *you* cry? I will stop. I will stop in a minute. This is not like a man. I am ashame of myself. I will stop now; please, lady . . .

[*Still crouching a little with pain, a hand clasped to his abdomen,* ALVARO *turns away from the wall. He blows his nose between two fingers.* SERAFINA *picks up a scrap of white voile and gives it to him to wipe his fingers*]

SERAFINA: Your jacket is torn.

ALVARO: [*Sobbing*] My company jacket is torn?

SERAFINA: Yes . . .

ALVARO: Where is it torn?

SERAFINA: [*Sobbing*] Down the—back.

ALVARO: Oh, Dio!

SERAFINA: Take it off. I will sew it up for you. I do—sewing.

ALVARO: Oh, Dio! [*Sobbing*] I got three dependents!

[*He holds up three fingers and shakes them violently at* SERAFINA]

SERAFINA: Give me—give me your jacket.

ALVARO: He took down my license number!

SERAFINA: People are always taking down license numbers and telephone numbers and numbers that don't mean nothing—all them numbers . . .

ALVARO: Three, three dependents! Not citizens, even! No relief checks, no nothing! [SERAFINA *sobs*] He is going to complain to the boss.

SERAFINA: I wanted to cry all day.

ALVARO: He said he would fire me if I don't stop fighting!

SERAFINA: Stop crying so I can stop crying.

ALVARO: I am a sissy. Excuse me. I am ashame.

SERAFINA: Don't be ashame of nothing, the world is too crazy for people to be ashame in it. I'm not ashame and I had two fights on the street and my daughter called me "disgusting." I got to sew this by hand; the machine is broke in a fight with two women.

ALVARO: That's what—they call a cat fight . . . [*He blows his nose*]

SERAFINA: Open the shutters, please, for me. I can't see to work.

[*She has crossed to her work table. He goes over to the window. As he opens the shutters, the light falls across his fine torso, the undershirt clinging wetly to his dark olive skin.* SERAFINA *is struck and murmurs:* "Ohhh . . ." *There is the sound of music*]

ALVARO: What, lady?

SERAFINA: [*In a strange voice*] The light on the body was like a man that lived here . . .

ALVARO: Che dice?

SERAFINA: Niente.—Ma com'è strano!—Lei è Napoletano?

[*She is threading a needle*]

ALVARO: Io sono Siciliano! [SERAFINA *sticks her finger with her needle and cries out*] Che fa?

SERAFINA: I—stuck myself with the needle!—You had—better wash up . . .

ALVARO: Dov'è il gabinetto?

SERAFINA: [*Almost inaudibly*] Dietro.

[*She points vaguely back*]

ALVARO: Con permesso! [*He moves past her. As he does so, she picks up a pair of broken spectacles on the work table. Holding them up by the single remaining side piece, like a lorgnette, she inspects his passing figure with an air of stupefaction. As he goes out, he says:*] A kick like that can have serious consequences!

[*He goes into the back of the house*]

SERAFINA: [*After a pause*] Madonna Santa!—*My husband's body,* with the head of a *clown!* [*She crosses to the Madonna*] O Lady, O Lady! [*She makes an imploring gesture*] Speak to me!—What are you saying?—Please, Lady, I can't hear you! Is it a sign? Is it a sign of something? What does it mean? Oh, *speak to me,* Lady!—Everything is too strange!

[*She gives up the useless entreaty to the impassive statue. Then she rushes to the cupboard, clambers up on a chair and seizes a bottle of wine from the top shelf. But she finds it impossible to descend from the chair. Clasping the dusty bottle to her breast, she crouches there, helplessly whimpering like a child, as* ALVARO *comes back in*]

ALVARO: Ciao!

SERAFINA: I can't get up.

ALVARO: You mean you can't get down?

SERAFINA: I mean I—can't get down . . .

ALVARO: Con permesso, Signora!

[*He lifts her down from the chair*]

SERAFINA: Grazie.

ALVARO: I am ashame of what happen. Crying is not like a man. Did anyone see me?

SERAFINA: Nobody saw you but me. To me it don't matter.

ALVARO: You are simpatica, molto!—It was not just the fight that makes me break down. I was like this all day!

[*He shakes his clenched fists in the air*]

SERAFINA: You and—me, too!—What was the trouble today?

ALVARO: My name is Mangiacavallo which means "Eat-a-horse."

It's a comical name, I know. Maybe two thousand and seventy years ago one of my grandfathers got so hungry that he ate up a horse! That ain't my fault. Well, today at the Southern Fruit Company I find on the pay envelope not "Mangiacavallo" but "EAT A HORSE" in big print! Ha, ha, ha, very funny!—I open the pay envelope! In it I find a notice.—The wages have been *garnishee*! You know what garnishee is? [SERAFINA *nods gravely*] Garnishee!—Eat a horse!—Road hog!—All in one day is too much! I go crazy, I boil, I cry, and I am ashame but I am not able to help it!—Even a Wop truck driver's a human being! And human beings must cry . . .

SERAFINA: Yes, they must cry. I couldn't cry all day but now I have cried and I am feeling much better.—I will sew up the jacket . . .

ALVARO: [*Licking his lips*] What is that in your hand? A bottle of vino?

SERAFINA: This is Spumanti. It comes from the house of the family of my husband. The Delle Rose! A very great family. I was a peasant, but I married a baron!—No, I still don't believe it! I married a baron when I didn't have shoes!

ALVARO: Excuse me for asking—but where is the Baron, now? [SERAFINA *points gravely to the marble urn*] Where did you say?

SERAFINA: Them're his ashes in that marble urn.

ALVARO: Ma! Scusatemi! Scusatemi! [*Crossing himself*]—I hope he is resting in peace.

SERAFINA: It's him you reminded me of—when you opened the shutters. Not the face but the body.—Please get me some ice from the icebox in the kitchen. I had a—very bad day . . .

ALVARO: Oh, ice! Yes—ice—I'll get some . . .

[*As he goes out, she looks again through the broken spectacles at him*]

SERAFINA: *Non posso crederlo!*—A clown of a face like that with my husband's body!

[*There is the sound of ice being chopped in the kitchen. She inserts a corkscrew in the bottle but her efforts to open it are clumsily unsuccessful.* ALVARO *returns with a little bowl of ice.*

He sets it down so hard on the table that a piece flies out. He scrambles after it, retrieves it and wipes it off on his sweaty undershirt]

SERAFINA: I think the floor would be cleaner!

ALVARO: Scusatemi!—I wash it again?

SERAFINA: Fa niente!

ALVARO: I am a—clean!—I . . .

SERAFINA: Fa niente, niente!—The bottle should be in the ice but the next best thing is to pour the wine over the bottle.

ALVARO: You mean over the ice?

SERAFINA: I mean over the . . .

ALVARO: Let me open the bottle. Your hands are not used to rough work.

[She surrenders the bottle to him and regards him through the broken spectacles again]

SERAFINA: These little bits of white voile on the floor are not from a snowstorm. I been making voile dresses for high school graduation.—One for my daughter and for thirteen other girls.—All of the work I'm not sure didn't kill me!

ALVARO: The wine will make you feel better.

[There is a youthful cry from outside]

SERAFINA: There is a wild bunch of boys and girls in this town. In Sicily the boys would dance with the boys because a girl and a boy could not dance together unless they was going to be married. But here they run wild on islands!—boys, girls, man-crazy teachers . . .

ALVARO: Ecco! *[The cork comes off with a loud pop.* SERAFINA *cries out and staggers against the table. He laughs. She laughs with him, helplessly, unable to stop, unable to catch her breath]*—I like a woman that laughs with all her heart.

SERAFINA: And a woman that cries with her heart?

ALVARO: I like everything that a woman does with her heart.

[Both are suddenly embarrassed and their laughter dies out.

SERAFINA *smooths down her rayon slip. He hands her a glass of the sparkling wine with ice in it. She murmurs "Grazie." Unconsciously the injured finger is lifted again to her lip and she wanders away from the table with the glass held shakily]*

ALVARO: [*Continuing nervously*] I see you had a bad day.

SERAFINA: Sono così—stanca . . .

ALVARO: [*Suddenly springing to the window and shouting*] Hey, you kids, git down off that truck! Keep your hands off them bananas! [*At the words "truck" and "bananas"* SERAFINA *gasps again and spills some wine on her slip*] Little buggers!—Scusatemi . . .

SERAFINA: You haul—you haul bananas?

ALVARO: Si, Signora.

SERAFINA: Is it a 10-ton truck?

ALVARO: An 8-ton truck.

SERAFINA: My husband hauled bananas in a 10-ton truck.

ALVARO: Well, he was a baron.

SERAFINA: Do you haul just bananas?

ALVARO: Just bananas. What else would I haul?

SERAFINA: My husband hauled bananas, but underneath the bananas was something else. He was—wild like a—Gypsy.—"Wild—like a—Gypsy?" Who said that?—I hate to start to remember, and then not remember . . .

[*The dialogue between them is full of odd hesitations, broken sentences and tentative gestures. Both are nervously exhausted after their respective ordeals. Their fumbling communication has a curious intimacy and sweetness, like the meeting of two lonely children for the first time. It is oddly luxurious to them both, luxurious as the first cool wind of evening after a scorching day.* SERAFINA *idly picks up a little Sicilian souvenir cart from a table]*

SERAFINA: The priest was against it.

ALVARO: What was the priest against?

SERAFINA: Me keeping the ashes. It was against the Church law. But I had to have something and that was all I could have.

[*She sets down the cart*]

ALVARO: I don't see nothing wrong with it.

SERAFINA: You don't?

ALVARO: No! Niente!—The body would've decayed, but ashes always stay clean.

SERAFINA: [*Eagerly*] Si, si, bodies decay, but ashes always stay clean! Come here. I show you this picture—my wedding. [*She removes a picture tenderly from the wall*] Here's me a bride of fourteen, and this—this—this! [*Drumming the picture with her finger and turning her face to* ALVARO *with great lustrous eyes*] My husband! [*There is a pause. He takes the picture from her hand and holds it first close to his eyes, then far back, then again close with suspirations of appropriate awe*] Annnh?—Annnnh?— Che dice!

ALVARO: [*Slowly, with great emphasis*] Che bell' uomo! Che bell' uomo!

SERAFINA: [*Replacing the picture*] A rose of a man. On his chest he had the tatto of a rose. [*Then, quite suddenly*]—Do you believe strange things, or do you doubt them?

ALVARO: If strange things didn't happen, I wouldn't be here. You wouldn't be here. We wouldn't be talking together.

SERAFINA: Davvero! I'll tell you something about the tattoo of my husband. My husband, he had this rose tattoo on his chest. One night I woke up with a burning pain on me here. I turn on the light. I look at my naked breast and on it I see the rose tattoo of my husband, on me, on *my* breast, *his* tattoo.

ALVARO: Strano!

SERAFINA: And that was the night that—I got to speak frankly to tell you . . .

ALVARO: Speak frankly! We're grown-up people.

SERAFINA: That was the night I conceived my son—the little boy that was lost when I lost my husband . . .

ALVARO: Che cosa—strana!—Would you be willing to show me the rose tattoo?

SERAFINA: Oh, it's gone now, it only lasted a moment. But I did see it. I saw it clearly.—Do you believe me?

ALVARO: Lo credo!

SERAFINA: I don't know why I told you. But I like what you said. That bodies decay but ashes always stay clean—immacolate!—But, you know, there are some people that want to make everything dirty. Two of them kind of people come in the house today and told me a terrible lie in front of the ashes.—So awful a lie that if I thought it was true—I would smash the urn—and throw the ashes away! [*She hurls her glass suddenly to the floor*] Smash it, *smash it like that!*

ALVARO: Ma!—Baronessa!

[SERAFINA *seizes a broom and sweeps the fragments of glass away*]

SERAFINA: And take this broom and sweep them out the back door like so much trash!

ALVARO: [*Impressed by her violence and a little awed*] What lie did they tell you?

SERAFINA: No, no, no! I don't want to talk about it! [*She throws down the broom*] I just want to forget it; it wasn't true, it was false, false, false!—as the hearts of the bitches that told it . . .

ALVARO: Yes. I would forget anything that makes you unhappy.

SERAFINA: The memory of a love don't make you unhappy unless you believe a lie that makes it dirty. I don't believe in the lie. The ashes are clean. The memory of the rose in my heart is perfect!— Your glass is weeping . . .

ALVARO: *Your* glass is weeping too.

[*While she fills his glass, he moves about the room, looking here and there. She follows him. Each time he picks up an article for inspection she gently takes it from him and examines it herself with fresh interest*]

ALVARO: Cozy little homelike place you got here.

SERAFINA: Oh, it's—molto modesto.—You got a nice place, too?

ALVARO: I got a place with three dependents in it.

SERAFINA: What—dependents?

ALVARO: [*Counting them on his fingers*] One old maid sister, one feeble-minded grandmother, one lush of a pop that's not worth the powder it takes to blow him to hell.—They got the parchesi habit. They play the game of parchesi, morning, night, noon. Passing a bucket of beer around the table . . .

SERAFINA: They got the beer habit, too?

ALVARO: Oh, yes. And the numbers habit. This spring the old maid sister gets female trouble—mostly mental, I think—she turns the housekeeping over to the feeble-minded grandmother, a very sweet old lady who don't think it is necessary to pay the grocery bill so long as there's money to play the numbers. She plays the numbers. She has a perfect system except it don't ever work. And the grocery bill goes up, up, up, up, up!—so high you can't even see it!— Today the Ideal Grocery Company garnishees my wages . . . There, now! I've told you my life . . . [*The parrot squawks. He goes over to the cage*] Hello, Polly, how's tricks?

SERAFINA: The name ain't Polly. It ain't a she; it's a he.

ALVARO: How can you tell with all them tail feathers? [*He sticks his finger in the cage, pokes at the parrot and gets bitten*] Owww!

SERAFINA: [*Vicariously*] Ouuu . . . [ALVARO *sticks his injured finger in his mouth.* SERAFINA *puts her corresponding finger in her mouth. He crosses to the telephone*] I told you watch out.— What are you calling, a doctor?

ALVARO: I am calling my boss in Biloxi to explain why I'm late.

SERAFINA: The call to Biloxi is a ten-cent call.

ALVARO: Don't worry about it.

SERAFINA: I'm not worried about it. You will pay it.

ALVARO: You got a sensible attitude toward life . . . Give me the Southern Fruit Company in Biloxi—seven-eight-seven!

SERAFINA: You are a bachelor. With three dependents?

[*She glances below his belt*]

ALVARO: I'll tell you my hopes and dreams!

SERAFINA: Who? Me?

ALVARO: I am hoping to meet some sensible older lady. Maybe a
lady a little bit older than me.—I don't care if she's a little too
plump or not such a stylish dresser! [SERAFINA *self-consciously
pulls up a dangling strap*] The important thing in a lady is understanding. Good sense. And I want her to have a well-furnished
house and a profitable little business of some kind . . .

[*He looks about him significantly*]

SERAFINA: And such a lady, with a well-furnished house and business, what does she want with a man with three dependents with
the parchesi and the beer habit, playing the numbers!

ALVARO: Love and affection!—in a world that is lonely—and cold!

SERAFINA: It might be lonely but I would not say "cold" on this
particular day!

ALVARO: Love and affection is what I got to offer on hot or cold
days in this lonely old world and is what I am looking for. I got
nothing else. Mangiacavallo has nothing. In fact, he is the grandson of the village idiot of Ribera!

SERAFINA: [*Uneasily*] I see you like to make—jokes!

ALVARO: No, no joke!—Davvero!—He chased my grandmother in a
flooded rice field. She slip on a wet rock.—Ecco! Here I am.

SERAFINA: You ought to be more respectful.

ALVARO: What have I got to respect? The rock my grandmother
slips on?

SERAFINA: Yourself at least! Don't you work for a living?

ALVARO: If I *don't* work for a living I would respect myself *more*.
Baronessa, I am a healthy young man, existing without no love
life. I look at the magazine pictures. Them girls in the advertise-

ment—you know what I mean? A little bitty thing here? A little bitty thing there?

[*He touches two portions of his anatomy. The latter portion embarrasses* SERAFINA, *who quietly announces:*]

SERAFINA: The call is ten cents for three minutes. Is the line busy?

ALVARO: Not the line, but the boss.

SERAFINA: And the charge for the call goes higher. That ain't the phone of a millionaire you're using!

ALVARO: I think you talk a poor mouth. [*He picks up the piggy bank and shakes it*] This pig sounds well-fed to me.

SERAFINA: Dimes and quarters.

ALVARO: Dimes and quarters're better than nickels and dimes. [SERAFINA *rises severely and removes the piggy bank from his grasp*] Ha, ha, ha! You think I'm a bank robber?

SERAFINA: I think you are maleducato! Just get your boss on the phone or hang the phone up.

ALVARO: What, what! Mr. Siccardi? How tricks at the Southern Fruit Comp'ny this hot afternoon? Ha, ha, ha!—Mangiacavallo!— What? You got the complaint already? Sentite, per favore! This road hog was—Mr. Siccardi? [*He jiggles the hook; then slowly hangs up*] A man with three dependents!—out of a job . . .

[*There is a pause*]

SERAFINA: Well, you better ask the operator the charges.

ALVARO: Oofla! A man with three dependents—out of a job!

SERAFINA: I can't see to work no more. I got a suggestion to make. Open the bottom drawer of that there bureau and you will find a shirt in white tissue paper and you can wear that one while I am fixing this. And call for it later. [*He crosses to the bureau*]—It was made for somebody that never called for it. [*He removes the package*] Is there a name pinned to it?

ALVARO: Yes, it's . . .

SERAFINA: [*Fiercely, but with no physical movement*] Don't tell me the name! Throw it away, out the window!

ALVARO: Perchè?

SERAFINA: Throw it, throw it away!

ALVARO: [Crumpling the paper and throwing it through the window] Ecco fatto! [There is a distant cry of children as he unwraps the package and holds up the rose silk shirt, exclaiming in Latin delight at the luxury of it] Colore di rose! Seta! Seta pura! —Oh, this shirt is too good for Mangiacavallo! Everything here is too good for Mangiacavallo!

SERAFINA: Nothing's too good for a man if the man is good.

ALVARO: The grandson of a village idiot is not that good.

SERAFINA: No matter whose grandson you are, put it on; you are welcome to wear it.

ALVARO: [Slipping voluptuously into the shirt] Sssssssss!

SERAFINA: How does it feel, the silk, on you?

ALVARO: It feels like a girl's hands on me!

[There is a pause, while he shows her the whiteness of his teeth]

SERAFINA: [Holding up her broken spectacles] It will make you less trouble.

ALVARO: There is nothing more beautiful than a gift between people!—Now you are smiling!—You like me a little bit better?

SERAFINA: [Slowly and tenderly] You know what they should of done when you was a baby? They should of put tape on your ears to hold them back so when you grow up they wouldn't stick out like the wings of a little kewpie!

[She touches his ear, a very slight touch, betraying too much of her heart. Both laugh a little and she turns away, embarrassed.
Outside the goat bleats and there is the sound of splintering timber. One of the children races into the front yard, crying out]

SALVATORE: Mizz' Dell' Rose! The black goat's in your yard!

SERAFINA: Il becco della strega!

[SERAFINA *dashes to the window, throws the shutters vio-lently open and leans way out. This time, she almost feels re-lief in this distraction. The interlude of the goat chase has a quality of crazed exaltation. Outside is heard the wild bleat-ing of the goat and the jingling of his harness*]

SERAFINA: Miei pomodori! Guarda i miei pomodori!

THE STREGA: [*Entering the front yard with a broken length of rope, calling out*] Heyeh, Billy! Heyeh. Heyeh, Billy!

SERAFINA: [*Making the sign of horns with her fingers*] There is the Strega! She lets the goat in my yard to eat my tomatoes! [*Backing from the window*] She has the eye; she has the malocchio, and so does the goat! The goat has the evil eye, too. He got in my yard the night that I lost Rosario and my boy! Madonna, Madonna mia! Get that goat out of my yard!

[*She retreats to the Madonna, making the sign of the horns with her fingers, while the goat chase continues outside*]

ALVARO: Now take it easy! I will catch the black goat and give him a kick that he will never forget!

[ALVARO *runs out the front door and joins in the chase. The little boy is clapping together a pair of tin pan lids which sound like cymbals. The effect is weird and beautiful with the wild cries of the children and the goat's bleating.* SERAFINA *remains anxiously half way between the shutters and the pro-tecting Madonna. She gives a furious imitation of the bleat-ing goat, contorting her face with loathing. It is the fury of a woman at the desire she suffers. At last the goat is cap-tured*]

BRUNO: Got him, got him, got him!

ALVARO: Vieni presto, Diavolo!

[ALVARO *appears around the side of the house with a tight hold on the broken rope around the goat's neck. The boy fol-lows behind, gleefully clapping the tin lids together, and fur-ther back follows the* STREGA, *holding her broken length of rope, her grey hair hanging into her face and her black skirts*

caught up in one hand, revealing bare feet and hairy legs.
SERAFINA *comes out on the porch as the grotesque little procession passes before it, and she raises her hand with the
fingers making horns as the goat and the* STREGA *pass her.*
ALVARO *turns the goat over to the* STREGA *and comes panting
back to the house*]

ALVARO: Niente paura!—I got to go now.—You have been troppo
gentile, Mrs. . . .

SERAFINA: I am the widow of the Baron Delle Rose.—Excuse the
way I'm—not dressed . . . [*He keeps hold of her hand as he
stands on the porch steps. She continues very shyly, panting a
little*] I am not always like this.—Sometimes I fix myself up!—
When my husband was living, when my husband comes home,
when he was living—I had a clean dress on! And sometimes even,
I—put a rose in my hair . . .

ALVARO: A rose in your hair would be pretty!

SERAFINA: But for a widow—it ain't the time of roses . . .

[*The sound of music is heard, of a mandolin playing*]

ALVARO: Naw, you make a mistake! It's always for everybody the
time of roses! The rose is the heart of the world like the heart is
the—heart of the—body! But you, Baronessa—you know what I
think you have done?

SERAFINA: What—what have I—done?

ALVARO: You have put your heart in the marble urn with the ashes.
[*Now singing is heard along with the music, which continues to
the end of the scene*] And if in a storm sometime, or sometime
when a 10-ton truck goes down the highway—the marble urn was
to break! [*He suddenly points up at the sky*] Look! Look,
Baronessa!

SERAFINA: [*Startled*] Look? Look? I don't see!

ALVARO: I was pointing at your heart, broken out of the urn and
away from the ashes!—*Rondinella felice!*

[*He makes an airy gesture toward the fading sky*]

SERAFINA: Oh! [*He whistles like a bird and makes graceful wing-*

like motions with his hands] Buffone, buffone—piantatela! I take you serious—then you make it a joke . . .

[*She smiles involuntarily at his antics*]

ALVARO: When can I bring the shirt back?

SERAFINA: When do you pass by again?

ALVARO: I will pass by tonight for supper. Volete?

SERAFINA: Then look at the window tonight. If the shutters are open and there is a light in the window, you can stop by for your —jacket—but if the shutters are closed, you better not stop because my Rosa will be home. Rosa's my daughter. She has gone to a picnic—maybe—home early—but you know how picnics are. They—wait for the moon to—start singing.—Not that there's nothing wrong in two grown-up people having a quiet conversation!—but Rosa's fifteen—I got to be careful to set her a perfect example.

ALVARO: I will look at the window.—I will look at the win-dooow!

[*He imitates a bird flying off with gay whistles*]

SERAFINA: Buffone!

ALVARO: [*Shouting from outside*] Hey, you little buggers, climb down off that truck! Lay offa them bananas!

[*His truck is heard starting and pulling away.* SERAFINA *stands motionless on the porch, searching the sky with her eyes*]

SERAFINA: Rosario, forgive me! Forgive me for thinking that awful lie could be true!

[*The light in the house dims out. A little boy races into the yard holding triumphantly aloft a great golden bunch of bananas. A little girl pursues him with shrill cries. He eludes her. They dash around the house. The light fades and the curtain falls*]

ACT THREE

It is the evening of the same day. The neighborhood children are playing games around the house. One of them is counting by fives to a hundred, calling out the numbers, as he leans against the palm tree.
SERAFINA *is in the parlor, sitting on the sofa. She is seated stiffly and formally, wearing a gown that she has not worn since the death of her husband, and with a rose in her hair. It becomes obvious from her movements that she is wearing a girdle that constricts her unendurably.*

[*There is the sound of a truck approaching up on the highway.* SERAFINA *rises to an odd, crouching position. But the truck passes by without stopping. The girdle is becoming quite intolerable to* SERAFINA *and she decides to take it off, going behind the sofa to do so. With much grunting, she has gotten it down as far as her knees, when there is the sound outside of another truck approaching. This time the truck stops up on the highway, with a sound of screeching brakes. She realizes that* ALVARO *is coming, and her efforts to get out of the girdle, which is now pinioning her legs, become frantic. She hobbles from behind the sofa as* ALVARO *appears in front of the house*]

ALVARO: [*Gaily*] Rondinella felice! I will look at win-dooooo! Signora Delle Rose!

[SERAFINA's *response to this salutation is a groan of anguish. She hobbles and totters desperately to the curtains between the rooms and reaches them just in time to hide herself as*

ALVARO *comes into the parlor from the porch through the screen door. He is carrying a package and a candy box*]

ALVARO: C'è nessuno?

SERAFINA: [*At first inaudibly*] Si, si, sono qui. [*Then loudly and hoarsely, as she finally gets the girdle off her legs*] Si, si, sono qui!

[*To cover her embarrassment, she busies herself with fixing wine glasses on a tray*]

ALVARO: I hear the rattle of glasses! Let me help you!

[*He goes eagerly through the curtain but stops short, astonished*]

SERAFINA: Is—something the—matter?

ALVARO: I didn't expect to see you looking so pretty! You are **a** *young* little widow!

SERAFINA: You are—fix yourself up . . .

ALVARO: I been to The Ideal Barber's! I got the whole works!

SERAFINA: [*Faintly, retreating from him a little*] You got—rose oil —in your hair . . .

ALVARO: Olio di rose! You like the smell of it? [*Outside there is a wild, distant cry of children, and inside a pause.* SERAFINA *shakes her head slowly with the infinite wound of a recollection*]—You —don't—like—the smell of it? Oh, then I wash the smell *out*, I go and . . .

[*He starts toward the back. She raises her hand to stop him*]

SERAFINA: No, no, no, fa—niente.—I—*like* the smell of it . . .

[*A little boy races into the yard, ducks some invisible missile, sticks out his tongue and yells: "Yahhhhh!" Then he dashes behind the house*]

SERAFINA: Shall we—set down in the parlor?

ALVARO: I guess that's better than standing up in the dining room. [*He enters formally*]—Shall we set down on the sofa?

SERAFINA: You take the sofa. I will set down on this chair.

ALVARO: [*Disappointed*] You don't like to set on a sofa?

SERAFINA: I lean back too far on that sofa. I like a straight back behind me . . .

ALVARO: That chair looks not comfortable to me.

SERAFINA: This chair is a comfortable chair.

ALVARO: But it's more easy to talk with two on a sofa!

SERAFINA: I talk just as good on a chair as I talk on a sofa . . . [*There is a pause.* ALVARO *nervously hitches his shoulder*] Why do you hitch your shoulders like that?

ALVARO: Oh, that!—That's a—nervous—habit . . .

SERAFINA: I thought maybe the suit don't fit you good . . .

ALVARO: I bought this suit to get married in four years ago.

SERAFINA: But didn't get married?

ALVARO: I give her, the girl, a zircon instead of a diamond. She had it examined. The door was slammed in my face.

SERAFINA: I think that maybe I'd do the same thing myself.

ALVARO: Buy the zircon?

SERAFINA: No, slam the door.

ALVARO: Her eyes were not sincere looking. You've got sincere looking eyes. Give me your hand so I can tell your fortune! [*She pushes her chair back from him*] I see two men in your life. One very handsome. One not handsome. His ears are too big but not as big as his heart! He has three dependents.—In fact he has four dependents! Ha, ha, ha!

SERAFINA: What is the fourth dependent?

ALVARO: The one that every man's got, his biggest expense, worst troublemaker and chief liability! Ha, ha, ha!

SERAFINA: I hope you are not talking vulgar. [*She rises and turns her back to him. Then she discovers the candy box*] What's that fancy red box?

ALVARO: A present I bought for a nervous but nice little lady!

SERAFINA: Chocolates? Grazie! Grazie! But I'm too fat.

ALVARO: You are not fat, you are just pleasing and plump.

[*He reaches way over to pinch the creamy flesh of her upper arm*]

SERAFINA: No, please. Don't make me nervous. If I get nervous again I will start to cry . . .

ALVARO: Let's talk about something to take your mind off your troubles. You say you got a young daughter?

SERAFINA: [*In a choked voice*] Yes. I got a young daughter. Her name is Rosa.

ALVARO: Rosa, Rosa! She's pretty?

SERAFINA: She has the eyes of her father, and his wild, stubborn blood! Today was the day of her graduation from high school. She looked so pretty in a white voile dress with a great big bunch of—roses . . .

ALVARO: Not no prettier than her Mama, I bet—with that rose in your hair!

SERAFINA: She's only fifteen.

ALVARO: Fifteen?

SERAFINA: [*Smoothing her blue silk lap with a hesitant hand*] Yes, only fifteen . . .

ALVARO: But has a boyfriend, does she?

SERAFINA: She met a sailor.

ALVARO: Oh, Dio! No wonder you seem to be nervous.

SERAFINA: I didn't want to let her go out with this sailor. He had a gold ring in his ear.

ALVARO: Madonna Santa!

SERAFINA: This morning she cut her wrist—not much but enough to bleed—with a kitchen knife!

ALVARO: Tch, tch! A very wild girl!

SERAFINA: I had to give in and let her bring him to see me. He said he was Catholic. I made him kneel down in front of Our Lady there and give Her his promise that he would respect the innocence of my Rosa!—But how do I know that he was a Catholic, *really?*

ALVARO: [*Taking her hand*] Poor little worried lady! But you got to face facts. Sooner or later the innocence of your daughter cannot be respected.—Did he—have a—tattoo?

SERAFINA: [*Startled*] Did who have—what?

ALVARO: The sailor friend of your daughter, did he have a tattoo?

SERAFINA: Why do you ask me that?

ALVARO: Just because most sailors have a tattoo.

SERAFINA: How do I know if he had a tattoo or not!

ALVARO: *I* got a tattoo!

SERAFINA: *You* got a tattoo?

ALVARO: Si, si, veramente!

SERAFINA: What kind of tattoo you got?

ALVARO: What kind you think?

SERAFINA: Oh, I think—you have got—a South Sea girl without clothes on . . .

ALVARO: No South Sea girl.

SERAFINA: Well, maybe a big red heart with MAMA written across it.

ALVARO: Wrong again, Baronessa.

[*He takes off his tie and slowly unbuttons his shirt, gazing at her with an intensely warm smile. He divides the unbuttoned shirt, turning toward her his bare chest. She utters a gasp and rises*]

SERAFINA: No, no, no!—*Not a rose!*

[*She says it as if she were evading her feelings*]

ALVARO: Si, si, una rosa!

SERAFINA: I—don't feel good! The air is . . .

ALVARO: Che fate, che fate, che dite?

SERAFINA: The house has a tin roof on it!—The air is—I got to go outside the house to breathe! Scu—scusatemi!

[*She goes out onto the porch and clings to one of the spindling porch columns for support, breathing hoarsely with a hand to her throat. He comes out slowly*]

ALVARO: [*Gently*] I didn't mean to surprise you!—Mi dispiace molto!

SERAFINA: [*With enforced calm*] Don't—talk about it! Anybody could have a rose tattoo.—It don't mean nothing.—You know how a tin roof is. It catches the heat all day and it don't cool off until—midnight . . .

ALVARO: No, no, not until midnight. [*She makes a faint laughing sound, is quite breathless and leans her forehead against the porch column. He places his fingers delicately against the small of her back*] It makes it hot in the bedroom—so that you got to sleep without nothing on you . . .

SERAFINA: No, you—can't stand the covers . . .

ALVARO: You can't even stand a—*nightgown!*

[*His fingers press her back*]

SERAFINA: Please. There is a strega next door; she's always watching!

ALVARO: It's been so long since I felt the soft touch of a woman! [*She gasps loudly and turns to the door*] Where are you going?

SERAFINA: I'm going back in the house!

[*She enters the parlor again, still with forced calm*]

ALVARO: [*Following her inside*] Now, now, what is the matter?

SERAFINA: I got a feeling like I have—forgotten something.

ALVARO: What?

SERAFINA: I can't remember.

ALVARO: It couldn't be nothing important if you can't remember. Let's open the chocolate box and have some candy.

SERAFINA: [*Eager for any distraction*] Yes! Yes, open the box!

[ALVARO *places a chocolate in her hand. She stares at it blankly*]

ALVARO: Eat it, eat the chocolate. If you don't eat it, it will melt in your hand and make your fingers all gooey!

SERAFINA: Please, I . . .

ALVARO: Eat it!

SERAFINA: [*Weakly and gagging*] I can't, I can't, I would choke! Here, you eat it.

ALVARO: Put it in my mouth! [*She puts the chocolate in his mouth*] Now, look. Your fingers are gooey!

SERAFINA: Oh!—I better go wash them!

[*She rises unsteadily. He seizes her hands and licks her fingers*]

ALVARO: Mmmm! Mmmmm! Good, very good!

SERAFINA: Stop that, stop that, stop that! That—ain't—nice . . .

ALVARO: I'll lick off the chocolate for you.

SERAFINA: No, no, no!—I am the mother of a fifteen-year-old girl!

ALVARO: You're as old as your arteries, Baronessa. Now set back down. The fingers are now white as snow!

SERAFINA: You don't—understand—how I feel . . .

ALVARO: You don't understand how *I* feel.

SERAFINA: [*Doubtfully*] How do you—feel? [*In answer, he stretches the palms of his hands out toward her as if she were a fireplace in a freezing-cold room*]—What does—that—mean?

ALVARO: The night is warm but I feel like my hands are—freezing!

SERAFINA: Bad—circulation . . .

ALVARO: No, too *much* circulation! [ALVARO *becomes tremulously pleading, shuffling forward a little, slightly crouched like a beggar]* Across the room I feel the sweet warmth of a lady!

SERAFINA: [*Retreating, doubtfully*] Oh, you talk a sweet mouth. I think you talk a sweet mouth to fool a woman.

ALVARO: No, no, I know—I know that's what warms the world, that is what makes it the summer! [*He seizes the hand she holds defensively before her and presses it to his own breast in a crushing grip*] Without it, the rose—the rose would not grow on the bush; the fruit would not grow on the tree!

SERAFINA: I know, and the truck—the truck would not haul the bananas! But, Mr. Mangiacavallo, that is my hand, not a sponge. I got bones in it. Bones break!

ALVARO: Scusatemi, Baronessa! [*He returns her hand to her with a bow*] For me it is winter, because I don't have in my life the sweet warmth of a lady. I live with my hands in my pockets! [*He stuffs his hands violently into his pants' pockets, then jerks them out again. A small cellophane-wrapped disk falls on the floor, escaping his notice, but not* SERAFINA's]—You don't like the poetry! —How can a man talk to you?

SERAFINA: [*Ominously*] I like the poetry good. Is that a piece of the poetry that you dropped out of your pocket? [*He looks down*]—No, no, right by your foot!

ALVARO: [*Aghast as he realizes what it is that she has seen*] Oh, that's—that's nothing!

[*He kicks it under the sofa*]

SERAFINA: [*Fiercely*] You talk a sweet mouth about women. Then drop such a thing from your pocket?—Va via, vigliacco!

[*She marches grandly out of the room, pulling the curtains together behind her. He hangs his head despairingly between his hands. Then he approaches the curtains timidly*]

ALVARO: [*In a small voice*] Baronessa?

SERAFINA: Pick up what you dropped on the floor and go to the Square Roof with it. Buona notte!

ALVARO: Baronessa!

[*He parts the curtains and peeks through them*]

SERAFINA: I told you good night. Here is no casa privata. Io, non sono puttana!

ALVARO: Understanding is—very—necessary!

SERAFINA: I understand plenty. You think you got a good thing, a thing that is cheap!

ALVARO: You make a mistake, Baronessa! [*He comes in and drops to his knees beside her, pressing his cheek to her flank. He speaks rhapsodically*] So soft is a lady! So, so, so, so, so *soft*—is a lady!

SERAFINA: Andate via, sporcaccione, andate a casa! Lasciatemi! Lasciatemi stare!

[*She springs up and runs into the parlor. He pursues. The chase is grotesquely violent and comic. A floor lamp is overturned. She seizes the chocolate box and threatens to slam it into his face if he continues toward her. He drops to his knees, crouched way over, and pounds the floor with his fists, sobbing*]

ALVARO: Everything in my life turns out like this!

SERAFINA: Git up, git up, git up!—you village idiot's grandson! There is people watching you through that window, the—strega next door . . . [*He rises slowly*] And where is the shirt that I loaned you?

[*He shuffles abjectly across the room, then hands her a neatly wrapped package*]

ALVARO: My sister wrapped it up for you.—My sister was very happy I met this *nice* lady!

SERAFINA: Maybe she thinks I will pay the grocery bill while she plays the numbers!

ALVARO: She don't think nothing like that. She is an old maid, my sister. She wants—nephews—nieces . . .

SERAFINA: You tell her for me I don't give nephews and nieces!

[ALVARO *hitches his shoulders violently in his embarrassment and shuffles over to where he had left his hat. He blows the dust off it and rubs the crown on his sleeve.* SERAFINA *presses a knuckle to her lips as she watches his awkward gestures. She is a little abashed by his humility. She speaks next with the great dignity of a widow whose respectability has stood the test*]

SERAFINA: Now, Mr. Mangiacavallo, please tell me the truth about something. When did you get the tattoo put on your chest?

ALVARO: [*Shyly and sadly, looking down at his hat*] I got it tonight—after supper . . .

SERAFINA: That's what I thought. You had it put on because I told you about my husband's tattoo.

ALVARO: I wanted to be—close to you . . . to make you—happy . . .

SERAFINA: Tell it to the marines! [*He puts on his hat with an apologetic gesture*] You got the tattoo and the chocolate box after supper, and then you come here to fool me!

ALVARO: I got the chocolate box a long time ago.

SERAFINA: How long ago? If that is not too much a personal question!

ALVARO: I got it the night the door was slammed in my face by the girl that I give—the zircon . . .

SERAFINA: Let that be a lesson. Don't try to fool women. You are not smart enough!—Now take the shirt back. You can keep it.

ALVARO: Huh?

SERAFINA: Keep it. I don't want it back.

ALVARO: You just now said that you did.

SERAFINA: It's a man's shirt, ain't it?

ALVARO: You just now accused me of trying to steal it off you.

SERAFINA: Well, you been making me nervous!

ALVARO: Is it my fault you been a widow too long?

SERAFINA: You make a mistake!

ALVARO: *You* make a mistake!

SERAFINA: Both of us make a mistake!

[*There is a pause. They both sigh profoundly*]

ALVARO: We should of have been friends, but I think we meet the wrong day.—Suppose I go out and come in the door again and we start all over?

SERAFINA: No, I think it's no use. The day was wrong to begin with, because of two women. Two women, they told me today that my husband had put on my head the nanny-goat's horns!

ALVARO: How is it possible to put horns on a widow?

SERAFINA: That was before, before! They told me my husband was having a steady affair with a woman at the Square Roof. What was the name on the shirt, on the slip of paper? Do you remember the name?

ALVARO: You told me to . . .

SERAFINA: Tell me! Do you remember?

ALVARO: I remember the name because I know the woman. The name was Estelle Hohengarten.

SERAFINA: Take me there! Take me to the Square Roof!—Wait, wait!

[*She plunges into the dining room, snatches a knife out of the sideboard drawer and thrusts it in her purse. Then she rushes back, with the blade of the knife protruding from the purse*]

ALVARO: [*Noticing the knife*] They—got a cover charge there . . .

SERAFINA: I will charge them a cover! Take me there now, this minute!

ALVARO: The fun don't start till midnight.

SERAFINA: I will start the fun sooner.

ALVARO: The floor show commences at midnight.

SERAFINA: I will commence it! [*She rushes to the phone*] Yellow
Cab, please, Yellow Cab. I want to go to the Square Roof out of
my house! Yes, you come to my house and take me to the Square
Roof right this minute! My number is—what is my number? Oh
my God, what is my number?—64 is my number on Front Street!
Subito, subito—quick!

[*The goat bleats outside*]

ALVARO: Baronessa, the knife's sticking out of your purse. [*He
grabs the purse*] What do you want with this weapon?

SERAFINA: To cut the lying tongue out of a woman's mouth! Saying
she has on her breast the tattoo of my husband because he had put
on me the horns of a goat! I cut the heart out of that woman, she
cut the heart out of me!

ALVARO: Nobody's going to cut the heart out of nobody!

[*A car is heard outside, and* SERAFINA *rushes to the porch*]

SERAFINA: [*Shouting*] Hey, Yellow Cab, Yellow Cab, Yellow—
Cab . . . [*The car passes by without stopping. With a sick moan
she wanders into the yard. He follows her with a glass of wine*]—
Something hurts—in my heart . . .

ALVARO: [*Leading her gently back to the house*] Baronessa, drink
this wine on the porch and keep your eyes on that star. [*He leads
her to a porch pillar and places the glass in her trembling hand.
She is now submissive*] You know the name of that star? That
star is Venus. She is the only female star in the sky. Who put her
up there? Mr. Siccardi, the transportation manager of the Southern Fruit Company? No. She was put there by God. [*He enters
the house and removes the knife from her purse*] And yet there's
some people that don't believe in nothing. [*He picks up the
telephone*] Esplanade 9-7-0.

SERAFINA: What are you doing?

ALVARO: Drink that wine and I'll settle this whole problem for you.
[*On the telephone*] I want to speak to the blackjack dealer,
please, Miss Estelle Hohengarten . . .

SERAFINA: Don't talk to that woman, she'll lie!

ALVARO: Not Estelle Hohengarten. She deals a straight game of cards.—Estelle? This is Mangiacavallo. I got a question to ask you which is a personal question. It has to do with a very goodlooking truckdriver, not living now but once on a time thought to have been a very well-known character at the Square Roof. His name was . . . [*He turns questioningly to the door where Serafina is standing*] What was his name, Baronessa?

SERAFINA: [*Hardly breathing*] Rosario Delle Rose!

ALVARO: Rosario Delle Rose was the name. [*There is a pause*]—È vero?—Mah! Che peccato . . .

[SERAFINA *drops her glass and springs into the parlor with a savage outcry. She snatches the phone from* ALVARO *and screams into it*]

SERAFINA: [*Wildly*] This is the wife that's speaking! What do you know of my husband, what is the lie?

[*A strident voice sounds over the wire*]

THE VOICE: [*Loud and clear*] Don't you remember? I brought you the rose-colored silk to make him a shirt. You said, "For a man?" and I said, "Yes, for a man that's wild like a Gypsy!" But if you think I'm a liar, come here and let me show you his rose tattooed on my chest!

[SERAFINA *holds the phone away from her as though it had burst into flame. Then, with a terrible cry, she hurls it to the floor. She staggers dizzily toward the Madonna.* ALVARO *seizes her arm and pushes her gently onto the sofa*]

ALVARO: Piano, piano, Baronessa! This will be gone, this will pass in a moment.

[*He puts a pillow behind her, then replaces the telephone*]

SERAFINA: [*Staggering up from the sofa*] The room's—going round . . .

ALVARO: You ought to stay lying down a little while longer. I know, I know what you need! A towel with some ice in it to put on your forehead—Baronessa.—You stay right there while I fix it! [*He goes into the kitchen, and calls back*] Torno subito, Baronessa!

[*The little boy runs into the yard. He leans against the bending trunk of the palm, counting loudly*]

THE LITTLE BOY: Five, ten, fifteen, twenty, twenty-five, thirty . . .

[*There is the sound of ice being chopped in the kitchen*]

SERAFINA: Dove siete, dove siete?

ALVARO: In cucina!—Ghiaccio . . .

SERAFINA: Venite qui!

ALVARO: Subito, subito . . .

SERAFINA: [*Turning to the shrine, with fists knotted*] Non voglio, non voglio farlo!

[*But she crosses slowly, compulsively toward the shrine, with a trembling arm stretched out*]

THE LITTLE BOY: Seventy-five, eighty, eighty-five, ninety, ninety-five, one hundred! [*Then, wildly*] Ready or not you shall be caught!

[*At this cry, SERAFINA seizes the marble urn and hurls it violently into the furthest corner of the room. Then, instantly, she covers her face. Outside the mothers are heard calling their children home. Their voices are tender as music, fading in and out. The children appear slowly at the side of the house, exhausted from their wild play*]

GIUSEPPINA: Vivi! Vi-vi!

PEPPINA: Salvatore!

VIOLETTA: Bruno! Come home, come home!

[*The children scatter. ALVARO comes in with the ice-pick*]

ALVARO: I broke the point of the ice-pick.

SERAFINA: [*Removing her hands from her face*] I don't want ice . . . [*She looks about her, seeming to gather a fierce strength in her body. Her voice is hoarse, her body trembling with violence, eyes narrow and flashing, her fists clenched*] Now I show you how wild and strong like a man a woman can be! [*She crosses to the screen door, opens it and shouts*] Buona notte, Mr. Mangiacavallo!

ALVARO: You—you make me go *home*, now?

SERAFINA: No, no; senti, cretino! [*In a strident whisper*] You make out like you are going. You drive the truck out of sight where the witch can't see it. Then you come back and I leave the back door open for you to come in. Now, tell me good-bye so all the neighbors can hear you! [*She shouts*] Arrivederci!

ALVARO: Ha, ha! Capish! [*He shouts too*] Arrivederci!

[*He runs to the foot of the embankment steps*]

SERAFINA: [*Still more loudly*] Buona notte!

ALVARO: Buona notte, Baronessa!

SERAFINA: [*In a choked voice*] Give them my love; give everybody—my love . . . Arrivederci!

ALVARO: Ciao!

[ALVARO *scrambles on down the steps and goes off.* SERAFINA *comes down into the yard. The goat bleats. She mutters savagely to herself*]

SERAFINA: Sono una bestia, una bestia feroce!

[*She crosses quickly around to the back of the house. As she disappears, the truck is heard driving off; the lights sweep across the house.* SERAFINA *comes in through the back door. She is moving with great violence, gasping and panting. She rushes up to the Madonna and addresses her passionately with explosive gestures, leaning over so that her face is level with the statue's*]

SERAFINA: Ora, ascolta, Signora! You hold in the cup of your hand this little house and you smash it! You break this little house like the shell of a bird in your hand, because you hate Serafina?—Serafina that *loved* you!—No, no, no, you don't speak! I don't believe in you, Lady! You're just a poor little doll with the paint peeling off, and now I blow out the light and I forget you the way you forget Serafina! [*She blows out the vigil light*] Ecco—fatto!

[*But now she is suddenly frightened; the vehemence and boldness have run out. She gasps a little and backs away from the shrine, her eyes rolling apprehensively this way and that. The parrot squawks at her. The goat bleats. The night is full of sinister noises, harsh bird cries, the sudden flapping of wings in the cane-brake, a distant shriek of Negro laughter.* SERAFINA *retreats to the window and opens the shutters wider to admit the moonlight. She stands panting by the window with a fist pressed to her mouth. In the back of the house a door slams open.* SERAFINA *catches her breath and moves as though for protection behind the dummy of the bride.* ALVARO *enters through the back door, calling out softly and hoarsely, with great excitement*]

ALVARO: Dove? Dove sei, cara?

SERAFINA: [*Faintly*] Sono qui . . .

ALVARO: You have turn out the light!

SERAFINA: The moon is enough . . . [*He advances toward her. His white teeth glitter as he grins.* SERAFINA *retreats a few steps from him. She speaks tremulously, making an awkward gesture toward the sofa*] Now we can go on with our—conversation . . . [*She catches her breath sharply*]

[*The curtain comes down*]

SCENE TWO

It is just before daybreak of the next day. ROSA *and* JACK *appear at the top of the embankment steps.*

ROSA: I thought they would never leave. [*She comes down the steps and out in front of the house, then calls back to him*] Let's go down there.

[*He obeys hesitatingly. Both are very grave. The scene is played as close as possible to the audience. She sits very straight. He stands behind her with his hands on her shoulders*]

ROSA: [*Leaning her head back against him*] This was the happiest day of my life, and this is the saddest night . . .

[*He crouches in front of her*]

SERAFINA: [*From inside the house*] Aaaaaahhhhhhhh!

JACK: [*Springing up, startled*] What's that?

ROSA: [*Resentfully*] Oh! That's Mama dreaming about my father.

JACK: I—feel like a—*heel!* I feel like a rotten heel!

ROSA: Why?

JACK: That promise I made your mother.

ROSA: I hate her for it.

JACK: Honey—Rosa, she—wanted to protect you.

[*There is a long-drawn cry from the back of the house: "Ohhhh—Rosario!"*]

ROSA: She wanted me not to have what she's dreaming about . . .

JACK: Naw, naw, honey, she—wanted to—protect you . . .

[*The cry from within is repeated softly*]

ROSA: Listen to her making love in her sleep! Is that what she wants *me* to do, just—*dream* about it?

JACK: [*Humbly*] She knows that her Rosa *is* a rose. And she wants her rose to have someone—better than *me* . . .

ROSA: *Better* than—*you!*

[*She speaks as if the possibility were too preposterous to think of*]

JACK: You see me through—rose-colored—glasses . . .

ROSA: I see you with love!

JACK: Yes, but your Mama sees me with—common sense . . . [*SERAFINA cries out again*] I got to be going! [*She keeps a tight hold on him. A rooster crows*] Honey, it's so late the roosters are crowing!

ROSA: They're fools, they're fools, it's early!

JACK: Honey, on that island I almost forgot my promise. Almost, but not quite. Do you understand, honey?

ROSA: Forget the promise!

JACK: I made it on my knees in front of Our Lady. I've got to leave now, honey.

ROSA: [Clasping him fiercely] You'd have to break my arms to!

JACK: Rosa, Rosa! You want to drive me crazy?

ROSA: I want you not to remember.

JACK: You're a very young girl! Fifteen—fifteen is too young!

ROSA: Caro, caro, carissimo!

JACK: You got to save some of those feelings for when you're grown up!

ROSA: Carissimo!

JACK: Hold some of it back until you're grown!

ROSA: I have been grown for two years!

JACK: No, no, that ain't what I . . .

ROSA: Grown enough to be married, and have a—baby!

JACK: [Springing up] Oh, good—Lord! [He circles around her, pounding his palm repeatedly with his fist and champing his teeth together with a grimace. Suddenly he speaks] I got to be going!

ROSA: You want me to scream? [He groans and turns away from her to resume his desperate circle. ROSA is blocking the way with her body]—I know, I know! You don't want me! [Jack groans through his gritting teeth] No, no, you don't want me . . .

JACK: Now you listen to me! You almost got into trouble today on that island! You almost did, but not quite!—But it didn't quite happen and no harm is done and you can just—forget it . . .

ROSA: It is the only thing in my life that I want to remember!—When are you going back to New Orleans?

JACK: Tomorrow.

ROSA: When does your—ship sail?

JACK: Tomorrow.

ROSA: Where to?

JACK: Guatemala.

SERAFINA: [*From the house*] Aahh!

ROSA: Is that a long trip?

JACK: After Guatemala, Buenos Aires. After Buenos Aires, Rio. Then around the Straits of Magellan and back up the west coast of South America, putting in at three ports before we dock at San Francisco.

ROSA: I don't think I will—ever see you again . . .

JACK: The ship won't sink!

ROSA: [*Faintly and forlornly*] No, but—I think it could just happen once, and if it don't happen that time, it never can—later . . . [*A rooster crows. They face each other sadly and quietly*] You don't need to be very old to understand how it works out. One time, one time, only once, it could be—God!—to remember.—Other times? Yes—they'd be something.—But only once, God—to remember . . . [*With a little sigh she crosses to pick up his white cap and hand it gravely to him*]—I'm sorry to you it didn't—mean—that much . . .

JACK: [*Taking the cap and hurling it to the ground*] Look! Look at my knuckles! You see them scabs on my knuckles? You know how them scabs got there? They got there because I banged my knuckles that hard on the deck of the sailboat!

ROSA: Because it—didn't quite happen? [*JACK jerks his head up and down in grotesquely violent assent to her question. ROSA picks up his cap and returns it to him again*]—Because of the promise to Mama! I'll never forgive her . . . [*There is a pause*] What time in the afternoon must you be on the boat?

JACK: Why?

ROSA: Just tell me what time.

JACK: Five!—Why?

ROSA: What will you be doing till five?

JACK: Well, I could be a goddam liar and tell you I was going to—pick me a hatful of daisies in—Audubon Park.—Is that what you want me to tell you?

ROSA: No, tell me the truth.

JACK: All right, I'll tell you the truth. I'm going to check in at some flea-bag hotel on North Rampart Street. Then I'm going to get loaded! And then I'm going to get . . .

[*He doesn't complete the sentence but she understands him. She places the hat more becomingly on his blond head*]

ROSA: Do me a little favor. [*Her hand slides down to his cheek and then to his mouth*] Before you get loaded and before you—before you—

JACK: Huh?

ROSA: Look in the waiting room at the Greyhound bus station, please. At twelve o'clock, noon!

JACK: Why?

ROSA: You might find me there, waiting for you . . .

JACK: What—what good would that do?

ROSA: I never been to a hotel but I know they have numbers on doors and sometimes—numbers are—lucky.—Aren't they?—Sometimes?—Lucky?

JACK: You want to buy me a ten-year stretch in the brig?

ROSA: I want you to give me that little gold ring on your ear to put on my finger.—I want to give you my heart to keep forever! And ever! And ever! [*Slowly and with a barely audible sigh she leans her face against him*] Look for me! I will be there!

JACK: [*Breathlessly*] In all of my life, I never felt nothing so sweet as the feel of your little warm body in my arms . . .

[*He breaks away and runs toward the road. From the foot of the steps he glares fiercely back at her like a tiger through the bars of a cage. She clings to the two porch pillars, her body leaning way out*]

ROSA: Look for me! I will be there!

[JACK *runs away from the house.* ROSA *returns inside, List-lessly she removes her dress and falls on the couch in her slip, kicking off her shoes. Then she begins to cry, as one cries only once in a lifetime, and the scene dims out*]

SCENE THREE

The time is three hours later.
We see first the exterior view of the small frame building against a night sky which is like the starry blue robe of Our Lady. It is growing slightly paler.

[*The faint light discloses* ROSA *asleep on the couch. The covers are thrown back for it has been a warm night, and on the concave surface of the white cloth, which is like the dimly lustrous hollow of a shell, is the body of the sleeping girl which is clad only in a sheer white slip.*
A cock crows. A gentle wind stirs the white curtains inward and the tendrils of vine at the windows, and the sky lightens enough to distinguish the purple trumpets of the morning glory against the very dim blue of the sky in which the planet Venus remains still undimmed.
In the back of the cottage someone is heard coughing hoarsely and groaning in the way a man does who has drunk very heavily the night before. Bedsprings creak as a heavy figure rises. Light spills dimly through the curtains, now closed, between the two front rooms.
There are heavy, padding footsteps and ALVARO *comes stumbling rapidly into the dining room with the last bottle of Spumanti in the crook of an arm, his eyes barely open, legs rubbery, saying, "Wuh-wuh-wuh-wuh-wuh-wuh . . ." like the breathing of an old dog. The scene should be played with the pantomimic lightness, almost fantasy, of an early Chaplin comedy. He is wearing only his trousers and his chest is bare.*

As he enters he collides with the widow dummy, staggers
back, pats her inflated bosom in a timid, apologetic way, re-
marking:]

ALVARO: Scusami, Signora, I am the grandson of the village idiot of
Ribera!

[ALVARO *backs into the table and is propelled by the impact
all the way to the curtained entrance to the parlor. He draws
the curtains apart and hangs onto them, peering into the
room. Seeing the sleeping girl, he blinks several times, suddenly makes a snoring sound in his nostrils and waves one
hand violently in front of his eyes as if to dispel a vision. Outside the goat utters a long "Baaaaaaaaaaa!" As if in response,*
ALVARO *whispers, in the same basso key, "Che bella!" The
first vowel of "bella" is enormously prolonged like the "baaa"
of the goat. On his rubbery legs he shuffles forward a few
steps and leans over to peer more intently at the vision. The
goat bleats again.* ALVARO *whispers more loudly: "Che bel-la!"
He drains the Spumanti, then staggers to his knees, the empty
bottle rolling over the floor. He crawls on his knees to the
foot of the bed, then leans against it like a child peering into
a candy shop window, repeating: "Che bel-la, che bel-la!"
with antiphonal responses from the goat outside. Slowly, with
tremendous effort, as if it were the sheer side of a precipice,
he clambers upon the couch and crouches over the sleeping
girl in a leap-frog position, saying "Che bel-la!" quite loudly,
this time, in a tone of innocently joyous surprise. All at once*
ROSA *wakens. She screams, even before she is quite awake, and
springs from the couch so violently that* ALVARO *topples over
to the floor.*
SERAFINA *cries out almost instantly after* ROSA. *She lunges
through the dining room in her torn and disordered nightgown. At the sight of the man crouched by the couch a
momentary stupefaction turns into a burst of savage fury. She
flies at him like a great bird, tearing and clawing at his
stupefied figure. With one arm* ALVARO *wards off her blows,
plunging to the floor and crawling into the dining room. She
seizes a broom with which she flails him about the head, but-
tocks and shoulders while he scrambles awkwardly away. The
assault is nearly wordless. Each time she strikes at him she
hisses: "Sporcaccione!" He continually groans: "Dough,*

*dough, dough!" At last he catches hold of the widow dummy
which he holds as a shield before him while he entreats the
two women*]

ALVARO: Senti, Baronessa! Signorina! I didn't know what I was
doin', I was dreamin', I was just dreamin'! I got turn around in the
house; I got all twisted! I thought that you was your Mama!—
Sono ubriaco! Per favore!

ROSA: [*Seizing the broom*] That's enough, Mama!

SERAFINA: [*Rushing to the phone*] Police!

ROSA: [*Seizing the phone*] No, no, no, no, no, no!—You want everybody to know?

SERAFINA: [*Weakly*] Know?—Know *what*, cara?

ROSA: Just give him his clothes, now, Mama, and let him get out!

[*She is clutching a bedsheet about herself*]

ALVARO: Signorina—young lady! I swear I was *dreaming!*

SERAFINA: Don't speak to my daughter! [*Then, turning to* ROSA]—
Who is this man? How did this man get here?

ROSA: [*Coldly*] Mama, don't say any more. Just give him his
clothes in the bedroom so he can get out!

ALVARO: [*Still crouching*] I am so sorry, so sorry! I don't remember a thing but that I was dreaming!

SERAFINA: [*Shoving him toward the back of the room with her
broom*] Go on, go get your clothes on, you—idiot's grandson,
you!—Svelto, svelto, più svelto! [ALVARO *continues his apologetic
mumbling in the back room*] Don't talk to me, don't say nothing! Or I will kill you!

[*A few moments later* ALVARO *rushes around the side of the
house, his clothes half buttoned and his shirt-tails out*]

ALVARO: But, Baronessa, I *love* you! [*A tea kettle sails over his
head from behind the house. The* STREGA *bursts into laughter.
Despairingly* ALVARO *retreats, tucking his shirt-tails in and shaking
his head*] Baronessa, Baronessa, I love you!

[*As* ALVARO *runs off, the* STREGA *is heard cackling:*]

THE STREGA'S VOICE: The Wops are at it again. Had a truckdriver in the house all night!

[ROSA *is feverishly dressing. From the bureau she has snatched a shimmering white satin slip, disappearing for a moment behind a screen to put it on as* SERAFINA *comes padding sheepishly back into the room, her nightgown now covered by a black rayon kimona sprinkled with poppies, her voice tremulous with fear, shame and apology*]

ROSA: [*Behind the screen*] Has the man gone?

SERAFINA: That—man?

ROSA: Yes, "that man!"

SERAFINA: [*Inventing desperately*] I don't know how he got in. Maybe the back door was open.

ROSA: Oh, yes, maybe it was!

SERAFINA: Maybe he—climbed in a window . . .

ROSA: Or fell down the chimney, maybe!

[*She comes from behind the screen, wearing the white bridal slip*]

SERAFINA: Why you put on the white things I save for your wedding?

ROSA: Because I want to. That's a good enough reason.

[*She combs her hair savagely*]

SERAFINA: I want you to understand about that man. That was a man that—that was—that was a man that . . .

ROSA: You can't think of a lie?

SERAFINA: He was a—truckdriver, cara. He got in a fight, he was chase by—policemen!

ROSA: They chased him into your bedroom?

SERAFINA: I took pity on him, I give him first aid, I let him sleep on the floor. He give me his promise—he . . .

ROSA: Did he kneel in front of Our Lady? Did he promise that he would respect your innocence?

SERAFINA: Oh, cara, cara! [*Abandoning all pretense*] He was Sicilian; he had rose oil in his hair and the rose tattoo of your father. In the dark room I couldn't see his clown face. I closed my eyes and dreamed that he was your father! I closed my eyes! I dreamed that he was your father . . .

ROSA: Basta, basta, non voglio sentire più niente! The only thing worse than a liar is a liar that's also a hypocrite!

SERAFINA: Senti, per favore! [ROSA *wheels about from the mirror and fixes her mother with a long and withering stare.* SERAFINA *cringes before it.*] Don't look at me like that with the eyes of your father!

[*She shields her face as from a terrible glare*]

ROSA: Yes, I am looking at you with the eyes of my father. I see you the way *he* saw you. [*She runs to the table and seizes the piggy bank*] Like this, this *pig!* [SERAFINA *utters a long, shuddering cry like a cry of childbirth*] I need five dollars. I'll take it out of this! [ROSA *smashes the piggy bank to the floor and rakes some coins into her purse.* SERAFINA *stoops to the floor. There is the sound of a train whistle.* ROSA *is now fully dressed, but she hesitates, a little ashamed of her cruelty—but only a little.* SERAFINA *cannot meet her daughter's eyes. At last the girl speaks*]

SERAFINA: How beautiful—is my daughter! Go to the boy!

ROSA: [*As if she might be about to apologize*] Mama? He didn't touch me—he just said—"Che bella!"

[SERAFINA *turns slowly, shamefully, to face her. She is like a peasant in the presence of a young princess.* ROSA *stares at her a moment longer, then suddenly catches her breath and runs out of the house. As the girl leaves,* SERAFINA *calls:*]

SERAFINA: Rosa, Rosa, the—wrist watch! [SERAFINA *snatches up the little gift box and runs out onto the porch with it. She starts to call her daughter again, holding the gift out toward her, but her breath fails her*] Rosa, Rosa, the—wrist watch . . .

[*Her arms fall to her side. She turns, the gift still ungiven. Senselessly, absently, she holds the watch to her ear again. She shakes it a little, then utters a faint, startled laugh*]

[ASSUNTA *appears beside the house and walks directly in, as though* SERAFINA *had called her*]

SERAFINA: Assunta, the urn is broken. The ashes are spilt on the floor and I can't touch them.

[ASSUNTA *stoops to pick up the pieces of the shattered urn.* SERAFINA *has crossed to the shrine and relights the candle before the Madonna*]

ASSUNTA: There are no ashes.

SERAFINA: Where—where are they? Where have the ashes gone?

ASSUNTA: [*Crossing to the shrine*] The wind has blown them away.

[ASSUNTA *places what remains of the broken urn in* SERAFINA's *hands.* SERAFINA *turns it tenderly in her hands and then replaces it on the top of the prie-dieu before the Madonna*]

SERAFINA: A man, when he burns, leaves only a handful of ashes. No woman can hold him. The wind must blow him away.

[ALVARO's *voice is heard, calling from the top of the highway embankment*]

ALVARO'S VOICE: Rondinella felice!

[*The neighborhood women hear* ALVARO *calling, and there is a burst of mocking laughter from some of them. Then they all converge on the house from different directions and gather before the porch*]

PEPPINA: Serafina Delle Rose!

GIUSEPPINA: Baronessa! Baronessa Delle Rose!

PEPPINA: There is a man on the road without the shirt!

GIUSEPPINA: [*With delight*] Si, si! Senza camicia!

PEPPINA: All he got on his chest is a rose tattoo! [*To the women*] She lock up his shirt so he can't go to the high school?

[*The women shriek with laughter. In the house* SERAFINA *snatches up the package containing the silk shirt, while* ASSUNTA *closes the shutters of the parlor windows*]

SERAFINA: Un momento! [*She tears the paper off the shirt and rushes out onto the porch, holding the shirt above her head defiantly*] Ecco la camicia!

[*With a soft cry,* SERAFINA *drops the shirt, which is immediately snatched up by* PEPPINA. *At this point the music begins again, with a crash of percussion, and continues to the end of the play.* PEPPINA *flourishes the shirt in the air like a banner and tosses it to* GIUSEPPINA, *who is now on the embankment.* GIUSEPPINA *tosses it on to* MARIELLA, *and she in her turn to* VIOLETTA, *who is above her, so that the brilliantly colored shirt moves in a zig-zag course through the pampas grass to the very top of the embankment, like a streak of flame shooting up a dry hill. The women call out as they pass the shirt along:*]

PEPPINA: Guardate questa camicia! Coloro di rose!

MARIELLA: [*Shouting up to* ALVARO] Corragio, signor!

GIUSEPPINA: Avanti, avanti, signor!

VIOLETTA: [*At the top of the embankment, giving the shirt a final flourish above her*] Corragio, corragio! The Baronessa is waiting!

[*Bursts of laughter are mingled with the cries of the women. Then they sweep away like a flock of screaming birds, and* SERAFINA *is left upon the porch, her eyes closed, a hand clasped to her breast. In the meanwhile, inside the house,* ASSUNTA *has poured out a glass of wine. Now she comes to the porch, offering the wine to* SERAFINA *and murmuring:*]

ASSUNTA: Stai tranquilla.

SERAFINA: [*Breathlessly*] Assunta, I'll tell you something that maybe you won't believe.

ASSUNTA: [*With tender humor*] It is impossible to tell me anything that I don't believe.

SERAFINA: Just now I felt on my breast the burning again of the rose. I know what it means. It means that I have conceived! [*She lifts the glass to her lips for a moment and then returns it to* ASSUNTA] Two lives again in the body! Two, two lives again, two!

ALVARO'S VOICE: [*Nearer now, and sweetly urgent*] Rondinella felice!

[ALVARO *is not visible on the embankment but* SERAFINA *begins to move slowly toward his voice*]

ASSUNTA: Dove vai, Serafina?

SERAFINA: [*Shouting now, to* ALVARO] Vengo, vengo, amore!

[*She starts up the embankment toward* ALVARO *and the curtain falls as the music rises with her in great glissandi of sound*]

THE FOURPOSTER

Jan de Hartog

Jan de Hartog

One of the most difficult dramatic feats to carry off successfully is the two-character play that sustains audience interest and involvement throughout the evening. Not only did Jan de Hartog accomplish this feat with *The Fourposter*, he parlayed it into a 1952 Tony Award-winning play and one of the most appealing and enduring marital comedies of the modern theatre.

Unlike most other works of this genre, the author did not resort to such artificial devices as the constant and prolonged use of the telephone, a surplus of props or even offstage voices. Instead, he simply relied on two thoroughly human and spirited characters to relate his charming chronicle of three and a half decades of married life. The fourposter of the play's title is a kind of guardian symbol of marital solidity in times of joy and stress.

The majority of critics responded with enormous affection to both the play and its stars, Jessica Tandy and Hume Cronyn.

Brooks Atkinson of the New York *Times* termed it "The most civilized comedy we have had on marriage for years. Mr. de Hartog has written it with great understanding and skill . . . The writing is so compact and simple that you may not realize at once how good it is . . . So far *The Fourposter* is the pleasantest comedy of the season."

Walter Kerr noted in the New York *Herald Tribune*: "*The Four-poster* is Jan de Hartog's salute to an enduring marriage. He has written it as a two-character play, and he has hurdled this particular difficulty with remarkable skill."

Whitney Bolton of *The Morning Telegraph* lauded it as: "An uncommonly ingenious play . . . something to embrace and cherish . . . with its overwhelming tenderness, its superb wit and its wrenching drama. Wit it has in fullness. Tenderness is a constant emotion with it. Drama is its broad base. For these are completely right people, these characters. She is a bride and he is a bridegroom in which love and the agonies of embarrassment vie for conquest of the individual. Later, as they live out their lives, age and reach a new level in understanding, the shaping magic of a good marriage is plain to see . . . I don't know how, if you live, if you breathe, if you have ever loved anyone, how you can fail to fall under the spell of *The Fourposter* . . . It is worth a fortune, in chuckles and smiles and a few tears."

Other reviewers agreed that *The Fourposter* is "an irresistible comedy" that is "a mirror held up to life with the images lucidly reflected and undistorted," a work that is replete "with touches that ring the bell of truthful and humorous observations."

Named one of the ten best plays of the 1951–52 season, *The Fourposter* ran for 632 performances. Numerous road companies and summer stock productions followed and in 1952 it was made into a movie starring Rex Harrison and Lilli Palmer.

Yet there was more successful mileage ahead for the property. Tom Jones and Harvey Schmidt converted it into the musical *I Do! I Do!* which opened in New York in 1966 with Mary Martin and Roberton Preston. The two-character musical played for 560 performances and subsequently toured nationally.

Jan de Hartog was born on April 22, 1914, in Haarlem, Holland, and attended the Amsterdam Naval College. During World War II, he served with the Netherlands Merchant Marine and was awarded the Netherlands Cross of Merit.

In addition to *The Fourposter*, Mr. de Hartog's other plays include: *The End of the Liberty*; *This Time Tomorrow*; and *Skipper Next to God*.

He also has written a considerable number of screenplays, among them: *Somewhere in Holland*; *Skipper Next to God*; *The Fourposter*; *The Key*; *The Spiral Road*; and *Lisa*.

A novelist as well as playwright, his published works include: *Holland's Glory*; *The Lost Sea*; *The Distant Shore*; *The Little Ark*; *A Sailor's Life*; *The Spiral Road*; *The Inspector*; *Waters of the New World*; *The Artist*; and *The Hospital*.

The Fourposter was first presented by The Playwrights' Company on October 24, 1951, at the Ethel Barrymore Theatre, New York. The cast was as follows:

AGNES   *Jessica Tandy*
MICHAEL   *Hume Cronyn*

Directed by José Ferrer
Setting by Syrjala
Costumes by Lucinda Ballard

ACT ONE

Scene 1:   *1890.*
Scene 2:   *A year later.*

ACT TWO

Scene 1:   *1901.*
Scene 2:   *Seven years later.*

ACT THREE

Scene 1:   *1913.*
Scene 2:   *Twelve years later.*

ACT ONE

SCENE ONE

1890. Night. Bedroom. Fourposter. Door in arch center back wall, window in right; washstand and low chair down left. Wardrobe above washstand; bed table in front of window; bureau right of arch. Bed on dais left of arch; chest at foot of bed; arm chair and trunk, right center. Console table and two chairs in rear of hall. The room is dark. Low-burning gaslamps shimmer bluishly. The door is opened clumsily, and HE *enters, carrying her in his arms into the room out of the lighted passage.* HE *wears a top hat on the back of his head;* SHE *is in her bridal gown.* HE *stops in the moonlight, kisses her, whirls and carries her to bed.*

SHE: Oh, Micky, whoo! Hold me! Hold me tight! Whoo! Whoo! I'm falling. I can't—[HE *throws her onto the bed and tries to kiss her again*] Michael, the door! The door! [HE *runs to the door and closes it.* SHE *gets off the bed, straightens her hat and dress*] Oh, goodness, my hair—and look at my dress! [SHE *turns on the gas bracket on wall beside the bed.* HE *crosses and turns up gas bracket right of arch.* SHE *turns toward him.* HE *crosses to her, takes off gloves, puts one in each pocket and kneels before her*] What are you doing?

HE: I'm worshipping you.

SHE: Get up immediately! [*Tries to lift him up*] Michael, get up, I say!

HE: [*Kneeling, hands on her waist*] Can't I worship you?

SHE: Are you out of your senses? If our Lord should see you—

HE: He could only rejoice in such happiness.

SHE: Michael, you mustn't blaspheme. You know you mustn't. Just because you've had a little too much to drink.

HE: I haven't drunk a thing. [*Teeters on his knees*] If I'm drunk, I'm drunk only with happiness—

SHE: You wouldn't be praying with everything on if you weren't. . . . Oh! Goodness! I think I am, too.

HE: Happy?

SHE: Tipsy. Let me see if I can stand on one leg. [*Holding her hands out to him, tries and fails*] Whoo!

HE: [*Rises*] Angel!

[*Tries to kiss her, but* SHE *dodges*]

SHE: Michael, that hat—!

HE: What? Oh. [*Takes hat off*] What have you got in your hands?

SHE: A little rose—a little rose from our wedding cake.

HE: Let's eat it.

SHE: No—I want to keep it—always—

[SHE *puts it in her dress*]

HE: [*Puts hat on*] Agnes, Agnes, tell me that you are happy.

SHE: Please, Michael, do say something else for a change.

HE: I can't. I've only one word left to express what I feel; happy. Happy, happy, happy, happy—Happy!

[*Twirls and, stumbling against dais, sprawls back against bed*]

SHE: [*Crossing to him*] Are you all right?

HE: Happy!

SHE: I suddenly feel like saying all sorts of shocking things.

HE: Go on.

SHE: Listen—no, in your ear—[*He rises, crosses to her.* SHE *wants to whisper something but is checked by what she sees*] Oh! Michael—!

HE: [*Faces her*] What?

SHE: No, don't move. [*Looks at ear again*] Let me see the other one. [HE *turns his head and* SHE *looks at his other ear*] You pig!

HE: What is it?

SHE: Don't you ever wash?

HE: Every day.

SHE: All over?

HE: Oh, well—the main things.

SHE: What *are* the main things?

HE: [*Trying to kiss her*] My precious—

SHE: Your what?

HE: You are my precious. Wouldn't you like to kiss me?

SHE: I would like to go over you from top to bottom, with hot water and soap; that's what I would like to do.

HE: Please do.

SHE: Oh, well—don't let's dwell on it. [SHE *sits on trunk*] Ouch!

HE: Sweetheart! What's the matter?

SHE: Ouch! My shoes are hurting me. I must take them off or I'll faint.

HE: Let me do it! Please—

[SHE *puts out her foot.* HE *kneels and tenderly pulls her skirt back and kisses her shoe*]

SHE: Michael, please, they hurt me so.

HE: [*Kisses her foot again; when* SHE *wants to do it herself*] No, no, dearest! Let me do it, please let me do it.

[HE *takes her shoe again*]

SHE: But you take such a long time.

HE: [*Untying bow on shoe*] Isn't that heaven? I could spend the
whole night undressing you.

SHE: I didn't ask you to undress me. I only asked you to help me
out of my shoes.

HE: I would help you out of anything you ask, dear heart.

[*Takes off shoe*]

SHE: [*Withdraws her foot*] Now that's one, and now—[*As* SHE
*leans forward to take off other shoe herself, sees him, still on his
knees, leaning back and staring at her*] Please, Michael, don't
look at me so creepily. Please get undre—take your hat off!

HE: [*Takes hat off, puts it on trunk*] Agnes, do you remember
what I told you, when we first met?

SHE: No—?

HE: That we had met in a former existence.

SHE: Oh, that.

HE: I am absolutely certain of it now.

SHE: Of what?

HE: That moment, just now, I suddenly had the feeling of having
experienced all this before.

SHE: Did you really?

HE: You sitting here just as you are, I on my knees in front of you
in a hired suit, just before we—

SHE: What?

HE: [*Putting shoe down,* HE *leans against her knee*] Oh, darling,
I am happy.

SHE: *Must* you make me cry?

HE: You should, you know. This is a very sad occasion, really. Your
youth is over.

SHE: [*Pushing him back and getting up*] I want to go home.

HE: What—?

SHE: I can't! I want to go home!

HE: [*Still on knees*] Darling, what's the matter? What have I done?

SHE: [*Picks up shoe*] I want to go home. I should never have married you.

HE: [*Rises*] Agnes—

SHE: How can you! How dare you say such a thing!

HE: But what—? I haven't said a thing all night but that I was—

SHE: My youth over! That's what you would like! Undressing me, the whole night long, with your hat on and unwashed ears and—oh!

   [*Crosses to him and puts her arms around his neck and weeps*]

HE: [*Comforting her inexperiencedly*] That's right, darling; that's it; you cry, my dearest; that's the spirit.

SHE: That's—that's why you made me drink such a lot, taking nothing yourself all the time.

HE: Why, I've had at least three bottles.

SHE: [*Breaks away from him and backs up*] Then what did you say? What did you say, when you threw me on the bed?

HE: Threw?

SHE: "If I'm drunk, I'm drunk with happiness." That's what you said.

HE: But, darling, only a minute ago you said yourself—

SHE: I did not!

HE: Well, of all the—[*Takes her by the shoulders*] Here—smell! [*Breathes at her with his mouth wide open*] Ho, ho, ho!

SHE: [*Escaping the kiss she wants by hiding her face against his shoulder*] Oh, I'm so dizzy.

HE: I love you.

SHE: I'm so embarrassed.

HE: Why?

SHE: Because I'm so dizzy.

HE: So am I.

SHE: Dizzy?

HE: Embarrassed.

SHE: Why?

HE: [*Backs away from her*] Oh, well, you know. It would have been such a relief if I could have spent the whole night taking off your shoes.

SHE: And then have breakfast, straight away, yes?

HE: [*Picks up hat*] Yes. Agnes, I—I don't revolt you, do I?

SHE: [*Slips off other shoe, picks it up*] You? Why on earth should you?

HE: Well, I mean—those ears and—things, you know.

SHE: [*Puts shoes on chest at foot of bed*] But, darling, I said that only because of other people. What do I care?

HE: And Agnes—there's something I should tell you.

SHE: Why tell it just now?

HE: You're right. [*Puts hat on*] I'm such a fool that I—[SHE *frowns.* HE *takes hat off again and puts it on trunk*] Would you like something to drink?

SHE: Heavens, no. Don't talk about drinking.

HE: A glass of water, I mean. [*Picks up glass and carafe*] After all that champagne.

SHE: Michael, please talk about something else. I—I really couldn't just now, honestly.

HE: Well, I think I will.

[*Pours glass of water*]

SHE: Did you write a poem for tonight?

HE: No.

SHE: What a pity. I thought you would have written something beautiful for our wedding.

HE: [*Drinks*] No.

SHE: Nothing at all?

HE: [*Drinks again and puts glass down*] No.

SHE: You're blushing. Please read it to me.

HE: I haven't got one, darling, really, I haven't.

SHE: You're lying. I can tell by your eyes that you are lying.

HE: As a matter of fact, you wouldn't like it, darling; it's rather modern. There is another one I'm writing just now.

SHE: I want to hear the one about our wedding.

HE: Never before in my whole life have I told anybody anything about a poem I hadn't finished.

SHE: Is it in your pocket?

   [*Starts to pick his pockets*]

HE: [*Trying to keep her hands back, sits in chair*] Agnes, you can't have it. I think it's going to be wonderful. "The Fountain of the Royal Gardens."

SHE: Why may I not hear the one about our wedding?

HE: [*Takes her hands*] Darling, don't you think it much more special, just now, something nobody else has ever heard before?

SHE: Has anybody heard the one about our wedding, then?

HE: [*Takes poems from pocket*] Listen, tell me what you think of the permutation of the consonants, the onomatopoeia, I mean: "Hissing shoots the slender shower; out of shining, slimy stone—"

SHE: [*Steps back*] No.

HE: "Swaying shivers sparkling flower; rainbow shimmers in the foam. [SHE *starts to door*] Flashing, dashing, splashing, crashing

—" [SHE *hurries to the door, picking up suitcase from chest as she goes*] Where are you going?

SHE: [*Opens door, taking the key from the lock*] Back in a minute.

   [*Exits, shuts door, locks it*]

HE: Why are you taking your suitcase? [*Rises and runs to door; drops poems on chest as he goes*] Agnes, darling! Agnes! Agnes!

   [*Tries to open the locked door*]

   [HE *turns, sees her shoes, picks them up and smiles. Suddenly, a thought strikes him.* HE *drops the shoes, runs onto dais, picks up suitcase there, starts to put it on bed, stops, turns, then crosses and puts suitcase on arms of chair.* HE *opens the case, takes out nightcap and puts it on his head.* HE *rips off his coat and vest, shirt and tie. As* HE *starts to take his trousers off, he stops, listens, runs to door, listens again. He then hurries and takes the trousers off.* HE *takes nightshirt from case, crosses to foot of bed, throws nightshirt on bed and sits on chest and hurriedly takes off his shoes. Then* HE *pauses, looks toward the door in embarrassment.* HE *quickly puts the shoes back on again, gets into the nightshirt, pulls his trousers on over it; then his coat.* HE *moves a few steps, turns, sees his vest, shirt and tie on trunk where* HE *had thrown them.* HE *tosses them into the suitcase, fastens it, puts suitcase in wardrobe; starts to washstand, stops, looks toward door. Then quickly* HE *crosses down to washstand, picks up towel, dampens one corner of it in pitcher of water and starts to wash his right ear.*
   SHE *enters. As* HE *hears door open, he sits in chair and folds his arms.* SHE *closes the door and puts the key back in the lock. Her dress is changed somehow; it looks untidier and* SHE *has taken off her wedding hat.* SHE *turns from door, spots him sitting in the chair, the collar of his jacket upturned and the nightcap on his head*]

HE: Hullo.

SHE: What—what are you doing?

HE: Sitting.

SHE: What on earth is that?

HE: What?

SHE: On your head?

HE: Oh—why—

SHE: Do you wear a nightcap?

HE: Oh, no. Just now when there's a draft.

[*Rises, takes cap off and puts it in his pocket. Crosses to her*]

SHE: Is that a nightshirt?

HE: What have you got on?

SHE: My father has been wearing pajamas for ages.

HE: Oh, has he really? Well, I don't.

SHE: Why have you—changed?

HE: Why have you?

SHE: I? Oh—I'm sleepy.

HE: So am I.

SHE: Well, then, shall we—?

HE: Why, yes—let's.

SHE: All right. Which side do you want?

HE: I? Oh, well—I don't care, really. Any side that suits you is all right with me.

SHE: I think I would like the far side. Because of the door.

HE: The door?

SHE: [*Turns back quilt*] Because of breakfast, and in case somebody should knock. You could answer it.

HE: I see.

SHE: [*Picks up "God Is Love" pillow from bed*] What's this?

HE: What?

SHE: This little pillow? Did you put that there?

HE: Of course not! What's it got written on it?

SHE: "God Is Love." Oh, how sweet! Mother must have done that.
Wasn't that lovely of her?

       [*Puts pillow back on bed*]

HE: [*Looks at door*] Yes, charming.

       [SHE *turns away and starts undressing.* HE *takes off his coat.*
       SHE *turns. After an embarrassing moment in which neither of
       them can think of anything to say:*]

SHE: Michael, please turn 'round.

HE: Oh, I'm so sorry—I just didn't realize.

       [HE *sits down on the edge of the chest, putting his coat be-
       side him, and takes off his shoes and socks.* SHE *steps down
       from dais, steps out of dress and hangs it in wardrobe. Crosses
       back up onto dais*]

SHE: It's rather a pretty bed, isn't it?

HE: [*Picks up her shoes and places them next to his*] Yes, it is,
isn't it? It was my father's, you know.

SHE: Not your mother's?

HE: Yes, of course, my parents. I was born in it, you know.

SHE: [*Taking a step toward him*] Michael—

HE: [*Turning toward her*] Yes, darling?

SHE: [*Backing up*] No, don't look! Michael?

HE: [*Turning away*] Yes?

SHE: Tell me how much you love me, once more.

HE: I can't any more.

SHE: What?

HE: I can't love you any more than I'm doing. I wor—I'm the hap
—I'm mad about you.

SHE: That's what I am about you. Honestly.

HE: That is nice, dear.

SHE: I am so happy, I couldn't be happier.

HE: That is lovely, darling.

SHE: And I wouldn't want to be, either.

HE: What?

SHE: Happier.

HE: I see.

SHE: I wish that everything could stay as it was—before today. I couldn't stand any more—happiness. Could you?

HE: God, no.

SHE: How coldly you say that.

HE: But what the blazing hell do you expect me to say then?

SHE: Michael! Is that language for the wedding ni—before going to sleep? You ought to be ashamed of yourself!

HE: But damn it, Agnes—[*Sneezes*] I—I've got a splitting headache and I'm dying of cold feet.

   [*Takes nightcap from pocket and puts it on*]

SHE: [*Takes off her slippers*] Then why don't you get into bed, silly? [*He rises, crosses up onto dais*] No! A moment! A moment!

   [HE *turns away.* SHE *gets into bed, the "God Is Love" pillow beneath her head.* HE *stands for a moment in embarrassment, starts to take off his trousers, then realizing that the room is still brightly lit, he crosses to bracket and turns it off*]

HE: May I turn 'round now?

SHE: Yes. [HE *crosses up onto dais and reaches to turn down the left bracket but is stopped by her interruption*] Wait! It can't leak, can it? The lamp, I mean?

HE: Of course not.

SHE: But I think I smell gas.

HE: [*Reaches behind him and takes her hand*] Darling, listen.

You are an angel, and I'm madly in love with you, and I'm embarrassed to death and so are you, and that's the reason why we— Goodnight.

[HE *reaches up and turns down the bracket*]

SHE: Goodnight. [HE *steps down, takes off his trousers and puts them on chair*] Can you find your way?

HE: Yes, yes—[*Crossing back up to bed, stubs his toe on the dais*] Ouch!

SHE: Michael! What are you doing?

HE: Nothing. I hurt my toe.

[HE *gets into bed*]

SHE: Oh, I'm so sorry. [*Long silence*] Do get into bed carefully, won't you?

HE: I'm in it already.

SHE: Michael?

HE: Yes?

SHE: Michael, what was it you didn't want to tell me tonight?

HE: Ah—

SHE: You may tell me now, if you like. I'm not embarrassed any more, somehow.

HE: Well—

SHE: If you tell me what it was, I'll tell you something as well.

HE: What?

SHE: But you must tell me as well. Promise me.

HE: Yes.

SHE: No, promise me first.

HE: All right. I promise.

SHE: I—I've never seen a man—before—completely. Never.

HE: Oh, well—you haven't missed much.

SHE: And you?

HE: Oh.

SHE: Have you ever seen a woman before—completely?

HE: Well—

SHE: What does that mean?

HE: You know, I once had my fortune told by a gypsy.

SHE: Oh—

HE: She said I'd have a very happy married life, that I'd live to a ripe old age, and she said that everything would turn out all right.

SHE: And was she—naked?

HE: Of course not! She went from house to house with a goat.

SHE: Oh—Goodnight.

HE: Goodnight. [*Pause*] Are you comfy?

SHE: Oh, yes.

HE: Not too cold?

SHE: Heavens, no. I'm simply boiling. And you?

HE: Rather cold, really.

SHE: [*After a silence*] Michael!

HE: Yes?

SHE: Michael! Now I'm sure that I smell gas. [SHE *sits up*]

HE: That must be the drink.

SHE: Do you still smell of drink that much? I can't believe it.

HE: Yes.

SHE: Let me smell your breath again.

HE: Oh, please, Agnes, let's try to go to sleep.

SHE: No, Michael, I want to smell it. If it is the gas, we may be dead tomorrow, both of us.

HE: Oh, well—

SHE: Oh, well? Do you want to die?

HE: Sometimes.

SHE: Now?

HE: No, no.

SHE: Please, Michael, let me have a little sniff before I go to sleep; otherwise, I won't close an eye. [*Lies down*] Please, Michael.

HE: [*Sits up and leans over her*] Ho! Ho! Ho! [*Lies back on his pillow*] There.

SHE: [*Sits up and leans over him*] I don't smell a thing. Do it again.

HE: Ho! Ho!

SHE: *Again*—

HE: Ho, ho.

SHE: *Again*—

HE: [*Raises his arm to embrace her*] Ho—

CURTAIN

SCENE TWO

1891. Late afternoon. The same bedroom. Down right a bassinette. Right center chair is now down right. HE *is lying in the fourposter, with a towel wrapped around his head. The bed is strewn with books, papers, an over-sized dinner bell and his dressing gown. Heaps of books and papers are on the dais at foot of bed. When the curtain rises,* HE *awakens.*

HE: [*From beneath the blankets*] Agnes! Agnes! [*Sits up*] Agnes!

[*Picks up bell and rings loudly and insistently*]

SHE: [*Enters arch hurriedly carrying a pile of clean laundry.* SHE *is very pregnant*] Yes, yes, yes, yes, yes. What is it?

HE: I've got such a pain! [SHE *returns to door and closes it*] I can't stand it any longer!

SHE: [*Putting laundry on chest*] Now, come, come, darling. Don't dramatize. [*Takes towel from his head*] I'll soak your towel again.

HE: No! It isn't my head, it's shifted to here.

[*Puts his hand on his back*]

SHE: Where?

HE: Here! [*Leans forward. Places her hand on the painful spot*] Here! What is there? Do you feel anything?

SHE: You've got a pain there?

HE: As if I'd been stabbed. No, don't take your hand away—oh, that's nice.

SHE: [*Suspiciously*] But what sort of pain? Does it come in—in waves? First almost nothing and then growing until you could scream?

HE: That's right. How do you know—

SHE: Micky, that's impossible.

HE: What's impossible? Do you think I'm shamming?

SHE: You're having labor pains!

HE: You're crazy!

SHE: And all the time—all the time I've put up a brave front because I thought you were really ill!

[*Sits on chest, puts towel on chest*]

HE: But I *am* ill! What do you think? That I lay here groaning and sweating just for the fun of it?

SHE: All the time I've been thinking of *you!*

HE: I've done nothing else, day and night, but think of *you!* How else do you think I got the pains *you're* supposed to have? [SHE *sobs*] Oh hell! This is driving me mad!

[HE *jumps out of bed*]

SHE: Micky! [HE *tears open the wardrobe*] Micky, what are you doing?

HE: Where are my shoes?

SHE: Michael! You aren't running away, are you?

HE: [*Gets clothes from wardrobe*] I'm going to get that doctor.

SHE: [*Rises*] No, Michael, you mustn't.

HE: [*Puts clothes on chair*] If I drop dead on the pavement, I'm going to get that doctor. I'm not going to leave you in this condition a minute longer. He said so himself, the moment you got those pains.

[*Kneels, looks under bed*]

SHE: When *I* got them! Not when you got them!

HE: Don't you feel anything then?

SHE: Nothing! Nothing at all.

HE: Agnes, I don't understand why you were crying just now.

SHE: [*Helps him up*] Please darling, please go back to bed. You'll catch a cold with those bare feet and you're perspiring so freely. Please, darling.

HE: But I don't want to.

SHE: [*Pops him into bed*] I want you to. Uppy-pie, in you go!

HE: Anyone would think you wanted me to be ill.

SHE: No grumbling, no growling. [*Puts "God Is Love" pillow behind his head*] There! Comfy?

HE: No! [HE *throws pillow to floor.* SHE *picks up laundry, crosses to bureau and puts laundry in drawer. Closes drawer*] Agnes, I'm scared.

SHE: But what on earth of?

HE: Of—of the baby. Aren't you?

SHE: Good Heavens, no. Why should I? It's the most natural thing in the world, isn't it? And I'm feeling all right.

        [Picks up sewing]

HE: You have changed a lot, do you know that?

SHE: *[Starts sewing]* Since when?

HE: Since you became a mother.

SHE: But I'm not a mother yet.

HE: Then you don't even realize it yourself. Suddenly you have become a woman.

SHE: Have I ever been anything else?

HE: A silly child.

SHE: So that's what you thought of me when we married?

HE: When we married, my feet were off the ground.

SHE: Well, you've changed a lot, too.

HE: Of course I have. I have become a man.

SHE: Hah!

HE: Well, haven't I? Agnes, aren't I much more calm, composed—

SHE: *[Picks up rattle from bassinette and throws it to him]* You're a baby!

HE: *[Throws covers back and sits on edge of bed]* That's right! Humiliate me! Lose no opportunity of reminding me that I'm the male animal that's done its duty and now can be dismissed!

SHE: Michael!

HE: Yes! A drone, that's what I am! The one thing lacking is that you should devour me. The bees—

SHE: Michael, Michael, what's the matter?

        [Reaches out to him]

HE: I'm afraid!

SHE: But I'm not, Michael, honestly, not a bit.

HE: I'm afraid of something else.

SHE: What?

HE: That I've lost you.

SHE: [*Rises, crosses to him*] Michael, look at me—what did the doctor tell you?

HE: It's got nothing to do with the doctor. It's got nothing to do with you, either. It's got to do with me.

SHE: [*Puts arms about him*] But you're going to be all right, aren't you?

HE: [*Breaks away*] I'd never be all right again, if I've lost you.

SHE: But what are you talking about? You've got me right here, haven't you?

HE: But your heart, that's gone. I wish I was lying in that cradle.

SHE: [*Puts her arms around him again*] You fool—[*Kisses him*] —you can't be as stupid as all that. No, Michael.

HE: [*Breaks away, crossing to chest and picks up slippers*] I'm sorry I brought the subject up. Whatever did I do with my shoes?

SHE: Darling, do you mean that you haven't noticed how I've tried every day, all day long to prove to you how much I love you—and I don't understand why I should.

[*Sits on chest*]

HE: Listen! Before that cuckoo pushes me out of the nest, I want to tell you once more that I love you. Love you, just as you are— [*Sits on bed and puts on slippers*] I thought I loved you when I married you, but that wasn't you at all. That was a romantic illusion. I loved a sort of fairy princess with a doll's smile and a—well, anyway not a princess with hiccoughs and cold feet, scratching her stomach in her sleep—[*Takes her hand*] I thought I was marrying a princess and I woke up to find a friend, a wife—You know, sometimes when I lay awake longer than you, with my arm around your shoulder and your head on my chest, I thought with pity of all those lonely men staring at the ceiling or writing poems—pity, and such happiness that I knew at that very moment it wouldn't last. I was right, that's all.

[*Rises, picks up robe*]

SHE: Well, if you thought about a princess, I thought about a poet.

HE: [*Fixes sleeves in robe right side out*] Oh?

SHE: You didn't know that I had cold feet and every now and again I get an attack of hiccoughs—

HE: [*Putting on robe*] You don't do anything else the whole night long.

SHE: What?

HE: Scratch your stomach and sniff and snort and smack your lips, but go on, go on.

SHE: And you lie listening to all this without waking me up?

HE: Yes. Because I don't know anything in the world I'd rather listen to. [*Kisses her*] Got anything to say to that?

SHE: Yes, but I won't say it.

HE: Why not?

SHE: Never mind, darling, you stay just as you are.

HE: Miserable, deserted, alone? You do nothing else all day and night but fuss over that child—eight months now! First it was knitting panties, then sewing dresses, fitting out the layette, rigging the cradle—

[*Ties robe*]

SHE: And all this time you sat quietly in your corner, didn't you?

HE: I retired into the background as becomes a man who recognizes that he is one too many.

SHE: [*Rises, crossing to him*] Oh, angel! [*Puts her arms around his neck and kisses him*] Do you still not understand why I love you so much?

HE: You—you noticed how I blotted myself out?

SHE: Did I?

HE: I didn't think you did.

SHE: You helped me more than all model husbands put together. Without you I would have been frightened to death for eight whole months. But I simply had no time.

HE: [*Turns suddenly to her*] I believe you're teasing me.

SHE: I love you. Do you believe that?

HE: Of course.

SHE: Must I prove it to you?

HE: Oh, no. I'm perfectly prepared to take your word for it.

SHE: All right, if you like, we'll send the child to a home.

HE: What?

SHE: And then we'll go and look at it every Sunday.

HE: Agnes, why do you tease me?

SHE: Darling, I'm not teasing you. I'm telling you the truth. Even if I were going to have twenty children, you are my husband and I'd rather leave them as foundlings—

  [SHE *grasps at her back and turns upstage.* HE *stares at her in horror*]

HE: [*Crossing to her*] Darling, what—what is it? Agnes!

SHE: [*Clutching the bed post*] Oh!

HE: [*Picks up clothes, crossing to her*] The doctor! For God's sake, the doctor!

  [*Frantically unties robe*]

SHE: No—oh, oh! Don't—not the doctor. Stay here.

HE: [*Puts clothes back on chair, crossing to her*] Darling! darling! Angel! Agnes, my love! What must I do? For God's sake, I must do something!

SHE: [*Sings, convulsed by pain, loudly*]
  "*Yankee Doodle went to town,*
  Riding on a pony—"

HE: Agnes!

SHE: [Sings on]
"He stuck a feather in his hat,
And called it macaroni."

HE: [Takes her by shoulders] Agnes!

[HE slaps her cheek quickly several times]

SHE: [Regains her senses, slaps back at him] Oh, Micky—What are
you doing?

HE: I—I thought you were going mad.

SHE: I? Why?

HE: [Seats her on chest] You started to sing.

SHE: Oh, yes. The doctor said if those pains started, I had to sing.
That would help. I must have done it automatically.

HE: Are you all right now?

SHE: Oh yes, yes.

HE: Now you just sit here quietly. I'll get the doctor.

SHE: No, Michael, you mustn't. He said we weren't to bother him
until the pains came regularly.

HE: Regularly? But I won't be a minute.

[Picks up clothes]

SHE: Oh, please, please don't go away. Oh, I wish mother were
here.

HE: [Puts clothes on bed] Now, don't worry! This is the most
natural thing in the world. You just sit here quietly. I'll put some
clothes on and—

SHE: Oh no, no Micky, please, please don't fuss. I wish it didn't
have to happen so soon.

HE: [Turns upstage with back to audience, takes off pajama pants.
Puts on trousers] Yes.

SHE: [Picks up pajama pants] I'm not nearly ready for it yet—

HE: [*Taking off robe and putting it on bed*] Well, I am. Honestly, I am. I can't wait to—to go fishing with him, if it's a boy, and—and, if it's a girl, go for walks, nature rambles—

[*Crosses to wardrobe and gets tie from there*]

SHE: But that won't happen for years. First, there will be years of crying and diapers and bottles—

HE: [*Ties tie*] I don't mind, darling. Honestly, I don't. I'll—find something to do. I'll work and—and go fishing alone. You're never going to have to worry about—

SHE: [*In pain again*] Oh!

HE: [*Crossing to her, kneels*] Another one?

SHE No. No, I don't think so.

HE: Now, why don't you go to bed? [*Throws robe and coat on chest. Fixes bed linen*] You go to bed—I'll finish dressing and make you a nice cup of tea, yes?

SHE: No, no thank you, darling. I think I'll stay right where I am. Oh, I haven't done nearly all the things I should have done. [*Rises, crossing to door*] There's still half the laundry out on the roof and—

HE: [*Stops her*] Agnes, do stop worrying! As soon as I've finished dressing, I'll go to the roof and take the washing in for you.

[*Seats her on chest*]

SHE: [*Puts arms about his waist*] No, please don't leave me alone.

HE: [*Puts his arms about her shoulders*] All right, all right. There's nothing to be afraid of. This has been going on for millions and millions of years. Now what would you like? Shall I read you something? [*Picks up books*] "Schopenhauer," "Alice in Wonderland"?

SHE: No.

HE: I know. I've started a new book. It's only half a page. Shall I read you that? Yes?

[HE *picks up writing pad*]

SHE: [*Biting her lip*] Yes—

HE: [*Sits on front of bed*] It's going to be a trilogy. It's called "Burnt Corn, the Story of a Rural Love." Do you like that as a title?

SHE: [*Biting her lips*] I think that's wonderful.

HE: Now this is how it opens—[*Takes hold of her hand*] Are you all right?

SHE: Fine.

HE: [*Reads*] "When she entered the attic with the double bed, she bent her head, partly out of reverence for the temple where she had worshipped and sacrificed, partly because the ceiling was so low. It was not the first time she had returned to that shrine—" [SHE *has a pain*] Are you all right?

SHE: Oh, Micky, I love you so. Don't, don't let's ever—[SHE *has another pain.* HE *helps her like a sweet man.* HE *drops pad and kneels before her.* SHE *buries her head in his shoulder, then looks up*] Now—now, I think you'd better go and call him.

HE: I will, my darling. [*Puts on his coat. Crosses to door, stops, returns to her*] Now, you just sit tight.

[*Crosses to door, returns and kisses her. Crosses to door, turns, sees bassinette, runs to it and pulls it over close to her and exits as:*]

CURTAIN

ACT TWO

SCENE ONE

1901. *Night. The same room, ten years later. The only piece of furniture left from the preceding scene is the fourposter, but it has been fitted out with new brocade curtains. Paintings hang on the walls, expensive furniture crowds the room. Dressing table and chair up right; sofa right center; chair down right; sofa at foot of bed with tabouret below it; chairs left center and left. Bed table on dais at head of bed. Bureau in dressing room. No washstand any more, but a bathroom down left. Where the wardrobe stood in the preceding act, the wall has been removed and this has become an entrance to a dressing room. The whole thing is very costly, very grand and very new. Only one side of the bed has been made; there is only one pillow on the bed with the "God Is Love" pillow on top of it.*

AT RISE: *There is no one in the room.* SHE *enters door center and slams the door behind her.* SHE *stands at the foot of the bed, removing her evening gloves. Crosses to dressing table, throws gloves on the table, and is stopped by a knock at the door.* SHE *stands for a moment. The knock is repeated, more insistently.*

SHE: [*After a pause*] Come in.

HE: [*Enters, closes door*] Excuse me. [*Goes to the dressing room, gets his night clothes, re-enters and crosses to door*] Good night.

SHE: [*As* HE *opens door*] You were the life and soul of the party this evening, with your interminable little stories.

HE: [*Starts out, stops, turns*] My dear, if you don't enjoy playing second fiddle, I suggest you either quit the orchestra or form one of your own.

[*Goes out and shuts door*]

SHE: [*Mutters after a moment's stupefaction*] Now, I've had enough! [*Runs to door, rips it open, stands in hallway and calls off*] Michael! [*Then bellows*] Michael! Come here!

[*Re-enters, takes off evening wrap, throws it on bed*]

HE: [*Pops in. Has top hat and cane in hand and evening cape over arm*] Have you taken leave of your senses? The servants?

SHE: I don't care if the whole town hears it. [HE *exits*] Come back, I say!

HE: [*Re-enters*] All right. This situation is no longer bearable!

[*Closes door*]

SHE: What on earth is the matter with you?

HE: Now, let me tell you one thing, calmly. [SHE *crosses to dressing table. Takes off plume, throws it on table*] My greatest mistake has been to play up to you, plying you with presents—

SHE: I like that!

[*Picks up gloves*]

HE: Calmly! Do you know what I should have done? I should have packed you off to boarding school, big as you are, to learn deportment.

SHE: [*Turns to him*] Deportment for what?

HE: To be worthy of me.

SHE: The pompous ass whose book sold three hundred thousand copies!

HE: That is entirely beside the point.

SHE: It is right to the point! [*Carrying gloves*] Before you had written that cursed novel, the rest of the world helped me to keep you sane. Every time you had finished a book or a play or God knows what, and considered yourself to be the greatest genius since Shakespeare—[HE *says* "*Now really!*" HE *puts cape, hat, gloves on chair*]—I was frightened to death it might turn out to be a success. [SHE *crosses to him*] But, thank Heaven, it turned out to be such a thorough failure every time, that I won the battle with your megalomania. But now, now this book, the only book you ever confessed to be trash until you read the papers—oh, what's the use!

[*Rolls up gloves*]

HE: My dear woman, I may be vain, but you are making a tragic mistake.

SHE: [*Laughs*] Now listen! [*Laughs*] Just listen to him! To be married to a man for eleven years, and then to be addressed like a public meeting. [*Throws gloves on dressing table*] Tragic mistake! [HE *sits.* SHE *crosses down to him*] Can't you hear yourself, you poor darling idiot, that you've sold your soul to a sentimental novel?

HE: Agnes, are you going on like this, or must I—

SHE: Yes, yes, you must! You *shall* hear it. [HE *pounds floor with cane*] And don't interrupt me! There is only one person in this world who loves you in spite of what you are, and let me tell you—

HE: You are mistaken. There is a person in this world who loves me —because of what I am.

SHE: And what are you, my darling?

HE: Ask her.

SHE: Her—

HE: Yes.

SHE: Oh—[*Holds onto bed post*] Who is she?

HE: You don't know her.

SHE: Is she—young? How young?

HE: No. [*Rises. Picks up clothes*] I'll be damned if I go on with this. You look like a corpse.

SHE: A corpse?

HE: So pale, I mean. [*At door*] Agnes, I'm not such a monster, that—[*Crossing to her*] Sit down. Please, Agnes, do sit—Agnes!

SHE: [*Turns away*] No, no—it's nothing. I'm all right. What do you think? That I should faint in my thirty-first year because of something so—so ordinary?

HE: Ordinary?

SHE: With two children? I didn't faint when Robert had the mumps, did I?

HE: Don't you think this is a little different?

SHE: No, Michael. This belongs to the family medicine chest.

HE: I love her!

SHE: So, not me anymore? [HE *doesn't reply*] I don't mean as a friend, or as—as the mother of your children, but as a wife? You may tell me honestly, really. Is that why you've been sleeping in the study?

HE: I haven't slept a wink.

SHE: I see. It must be Cook who snores.

HE: [*Turns to her*] Since when do I snore?

SHE: Not you, dear, Cook. Every night when I went down the passage.

HE: [*Goes to the door, opens it*] Good night!

SHE: Sleep well.

HE: What was that?

SHE: Sleep well.

HE: Oh—[*Stops at door, then slams it shut*] No! [*Throws clothes down on sofa at foot of bed*] I'll be damned, I won't stand it!

SHE: What is the matter?

HE: Cook snores! Agnes, I love somebody else! It's driving me crazy! You, the children, she, the children, you—for three weeks I have lived through hell, and all you've got to say is "Cook snores!"

SHE: But darling—

HE: No, no, no, no! You are so damned sure of yourself that it
makes me sick! I know you don't take this seriously, but believe
me, I love that woman! I must have that woman or I'll go mad!

SHE: [*Turns to him*] Haven't you—had her yet?

HE: At last! Thank God, a sign of life. [SHE *sits on sofa at foot of
bed*] Why haven't you looked at me like that before? I have
begged, implored, crawled to you for a little understanding and
warmth, and love, and got nothing. Even my book, that was written inspired by you, longing for you—right from the beginning
you have seen it as a rival. Whatever I did, whatever I tried: a carriage, servants, money, dresses, paintings, everything—you hated
that book. And now? Now you have driven me into somebody
else's arms. Somebody else, who understands at least one thing
clearly: that she will have to share me with my work.

SHE: Does she understand that she will have to share you with other
women as well?

HE: She doesn't need to. At last I found a woman who'll live with
my work, and a better guarantee of my faithfulness nobody could
have.

SHE: But how does she live with it? What does she do?

HE: She listens. [*Sits on bed*] She encourages me—with a look, a
touch, a—well, an encouragement. When I cheer, she cheers with
me, when I meditate, she meditates with me—

SHE: And when you throw crockery, she throws crockery with you?

HE: [*Checks himself*] Haven't you understood one single word of
what I have been saying? Won't you, can't you see that I have
changed?

SHE: No.

HE: [*Rises*] Then you are blind, blind, blind! That's all I can say. At
any rate, *you've* changed.

SHE: I!

HE: No, don't let's start that.

SHE: Go on.

HE: No, it's senseless. No reason to torture you any longer, once I have—

SHE: Once you have tasted blood?

HE: Agnes, I'm sorry it was necessary for me to hurt you. It couldn't very well have been done otherwise. I'm at the mercy of a feeling stronger than I.

[*Sits on sofa*]

SHE: Rotten, isn't it.

HE: Horrible.

SHE: And yet—at the same time not altogether.

HE: No. On the other hand, it's delicious.

SHE: The greatest thing a human being can experience.

HE: I'm glad you understand it so well.

SHE: Understand?—why, of course. It's human, isn't it?

HE: How do you come to know that?

SHE: What?

HE: That it's—human?

SHE: Well, I'm a human being, aren't I?

HE: Agnes, I never heard you talk like this before. What's the matter with you?

SHE: Well, I might have my experience too, mightn't I? [*Rises. Picks up clock from bedtable*] Good night!

HE: [*Rises*] Just a minute! I want to hear a little more about this.

SHE: But I know it now, dear.

HE: Yes, you do! But I don't! What sort of experiences are you referring to?

SHE: [*Crossing to him. Puts clock on tabouret*] Now, listen, my little friend! You have dismissed me without notice, and I haven't complained once as any other housekeeper would have done. I have accepted the facts, because I know a human being is at the mercy of this feeling, however horrible and at the same time delicious it may be.

HE: Agnes!

SHE: I really don't understand you. I am not thwarting you in the least, and instead of your going away happily and relieved that you are not going to leave a helpless wreck behind—

HE: You might answer just one plain question before—we finish this business. Have you—aren't you going to be alone, if I leave you?

SHE: Alone? I've got the children, haven't I?

HE: That's not at all certain.

SHE: [After a shaky silence] You had better leave this room very quickly now, before you get to know a side of me that might surprise you a lot.

HE: [Crossing to her] I have, I'm afraid. I demand an answer. Have you a lover?

SHE: [Goes to door, opens it] Good night.

HE: For eleven long years I have believed in you! You were the purest, the noblest thing in my life!

SHE: [Interrupting, and with him]—the noblest thing in my life! Good night!

HE: If you don't answer my question, you'll never see me again.

SHE: Get out of here.

HE: [Sits on sofa] No.

SHE: All right. Then there's only one thing left to be done.

[SHE picks up wrap from bed and exits into dressing room]

HE: What? What did you want to say? [SHE does not answer. SHE returns with second wrap and overnight case; puts them both on chair and opens case] What's the meaning of that? [SHE goes on, crosses onto dais, picks up nightgown and negligee. Packs them in case] Darling, believe me, I won't blame you for anything, only tell me—[Rises]—where are you going?

SHE: [*Crossing to dressing table and getting brushes and comb*] Would you mind calling a cab for me?

HE: Agnes!

SHE: [*Packs brushes and comb in case*] Please, Michael, I can't arrive there too late. It is such an embarrassing time already. Pass me my alarm clock, will you?

HE: No, I can't have been mistaken about you that much! Only yesterday you said that I had qualities—

SHE: Excuse me.

[*Passes him, gets her alarm clock from the tabouret. Puts clock in case*]

HE: [*Wants to stop her when she passes, but checks himself*] All right. It *is* a solution, anyhow.

SHE: [*Closes overnight case, picks it up, puts wrap over arm, crosses to him and puts out her hand*] Goodbye, Michael.

[HE *refuses.* SHE *starts.* HE *blocks her way*]

HE: Do you really think I'm going to let you do this? Do you?

SHE: A gentleman does not use force when a lady wishes to leave the room.

HE: Oh, I'm so sorry.

SHE: Thank you. [*Crosses up toward door.* HE *grabs her arm and pulls her back.* SHE *drops her suitcase and wrap in the struggle.* HE *flings her up onto the bed*] Michael! Let me go! Let me go! I—

HE: Now look, I've put up with all the nonsense from you—[SHE *succeeds in tearing herself free, gets off the bed and kicks his shin*] Ouch!

[HE *grasps at his shinbone and limps down right, leans against arm of sofa*]

SHE: Get out!

HE: Right on my scar!

SHE: Get out! [HE *takes off his coat, throws it on chair. As* HE *starts toward her:*] I'll scream the house down if you dare come near me!

[SHE *scrambles back up onto bed*]

HE: Where's my pillow!

SHE: [*Reaching for bell pull*] Get out or I'll ring the bell!

HE: [*As* HE *exits to dressing room*] Make up that bed properly.

SHE: You're the vilest swine God ever created.

HE: [*Re-enters carrying pillow. Crossing to foot of bed*] If I have to make you hoarse and broken for the rest of your life, you'll know that I am a man. Make up that bed!

[*Throws pillow at her*]

SHE: I would rather—

HE: And shut up! Get off there!

SHE: [*Strikes at him with "God Is Love" pillow*] You are the silliest hack-writer I ever—

HE: [*Grabs "God Is Love" pillow and throws it aside*] Get off, or I'll drag you off!

SHE: [*Gets off bed*] And that book of yours is rubbish.

HE: What did I tell you after I finished it? Listening to me once in awhile wouldn't do you any harm. Here! [*Throws comforter at her*] Fold that!

SHE: [*Throws it back*] Fold it yourself!

HE: [*Throws it back*] Fold it!

[SHE *goes at him and* HE *grasps her hands.* SHE *still tries to flail him.* HE *slips in the struggle and sits on dais.* SHE *tries to pound his head.* HE *regains his feet and pinions her arms behind her*]

SHE: [*As* HE *grasps her face with left hand*] I'll bite you!

HE: Oh, no you won't. If you could see your eyes now, you'd close them. They're blinding.

SHE: With hatred!

HE: With love.

      [*Gives her a quick kiss;* SHE *breaks free.* HE *gets on guard*]

SHE: [*Looks at him speechless for a moment, then sits on the bed, away from him, sobbing*] I wish I were dead. I want to be dead, dead, dead—

HE: [*Sits on edge of bed, holding shin*] Before you die, look in my eyes, just once. Look! [*Turns her to him.* SHE *looks*] What do you see there?

SHE: Wrinkles!

HE: [*Picks up evening pumps which have come off in the scuffle*] That's how long it is since you last looked. [*Sits on bed and puts one pump on*] What else?

SHE: But—what about her?

HE: I was lonely.

SHE: [*Stands*] You'd better go now.

HE: Weren't you?

SHE: Please go.

HE: [*Picks up evening coat. Crosses up to door.* SHE *picks up his pillow and puts it on chair. At archway, as* HE *puts on other pump*] I've started writing a new book.

SHE: When?

HE: A couple of weeks ago.

SHE: And you haven't read me anything yet? Impossible.

HE: I read it to her.

SHE: Oh—and?

HE: She liked it all right. But she thought it a little—well, coarse.

SHE: You, coarse? What kind of sheep is she?

HE: Shall I go and get the manuscript?

SHE: [*Picks up his pillow*] Tomorrow.

HE: [*Moves quickly to door and puts hand on door knob*] No, now!

SHE: [*Crosses up onto dais, puts his pillow in bed*] Please, tomorrow—tomorrow.

[HE *throws coat onto sofa at foot of bed and crosses around onto dais and embraces her*]

CURTAIN

SCENE TWO

1908. 4:00 A.M. *to dawn. When the curtain rises, the stage is dark. The door is opened brusquely and* HE *enters, wearing an overcoat over his pajamas.* HE *is carrying a bourbon bottle and riding crop.* SHE *is asleep in the fourposter.*

HE: [*As* HE *enters*] Agnes! [*Crosses to dressing table and turns on dressing table lamps*] Agnes, Agnes, look at this!

[*Turns on bedtable lamp.* HE *shows her brown bourbon bottle.*]

SHE: [*Waking up and shielding her eyes with arm*] Hunh? What's the matter?

HE: In his drawer, behind a pile of junk—this!

SHE: What?

HE: He's seventeen—eighteen! And it's four o'clock in the morning! And—and now, this!

SHE: [*Sitting up*] What, for Heaven's sake?

HE: [*Hands her the bottle*] Look!

SHE: [*Takes bottle and looks at it*] Bourbon!

HE: Your son. The result of your modern upbringing.

SHE: But what—where—[*Puts bottle down in bed*]—what does all this mean? What's the time?

[*Leans over and picks up clock*]

HE: [*Exits into bathroom*] It's time I took over his education.

SHE: But he told you he would be late tonight. He specially asked permission to go to that dance—I gave him the key myself!

HE: [*Re-enters and exits again into dressing room*] Where did you put that thing?

SHE: What thing?

HE: My old shaving strop.

SHE: What do you want that for? [*Lying back in bed*] Come back to bed.

HE: [*Re-enters*] So you approve of all this? You think its perfectly natural that a child boozes in his bedroom and paints the town until four o'clock in the morning?

SHE: But darling, he told you! And surely the child has a right to a bit of gaiety.

HE: One day let me explain the difference to you between gaiety and delirium tremens!

SHE: What are you going to do, Michael?

HE: [*Turns round in the doorway*] I am going downstairs where I have been since one o'clock this morning. And when he comes home, I—

SHE: [*Climbs out of bed.* SHE *wears a slumber bonnet. Picks up robe*] I won't let you—if you are going to beat that child, you will have to do so over my dead body.

[*Putting on robe*]

HE: Don't interfere, Agnes.

SHE: I mean it, Michael! Whatever happens, even if he has taken to opium, I will not let you beat that child!

HE: All right. In that case, we had better call the police.

SHE: But you knew he was coming in late! These children's parties go on till dawn!

HE: [*With a politician's gesture of despair*] Now, in my young days, if I was told to be in at a certain hour—[*Turns to her for the beginning of a big speech*] I—[*Sees her for the first time*] What in the name of sanity have you got on your head?

SHE: Now, now, that's the very latest thing—everyone's wearing them—

HE: But what *is* it?

SHE: A slumber helmet.

HE: Slumber helmet! Bourbon in the bedroom, children's parties that go on till dawn and slumber helmets. All right. [*Throws riding crop on sofa at foot of bed and rips off overcoat*] I am going to bed.

SHE: [*Crossing to foot of bed*] Listen to me, will you?

HE: [*Steps out of slippers*] I have the choice between bed and the madhouse—I prefer bed. I have a life to live. Good night! [HE *gets into bed and pulls the blanket up. Then, suddenly sitting up*] I hope you enjoy being a drunkard's mother!

   [*Lies back*]

SHE: I don't want to spoil your performance as an irate father, but I can't help thinking what your attitude would be if it were not Robert, but Lizzie who stayed out late.

HE: [*Sits up*] Exactly the same! With this difference, that Lizzie would never do such a thing.

SHE: Ha!

HE: Because she happens to be the only sane member of this family. Except me, of course.

   [*Lies back*]

SHE: I could tell you something about her that would—no, I'd better not.

HE: [*Sits up*] If you think that I am going to fall for that stone-

age woman's trick of hinting at something and then stopping—
That child is as straight and as sensible as—as a glass of milk.

[*Lies back*]

SHE: Milk!

HE: [*Finds bottle in bed, sits up, puts bottle on bedtable, lies back*] At least she doesn't go to bed with a bottle of bourbon.

SHE: Hmm—

HE: [*Sitting up*] What—hmm?

SHE: Nothing, nothing. Nothing, nothing.

HE: Agnes, you aren't by any chance suggesting that she goes to bed with anything else, are you?

SHE: I am not suggesting anything. I am just sick and tired of your coming down like a ton of bricks on that poor boy every time, while she is allowed to do whatever she pleases.

HE: So! I have an unhealthy preference for my daughter. Is that it?

SHE: I am not saying that. I—

HE: All right, say it! Say it!

SHE: What?

HE: Oedipus! Oh! Leave me alone.

[*Under the blankets again*]

SHE: [*Sits on sofa*] In his drawer, did you say?

HE: Shut up.

SHE: Darling, I know you never concern yourself with the children's education except for an occasional bout of fatherly hysteria, but I think that this time you are going a little too far, if you don't mind my saying so.

[*Sits back with feet up on sofa*]

HE: [*Sitting up*] What else do you want me to do? I have to spend every waking hour earning money. Agnes, you are my second in command—I have to leave certain things to you; but, if I see that they are obviously going wrong, it is my duty to intervene.

SHE: If that is your conception of our relationship, then you ought to think of something better than a shaving crop and a riding strop.

HE: Riding crop! And it's not a matter of thinking of something better, it's—

[HE *stops, because* SHE *has suddenly got up and gone to the window, as if she heard something*]

SHE: Michael!

HE: Is that him?

[*As* SHE *does not answer,* HE *gets out of bed and grabs his overcoat*]

SHE: [*Peeking out the window*] I thought I heard the gate.

HE: [*From doorway*] Robert! [*Exits and calls offstage*] Is that you, Robert? [*No answer, so he comes back*] No.

[*Sits down on sofa*]

SHE: [*Sits at dressing table, opens powder box*] Why don't you go back to bed?

HE: Because I'm worried.

SHE: [*Picking up handmirror and puff and powdering face*] Why, that's nonsense!

HE: And so are you.

SHE: [*Turns profile*] What on earth gives you that idea?

HE: That you are powdering your face at four o'clock in the morning.

SHE: [*Puts down mirror, puff. Rises, realizes that there is no use pretending any longer, goes to the bottle and picks it up from bed-table*] What drawer was it?

HE: The one where he keeps all his junk.

SHE: I can't believe it. It can't be true.

HE: Well, there you are.

SHE: How did you find it?

HE: I was sitting downstairs waiting—I got more and more worried so I decided to go up to his room and see whether perhaps he had climbed in through the window, and then I happened to glance into an open drawer, and there it was.

SHE: [*Puts bottle on tabouret, and sits in chair*] But it isn't possible. A child can't be drinking on the sly without his mother knowing it.

HE: We'll have to face it, my dear. He is no longer a child. When I looked into that drawer and found his old teddy bears, his steam engine and then that bottle, I—I can't tell you what I felt.

SHE: Suppose—of course it isn't—but suppose—it is true, whatever shall we do?

HE: I don't know—see a doctor.

SHE: Nonsense. It's perfectly natural childish curiosity. A boy has to try everything once.

HE: [*Rises*] If that's going to be your attitude, he'll end by trying murder once. By the way, what were you going to say about Lizzie?

SHE: [*Smiles*] She is in love.

HE: What?

SHE: She's secretly engaged.

HE: To whom?

SHE: The boy next door.

HE: To that—ape? To that pie face?

SHE: I think it's quite serious.

HE: The child is only—nonsense!

SHE: She is not a child anymore. She's—well, the same thing Robert is, I suppose. I wouldn't be surprised if one of these days the boy came to see you to ask for her hand.

HE: If he does, I'll shoot him.

SHE: But darling—

HE: But she's only sixteen! Agnes, this is a nightmare!

SHE: But sweetheart—

HE: [*Turns to her*] She can't be in love and certainly not with *that!*

SHE: Why not?

HE: After spending her whole life with me, she can't fall in love with something hatched out of an egg.

SHE: Are you suggesting that the only person the child will be allowed to fall in love with is a young edition of yourself?

HE: Of course not. Don't be indecent. What I mean is that at least we should have given them taste! They should have inherited our taste.

SHE: Well, he seems to have inherited a taste for bourbon.

HE: I don't understand how you can joke about it. This happens to be the worst night of my life.

[*Crosses onto dais and gets slippers*]

SHE: I'm not joking, darling. I just don't think that there's much point in us sitting up all night worrying ourselves sick about something we obviously can't do anything about until the morning. [*Rises*] Come, go back to bed.

HE: You go to bed—I'll wait up for him.

SHE: Shall I make you a cup of tea?

HE: Tea! You know, we haven't had a single crisis in our life yet for which your ultimate solution wasn't a cup of tea.

SHE: [*Straightening bed linen*] I'm sorry. I was only trying to be sensible about it.

HE: [*Crossing to tabouret*] I know you are. I apologize if I've said things that I didn't mean. [*Picks up the bourbon bottle and uncorks it with his left hand*] I think what we both need is a swig of this. Have we got any glasses up here?

SHE: Only tooth-glasses. [HE *takes a swig, then with a horrified expression thrusts the bottle and cork into her hands and runs to the bathroom*] Michael.

[SHE *smells the bottle, grimaces*]

HE: [*Rushing out of bathroom with a nauseated look on his face*] What is that?

SHE: [*Corking bottle*] Cod liver oil!

HE: Ohhh—!!

[*Runs back into bathroom*]

SHE: [*Takes handkerchief from pocket, wipes bottle*] How on earth did it get into this bottle?

HE: God knows! [*Re-enters to just outside bathroom door.* HE *carries a glass of water*] Agnes, I think that little monster must have been trying to set a trap for me!

[*Runs back into bathroom*]

SHE: [*Holding bottle up, puzzling over contents*] Michael, wait a minute! [SHE *is interrupted by the sound of his gargling*] I know! Well, this is the limit!

HE: [*Re-enters, wiping mouth with towel*] What?

SHE: Do you remember three years ago that he had to take that spoonful of cod liver oil every night and that he didn't want to take it in my presence? Of course I measured the bottle every morning, but he poured it into this!

HE: Agnes, do you mean to say that that stuff I swallowed is three years old?

SHE: The little monkey! Oh, now I *am* going to wait till he gets home!

[*Sits on sofa*]

HE: I think perhaps we'd better call the doctor. This stuff must be putrid by now.

[*Throws towel into bathroom*]

SHE: [*Holding bottle*] You'll have to speak to him, Michael. This is one time that you'll have to speak to him. I—[*Hears something*] Michael, there he is! [*Rises, crosses up to door.* HE *rushes to door, stops, returns to sofa and picks up riding crop. Starts out.* SHE *stops him*] No, Michael, not that! Don't go that far!

HE: Three-year old cod liver oil!

[HE *whips the air with the riding crop. Exits*]

[SHE *listens for a moment, very worried. Then* SHE *runs into the bathroom and leaves the bottle there. Re-enters, crosses to door, listens, crosses down to sofa and sits, all the while muttering to herself.* HE *appears in the doorway, dejectedly holding his riding crop in his hand.* HE *looks offstage, incredulously.* SHE *turns to him*]

SHE: Well—what did you say?

HE: [*Closes door; distracted, turns to her*] I beg your pardon?

SHE: What did you *say* to him?

HE: Oh—er—"Good morning."

SHE: Is that all?

HE: [*Throws crop on sofa*] Yes.

SHE: [*Rises*] Well, I must say! To go through all this rigamarole and then to end up with—I honestly think you could have said something more.

HE: [*Sits on sofa*] I couldn't.

SHE: Why not?

HE: He was wearing a top hat.

[HE *makes a helpless gesture and rests his head in his hands.* SHE *laughs, crosses to him and puts her arms about him, then kisses him on the top of his head*]

CURTAIN

ACT THREE

1913. Late afternoon. The same bedroom. Dressing table and chair at window; tobacco stool at left of arch; sofa right center; bedtable as before; chairs center and left center. The bed canopy has been changed as have the drapes and articles of furniture. It is all in more conservative taste now. As the curtain rises, SHE *is seated at the dressing table, holding a wedding bouquet that matches her gown and hat. After a moment,* HE *is heard humming the Wedding March.*

HE: [*From dressing room*] Agnes! [*Hums a bit more, then whistles for her.* HE *enters arranging his smoking jacket. Crosses to foot of bed, humming again. Sees her*] Oh, there you are. Your hat still on? Agnes!

SHE: [*Starts*] Yes?

HE: Hey! Are you asleep?

SHE: [*Sighs and smiles absently*] Yes—

HE: [*Fixing scarf, looking in mirror of dressing table*] Come on, darling. The only thing to think is: little children grow up. Let's be glad she ended up so well.

SHE: Yes—

HE: Thank God, Robert is a boy. I couldn't stand to go through that a second time, to see my child abducted by such a—[*Crosses to smoking stand*] Oh, well, love is blind.

SHE: [*Putting down bouquet*] Michael.

HE: Yes? [*Opens humidor and picks up pipe*] What is the matter with you? The whole day long you've been so—so strange.

SHE: How?

HE: You aren't ill, are you?

SHE: No.

HE: That's all right then. [*Starts filling his pipe*] What did you want to say?

SHE: [*Rises*] Today is the first day of Lizzie's marriage.

HE: It is. And?

SHE: [*Sits on sofa*] And the last day of ours.

HE: Beg pardon?

SHE: [*Takes off gloves*] I waited to tell you, perhaps too long. I didn't want to spoil your fun.

HE: My *fun?*

SHE: Yes. I haven't seen you so cheerful for ages.

HE: Well—I'm—[*Closes humidor*] For your sake I have made a fool of myself. For your sake I have walked around all these days with the face of a professional comedian, with a flower in my buttonhole and death in my heart! Do you know what I would have liked to do? To hurl my glass in the pie face of that bore, take my child under my arm—and as for that couple of parents-in-law—[*Looks heavenward*] And now you start telling me that you didn't want to spoil my fun!

[*Searches pockets for match*]

SHE: With the information that I am going away.

HE: You are what—?

SHE: I'm going away.

HE: [*Feeling pockets for match*] Huh?

SHE: Away.

HE: How do you mean?

SHE: Can't you help me just a little by understanding quickly what I mean?

HE: But, darling—

SHE: Michael, I'll say it to you plainly once, and please try to listen quietly. If you don't understand me after having heard it once, I'll —I'll have to write it to you.

HE: But darling, we needn't make such a fuss about it. [*Sits on sofa*] You want to have a holiday now the children have left the house; what could be more sensible? No need to announce it to me like an undertaker.

SHE: Not for a holiday, Michael—forever.

HE: You want to move into another house?

SHE: I want to go away from *you*.

HE: From me?

SHE: Yes.

HE: You want to—visit friends, or something?

SHE: Please, darling, stop it. You knew ages ago what I meant; please don't try and play for time, it makes it all so—so difficult.

HE: I don't know a damn thing. What have I done?

SHE: Nothing, nothing. You are an angel. But I am—not.

HE: [*Rises*] Agnes, what is the matter with you?

SHE: I would appreciate it if you would stop asking me what is the matter with me. There never has been anything the matter with me, and there couldn't be less the matter with me now. The only thing is, I can't—

HE: Can't what?

SHE: Die behind the stove, like a domestic animal.

HE: Good Heavens—

SHE: You wouldn't understand. You are a man. You'll be able to do what you like until you are seventy.

HE: But my dear good woman—

SHE: I won't! Today I stopped being a mother; in a few years' time, perhaps next year even, I'll stop being a woman.

HE: And that's what you don't want?

SHE: I can't help it. That happens to be the way a benevolent Providence arranged things.

HE: But darling, then it's madness.

SHE: I want to be a woman just once, before—before I become a grandmother. Is that so unreasonable?

HE: But my angel—

SHE: [*Rises; takes off hat*] For Heaven's sake, stop angeling me! You treat me as if I were sitting in a wheel-chair already. I want to live, can't you understand that? [HE *backs up, leans on sofa.* SHE *puts hat and gloves on bed*] My life long I have been a mother, my life long I've had to be at somebody's beck and call; I've never been able to be really myself, completely, wholeheartedly. No, never! From the very first day you have handcuffed me and gagged me and shut me in the dark. When I was still a child who didn't even know what it meant to be a woman, you turned me into a mother.

HE: [*Steps toward her*] But darling, you wanted Robert—

SHE: No, not through Robert, not through Lizzie, through yourself, your selfishness, your—Oh, Michael. [*Crossing to him, puts her hand on his shoulder*] I didn't intend to say all this, honestly, I didn't. I only wanted to be honest and quiet and nice about it, but —but I can't help it. I can't! The mere way you look at me, now, this very moment! That amazement, that heartbreaking stupidity —don't you feel yourself that there is nothing between us anymore in the way of tenderness, of real feeling, of love; that we are dead, as dead as doornails, that we move and think and talk like—like puppets? [SHE *sits on chair*] Making the same gestures every day, the same words, the same kisses—[HE *sits on chair*] Today, in the carriage, it was sinister. The same, the same, everything was the same; the coachman's boots behind the little window, the sound of the hooves on the pavement, the scent of flowers, the—I wanted to throw open the door, jump out, fall, hurt myself, I don't know what—only to feel that I was alive! [SHE *rises*] I, I, not that innocent, gay child in front, who was ex-

periencing all this for the first time, who played the part I had re-
hearsed for her, but I couldn't. I said "yes" and "no" and "darling" and "isn't it cold," but I heard my own voice and saw my
own face mirrored in the little window, in the coachman's boots,
like a ghost, and as I put my hat straight, to prove to myself that I
wasn't a ghost, driving to my own burial, I looked at myself in exactly the same way, in the same window perhaps, to see if my
bridal veil—[*Her voice breaks;* SHE *covers her face with her
hands; crosses up onto dais and falls onto bed, weeping.* HE *rises,
puts his pipe into his pocket, crosses up onto dais and puts his
hands on her waist*] No! Don't touch me! [*Sits up, gets handkerchief from bedtable drawer and wipes her eyes*] Michael, I don't
want to, I don't want to blame you for anything. You've always
been an angel to me, you've always done whatever you could,
as much as you could—[HE *sits on bed*]—although you never
opened a door for me, always got on the street car first, never
bought me anything nice—oh yes, I know, darling, you have given
me many beautiful presents. But something real—if it had only
been one book you didn't want to read yourself; or one box of
chocolates you didn't like yourself, but nothing. Absolutely nothing. [*Shows him her hands*] Look, just look! Only wrinkles and a
wedding ring, and a new cash book for the household every year.
[HE *takes her hand, raises it to his lips, kisses the palm of her
hand*] No, Michael. [SHE *crosses down*] That's so easy, so mean,
really. You've always known how to make that one little gesture,
say that one little word—but now it doesn't work anymore. This is
what I've been trying to tell you all along. It's the most difficult
part of all, and I don't know if I—no, I can't.

   [*Sits on sofa*]

HE: Say it.

SHE: I don't think—I'm sure I don't love you any more. I don't say
this to hurt you, darling, honestly I don't. I only want you to understand. [*Turns to him*] Do you? Do you a little?

HE: Yes. I think so.

SHE: I even remember the moment I realized I didn't love you.
One clear, terrible moment.

HE: When was that?

SHE: It was about a month ago, one Sunday morning in the bathroom. I came in to bring you your coffee and you were rubbing your head with your scalp lotion. I said something about that boy's poems that you had given me to read; I don't remember what I said—and then you said, "I could tell him where to put them"—with both hands on your head. [*Puts hands on her head*] And then—then it was suddenly as if I were seeing you for the first time. It was horrible.

HE: [*After a silence*] Where had you thought of going?

SHE: Oh, I don't know. I thought a room in a boarding house somewhere.

HE: Not a trip, abroad for instance?

SHE: Good Heavens, no.

HE: Why not?

SHE: Because I don't feel like it—[*Turns to him*]—you don't think that I—that there is something the matter with me?

HE: No.

SHE: Do you understand now why I *must* go away?

HE: Well, if I were to come into the bathroom with my head full of love lyrics, like you, only to see you rubbing your face with skin food or shaving your arm pits, I don't think I'd have been overcome by any wave of tenderness for you—but I wouldn't go and live in a boarding house.

SHE: That was not the point. The point was what you said.

HE: "I could tell him where to put them." [*Rises*] H'mm. You're sure that was the point?

SHE: Why?

HE: Who wrote those poems you were talking about?

SHE: Well, that boy—that boy, who keeps asking you what you think about his work.

HE: You liked what he wrote, didn't you?

SHE: Oh, yes. I thought it young, promising—honestly. It had something so—so—

HE: So—well?

SHE: Well, what?

HE: Well, I seem to remember this same description twenty-three years ago.

SHE: You aren't trying to tell me that I'm in love? I won't say another word to you! The very idea that I, with a boy like that, such a—such—It's just that the boy has talent! At least as much as you had, when you were still rhyming about gazelles with golden horns.

HE: I was rhyming about you.

SHE: He must be rhyming about somebody as well, but—

HE: Of course he is. About you, too.

SHE: Me?

HE: What did he write on the title page—"Dedicated in reverent admiration to the woman who inspired my master." Well, I have been his master only insofar that I wrote him a letter: "Dear Sir, I have read your poems twice. I would advise you to do the same." Still, I don't know. Perhaps I'm growing old-fashioned. After all, he's new-school and all that. I should like to read those poems again. Have you got them here?

SHE: Yes.

HE: Where are they?

SHE: [*Gets poems from lower drawer of bedtable and starts to hand him the poems, then stops*] You aren't going to make fun of them, are you?

HE: [*Takes out glasses, puts them on, takes poems from her*] Fun? Why should I? I think this occasion is serious enough for both of us to find out what exactly we're talking about. Perhaps you're right. Perhaps I need this lesson. Well, let's have it. [*Reads the title*] "Flashing Foam—Jetsam on the Beach of Youth." H'm. That seems to cover quite a lot. First Sonnet: "Nocturnal Embrace."

SHE: Michael, if you're going to make a fool of this poor boy who is just starting, only because you—

HE: Who is doing the starting here? Me! After thirty years I'm just starting to discover how difficult it is to write something that is worth reading, and I *shall* write something worth reading one day unless—well, "Nocturnal Embrace." [*Reads*]

"We are lying in the double bed,
  On the windows have thrown a net
    The dead leaves of an acorn tree."

Do you understand why it has to be an acorn tree? Why not an oak?

SHE: [*Leaning against bedpost*] Because it's beautiful. Because it gives atmosphere.

HE: I see. I'm sorry. [HE *reads*]
"From a church tower far unseen,
  A solemn bell strikes twelve."

Well, now that rhyme could definitely be improved.
"From a church tower far unseen,
  A solemn bell strikes just thirteen."

[SHE *doesn't answer.* HE *reads on*]
"Strikes twelve,
  O'er the darkened fields,
  The silent sea.
  But then we start and clasp
  A frightened, sickening gasp,
  For a foot has stopped behind the door."

Now this I understand. [*Crossing to her*] No wonder they are startled. Suppose you're just busy clasping each other, and then a foot walks along the corridor and stops right outside your door—[HE *shudders*]

SHE: I'm not laughing, if that's what you're after.

HE: That's not what he was after in any case, but let's see how it ends. [HE *reads*]
"For a foot has stopped behind the door.
  Silence. Thumping. It's our hearts
  Waiting with our breath—"

Wondering where the other foot's got to, I suppose—

SHE: Michael, please stop it!

HE: Why? Am I his master or am I not? And has he got the cheek to dedicate this bad pornography to my Agnes or has he not?

SHE: He meant it for the best.

HE: Oh now, did he really? [*Throws poems on sofa*] Do you call that for the best, to turn the head of a woman, the best wife any man could wish himself, at the moment when she's standing empty-handed because she imagines her job is over? To catch her at a time when she can't think of anything better to do than to become young again and wants to start for a second time fashioning the first damn fool at hand into a writer like me?

SHE: But you don't need me anymore.

HE: Oh no? Well, let me tell you something. People may buy my books by the thousands, they may write me letters and tell me how I broke their hearts and made them bawl their damn heads off, but I know the truth alright. It's *you* who makes me sing—and if I sing like a frog in a pond, it's not my fault.

    [*Sits on sofa. Takes off glasses*]

SHE: [*Is so amused and relieved that* SHE *cries and laughs at the same time. The laughter gets the upper hand*] Oh, Michael!

HE: What are you laughing at?

SHE: [*Crossing to him and sitting on sofa beside him*] Oh, Michael—I'm not laughing—I'm not laughing. [SHE *embraces him and sobs on his shoulder*]

HE: [*Comforts her like a man who suddenly feels very tired*] I'll be damned if I understand that. [*Rests his head on her shoulder*]

CURTAIN

SCENE TWO

1925. Dawn. Same bedroom, twelve years later. It is apparent that they are moving out—pictures have been taken off the walls, leaving discolored squares on the wallpaper; a step ladder leans against the right wall of archway; all drapes have

been removed with the exception of the bed canopy and
spread on the fourposter which is the only piece of furniture
remaining in the room. Several large suitcases, packed and
closed, are sitting down right center; a trunk at right.

AT RISE: HE *is heard messing about in the bathroom. Then*
HE *comes out, humming and carrying toilet articles.* HE *goes*
to the suitcases, finds them shut, carries the stuff to the bed.
HE *crosses again to the suitcases, opens one. It is full.* HE *slams*
the lid shut and fastens the locks, at the same time noticing
that a small piece of clothing is left hanging out. HE *disre-*
gards it and drags a second case on top of the first one, opens
it, finds that it is fully packed as well. However, HE *rearranges*
the contents to make room for his toilet articles. As HE *starts*
back to bed, he again notices the piece of clothing hanging
out of the bottom case. HE *looks toward door, then leans*
down and rips off the piece of material, puts it in his pocket
and crosses up onto dais. HE *picks up his toilet articles from*
the bed, turns, then drops them on the floor. HE *mutters,*
"Damn!" and gets down on his hands and knees to pick them
up. At that moment, when HE *is out of sight,* SHE *comes in*
carrying the little "God Is Love" pillow. The moment SHE *real-*
izes he is there, SHE *quickly hides the pillow behind her back.*

SHE: What are you doing?

HE: [*Rises*] Packing.

SHE: [*Picks up knitting bag from floor at foot of bed and puts it
near suitcases*] Well, hurry up, darling. The car comes at eight
and it's almost twenty of. What have you been doing all this
time?

HE: Taking down the soap dish in the bathroom.

SHE: The soap dish? What on earth for?

HE: I thought it might come in useful.

SHE: But darling, you mustn't. It's a fixture.

HE: Nonsense. Anything that is screwed on isn't a fixture. Only
things that are nailed.

SHE: That's not true at all. The agent explained it most carefully.
Anything that's been fixed for more than twenty-five years is a
fixture.

HE: [*Hands her the soap dish*] Then I'm a fixture, too.

SHE: [*Crosses to bathroom*] Don't be witty, darling. There isn't time.

HE: [*Seeing little pillow under her arm*] Hey! Hey! Hey! [SHE *stops*] We don't have to take that little horror with us, do we?

SHE: No. [*Exits into bathroom*]

HE: [*Picks up part of his toilet things*] What about the bed?

SHE: [*Off*] What?

HE: [*Crossing to suitcases*] Are you going to unmake the bed or have we sold the blankets and the sheets with it? [*Starts packing toilet things*]

SHE: [*Off*] What is it, dear?

HE: Have we only sold the horse or the saddle as well?

SHE: [*Re-enters, stands holding the little pillow*] Horse, what horse?

HE: What's to become of those things? Have we sold the bed-clothes or haven't we?

SHE: Oh, no dear. Only the spread. I'll pack the rest. [*Crosses onto dais. Puts little pillow under arm and strips pillow cases*]

HE: In what? These suitcases are landmines. Why are you nursing that thing? [SHE *mumbles something and tucks little pillow more firmly under her arm.* HE *crosses up to her*] Just what are you planning to do with it?

SHE: I thought I'd leave it as a surprise.

HE: A surprise?

SHE: Yes, for the new tenants. Such a nice young couple. [*Places pillow*]

HE: Have you visualized that surprise, may I ask?

SHE: Why?

HE: Two young people entering the bedroom on their first night of their marriage, uncovering the bed and finding a pillow a foot across with "God Is Love" written on it.

SHE: [*Picks up rest of toilet articles and newspaper from bed. Puts them down on dais, the newspaper on top*] You've got nothing to do with it.

HE: Oh, I haven't, have I? Well, I have. I've only met those people once, but I'm not going to make a fool of myself.

SHE: But, darling—

HE: There's going to be no arguing about it, and that's final. [*Snatches pillow, throws it on trunk. Mutters*] God is Love!

SHE: [*Stripping blanket and sheets from bed*] All right. Now, why don't you run downstairs and have a look at the cellar.

HE: Why?

SHE: [*Stuffs bed linen in pillow case*] To see if there's anything left there.

HE: Suppose there is something left there, what do you suggest we do with it? Take it with us? You don't seem to realize that the apartment won't hold the stuff from one floor of this house.

SHE: Please, darling, don't bicker. We agreed that it was silly to stay on here with all these empty rooms.

HE: But where are we going to put all this stuff?

SHE: Now, I've arranged all that. Why don't you go down and see if there's anything left in the wine cellar?

HE: Ah, now you're talking!

[HE *goes out*]

[SHE *twirls the pillow case tight, and leaves it by the suitcases. Picks up the "God Is Love" pillow, returns to the bed, and places it on top of the regular bed pillows, then stands back and admires it. With one hand on bedpost,* SHE *glances over the entire bed and smiles fondly. Then straightens the spread, moves around to upstage side, smooths out the cover, goes to foot of bed, stops, hears him coming; crosses around to upstage side again and quickly covers the "God Is Love" pillow with spread*]

HE: [*Entering with champagne bottle*] Look what I've found!

SHE: What?

HE: Champagne! [*Blows dust from bottle*] Must be one that was left over from Robert's wedding.

SHE: Oh.

HE: Have we got any glasses up here?

SHE: Only the tooth-glasses.

HE: [*Sits on edge of bed*] All right, get them.

SHE: You aren't going to drink it now?

HE: Of course. Now, don't tell me this is a fixture!

[*Tears off foil from bottle*]

SHE: But darling, we can't drink champagne at eight o'clock in the morning.

HE: Why not?

SHE: We'll be reeling about when we get to that place. That would be a nice first impression to make on the landlady!

HE: I'd be delighted. I'd go up to that female sergeant major and say, "Hiya! Hah! Hah!"

[*Blows his breath in her face as in the First Act*]

[*The memory strikes them both.* THEY *stay for a moment motionless.* SHE *pats his cheek lovingly*]

SHE: I'll go get those glasses.

[SHE *exits into bathroom*]

[HE *rises, throws the foil into the wastebasket at foot of bed and puts bottle on floor. Goes back to bed and looks for the rest of his toilet articles.* HE *pulls back the spread, picks up the "God Is Love" pillow, looks under it, tosses it back, looks under the other pillows, then suddenly realizes that the "God Is Love" pillow has been put back in the bed. Picks it up and calls:*]

HE: Agnes.

SHE: [*Off*] What?

HE: Agnes.

SHE: [*Re-enters carrying towel and two glasses*] What? Oh—

[SHE *is upset when she sees what it is, and very self-conscious*]

HE: Agnes, did you put this back in the bed?

SHE: Yes.

HE: Why, for Heaven's sake?

SHE: I told you—I wanted to leave something—friendly for that young couple—a sort of message.

HE: What message?

SHE: I'd like to tell them how happy we'd been—and that it was a very good bed—I mean, it's had a very nice history, and that—marriage was a good thing.

HE: Well, believe me, that's not the message they'll read from this pillow. Agnes, we'll do anything you like, we'll write them a letter, or carve our initials in the bed, but I won't let you do this to that boy—

SHE: Why not? [SHE *puts glasses and towel on floor beside knitting bag, takes little pillow from him and crosses up to bed*] When I found this very same little pillow in this very same bed on the first night of our marriage, I nearly burst into tears!

HE: Oh, you did, did you? Well, so did I! And it's time you heard about it! When, on that night, at that moment, I first saw that pillow, I suddenly felt as if I'd been caught in a world of women. Yes, women! I suddenly saw loom up behind you the biggest trade union in existence, and if I hadn't been a coward in long woolen underwear with my shoes off, I would have made a dive for freedom.

SHE: That's a fine thing to say! After all these years—

HE: Now, we'll have none of that. You can burst into tears, you can stand on your head, you can divorce me, but I'm not going to let you paralyze that boy at a crucial moment.

SHE: But it isn't a crucial moment!

HE: It is *the* crucial moment!

SHE: It is not! She would find it before, when she made the bed. That's why I put it there. It is meant for her, not for him, not for you, for her from me!

[*Puts little pillow on bed as before*]

HE: Whomever it's for, the answer is NO! [HE *takes the little pillow and puts it on the trunk again.* SHE *pulls the spread up over the bed pillows*] Whatever did I do with the rest of my toilet things?

[SHE *picks them up from floor by bed, crosses to him, hands them to him, puts newspaper in wastebasket.* HE *is very carefully packing his things. When* HE *is finished, he closes the lid to the suitcase*]

You'll have to sit on this with me. I'll never get it shut alone. [SHE *sits down beside him*] Now, get hold of the lock and when I say "Yes," we'll both do—that. [HE *bounces on the suitcase*] Ready? Yes! [*They bounce.* HE *fastens his lock*] Is it shut?

SHE: [*Trying to fix catch*] Not quite.

HE: What do you mean, not quite? Either it's shut or it isn't.

SHE: It isn't.

HE: All right. Here we go again. Ready? Yes! [*They bounce again*] All right?

SHE: Yes.

HE: [*Picks up champagne bottle*] Now, do we drink this champagne or don't we?

SHE: [*Picks up glasses, towel, packs them in knitting bag*] No.

HE: All right. I just thought it would be a nice idea. Sort of round things off. [*Puts champagne bottle back on floor*] Well, what do we do? Sit here on the suitcase till the car comes, or go downstairs and wait in the hall?

SHE: I don't know.

HE: [*Looks at her, then at the little pillow on trunk, then smiles at her anger*] It's odd, you know, how after you have lived in a place for so long, a room gets full of echoes. Almost everything we've said this morning we have said before. It's the bed—[SHE *lays her head on his shoulder*]—it's the bed, really, that I regret most. Pity it wouldn't fit. I wonder how the next couple will get along. Do you know what he does?

SHE: He's a salesman.

HE: A salesman, eh? Well, why not? So was I. Only I realized it too late. The nights that I lay awake in that bed thinking how I'd beat Shakespeare at the game—

SHE: Never mind, darling, you've given a lot of invalids a very nice time.

[*In his reaction, as* HE *turns to reply: doorbell rings twice.* HE *rises and looks out window. Crosses to door, opens it.* SHE *rises and turns top suitcase up.* HE *crosses, puts bed linen under left arm, picks up top suitcase in left hand.* SHE *turns up the other suitcase and* HE *picks that one up in his right hand; turns to go.* SHE *quickly gets the knitting bag, stops him and tucks it under his right arm.* HE *exits.*

SHE *picks up purse, gloves, from off of trunk, then quickly takes the little pillow and crosses to bed but stops suddenly, hearing him return, and hides the pillow under her coat.* HE *crosses to trunk, leans over to grasp its handle, sees that the little pillow is not there, but proceeds to drag the trunk out. At the door, as* HE *swings trunk around,* HE *looks back at her.* SHE *is standing, leaning against the bedpost, pulling on her gloves. As soon as* HE *is out of sight,* SHE *hurriedly puts the pillow back into the bed and covers it.*

HE *re-enters, wearing his hat, picks up bottle of champagne, crosses up to bed, drops hat on foot of bed, flings back the covers, picks up the little pillow and throws it to her side of the bed; then throws the bottle of champagne down on the pillow on his side and flips the spread back into place.* HE *picks up his hat and crosses to her. They stand there for a moment, looking about the room.* HE *puts his hat on, smiles, leans down and hesitantly, but surely, picks her up.* SHE *cries, "Michael!"* HE *stands there for a moment, kisses her, then turns and carries her out of the room*]

CURTAIN

THE TEAHOUSE OF THE AUGUST MOON

John Patrick

(Based on the Novel by Vern Sneider)

John Patrick

Without hesitation, *The Teahouse of the August Moon* can be described as the most honored comedy of the 1950s. In addition to being named the 1954 Tony Award play, John Patrick's dramatization of Vern Sneider's novel received the 1953–54 Pulitzer Prize, the same season's New York Drama Critics' Circle Award, the Aegis Club Award, and the Donaldson Award.

Running in New York for 1,027 performances, the Maurice Evans and George Schaefer production accumulated four additional Tonys: for the author, the producers, actor David Wayne, and scenic designer Peter Larkin.

Not only was the public immediately (and for almost three years thereafter) attracted to the varied enchantments of the comedy, but the professional appraisers were equally dazzled by the glow of that incandescent August Moon.

Richard Watts, Jr., stated in the New York *Post*: "A warm, charming and thoroughly delightful comedy has been made by John Patrick out of *The Teahouse of the August Moon*, Vern Sneider's novel about the American wartime occupation of the embattled island of Okinawa . . . The result is a wise, gently satirical and beautifully understanding dramatic fantasy concerning the impact on each other of East and West . . . The new play offers the most complete joy the theatre has provided for many a month . . . Over and beyond its rich and deliciously humorous and touching qualities as sheer entertainment, I think the most enchanting quality of *The Teahouse of the August Moon* is its gay, smiling tribute to the human spirit and the capacity of mankind for mutual understanding."

Brooks Atkinson described it in the New York *Times* as: "Completely captivating . . . a piece of exotic make-believe in a style as intimate as a fairy story. What Mr. Patrick says is interesting. How he says it is imaginative and original . . . A delightful comedy and an ingratiating play."

Fellow aisle-sitters joined in the chorus of critical hosannas: "A play of enchantment and wit, of satire and philosophy put together with loving hands and great perceptiveness . . . it is a full, rewarding and utterly magic event."

"A thoroughly enchanting play filled with the most extraordinary good sense about human and international relations" that "beautifully blends satire, robust comedy and heart" and has "a wistful undertone which enhances its enjoyment."

"Funny, humane and wise, charming and touching, shrewdly, good-naturedly satirical and lyrically beautiful, altogether it is one of the happiest things to have happened to Broadway in years."

A screen version of *The Teahouse of the August Moon* was released in 1956 with Marlon Brando, Glenn Ford, Eddie Albert, and Paul Ford repeating his stage role of the blustering Colonel Wainwright Purdy III.

John Patrick was born in Louisville, Kentucky, on May 17, 1907. He was educated at Holy Cross College, Harvard and Columbia universities.

He began his professional career by writing radio scripts in San Francisco; then, subsequently, came to Hollywood where he was engaged as a screen writer.

During World War II, he joined the American Field Service and served overseas as a captain with a British ambulance unit in Egypt, India, Burma, and Syria.

A prolific writer, Mr. Patrick first came to Broadway's attention with the 1935 production of his play, *Hell Freezes Over*. Many others were to follow, including: *The Willow and I* (1942); *The Hasty Heart*, selected as one of the ten best plays of the season, (1945); *The Story of Mary Surratt* (1947); *The Curious Savage* (1950); *Lo and Behold!* (1951); *The Teahouse of the August Moon* (1953); *Good as Gold*, based on Alfred Toombs's book (1957); *Juniper and the Pagans* (1959); *Everybody Loves Opal* (1961); *Everybody's Girl* (1967); *Scandal Point, A Barrelful of Pennies* (1968); *Love Is a Time of Day* (1969); and the book for *Lovely Ladies, Kind Gentlemen*, a musical based on *The Teahouse of the August Moon* (1970).

A phenomenally popular author with summer stock, dinner and community theatre audiences throughout the nation, Mr. Patrick has written, especially for this market, three sequels to his 1961 comedy, *Everybody Loves Opal*: *Opal's Husband*; *Opal's Baby*; and *Opal*

Is a Diamond. His other recent stage works include: *A Bad Year for Tomatoes; The Dancing Mice; The Enigma;* and *The Savage Dilemma.*

In addition to his extensive work in the theatre, Mr. Patrick has written some thirty screenplays. To name some in nonchronological order: *Three Coins in the Fountain; Love Is a Many-Splendored Thing; The Teahouse of the August Moon; High Society; The World of Suzie Wong; The Shoes of the Fisherman; Some Came Running;* and *Les Girls.* The latter (which had a Cole Porter score and starred Gene Kelly, Mitzi Gaynor, and Kay Kendall) brought him both a Screen Writers' Guild and Foreign Correspondents' Award for the year's best screenplay.

The Teahouse of the August Moon was first presented by Maurice Evans, in association with George Schaefer, on October 15, 1953, at the Martin Beck Theatre, New York. The cast was as follows:

SAKINI	*David Wayne*
SERGEANT GREGOVICH	*Harry Jackson*
COL. WAINWRIGHT PURDY III	*Paul Ford*
CAPTAIN FISBY	*John Forsythe*
OLD WOMAN	*Naoe Kondo*
OLD WOMAN'S DAUGHTER	*Mara Kim*
THE DAUGHTER'S CHILDREN	*Moy Moy Thom, Joyce Chen and Kenneth Wong*
LADY ASTOR	*Saki*
ANCIENT MAN	*Kame Ishikawa*
MR. HOKAIDA	*Chuck Morgan*
MR. OMURA	*Kuraji Seida*
MR. SUMATA	*Kaie Deei*
MR. SUMATA'S FATHER	*Kikuo Hiromura*
MR. SEIKO	*Haim Winant*
MISS HIGA JIGA	*Shizu Moriya*
MR. KEORA	*Yuki Shimoda*
MR. OSHIRA	*William Hansen*
VILLAGERS	*Jerry Fujikawa, Frank Ogawa, Richard Akagi, Laurence Kim and Norman Chi*
LADIES' LEAGUE FOR DEMOCRATIC ACTION	*Vivian Thom, Naoe Kondo, Mary Anne Reeve and Mara Kim*
LOTUS BLOSSOM	*Mariko Niki*
CAPTAIN MC LEAN	*Larry Gates*

Directed by Robert Lewis
Settings and Lighting by Peter Larkin
Costumes by Noel Taylor
Music by Dai-Keong Lee

ACT ONE

Scene 1: *Okinawa. Colonel Purdy's Office, GHQ.*
Scene 2: *Outside Captain Fisby's Quarters, GHQ.*
Scene 3: *Tobiki Village.*

ACT TWO

Scene 1: *Tobiki Village.*
Scene 2: *Colonel Purdy's Office, GHQ.*
Scene 3: *Captain Fisby's Office, Tobiki.*
Scene 4: *Tobiki Village.*

ACT THREE

Scene 1: *The Teahouse of the August Moon.*
Scene 2: *Captain Fisby's Office, Tobiki.*
Scene 3: *The Teahouse of the August Moon.*

ACT ONE

SCENE ONE

Directly behind the house curtain is a second curtain consisting of four panels of split bamboo. Each of these sections can be raised and lowered individually.

As the house lights dim, the Oriental strains from a stringed instrument can be heard playing softly in the background. A pool of light picks up SAKINI *standing framed against the bamboo backing. He wears a pair of tattered shorts and a native shirt. His shoes, the gift of a G.I., are several sizes too large. His socks are also too large and hang in wrinkles over his ankles. He is an Okinawan who might be any age between thirty and sixty. In repose his face betrays age, but the illusion is shattered quickly by his smile of childlike candor.*

With hands together in prayer-like supplication, he walks down to the footlights and bows to the audience center in solemn ritual. Then he bows from the waist—to the left and to the right.

Straightening up, he examines the audience seated before him with open curiosity. The music ceases. As it ceases, SAKINI *begins to work his jaws vigorously.*

SAKINI: Tootie-fruitie.

> [*He takes the gum from his mouth and, wrapping it carefully in a piece of paper, puts it in a matchbox and restores it to a pocket in his shirt*]

Most generous gift of American sergeant.

> [*He resumes his original posture of dignity*]

Lovely ladies, kind gentlemen:
Please to introduce myself.
Sakini by name.
Interpreter by profession.
Education by ancient dictionary.
Okinawan by whim of gods.
History of Okinawa reveal distinguished record of conquerors.
We have honor to be subjugated in fourteenth century by Chinese pirates.
In sixteenth century by English missionaries.
In eighteenth century by Japanese war lords.
And in twentieth century by American Marines.
Okinawa very fortunate.
Culture brought to us. . . . Not have to leave home for it.
Learn many things.
Most important that rest of world not like Okinawa.
World filled with delightful variation.
Illustration.
In Okinawa . . . no locks on doors.
Bad manners not to trust neighbors.
In America . . . lock and key big industry.
Conclusion?
Bad manners good business.
In Okinawa . . . wash self in public bath with nude lady quite proper.
Picture of nude lady in private home . . . quite improper.
In America . . . statue of nude lady in park win prize.
But nude lady in flesh in park win penalty.
Conclusion?
Pornography question of geography.
But Okinawans most eager to be educated by conquerors.
Deep desire to improve friction.
Not easy to learn.
Sometimes painful.
But pain makes man think.
Thought makes man wise.
Wisdom makes life endurable.
So . . .

[*He crosses back to the left of the first of the panels*]

We tell little story to demonstrate splendid example of benevolent assimilation of democracy by Okinawa.

[*He claps his hands, signaling the stagehand to raise the first of the four panels. Flush against the curtain is revealed a sign nailed onto a denuded palm stump. It points toward the other side of the stage and reads:* COL. WAINWRIGHT PURDY III]

Boss by name of Colonel Purdy—Three. Number three after name indicate he is a son of a son of a son.

[*He steps to the next panel and claps again. The screen rolls up revealing a laundry line tied to a second denuded stump. As these panels are raised the background is revealed in sections. It includes a jeep parked against a pile of empty gasoline drums, trees ripped of foliage by recent gunfire—all creating an impression of general destruction. There are several articles of wearing apparel hanging on the laundry line, foremost of which is a pair of khaki pants size forty*]

Colonel Purdy, Three, displays splendid example of cleanliness for native population to follow. But native population cannot follow. Native not *have* two pairs of pants.

[*He then claps for the next screen to rise, revealing more of the laundry. To the extreme right is seen the outside of* COLONEL PURDY'S *Quonset office. Nailed on the post holding the other end of the line is a sign reading:* OFFICERS' LAUNDRY ONLY]

Colonel Purdy put up many signs. This exceedingly civilized. Make it very easy for uncivilized to know what *not* to do. Here laundry of officer not to fraternize with laundry of enlisted man.

[SAKINI *now signals for the last panel to be raised, revealing the inside of the hut.* COLONEL PURDY'S *vacant desk is beside the door. A sign denotes his proprietorship. Another sign admonishes the visitor to* THINK! *The office is small and sparse. A bulletin board for "Daily Orders" hangs on the upstage wall. Against this wall is the desk of* SERGEANT GREGOVICH. *Behind a sign denoting his rating sits the*

SERGEANT. *His posture is frozen—as if awaiting a signal to come to life.* SAKINI *crosses down center to explain to his audience*]

This gentleman honorable Sergeant Gregovich—assistant to Colonel Purdy. Not son of a son of a son.

[*He turns toward the* SERGEANT]

Play has begun, Sergeant.

[GREGOVICH *now comes to life. He begins to chew his gum vigorously and to look about the office. He rises and crosses down to* COLONEL PURDY'S *desk. He gets down on his hands and knees in front of desk and reaches under it*]

Oh, you know what he is doing? Explanation. Colonel Purdy great student of history. Every month wife of Colonel Purdy send him magazine called *Adventure Magazine.* Cover has picture of pirate with black patch over eye. Everybody try to steal magazine. Colonel hide under desk so he can read first.

[GREGOVICH *rises triumphantly with the magazine*]

But Sergeant always find. Smart mouse.

[GREGOVICH *returns to his desk and buries himself behind the pages of the magazine. At this point* COLONEL PURDY *himself enters from the left. As his laundry has indicated. he is a man of proportions. The worries of the world in general and the Army of Occupation in particular weigh heavily on his shoulders. He stops to glance at the nearest official sign. He takes out a small notebook to make an entry.* SAKINI'S *presence is not recognized until indicated*]

This gentleman exalted boss—Colonel Purdy, Three. Subject of sovereign American city of Pottawattamie, Michigan.

[COLONEL PURDY *hiccups and taps his chest*]

Also subject to indignity of indigestion. Colonel Purdy explain this by saying—

PURDY: [*Clears his throat and says to himself*] An occupational disorder of the Army of Occupation.

[*He taps his chest again and puts the notebook away*]

SAKINI: Colonel Purdy very wise man. Always hit nail on head. Every morning, look at sky—[COLONEL PURDY *puts his hands on his hips and glances skyward*] And make prophecy.

PURDY: It's not going to rain today.

SAKINI: And you know what? Not rain. Of course, not rain here this time of year in whole history of Okinawa. But Colonel not make mistake. [COLONEL PURDY *goes down the laundry line and stops to button the top of a pair of shorts*] Colonel Purdy gentleman of propriety. [PURDY *goes back to count articles of clothing*] And precision. Always count laundry.

PURDY: [*Counts aloud*] Un—deux—trois.

SAKINI: Explanation. Army teach Colonel French for invasion of Europe. Then send to Okinawa instead.

PURDY: . . . quatre—cinq—six—sept.

[*He beams with satisfaction*]

SAKINI: Very good. Colonel count in French and not notice one pair shorts missing in Okinawa.

PURDY: [*His expression quickly changes*] What? [*He goes down the line and counts again in English*] One, two, three, four, five, six, seven!

[*He inhales deeply for an explosion*]

SAKINI: [*Rushes down to the footlights*] Oh—ladies please close ears unless want to hear unladylike oath.

[*He puts his hands over his own ears*]

PURDY: [*Explodes*] Damitohell! Damitohell! Damitohell!

SAKINI: Now Colonel yell loud for Sakini. But Sakini hide. Pretend to be asleep.

[*He promptly curls up on the ground beside the office, with his back to the* COLONEL]

PURDY: Sakini! [SAKINI *snores.* PURDY *strides over to tower above him*] Sakini!

SAKINI: [*Rises quickly*] Oh—oh. Good morning, boss. You sure surprise me.

PURDY: *Where* is the boy that does my laundry!

SAKINI: Bring laundry back and go home to sleep, boss.

PURDY: I want you to find out why my laundry comes back every week with one piece missing!

SAKINI: Gets lost, boss.

PURDY: I *know* it gets lost. What I want to find out is *how* it gets lost.

SAKINI: Very simple. Boy takes laundry to top of mountain stream and throws in water. Then runs down hill fast as dickens to catch laundry at bottom. Sometimes not run fast enough.

PURDY: [*Heaves a martyr's sigh*] No wonder you people were subjugated by the Japanese. If you're not sleeping you're running away from work. Where is your "get-up-and-go"?

SAKINI: Guess "get-up-and-go" went.

          [SAKINI *starts to sit on the ground*]

PURDY: Well, get up and go over to the mess and see if Captain Fisby has arrived. If he has, tell him to report to me at once. Hurry! [*As* SAKINI *starts across the stage* PURDY *looks with annoyance at the G.I. socks that hang down over* SAKINI's *ankles*] Sakini!

SAKINI: [*Stops*] Yes, boss?

PURDY: You're a civilian employee in the pay of the United States Army. And should dress accordingly. *Pull Your Socks Up!*

SAKINI: Yes, boss. [*He leans over and pulls up his socks—not a great improvement*] Anything else, boss?

PURDY: That will be all. [SAKINI *ambles across the stage so slowly that the* COLONEL *explodes in exasperation*] Is that as *fast* as you can walk!

SAKINI: Oh no, boss. But if I walk any faster—socks fall down.

          [*As* SAKINI *exits,* COLONEL PURDY *closes his eyes and counts to ten in vehement French.* PURDY *remains arrested in this position.* SAKINI *re-enters downstage. He signals the closing of the panels left, shutting out the* COLONEL]

SAKINI: Introduction now over. Kindly direct attention to office. [*He leans out toward the footlights and calls across stage*] Oh, Honorable Sergeant—ready now to continue.

[SERGEANT GREGOVICH *again comes to life. He glances out the office door and quickly hides the* Adventure *Magazine. He stands at attention as* COLONEL PURDY *enters.* SAKINI *exits into the wings*]

GREGOVICH: Good morning, sir.

PURDY: At ease. [COLONEL PURDY *sits down behind his desk and begins searching through the papers on it*] I'm thinking of getting rid of that interpreter. He doesn't set a good example.

GREGOVICH: We've got to have someone around that speaks the language, sir.

PURDY: You're quite right, Sergeant. You're quite right. It isn't often I make a mistake, but when I do—

GREGOVICH: It's a beaut?

PURDY: [*Stiffly*] I wasn't going to say that. I was going to say—I admit it.

GREGOVICH: Sorry, sir.

PURDY: We've got a new officer reporting this morning. He's been transferred to us from "Psychological Warfare." [*Benevolently*] I don't suppose you happen to know who *they* are?

GREGOVICH: Aren't they something at the rear of the Rear Echelon?

PURDY: They're just the cream of the Army's geniuses. They're just the brains behind the fighting heart. Every man jack of them has a mind like a steel trap. And we are lucky to be getting one of their officers.

GREGOVICH: I'll watch my step, sir.

PURDY: While we're waiting for Captain Fisby, I want you to make a note of some new signs I want painted.

GREGOVICH: [*Takes up a pad*] The painter hasn't finished the ones you ordered yesterday, sir.

PURDY: There's only one answer to that. Put on another sign painter. Now. I noticed the men were dancing with each other in the canteen the other night.

GREGOVICH: Yes, sir. [*He writes on his pad*] "No dancing allowed."

PURDY: [*Annoyed*] I didn't say that, Gregovich! I don't object to the men dancing. I want them to enjoy themselves. But it doesn't set a good example for the natives to see noncoms dancing with enlisted men. So have a sign posted saying, "Sergeants Are Forbidden to Dance with Privates."

GREGOVICH: Yes, sir.

PURDY: Have another sign put up beside that clear pool of water just below the falls—"For Officers Only."

GREGOVICH: Where will the men bathe, sir?

PURDY: There is another pool just below it they can use.

GREGOVICH: If you'll pardon me, sir—they're not going to like that. They'll be bathing in water the officers have already bathed in.

PURDY: That's a valid objection, Gregovich. We don't want to do anything unreasonable. [*He concentrates for a moment*] How far is the second pool below the first?

GREGOVICH: About three hundred yards.

PURDY: [*Satisfied*] Then it's quite all right. Water purifies itself every two hundred feet.

GREGOVICH: Do you think that will satisfy the men, sir?

PURDY: I don't see why it shouldn't. It satisfies science. Well, you might as well take those memos to the sign painter now.

GREGOVICH: Yes, sir.

[*He goes out. As soon as he is gone,* COLONEL PURDY *moves around to the front of his desk and feels under it for his Adventure Magazine. When he fails to find it, he kneels down on all fours to peer under the desk.* SAKINI *enters and looks around. He steps over and taps the nearest part of* COLONEL PURDY—*his ample rear end*]

SAKINI: Sakini here, boss.

PURDY: [*Glances around indignantly*] Don't *ever* put your finger on an officer!

SAKINI: Not right, boss?

PURDY: No! If you want to announce your presence—knock! [*He peers under the desk again*] Can't you natives learn anything about custom? [SAKINI *stands unhappily a moment, then leans forward and knocks gently on the* COLONEL. PURDY *rises in wrath*] What do you think you're doing?

SAKINI: Not know, boss. Do what you ask.

PURDY: [*Moves behind his desk*] Everything in this Godforsaken country conspires to annoy me. [*He turns to* SAKINI] Well, where is Captain Fisby?

SAKINI: [*Points out the door*] He come now. I run ahead. [*He points to his ankles*] Socks fall down.

[*He then steps back to allow* CAPTAIN FISBY *to enter.* CAPTAIN FISBY *is in his late twenties, nice-looking and rather on the earnest side. He is nervous and eager to make a good impression. He salutes smartly*]

CAPTAIN FISBY: Captain Fisby reporting, sir.

PURDY: [*Returns the salute*] Welcome to Team 147, Captain.

[*He puts out his hand*]

FISBY: [*Shakes hands*] Thank you, sir.

PURDY: I can't tell you how glad I am to have you, Captain. Frankly, we're so desperate for officer personnel I'd be glad to see you even if you had two heads. [SAKINI *breaks into gales of laughter.* PURDY *turns to him icily*] That will be all, Sakini. You can wait outside.

SAKINI: [*Bows*] I sit by door. Not sleep!

[*He exits*]

PURDY: Sit down, Captain, sit down. [FISBY *sits facing* PURDY] Have you unpacked?

FISBY: [*Proudly*] Yes *sir!* I got in last night and unpacked at once.

PURDY: Well, that's too bad, because you'll have to pack again. I'm sending you to Tobiki at once. We need a man of your caliber up there right away.

[*He laughs with forced heartiness*]

FISBY: [*Forces a laugh in return*] Thank you.

PURDY: I'm informed, Captain, that you requested this transfer from "Psychological Warfare" to *my* outfit. May I say that I am honored.

FISBY: Well—in all fairness, sir—I think I should tell you . . . the information is only partly true.

PURDY: [*Pauses*] You *didn't* request this transfer to me?

FISBY: I was *requested* to request it, sir.

PURDY: Oh. [*He blinks to aid his digestion of this information*] May I ask why?

FISBY: Well, my propaganda to undermine enemy morale always seemed to undermine the staff's morale instead, sir.

PURDY: *How* did you get into "Psychological Warfare" in the *first* place?

FISBY: I had been requested to request a transfer.

PURDY: From what?

FISBY: Paymaster General's office.

PURDY: What was your duty there?

FISBY: I was in charge of the payroll computation machine until— until—

[*He flounders unhappily*]

PURDY: Until *what*?

FISBY: Well, sir, machines have always been my mortal enemies. I don't think they're inanimate at all. I think they're full of malice and ill will. They—

PURDY: I *asked* you what happened, Captain.

FISBY: Well, this computation machine made a mistake of a quarter of a million dollars on the payroll. Unfortunately, the men were paid *before* the mistake was discovered.

PURDY: What did they do to you?

FISBY: For a while I was given a job licking envelopes.

PURDY: Then you asked for a transfer?

FISBY: No, sir, I developed an allergy to glue.

PURDY: How many outfits in this man's army have you been in, Captain?

FISBY: How many are there, sir?

PURDY: Never mind. I admit disappointment but not defeat. I'd thought you were given to me in recognition of my work here. Frankly, I expect to be made a general soon, and I want that star for my wife's crown. Naturally, that's very hush-hush.

FISBY: [*Nods*] Naturally. Maybe I just wasn't cut out to be a soldier.

PURDY: Captain, none of us was cut out to be a soldier. But we do the job. We adjust. We adapt. We roll with the punch and bring victory home in our teeth. Do you know what *I* was before the war?

FISBY: [*Hesitates unhappily*] A football coach?

PURDY: I was the Purdy Paper Box Company of Pottawattamie. What did I know about foreigners? But my job is to teach these natives the meaning of democracy, and they're going to learn democracy if I have to shoot every one of them.

FISBY: I'm sure your wife wouldn't want her star that way, sir.

PURDY: What did you do before the war?

FISBY: I was an associate professor at Muncie.

PURDY: What did you teach?

FISBY: The humanities.

PURDY: Captain, you are finally getting a job you're qualified by training to handle—teaching these natives how to act human.

FISBY: The humanities isn't quite that, sir.

PURDY: If you can teach one thing you can teach another. Your job at Tobiki will be to teach the natives democracy and make them self-supporting. Establish some sort of industry up there.

FISBY: Is there a general plan?

PURDY: There is a specific plan. [*He extends a document the size of a telephone book*] Washington has drawn up full instructions pertaining to the welfare and recovery of these native villages. *This* is Plan B. Consider it your *Bible*, Captain.

FISBY: I'll study it carefully, sir. There might be some questions I'd like to ask you.

PURDY: [*Points to Plan B*] Washington has anticipated all your questions.

FISBY: But I was thinking—

PURDY: You don't even have to think, Captain. This document relieves you of that responsibility.

FISBY: But in dealing with the natives, sir—

PURDY: [*Interrupts*] It's all covered in Section Four: "Orienting the Oriental." How is your Luchuan?

FISBY: I don't know, sir. What is it?

PURDY: It's the native dialect. Well, I can see you'll need an interpreter. [*His eyes light up and he slaps his desk*] I have just the man for you! [*He turns and calls out the door*] Sakini!

FISBY: I could study the dialect, sir.

PURDY: No need. We won the war. I'll give you my own interpreter.

FISBY: Oh, I wouldn't want to deprive you of—

PURDY: I insist.

[SAKINI *enters. He bows—and then remembers. He leans forward and politely knocks on the desk*]

SAKINI: Sakini present. Socks up. Not sleeping.

PURDY: Sakini, this is Captain Fisby.

FISBY: Hello, Sakini.

SAKINI: [*Bows, then turns to* PURDY] We meet already. [*He smiles in comradeship*] You forget, boss?

PURDY: [*Covers his face, counts to ten, then looks up*] I am assigning you to Captain Fisby. He's going to take charge of a village at the top of Okinawa—a village called Tobiki.

SAKINI: Oh! Tobiki very nice place, boss. But not at top of Okinawa. At bottom.

PURDY: Don't tell me where the villages under my command are located. I happen to have looked at the map.

SAKINI: So sorry, boss. But I happen to get born in Tobiki. Is at bottom.

PURDY: [*Whips a map out of his desk*] Then it's time you learned where you were born. I also happen to give a course in map reading.

SAKINI: [*Looks at map*] So sorry, boss. But map upside down.

FISBY: [*Looks at map*] He's right.

PURDY: [*Looks at map—turns it around*] Why in hell doesn't the Army learn how to draw a map properly! [*Turns to* SAKINI] That will be all, Sakini. Find Sergeant Gregovich and have him assign a jeep to Captain Fisby. Then load supplies and the captain's gear in the jeep. You will be leaving at once. I'll send rice rations later.

SAKINI: [*Takes the* COLONEL's *hand and pumps it*] Oh, thank you, boss. You very kind to send me home. I mention you in prayer to gods. [*He turns to* FISBY] I wait at jeep for you, Captain. [*He starts to run, then slows down quickly*] Very happy, sir. Socks up.

[*He goes out.* PURDY *turns wearily to* FISBY]

PURDY: I sometimes think we Occupation Teams have it tougher than combat troops. [*He quickly holds up a protesting hand*] Granted they have it rough for a while. But we have the killing daily grind, with no glory in it.

FISBY: Yes, sir, I know what you mean. Life itself is a battlefield with its own obscure heroes.

PURDY: [*Looks at* FISBY *with surprise*] I consider that poetry, Captain.

FISBY: I'm afraid it's just prose, sir. And it isn't mine, it's Victor Hugo's.

PURDY: [*Corrected*] Oh, yes. Victor Hugo! How I loved *Tale of Two Cities*.

FISBY: Isn't that Dickens, sir?

PURDY: I guess I was thinking of the movie. Well! To get back to Tobiki. Your first job when you get there will be to establish a municipal government and build a school.

FISBY: A school?

PURDY: It's all in Plan B. I'll see that cement and lumber are sent down to you. Plan B calls for the schoolhouse to be pentagon-shaped.

FISBY: If you say so, sir.

PURDY: When the school is built, you will organize a Ladies' League for Democratic Action. You will deliver a series of lectures on democracy as outlined in the outline. Captain, this is a chance for you to make a name for yourself.

FISBY: I will, sir. You see, I feel that I've personally delayed victory at least a year, and I have to vindicate myself.

PURDY: That's the kind of talk I like to hear from my officers. Well, I won't detain you then. [*He rises*] My only order to you is: Put that village on the map.

FISBY: Yes, sir.

PURDY: Send me a bimonthly Progress Report—in triplicate.

FISBY: Yes, sir.

PURDY: Don't duplicate your work.

FISBY: No, sir.

PURDY: Fire those natives with the Spirit of Occupation.

FISBY: Yes, sir.

PURDY: And remember—that the eyes of Washington are on our Occupation Teams. And the eyes of the world are on Washington.

FISBY: I'll keep the eyes in mind, sir.

PURDY: Good-bye, Captain. [FISBY *salutes smartly and goes out.* PURDY *stands for a moment, moved by the vastness of the canvas. Then he turns to his desk*] Where the hell is my *Adventure Magazine!*

THE SCENE BLACKS OUT QUICKLY

SCENE TWO

Outside CAPTAIN FISBY'S *quarters.*
A few minutes later.
CAPTAIN FISBY *and* SAKINI *enter from left and cross before the panels, all of which are now down.*

SAKINI: Everything all ready, boss. We go to Tobiki now?

FISBY: I guess so. Well, wish me luck, Sakini. I'm going out to spread the gospel of Plan B.

SAKINI: You already lucky, boss. You got me.

FISBY: [*Smiles*] Thanks . . . do you know the road?

SAKINI: No road, boss—just path for wagon cart and goat.

FISBY: Will a jeep make it?

SAKINI: We find out, boss.

FISBY: Naturally. How long will it take us?

SAKINI: Oh—not know until we arrive, boss.

FISBY: Naturally. Well, we might as well get started. I'll drive and you give directions.

SAKINI: Oh, very happy to go home.

FISBY: Where is the jeep?

SAKINI: Right here, boss.

[*He turns and claps his hands. The panels go up. The laundry line has been removed and the jeep pulled down center. The jeep is piled with* FISBY's *belongings. Perched high on the top of this pyramid sits a very old and very wrinkled* NATIVE WOMAN. SAKINI *pays no attention to her as he goes around the jeep test-kicking the tires. And the* OLD WOMAN *sits disinterested and aloof from what goes on below her*]

FISBY: Hey, wait a minute! What's she doing up there?

[*He points to her. The* OLD WOMAN *sits with hands folded serenely, looking straight ahead*]

SAKINI: She nice old lady hear we go to Tobiki village. She think she go along to visit grandson.

FISBY: Oh, she does. Well, you explain that I'm very sorry but she'll have to take a bus.

SAKINI: No buses to Tobiki. People very poor—can only travel on generosity.

FISBY: I'm sorry, but it's against regulations.

SAKINI: She not fall off, boss. She tied on.

FISBY: Well, untie her and get her down. She'll just have to find some other way to visit her grandson.

SAKINI: Her grandson mayor of Tobiki village. You make him lose face if you kick old grandmother off jeep.

FISBY: She's the mayor's grandmother?

SAKINI: Oh yes, boss.

FISBY: Well, since she's already tied on, I guess we can take her. [*He looks at the bundles*] Are all those *mine*?

SAKINI: Oh, no. Most of bundles belong to old lady. She think she visit three or four months so she bring own bed and cooking pots.

FISBY: Well, tell her to yell out if she sees any low branches coming. [*He starts to get in*] Let's get started.

SAKINI: Oh, can't go yet, boss.

FISBY: Why not?

SAKINI: Old lady's daughter not here.

FISBY: [*Glances at watch*] We can't wait for a lot of good-byes, Sakini!

SAKINI: [*Looking behind* FISBY] Oh, she come now—right on dot you bet.

[CAPTAIN FISBY *turns to witness a squat young* NATIVE WOMAN *come on pushing a wheelbarrow loaded with bundles. She stops long enough to bow low to* FISBY—*then begins to tie bundles onto the jeep*]

FISBY: Sakini, can't the old lady leave some of that stuff behind?

SAKINI: Not her things, boss. Belong to daughter.

FISBY: Wait a minute. Is the daughter planning on going with us, too?

SAKINI: Old lady very old. Who take care of her on trip?

FISBY: Well, I—[*The* DAUGHTER *takes the wheelbarrow and hurries off*] Hey—you come back! Sakini—tell her to come back. We can't carry any more bundles.

SAKINI: [*Calmly*] Oh, she not go to get bundles, boss. She go to get children.

FISBY: Come here, Sakini. Now look—this sort of thing is always happening to me and I have to put a stop to it some place. This time I'm determined to succeed. It's not that I don't *want* to take them. But you can see for yourself, *there's no room left for kids!*

SAKINI: But daughter not go without children and old lady not go without daughter. And if old lady not go, mayor of Tobiki be mad at you.

[*Turns to see the* DAUGHTER *hurry back with three* CHILDREN *in tow. They all bow politely to* FISBY. *Their mother then piles them on the hood of the jeep*]

FISBY: For Pete's sake, Sakini, how does she expect me to see how to drive!

SAKINI: Old lady got very good eyesight. She sit on top and tell us when to turn.

[*At this point one of the* CHILDREN *climbs off the hood and points offstage*]

CHILD: A! Wasureta!

DAUGHTER: Wasureta? Nanisa?

CHILD: Fija dayo.

[*The* CHILD *dashes offstage*]

FISBY: Now, where's he going?

SAKINI: [*To* DAUGHTER] Doshtano?

DAUGHTER: Fija turete kurendes!

SAKINI: [*To* FISBY] He go to get goat.

FISBY: A goat!

SAKINI: Can't go and leave poor goat behind.

DAUGHTER: [*Waves gaily to the* OLD WOMAN *on top of the jeep*] Okasan daijobu!

[*She climbs the pyramid of bundles to settle beside her*]

FISBY: Well, right here is where we start seeing who's going to lose face. No goat is going to travel on this jeep.

SAKINI: You not like goats, boss?

FISBY: It has nothing to do with whether I like goats or not. I'm positive the colonel wouldn't like it.

SAKINI: But children not go without goat, mother not go without children, old lady not go without daughter—

FISBY: [*Repeats with* SAKINI]—and if old lady not go, the mayor of

NOTE: The Luchuan dialect used throughout the play is merely a phonetic approximation.

Tobiki be mad at you! [FISBY *sees the goat being led on by the* SMALL BOY] Oh, no!

SAKINI: Everybody here, boss. Goat not got children. Goat unmarried lady goat.

FISBY: All right, all right. Put it on the hood with the kids. [*The goat is placed on the hood and held by the* CHILDREN] We've got to get started or we'll never get off the ground.

SAKINI: All ready to go, boss. You get in now. Nobody else going.

[*But before* FISBY *can climb in an* OLD MAN *comes hurrying in and, without looking to the right or left, climbs on the back of the jeep and settles down*]

FISBY: Now who the hell is he?

SAKINI: [*Looks at* OLD MAN] Now who the hell is he? [*Back to* FISBY] Not know, boss, never see before.

FISBY: Is he a relation of theirs?

SAKINI: [*To the woman on top of the jeep*] Kore dare?

MOTHER: Mitakoto nai hito desu.

SAKINI: She say she never see him before, boss.

FISBY: Well, ask him what he's doing here!

SAKINI: [*Goes to the* OLD MAN] Ojisan, doshtano?

OLD MAN: Washimo notte ikuyo.

SAKINI: He say he see people going somewhere on trip and he think maybe he like to go somewhere, too.

FISBY: Tell him to get off and get off quick!

SAKINI: Dame dayo, ojisan, orina, orina!

OLD MAN: [*Angrily*] Fija noserunnera washimo noruyo!

SAKINI: He say why not take him? You take goat. He say maybe you think he not as good as goat?

FISBY: Look, Sakini, explain to him that the eyes of the world are on Washington and the eyes of Washington are on me. I can't be responsible for—

[*But before this can be translated,* COLONEL PURDY *stalks on and comes to an abrupt halt*]

PURDY: Captain Fisby!

FISBY: Yes, sir.

PURDY: What in the name of Occupation do you think you're doing!

FISBY: It's hard to explain, sir. . . . I, ah . . . ah . . .

[*As he flounders, the* OLD LADY *on top of the bundles comes to life. She looks down and screams shrilly*]

OLD LADY: Yakamashii oyajijana, hayo *iko, iko!*

PURDY: What is *she* saying?

SAKINI: She say . . . tell fat old man to shut up so we can get started!

[*As* COLONEL PURDY's *jaw drops, the panels drop also*]

BLACKOUT

SCENE THREE

Tobiki village.
Ten days later.
All the bamboo panels are down. SAKINI *walks in front of them to the center of the stage from the wings.*

SAKINI: [*Bows*]
Distance from Headquarters to Tobiki village by map . . . two inches.
By horse . . . three days.
By foot . . . four days.

By jeep . . . ten days.
Explanation:
Captain want to go to Tobiki
Children want to go ocean. Never see ocean.
We see ocean.
Captain want to go to Tobiki.
Old lady's daughter want to visit Awasi.
We go Awasi.
Old lady make second mistake.
Captain demand we go Tobiki.
Ancient man have cousin in Yatoda.
We go Yatoda.
Damn fool old lady not know one road from another.
Now we arrive Tobiki.
Tobiki welcome rice and democracy.

> [*He claps his hands for the panels to be raised, then walks into the scene. The destitute village of Tobiki is revealed with its sagging huts and its ragged villagers grouped in the square just outside of* CAPTAIN FISBY'S *office. This is a small bamboo structure with a thatched roof. It has a makeshift desk and field telephone. There is a cot crowded against the upper wall.* FISBY, *his glasses on, sits studying Plan B. He puts the document down, and, taking off his glasses, calls to* SAKINI]

FISBY: Sakini!

SAKINI: Right here, boss. Not asleep, boss.

FISBY: Good. According to Plan B, my first job here is to hold a public meeting.

SAKINI: Public waiting in public square . . . eager to meet new boss, boss.

FISBY: Good. Now, Plan B calls for a lecture on the ABC's of democracy. [*He turns to* SAKINI] Make sure they understand that I come as friend of the people. That we intend to lift the yoke of oppression from their shoulders.

SAKINI: Oh, they like that, boss. This their favorite speech.

FISBY: What do you mean, their favorite speech?

SAKINI: Oh, Japanese say same things when they come, boss. Then take everything.

FISBY: Well, we're not here to *take* anything.

SAKINI: They got nothing left to take away, boss.

FISBY: [*Annoyed*] Well, if they *did* have, we wouldn't take it. We're here to *give* them something.

SAKINI: Oh, not get angry, boss. We not mind. After eight centuries we get used to it. When friends come now, we hide things quick as the dickens.

FISBY: [*Rises, a little upset*] Well, I guess it's up to me to convince them we really are friends. Let's meet the villagers. [*He picks up his papers*] And let them meet Plan B.

[*As they step out the door to the office, the* VILLAGERS *rise and bow respectfully in unison.* FISBY *surveys them*]

SAKINI: [*Introducing* FISBY] Amerikano Taisho-san, Captain Fisby.

FISBY: [*Bows in return*] Well, we might as well get started, Sakini. [*He finds a box and stands on it. He glances into Plan B and clears his throat*] Citizens of Tobiki village. I—

SAKINI: [*Interrupts him*] Sorry, boss. Can't begin lecture yet.

FISBY: Why not?

SAKINI: Not good manners. People bring you gifts. You must accept gifts first.

FISBY: But I'm here to bring gifts from my government to them.

SAKINI: Very rude to make people feel poor, boss.

FISBY: I don't want to make anyone feel poor, but—

SAKINI: You make them lose face if you refuse, boss. They not accept democracy from you.

FISBY: All right. All right, then. Say to them that I'll accept their gifts in the name of the United States Occupation Forces.

SAKINI: [*Turns to the* VILLAGERS] Soreja moratte okuyo!

[MR. HOKAIDA, *an enormous villager in tattered peasant clothes, steps forward*]

MR. HOKAIDA: [*Bows diffidently and offers his present to* FISBY] Amerika-san, korewo dozo.

SAKINI: This Mr. Hokaida, boss. He give you fine present.

FISBY: Thank you. Thank you very much. [*He takes it and turns to* SAKINI *puzzled*] What is it?

SAKINI: You not know?

FISBY: No.

SAKINI: Oh, where you been all your life, boss?

FISBY: Living without one of these, I guess.

SAKINI: Is very splendid cricket cage, boss.

FISBY: What's it used for?

SAKINI: Keep cricket in.

FISBY: Why?

SAKINI: So Fortune smile on you. Cricket very good luck.

FISBY: But there's no cricket in it.

SAKINI: Bad luck to give cricket. You must catch your own fortune. No one can get it for you.

FISBY: [*Considers this*] Thank him and tell him I'll keep my eye out for a cricket.

SAKINI: Ya, arigato. [MR. HOKAIDA *bows away as an* ANCIENT NATIVE *steps forward and bows*] This Mr. Omura. He bring you gift of chopsticks.

MR. OMURA: Korede mainichi gochiso wo, dozo.

SAKINI: He say: May only food of gods touch your lips.

[*As* FISBY *bows*, MR. SUMATA, *a nervous citizen in a torn straw hat, pushes his way toward* SAKINI]

MR. SUMATA: Sugu modotte kuruyo!

SAKINI: Doshtandes?

MR. SUMATA: Ima sugu presento motte kuruyo.

[*He turns and runs hurriedly off stage right*]

FISBY: What was that?

SAKINI: That Mr. Sumata. He have present at home for you. He say not go away until he get.

[*A rather handsome young Tobikian,* MR. SEIKO, *now steps forward and extends a pair of wooden sandals*]

MR. SEIKO: Dozo korewo chakini.

SAKINI: This Mr. Seiko. He brings you geta.

FISBY: Geta?

SAKINI: Wooden sandals. Very comfortable for tired feet. He say: May you walk in prosperity.

FISBY: Tell him I shall walk in the—the cool—meadow—of—of pleasant memories. Is that all right?

SAKINI: Oh, that's very pretty, boss. [*He turns to* MR. SEIKO] Ya, arigato, Seiko-san.

MR. SEIKO: [*Beams, bows, and backs away*] Iya, kosi no itari desu.

SAKINI: He say you do him honor. [*Here a chunky, flat-faced, aggressive* YOUNG WOMAN *with heavy glasses pushes forward with her present*] Oh, this Miss Higa Jiga—unmarried lady. She bring you three eggs.

FISBY: Tell her I shall eat them for breakfast.

[*He bows to her*]

SAKINI: Captain-san, daisuki desu.

MISS HIGA JIGA: Kame no tamago desu.

[*She bows away*]

SAKINI: She say she hope you enjoy turtle eggs.

FISBY: [*Grins and bows to her*] She'll never know.

SAKINI: You very big success. They sure like you already. [*Another*

VILLAGER *steps forward and offers a gift*] This Mr. Keora. He bring you another cricket cage. Minus cricket.

FISBY: Say to him—that my prospects of good fortune are doubled.

[*He looks rather pleased with himself*]

SAKINI: Kagowa futatsu de, un wa bai!

MR. KEORA: Hoho! Naka naka shiteki desna!

[*He bows away*]

SAKINI: He say you are inspired poet.

FISBY: [*Modestly*] It's all in getting the hang of it.

SAKINI: [*Introducing the next citizen, a very* OLD MAN *leaning on a stick*] This old man Mr. Oshira. He bring you fine lacquered cup he make himself.

FISBY: Tell him I'm forever in his debt for such a beautiful gift.

OSHIRA: You are most welcome, Captain.

FISBY: [*Turns to him in surprise*] You speak English!

SAKINI: Mr. Oshira teach me English when I am little boy in Tobiki.

OSHIRA: In my youth I work in Manila. How is Mr. McKinley?

FISBY: [*Puzzled for a moment*] Who? Oh—President McKinley. I'm afraid someone shot him.

OSHIRA: I am sad.

FISBY: It was a long time ago.

OSHIRA: Yes, a long time. [*He indicates the cup*] May August moon fill your cup.

FISBY: May I ask, why an August moon?

OSHIRA: All moons good, but August moon little older, little wiser.

FISBY: Did Sakini say you made this cup yourself?

OSHIRA: Oh, yes. I learned from my father before me who learned from his father before him. Is our heritage.

SAKINI: Look, boss, this cup thin as paper, carved from one block of wood. Then painted many times with red lacquer.

FISBY: And did you paint the gold fish inside?

OSHIRA: [Nods] It is imperfect.

SAKINI: When Mr. Oshira little boy, he work ten years to learn how to paint gold fish exactly like his papa paint.

FISBY: It's just beautiful! Can you still make things like this?

OSHIRA: One does not forget.

FISBY: Sakini, here's an industry we can start right away. This is a lost art. [Turns to OSHIRA] Is there any way we could mass-produce these?

OSHIRA: Mass-produce?

FISBY: You know—set up machines and turn them out by the gross.

OSHIRA: [Shakes his head] I take pride in making one cup at time, Captain. How can I take pride in work of machine?

FISBY: How many of these could you turn out in a day?

OSHIRA: If I work hard, maybe one or two a week.

FISBY: [Disappointed] Well, it's a start. Make as many as you can. We'll send them up to the American Post Exchange and sell them as fast as you can turn them out.

OSHIRA: I shall do my best. The swiftness of my youth has deserted me, sir. [He bows and moves back] But I shall make fewer mistakes.

FISBY: [Excitedly] Sakini, tell Mr. Omura to make up a batch of chopsticks. Have everybody get to work making cricket cages, wooden sandals and—[Pointing]—these straw hats. We'll put this village in the souvenir business.

SAKINI: We all make money, boss?

FISBY: If they can turn out enough of these things, I guarantee the recovery of Tobiki village. Tell them.

SAKINI: Kore dondon tsukuru yoni . . . [There is a general ex-

change of chatter and approval] They say they make everything, fast as the dickens, boss.

FISBY: Good. We're in business. Now ask them if they'd mind postponing the rest of the gifts until later. I'd like to tell them what *we're* planning for *them*.

SAKINI: Sa, sono hanashi shiyo.

CITIZENS: No agerumono naiyo! Hanashi wo kiko.

SAKINI: They say sure. They got no more presents anyhow.

FISBY: Good. First I want to tell them about the school we're going to build for their children. All set to translate?

SAKINI: All set.

FISBY: All right. [*He consults Plan B*] Plan B says the direct approach is most effective. This is it. [*He steps back up on a box and looks forcefully at his listeners. Then he points a dramatic finger at them*] Do you want to be ignorant?

SAKINI: [*Also points a finger*] Issho bakaja dame daro?

[*The* CITIZENS *make a noise that sounds like "Hai"*]

FISBY: What did they say?

SAKINI: They say "Yes."

FISBY: What do you mean, "yes"? They *want* to be ignorant?

SAKINI: No, boss. But in Luchuan "yes" means "no." They say "yes," they *not* want to be ignorant.

FISBY: Oh. [*He turns back to his rapt audience and assumes his forensic posture*] Do you want your *children* to be ignorant?

SAKINI: Issho kodomotachi mo bakaja dame daro?

[*The* VILLAGERS *respond with a noise that sounds like "Iie"*]

FISBY: What did they say then?

SAKINI: They say "No."

FISBY: "No" they do, or "No" they don't?

SAKINI: Yes, they not want no ignorant children.

FISBY: Good. [*He turns back to the* VILLAGERS] Then this is what my government is planning to do for you. First there will be daily issues of rice for everyone.

SAKINI: Mazu kome no hykyu!

[*The* VILLAGERS *cheer*]

FISBY: We will build a fine new school here for your children. [*Then recalling* COLONEL PURDY's *dictum*] Pentagon-shaped.

SAKINI: Gakko taterundayo katachi wa—[*He flounders*] Ah—Pentagon.

[*The* CITIZENS *look at each other, puzzled*]

MISS HIGA JIGA: Nandesutte?

SAKINI: Pentagon.

MISS HIGA JIGA: Sore wa nandesuka?

SAKINI: They say what is Pentagon? Never hear before.

FISBY: Never heard of the *Pentagon!*

SAKINI: No, boss.

FISBY: Well, they certainly do need a school here. The Pentagon is —is—[*He looks down at their eager faces*] Well, it really means five-sided.

SAKINI: Kabega itsutsusa, ii, ni, san, yon, go.

[*Holds up five fingers. There is a burst of laughter from the* CITIZENS]

MISS HIGA JIGA: [*Giggling*] Ara, gokakuno kodomo nante arimasenyo.

SAKINI: They say no children in Tobiki got five sides.

FISBY: The *school* will be five-sided—like a building in Washington.

SAKINI: [*Explains*] Chigauyo, chigauyo, onaji mono arundes yo, Washington ni. [*There is a decided reaction of approval.* SAKINI *turns back to* FISBY] They very impressed.

FISBY: [*Continuing*] Everyone will learn about democracy.

SAKINI: Mazu minshu shugi bera-bera bera-bera.

MISS HIGA JIGA: Minshu shugi bera-bera bera-bera?

SAKINI: They say: Explain what is democracy. They know what rice is.

FISBY: Oh. [*He scratches his head*] Well, it's a system of self-determination. It's—it's the right to make the wrong choice.

SAKINI: Machigattemo iindayo.

[*They look up blankly, silently*]

FISBY: I don't think we're getting the point over. Explain that if I don't like the way Uncle Sam treats me, I can write the President himself and tell him so.

SAKINI: Daitoryo ni tegami kaitemo iinosa.

[*The* VILLAGERS *all laugh heartily*]

MISS HIGA JIGA: Masaka soonakoto!

SAKINI: [*Triumphantly*] They say: But do you *send* the letters?

FISBY: Let's get on with the lecture. [*He turns back to the* CITIZENS *and reads from Plan B*] Tell them hereafter all men will be free and equal. . . .

SAKINI: Subete, jiyuu, to byodo, de ar, de ar.

FISBY: [*Increases his tempo and volume*] Without discrimination . . .

SAKINI: [*Taking* FISBY's *tone*] Sabetsu taigoo haishi de ar.

FISBY: The will of the majority will rule!

SAKINI: Subete minna de kime, de ar!

FISBY: [*Finishing with a flourish*] And Tobiki village will take its place in the brotherhood of democratic peoples the world over!

SAKINI: [*Rising to new demagogic heights*] Koshite, Tobiki, jiyuu, Okinawa, byodo sabetsu, taigu—haishi, jiyuu, byodo de ar, de ar. [*A great burst of applause greets* SAKINI's *performance. He turns to* FISBY] We going over big, boss.

FISBY: [*Agrees with a nod*] Now to get this village organized. Is the mayor here?

SAKINI: [*Points*] Mr. Omura is mayor, boss. [MR. OMURA *steps forward*] He only one in Tobiki with white coat.

FISBY: [*Glances at the worn, ragged coat*] It looks to me as if you'll have to get a new coat or a new mayor soon.

SAKINI: Better keep mayor, boss. Impossible to get white coat.

FISBY: Well, since we've got a mayor, we only have to find a Chief of Agriculture and a Chief of Police. That's going to present a problem.

SAKINI: No problem, boss. You just look over gifts and see who give you best gift. Then you give him best job.

FISBY: Sakini, that is *not* the democratic way. The people themselves must choose the man best qualified. Tell them they are to elect their own Chief of Agriculture.

SAKINI: Sah! Senkyo desu. Mazu Chief of Agriculture.

WOMEN VILLAGERS: [*Push* MR. SIEKO *forward shouting*] Seiko-san, Seiko-san ga ii, Seiko-san!

SAKINI: They say they elect Mr. Seiko. He best qualified for agriculture.

FISBY: He's an experienced farmer?

SAKINI: No, boss. He's artist. He draw lovely picture of golden wheat stalk with pretty green butterfly.

FISBY: Drawing pictures of wheat doesn't make him a wheat expert.

SAKINI: Wheat not grow here anyhow, boss. Only sweet potatoes.

FISBY: All right, all right! If he's their choice.

SEIKO: Ano! Watashimo shiroi koto wo.

SAKINI: He say do he get white coat like the mayor?

FISBY: Tell him I'll get him a helmet that says "Chief of Agriculture" on it.

SAKINI: Yoshi, yoshi, kammuri ageruyo.

[SEIKO *bows and backs away*]

FISBY: Next we want to elect a Chief of Police.

SAKINI: Kondowa Chief of Police!

VILLAGERS: [*Clamor and push the fat* MR. HOKAIDA *forward*]
Hokaida-san. Soda, soda. Hokaida-san.

FISBY: What are *his* qualifications for office?

SAKINI: People afraid of him. He champion wrestler.

[MR. HOKAIDA *flexes his muscles*]

FISBY: Well, no one can say this isn't self-determination.

MR. HOKAIDA: Washime ano kammuri wo.

SAKINI: He say do he get helmet, too?

FISBY: [*Nods*] I'll requisition another helmet.

SAKINI: Agemasuyo.

MR. HOKAIDA: [*Bows smiling*] Ya, doomo.

FISBY: Now for the ladies. We intend to organize a Ladies' League
for Democratic Action. We'll want to elect a League President.

SAKINI: Oh, ladies never vote before—they like that. [*He turns to
the* LADIES] Kondowa Ladies' League for Democratic Action!

[*This announcement is greeted by excited chatter. The* LADIES
push MISS HIGA JIGA *forward*]

LADIES: Higa-Jiga-san—Higa-Jiga-san!

SAKINI: They say they elect Miss Higa Jiga. They think she make
classy president.

MISS HIGA JIGA: [*Points to her head*] Ano, watashi nimo ano
booshio . . .

FISBY: [*Laughs*] All right, I'll see that she gets a helmet, too.
Now ask them if they have any question they'd like to ask *me*.

SAKINI: Sa, nanka kikitai koto ga attara.

OLD WOMAN: Sakini-san, ima nanji kaina?

SAKINI: They say they like to know what time is it?

SAKINI: [*Puzzled*] Time? [*Glances at his watch*] Quarter of five, why?

SAKINI: They say they got to hurry then. They not like to miss sunset. This is time of day they sit in pine grove, sip tea and watch sun go down.

FISBY: All right, thank them and tell them they can go have tea in the pine grove.

SAKINI: Ya, minna kaette mo iiyo.

[*They bow and, chattering happily among themselves, go off right.* FISBY *gathers up his gifts*]

FISBY: How do you think we did, Sakini?

SAKINI: They cooperate, boss. Future look very rosy.

FISBY: Where do you think I can find a cricket?

SAKINI: One come along. May have one in house now and not know it.

FISBY: Well, I'll take these things in and get started on my Progress Report.

[*He goes to the office hut*]

SAKINI: I take a little snooze then. Public speaking very exhausting.

FISBY: [*As he goes inside*] I think I handled it pretty well.

[*He sits down at his desk. He examines his gifts and then, putting on his glasses, begins to study Plan B again. After a moment,* MR. SUMATA *enters from the right. He carries a couple of battered suitcases. He is followed by* LOTUS BLOSSOM, *a petite and lovely geisha girl in traditional costume. When they are about center stage, young* MR. SEIKO *runs up after the geihsa girl. She turns to him*]

SEIKO: Ano, chotto . . .

LOTUS BLOSSOM: Ara! Nani?

SUMATA: [*Steps in front of* SEIKO *and points an angry finger under his nose*] Dame, dame, atchi ike. [SEIKO *bows head and retreats.* MR. SUMATA *then turns to* SAKINI] Amerika-san doko?

SAKINI: [*Indicates the office*] Asco.

SUMATA: [*Indicates geisha girl*] Kore tsurete kitandayo.

SAKINI: Oh? Do-sunno?

SUMATA: Kore Taisho-san ni agetainja.

[*He bows and goes off quickly, almost running. The* GEISHA *remains with* SAKINI. SAKINI *smiles and steps inside the office. He stands behind* FISBY]

SAKINI: You busy, boss?

FISBY: [*Without turning around to him*] Yes, but what is it?

SAKINI: Mr. Sumata leave present for you, boss.

FISBY: Put it on the shelf where it'll be out of the way.

SAKINI: [*Glances back outside*] Not able to do, boss. Present get mad.

FISBY: [*Turns around*] What's this about, Sakini?

SAKINI: [*Motions to the* GEISHA, *who steps inside smiling. She bows*] Here you are, boss.

FISBY: [*Rising*] Who is *she*?

SAKINI: Souvenir.

FISBY: What are you talking about?

SAKINI: Present from Mr. Sumata.

FISBY: Wait a minute. Is he kidding? I can't accept a human present.

SAKINI: Oh, human present very lovely. Introducing Lotus Blossom, geisha girl first class. [*He turns to* LOTUS BLOSSOM] Amerika-san no Captain Fisby.

LOTUS BLOSSOM: [*Smiling happily*] Ara, ii otokomaene! Watashi sukidawa.

SAKINI: She say she very happy to belong to handsome captain. She say she serve you well.

FISBY: She's not going to serve me at all. You get that Mr. Sumata and tell him I'm returning his present.

SAKINI: Impossible to do, boss. Mr. Sumata leave present and go up mountains to visit cousin. He say good-bye and wish you much success in Tobiki.

LOTUS BLOSSOM: [*Sweetly*] Watashi kokoni sumun desho?

SAKINI: She say, where do you want her to stay, boss?

FISBY: You tell her I don't care where she stays. She can't stay here.

SAKINI: [*Shocked*] Where she go then? She got no home. Mr. Sumata already gone away.

FISBY: Well, find her a place for the time being.

SAKINI: [*Grins*] Plenty of room in my house, boss. Just me and my grandpapa.

FISBY: No, I can't do that. Sit her over on that box until I can think where to put her.

SAKINI: You can put her in business, boss.

FISBY: You keep a civil tongue in your head, Sakini.

LOTUS BLOSSOM: [*Comes over to* FISBY, *whom she has been watching with great interest*] Okimono to ozohri motte kimasune.

SAKINI: She like to put on your sandals and kimono for you. She trained to please you, boss.

FISBY: I know what she's trained to do. And I don't need any translation. [*He sits down at his desk again*] Sakini . . . take my supplies out of the shack and bring them over here. We'll set her up there where I can keep an eye on her.

SAKINI: Not very democratic, boss. You make her lose face if she not make you comfortable, boss. She think she bad geisha girl.

FISBY: You tell her . . . I've got some face to save, too . . . so she can just forget this Oriental hanky-panky.

SAKINI: Anta irantesa!

LOTUS BLOSSOM: [*Waves him away*] Ara, nani ittennoyo. Imasara ikettatte ikarenai desho.

FISBY: Well, what did she say?

SAKINI: She say for me to go on home to grandpapa . . . she first-class geisha girl . . . she know her business. Good night, boss.

[FISBY *stands eyeing* LOTUS BLOSSOM *as* SAKINI *goes out. The lights go down quickly. During the brief blackout, the two center panels are lowered, shutting out the village street. The office of* COLONEL PURDY *is swung into place in the last panel right. The lights come up on* PURDY *twisting the bell on his field telephone*]

PURDY: What do you mean . . . there's no answer? Well, keep trying. I'm not the kind of a man to take "no answer" for an answer.

[*The lights come up on the opposite side of the stage in* FISBY's *office.* FISBY *is holding onto his jacket buttons.* LOTUS BLOSSOM *stands in front of him holding out his robe. She is gently persistent and puzzled at his reticence*]

FISBY: It's *not* a kimono . . . it's a bathrobe. And I don't *want* to put it on.

LOTUS BLOSSOM: [*Reaches to unbutton his jacket*] Sa! Shizukani shimasho ne.

FISBY: No, it's against regulations. [*Phone rings. He takes the robe away from* LOTUS BLOSSOM *and sits on it. Then he picks up the phone*] Hello!

PURDY: [*Jumps*] You don't have to shout. I can hear you. This is Colonel Purdy.

FISBY: [*Leaps to his feet and pushes* LOTUS BLOSSOM *behind him as if to hide her*] Yes, sir.

PURDY: Just thought I'd check up on you. How are things going?

[LOTUS BLOSSOM *begins to fan her master*]

FISBY: Well, everything seems to be under control at the moment.

[*He sits down and takes out a cigarette.* LOTUS BLOSSOM *promptly lights it for him*]

PURDY: Anything *I* can do for you?

FISBY: [*Pauses*] I can't think of anything, sir.

PURDY: I realize it's bound to get lonely for you down there . . . so you know what I'm going to do, my boy?

FISBY: [LOTUS BLOSSOM *gets the geta and kneels before him.* FISBY *watches her apprehensively and asks . . .*] What are you going to do?

PURDY: I'll tell you. I'm going to send you some of my old *Adventure Magazines.*

FISBY: [*As* LOTUS BLOSSOM *starts to take off his shoes*] No, *no.* I don't want them. [*Into the phone*] I mean . . . yes . . . thank you. [*He rises and twists about trying to pull his foot away from* LOTUS BLOSSOM] I'd like something to read.

PURDY: How are you getting along with the natives?

FISBY: [*His leg over the chair*] The problem here, sir, is a very old one. It seems to be a question of who's going to lose face.

PURDY: I understand. As Mrs. Purdy says, "East is East and West is West, and there can be no Twain." But you're making progress?

FISBY: Nothing I'd like to put on paper, sir.

[LOTUS BLOSSOM *gets his shoes off and slips the sandals on*]

PURDY: Well, when things get moving down there, send in a detailed Progress Report.

FISBY: If that's what you want, sir.

[LOTUS BLOSSOM *recovers the robe. She reaches out to unbutton his jacket*]

PURDY: You'll find these people lack the capacity for sustained endeavor. Don't hesitate to build a fire under them.

FISBY: [*Struggling to keep his jacket on*] That won't be necessary, sir.

PURDY: Don't forget . . . the eyes of Washington are on you, Fisby.

FISBY: [*As* LOTUS BLOSSOM *tries to pull his jacket over his head*] I hope not, sir.

PURDY: [*Ponders*] Fisby, it just occurred to me. Have you given any thought to physical education?

FISBY: If I may say so, sir [LOTUS BLOSSOM *gets one arm out*] I consider the suggestion . . . [*He hugs the other sleeve*] a masterpiece of timeliness.

[*He gets down on one knee*]

PURDY: Thank you, my boy. [*Pauses*] Could you use a deck of cards? Hello? Hello, Fisby . . . you're getting weak.

[*As* FISBY *looks back at the telephone and nods in complete agreement, the two scenes black out simultaneously. The panels fall. A spot picks up* SAKINI *as he steps from the wings*]

SAKINI:
Discreet place to stop now and sip soothing cup of jasmine tea.
Conclusion?
Not yet.
Continuation shortly.
Lotus Blossom not lose face!

[*He bows*]

THE CURTAIN FALLS

ACT TWO

Tobiki village.
A few days later.
All the panels are down. SAKINI *enters from the wings and crosses down to the footlights center. He bows to the audience.*

SAKINI:

Lovely ladies, kind gentlemen:

Most traveled person in history of world is summer sun.

Each day must visit each man no matter where he live on globe.

Always welcome visitor.

Not bring gossip.

Not stay too long.

Not depart leaving bad taste of rude comment.

But summer sun never tell topside of world what bottomside like.

So bottomside must speak for itself.

We continue with little story of Tobiki.

Center of industry.

Seat of democracy.

[*He beams*]

Home of geisha girl.

[*He goes to the right proscenium arch as all the panels are raised, revealing the empty street outside of* FISBY's *office.* FISBY *enters, starts across stage,* SAKINI *falling in step behind him*]

Was wondering what happened to you, boss?

FISBY: [*Stops*] I went down to inspect the sweet-potato fields. Sakini, no one was there. The potatoes were piled up, but no one was working.

SAKINI: Very hot day, boss.

FISBY: But I can't find my Chief of Agriculture. Or the Mayor, or the Chief of Police. Where is everybody?

SAKINI: Lotus Blossom leave belongings over at Awasi—got no way to bring things here. So—everybody take wheelbarrow to help move Lotus Blossom to Tobiki.

FISBY: And has she got so many things that it takes my entire staff to move her to this village?

SAKINI: No, boss, but Chief of Police not trust Chief of Agriculture, and Mayor not trust Mr. Oshira, so all go.

FISBY: Mr. Oshira? That old man!

SAKINI: He's old, boss, but not dead.

FISBY: A fine way for officials to behave! You tell them I want to see them the moment they come back. [*He starts for his office*] A fine thing!

SAKINI: Nothing to worry about, boss. They not beat your time. You own Lotus Blossom.

FISBY: I do *not* own her. It's not a question of—of—[*He sits down at his desk*] Well, this sort of nonsense isn't going to stop my work. [*He shifts the papers on his desk*] I intend to get started on that schoolhouse today. We've got the materials, so all we need now is some good carpenters. [*He turns to* SAKINI, *who has followed him inside*] Who is the best carpenter in the village?

SAKINI: Mr. Sumata.

FISBY: Fine. Get hold of him. Wait a minute! Isn't he the joker who gave me Lotus Blossom?

SAKINI: Mr. Sumata has finger in lots of pies, boss.

FISBY: Well, since he's vanished, who is the next best carpenter?

SAKINI: Father of Mr. Sumata.

FISBY: Where is he?

SAKINI: Go on vacation with Mr. Sumata.

FISBY: [*Beginning to get annoyed*] Well, who is the *third* best carpenter then?

SAKINI: No more, boss. Only Sumata and son. They have what you call monopoly.

FISBY: There's something fishy about their disappearing.

[MISS HIGA JIGA, *wearing a red helmet with flowers, followed by several other* LADIES, *comes storming across the stage to the office door.* SAKINI *hears them and goes to the door*]

MISS HIGA JIGA: [*Angrily*] Watashitachi sabetsu taigu desyo!

FISBY: [*Goes to the door also*] What's the matter with her?

SAKINI: Miss Higa Jiga say do you know what we got in this village, boss? Discrimination.

FISBY: [*Wearily*] Where?

[SAKINI *turns to* MISS HIGA JIGA]

MISS HIGA JIGA: [*Indignantly*] Watashitachi hykyu matte itara Lotus Blossom ga kite clarku ga anata desuka ma dozo kochirae watashitachi nijikan mo machi mashita yo.

SAKINI: She say that Ladies' League for Democratic Action wait in line for rice rations. Along come Lotus Blossom and ration clerks say, "Oh, how do you do? Oh, please don't stand in line. You come inside and have cup of tea." Then clerks shut up warehouse and leave Ladies' League waiting in sun two hours.

FISBY: It's things like this that undermine the democratic ideal. You tell Miss Higa Jiga I intend to do something about it.

[*He storms into his office*]

SAKINI: [*Turns to* MISS HIGA JIGA] Nantoka shimasuyo.

FISBY: I can see right now we're going to have to get rid of the disrupting factor in our recovery. [*He picks up the field telephone and twists the handle*] Get me Major McEvoy at Awasi.

SAKINI: [*Follows* FISBY *inside*] What are you going to do, boss?

FISBY: This village isn't big enough for Plan B and a geisha girl.

SAKINI: Oh, boss, Tobiki never have geisha girl before. We like very much.

FISBY: She has to go. [*Then into the telephone*] Major McEvoy? Captain Fisby at Tobiki. I have a request from one of my people to transfer to your village. Yes, it's a female citizen. Profession? Well . . .

[*He looks at* SAKINI]

SAKINI: Oh, please not send her away, boss. Not democratic.

FISBY: As a matter of fact her name *is* Lotus Blossom. *How* did *you* know? What do you mean, what am I trying to put over on you? Oh, you did?

[*He hangs up. Then he glares at* SAKINI]

SAKINI: [*With great innocence*] He knows Lotus Blossom, boss?

FISBY: Very well. She was at Awasi and damn near wrecked his whole plan for recovery. She's been booted out of every village by every commander on the island.

SAKINI: Oh, poor little Lotus Blossom.

FISBY: Poor little Lotus Blossom my eye. She upsets every village she's in.

SAKINI: Not her fault she beautiful, boss.

FISBY: No wonder that Mr. Sumata disappeared. The major paid him a hundred yen to get her out of his village.

SAKINI: [*Eagerly*] You keep her now, boss?

FISBY: I have to. [*He points a finger at* SAKINI] Well, she's not going to get away with causing dissension in *my* village!

[MISS HIGA JIGA, *weary of waiting outside, storms in*]

MISS HIGA JIGA: Doshte itadakemasno Daitoryo ni tegami wo kakimasawayo.

FISBY: [*Pleads*] Tell her to go away.

SAKINI: She say she waiting for some democratic action. She say if she don't get it, she thinks she write this Uncle Sam you talk about.

FISBY: Now, look. I don't want complaints going into Headquarters. Tell her discrimination is being eliminated.

SAKINI: Sabetsu yamemasyo.

MISS HIGA JIGA: Yamenakutemo iinoyo, watashitachi nimo wakete itadakeba.

SAKINI: Miss Higa Jiga say please not eliminate discrimination. She say just give her some, too.

FISBY: And just what does she mean by that?

SAKINI: She say Lotus Blossom unfair competition.

FISBY: Granted.

SAKINI: She say you promise everybody going to be equal.

FISBY: I intend to keep my word.

SAKINI: Well, she say she can't be equal unless she has everything Lotus Blossom has.

FISBY: What Lotus Blossom's got, the Government doesn't issue.

SAKINI: [*Taking a piece of paper which* MISS HIGA JIGA *waves*] She make list, boss. Shall I read, boss?

FISBY: Go ahead.

SAKINI: She wants you to get her and ladies in League following items:
A. Red stuff to put on lips like geisha.
B. Stuff that smell pretty—

FISBY: Now, *just* wait a minute. What would H.Q. think if I requisitioned lipstick!

SAKINI: [*Hands list back to* MISS HIGA JIGA] Dame desuyo.

MISS HIGA JIGA: Jaa Daitoryo ni tegami wo dashimaswa.

SAKINI: She say she sorry, but now she guess she just have to write this letter to Uncle Samuel after all.

FISBY: [*Throws up his hands*] All right. *All Right!* Tell her I'll call up the post exchange at Awasi and see if they have any shaving powder and toilet water.

SAKINI: Ya, katte agemasuyo.

MISS HIGA JIGA: [*Beams*] Ano wasure naidene bobby pin.

SAKINI: She say not forget bobby pins for hair.

FISBY: I think I might have been happier in the submarine command.

MISS HIGA JIGA: [*Stops as she is about to go*] Mohitotsu onegai watashitachi mo mina geisha ni.

SAKINI: She say one more thing. Can you get Lotus Blossom to teach Ladies' League all to be geisha girls?

FISBY: [*Leaps to his feet*] Teach the innocent women of this village to be—No! [MISS HIGA JIGA *shrugs and goes outside. As* FISBY *sinks back at his desk,* MISS HIGA JIGA *talks excitedly to the* WOMEN *gathered outside. They run off giggling.* FISBY *sits at his desk and picks up Plan B*] Plan B! [*He thumbs through its pages*] Let's just see if Washington anticipated *this.*

[*He buries his chin in his hands.* SAKINI *sits quietly watching him. Outside in the village street,* LOTUS BLOSSOM *enters and starts daintily toward the office. She has only gotten halfway when* SEIKO *overtakes her*]

SEIKO: [*Panting*] Ano, chotto.

LOTUS BLOSSOM: [*Stops and looks at him archly*] Nani?

SEIKO: [*Takes a chrysanthemum bud from his waist*] Ano korewo dozo.

LOTUS BLOSSOM: [*Takes it indifferently*] Ara, so arigato.

SEIKO: [*Strikes his heart passionately*] Boku no, kono, hato, o.

LOTUS BLOSSOM: [*Flicks her finger*] Anato no hahto? Ara shinzo ne.

SEIKO: [*Disembowels himself with an imaginary knife*] Harakitte shinimas.

LOTUS BLOSSOM: [*Yawns*] Imagoro sonnano hayaranai noyo.

SEIKO: [*Points toward* FISBY's *office*] Soka Amerika-san ga iinoka?

LOTUS BLOSSOM: [*Haughtily*] Nandeste! Sonnakoto yokeina osowa.

SEIKO: [*Laughs decisively*] Nanda rashamon janaika.

LOTUS BLOSSOM: [*Backs him up with an angry finger*] Watashimo kotoni kansho shinaideyo.

SEIKO: [*Bows his head*] Gomen nasai iisugi deshta.

LOTUS BLOSSOM: [*Points away*] Atchi, itte. [SEIKO *sighs, turns and plods off toward the sweet-potato fields, crushed and dejected.* LOTUS BLOSSOM *tidies her hair and continues to the office. She calls in coyly*] Fuisbee-san!

SAKINI: [*Rises and looks out the door*] Oh, what do you think, boss? Lotus Blossom back. She come to see you.

FISBY: And high time. [*He turns to face the door as* LOTUS BLOSSOM *enters and bows*] Where have *you* been all day? Never mind, I know—upsetting the agricultural horse cart.

LOTUS BLOSSOM: Fu-san no kao nikkori nasaruto totemo kawaii wa.

SAKINI: She say sun burst through the clouds now that you smile on her.

FISBY: I'm not smiling. [*She hands him* SEIKO's *chrysanthemum bud*]

SAKINI: Oh, boss, you know what she give you?

FISBY: The works.

SAKINI: When lady give gentleman chrysanthemum bud, in Okinawa that means her heart is ready to unfold.

FISBY: Well, this is one bud that's not going to flower.

LOTUS BLOSSOM: [*Offering a box she has brought*] Kore otsukemono yo. Dozo.

SAKINI: She say you like to eat some tsukemono? Tsukemono nice thing to eat between meals.

FISBY: No.

LOTUS BLOSSOM: [*Takes geta and kneels beside him*] Dozo ohaki osobase.

FISBY: Tell her to *leave my feet* alone.

LOTUS BLOSSOM: [*Studies* FISBY] Kasa kaburu. Nisshabyo nanoyo.

SAKINI: She worried about you, boss. She say when you go in hot sun, should wear *kasa*—that straw hat—on head.

FISBY: Tell her never mind about my feet or my head. I want her to stop interfering with the recovery program. To stop causing rebellion and making the men—ah—ah—discontented.

SAKINI: [*Turns to* LOTUS BLOSSOM] Jama shicha dame dayo.

LOTUS BLOSSOM: [*Smiles*] Fu-san ocha ikaga?

SAKINI: She say you want some tea?

FISBY: [*Throwing himself down on his cot*] No.

LOTUS BLOSSOM: Shami demo hikimashoka?

SAKINI: She say you want some music?

FISBY: No.

LOTUS BLOSSOM: [*Giggles*] Ara Fu-san-tara yaiteruno.

SAKINI: She say you jealous, boss?

FISBY: [*Mirthlessly*] Ha!

LOTUS BLOSSOM: Honto ni doshita no?

SAKINI: She say you want to tell her your troubles, boss?

FISBY: Why should I tell her my troubles?

SAKINI: She geisha girl, that's her *business*, boss.

FISBY: Some business.

LOTUS BLOSSOM: Shoga naiwane. Mah soshite irasshai yo.

SAKINI: She say she hear about lack of cooperation here. She feel very bad. She say she want to help because you best boss she ever had. You not make her work and you not take money from her.

FISBY: [*Sits up on his cot*] Did the other men who owned her . . . hire her out and then take money from her?

SAKINI: Oh, sure.

FISBY: Well, where I come from we have a name for men who—who—do *that* sort of thing.

SAKINI: You have geisha business in America, too?

FISBY: [*Rises*] No! Sakini, you give her to understand I have no intention of putting her to—to work.

SAKINI: Why not, boss? She pay all her dues to Geisha Guild. She member in good standing.

FISBY: You mean they've got a union for this sort of thing?

SAKINI: Geisha girl have to be protected, boss. Must keep up rates.

FISBY: This is the most immoral thing I've ever heard of. Haven't you people any sense of shame?

SAKINI: We bad not to be ashamed, boss?

FISBY: Obviously, there is a fundamental difference between us that can't be reconciled. I don't say that where I come from there's no such thing as prostitution. But, by God, we don't have unions, set rates and collect dues!

SAKINI: But geisha girl not prostitute, boss.

FISBY: At least we have the decency—[*He stops*] What do you mean, geisha girls aren't prostitutes? Everybody knows what they do.

SAKINI: Then everybody wrong, boss.

FISBY: Well, what do they get paid for, then?

SAKINI: Hard to explain fundamental difference. Poor man like to feel rich. Rich man like to feel wise. Sad man like to feel happy. All go to geisha house and tell troubles to geisha girl. She listen politely and say, "Oh, that's too bad." She very pretty. She make tea, she sing, she dance, and pretty soon troubles go away. Is not worth something, boss?

FISBY: And that's *all* they do?

SAKINI: Very ancient and honorable profession.

FISBY: Look, Sakini, I apologize. I guess I jumped the gun. And I'm glad you explained. It sort of puts a new light on things.

[*He turns to* LOTUS BLOSSOM *and grins.*]

LOTUS BLOSSOM: Ara, kyuni nikkorisite, mada okotteru no.

SAKINI: She say why are you smiling at her all of a sudden? You mad or something?

FISBY: Tell her that I'm a dope. That I have a coconut for a head.

SAKINI: No use, boss. She not believe.

FISBY: Then will you ask her if she'd be kind enough to give geisha lessons to the Ladies' League for Democratic Action?

SAKINI: Odori ya shami Ladies' League ni oshiete?

LOTUS BLOSSOM: Er iiwa, demo kumiaiaga kowaiwane.

SAKINI: She say Geisha Guild closed shop, but she teach if you not report her.

[*At this point the men of the village come across the square and stop before the office.* LOTUS BLOSSOM *goes to the door. Immediately there are* ohs *and* ahs *from the men*]

FISBY: What is that?

SAKINI: Sound like Okinawan wolf call, boss.

FISBY: Well, let's find out. [*He goes outside to face the group, followed by* SAKINI] Ask what's the matter.

SAKINI: Doshtano?

MR. KEORA: Minna gakko nanka yori chaya go ii soda.

SAKINI: They say they just held meeting in democratic fashion and majority agree on resolution. They want you to build them cha ya.

FISBY: A what?

SAKINI: Cha ya. That's teahouse, boss.

FISBY: A teahouse?

SAKINI: Yes, boss. They say now that this village have geisha girl just like big city, they should have teahouse like big city, too.

FISBY: But I can't build them a teahouse . . . I have no authority to do that.

SAKINI: But you tell them will of majority is law. You going to break law?

FISBY: They're going to get a school . . . that's enough.

SAKINI: But majority too old to go to school . . . they want teahouse.

FISBY: There is no provision in Plan B for a teahouse.

LOTUS BLOSSOM: Ano . . . ochaya sae tatereba mondai naija nai no.

SAKINI: Lotus Blossom say teahouse in Tobiki make recovery program work. Everybody make geta and cricket cages like crazy so they can spend money at teahouse.

FISBY: I haven't got any materials to build a teahouse.

SAKINI: Zairyo ga naiyo.

LOTUS BLOSSOM: Ara, kinoo renga ya zaimoku takusan kite orimashitayo.

SAKINI: She say Army truck come yesterday and leave beautiful brick and lovely paint.

FISBY: For the new *schoolhouse*. Tell them . . . it just can't be done.

SAKINI: Dame, dame, dame desuyo!

[FISBY *looks down into the disappointed faces of the* VILLAGERS]

VILLAGERS: Achara-san, iijiwaru dane.

SAKINI: They say you very mean to them after *all* the nice presents they give you.

FISBY: I'm sorry.

SAKINI: They very sorry too, boss. You know why?

FISBY: I think I do.

SAKINI: No, boss. When you leave here . . . Tobiki be forgotten village. Not have park, not have statue . . . not even lovely jail. Tobiki like to be proud. Teahouse give them face.

FISBY: It's going to be a fine schoolhouse. Five sides.

OSHIRA: May I speak, Captain-san?

FISBY: Of course, Mr. Oshira.

OSHIRA: There are lovely teahouses in the big cities. But the men of Tobiki have never been inside them. We are too poor and our clothes are too ragged. All of my life I have dreamed of visiting a teahouse where paper lanterns cast a light in the lotus pond and bamboo bells hanging in the pines tinkle as the breezes brush them. But this picture is only in my heart . . . I may never see it. I am an old man, sir. I shall die soon. It is evil for the soul to depart this world laden with envy or regret. Give us our teahouse, sir. Free my soul for death.

FISBY: [*Unhappily*] But . . . we haven't got any carpenters!

SAKINI: [*Calls over the heads of the group*] Oi! Daiku-san! Daiku-san! [MR. SUMATA *and* HIS FATHER *come trotting across the stage carrying their carpenter boxes.* SAKINI *turns to* FISBY] Oh, what you think? Mr. Sumata and his papa just come down from mountains!

FISBY: [*Gives* SAKINI *a penetrating but defeated look*] All right. All right! I haven't got a chance. I guess Uncle Sam is going into the teahouse business.

[*He turns and goes back into his office, followed by* LOTUS BLOSSOM. *He picks up Plan B.* SAKINI *announces the decision from the steps*]

SAKINI: Cha ya, tatete iiyo!

[*There is an outburst of cheers from the* VILLAGERS. *It sounds very much like* "Fisby-san, Banzai, Uncle Sam, Banzai!" *Inside* FISBY *begins tearing up Plan B.* LOTUS BLOSSOM *kneels before him, geta in hand.* FISBY *extends his feet and smiles down at her. The cheering outside continues. As the panels descend—*]

THE SCENE BLACKS OUT QUICKLY

SCENE TWO

COLONEL PURDY's *office.*
A *few weeks later.*
The right panel is lifted. A light picks up COLONEL PURDY. *He sits at his desk fuming over a report. The rest of the stage remains dark. He calls* GREGOVICH *on his office inter-com.*

PURDY: Gregovich!

GREGOVICH'S VOICE: Yes, sir?

PURDY: Get me Captain Fisby at Tobiki.

GREGOVICH: Yes, sir.

[*The extreme left panel rises leaving the intervening panels lowered.* FISBY *sits with his feet propped up on his desk. He is wearing his bathrobe "kimono."* LOTUS BLOSSOM *stands at his side fanning him. Over the scene, the sound of hammering and sawing can be heard. Over this the phone can be heard to ring.* FISBY *lifts the receiver*]

FISBY: Captain Fisby.

PURDY: Colonel Purdy.

FISBY: [*Over noise*] Who?

PURDY: Colonel Purdy!

FISBY: I can't hear you. Hold on a minute. [*He turns to* LOTUS BLOSSOM] See if you can stop that hammering on the teahouse for a minute.

[*He goes through the motions.* LOTUS BLOSSOM *nods understandingly and goes out*]

PURDY: What's going on down there, Fisby?

FISBY: [*As the noises cease*] Now, who is it?

PURDY: Colonel Purdy.

FISBY: [*Wraps his robe about his legs quickly*] Oh, good afternoon, Colonel.

PURDY: I want to talk to you about your Progress Report.

FISBY: I sent it in.

PURDY: I have it. I have it right in front of me. I've read it twice. Now, suppose *you* tell *me* what it says.

FISBY: What would you like to have me explain, sir?

PURDY: I'd like you to explain why there's nothing in here about the schoolhouse. Didn't you get the lumber?

FISBY: [*Uneasily*] Yes, sir . . . it's being used right now. But we'll need some more, I'm afraid.

PURDY: I sent ample according to specifications. How big a structure are you building?

FISBY: Well . . . we ought to consider expansion. Populations increase.

PURDY: We don't need to consider expansion. Our troops will be out of here by the next generation. Which brings me to another point. [*He refers to the report*] What's this about six kids being born last week?

FISBY: Well, there wasn't much else to fill the Progress Report, sir.

PURDY: Then you've failed at your indoctrination. Don't you know yet that births are entered under "Population Increases"? They are not considered progress.

FISBY: But they weren't children, sir. They were kids . . . goats.

PURDY: There must be something wrong with this connection. It sounded just as if you said "goats."

FISBY: I did, sir. Kids . . . goats. You see, we're trying to increase the livestock herd down here. I thought . . .

PURDY: Goats! I don't care what you thought. Look here, Fisby. Suppose some congressman flew in to inspect our team. How would I explain such a report?

FISBY: Well, goats will breed, sir. Congress can't stop that. And I've been concerned with . . .

PURDY: The population of civilians alone concerns us. I want to know exactly what progress you've made as outlined in Plan B.

FISBY: Well . . . I'm getting along fine with the people.

PURDY: In other words, nothing. Listen to me. Do you realize what Major McEvoy has accomplished in his village?

FISBY: No, sir.

PURDY: Well, I'll tell you. His fourth-graders know the alphabet through "M," and his whole village can sing "God Bless America" in English.

FISBY: Yes, sir. That's real progress, sir. I wish I could say the same.

PURDY: See that you do. I don't want any rotten apples in my barrel. Now . . . I want to know exactly what you have accomplished in the five weeks you've been down there.

FISBY: Well, sir . . . I've started an industry. I'm sending our first shipment out for sale this week.

PURDY: What are you making?

FISBY: [*Looks down at his feet*] Oh, getas and . . .

PURDY: Wait a minute . . . what in God's name is a *geta*?

FISBY: Not "a" geta . . . *getas* . . . you have to have two.

PURDY: Are you breeding some *other* kind of animal?

FISBY: You wear them on your feet, sir. Excellent for strengthening the metatarsal muscles. Then . . . I have a group busy building cricket cages. . . .

PURDY: Captain Fisby!

FISBY: Yes, sir.

PURDY: What kind of cages did you say?

FISBY: Cricket. Like in cricket on the hearth. I think we'll find a great market for them. Of course, we don't supply the crickets.

PURDY: Naturally not. Captain Fisby . . . have you been taking your salt pills?

FISBY: Yes, sir . . . I take them at cha ya . . . with my tea.

PURDY: Have you been going out in the sun without your helmet?

FISBY: I wear a kasa, sir . . . it's more practical . . . wind can blow through the straw.

PURDY: I see. I see. That will be all, Captain.

[*He hangs up quickly*]

FISBY: Hello . . . hello . . .

[*He hangs up and sits looking at the phone rather puzzled. The lights go down in his office and the panel descends.* COLONEL PURDY *also sits looking at the phone in his office. He calls* SERGEANT GREGOVICH *on the inter-com*]

PURDY: Sergeant! What is the name of that psychiatrist over at Awasi?

GREGOVICH: Captain McLean?

PURDY: Get him on the phone. My man at Tobiki has gone completely off his rocker!

THE SCENE BLACKS OUT QUICKLY

SCENE THREE

CAPTAIN FISBY's *office.*
A *few days later.*
The office is empty as the panel rises. After a moment CAP-

TAIN MC LEAN *enters. He is an intense, rather wild-eyed man in his middle forties. He glances about furtively, then begins to examine the papers on* FISBY's *desk. He makes several notes in a notebook. He picks up* FISBY's *cricket cage and is examining it intently when* FISBY *enters behind him. He halts upon seeing* MC LEAN. FISBY *is wearing his blue bathrobe, his geta and a native straw hat.*

FISBY: Well, who are you?

MC LEAN: [*Gasps in surprise*] Oh, you startled me.

FISBY: Can I do anything for you? I'm Captain Fisby.

MC LEAN: I'm Captain McLean. There was no one here . . . so I came in.

FISBY: [*He looks at his insignia*] Oh, medical corps. What brings you to Tobiki?

MC LEAN: Well, I'm—I'm on leave. Thought I'd spend it making some—some—ethnological studies. [*He adds quickly*] Of the natives.

FISBY: Well, you couldn't have come to a more interesting spot. Sit down, Captain.

MC LEAN: [*Sits*] Thank you. Would you have any objection to my spending a week or so making my studies, Captain?

FISBY: Not at all. Make yourself at home. I'll take that if it's in your way.

[*He reaches out to relieve* MC LEAN *of the cricket cage he still holds*]

MC LEAN: [*Glances at the cage in his hand and laughs awkwardly*] Oh, yes. I was just examining it.

FISBY: [*Pleased at his authority on the subject*] It's a cricket cage.

MC LEAN: [*Pauses*] You . . . like crickets?

FISBY: I haven't found one yet. But at least I've got the cage. I've got two . . . if you want one.

MCLEAN: Thank you, no. Thank you very much. [*He looks at* FISBY's *attire*] What happened to your uniform, Captain?

FISBY: It's around. I find getas and a kimono much more comfortable in this climate.

MCLEAN: But isn't that a bathrobe?

FISBY: [*Shrugs*] It passes for a kimono. Would you like to take off your shoes, Captain?

MCLEAN: Thank you . . . no. I'll keep them on if you don't mind.

FISBY: Can I offer you some tsukemono? You eat these during the day between meals. [*He extends a platter*] Tsukemono means fragrant things.

MCLEAN: I just had a chocolate bar, thank you. [*He rises and looks out the door*] May I ask what you're building down the road?

FISBY: [*Proudly*] That's my cha ya. [*He pops a few tsukemonos into his mouth*] It's really going to be something to write home about.

MCLEAN: Cha ya?

FISBY: Well, it just so happens, Captain, that I own a geisha girl. That might sound strange to you, but you get used to these things after a while. And if you have a geisha, you've got to have a cha ya. Sure you don't want some tsukemono?

MCLEAN: I really couldn't eat a thing. [*He glances out the door again*] May I ask what the men are doing down there wading in that irrigation ditch?

FISBY: They're not wading, they're building a lotus pond. You can't have a cha ya without a lotus pond.

MCLEAN: [*Sits opposite* FISBY] How have you felt lately, Fisby?

FISBY: McLean, I'll tell you something. I've never been happier. I feel reckless and free. And it all happened the moment I decided not to build that damned pentagon-shaped school.

MCLEAN: That what?

FISBY: The good colonel ordered me to build a pentagon-shaped schoolhouse down here. But the people wanted a teahouse. Believe it or not, someone gave me a geisha girl. So I'm giving this village what it wants. That must all sound pretty crazy to you, Mac.

MC LEAN: Well, yes and no.

FISBY: These are wonderful people with a strange sense of beauty. And hard-working . . . when there's a purpose. You should have seen them start out day before yesterday, great bundles of things they'd made piled high on their heads. Getas, cricket cages, lacquer ware—things to sell as souvenirs up north. Don't let anyone tell you these people are lazy.

MC LEAN: Oh. I see. I see.

FISBY: No, you don't. But you'll have a chance to study them.

MC LEAN: So you're building them a teahouse.

FISBY: Next thing I'm going to do for them is find out if this land here will grow anything besides sweet potatoes. I'm going to send for fertilizers and DDT and—

MC LEAN: [Leaps to his feet] Chemicals!

FISBY: Sure, why not?

MC LEAN: Do you want to poison these people?

FISBY: No, but—

MC LEAN: Now you've touched on a subject that is very close to me. For years I've planned to retire and buy a farm—raise specialties for big restaurants. So let me tell you this. Chemicals will kill all your earthworms, and earthworms aerate your soil.

FISBY: They do?

MC LEAN: Do you know an earthworm leaves castings eight times its own weight every day?

FISBY: That much!

MC LEAN: Organic gardening is the only thing. Nature's way—compost, manure, but no chemicals.

FISBY: Hey! You know a lot about this.

MC LEAN: [*Modestly*] I should. I've subscribed to all the farm journals for years.

FISBY: Say, you could help these people out while you're here—if you would. Do you think you could take over supervision—establish a sort of experimental station for them?

MC LEAN: Well, I—no—no—I haven't time.

FISBY: Take time. This is a chance for you to put some of your theories into practice.

MC LEAN: [*Haughtily*] They are not theories. They are proven facts.

FISBY: I'll give you a couple of men to help, and all you'd have to do is tell us how.

MC LEAN: [*Hesitates*] Is your soil acid or alkaline?

FISBY: Gosh, I don't know.

MC LEAN: Well, that's the very *first* thing you have to find out. Do you have bees?

FISBY: I haven't seen any.

MC LEAN: [*Shakes his head sadly*] People always underestimate the importance of bees for pollinating.

FISBY: [*Slaps him on the back*] Mac, you're just the man we've needed down here. You're a genius!

MC LEAN: I'll want plenty of manure.

FISBY: You'll get it.

MC LEAN: And I'll want to plan this program scientifically. I wish I had some of my books . . . and my seed catalogues. [*He measures from the floor*] I've got a stack of catalogues that high.

FISBY: Why don't you make a list, and I'll get the boys over at the airstrip to fly us in seeds from the States.

MC LEAN: [*The gardener fever possesses the doctor as he begins to make his list*] Every spring I've made lists of seeds and never had any soil to put them in. And now . . . I could actually germinate. [*He writes*] Corn—Golden Bantam. [*Then adds enthusiastically*] And Country Gentleman! Hybrid.

FISBY: Why don't I just leave you with your list while I check on the lotus pond? [MC LEAN *doesn't hear him*] Well, I'll be back for tea. We have tea in the pine grove and watch the sun go down.

[*He goes out*]

MC LEAN: [*Continues with his list reading aloud*] Cucumbers—Extra Early Green Prolific. [*His enthusiasm mounts*] Radishes—Crimson Giant! [*The telephone begins to ring; he ignores it as he writes*] Tomatoes—Ponderosa Earliana. [*The telephone rings insistently*] Watermelon!

[*He closes his eyes ecstatically*]

[*The panel rises on the opposite side of the stage revealing* COLONEL PURDY's *office. The intervening panel remains down.* COLONEL PURDY *sits at his desk jiggling his telephone hook*]

PURDY: What's the matter with this connection! Ring again!

MC LEAN: [*Ignores the ringing*] Watermelon—All-American Gold Medal! [*He writes it down as the phone rings. He looks up impatiently and lifts the receiver*] Hello!

PURDY: [*Confidentially*] Who is this?

MC LEAN: This is Captain McLean.

PURDY: This is Colonel Purdy. Can you talk?

MC LEAN: Why not?

PURDY: I was anxious to hear your report on you-know-who.

MC LEAN: On *who?*

PURDY: *Captain Fisby!* The man I sent you down to examine.

MC LEAN: Oh. [*He weighs his problem quickly*] Oh. Well . . . I'll have to stay down here several weeks for some . . .

PURDY: Several weeks!

MC LEAN: Rome wasn't built in a day.

PURDY: What?

MC LEAN: I said, Rome wasn't built in a day.

PURDY: [*Digests this*] Well . . . you're the doctor.

MC LEAN: I'll send in a report . . . from time to time. I can tell you now I expect to work miracles down here.

PURDY: Splendid . . . splendid. Is there anything I can send? Some old *Adventure Magazines* or anything?

MC LEAN: There are a couple of books I'd like, but I don't think you could get them.

PURDY: [*Picks up pencil*] You name them.

MC LEAN: Well . . . one is *Principles of Pea Production,* and the other is *Do's and Don'ts of Cabbage Culture.* [PURDY *starts to write . . . then stops*] And do you think you could lay your hands on a soil test kit?

PURDY: [*Looks at earphone*] A what?

MC LEAN: [*Enunciating*] A *soil test kit.* I want to see if the soil is sour down here.

PURDY: Sour, did you say?

MC LEAN: Yes . . . if your soil is sour your seeds won't germinate. And I sure wish I had some bees.

PURDY: There *is* something wrong with this connection!

MC LEAN: I'm going to take time out here to build up the soil with manure.

PURDY: [*Unbelieving*] Did you say manure?

MC LEAN: I've lost faith in chemicals. You kill all your worms. I can tell you, when you kill a worm, Colonel . . . you're killing a friend. [*There is a long pause*] Hello . . . hello.

PURDY: [*Puts down the phone and turns to the squawk box*] Gregovich, where is Plan B!

GREGOVICH'S VOICE: What did you want, sir?

PURDY: I want to see who I send to analyze an analyst.

THE PANELS FALL QUICKLY ON EACH SIDE
OF THE STAGE

SCENE FOUR

Village square.
A few weeks later.
The panels rise to reveal the village square and FISBY'S *office.*
Natives are seated in the square, great bundles beside them.
Others arrive and sink into positions of dejection. FISBY *works*
at his desk. SAKINI *enters and looks at the* VILLAGERS.

SAKINI: [*To* MR. KEORA] Doshtano?

KEORA: Hitotsu mo unremasenna.

SAKINI: Oh, oh, . . . too bad. [SAKINI *crosses and enters* FISBY'S
office] Boss!

FISBY: Yes?

SAKINI: Mr. Keora and everybody back from Big Koza.

FISBY: Good. Let's see how they made out. [*He steps outside fol-*
lowed by SAKINI. *He stops as he sees his* VILLAGERS *sitting deject-*
edly before their large bundles. He turns to SAKINI] What's the
matter?

SAKINI: Mr. Keora very tired. Walk two days with bundle on back
to sell straw hats to American soldiers at Big Koza. Nobody buy,
so walk back. Too many damn hats now, boss.

FISBY: He couldn't sell *any*? [SAKINI *shakes his head*] Why not?

SAKINI: [*Shrugs*] Soldiers not want. Soldiers say . . . what you think
we are . . . hayseed? So come home.

FISBY: [*Sees old* MR. OSHIRA *and crosses to him.* OSHIRA *rises*] Mr. Oshira . . . did you take your lacquer ware to Yatoda?

OSHIRA: Oh, yes . . . but come back . . not go again.

FISBY: But I don't understand. . . . The Navy always spends money.

OSHIRA: Sailors say, "Oh, pretty good . . . how much you want?" I say, "Twenty-five yen." They say, "Oh, too much . . . can get better in five-and-ten-cent store. Give you one nickel."

FISBY: Did you explain how many years it took you to learn how to turn out such work?

OSHIRA: [*Nods*] They say, "What you want us to do, cry?"

FISBY: [*Angrily*] Damn stupid morons! [*He turns back to* OSHIRA] Did you tell them that each cup was handmade?

OSHIRA: They say . . . not care. They say . . . at home have big machines that turn out ten cups every minute. They say . . . take nickel or jump in lake.

FISBY: [*Unhappily*] So you had to carry them all the way back?

SAKINI: Poor Mr. Oshira. No one want his lacquer ware.

FISBY: Well, he's wrong. He's a great artist and I'll buy everything he's made myself.

SAKINI: But you not able to buy everything from everybody in Tobiki, boss.

FISBY: [*Sits down on steps*] Tell them that they should all be proud of their work. And that I'm proud of all of them.

SAKINI: Gokro, gokro san.

FISBY: I'll think of something . . . I'll hit on an idea to bring money to this village yet.

SAKINI: Boss . . . you stop work on teahouse now?

FISBY: No! You'll get a teahouse if I give you nothing else.

SAKINI: They sure wish they could make some money to spend at teahouse, boss. Not like to go like beggars.

FISBY: Give me a little time, Sakini.

[*As they sit around, each deep in his personal problems,* MC LEAN *enters. His uniform is gone. He is wearing his bathrobe, a straw hat and geta*]

MC LEAN: Fisby! You're just the man I want to see. Can I have a couple of boys to help me? The damn Japanese beetles are eating up my Chinese peas.

FISBY: [*Dispiritedly*] Sure . . . I'll get a couple for you.

MC LEAN: [*Looks around*] What's the matter?

FISBY: There's no market for our products.

MC LEAN: Oh . . . that's too bad. What are you going to do?

[*He sits down*]

FISBY: Try to think of something.

OSHIRA: The world has left us behind.

[*The* VILLAGERS *begin to rise and pick up their handiwork*]

SEIKO: Amerika-san no seija naiyo. Sa, sa, kaette yakezake da!

SAKINI: They say . . . tell you not your fault no one wants to buy, boss. They say guess they go home now and get drunk.

FISBY: Tell them I don't blame them. If I had anything to drink . . . I'd do the same. [*As they start to file out, both* MC LEAN *and* FISBY *have a delayed reaction. They leap to their feet together*] Wait a minute! [*The* VILLAGERS *stop*] What are they going to get drunk *on?*

SAKINI: They got nothing but brandy.

MC LEAN: Nothing but *brandy!*

FISBY: How did they manage to get brandy?

SAKINI: We make very fine brandy here, from sweet potatoes. Been making for generations.

FISBY: You make a brandy *yourselves?*

SAKINI: Oh, yes. We make for weddings and funerals.

FISBY: [*Looks at* MC LEAN] What does it taste like?

SAKINI: You want some, boss? [*He turns to* HOKAIDA] Imozake, skoshi!

FISBY: Sakini, if this stuff is any good at all, we're in business. This is one thing I *know* our men will buy.

SAKINI: Oh . . . I think we not like to sell brandy. Only make for ceremony.

MC LEAN: It may not be any good anyhow. There are some things even the troops won't drink.

HOKAIDA: [*Returns with an earthen jug*] Hai, imozake.

[*He hands the jug to* FISBY]

SAKINI: There you are, boss. You like taste now?

FISBY: I'd like to smell it first.

[*He gives it a sniff and jerks his head back*]

MC LEAN: Obviously, it has a kick.

FISBY: How old is this brandy, Sakini?

SAKINI: [*Turns to* HOKAIDA] Kore itsuno?

HOKAIDA: [*Holds up seven fingers*] Issukan mae dayo.

FISBY: Seven years old?

SAKINI: Oh, no, boss. He make last week.

FISBY: It couldn't smell like that in only a week.

SAKINI: Is village secret. You try now?

FISBY: [*Hands it to* MC LEAN] You try it, Mac. You're a medical man.

MC LEAN: [*Backs away*] You first.

FISBY: I insist. You're my guest.

MC LEAN: I waive the honor.

FISBY: [*Turns to* SAKINI] Has anyone ever gone blind or died from this?

MC LEAN: He said they make it for funerals.

SAKINI: Oh, no, boss. We not blind. We not dead.

FISBY: There, you see.

MC LEAN: They've worked up an immunity over the years.

FISBY: Well, I don't want to kill any of my countrymen. Couldn't you make some sort of test, Doc? [As MC LEAN *considers this, the bleat of a goat is heard offstage.* FISBY *and* MC LEAN *exchange looks and nod*] Sakini, get Lady Astor. [To MC LEAN] That's Miss Higa Jiga's goat. She asked me to give it a classy name.

[SAKINI *goes to get* LADY ASTOR]

MC LEAN: I'm not sure what we'll prove. Goats have hardy stomachs.

SAKINI: [*Returns leading a goat*] Boss, you make guinea pig of goat?

FISBY: If this passes the goat-test, it's all right. No Marine would ever admit he had a weaker stomach than a goat.

MC LEAN: May I borrow this a moment?

[*He takes* MR. HOKAIDA'S *red helmet and pours into it from the jug*]

SAKINI: Lady Astor very lucky goat.

FISBY: You hold her, Sakini. Proceed, Doctor . . . in the name of science. [*The goat sniffs the contents of the helmet*] We're either going to have an industry or goat meat for dinner.

[LADY ASTOR *begins to drink the concoction. They watch her lap up the liquor and lick her lips with relish*]

MC LEAN: [*Stands back*] It doesn't seem to affect her. [*Draws his fingers back and forth in front of the goat's eyes*] Reflexes all right.

FISBY: Let's watch her a minute. The future of Tobiki and the health of the Army are at stake here. [FISBY *and* MC LEAN *and the* VILLAGERS *stand watching the goat.* LADY ASTOR *is quite content.* FISBY *rises*] Well, here goes. [*He takes the jug and samples the contents himself.* MC LEAN *watches him. Then he, too, tests from the jug. They look at each other and grin*] Whee!

[*He dashes for his office*]

SAKINI: [*Follows*] What you going to do, boss?

FISBY: I am about to form the Cooperative Brewing Company of Tobiki. [FISBY *is followed by* SAKINI, MC LEAN, *and some of the* VILLAGERS. *He picks up the phone*] Get me the Officers' Club at Awasi.

SAKINI: We going to make brandy, boss?

FISBY: I'll tell you in a minute. [*He turns back to telephone*] Hello . . . Officers' Club, Awasi? This is Captain Fisby at Tobiki. Oh, hello, Major, how are you? Major, when I was with your unit, you could never keep a supply of liquor in the club, and I stumbled onto something and wondered if you'd be interested. Tobiki, as you know, is the heart of the brandy industry and—[*He takes the phone away from his ear as the word brandy is shouted back at him*] Yes . . . brandy. . . . [*He turns to* MC LEAN] Doc, look up the word "sweet potato" and see if it has another fancier name. [*He turns back to the phone*] Yes . . . I'm here . . . yes . . . I could get you some if you could pay their price and keep the source secret. Oh, yes, it's been made here for generations. Why, you never tasted anything like it.

MC LEAN: The Haitian word for sweet potato is *b-a-t-a-t-a*.

[*He spells it out*]

FISBY: [*Into the phone*] You've heard of Seven Star Batata, haven't you? Well, Tobiki is where it's made. [*He turns to* MC LEAN] The Seven Star did it.

SAKINI: Brandy much better if eight or ten days old, boss.

FISBY: We also have Eight Star and Ten Star. Well, naturally the Ten Star comes a little higher. It sells for—[*He looks at* SAKINI *desperately.* SAKINI *holds up ten fingers*] A hundred occupation yen a gallon.

SAKINI: I mean *ten* yen, boss.

FISBY: Delivered. All right, we'll send up five gallons in about a week. It'll be delivered by our Department of Agriculture. You're welcome. [*He hangs up and turns to* SAKINI] Sakini, if every family in Tobiki starts making brandy, how much can we turn out in a week?

SAKINI: Oh, maybe . . . forty . . . fifty gallons.

FISBY: Better aim for eighty. [*He lifts the receiver again*] I'd like to get the naval base at Big Koza, Officers' Club, Commander Myers.

SAKINI: Maybe if everybody build private stills, Tobiki can turn out hundred gallon.

FISBY: I'll know better after I talk to the Navy. [*He speaks into the phone*] Commander Myers? Captain Fisby at Tobiki. Commander, we've got a surplus of brandy down here and I was wondering . . . [*Again he takes the phone away from his ear as the word brandy is blasted back*] Yes. Brandy. Ten Star Batata. Well, Lady Astor won't drink anything else. Oh . . . we could supply you with as much as you want at a hundred yen a gallon. Fifteen gallons? Right! It will be delivered Horse Cart Special in ten days. [*He hangs up and turns to the others crowding into his office*] Sakini, tell them to all start making brandy, and in a week or two everyone in this village is going to have more money than he ever dreamed of.

SAKINI: Ah, dondon kaseide sake tsukreba minna kanega mokaruyo!

MR. KEORA: Minna shiroi koto katte moii darone?

SAKINI: They say . . . if they work like the dickens, can they all have white coats like the mayor?

FISBY: Yes. I'll get the cloth somewhere. That's a promise. [*The telephone rings*] Wait a minute. Hello? Well, word gets around fast. [*He picks up his order blank*] Twenty gallons? PX, GHQ, C.O.D. O.K. [*He hangs up*] Get to work, boys! [*As they turn to leave,* FISBY *suddenly leaps to his feet*] Wait! *They stand frozen as he crouches and starts toward them. He slaps his hand on the floor and then rises triumphantly*] I got my cricket!

[*The* VILLAGERS *cheer for* FISBY]

THE PANELS FALL QUICKLY

ACT THREE

SCENE ONE

Teahouse of the August Moon.
Several weeks later.
All the panels are down. SAKINI *steps from the wings to address the audience.*

SAKINI: [*Bows*]

Ability of Americans for mass production equaled only by American capacity for consumption.

Fortune often comes in back door while we look out front window.

Prosperity not only smile on Tobiki.

Prosperity giggle like silly girl.

Very strange.

Things we do best . . . not wanted.

Things we think least of . . . wanted most.

No conclusion.

Tobiki now village of beautiful houses.

But loveliest of all is Teahouse of August Moon.

[*He goes off extreme left, signaling for the panels to rise. Offstage the music of string instruments can be heard playing softly. The panels go up. The ugly thatched huts are gone. In the center of the stage, exquisite in its simplicity, stands the teahouse. Small bells tinkle from its pagoda roof. Soft lights glow through the colored paper panels. Dwarf pines edge the walk leading to a small bridge. An August moon hangs in the autumn sky. The silhouette of* LOTUS BLOSSOM *is framed in the center panel by the soft back lighting. She slides the panel open and steps into the almost bare center room of the teahouse. She crosses and lights the lanterns hanging from the eave extensions. As she goes through this ceremony, the* GUESTS *wander in. Before they enter the teahouse, they remove their shoes and rinse their fingers in the ceremonial bamboo basin. Then they enter and seat themselves on green floor mats. The* WOMEN *are dressed in silk kimonos of varying hues and the majority of the* MEN *wear spotless white suits.* LOTUS BLOSSOM *bows to them and returns through the sliding door again.* FISBY *and* MC LEAN, *followed by* SAKINI, *enter.* SAKINI *wears a white suit and the* AMERICANS *wear their bathrobes and geta. They are greeted enthusiastically by the* GUESTS]

SAKINI: I tell Lotus Blossom you here, boss.

[*He disappears through the sliding panel in the center of the teahouse*]

FISBY: [*As they walk around inspecting the grounds*] It's really something, isn't it?

MC LEAN: Where did they all get their white suits?

FISBY: They made them.

MC LEAN: Where'd they get the cloth?

FISBY: I got it from the naval base at Awasi for ten gallons of brandy. It's target cloth.

MC LEAN: Those kimonos aren't target cloth.

FISBY: Parachute silk. Six gallons' worth.

[LOTUS BLOSSOM *enters, followed by* SAKINI. *She hurries down to* FISBY *and bows. She extends a yellow chrysanthemum to him*]

SAKINI: Chrysanthemum bud in full bloom, boss.

LOTUS BLOSSOM: [*She bows as* FISBY *accepts the gift*] Hop-pee.

[*Her eyes almost disappear in a great smile of pride*]

FISBY: What did she say?

SAKINI: I try like the dickens to teach her to say "happy birthday," but she can't say "birthday," boss.

LOTUS BLOSSOM: Hop-pee.

FISBY: Well . . . I'm floored! [*He bows to her*] Thank you, Lotus Blossom. [*To* SAKINI] How did you know?

MC LEAN: I gave you away.

SAKINI: Everybody in village like to show appreciation, boss.

FISBY: I should have had a kimono made. When you said "formal," I thought this would do.

LOTUS BLOSSOM: Hop-pee. Hop-pee.

FISBY: And a hop-pee hop-pee to you.

GUESTS: [*Murmur in the background*] Hayaku oiwai hajimeyo, soda, soda.

SAKINI: Everybody impatient to get on with the party, boss.

LOTUS BLOSSOM: Hop-pee.

[*She indicates the center mat*]

SAKINI: You sit down now, boss. Lotus Blossom going to dance in your honor.

FISBY: You hear that. . . . She's going to dance! [*Quickly sits down*] Sit down, you farmer. . . . This is in my honor.

MC LEAN: My, my! How am I going to stall Purdy so I can stay down here?

FISBY: I'll have a relapse for you. [*They turn to watch* LOTUS BLOSSOM *as she takes her position and the first notes are struck by the musicians present.* LOTUS BLOSSOM *performs for them a traditional dance of infinite grace and delicacy. She finishes, concluding her performance in front of* FISBY, *who rises and bows to her*] What a lovely little thing you are! This belongs to you.

[*He returns the chrysanthemum with a flourish.* LOTUS BLOS- SOM *accepts it and seats herself quickly on a mat and hides her head*]

SAKINI: Oh, boss . . . you know what you do!

FISBY: It called for flowers.

SAKINI: That mean you give your heart to her.

FISBY: [*Lightly*] Well, I do. We all do. [*Turns to* MC LEAN] Wasn't that beautiful, Mac!

MC LEAN: She can dance in my cha ya any day.

SAKINI: You sit beside Lotus Blossom now, boss. You guest of honor and referee.

FISBY: [*Starts to sit down*] Referee! I thought this was a birthday party.

SAKINI: Lotus Blossom now putting on wrestling match for you, boss.

FISBY: Wrestling match?

LOTUS BLOSSOM: [*Stands and claps hands*] Sa, osumo hajime mashoyo.

[*Immediately two men bring in four poles which they set up downstage center to mark a square. Each pole has colored cloth hanging from it*]

MC LEAN: Who is wrestling?

[*He sits next to* FISBY]

SAKINI: Wrestling match between Chief of Agriculture and Chief of Police.

FISBY: [*To* LOTUS BLOSSOM] Hokaida and Seiko?

[*She nods*]

SAKINI: Grudge fight, boss.

FISBY: Really?

SAKINI: Whoever win match get to haul sweet potatoes for Lotus Blossom.

FISBY: [*Watching the poles being set up, he indicates them to* LOTUS BLOSSOM] Why have they wrapped colored cloth around the poles?

LOTUS BLOSSOM: Kuro wa fuyu, Ao wa haru, Akaga natsu de, Shirowa akiyo. Wakkatta?

SAKINI: She explain, boss, that black cloth remind us of winter, green cloth remind us of spring, red is the summer and white the autumn.

LOTUS BLOSSOM: [*Claps her hands*] Osumo, osumo!

[MR. HOKAIDA, *bare except for a pair of black shorts, enters and crosses to one corner of the ring, where he squats on his heels. An outburst of approval greets his entrance. He smiles with fatuous pleasure, and makes a desperate effort to hold in his fat stomach*]

MC LEAN: Do his black shorts mean anything?

SAKINI: Just easy to clean.

[LOTUS BLOSSOM *claps her dainty hands again.* MR. SEIKO *enters, lean and wiry, also wearing black shorts and a sweat shirt reading* U.S.S. Princeton]

FISBY: Where did he get *that?*

SAKINI: Sailor at naval base. Some class, eh? [MR. SEIKO *peels off the shirt to great applause and squats in the opposite corner. He glares across at* HOKAIDA, *who thrusts his jaw forward*] They waiting on you to give signal now, boss.

FISBY: Waiting on *me?*

SAKINI: Oh, yes . . . you are Honorable Referee.

LOTUS BLOSSOM: [*Hands her fan to* FISBY] Korede aizu shite kudasai.

FISBY: What do I do with this?

SAKINI: Now you cover face with fan.

FISBY: Why?

SAKINI: That mean you not take sides. Now you go to center of ring and drop fan from face.

MC LEAN: And get the hell out in a hurry.

FISBY: How many falls?

SAKINI: No falls, boss. First one to throw other out of ring—winner.

[FISBY *covers his face with the fan and walks down center. The two wrestlers crouch, poised to leap, their eyes on the fan.* FISBY *whips the fan away from his face and dashes back out of range. The protagonists circle each other slowly. Suddenly all hell breaks loose. The teahouse guests cheer their favorite. The fat* MR. HOKAIDA *picks up* MR. SEIKO *and subjects him to a series of head spins and thumpings. But he exhausts himself; and it is* SEIKO *who ends by tossing* HOKAIDA *out of the ring. A cheer rises from the guests.* FISBY *sighs with relief*]

Now the judges must decide who win.

FISBY: Decide! Is there any doubt?

[*The three judges confer. They then turn to* MR. HOKAIDA *and bow*]

SAKINI: Mr. Hokaida! The winner . . .

[*This startling announcement is greeted with approval.* SEIKO *beats his head and wails*]

FISBY: How *could* he be the winner! He was thrown out of the ring.

SAKINI: Maybe so, but judges all cousins of Mr. Hokaida.

FISBY: But the judges are wrong.

SAKINI: [*Confidentially*] We know who really win . . . but this way nobody lose face.

[SEIKO *and* HOKAIDA *exit*]

LOTUS BLOSSOM: Sa kondo wa Fu-san no ban yo.

SAKINI: Lotus Blossom say guests now wish *you* to perform.

FISBY: Perform what?

SAKINI: They like now for you and doctor to sing song or something.

FISBY: Sing!

SAKINI: Must do, boss. Bad manners to refuse.

FISBY: [*Repeats in alarm*] Sing! [*He turns to* MC LEAN] Get on your feet, Mac, we've got to sing something.

MC LEAN: What?

FISBY: We could sing the national anthem.

MC LEAN: No, we couldn't—I don't know the words.

FISBY: How about "Deep in the Heart of Texas"?

MC LEAN: Why not? There're no Texans here.

[*They step forward*]

FISBY: Mac, let's have some fun. [*He turns to* SAKINI] Sakini, you tell them they must all help us. They must clap and sing "Deep in the Heart of Texas" every time *we* do.

SAKINI: [*Beaming*] Tewo tataite Deep in the Heart of Texas. [*Demonstrates clapping*] Koshte, Deep in the Heart of Texas.

[*The* VILLAGERS *chatter and agree with enthusiasm.* FISBY *and* MC LEAN *stand close together and begin singing. Each time they come to the designated phrase,* SAKINI *gives a signal and the* VILLAGERS *join in lustily. Lost in their eager concentration, no one observes the entrance of* COLONEL PURDY. *He looks from the "kimono"-clad figures of* FISBY *and* MC LEAN *to the assemblage. As he shouts at* FISBY, *his voice is drowned out by the chorus of "Deep in the Heart of Texas." The song continues.* PURDY *signals offstage.* GREGOVICH *enters and is instructed by* COLONEL PURDY *to end the objectionable noises*]

GREGOVICH: Captain Fisby!

[*Again the voice coincides with the shouts of "Deep in the Heart of Texas" and is lost.* COLONEL PURDY *stalks downstage center, followed by* GREGOVICH]

PURDY: Captain Fisby! What in the name of Occupation is going on here?

[FISBY *gasps and backs away. Suddenly aware of his bathrobe, he stoops down to cover his bare legs.* MC LEAN *sur-*

renders completely to panic. He runs to hide behind guests.
The GUESTS, *alarmed by the sudden intrusion, scatter in all di-*
rections. In the midst of this bedlam—]

THE PANELS ARE LOWERED

SCENE TWO

Office of CAPTAIN FISBY.
Next morning.
The four bamboo panels are down. SAKINI *enters from the*
wings right and crosses down to the footlights.

SAKINI: [*Bows*]
When present is blackest,
Future can only be brighter.
Okinawa invaded many times.
Not sink in ocean yet.
Survive Chinese.
Survive Japanese.
Survive missionaries and Americans.
Invaded by typhoon.
Invaded by locust.
Invaded by cockroach and sweet-potato moth.
Tobiki now invaded by Honorable Colonel.
Not sink in ocean.

[*He goes to the left side of the stage and raises the panels in*
front of FISBY's *office. He then exits.* COLONEL PURDY *is seated*
at FISBY's *desk going through his papers.* FISBY *stands behind*
him nervously watching. MCLEAN *sits on the cot biting his*
nails. He rises]

PURDY: [*Without looking up*] Sit down! [MCLEAN *sits down*
again. PURDY *turns to* FISBY *and glares at him*] Where are your
bimonthly Progress Reports?

FISBY: I—I think they should be right here under the cricket cage, sir.

PURDY: [*Takes some papers from under the cage and glances at them*] These are all completely blank. [*He turns to* FISBY] Fisby, you can't convince me that you've been down here for two months doing absolutely nothing.

FISBY: Oh, no, sir. I mean yes, sir. I have not been doing "nothing."

PURDY: You're beginning to sound like a native.

MC LEAN: [*Rises*] The tendency is always to descend to the level of the environment, sir. It's a primary postulate of psychology.

PURDY: [*Turns on him*] Well, it's a primary regulation of the Army to make out reports! [*Back to* FISBY] Now, I want to know exactly what you've accomplished here from the moment you arrived.

FISBY: Well, let me think. . . .

MC LEAN: Could I—

PURDY: Sit down! [*He turns to* FISBY] How many lectures have you delivered to the village children on democratic theory?

FISBY: Well, let me see.

PURDY: Four—five?

FISBY: [*Thinks*] Not that many, sir.

PURDY: Three?

MC LEAN: [*Hopefully*] Two?

FISBY: N-no.

PURDY: You only delivered *one* lecture?

FISBY: None, sir.

PURDY: Don't tell me you haven't delivered a single lecture!

FISBY: Yes, sir, I haven't delivered no lecture. I mean . . . any lecture.

PURDY: Did you organize a Ladies' League for Democratic Action?

FISBY: [*Beaming*] Yes, sir. I sure did. I did that all right!

PURDY And how many lectures on democratic theory have you given *them?*

FISBY: [*Deflated again*] None, sir.

PURDY: You can't mean none. You must mean one or two.

FISBY: No, sir, none.

PURDY: I refuse to believe it.

FISBY: I'm glad, sir.

MC LEAN: [*Rises in desperation*] Sir, I *must* go.

PURDY: Where!

MC LEAN: My *seedlings* are wilting. I have to transplant them.

PURDY: Captain, you will pack your gear and transplant yourself to your unit at once.

MC LEAN: Yes, sir. [*He turns to* FISBY] They'll die. It's murder. [*He goes to the door and turns sadly to* FISBY *again*] Please take care of my beans.

[*He exits*]

PURDY: [*Turns back to* FISBY] Now! Is the schoolhouse finished?

FISBY: [*Sighs*] No, sir.

PURDY: *Why* isn't it finished?

FISBY: It isn't finished, sir, because it isn't started.

PURDY: I have a splitting headache, Fisby. I ask you not to provoke me needlessly. Now, where is the schoolhouse?

FISBY: I never built it.

PURDY: Don't stand there and tell me you never built it. I sent the lumber down two months ago.

FISBY: [*Impressed*] Is it *that* long, sir?

PURDY: What did you do with the lumber I sent?

FISBY: Well, I built a teahouse.

PURDY: [*Stares at him*] I don't suppose you have any aspirin here?

FISBY: No, sir, I haven't.

PURDY: Now, sit down, Fisby. I want to be fair. [FISBY *sits down*] I'm a patient man. When I run into something that defies reason, I like to find the reason. [*Explodes*] What in the name of Occupation do you mean by saying you built a *teahouse* instead of a *schoolhouse!*

FISBY: It's a little hard to explain, sir. Everybody in the village wanted one . . . and Lotus Blossom needed it for her work.

PURDY: And just what is your relationship with this woman?

FISBY: Well, she was a present. So to speak. She's a geisha girl—after a fashion.

PURDY: You built this teahouse—this place for her to ply her trade —with lumber belonging to the Army of Occupation of the United States Government?

FISBY: Well, it just seemed like lumber at the time.

PURDY: Fisby, are you operating a house of prostitution here on Government rice?

FISBY: No, sir! Geishas aren't what you think.

PURDY: Don't tell me what to think. Army Intelligence warned me I'd find something mighty peculiar going on in Tobiki.

FISBY: What's Army Intelligence got to do with it, sir?

PURDY: You're not very cunning, Fisby. With all the Occupation money on the island finding its way to this village, did you think it wouldn't come to the attention of Intelligence?

FISBY: Oh.

PURDY: Why did you do it, Fisby, why!

FISBY: Well, Lotus Blossom had to have a place to teach the Ladies' League how to become geishas and—

PURDY: Fisby! You mean to say you've turned all the decent women of this village into professional . . . [*He slumps into the chair*] How could you sink to such depths, man!

FISBY: I was only giving in to what the majority wanted, sir.

PURDY: I don't doubt that statement—not at all. It is a sad thing that it took a war to convince me that most of the human race is degenerate. Thank God I come from a country where the air is clean, where the wind is fresh, where—

FISBY: [*Interrupts*] For heaven's sake, sir, would you please listen to me instead of yourself! There is not a thing goes on in that teahouse that your mother couldn't watch.

PURDY: [*Leaps to his feet and points a warning finger*] You be careful how you use my mother's name, Fisby.

FISBY: Well, *my* mother then. I swear there's nothing immoral about our teahouse.

PURDY: Then answer me this. What is bringing all that Occupation money to this particular village? There is only one thing that attracts that kind of money.

FISBY: Well, evidently there are two things.

PURDY: And if it isn't honor that you sell here, what is it?

FISBY: [*Sighs unhappily*] We . . . make things.

PURDY: What?

FISBY: Mats . . . and hats . . . and cricket cages.

PURDY: One hundred and fifty thousand yen finds its way to this village every month. You can't convince me that the American soldier is spending that much on "cricket cages."

FISBY: Well, naturally . . . not all of it.

[*The telephone rings.* FISBY *looks at it apprehensively*]

PURDY: Answer it.

FISBY: [*Pauses*] It's nothing important, sir.

PURDY: It might be for me. Answer it.

FISBY: [*Airily*] Oh, it rings all day, sir. Pay no attention.

PURDY: Then I'll *answer* it! [*He picks up the telephone.* FISBY *covers his face*] Hello? *What* do you want? Who is this? Well, Commander Myers, I think you have the wrong connection. This is not a brewery. Yes . . . yes . . . yes! [*He turns to look at* FISBY] Oh . . . I see. I see. I see.

[*He hangs up. He turns to* FISBY, *who smiles weakly*]

FISBY: It was the only thing we could make that anyone wanted to buy, sir.

PURDY: Brandy! [*Sadly*] I don't know which is worse. Putting your country in the white slave trade or the wholesale liquor business. Congress will have to decide.

FISBY: We've the most prosperous village on the island, sir.

PURDY: This ends my Army career. I promised Mrs. Purdy I'd come out a general. You've broken a fine woman's heart, Fisby.

FISBY: You said to make the village self-supporting, sir.

PURDY: I didn't tell you to encourage lewdness and drunkenness. You've sullied the reputation of your nation and all the tears—

FISBY: All right, sir, shall I kill myself?

PURDY: Oh, don't minimize this. You don't know the enemy's genius for propaganda.

FISBY: Does anyone have to know, sir? We're doing all right.

PURDY: [*Explodes*] Yes, they have to know! I requested an investigation myself. I've notified the Inspector General. Now I'll have to radio the whole story to Washington.

FISBY: Oh.

PURDY: [*Calmer*] Well, what have you done with all this money you've made so dishonestly?

FISBY: Banked it in Seattle.

PURDY: Oh, that's despicable—making a personal fortune off the labor of these ignorant people.

FISBY: I haven't touched a cent for myself, sir. It's been deposited in the name of the Tobiki Cooperative. The whole village are equal partners. Share and share alike.

PURDY: [*Leaps up*] That's *Communism!*

FISBY: Is it?

PURDY: [*Sinks down again*] I'll be lucky to get out of this war a private. [*He is a beaten man*] Well, there is only one thing for me to do.

FISBY: What is that, sir?

PURDY: First, you are to consider yourself under technical arrest. You will proceed to H.Q. at once to await court-martial.

FISBY: Yes, sir.

PURDY: [*Steps to the door*] Gregovich! [*He turns back to* FISBY] I must go on to Awasi this afternoon on an inspection tour. But before I leave, I intend to wipe this stain from our country's honor.

[SERGEANT GREGOVICH *enters and salutes*]

GREGOVICH: You called, sir?

PURDY: I did. We have some business to attend to here before going on to Awasi.

GREGOVICH: Yes, sir. I'm glad to hear it. [*He turns to* FISBY] May I congratulate you on what you've done to this village, sir. It's a dream.

FISBY: Thank you, Sergeant.

PURDY: It is an alcoholic dream. It is one vast distillery. I want you to take a detail and some axes and smash every still in this village.

GREGOVICH: Destroy them?

PURDY: Beyond repair. I want you to take another detail and rip down that teahouse.

GREGOVICH: But, Colonel—

PURDY: Pile the lumber beside the warehouse. That is an order. Do you understand?

GREGOVICH: Yes, sir!

[*As he turns to follow orders,* FISBY *sinks into his chair and the scene blacks out quickly*]

CURTAIN

SCENE THREE

Teahouse of the August Moon.
A few hours later.
All the panels are down. Behind the scenes can be heard the destruction of the stills and the dismantling of the teahouse. SAKINI *comes out from the wings and crosses down to the footlights. He flinches at the sound of an ax falling on wood.*

SAKINI: [*Sadly*] Oh, no comment.

[*He walks back into the wings as all the panels are raised simultaneously. Only the frame of the teahouse has been spared. The paper panels have disappeared, the pagoda roof is gone with its tinkling bells. There are no colored lanterns and no dwarf pines to grace the path. The bare supports stand stark and ugly. Resting at the edge of the frame is a wheelbarrow.* LOTUS BLOSSOM *is collecting the last of her possessions. She takes a brass brazier down to place in the wheelbarrow. Then she stands with her back to the audience surveying all that remains of the teahouse.* FISBY *comes on, and, seeing* LOTUS BLOSSOM, *hesitates. Then he crosses to stand beside her. He takes her hand, and the two of them stand looking at the ruins.* LOTUS BLOSSOM *walks to the center of the teahouse and sits on the bare floor.* FISBY *comes up and sits on the floor facing her. She goes through the ceremony of pouring him an imaginary cup of tea.* FISBY *accepts with mock formality. As he takes the cup and pretends to drink it,* LOTUS BLOSSOM *covers her face with her hands.* FISBY *sits watching her mutely*]

SAKINI: [*Entering*] Jeep all loaded, boss.

FISBY: I'll be along in a minute.

SAKINI: Oh, pretty soon have nice schoolhouse here.

FISBY: [*Bitterly*] Pentagon-shaped.

SAKINI: Not be too bad. You take Lotus Blossom with you?

FISBY: No.

SAKINI: What happen to her then?

FISBY: What would have happened to her if we'd never come along?

SAKINI: Not know. Maybe someday she meet nice man and give up Geisha Guild.

FISBY: Ask her if there is anything I can do for her before I go.

SAKINI: [*Comes up to stand behind them*] Nanika iitai?

LOTUS BLOSSOM: [*Softly*] Fu-san, watashito kekkon shite chodai.

SAKINI: [*Scolding*] Sonna bakana koto.

LOTUS BLOSSOM: [*Persistent*] Iikara hayaku itte!

FISBY: What does she want?

SAKINI: Oh, that crazy Lotus Blossom. She want you to marry her.

FISBY: Why should she want to marry me?

SAKINI: She think you nicest man she ever see, boss.

FISBY: Tell her that I am clumsy, that I seem to have a gift for destruction. That I'd disillusion her as I have disillusioned her people.

SAKINI: Kokai suruyo.

LOTUS BLOSSOM: Ikitai noyo. Amerika ni. Ikitai noyo.

SAKINI: She say she think she like to go to America. There everybody happy. Sit around and drink tea while machines do work.

FISBY: She wouldn't like it, Sakini. I should hate to see her wearing sweaters and sports shoes and looking like an American looking like an Oriental.

SAKINI: But she want to be an American, boss. She never see an American she not like, boss.

FISBY: Some of them wouldn't like her, Sakini. In the small town where I live, there'd be some who would make her unhappy.

SAKINI: Why, boss?

FISBY: She'd be different.

SAKINI: Dame dayo.

LOTUS BLOSSOM: [Takes FISBY's hand] Sonna koto naiwa, Ameri-katte minshu shugi desumono ne.

SAKINI: She say not believe that. In America everybody love everybody. Everybody help everybody; that's democracy.

FISBY: No. That's faith. Explain to her that democracy is only a method—an ideal system for people to get together. But that unfortunately . . . the people who get together . . . are not always ideal.

SAKINI: That's very hard to explain, boss. She girl in love. She just want to hear pretty things.

FISBY: Then tell her that I love what she is, and that it would be wrong to change that. To impose my way of life on her.

SAKINI: Tassha dene!

FISBY: Tell her that I shall never forget her. Nor this village. Tell her that in the autumn of my life—on the other side of the world —when an August moon rises from the east, I will remember what was beautiful in my youth, and what I was wise enough to leave beautiful.

SAKINI: Issho wasurenai kara ne. Mangetsu no yoru niwa anata o omoidashimasu.

LOTUS BLOSSOM: [Remains silent a moment] Watashi mo Fu-san no koto issho wasurenaiwa. Fu-san no koto uta ni shite, Okinawaju ni hirome masu.

SAKINI: She say she always remember you, boss. She say she guess maybe she be what she is—first-class geisha girl. She want you to know she make up long song-story about you to sing in teahouse. And maybe hundred years from now, you be famous all over Okinawa.

FISBY: [*Rises*] I'd like that.

LOTUS BLOSSOM: [*Rises*] Iinoyo. Fu-san damedemo Seiko-san ga irun dakara.

SAKINI: She say since you not marry her, maybe you suggest some-body here. [FISBY *laughs*] She say that Mr. Seiko been looking at her like sick goat. She say what you think of him?

FISBY: Well, he took an awful beating just so he could carry her sweet potatoes.

LOTUS BLOSSOM: Fu-san, Seiko-san iito omouno?

SAKINI: She say you think she ought to marry him?

FISBY: I think she ought to decide for herself.

[*And* MR. SEIKO *enters. He is dressed in his white suit and his hair is slicked down tight. He crosses to* LOTUS BLOSSOM. *They all turn to look at him*]

SEIKO: [*Bows to* LOTUS BLOSSOM] A, boku, oshimasho.

SAKINI: [*To* FISBY] Mr. Seiko tell Lotus Blossom he sure like to push her wheelbarrow for her.

LOTUS BLOSSOM: Iikara sakini itte chodai.

SAKINI: She say oh, all right, but not to think that means she's his property.

[MR. SEIKO *beams like a schoolboy and, picking up the han-dles of the wheelbarrow, he trots offstage with* LOTUS BLOS-SOM's *possessions. She turns to* FISBY *and hands him her fan*]

LOTUS BLOSSOM: Korede aizu shite chodai. Soremade watashi doko-nimo ikimasen kara.

SAKINI: She say she go now, but you still her boss. She not go until you give signal.

[FISBY *takes the fan and puts it before his eyes. Without waiting for him to drop it,* LOTUS BLOSSOM *runs off right. When he lowers the fan, he knows she's gone. He sits down on the platform that had been the teahouse veranda*]

SAKINI: You go now, boss?

FISBY: Shortly.

SAKINI: Since you not take Lotus Blossom, maybe you take me, boss?

FISBY: Major McEvoy is coming down to take charge. You'll work with him.

SAKINI: Would rather work with you.

FISBY: You'll like Major McEvoy.

SAKINI: I'll work for you for half price, boss.

FISBY: Major McEvoy will need your help in getting this village on its feet again.

SAKINI: You very hard man to bargain with, boss. If you want, I work for rice rations only.

FISBY: No.

SAKINI: You mean you going to make me work for *nothing*, boss?

FISBY: I mean *yes*, you're *not* going to work for me at all. And you belong here.

SAKINI: You know what I think happen when Americans leave Okinawa?

FISBY: What?

SAKINI: [*Grins*] I think maybe we use pentagon-shaped school-house for teahouse.

[FISBY *laughs. He gives* SAKINI *a slap on the shoulder*]

FISBY: Good-bye, Sakini, you're a rare rascal and I'll miss you.

SAKINI: Good-bye, boss.

[FISBY *starts off left. He has gone halfway when* SAKINI *calls*]

Boss—

FISBY: [*Stops*] Yes?

SAKINI: You not failure.

FISBY: [*Laughs*] I'll tell you something, Sakini. I used to worry a lot about not being a big success. I must have felt as you people felt at always being conquered. Well, now I'm not so sure who's the conqueror and who the conquered.

SAKINI: Not understand, boss.

FISBY: It's just that I've learned from Tobiki the wisdom of gracious acceptance. I don't want to be a world leader. I'm making peace with myself somewhere between my ambitions and my limitations.

SAKINI: That's good?

FISBY: It's a step backward in the right direction. [*He throws* SAKINI *a salute*] Take care.

   [*He walks off and* SAKINI *watches him go. Then, with a sigh,* SAKINI *turns to survey the skeleton of the teahouse. The silence is broken by the stormy entrance of* COLONEL PURDY]

PURDY: Sakini! Where is Captain Fisby?

SAKINI: [*Points*] Just leaving, boss.

PURDY: [*Shouts*] Fisby! Fisby! [*Gestures frantically*] Come back here at once! [*He goes to the platform and sinks down gasping*] I'm not in shape—too much paper work. [FISBY *returns from the left*] Where in hell have you been, Fisby? I've been looking all over for you.

FISBY: I'm ready to leave, sir.

PURDY: You can't leave. You've got to stay here. You've got to help me, Fisby.

FISBY: Help doing what, sir?

PURDY: Pulling this village back together again. All hell has broken loose, Fisby. [*He sits down to wipe his brow*] Where is Gregovich!

FISBY: Breaking up the last of the stills, sir.

PURDY: Oh, *no!*

[*He holds his head*]

FISBY: What's happened, sir?

PURDY: I radioed the report to Washington. Some fool senator mis-understood. He's using this village as an example of American "get-up-and-go" in the recovery program. The Pentagon is boasting. Congress is crowing. We're all over the papers.

FISBY: But that's wonderful, sir.

PURDY: No, it's not wonderful. A Congressional Committee is flying over to study our methods. They are bringing in photographers for a magazine spread. Today, Fisby, today!

FISBY: Oh, that's bad, sir.

PURDY: [*Wails*] Gregovich!

FISBY: Isn't there any way to stall them off, sir? Quarantine the place or something?

PURDY: You can't quarantine a congressman. They have immunity or something. [*He takes* FISBY *by the jacket*] Fisby, help me. I don't ask it for my sake. I ask it for Mrs. Purdy. I could be a brigadier yet.

[*Before* FISBY *can answer,* GREGOVICH *comes in from the left and salutes*]

GREGOVICH: You called, sir?

PURDY: [*Hurries over to him*] Gregovich! Gregovich! You haven't destroyed all the stills, have you, Gregovich? No, of course you haven't.

GREGOVICH: Yes, sir, I have. I carried out orders to the letter.

PURDY: [*Turns away shouting*] Why can't someone disobey orders once in a while! What has happened to the American spirit of rebellion! [GREGOVICH *hiccups, smiles sillily and folds up on the floor.* FISBY *and* PURDY *race over to kneel beside him*] Sunstroke?

FISBY: Potato brandy.

PURDY: Sergeant, wake up. Do you hear me? That's an order.

FISBY: I'm afraid he's passed out, sir.

PURDY: It's desertion. I need every man. Gregovich, get to your feet!

[*With* FISBY's *help he gets* GREGOVICH *to his feet*]

GREGOVICH: Sorry, sir.

PURDY: I want to ask you some questions. Stop weaving.

GREGOVICH: *You're* weaving sir. *I'm* perfectly still.

PURDY: You smell like a brewery.

GREGOVICH: I fell in a vat.

PURDY: You got drunk.

GREGOVICH: No, sir. I fell in a vat. Naturally, I had to open my mouth to yell for help.

PURDY: Go to the office and sober up at once.

GREGOVICH: Yes, sir.

[*He salutes with a happy smile, jogs off*]

PURDY: I'm a sinking ship . . . scuttled by my own men.

[*He sinks.* SAKINI, *who has been sitting with arms folded and a fatuous grin on his face, speaks up*]

SAKINI: Colonel Purdy?

PURDY: Don't bother me.

SAKINI: Stills not all destroyed.

PURDY: I haven't got time to . . . What did you say?

SAKINI: We not born yesterday. Get sergeant drunk . . . and give him water barrels to break.

PURDY: Sakini, my friend, you're not just saying that to make me feel better?

SAKINI: Oh, stills all good as ever. Production not cease yet.

FISBY: [*Fondly*] You really are a rogue, Sakini.

PURDY: No . . . he's really an American. He has get-up-and-go.

FISBY: Sakini, if everybody in the village worked together . . . how long would it take to rebuild the teahouse?

PURDY: We don't ask the impossible.

SAKINI: Oh, maybe three minutes . . . maybe five.

PURDY: That's impossible.

SAKINI: We not destroy. Just take away and hide. You watch now, boss. [*He turns and calls*] Oi, mo iiyo, mo iiyo. [*From the wings, right and left, the* VILLAGERS *steps out*] Oi, haba, haba. [*The* VILLAGERS *respond with happy cries and dash off*] Country that has been invaded many times soon master art of hiding things.

PURDY: You think we can pull it off, Sakini?

SAKINI: You watch now.

[*And even as he speaks, the sections of the teahouse are carried in and the swift work of putting them together progresses before our eyes. Music is heard in the background. The pagoda roof with its tinkling bells is lowered. The dwarf pines and the arched bridge are brought back. The colored panels are slipped into place and the lanterns are hung.* LOTUS BLOSSOM *comes on with flowers which she arranges.* SAKINI *snaps his fingers and the August moon is magically turned on in the sky. When the final lantern is hung,* MC LEAN *comes in. He stops. His mouth falls open*]

PURDY: Close your mouth, Captain—haven't you ever seen a cha ya before? [*He turns back to* FISBY] Fisby, this is a land of adventure . . . a land of jade and spices . . . of Chinese junks and river pirates. . . . Makes a man's blood pound.

FISBY: Colonel . . . I consider what you just said pure . . . [*He pauses*] . . . poetry.

PURDY: Thank you . . . thank you, boy. [*He sighs ecstatically*] It's the mystery of the Orient.

FISBY: It's beautiful. Simply beautiful.

PURDY: There's only one thing wrong. It needs a sign to tell people what it is. And I think we ought to put a sign up over there naming this Grace Purdy Avenue. And another sign . . .

FISBY: Colonel Purdy. Won't you have a cup of tea? [*He takes his arm. As he propels him toward the teahouse, he speaks over his shoulder to* SAKINI] Twenty Star for the colonel, Sakini.

[*As the bamboo panels begin to descend on the teahouse,* SAKINI *steps down to the audience*]

SAKINI:
Little story now concluded.
History of world unfinished.
Lovely ladies . . . kind gentlemen—
Go home to ponder.
What was true at the beginning remains true.
Pain makes man think.
Thought makes man wise.
Wisdom makes life endurable.
Our play has ended.
May August moon bring gentle sleep.

[*He bows*]

THE CURTAIN FALLS

THE DIARY OF ANNE FRANK

Frances Goodrich and Albert Hackett

*(Based on the Book
Anne Frank: The Diary of a Young Girl)*

CAUTION: Professionals and amateurs are hereby warned that *The Diary of Anne Frank,* being fully protected under the Copyright Laws of the United States of America, the British Commonwealth, including the Dominion of Canada, and all other countries of the International Copyright Union and the Universal Copyright Convention, is subject to royalty. All rights, including professional, amateur, motion picture, recitation, lecturing, public reading, radio and television broadcasting, and the rights of translation into foreign languages, are strictly reserved. Particular emphasis is laid on the question of readings, permission for which must be secured from the author's agent in writing.

The stock performance rights of *The Diary of Anne Frank* are controlled by Samuel French, Inc., 25 West 45th Street, New York, New York 10036, without whose permission in writing no performance of it may be made.

The amateur acting rights of *The Diary of Anne Frank* are controlled exclusively by the Dramatists Play Service, Inc., 440 Park Avenue South, New York, New York 10016, without whose permission in writing no amateur performance of it may be made.

The guidance of Mr. Otto H. Frank, Dr. L. de Jong, Miss Lidia Winkle, and The Netherlands State Institute for War Documentation, Amsterdam, is gratefully acknowledged.

Frances Goodrich and Albert Hackett

Not only was *The Diary of Anne Frank* the dramatic highlight of the 1955–56 Broadway season, it also garnered the theatre's three top honors: a Tony Award, the Pulitzer Prize, and the New York Drama Critics' Circle Award. Dramatized by Frances Goodrich and Albert Hackett (Mr. and Mrs. Hackett) from the moving and widely read book *Anne Frank: The Diary of a Young Girl*, published in an English translation in America in 1952, it ran for 717 capacity performances.

The critics extolled it as "a monument to the unconquerable spirit of Anne Frank, and as a reminder of man's inhumanity to man."

John McClain of the New York *Journal-American* called it "a searing study of the suspense and torture visited upon a group of Jewish people hiding out from the Nazis in Amsterdam during World War II."

Walter Kerr reported in the New York *Herald Tribune*: "Frances Goodrich and Albert Hackett have fashioned a wonderfully sensitive and theatrically craftsmanlike narrative out of the real-life legacy left us by a spirited and straightforward Jewish girl."

"There is so much beauty, warm humor, gentle pity and cold horror in *The Diary of Anne Frank*," wrote John Chapman in the New York *Daily News*, "that it is difficult to imagine how this play could be contained in one set on one stage."

It was a view confirmed by other members of the press corps who described it as "theatre at its powerful best . . . which endows the deeper grief of its subject with a shining and even triumphant humanity . . . It is an agonizingly correct restoration to speaking life of a fated young girl's noble diary . . . yet amidst such uncertainty and danger, the spirit of man, including his comic spirit, is by no means extinguished!"

Brilliantly directed by Garson Kanin and performed by a remarkable company, Brooks Atkinson observed in his foreword to the original published edition of the play: "Combining instinct for the theatre with precise knowledge of the theme, Mr. Kanin was able to cast the play flawlessly. When it opened in the autumn of 1955, the performance was especially notable for two of the actors who were in it. Joseph Schildkraut, who played the part of Anne's father, gave the performance a solid underpinning by his quiet command of the whole situation and his restrained gentleness. In her first Broadway part, Susan Strasberg, seventeen years of age, played Anne with mercurial spontaneity and purity of soul that gave the performance exaltation and beauty. Like the work as a whole, her performance was overflowing with life but never self-conscious. The play deserved this sort of acting.

"Through every line of it shines the spirit of Anne Frank. For the most part, it is a smiling spirit. By preserving it so delicately, Mr. and Mrs. Hackett have let a clean, young mind address the conscience of the world."

According to Abe Laufe in his highly informative book *Anatomy of a Hit:* "The popularity of *The Diary of Anne Frank* was not limited to New York audiences. In other cities in the United States and in European countries, the play attracted audiences, for it was effective and emotionally sound drama and engendered sympathy for the victims hopelessly trapped in their attic. The drama was extremely effective in Germany . . . Critics who saw both the New York and German productions reported that the impact upon spectators in Germany was even greater than in New York; for the stunned audiences, at the end of the play, did not applaud and left the theatre silently."

Miss Goodrich was born in Belleville, New Jersey, and studied at Vassar College and the New York School of Social Service. Mr. Hackett was born in New York City, the son of professional parents (the family ran and acted in a well-known stock company in Philadelphia) and was educated privately and at the Professional Children's School. Both began their theatrical careers as actors.

As a writing team, Frances Goodrich and Albert Hackett achieved a productive and eminently successful record. The first result of their collaboration to be presented on Broadway was the comedy *Up Pops the Devil* (1930). Later, it was to be the basis of the musical *Everybody's Welcome,* which introduced the song "As Time Goes By." Other plays that followed were *Bridal Wise* (1932); *The Great Big Doorstep* (1942); and, of course, *The Diary of Anne Frank.*

As screen writers, they have a truly imposing list of films to their credit, including: *The Thin Man; Ah, Wilderness!; Naughty Marietta; Rose Marie; After the Thin Man; Lady in the Dark; Father of the Bride; Too Young to Kiss; It's a Wonderful Life; In the Good Old Summertime; Gaby; The Pirate; Father's Little Dividend; The Virginian; The Long, Long, Trailer; A Certain Smile; Easter Parade; Seven Brides for Seven Brothers; The Diary of Anne Frank; and Five Finger Exercise.*

In 1950, Mr. and Mrs. Hackett received the Screen Writers' Guild Award for their screenplay *Father of the Bride* and once again, in 1954, for *Seven Brides for Seven Brothers.*

THE DIARY OF ANNE FRANK was first presented by Kermit Bloomgarden on October 5, 1955, at the Cort Theatre, New York. The cast was as follows:

MR. FRANK	*Joseph Schildkraut*
MIEP	*Gloria Jones*
MRS. VAN DAAN	*Dennie Moore*
MR. VAN DAAN	*Lou Jacobi*
PETER VAN DAAN	*David Levin*
MRS. FRANK	*Gusti Huber*
MARGOT FRANK	*Eva Rubinstein*
ANNE FRANK	*Susan Strasberg*
MR. KRALER	*Clinton Sundberg*
MR. DUSSEL	*Jack Gilford*

Directed by Garson Kanin
Production Designed by Boris Aronson
Costumes by Helene Pons
Lighting by Leland Watson

THE TIME: *During the years of World War II and immediately thereafter.*

THE PLACE: *Amsterdam*

ACT ONE

SCENE ONE

The scene remains the same throughout the play. It is the top floor of a warehouse and office building in Amsterdam, Holland. The sharply peaked roof of the building is outlined against a sea of other rooftops, stretching away into the distance. Nearby is the belfry of a church tower, the Wester-toren, whose carillon rings out the hours. Occasionally faint sounds float up from below: the voices of children playing in the street, the tramp of marching feet, a boat whistle from the canal.

The three rooms of the top floor and a small attic space above are exposed to our view. The largest of the rooms is in the center, with two small rooms, slightly raised, on either side. On the right is a bathroom, out of sight. A narrow steep flight of stairs at the back leads up to the attic. The rooms are sparsely furnished with a few chairs, cots, a table or two. The windows are painted over, or covered with makeshift blackout curtains. In the main room there is a sink, a gas ring for cooking and a woodburning stove for warmth.

The room on the left is hardly more than a closet. There is a skylight in the sloping ceiling. Directly under this room is a small steep stairwell, with steps leading down to a door. This is the only entrance from the building below. When the door is opened we see that it has been concealed on the outer side by a bookcase attached to it.

The curtain rises on an empty stage. It is late afternoon November, 1945.

The rooms are dusty, the curtains in rags. Chairs and tables are overturned.

The door at the foot of the small stairwell swings open. MR. FRANK *comes up the steps into view. He is a gentle, cultured*

European in his middle years. There is still a trace of a German accent in his speech.
He stands looking slowly around, making a supreme effort at self-control. He is weak, ill. His clothes are threadbare.
After a second he drops his rucksack on the couch and moves slowly about. He opens the door to one of the smaller rooms, and then abruptly closes it again, turning away. He goes to the window at the back, looking off at the Westertoren as its carillon strikes the hour of six, then he moves restlessly on.
From the street below we hear the sound of a barrel organ and children's voices at play. There is a many-colored scarf hanging from a nail. MR. FRANK *takes it, putting it around his neck. As he starts back for his rucksack, his eye is caught by something lying on the floor. It is a woman's white glove. He holds it in his hand and suddenly all of his self-control is gone. He breaks down, crying.*
We hear footsteps on the stairs. MIEP GIES *comes up, looking for* MR. FRANK. MIEP *is a Dutch girl of about twenty-two. She wears a coat and hat, ready to go home. She is pregnant. Her attitude toward* MR. FRANK *is protective, compassionate.*

MIEP: Are you all right, Mr. Frank?

MR. FRANK: [*Quickly controlling himself*] Yes, Miep, yes.

MIEP: Everyone in the office has gone home . . . It's after six. [*Then pleading*] Don't stay up here, Mr. Frank. What's the use of torturing yourself like this?

MR. FRANK: I've come to say good-bye . . . I'm leaving here, Miep.

MIEP: What do you mean? Where are you going? Where?

MR. FRANK: I don't know yet. I haven't decided.

MIEP: Mr. Frank, you can't leave here! This is your home! Amsterdam is your home. Your business is here, waiting for you . . . You're needed here . . . Now that the war is over, there are things that . . .

MR. FRANK: I can't stay in Amsterdam, Miep. It has too many memories for me. Everywhere there's something . . . the house we lived in . . . the school . . . that street organ playing out there

. . . I'm not the person you used to know, Miep. I'm a bitter old man. [*Breaking off*] Forgive me. I shouldn't speak to you like this . . . after all that you did for us . . . the suffering . . .

MIEP: No. No. It wasn't suffering. You can't say we suffered.

[*As she speaks, she straightens a chair which is overturned*]

MR. FRANK: I know what you went through, you and Mr. Kraler. I'll remember it as long as I live. [*He gives one last look around*] Come, Miep.

[*He starts for the steps, then remembers his rucksack, going back to get it*]

MIEP: [*Hurrying up to a cupboard*] Mr. Frank, did you see? There are some of your papers here. [*She brings a bundle of papers to him*] We found them in a heap of rubbish on the floor after . . . after you left.

MR. FRANK: Burn them.

[*He opens his rucksack to put the glove in it*]

MIEP: But, Mr. Frank, there are letters, notes . . .

MR. FRANK: Burn them. All of them.

MIEP: Burn *this?*

[*She hands him a paperbound notebook*]

MR. FRANK: [*Quietly*] Anne's diary. [*He opens the diary and begins to read*] "Monday, the sixth of July, nineteen forty-two." [*To* MIEP] Nineteen forty-two. Is it possible, Miep? . . . Only three years ago. [*As he continues his reading, he sits down on the couch*] "Dear Diary, since you and I are going to be great friends, I will start by telling you about myself. My name is Anne Frank. I am thirteen years old. I was born in Germany the twelfth of June, nineteen twenty-nine. As my family is Jewish, we emigrated to Holland when Hitler came to power."

[*As* MR. FRANK *reads on, another voice joins his, as if coming from the air. It is* ANNE'S VOICE]

MR. FRANK AND ANNE: "My father started a business, importing spice and herbs. Things went well for us until nineteen forty.

Then the war came, and the Dutch capitulation, followed by the arrival of the Germans. Then things got very bad for the Jews."

[MR. FRANK'S VOICE *dies out.* ANNE'S VOICE *continues alone. The lights dim slowly to darkness. The curtain falls on the scene*]

ANNE'S VOICE: You could not do this and you could not do that. They forced Father out of his business. We had to wear yellow stars. I had to turn in my bike. I couldn't go to a Dutch school any more. I couldn't go to the movies, or ride in an automobile, or even on a streetcar, and a million other things. But somehow we children still managed to have fun. Yesterday Father told me we were going into hiding. Where, he wouldn't say. At five o'clock this morning Mother woke me and told me to hurry and get dressed. I was to put on as many clothes as I could. It would look too suspicious if we walked along carrying suitcases. It wasn't until we were on our way that I learned where we were going. Our hiding place was to be upstairs in the building where Father used to have his business. Three other people were coming in with us . . . the Van Daans and their son Peter . . . Father knew the Van Daans but we had never met them . . .

[*During the last lines the curtain rises on the scene. The lights dim on.* ANNE'S VOICE *fades out*]

SCENE TWO

It is early morning, July, 1942. The rooms are bare, as before, but they are now clean and orderly.
MR. VAN DAAN, *a tall, portly man in his late forties, is in the main room, pacing up and down, nervously smoking a cigarette. His clothes and overcoat are expensive and well cut.*
MRS. VAN DAAN *sits on the couch, clutching her possessions, a hatbox, bags, etc. She is a pretty woman in her early forties. She wears a fur coat over her other clothes.*
PETER VAN DAAN *is standing at the window of the room on the right, looking down at the street below. He is a shy, awkward*

boy of sixteen. He wears a cap, a raincoat, and long Dutch trousers, like "plus fours." At his feet is a black case, a carrier for his cat.
The yellow Star of David is conspicuous on all of their clothes.

MRS. VAN DAAN: [*Rising, nervous, excited*] Something's happened to them! I know it!

MR. VAN DAAN: Now, Kerli!

MRS. VAN DAAN: Mr. Frank said they'd be here at seven o'clock. He said . . .

MR. VAN DAAN: They have two miles to walk. You can't expect . . .

MRS. VAN DAAN: They've been picked up. That's what's happened. They've been taken . . .

[MR. VAN DAAN *indicates that he hears someone coming*]

MR. VAN DAAN: You see?

[PETER *takes up his carrier and his schoolbag, etc., and goes into the main room as* MR. FRANK *comes up the stairwell from below.* MR. FRANK *looks much younger now. His movements are brisk, his manner confident. He wears an overcoat and carries his hat and a small cardboard box. He crosses to the* VAN DAANS, *shaking hands with each of them*]

MR. FRANK: Mrs. Van Daan, Mr. Van Daan, Peter. [*Then, in explanation of their lateness*] There were too many of the Green Police on the streets . . . we had to take the long way around.

[*Up the steps come* MARGOT FRANK, MRS. FRANK, MIEP (*not pregnant now*) *and* MR. KRALER. *All of them carry bags, packages, and so forth. The Star of David is conspicuous on all of the* FRANKS' *clothing.* MARGOT *is eighteen, beautiful, quiet, shy.* MRS. FRANK *is a young mother, gently bred, reserved. She, like* MR. FRANK, *has a slight German accent.* MR. KRALER *is a Dutchman, dependable, kindly.*
As MR. KRALER *and* MIEP *go upstage to put down their parcels,* MRS. FRANK *turns back to call* ANNE]

MRS. FRANK: Anne?

[ANNE *comes running up the stairs. She is thirteen, quick in her movements, interested in everything, mercurial in her emotions. She wears a cape, long wool socks and carries a schoolbag*]

MR. FRANK: [*Introducing them*] My wife, Edith. Mr. and Mrs. Van Daan [MRS. FRANK *hurries over, shaking hands with them*] . . . their son, Peter . . . my daughters, Margot and Anne.

[ANNE *gives a polite little curtsy as she shakes* MR. VAN DAAN'*s hand. Then she immediately starts off on a tour of investigation of her new home, going upstairs to the attic room.* MIEP *and* MR. KRALER *are putting the various things they have brought on the shelves*]

MR. KRALER: I'm sorry there is still so much confusion.

MR. FRANK: Please. Don't think of it. After all, we'll have plenty of leisure to arrange everything ourselves.

MIEP: [*To* MRS. FRANK] We put the stores of food you sent in here. Your drugs are here . . . soap, linen here.

MRS. FRANK: Thank you, Miep.

MIEP: I made up the beds . . . the way Mr. Frank and Mr. Kraler said. [*She starts out*] Forgive me. I have to hurry. I've got to go to the other side of town to get some ration books for you.

MRS. VAN DAAN: Ration books? If they see our names on ration books, they'll know we're here.

MR. KRALER: There isn't any-thing . . .

MIEP: Don't worry. Your names won't be on them. [*As she hurries out*] I'll be up later.

MR. FRANK: Thank you, Miep.

MRS. FRANK: [*To* MR. KRALER] It's illegal, then, the ration books? We've never done anything illegal.

MR. FRANK: We won't be living here exactly according to regulations.

[*As* MR. KRALER *reassures* MRS. FRANK, *he takes various small things, such as matches, soap, etc., from his pockets, handing them to her*]

MR. KRALER: This isn't the black market, Mrs. Frank. This is what we call the white market . . . helping all of the hundreds and hundreds who are hiding out in Amsterdam.

[*The carillon is heard playing the quarter-hour before eight.* MR. KRALER *looks at his watch.* ANNE *stops at the window as she comes down the stairs*]

ANNE: It's the Westertoren!

MR. KRALER: I must go. I must be out of here and downstairs in the office before the workmen get here. [*He starts for the stairs leading out*] Miep or I, or both of us, will be up each day to bring you food and news and find out what your needs are. Tomorrow I'll get you a better bolt for the door at the foot of the stairs. It needs a bolt that you can throw yourself and open only at our signal. [*To* MR. FRANK] Oh . . . You'll tell them about the noise?

MR. FRANK: I'll tell them.

MR. KRALER: Good-bye then for the moment. I'll come up again, after the workmen leave.

MR. FRANK: Good-bye, Mr. Kraler.

MRS. FRANK: [*Shaking his hand*] How can we thank you?

[*The others murmur their good-byes*]

MR. KRALER: I never thought I'd live to see the day when a man like Mr. Frank would have to go into hiding. When you think—

[*He breaks off, going out.* MR. FRANK *follows him down the steps, bolting the door after him. In the interval before he returns,* PETER *goes over to* MARGOT, *shaking hands with her. As* MR. FRANK *comes back up the steps,* MRS. FRANK *questions him anxiously*]

MRS. FRANK: What did he mean, about the noise?

MR. FRANK: First let us take off some of these clothes.

[*They all start to take off garment after garment. On each of*

their coats, sweaters, blouses, suits, dresses, is another yellow
Star of David. MR. *and* MRS. FRANK *are underdressed quite*
simply. The others wear several things, sweaters, extra dresses,
bathrobes, aprons, nightgowns, etc.]

MR. VAN DAAN: It's a wonder we weren't arrested, walking along the
streets . . . Petronella with a fur coat in July . . . and that cat of
Peter's crying all the way.

ANNE: [*As she is removing a pair of panties*] A cat?

MRS. FRANK: [*Shocked*] Anne, please!

ANNE: It's all right. I've got on three more.

[*She pulls off two more. Finally, as they have all removed*
their surplus clothes, they look to MR. FRANK, *waiting for him*
to speak]

MR. FRANK: Now. About the noise. While the men are in the building below, we must have complete quiet. Every sound can be
heard down there, not only in the workrooms, but in the offices,
too. The men come at about eight-thirty, and leave at about five-
thirty. So, to be perfectly safe, from eight in the morning until six
in the evening we must move only when it is necessary, and then
in stockinged feet. We must not speak above a whisper. We must
not run any water. We cannot use the sink, or even, forgive me,
the w.c. The pipes go down through the workrooms. It would be
heard. No trash . . . [MR. FRANK *stops abruptly as he hears the*
sound of marching feet from the street below. Everyone is motion-
less, paralyzed with fear. MR. FRANK *goes quietly into the room on*
the right to look down out of the window. ANNE *runs after him,*
peering out with him. The tramping feet pass without stopping.
The tension is relieved. MR. FRANK, *followed by* ANNE, *returns to*
the main room and resumes his instructions to the group] . . .
No trash must ever be thrown out which might reveal that someone is living up here . . . not even a potato paring. We must burn
everything in the stove at night. This is the way we must live until
it is over, if we are to survive.

[*There is silence for a second*]

MRS. FRANK: Until it is over.

MR. FRANK: [*Reassuringly*] After six we can move about . . . we can talk and laugh and have our supper and read and play games . . . just as we would at home. [*He looks at his watch*] And now I think it would be wise if we all went to our rooms, and were settled before eight o'clock. Mrs. Van Daan, you and your husband will be upstairs. I regret that there's no place up there for Peter. But he will be here, near us. This will be our common room, where we'll meet to talk and eat and read, like one family.

MR. VAN DAAN: And where do you and Mrs. Frank sleep?

MR. FRANK: This room is also our bedroom.

MRS. VAN DAAN: That isn't right.   MR. VAN DAAN: It's your place. We'll sleep here and you take the room upstairs.

MR. FRANK: Please. I've thought this out for weeks. It's the best arrangement. The only arrangement.

MRS. VAN DAAN: [*To* MR. FRANK] Never, never can we thank you. [*Then to* MRS. FRANK] I don't know what would have happened to us, if it hadn't been for Mr. Frank.

MR. FRANK: You don't know how your husband helped me when I came to this country . . . knowing no one . . . not able to speak the language. I can never repay him for that. [*Going to* VAN DAAN] May I help you with your things?

MR. VAN DAAN: No. No. [*To* MRS. VAN DAAN] Come along, *liefje*.

MRS. VAN DAAN: You'll be all right, Peter? You're not afraid?

PETER: [*Embarrassed*] Please, Mother.

[*They start up the stairs to the attic room above.* MR. FRANK *turns to* MRS. FRANK]

MR. FRANK: You too must have some rest, Edith. You didn't close your eyes last night. Nor you, Margot.

ANNE: I slept, Father. Wasn't that funny? I knew it was the last night in my own bed, and yet I slept soundly.

MR. FRANK: I'm glad, Anne. Now you'll be able to help me straighten things in here. [*To* MRS. FRANK *and* MARGOT] Come with me . . . You and Margot rest in this room for the time being.

[*He picks up their clothes, starting for the room on the right*]

MRS. FRANK: You're sure . . . ? I could help . . . And Anne hasn't had her milk . . .

MR. FRANK: I'll give it to her. [*To* ANNE *and* PETER] Anne, Peter . . . it's best that you take off your shoes now, before you forget.

[*He leads the way to the room, followed by* MARGOT]

MRS. FRANK: You're sure you're not tired, Anne?

ANNE: I feel fine. I'm going to help Father.

MRS. FRANK: Peter, I'm glad you are to be with us.

PETER: Yes, Mrs. Frank.

[MRS. FRANK *goes to join* MR. FRANK *and* MARGOT]

[*During the following scene* MR. FRANK *helps* MARGOT *and* MRS. FRANK *to hang up their clothes. Then he persuades them both to lie down and rest. The* VAN DAANS *in their room above settle themselves. In the main room* ANNE *and* PETER *remove their shoes.* PETER *takes his cat out of the carrier*]

ANNE: What's your cat's name?

PETER: Mouschi.

ANNE: Mouschi! Mouschi! Mouschi! [*She picks up the cat, walking away with it. To* PETER] I love cats. I have one . . . a darling little cat. But they made me leave her behind. I left some food and a note for the neighbors to take care of her . . . I'm going to miss her terribly. What is yours? A him or a her?

PETER: He's a tom. He doesn't like strangers.

[*He takes the cat from her, putting it back in its carrier*]

ANNE: [*Unabashed*] Then I'll have to stop being a stranger, won't I? Is he fixed?

PETER: [*Startled*] Huh?

ANNE: Did you have him fixed?

PETER: No.

ANNE: Oh, you ought to have him fixed—to keep him from—you know, fighting. Where did you go to school?

PETER: Jewish Secondary.

ANNE: But that's where Margot and I go! I never saw you around.

PETER: I used to see you . . . sometimes . . .

ANNE: You did?

PETER: . . . in the schoolyard. You were always in the middle of a bunch of kids.

[*He takes a penknife from his pocket*]

ANNE: Why didn't you ever come over?

PETER: I'm sort of a lone wolf.

[*He starts to rip off his Star of David*]

ANNE: What are you doing?

PETER: Taking it off.

ANNE: But you can't do that. They'll arrest you if you go out without your star.

[*He tosses his knife on the table*]

PETER: Who's going out?

ANNE: Why, of course! You're right! Of course we don't need them any more. [*She picks up his knife and starts to take her star off*] I wonder what our friends will think when we don't show up today?

PETER: I didn't have any dates with anyone.

ANNE: Oh, I did. I had a date with Jopie to go and play ping-pong at her house. Do you know Jopie de Waal?

PETER: No.

ANNE: Jopie's my best friend. I wonder what she'll think when she telephones and there's no answer? . . . Probably she'll go over to the house . . . I wonder what she'll think . . . we left everything as if we'd suddenly been called away . . . breakfast dishes in the sink . . . beds not made . . . [*As she pulls off her star the cloth underneath shows clearly the color and form of the star*] Look! It's still there! [PETER *goes over to the stove with his star*] What're you going to do with yours?

PETER: Burn it.

ANNE: [*She starts to throw hers in, and cannot*] It's funny, I can't throw mine away. I don't know why.

PETER: You can't throw . . . ? Something they branded you with . . . ? That they made you swear so they could spit on you?

ANNE: I know. I know. But after all, it *is* the Star of David, isn't it?

[*In the bedroom, right,* MARGOT *and* MRS. FRANK *are lying down.* MR. FRANK *starts quietly out*]

PETER: Maybe it's different for a girl.

[MR. FRANK *comes into the main room*]

MR. FRANK: Forgive me, Peter. Now let me see. We must find a bed for your cat. [*He goes to a cupboard*] I'm glad you brought your cat. Anne was feeling so badly about hers. [*Getting a used small washtub*] Here we are. Will it be comfortable in that?

PETER: [*Gathering up his things*] Thanks.

MR. FRANK: [*Opening the door of the room on the left*] And here is your room. But I warn you, Peter, you can't grow any more. Not an inch, or you'll have to sleep with your feet out of the skylight. Are you hungry?

PETER: No.

MR. FRANK: We have some bread and butter.

PETER: No, thank you.

MR. FRANK: You can have it for luncheon then. And tonight we will have a real supper . . . our first supper together.

PETER: Thanks. Thanks.

[*He goes into his room. During the following scene he arranges his possessions in his new room*]

MR. FRANK: That's a nice boy, Peter.

ANNE: He's awfully shy, isn't he?

MR. FRANK: You'll like him, I know.

ANNE: I certainly hope so, since he's the only boy I'm likely to see for months and months.

[MR. FRANK *sits down, taking off his shoes*]

MR. FRANK: Annele, there's a box there. Will you open it?

[*He indicates a carton on the couch.* ANNE *brings it to the center table. In the street below there is the sound of children playing*]

ANNE: [*As she opens the carton*] You know the way I'm going to think of it here? I'm going to think of it as a boarding house. A very peculiar summer boarding house, like the one that we—[*She breaks off as she pulls out some photographs*] Father! My movie stars! I was wondering where they were! I was looking for them this morning . . . and Queen Wilhelmina! How wonderful!

MR. FRANK: There's something more. Go on. Look further.

[*He goes over to the sink, pouring a glass of milk from a thermos bottle*]

ANNE: [*Pulling out a pasteboard-bound book*] A diary! [*She throws her arms around her father*] I've never had a diary. And I've always longed for one. [*She looks around the room*] Pencil, pencil, pencil, pencil. [*She starts down the stairs*] I'm going down to the office to get a pencil.

MR. FRANK: Anne! No!

[*He goes after her, catching her by the arm and pulling her back*]

ANNE: [*Startled*] But there's no one in the building now.

MR. FRANK: It doesn't matter. I don't want you ever to go beyond that door.

ANNE: Never . . . ? Not even at nighttime, when everyone is gone? Or on Sundays? Can't I go down to listen to the radio?

MR. FRANK: Never. I am sorry, Anneke. It isn't safe. No, you must never go beyond that door.

[*For the first time* ANNE *realizes what "going into hiding" means*]

ANNE: I see.

MR. FRANK: It'll be hard, I know. But always remember this, Anneke. There are no walls, there are no bolts, no locks that anyone can put on your mind. Miep will bring us books. We will read history, poetry, mythology. [*He gives her the glass of milk*] Here's your milk. [*With his arm about her, they go over to the couch, sitting down side by side*] As a matter of fact, between us, Anne, being here has certain advantages for you. For instance, you remember the battle you had with your mother the other day on the subject of overshoes? You said you'd rather die than wear overshoes? But in the end you had to wear them? Well now, you see, for as long as we are here you will never have to wear overshoes! Isn't that good? And the coat that you inherited from Margot, you won't have to wear that any more. And the piano! You won't have to practice on the piano. I tell you, this is going to be a fine life for you!

[ANNE's *panic is gone.* PETER *appears in the doorway of his room, with a saucer in his hand. He is carrying the cat*]

PETER: I . . . I . . . I thought I'd better get some water for Mouschi before . . .

MR. FRANK: Of course.

[*As he starts toward the sink the carillon begins to chime the hour of eight. He tiptoes to the window at the back and looks down at the street below. He turns to* PETER, *indicating in pantomine that it is too late.* PETER *starts back for his room. He steps on a creaking board. The three of them are frozen for a minute in fear. As* PETER *starts away again,* ANNE *tiptoes over to him and pours some of the milk from her glass into the saucer for the cat.* PETER *squats on the floor, putting the milk before the cat.* MR. FRANK *gives* ANNE *his fountain pen, and then goes into the room at the right. For a second* ANNE

*watches the cat, then she goes over to the center table, and
opens her diary.*

In the room at the right, MRS. FRANK *has sat up quickly at the
sound of the carillon.* MR. FRANK *comes in and sits down beside her on the settee, his arm comfortingly around her.*

Upstairs, in the attic room, MR. *and* MRS. VAN DAAN *have
hung their clothes in the closet and are now seated on the
iron bed.* MRS. VAN DAAN *leans back exhausted.* MR. VAN DAAN
fans her with a newspaper.

ANNE *starts to write in her diary. The lights dim out, the curtain falls.*

In the darkness ANNE'S VOICE *comes to us again, faintly at
first, and then with growing strength*]

ANNE'S VOICE: I expect I should be describing what it feels like to
go into hiding. But I really don't know yet myself. I only know it's
funny never to be able to go outdoors . . . never to breathe fresh
air . . . never to run and shout and jump. It's the silence in the
nights that frightens me most. Every time I hear a creak in the
house, or a step on the street outside, I'm sure they're coming for
us. The days aren't so bad. At least we know that Miep and Mr.
Kraler are down there below us in the office. Our protectors, we
call them. I asked Father what would happen to them if the Nazis
found out they were hiding us. Pim said that they would suffer the
same fate that we would . . . Imagine! They know this, and yet
when they come up here, they're always cheerful and gay as if
there were nothing in the world to bother them . . . Friday, the
twenty-first of August, nineteen forty-two. Today I'm going to tell
you our general news. Mother is unbearable. She insists on treating me like a baby, which I loathe. Otherwise things are going better. The weather is . . .

[*As* ANNE'S VOICE *is fading out, the curtain rises on the
scene*]

SCENE THREE

It is a little after six o'clock in the evening, two months later.
MARGOT *is in the bedroom at the right, studying.* MR. VAN

DAAN *is lying down in the attic room above.*
The rest of the "family" is in the main room. ANNE *and* PETER
*sit opposite each other at the center table, where they have
been doing their lessons.* MR. FRANK *is on the couch.* MRS. VAN
DAAN *is seated with her fur coat, on which she has been sewing, in her lap. None of them are wearing their shoes.*
Their eyes are on MR. FRANK, *waiting for him to give them
the signal which will release them from their day-long quiet.*
MR. FRANK, *his shoes in his hand, stands looking down out of
the window at the back, watching to be sure that all of the
workmen have left the building below.*
After a few seconds of motionless silence, MR. FRANK *turns
from the window.*

MR. FRANK: [*Quietly, to the group*] It's safe now. The last work-
man has left.

[*There is an immediate stir of relief*]

ANNE: [*Her pent-up energy explodes*] WHEE!

MRS. FRANK: [*Startled, amused*] Anne!

MRS. VAN DAAN: I'm first for the w.c.

[*She hurries off to the bathroom.* MRS. FRANK *puts on her
shoes and starts up to the sink to prepare supper.* ANNE *sneaks*
PETER'S *shoes from under the table and hides them behind
her back.* MR. FRANK *goes in to* MARGOT'S *room*]

MR. FRANK: [*To* MARGOT] Six o'clock. School's over.

[MARGOT *gets up, stretching.* MR. FRANK *sits down to put on
his shoes. In the main room* PETER *tries to find his*]

PETER: [*To* ANNE] Have you seen my shoes?

ANNE: [*Innocently*] Your shoes?

PETER: You've taken them, haven't you?

ANNE: I don't know what you're talking about.

PETER: You're going to be sorry!

ANNE: Am I?

[PETER *goes after her.* ANNE, *with his shoes in her hand, runs from him, dodging behind her mother*]

MRS. FRANK: [*Protesting*] Anne, dear!

PETER: Wait till I get you!

ANNE: I'm waiting! [PETER *makes a lunge for her. They both fall to the floor.* PETER *pins her down, wrestling with her to get the shoes*] Don't! Don't! Peter, stop it. Ouch!

MRS. FRANK: Anne! . . . Peter!

[*Suddenly* PETER *becomes self-conscious. He grabs his shoes roughly and starts for his room*]

ANNE: [*Following him*] Peter, where are you going? Come dance with me.

PETER: I tell you I don't know how.

ANNE: I'll teach you.

PETER: I'm going to give Mouschi his dinner.

ANNE: Can I watch?

PETER: He doesn't like people around while he eats.

ANNE: Peter, please.

PETER: No!

[*He goes into his room.* ANNE *slams his door after him*]

MRS. FRANK: Anne, dear, I think you shouldn't play like that with Peter. It's not dignified.

ANNE: Who cares if it's dignified? I don't want to be dignified.

[MR. FRANK *and* MARGOT *come from the room on the right.* MARGOT *goes to help her mother.* MR. FRANK *starts for the center table to correct* MARGOT's *school papers*]

MRS. FRANK: [*To* ANNE] You complain that I don't treat you like a grownup. But when I do, you resent it.

ANNE: I only want some fun . . . someone to laugh and clown with . . . After you've sat all day and hardly moved, you've got to have some fun. I don't know what's the matter with that boy.

MR. FRANK: He isn't used to girls. Give him a little time.

ANNE: Time? Isn't two months time? I could cry. [*Catching hold of* MARGOT] Come on, Margot . . . dance with me. Come on, please.

MARGOT: I have to help with supper.

ANNE: You know we're going to forget how to dance . . . When we get out we won't remember a thing.

[*She starts to sing and dance by herself.* MR. FRANK *takes her in his arms, waltzing with her.* MRS. VAN DAAN *comes in from the bathroom*]

MRS. VAN DAAN: Next? [*She looks around as she starts putting on her shoes*] Where's Peter?

ANNE: [*As they are dancing*] Where would he be!

MRS. VAN DAAN: He hasn't finished his lessons, has he? His father'll kill him if he catches him in there with that cat and his work not done. [MR. FRANK *and* ANNE *finish their dance. They bow to each other with extravagant formality*] Anne, get him out of there, will you?

ANNE: [*At* PETER'S *door*] Peter? Peter?

PETER: [*Opening the door a crack*] What is it?

ANNE: Your mother says to come out.

PETER: I'm giving Mouschi his dinner.

MRS. VAN DAAN: You know what your father says.

[*She sits on the couch, sewing on the lining of her fur coat*]

PETER: For heaven's sake, I haven't even looked at him since lunch.

MRS. VAN DAAN: I'm just telling you, that's all.

ANNE: I'll feed him.

PETER: I don't want you in here.

MRS. VAN DAAN: Peter!

PETER: [*To* ANNE] Then give him his dinner and come right out, you hear?

[*He comes back to the table.* ANNE *shuts the door of* PETER's *room after her and disappears behind the curtain covering his closet*]

MRS. VAN DAAN: [*To* PETER] Now is that any way to talk to your little girl friend?

PETER: Mother . . . for heaven's sake . . . will you please stop saying that?

MRS. VAN DAAN: Look at him blush! Look at him!

PETER: Please! I'm not . . . anyway . . . let me alone, will you?

MRS. VAN DAAN: He acts like it was something to be ashamed of. It's nothing to be ashamed of, to have a little girl friend.

PETER: You're crazy. She's only thirteen.

MRS. VAN DAAN: So what? And you're sixteen. Just perfect. Your father's ten years older than I am. [*To* MR. FRANK] I warn you, Mr. Frank, if this war lasts much longer, we're going to be related and then . . .

MR. FRANK: *Mazeltov!*

MRS. FRANK: [*Deliberately changing the conversation*] I wonder where Miep is. She's usually so prompt.

[*Suddenly everything else is forgotten as they hear the sound of an automobile coming to a screeching stop in the street below. They are tense, motionless in their terror. The car starts away. A wave of relief sweeps over them. They pick up their occupations again.* ANNE *flings open the door of* PETER's *room, making a dramatic entrance. She is dressed in* PETER's *clothes.* PETER *looks at her in fury. The others are amused*]

ANNE: Good evening, everyone. Forgive me if I don't stay. [*She jumps up on a chair*] I have a friend waiting for me in there. My friend Tom. Tom Cat. Some people say that we look alike. But

Tom has the most beautiful whiskers, and I have only a little fuzz. I am hoping . . . in time . . .

PETER: All right, Mrs. Quack Quack!

ANNE: [*Outraged—jumping down*] Peter!

PETER: I heard about you . . . How you talked so much in class they called you Mrs. Quack Quack. How Mr. Smitter made you write a composition . . . " 'Quack, quack,' said Mrs. Quack Quack."

ANNE: Well, go on. Tell them the rest. How it was so good he read it out loud to the class and then read it to all his other classes!

PETER: Quack! Quack! Quack . . . Quack . . . Quack . . .

[ANNE *pulls off the coat and trousers*]

ANNE: You are the most intolerable, insufferable boy I've ever met!

[*She throws the clothes down the stairwell.* PETER *goes down after them*]

PETER: Quack, quack, quack!

MRS. VAN DAAN: [*To* ANNE] That's right, Anneke! Give it to him!

ANNE: With all the boys in the world . . . Why I had to get locked up with one like you! . . .

PETER: Quack, quack, quack, and from now on stay out of my room!

[*As* PETER *passes her,* ANNE *puts out her foot, tripping him. He picks himself up, and goes on into his room*]

MRS. FRANK: [*Quietly*] Anne, dear . . . your hair. [*She feels* ANNE's *forehead*] You're warm. Are you feeling all right?

ANNE: Please, Mother.

[*She goes over to the center table, slipping into her shoes*]

MRS. FRANK: [*Following her*] You haven't a fever, have you?

ANNE: [*Pulling away*] No. No.

MRS. FRANK: You know we can't call a doctor here, ever. There's only one thing to do . . . watch carefully. Prevent an illness before it comes. Let me see your tongue.

ANNE: Mother, this is perfectly absurd.

MRS. FRANK: Anne, dear, don't be such a baby. Let me see your tongue. [*As* ANNE *refuses*, MRS. FRANK *appeals to* MR. FRANK] Otto . . . ?

MR. FRANK: You hear your mother, Anne.

[ANNE *flicks out her tongue for a second, then turns away*]

MRS. FRANK: Come on—open up! [*As* ANNE *opens her mouth very wide*] You seem all right . . . but perhaps an aspirin . . .

MRS. VAN DAAN: For heaven's sake, don't give that child any pills. I waited for fifteen minutes this morning for her to come out of the W.C.

ANNE: I was washing my hair!

MR. FRANK: I think there's nothing the matter with our Anne that a ride on her bike, or a visit with her friend Jopie de Waal wouldn't cure. Isn't that so, Anne?

[MR. VAN DAAN *comes down into the room. From outside we hear faint sounds of bombers going over and a burst of ack-ack*]

MR. VAN DAAN: Miep not come yet?

MRS. VAN DAAN: The workmen just left, a little while ago.

MR. VAN DAAN: What's for dinner tonight?

MRS. VAN DAAN: Beans.

MR. VAN DAAN: Not again!

MRS. VAN DAAN: Poor Putti! I know. But what can we do? That's all that Miep brought us.

[MR. VAN DAAN *starts to pace, his hands behind his back.* ANNE *follows behind him, imitating him*]

ANNE: We are now in what is known as the "bean cycle." Beans boiled, beans en casserole, beans with strings, beans without strings . . .

[PETER *has come out of his room. He slides into his place at the table, becoming immediately absorbed in his studies*]

MR. VAN DAAN: [*To* PETER] I saw you . . . in there, playing with your cat.

MRS. VAN DAAN: He just went in for a second, putting his coat away. He's been out here all the time, doing his lessons.

MR. FRANK: [*Looking up from the papers*] Anne, you got an excellent in your history paper today . . . and very good in Latin.

ANNE: [*Sitting beside him*] How about algebra?

MR. FRANK: I'll have to make a confession. Up until now I've managed to stay ahead of you in algebra. Today you caught up with me. We'll leave it to Margot to correct.

ANNE: Isn't algebra *vile*, Pim!

MR. FRANK: Vile!

MARGOT: [*To* MR. FRANK] How did I do?

ANNE: [*Getting up*] Excellent, excellent, excellent, excellent!

MR. FRANK: [*To* MARGOT] You should have used the subjunctive here . . .

MARGOT: Should I? . . . I thought . . . look here . . . I didn't use it here . . .

[*The two become absorbed in the papers*]

ANNE: Mrs. Van Daan, may I try on your coat?

MRS. FRANK: No, Anne.

MRS. VAN DAAN: [*Giving it to* ANNE] It's all right . . . but careful with it. [ANNE *puts it on and struts with it*] My father gave me that the year before he died. He always bought the best that money could buy.

ANNE: Mrs. Van Daan, did you have a lot of boy friends before you were married?

MRS. FRANK: Anne, that's a personal question. It's not courteous to ask personal questions.

MRS. VAN DAAN: Oh, I don't mind. [*To* ANNE] Our house was always swarming with boys. When I was a girl we had . . .

MR. VAN DAAN: Oh, God. Not again!

MRS. VAN DAAN: [*Good-humored*] Shut up! [*Without a pause, to* ANNE. MR. VAN DAAN *mimics* MRS. VAN DAAN, *speaking the first few words in unison with her*] One summer we had a big house in Hilversum. The boys came buzzing round like bees around a jam pot. And when I was sixteen! . . . We were wearing our skirts very short those days and I had good-looking legs. [*She pulls up her skirt, going to* MR. FRANK] I still have 'em. I may not be as pretty as I used to be, but I still have my legs. How about it, Mr. Frank?

MR. VAN DAAN: All right. All right. We see them.

MRS. VAN DAAN: I'm not asking you. I'm asking Mr. Frank.

PETER: Mother, for heaven's sake.

MRS. VAN DAAN: Oh, I embarrass you, do I? Well, I just hope the girl you marry has as good. [*Then to* ANNE] My father used to worry about me, with so many boys hanging round. He told me, if any of them gets fresh, you say to him . . . "Remember, Mr. So-and-So, remember I'm a lady."

ANNE: "Remember, Mr. So-and-So, remember I'm a lady."

[*She gives* MRS. VAN DAAN *her coat*]

MR. VAN DAAN: Look at you, talking that way in front of her! Don't you know she puts it all down in that diary?

MRS. VAN DAAN: So, if she does? I'm only telling the truth!

[ANNE *stretches out, putting her ear to the floor, listening to what is going on below. The sound of the bombers fades away*]

MRS. FRANK: [*Setting the table*] Would you mind, Peter, if I moved you over to the couch?

ANNE: [*Listening*] Miep must have the radio on.

[PETER *picks up his papers, going over to the couch beside* MRS. VAN DAAN]

MR. VAN DAAN: [*Accusingly, to* PETER] Haven't you finished yet?

PETER: No.

MR. VAN DAAN: You ought to be ashamed of yourself.

PETER: All right. All right. I'm a dunce. I'm a hopeless case. Why do I go on?

MRS. VAN DAAN: You're not hopeless. Don't talk that way. It's just that you haven't anyone to help you, like the girls have. [*To* MR. FRANK] Maybe you could help him, Mr. Frank?

MR. FRANK: I'm sure that his father . . . ?

MR. VAN DAAN: Not me. I can't do anything with him. He won't listen to me. You go ahead . . . if you want.

MR. FRANK: [*Going to* PETER] What about it, Peter? Shall we make our school coeducational?

MRS. VAN DAAN: [*Kissing* MR. FRANK] You're an angel, Mr. Frank. An angel. I don't know why I didn't meet you before I met that one there. Here, sit down, Mr. Frank . . . [*She forces him down on the couch beside* PETER] Now, Peter, you listen to Mr. Frank.

MR. FRANK: It might be better for us to go into Peter's room.

[PETER *jumps up eagerly, leading the way*]

MRS. VAN DAAN: That's right. You go in there, Peter. You listen to Mr. Frank. Mr. Frank is a highly educated man.

[*As* MR. FRANK *is about to follow* PETER *into his room,* MRS. FRANK *stops him and wipes the lipstick from his lips. Then she closes the door after them*]

ANNE: [*On the floor, listening*] Shh! I can hear a man's voice talking.

MR. VAN DAAN: [*To* ANNE] Isn't it bad enough here without your sprawling all over the place?

[ANNE *sits up*]

MRS. VAN DAAN: [*To* MR. VAN DAAN] If you didn't smoke so much, you wouldn't be so bad-tempered.

MR. VAN DAAN: Am I smoking? Do you see me smoking?

MRS. VAN DAAN: Don't tell me you've used up all those cigarettes.

MR. VAN DAAN: One package. Miep only brought me one package.

MRS. VAN DAAN: It's a filthy habit anyway. It's a good time to break yourself.

MR. VAN DAAN: Oh, stop it, please.

MRS. VAN DAAN: You're smoking up all our money. You know that, don't you?

MR. VAN DAAN: Will you shut up? [*During this*, MRS. FRANK *and* MARGOT *have studiously kept their eyes down. But* ANNE, *seated on the floor, has been following the discussion interestedly.* MR. VAN DAAN *turns to see her staring up at him*] And what are you staring at?

ANNE: I never heard grownups quarrel before. I thought only children quarreled.

MR. VAN DAAN: This isn't a quarrel! It's a discussion. And I never heard children so rude before.

ANNE: [*Rising, indignantly*] I, rude!

MR. VAN DAAN: Yes!

MRS. FRANK: [*Quickly*] Anne, will you get me my knitting? [ANNE *goes to get it*] I must remember, when Miep comes, to ask her to bring me some more wool.

MARGOT: [*Going to her room*] I need some hairpins and some soap. I made a list.

[*She goes into her bedroom to get the list*]

MRS. FRANK: [*To* ANNE] Have you some library books for Miep when she comes?

ANNE: It's a wonder that Miep has a life of her own, the way we make her run errands for us. Please, Miep, get me some starch. Please take my hair out and have it cut. Tell me all the latest news, Miep. [*She goes over, kneeling on the couch beside* MRS. VAN DAAN] Did you know she was engaged? His name is Dirk, and Miep's afraid the Nazis will ship him off to Germany to work in one of their war plants. That's what they're doing with some of the young Dutchmen . . . they pick them up off the streets—

MR. VAN DAAN: [*Interrupting*] Don't you ever get tired of talking? Suppose you try keeping still for five minutes. Just five minutes.

[*He starts to pace again. Again* ANNE *follows him, mimicking him.* MRS. FRANK *jumps up and takes her by the arm up to the sink, and gives her a glass of milk*]

MRS. FRANK: Come here, Anne. It's time for your glass of milk.

MR. VAN DAAN: Talk, talk, talk. I never heard such a child. Where is my . . . ? Every evening it's the same, talk, talk, talk. [*He looks around*] Where is my . . . ?

MRS. VAN DAAN: What're you looking for?

MR. VAN DAAN: My pipe. Have you seen my pipe?

MRS. VAN DAAN: What good's a pipe? You haven't got any tobacco.

MR. VAN DAAN: At least I'll have something to hold in my mouth! [*Opening* MARGOT'S *bedroom door*] Margot, have you seen my pipe?

MARGOT: It was on the table last night.

[ANNE *puts her glass of milk on the table and picks up his pipe, hiding it behind her back*]

MR. VAN DAAN: I know. I know. Anne, did you see my pipe? . . . Anne!

MRS. FRANK: Anne, Mr. Van Daan is speaking to you.

ANNE: Am I allowed to talk now?

MR. VAN DAAN: You're the most aggravating . . . The trouble with you is, you've been spoiled. What you need is a good old-fashioned spanking.

ANNE: [*Mimicking* MRS. VAN DAAN] "Remember, Mr. So-and-So, remember I'm a lady." [*She thrusts the pipe into his mouth, then picks up her glass of milk*]

MR. VAN DAAN: [*Restraining himself with difficulty*] Why aren't you nice and quiet like your sister Margot? Why do you have to show off all the time? Let me give you a little advice, young lady. Men don't like that kind of thing in a girl. You know that? A man likes a girl who'll listen to him once in a while . . . a domestic girl, who'll keep her house shining for her husband . . . who loves to cook and sew and . . .

ANNE: I'd cut my throat first! I'd open my veins! I'm going to be remarkable! I'm going to Paris . . .

MR. VAN DAAN: [*Scoffingly*] Paris!

ANNE: . . . to study music and art.

MR. VAN DAAN: Yeah! Yeah!

ANNE: I'm going to be a famous dancer or singer . . . or something wonderful.

[*She makes a wide gesture, spilling the glass of milk on the fur coat in* MRS. VAN DAAN'S *lap.* MARGOT *rushes quickly over with a towel.* ANNE *tries to brush the milk off with her skirt*]

MRS. VAN DAAN: Now look what you've done . . . you clumsy little fool! My beautiful fur coat my father gave me . . .

ANNE: I'm so sorry.

MRS. VAN DAAN: What do you care? It isn't yours . . . So go on, ruin it! Do you know what that coat cost? Do you? And now look at it! Look at it!

ANNE: I'm very, very sorry.

MRS. VAN DAAN: I could kill you for this. I could just kill you!

[MRS. VAN DAAN *goes up the stairs, clutching the coat.* MR. VAN DAAN *starts after her*]

MR. VAN DAAN: Petronella . . . *liefje! Liefje!* . . . Come back . . . the supper . . . come back!

MRS. FRANK: Anne, you must not behave in that way.

ANNE: It was an accident. Anyone can have an accident.

MRS. FRANK: I don't mean that. I mean the answering back. You must not answer back. They are our guests. We must always show the greatest courtesy to them. We're all living under terrible tension. [*She stops as* MARGOT *indicates that* VAN DAAN *can hear. When he is gone, she continues*] That's why we must control ourselves . . . You don't hear Margot getting into arguments with them, do you? Watch Margot. She's always courteous with them. Never familiar. She keeps her distance. And they respect her for it. Try to be like Margot.

ANNE: And have them walk all over me, the way they do her? No, thanks!

MRS. FRANK: I'm not afraid that anyone is going to walk all over you, Anne. I'm afraid for other people, that you'll walk on them. I don't know what happens to you, Anne. You are wild, self-willed. If I had ever talked to my mother as you talk to me . . .

ANNE: Things have changed. People aren't like that any more. "Yes, Mother." "No, Mother." "Anything you say, Mother." I've got to fight things out for myself! Make something of myself!

MRS. FRANK: It isn't necessary to fight to do it. Margot doesn't fight, and isn't she . . . ?

ANNE: [Violently rebellious] Margot! Margot! Margot! That's all I hear from everyone . . . how wonderful Margot is . . . "Why aren't you like Margot?"

MARGOT: [Protesting] Oh, come on, Anne, don't be so . . .

ANNE: [Paying no attention] Everything she does is right, and everything I do is wrong! I'm the goat around here! . . . You're all against me! . . . And you worst of all!

[She rushes off into her room and throws herself down on the settee, stifling her sobs. MRS. FRANK sighs and starts toward the stove]

MRS. FRANK: [To MARGOT] Let's put the soup on the stove . . . if there's anyone who cares to eat. Margot, will you take the bread out? [MARGOT gets the bread from the cupboard] I don't know how we can go on living this way . . . I can't say a word to Anne . . . she flies at me . . .

MARGOT: You know Anne. In half an hour she'll be out here, laughing and joking.

MRS. FRANK: And . . . [She makes a motion upwards, indicating the VAN DAANS] . . . I told your father it wouldn't work . . . but no . . . no . . . he had to ask them, he said . . . he owed it to him, he said. Well, he knows now that I was right! These quarrels! . . . This bickering!

MARGOT: [*With a warning look*] Shush. Shush.

[*The buzzer for the door sounds.* MRS. FRANK *gasps, startled*]

MRS. FRANK: Every time I hear that sound, my heart stops!

MARGOT: [*Starting for* PETER's *door*] It's Miep. [*She knocks at the door*] Father?

[MR. FRANK *comes quickly from* PETER's *room*]

MR. FRANK: Thank you, Margot. [*As he goes down the steps to open the outer door*] Has everyone his list?

MARGOT: I'll get my books. [*Giving her mother a list*] Here's your list. [MARGOT *goes into her and* ANNE's *bedroom on the right.* ANNE *sits up, hiding her tears, as* MARGOT *comes in*] Miep's here.

[MARGOT *picks up her books and goes back.* ANNE *hurries over to the mirror, smoothing her hair*]

MR. VAN DAAN: [*Coming down the stairs*] Is it Miep?

MARGOT: Yes. Father's gone down to let her in.

MR. VAN DAAN: At last I'll have some cigarettes!

MRS. FRANK: [*To* MR. VAN DAAN] I can't tell you how unhappy I am about Mrs. Van Daan's coat. Anne should never have touched it.

MR. VAN DAAN: She'll be all right.

MRS. FRANK: Is there anything I can do?

MR. VAN DAAN: Don't worry.

[*He turns to meet* MIEP. *But it is not* MIEP *who comes up the steps. It is* MR. KRALER, *followed by* MR. FRANK. *Their faces are grave.* ANNE *comes from the bedroom.* PETER *comes from his room*]

MRS. FRANK: Mr. Kraler!

MR. VAN DAAN: How are you, Mr. Kraler?

MARGOT: This is a surprise.

MRS. FRANK: When Mr. Kraler comes, the sun begins to shine.

MR. VAN DAAN: Miep is coming?

MR. KRALER: Not tonight.

[KRALER *goes to* MARGOT *and* MRS. FRANK *and* ANNE, *shaking hands with them*]

MRS. FRANK: Wouldn't you like a cup of coffee? . . . Or, better still, will you have supper with us?

MR. FRANK: Mr. Kraler has something to talk over with us. Something has happened, he says, which demands an immediate decision.

MRS. FRANK: [*Fearful*] What is it?

[MR. KRALER *sits down on the couch. As he talks he takes bread, cabbages, milk, etc., from his briefcase, giving them to* MARGOT *and* ANNE *to put away*]

MR. KRALER: Usually, when I come up here, I try to bring you some bit of good news. What's the use of telling you the bad news when there's nothing that you can do about it? But today something has happened . . . Dirk . . . Miep's Dirk, you know, came to me just now. He tells me that he has a Jewish friend living near him. A dentist. He says he's in trouble. He begged me, could I do anything for this man? Could I find him a hiding place? . . . So I've come to you . . . I know it's a terrible thing to ask of you, living as you are, but would you take him in with you?

MR. FRANK: Of course we will.

MR. KRALER: [*Rising*] It'll be just for a night or two . . . until I find some other place. This happened so suddenly that I didn't know where to turn.

MR. FRANK: Where is he?

MR. KRALER: Downstairs in the office.

MR. FRANK: Good. Bring him up.

MR. KRALER: His name is Dussel . . . Jan Dussel.

MR. FRANK: Dussel . . . I think I know him.

MR. KRALER: I'll get him.

[*He goes quickly down the steps and out.* MR. FRANK *suddenly becomes conscious of the others*]

MR. FRANK: Forgive me. I spoke without consulting you. But I knew you'd feel as I do.

MR. VAN DAAN: There's no reason for you to consult anyone. This is your place. You have a right to do exactly as you please. The only thing I feel . . . there's so little food as it is . . . and to take in another person . . .

[PETER *turns away, ashamed of his father*]

MR. FRANK: We can stretch the food a little. It's only for a few days.

MR. VAN DAAN: You want to make a bet?

MRS. FRANK: I think it's fine to have him. But, Otto, where are you going to put him? Where?

PETER: He can have my bed. I can sleep on the floor. I wouldn't mind.

MR. FRANK: That's good of you, Peter. But your room's too small . . . even for *you.*

ANNE: I have a much better idea. I'll come in here with you and Mother, and Margot can take Peter's room and Peter can go in our room with Mr. Dussel.

MARGOT: That's right. We could do that.

MR. FRANK: No, Margot. You mustn't sleep in that room . . . neither you nor Anne. Mouschi has caught some rats in there. Peter's brave. He doesn't mind.

ANNE: Then how about *this?* I'll come in here with you and Mother, and Mr. Dussel can have my bed.

MRS. FRANK: No. No. *No!* Margot will come in here with us and he can have her bed. It's the only way, Margot, bring your things in here. Help her, Anne.

[MARGOT *hurries into her room to get her things*]

ANNE: [*To her mother*] Why Margot? Why can't I come in here?

MRS. FRANK: Because it wouldn't be proper for Margot to sleep with a . . . Please, Anne. Don't argue. Please.

[ANNE *starts slowly away*]

MRS. FRANK: [*To* ANNE] You don't mind sharing your room with Mr. Dussel, do you, Anne?

ANNE: No. No, of course not.

MR. FRANK: Good. [ANNE *goes off into her bedroom, helping* MARGOT. MR. FRANK *starts to search in the cupboards*] Where's the cognac?

MRS. FRANK: It's there. But, Otto, I was saving it in case of illness.

MR. FRANK: I think we couldn't find a better time to use it. Peter, will you get five glasses for me?

[PETER *goes for the glasses.* MARGOT *comes out of her bedroom, carrying her possessions, which she hangs behind a curtain in the main room.* MR. FRANK *finds the cognac and pours it into the five glasses that* PETER *brings him.* MR. VAN DAAN *stands looking on sourly.* MRS. VAN DAAN *comes downstairs and looks around at all the bustle*]

MRS. VAN DAAN: What's happening? What's going on?

MR. VAN DAAN: Someone's moving in with us.

MRS. VAN DAAN: In here? You're joking.

MARGOT: It's only for a night or two . . . until Mr. Kraler finds him another place.

MR. VAN DAAN: Yeah! Yeah!

[MR. FRANK *hurries over as* MR. KRALER *and* DUSSEL *come up.* DUSSEL *is a man in his late fifties, meticulous, finicky . . . bewildered now. He wears a raincoat. He carries a briefcase, stuffed full, and a small medicine case*]

MR. FRANK: Come in, Mr. Dussel.

MR. KRALER: This is Mr. Frank.

DUSSEL: Mr. Otto Frank?

MR. FRANK: Yes. Let me take your things. [*He takes the hat and briefcase, but* DUSSEL *clings to his medicine case*] This is my wife Edith . . . Mr. and Mr. Van Daan . . . their son, Peter . . . and my daughters, Margot and Anne.

[DUSSEL *shakes hands with everyone*]

MR. KRALER: Thank you, Mr. Frank. Thank you all. Mr. Dussel, I leave you in good hands. Oh . . . Dirk's coat.

[DUSSEL *hurriedly takes off the raincoat, giving it to* MR. KRALER. *Underneath is his white dentist's jacket, with a yellow Star of David on it*]

DUSSEL: [*To* MR. KRALER] What can I say to thank you . . . ?

MR. FRANK: [*To* DUSSEL] Mr. Kraler and Miep . . . They're our life line. Without them we couldn't live.

MR. KRALER: Please. Please. You make us seem very heroic. It isn't that at all. We simply don't like the Nazis. [*To* MR. FRANK, *who offers him a drink*] No, thanks. [*Then going on*] We don't like their methods. We don't like . . .

MR. FRANK: [*Smiling*] I know. I know. "No one's going to tell us Dutchmen what to do with our damn Jews!"

MR. KRALER: [*To* DUSSEL] Pay no attention to Mr. Frank. I'll be up tomorrow to see that they're treating you right. [*To* MR. FRANK] Don't trouble to come down again. Peter will bolt the door after me, won't you, Peter?

PETER: Yes, sir.

MR. FRANK: Thank you, Peter. I'll do it.

MR. KRALER: Good night. Good night.

GROUP: Good night, Mr. Kraler. We'll see you tomorrow, etc., etc.

[MR. KRALER *goes out with* MR. FRANK. MRS. FRANK *gives each one of the "grownups" a glass of cognac*]

MRS. FRANK: Please, Mr. Dussel, sit down.

[MR. DUSSEL *sinks into a chair.* MRS. FRANK *gives him a glass of cognac*]

DUSSEL: I'm dreaming. I know it. I can't believe my eyes. Mr. Otto Frank here! (*To* MRS. FRANK] You're not in Switzerland then? A woman told me . . . She said she'd gone to your house . . . the door was open, everything was in disorder, dishes in the sink. She said she found a piece of paper in the wastebasket with an address scribbled on it . . . an address in Zurich. She said you must have escaped to Zurich.

ANNE: Father put that there purposely . . . just so people would think that very thing!

DUSSEL: And you've been *here* all the time?

MRS. FRANK: All the time . . . ever since July.

[ANNE *speaks to her father as he comes back*]

ANNE: It worked, Pim . . . the address you left! Mr. Dussel says that people believe we escaped to Switzerland.

MR. FRANK: I'm glad. . . . And now let's have a little drink to welcome Mr. Dussel. [*Before they can drink,* MR. DUSSEL *bolts his drink.* MR. FRANK *smiles and raises his glass*] To Mr. Dussel. Welcome. We're very honored to have you with us.

MRS. FRANK: To Mr. Dussel, welcome.

[*The* VAN DAANS *murmur a welcome. The "grownups" drink*]

MRS. VAN DAAN: Um. That was good.

MR. VAN DAAN: Did Mr. Kraler warn you that you won't get much to eat here? You can imagine . . . three ration books among the seven of us . . . and now you make eight.

[PETER *walks away, humiliated. Outside a street organ is heard dimly*]

DUSSEL: [*Rising*] Mr. Van Daan, you don't realize what is happening outside that you should warn me of a thing like that. You don't realize what's going on . . . [*As* MR. VAN DAAN *starts his characteristic pacing,* DUSSEL *turns to speak to the others*] Right here in Amsterdam every day hundreds of Jews disappear . . . They surround a block and search house by house. Children come home from school to find their parents gone. Hundreds are being deported . . . people that you and I know . . . the Hallensteins . . . the Wessels . . .

MRS. FRANK: [*In tears*] Oh, no. No!

DUSSEL: They get their call-up notice . . . come to the Jewish theatre on such and such a day and hour . . . bring only what you can carry in a rucksack. And if you refuse the call-up notice, then they come and drag you from your home and ship you off to Mauthausen. The death camp!

MRS. FRANK: We didn't know that things had got so much worse.

DUSSEL: Forgive me for speaking so.

ANNE: [*Coming to* DUSSEL] Do you know the de Waals? . . . What's become of them? Their daughter Jopie and I are in the same class. Jopie's my best friend.

DUSSEL: They are gone.

ANNE: Gone?

DUSSEL: With all the others.

ANNE: Oh no. Not Jopie!

[*She turns away, in tears.* MRS. FRANK *motions to* MARGOT *to comfort her.* MARGOT *goes to* ANNE, *putting her arms comfortingly around her*]

MRS. VAN DAAN: There were some people called Wagner. They lived near us . . . ?

MR. FRANK: [*Interrupting, with a glance at* ANNE] I think we should put this off until later. We all have many questions we want to ask . . . But I'm sure that Mr. Dussel would like to get settled before supper.

DUSSEL: Thank you. I would. I brought very little with me.

MR. FRANK: [*Giving him his hat and briefcase*] I'm sorry we can't give you a room alone. But I hope you won't be too uncomfortable. We've had to make strict rules here . . . a schedule of hours . . . We'll tell you after supper. Anne, would you like to take Mr. Dussel to his room?

ANNE: [*Controlling her tears*] If you'll come with me, Mr. Dussel?

[*She starts for her room*]

DUSSEL: [*Shaking hands with each in turn*] Forgive me if I haven't really expressed my gratitude to all of you. This has been such a shock to me. I'd always thought of myself as Dutch. I was born in Holland, and my grandfather. And now . . . after all these years . . . [*He breaks off*] If you'll excuse me.

[DUSSEL *gives a little bow and hurries off after* ANNE. MR. FRANK *and the others are subdued*]

ANNE: [*Turning on the light*] Well, here we are.

[DUSSEL *looks around the room. In the main room* MARGOT *speaks to her mother*]

MARGOT: The news sounds pretty bad, doesn't it? It's so different from what Mr. Kraler tells us. Mr. Kraler says things are improving.

MR. VAN DAAN: I like it better the way Kraler tells it.

[*They resume their occupations, quietly.* PETER *goes off into his room. In* ANNE'S *room,* ANNE *turns to* DUSSEL]

ANNE: You're going to share the room with me.

DUSSEL: I'm a man who's always lived alone. I haven't had to adjust myself to others. I hope you'll bear with me until I learn.

ANNE: Let me help you. [*She takes his briefcase*] Do you always live all alone? Have you no family at all?

DUSSEL: No one.

[*He opens his medicine case and spreads his bottles on the dressing table*]

ANNE: How dreadful. You must be terribly lonely.

DUSSEL: I'm used to it.

ANNE: I don't think I could ever get used to it. Didn't you even have a pet? A cat, or a dog?

DUSSEL: I have an allergy for fur-bearing animals. They give me asthma.

ANNE: Oh, dear. Peter has a cat.

DUSSEL: Here? He has it here?

ANNE: Yes. But we hardly ever see it. He keeps it in his room all the time. I'm sure it will be all right.

DUSSEL: Let us hope so.

[*He takes some pills to fortify himself*]

ANNE: That's Margot's bed, where you're going to sleep. I sleep on the sofa there. [*Indicating the clothes hooks on the wall*] We cleared these off for your things. [*She goes over to the window*] The best part about this room . . . you can look down and see a bit of the street and the canal. There's a houseboat . . . you can see the end of it . . . a bargeman lives there with his family . . . They have a baby and he's just beginning to walk and I'm so afraid he's going to fall into the canal some day. I watch him. . . .

DUSSEL: [*Interrupting*] Your father spoke of a schedule.

ANNE: [*Coming away from the window*] Oh, yes. It's mostly about the times we have to be quiet. And times for the w.c. You can use it now if you like.

DUSSEL: [*Stiffly*] No, thank you.

ANNE: I suppose you think it's awful, my talking about a thing like that. But you don't know how important it can get to be, especially when you're frightened . . . About this room, the way Margot and I did . . . she had it to herself in the afternoons for studying, reading . . . lessons, you know . . . and I took the mornings. Would that be all right with you?

DUSSEL: I'm not at my best in the morning.

ANNE: You stay here in the mornings then. I'll take the room in the afternoons.

DUSSEL: Tell me, when you're in here, what happens to me? Where am I spending my time? In there, with all the people?

ANNE: Yes.

DUSSEL: I see. I see.

ANNE: We have supper at half past six.

DUSSEL: [*Going over to the sofa*] Then, if you don't mind . . . I like to lie down quietly for ten minutes before eating. I find it helps the digestion.

ANNE: Of course. I hope I'm not going to be too much of a bother to you. I seem to be able to get everyone's back up.

[DUSSEL *lies down on the sofa, curled up, his back to her*]

DUSSEL: I always get along very well with children. My patients all bring their children to me, because they know I get on well with them. So don't worry about that.

[ANNE *leans over him, taking his hand and shaking it gratefully*]

ANNE: Thank you. Thank you, Mr. Dussel.

[*The lights dim to darkness. The curtain falls on the scene.* ANNE'S VOICE *comes to us faintly at first, and then with increasing power*]

ANNE'S VOICE: . . . And yesterday I finished Cissy Van Marxvelt's latest book. I think she is a first-class writer. I shall definitely let my children read her. Monday the twenty-first of September, nineteen forty-two. Mr. Dussel and I had another battle yesterday. Yes, Mr. Dussel! According to him, nothing, I repeat . . . nothing, is right about me . . . my appearance, my character, my manners. While he was going on at me I thought . . . sometime I'll give you such a smack that you'll fly right up to the ceiling! Why is it that every grownup thinks he knows the way to bring up children? Particularly the grownups that never had any. I keep wishing that Peter was a girl instead of a boy. Then I would have someone to talk to. Margot's a darling, but she takes everything too seriously. To pause for a moment on the subject of Mrs. Van Daan. I must tell you that her attempts to flirt with father are getting her nowhere. Pim, thank goodness, won't play.

[*As she is saying the last lines, the curtain rises on the darkened scene.* ANNE'S VOICE *fades out*]

SCENE FOUR

It is the middle of the night, several months later. The stage is dark except for a little light which comes through the skylight in PETER's *room.*

Everyone is in bed. MR. *and* MRS. FRANK *lie on the couch in the main room, which has been pulled out to serve as a make-shift double bed.*

MARGOT *is sleeping on a mattress on the floor in the main room, behind a curtain stretched across for privacy. The others are all in their accustomed rooms.*

From outside we hear two drunken soldiers singing "Lili Marlene." A girl's high giggle is heard. The sound of running feet is heard coming closer and then fading in the distance. Throughout the scene there is the distant sound of airplanes passing overhead.

A match suddenly flares up in the attic. We dimly see MR. VAN DAAN. *He is getting his bearings. He comes quickly down the stairs, and goes to the cupboard where the food is stored. Again the match flares up, and is as quickly blown out. The dim figure is seen to steal back up the stairs.*

There is quiet for a second or two, broken only by the sound of airplanes, and running feet on the street below.

Suddenly, out of the silence and the dark, we hear ANNE *scream.*

ANNE: [*Screaming*] No! No! Don't . . . don't take me!

[*She moans, tossing and crying in her sleep. The other people wake, terrified.* DUSSEL *sits up in bed, furious*]

DUSSEL: Shush! Anne! Anne, for God's sake, shush!

ANNE: [*Still in her nightmare*] Save me! Save me!

[*She screams and screams.* DUSSEL *gets out of bed, going over to her, trying to wake her*]

DUSSEL: For God's sake! Quiet! Quiet! You want someone to hear?

[*In the main room* MRS. FRANK *grabs a shawl and pulls it around her. She rushes in to* ANNE, *taking her in her arms.* MR. FRANK *hurriedly gets up, putting on his overcoat.* MARGOT *sits up, terrified.* PETER's *light goes on in his room*]

MRS. FRANK: [*To* ANNE, *in her room*] Hush, darling, hush. It's all right. It's all right. [*Over her shoulder to* DUSSEL] Will you be kind enough to turn on the light, Mr. Dussel? [*Back to* ANNE] It's nothing, my darling. It was just a dream.

[DUSSEL *turns on the light in the bedroom.* MRS. FRANK *holds* ANNE *in her arms. Gradually* ANNE *comes out of her nightmare, still trembling with horror.* MR. FRANK *comes into the room, and goes quickly to the window, looking out to be sure that no one outside has heard* ANNE's *screams.* MRS. FRANK *holds* ANNE, *talking softly to her. In the main room* MARGOT *stands on a chair, turning on the center hanging lamp. A light goes on in the* VAN DAAN's *room overhead.* PETER *puts his robe on, coming out of his room*]

DUSSEL: [*To* MRS. FRANK, *blowing his nose*] Something must be done about that child, Mrs. Frank. Yelling like that! Who knows but there's somebody on the streets? She's endangering all our lives.

MRS. FRANK: Anne, darling.

DUSSEL: Every night she twists and turns. I don't sleep. I spend half my night shushing her. And now it's nightmares!

[MARGOT *comes to the door of* ANNE's *room, followed by* PETER. MR. FRANK *goes to them, indicating that everything is all right.* PETER *takes* MARGOT *back*]

MRS. FRANK: [*To* ANNE] You're here, safe, you see? Nothing has happened. [*To* DUSSEL] Please, Mr. Dussel, go back to bed. She'll be herself in a minute or two. Won't you, Anne?

DUSSEL: [*Picking up a book and a pillow*] Thank you, but I'm going to the w.c. The one place where there's peace!

[*He stalks out.* MR. VAN DAAN, *in underwear and trousers, comes down the stairs*]

MR. VAN DAAN: [*To* DUSSEL] What is it? What happened?

DUSSEL: A nightmare. She was having a nightmare!

MR. VAN DAAN: I thought someone was murdering her.

DUSSEL: Unfortunately, no.

[*He goes into the bathroom.* MR. VAN DAAN *goes back up the stairs.* MR. FRANK, *in the main room, sends* PETER *back to his own bedroom*]

MR. FRANK: Thank you, Peter. Go back to bed.

[PETER *goes back to his room.* MR. FRANK *follows him, turning out the light and looking out the window. Then he goes back to the main room, and gets up on a chair, turning out the center hanging lamp*]

MRS. FRANK: [*To* ANNE] Would you like some water? [ANNE *shakes her head*] Was it a very bad dream? Perhaps if you told me . . . ?

ANNE: I'd rather not talk about it.

MRS. FRANK: Poor darling. Try to sleep then. I'll sit right here beside you until you fall asleep.

[*She brings a stool over, sitting there*]

ANNE: You don't have to.

MRS. FRANK: But I'd like to stay with you . . . very much. Really.

ANNE: I'd rather you didn't.

MRS. FRANK: Good night, then. [*She leans down to kiss* ANNE. ANNE *throws her arm up over her face, turning away.* MRS. FRANK, *hiding her hurt, kisses* ANNE'S *arm*] You'll be all right? There's nothing that you want?

ANNE: Will you please ask Father to come.

MRS. FRANK: [*After a second*] Of course, Anne dear. [*She hurries out into the other room.* MR. FRANK *comes to her as she comes in*] Sie verlangt nach Dir!

MR. FRANK: [*Sensing her hurt*] Edith, *Liebe, shau* . . .

MRS. FRANK: *Es macht nichts! Ich danke dem lieben Herrgott, dass sie sich wenigstens an Dich wendet, wenn sie Trost braucht! Geh hinein, Otto, sie ist ganz hysterisch vor Angst.* [*As* MR. FRANK *hesitates*] *Geh zu ihr.* [*He looks at her for a second and then goes to get a cup of water for* ANNE. MRS. FRANK *sinks down on the bed, her face in her hands, trying to keep from sobbing aloud.* MARGOT *comes over to her, putting her arms around her*] She wants nothing of me. She pulled away when I leaned down to kiss her.

MARGOT: It's a phase . . . You heard Father . . . Most girls go through it . . . they turn to their fathers at this age . . . they give all their love to their fathers.

MRS. FRANK: You weren't like this. You didn't shut me out.

MARGOT: She'll get over it . . .

[*She smooths the bed for* MRS. FRANK *and sits beside her a moment as* MRS. FRANK *lies down. In* ANNE'S *room* MR. FRANK *comes in, sitting down by* ANNE. ANNE *flings her arms around him, clinging to him. In the distance we hear the sound of ack-ack*]

ANNE: Oh, Pim. I dreamed that they came to get us! The Green Police! They broke down the door and grabbed me and started to drag me out the way they did Jopie.

MR. FRANK: I want you to take this pill.

ANNE: What is it?

MR. FRANK: Something to quiet you.

[*She takes it and drinks the water. In the main room* MARGOT *turns out the light and goes back to her bed*]

MR. FRANK: [*To* ANNE] Do you want me to read to you for a while?

ANNE: No. Just sit with me for a minute. Was I awful? Did I yell terribly loud? Do you think anyone outside could have heard?

MR. FRANK: No. No. Lie quietly now. Try to sleep.

ANNE: I'm a terrible coward. I'm so disappointed in myself. I think I've conquered my fear . . . I think I'm really grown-up . . . and then something happens . . . and I run to you like a baby . . . I love you, Father. I don't love anyone but you.

MR. FRANK: [*Reproachfully*] Annele!

ANNE: It's true. I've been thinking about it for a long time. You're the only one I love.

MR. FRANK: It's fine to hear you tell me that you love me. But I'd be happier if you said you loved your mother as well . . . She needs your help so much . . . your love . . .

ANNE: We have nothing in common. She doesn't understand me. Whenever I try to explain my views on life to her she asks me if I'm constipated.

MR. FRANK: You hurt her very much just now. She's crying. She's in there crying.

ANNE: I can't help it. I only told the truth. I didn't want her here . . . [*Then, with sudden change*] Oh, Pim, I was horrible, wasn't I? And the worst of it is, I can stand off and look at myself doing it and know it's cruel and yet I can't stop doing it. What's the matter with me? Tell me. Don't say it's just a phase! Help me.

MR. FRANK: There is so little that we parents can do to help our children. We can only try to set a good example . . . point the way. The rest you must do yourself. You must build your own character.

ANNE: I'm trying. Really I am. Every night I think back over all of the things I did that day that were wrong . . . like putting the wet mop in Mr. Dussel's bed . . . and this thing now with Mother. I say to myself, that was wrong. I make up my mind, I'm never going to do that again. Never! Of course I may do something worse . . . but at least I'll never do *that* again! . . . I have a nicer side, Father . . . a sweeter, nicer side. But I'm scared to show it. I'm afraid that people are going to laugh at me if I'm serious. So the mean Anne comes to the outside and the good Anne stays on the inside, and I keep on trying to switch them around and have the good Anne outside and the bad Anne inside and be what I'd like to be . . . and might be . . . if only . . . only . . .

[*She is asleep.* MR. FRANK *watches her for a moment and then turns off the light, and starts out. The lights dim out.*

The curtain falls on the scene. ANNE'S VOICE *is heard dimly at first, and then with growing strength]*

ANNE'S VOICE: . . . The air raids are getting worse. They come over day and night. The noise is terrifying. Pim says it should be music to our ears. The more planes, the sooner will come the end of the war. Mrs. Van Daan pretends to be a fatalist. What will be, will be. But when the planes come over, who is the most frightened? No one else but Petronella! . . . Monday, the ninth of November, nineteen forty-two. Wonderful news! The Allies have landed in Africa. Pim says that we can look for an early finish to the war. Just for fun he asked each of us what was the first thing we wanted to do when we got out of here. Mrs. Van Daan longs to be home with her own things, her needle-point chairs, the Beckstein piano her father gave her . . . the best that money could buy. Peter would like to go to a movie. Mr. Dussel wants to get back to his dentist's drill. He's afraid he is losing his touch. For myself, there are so many things . . . to ride a bike again . . . to laugh till my belly aches . . . to have new clothes from the skin out . . . to have a hot tub filled to overflowing and wallow in it for hours . . . to be back in school with my friends . . .

[*As the last lines are being said, the curtain rises on the scene. The lights dim on as* ANNE'S VOICE *fades away]*

SCENE FIVE

It is the first night of the Hanukkah celebration. MR. FRANK *is standing at the head of the table on which is the Menorah. He lights the Shamos, or servant candle, and holds it as he says the blessing. Seated listening is all of the "family," dressed in their best. The men wear hats,* PETER *wears his cap.*

MR. FRANK: [*Reading from a prayer book*] "Praised be Thou, oh Lord our God, Ruler of the universe, who has sanctified us with Thy commandments and bidden us kindle the Hanukkah lights. Praised be Thou, oh Lord our God, Ruler of the universe, who has wrought wondrous deliverances for our fathers in days of old. Praised be Thou, oh Lord our God, Ruler of the universe, that Thou has given us life and sustenance and brought us to this happy season." [MR. FRANK *lights the one candle of the Menorah as he continues*] "We kindle this Hanukkah light to celebrate the great and wonderful deeds wrought through the zeal with which God filled the hearts of the heroic Maccabees, two thousand years ago. They fought against indifference, against tyranny and oppression, and they restored our Temple to us. May these lights remind us that we should ever look to God, whence cometh our help." Amen. [Pronounced O-mayn]

ALL: Amen.

[MR. FRANK *hands* MRS. FRANK *the prayer book*]

MRS. FRANK: [*Reading*] "I lift up mine eyes unto the mountains, from whence cometh my help. My help cometh from the Lord who made heaven and earth. He will not suffer thy foot to be moved. He that keepeth thee will not slumber. He that keepeth Israel doth neither slumber nor sleep. The Lord is thy keeper. The Lord is thy shade upon thy right hand. The sun shall not smite thee by day, nor the moon by night. The Lord shall keep thee from all evil. He shall keep thy soul. The Lord shall guard thy going out and thy coming in, from this time forth and forevermore." Amen.

ALL: Amen.

[MRS. FRANK *puts down the prayer book and goes to get the food and wine.* MARGOT *helps her.* MR. FRANK *takes the men's hats and puts them aside*]

DUSSEL: [*Rising*] That was very moving.

ANNE: [*Pulling him back*] It isn't over yet!

MRS. VAN DAAN: Sit down! Sit down!

ANNE: There's a lot more, songs and presents.

DUSSEL: Presents?

MRS. FRANK: Not this year, unfortunately.

MRS. VAN DAAN: But always on Hanukkah everyone gives presents . . . everyone!

DUSSEL: Like our St. Nicholas' Day.

[*There is a chorus of "no's" from the group*]

MRS. VAN DAAN: No! Not like St. Nicholas! What kind of a Jew are you that you don't know Hanukkah?

MRS. FRANK: [*As she brings the food*] I remember particularly the candles . . . First one, as we have tonight. Then the second night you light two candles, the next night three . . . and so on until you have eight candles burning. When there are eight candles it is truly beautiful.

MRS. VAN DAAN: And the potato pancakes.

MR. VAN DAAN: Don't talk about them!

MRS. VAN DAAN: I make the best *latkes* you ever tasted!

MRS. FRANK: Invite us all next year . . . in your own home.

MR. FRANK: God willing!

MRS. VAN DAAN: God willing.

MARGOT: What I remember best is the presents we used to get when we were little . . . eight days of presents . . . and each day they got better and better.

MRS. FRANK: [*Sitting down*] We are all here, alive. That is present enough.

ANNE: No, it isn't. I've got something . . .

[*She rushes into her room, hurriedly puts on a little hat improvised from the lamp shade, grabs a satchel bulging with parcels and comes running back*]

MRS. FRANK: What is it?

ANNE: Presents!

MRS. VAN DAAN: Presents!

DUSSEL: Look!

MR. VAN DAAN: What's she got on her head?

PETER: A lamp shade!

ANNE: [*She picks out one at random*] This is for Margot. [*She hands it to* MARGOT, *pulling her to her feet*] Read it out loud.

MARGOT: [*Reading*]

"You have never lost your temper.
You never will, I fear,
You are so good.
But if you should,
Put all your cross words here."

[*She tears open the package*] A new crossword puzzle book! Where did you get it?

ANNE: It isn't new. It's one that you've done. But I rubbed it all out, and if you wait a little and forget, you can do it all over again.

MARGOT: [*Sitting*] It's wonderful, Anne. Thank you. You'd never know it wasn't new.

[*From outside we hear the sound of a streetcar passing*]

ANNE: [*With another gift*] Mrs. Van Daan.

MRS. VAN DAAN: [*Taking it*] This is awful . . . I haven't anything for anyone . . . I never thought . . .

MR. FRANK: This is all Anne's idea.

MRS. VAN DAAN: [*Holding up a bottle*] What is it?

ANNE: It's hair shampoo. I took all the odds and ends of soap and mixed them with the last of my toilet water.

MRS. VAN DAAN: Oh, Anneke!

ANNE: I wanted to write a poem for all of them, but I didn't have time. [*Offering a large box to* MR. VAN DAAN] Yours, Mr. Van Daan, is *really* something . . . something you want more than anything. [*As she waits for him to open it*] Look! Cigarettes!

MR. VAN DAAN: Cigarettes!

ANNE: Two of them! Pim found some old pipe tobacco in the pocket lining of his coat . . . and we made them . . . or rather, Pim did.

MRS. VAN DAAN: Let me see . . . Well, look at that! Light it, Putti! Light it.

[MR. VAN DAAN *hesitates*]

ANNE: It's tobacco, really it is! There's a little fluff in it, but not much.

[*Everyone watches intently as* MR. VAN DAAN *cautiously lights it. The cigarette flares up. Everyone laughs*]

PETER: It works!

MRS. VAN DAAN: Look at him.

MR. VAN DAAN: [*Spluttering*] Thank you, Anne. Thank you.

[ANNE *rushes back to her satchel for another present*]

ANNE: [*Handing her mother a piece of paper*] For Mother, Hanukkah greeting.

[*She pulls her mother to her feet*]

MRS. FRANK: [*She reads*]
"Here's an I.O.U. that I promise to pay.
Ten hours of doing whatever you say.
                    Signed, Anne Frank."

[MRS. FRANK, *touched, takes* ANNE *in her arms, holding her close*]

DUSSEL: [*To* ANNE] Ten hours of doing what you're told? Any-thing you're told?

ANNE: That's right.

DUSSEL: You wouldn't want to sell that, Mrs. Frank?

MRS. FRANK: Never! This is the most precious gift I've ever had!

[*She sits, showing her present to the others.* ANNE *hurries back to the satchel and pulls out a scarf, the scarf that* MR. FRANK *found in the first scene*]

ANNE: [*Offering it to her father*] For Pim.

MR. FRANK: Anneke . . . I wasn't supposed to have a present!

[*He takes it, unfolding it and showing it to the others*]

ANNE: It's a muffler . . . to put round your neck . . . like an ascot, you know. I made it myself out of odds and ends . . . I knitted it in the dark each night, after I'd gone to bed. I'm afraid it looks better in the dark!

MR. FRANK: [*Putting it on*] It's fine. It fits me perfectly. Thank you, Annele.

[ANNE *hands* PETER *a ball of paper, with a string attached to it*]

ANNE: That's for Mouschi.

PETER: [*Rising to bow*] On behalf of Mouschi, I thank you.

ANNE: [*Hesitant, handing him a gift*] And . . . this is yours . . . from Mrs. Quack Quack. [*As he holds it gingerly in his hands*] Well . . . open it . . . Aren't you going to open it?

PETER: I'm scared to. I know something's going to jump out and hit me.

ANNE: No. It's nothing like that, really.

MRS. VAN DAAN: [*As he is opening it*] What is it, Peter? Go on. Show it.

ANNE: [*Excitedly*] It's a safety razor!

DUSSEL: A what?

ANNE: A razor!

MRS. VAN DAAN: [*Looking at it*] You didn't make that out of odds and ends.

ANNE: [*To* PETER] Miep got it for me. It's not new. It's second-hand. But you really do need a razor now.

DUSSEL: For what?

ANNE: Look on his upper lip . . . you can see the beginning of a mustache.

DUSSEL: He wants to get rid of that? Put a little milk on it and let the cat lick it off.

PETER: [*Starting for his room*] Think you're funny, don't you.

DUSSEL: Look! He can't wait! He's going to try it!

PETER: I'm going to give Mouschi his present!

[*He goes into his room, slamming the door behind him*]

MR. VAN DAAN: [*Disgustedly*] Mouschi, Mouschi, Mouschi.

[*In the distance we hear a dog persistently barking.* ANNE *brings a gift to* DUSSEL]

ANNE: And last but never least, my roommate, Mr. Dussel.

DUSSEL: For me? You have something for me?

[*He opens the small box she gives him*]

ANNE: I made them myself.

DUSSEL: [*Puzzled*] Capsules! Two capsules!

ANNE: They're ear-plugs!

DUSSEL: Ear-plugs?

ANNE: To put in your ears so you won't hear me when I thrash around at night. I saw them advertised in a magazine. They're not real ones . . . I made them out of cotton and candle wax. Try them . . . See if they don't work . . . see if you can hear me talk . . .

DUSSEL: [*Putting them in his ears*] Wait now until I get them in . . . so.

ANNE: Are you ready?

DUSSEL: Huh?

ANNE: Are you ready?

DUSSEL: Good God! They've gone inside! I can't get them out! [*They laugh as* MR. DUSSEL *jumps about, trying to shake the plugs out of his ears. Finally he gets them out. Putting them away*] Thank you, Anne! Thank you!

MR. VAN DAAN:	MRS. VAN DAAN:	MRS. FRANK:	MARGOT: I
A real Hanuk-	Wasn't it cute	I don't know	love my pres-
kah!	of her?	when she did	ent.
		it.	

ANNE: [*Sitting at the table*] And now let's have the song, Father . . . please . . . [*To* DUSSEL] Have you heard the Hanukkah song, Mr. Dussel? The song is the whole thing! [*She sings*] "Oh, Hanukkah! Oh, Hanukkah! The sweet celebration . . ."

MR. FRANK: [*Quieting her*] I'm afraid, Anne, we shouldn't sing that song tonight. [*To* DUSSEL] It's a song of jubilation, of rejoicing. One is apt to become too enthusiastic.

ANNE: Oh, please, please. Let's sing the song. I promise not to shout!

MR. FRANK: Very well. But quietly now . . . I'll keep an eye on you and when . . .

[*As* ANNE *starts to sing, she is interrupted by* DUSSEL, *who is snorting and wheezing*]

DUSSEL: [*Pointing to* PETER] You . . . You! [PETER *is coming from his bedroom, ostentatiously holding a bulge is his coat as if he were holding his cat, and dangling* ANNE's *present before it*] How many times . . . I told you . . . Out! Out!

MR. VAN DAAN: [*Going to* PETER] What's the matter with you? Haven't you any sense? Get that cat out of here.

PETER: [*Innocently*] Cat?

MR. VAN DAAN: You heard me. Get it out of here!

PETER: I have no cat.

[*Delighted with his joke, he opens his coat and pulls out a bath towel. The group at the table laugh, enjoying the joke*]

DUSSEL: [*Still wheezing*] It doesn't need to be the cat . . . his clothes are enough . . . when he comes out of that room . . .

MR. VAN DAAN: Don't worry. You won't be bothered any more. We're getting rid of it.

DUSSEL: At last you listen to me.

[*He goes off into his bedroom*]

MR. VAN DAAN: [*Calling after him*] I'm not doing it for you. That's all in your mind . . . all of it! [*He starts back to his place at the table*] I'm doing it because I'm sick of seeing that cat eat all our food.

PETER: That's not true! I only give him bones . . . scraps . . .

MR. VAN DAAN: Don't tell me! He gets fatter every day! Damn cat looks better than any of us. Out he goes tonight!

PETER: No! No!

ANNE: Mr. Van Daan, you can't do that! That's Peter's cat. Peter loves that cat.

MRS. FRANK: [*Quietly*] Anne.

PETER: [*To* MR. VAN DAAN] If he goes, I go.

MR. VAN DAAN: Go! Go!

MRS. VAN DAAN: You're not going and the cat's not going! Now please . . . this is Hanukkah . . . Hanukkah . . . this is the time to celebrate . . . What's the matter with all of you? Come on, Anne. Let's have the song.

ANNE: [*Singing*]
"*Oh, Hanukkah! Oh, Hanukkah!
The sweet celebration.*"

MR. FRANK: [*Rising*] I think we should first blow out the candle . . . then we'll have something for tomorrow night.

MARGOT: But, Father, you're supposed to let it burn itself out.

MR. FRANK: I'm sure that God understands shortages. [*Before blowing it out*]"Praised be Thou, oh Lord our God, who hast sustained us and permitted us to celebrate this joyous festival."

[*He is about to blow out the candle when suddenly there is a crash of something falling below. They all freeze in horror, motionless. For a few seconds there is complete silence.* MR. FRANK *slips off his shoes. The others noiselessly follow his ex-*

ample. MR. FRANK *turns out a light near him. He motions to* PETER *to turn off the center lamp.* PETER *tries to reach it, realizes he cannot and gets up on a chair. Just as he is touching the lamp he loses his balance. The chair goes out from under him. He falls. The iron lamp shade crashes to the floor. There is a sound of feet below, running down the stairs*]

MR. VAN DAAN: [*Under his breath*] God Almighty! [*The only light left comes from the Hanukkah candle.* DUSSEL *comes from his room.* MR. FRANK *creeps over to the stairwell and stands listening. The dog is heard barking excitedly*] Do you hear anything?

MR. FRANK: [*In a whisper*] No. I think they've gone.

MRS. VAN DAAN: It's the Green Police. They've found us.

MR. FRANK: If they had, they wouldn't have left. They'd be up here by now.

MRS. VAN DAAN: I know it's the Green Police. They've gone to get help. That's all. They'll be back!

MR. VAN DAAN: Or it may have been the Gestapo, looking for papers . . .

MR. FRANK: [*Interrupting*] Or a thief, looking for money.

MRS. VAN DAAN: We've got to do something . . . Quick! Quick! Before they come back.

MR. VAN DAAN: There isn't anything to do. Just wait.

[MR. FRANK *holds up his hand for them to be quiet. He is listening intently. There is complete silence as they all strain to hear any sound from below. Suddenly* ANNE *begins to sway. With a low cry she falls to the floor in a faint.* MRS. FRANK *goes to her quickly, sitting beside her on the floor and taking her in her arms*]

MRS. FRANK: Get some water, please! Get some water!

[MARGOT *starts for the sink*]

MR. VAN DAAN: [*Grabbing* MARGOT] No! No! No one's going to run water!

MR. FRANK: If they've found us, they've found us. Get the water. [MARGOT *starts again for the sink.* MR. FRANK, *getting a flashlight*] I'm going down.

> [MARGOT *rushes to him, clinging to him.* ANNE *struggles to consciousness*]

MARGOT: No, Father, no! There may be someone there, waiting . . . It may be a trap!

MR. FRANK: This is Saturday. There is no way for us to know what has happened until Miep or Mr. Kraler comes on Monday morning. We cannot live with this uncertainty.

MARGOT: Don't go, Father!

MRS. FRANK: Hush, darling, hush. [MR. FRANK *slips quietly out, down the steps and out through the door below*] Margot! Stay close to me.

> [MARGOT *goes to her mother*]

MR. VAN DAAN: Shush! Shush!

> [MRS. FRANK *whispers to* MARGOT *to get the water.* MARGOT *goes for it*]

MRS. VAN DAAN: Putti, where's our money? Get our money. I hear you can buy the Green Police off, so much a head. Go upstairs quick! Get the money!

MR. VAN DAAN: Keep still!

MRS. VAN DAAN: [*Kneeling before him, pleading*] Do you want to be dragged off to a concentration camp? Are you going to stand there and wait for them to come up and get you? Do something, I tell you!

MR. VAN DAAN: [*Pushing her aside*] Will you keep still!

> [*He goes over to the stairwell to listen.* PETER *goes to his mother, helping her up onto the sofa. There is a second of silence, then* ANNE *can stand it no longer*]

ANNE: Someone go after Father! Make Father come back!

PETER: [*Starting for the door*] I'll go.

MR. VAN DAAN: Haven't you done enough?

[*He pushes* PETER *roughly away. In his anger against his father* PETER *grabs a chair as if to hit him with it, then puts it down, burying his face in his hands.* MRS. FRANK *begins to pray softly*]

ANNE: Please, please, Mr. Van Daan. Get Father.

MR. VAN DAAN: Quiet! Quiet!

[ANNE *is shocked into silence.* MRS. FRANK *pulls her closer, holding her protectively in her arms*]

MRS. FRANK: [*Softly, praying*] "I lift up mine eyes unto the mountains, from whence cometh my help. My help cometh from the Lord who made heaven and earth. He will not suffer thy foot to be moved . . . He that keepeth thee will not slumber . . ."

[*She stops as she hears someone coming. They all watch the door tensely.* MR. FRANK *comes quietly in.* ANNE *rushes to him, holding him tight*]

MR. FRANK: It was a thief. That noise must have scared him away.

MRS. VAN DAAN: Thank God.

MR. FRANK: He took the cash box. And the radio. He ran away in such a hurry that he didn't stop to shut the street door. It was swinging wide open. [*A breath of relief sweeps over them*] I think it would be good to have some light.

MARGOT: Are you sure it's all right?

MR. FRANK: The danger has passed. [MARGOT *goes to light the small lamp*] Don't be so terrified, Anne. We're safe.

DUSSEL: Who says the danger has passed? Don't you realize we are in greater danger than ever?

MR. FRANK: Mr. Dussel, will you be still!

[MR. FRANK *takes* ANNE *back to the table, making her sit down with him, trying to calm her*]

DUSSEL: [*Pointing to* PETER] Thanks to this clumsy fool, there's someone now who knows we're up here! Someone now knows we're up here, hiding!

MRS. VAN DAAN: [*Going to* DUSSEL] Someone knows we're here, yes. But who is the someone? A thief! A thief! You think a thief is going to go to the Green Police and say . . . I was robbing a place the other night and I heard a noise up over my head? You think a thief is going to do that?

DUSSEL: Yes. I think he will.

MRS. VAN DAAN: [*Hysterically*] You're crazy!

[*She stumbles back to her seat at the table.* PETER *follows protectively, pushing* DUSSEL *aside*]

DUSSEL: I think some day he'll be caught and then he'll make a bargain with the Green Police . . . if they'll let him off, he'll tell them where some Jews are hiding!

[*He goes off into the bedroom. There is a second of appalled silence*]

MR. VAN DAAN: He's right.

ANNE: Father, let's get out of here! We can't stay here now . . . Let's go . . .

MR. VAN DAAN: Go! Where?

MRS. FRANK: [*Sinking into her chair at the table*] Yes. Where?

MR. FRANK: [*Rising, to them all*] Have we lost all faith? All courage? A moment ago we thought that they'd come for us. We were sure it was the end. But it wasn't the end. We're alive, safe. [MR. VAN DAAN *goes to the table and sits,* MR. FRANK *prays*] "We thank Thee, oh Lord our God, that in Thy infinite mercy Thou hast again seen fit to spare us." [*He blows out the candle, then turns to* ANNE] Come on, Anne. The song! Let's have the song!

[*He starts to sing.* ANNE *finally starts falteringly to sing, as* MR. FRANK *urges her on. Her voice is hardly audible at first*]

ANNE: [*Singing*]
"Oh, Hanukkah! Oh, Hanukkah!
The sweet . . . celebration . . ."

[*As she goes on singing, the others gradually join in, their voices still shaking with fear.* MRS. VAN DAAN *sobs as she sings*]

GROUP

"Around the feast . . . we . . . gather
In complete . . . jubilation . . .
Happiest of sea . . . sons
Now is here.
Many are the reasons for good cheer."

[DUSSEL comes from the bedroom. He comes over to the table, standing beside MARGOT, listening to them as they sing]

"Together
We'll weather
Whatever tomorrow may bring."

[As they sing on with growing courage, the lights start to dim]

"So hear us rejoicing
And merrily voicing
The Hanukkah song that we sing.
Hoy!"

[The lights are out. The curtain starts slowly to fall]

"Hear us rejoicing
And merrily voicing
The Hanukkah song that we sing."

[They are still singing, as the curtain falls]

CURTAIN

ACT TWO

SCENE ONE

In the darkness we hear ANNE'S VOICE, *again reading from the diary.*

ANNE'S VOICE: Saturday, the first of January, nineteen forty-four. Another new year has begun and we find ourselves still in our hiding place. We have been here now for one year, five months and twenty-five days. It seems that our life is at a standstill.

[*The curtain rises on the scene. It is late afternoon. Everyone is bundled up against the cold. In the main room* MRS. FRANK *is taking down the laundry which is hung across the back.* MR. FRANK *sits in the chair down left, reading.* MARGOT *is lying on the couch with a blanket over her and the many-colored knitted scarf around her throat.* ANNE *is seated at the center table, writing in her diary.* PETER, MR. *and* MRS. VAN DAAN *and* DUSSEL *are all in their own rooms, reading or lying down.*

As the lights dim on, ANNE'S VOICE *continues, without a break*]

ANNE'S VOICE: We are all a little thinner. The Van Daans' "discussions" are as violent as ever. Mother still does not understand me. But then I don't understand her either. There is one great change, however. A change in myself. I read somewhere that girls of my age don't feel quite certain of themselves. That they become quiet within and begin to think of the miracle that is taking place in their bodies. I think that what is happening to me is so wonderful . . . not only what can be seen, but what is taking place inside. Each time it has happened I have a feeling that I have a sweet secret. [*We hear the chimes and then a hymn being played on the carillon outside*] And in spite of any pain, I long for the time when I shall feel that secret within me again.

[*The buzzer of the door below suddenly sounds. Everyone is startled,* MR. FRANK *tiptoes cautiously to the top of the steps and listens. Again the buzzer sounds, in* MIEP's *V-for-Victory signal*]

MR. FRANK: It's Miep!

[*He goes quickly down the steps to unbolt the door.* MRS. FRANK *calls upstairs to the* VAN DAANS *and then to* PETER]

MRS. FRANK: Wake up, everyone! Miep is here! [ANNE *quickly puts her diary away.* MARGOT *sits up, pulling the blanket around her shoulders.* MR. DUSSEL *sits on the edge of his bed, listening, disgruntled.* MIEP *comes up the steps, followed by* MR. KRALER. *They bring flowers, books, newspapers, etc.* ANNE *rushes to* MIEP, *throwing her arms affectionately around her*] Miep . . . and Mr. Kraler . . . What a delightful surprise!

MR. KRALER: We came to bring you New Year's greetings.

MRS. FRANK: You shouldn't . . . you should have at least one day to yourselves.

[*She goes quickly to the stove and brings down teacups and tea for all of them*]

ANNE: Don't say that, it's so wonderful to see them! [*Sniffing at* MIEP's *coat*] I can smell the wind and the cold on your clothes.

MIEP: [*Giving her the flowers*] There you are. [*Then to* MARGOT, *feeling her forehead*] How are you, Margot? . . . Feeling any better?

MARGOT: I'm all right.

ANNE: We filled her full of every kind of pill so she won't cough and make a noise.

[*She runs into her room to put the flowers in water.* MR. *and* MRS. VAN DAAN *come from upstairs. Outside there is the sound of a band playing*]

MRS. VAN DAAN: Well, hello, Miep. Mr. Kraler.

MR. KRALER: [*Giving a bouquet of flowers to* MRS. VAN DAAN] With my hope for peace in the New Year.

PETER: [*Anxiously*] Miep, have you seen Mouschi? Have you seen him anywhere around?

MIEP: I'm sorry, Peter. I asked everyone in the neighborhood had they seen a gray cat. But they said no.

[MRS. FRANK *gives* MIEP *a cup of tea.* MR. FRANK *comes up the steps, carrying a small cake on a plate*]

MR. FRANK: Look what Miep's brought for us!

MRS. FRANK: [*Taking it*] A cake!

MR. VAN DAAN: A cake! [*He pinches* MIEP's *cheeks gaily and hurries up to the cupboard*] I'll get some plates.

[DUSSEL, *in his room, hastily puts a coat on and starts out to join the others*]

MRS. FRANK: Thank you, Miepia. You shouldn't have done it. You must have used all of your sugar ration for weeks. [*Giving it to* MRS. VAN DAAN] It's beautiful, isn't it?

MRS. VAN DAAN: It's been ages since I even saw a cake. Not since you brought us one last year. [*Without looking at the cake, to* MIEP] Remember? Don't you remember, you gave us one on New Year's Day? Just this time last year? I'll never forget it because you had "Peace in nineteen forty-three" on it. [*She looks at the cake and reads*] "Peace in nineteen forty-four!"

MIEP: Well, it has to come sometime, you know. [*As* DUSSEL *comes from his room*] Hello, Mr. Dussel.

MR. KRALER: How are you?

MR. VAN DAAN: [*Bringing plates and a knife*] Here's the knife, liefje. Now, how many of us are there?

MIEP: None for me, thank you.

MR. FRANK: Oh, please. You must.

MIEP: I couldn't.

MR. VAN DAAN: Good! That leaves one . . . two . . . three . . . seven of us.

DUSSEL: Eight! Eight! It's the same number as it always is!

MR. VAN DAAN: I left Margot out. I take it for granted Margot won't eat any.

ANNE: Why wouldn't she!

MRS. FRANK: I think it won't harm her.

MR. VAN DAAN: All right! All right! I just didn't want her to start coughing again, that's all.

DUSSEL: And please, Mrs. Frank should cut the cake.

MR. VAN DAAN: What's the dif-   MRS. VAN DAAN: It's not Mrs.
ference?   Frank's cake, is it, Miep? It's for all of us.

DUSSEL: Mrs. Frank divides things better.

MRS. VAN DAAN: [Going to   MR. VAN DAAN: Oh, come on!
DUSSEL] What are you trying   Stop wasting time!
to say?

MRS. VAN DAAN: [To DUSSEL] Don't I always give everybody exactly the same? Don't I?

MR. VAN DAAN: Forget it, Kerli.

MRS. VAN DAAN: No. I want an answer! Don't I?

DUSSEL: Yes. Yes. Everybody gets exactly the same . . . except Mr. Van Daan always gets a little bit more.

[VAN DAAN advances on DUSSEL, the knife still in his hand]

MR. VAN DAAN: That's a lie!

[DUSSEL retreats before the onslaught of the VAN DAANS]

MR. FRANK: Please, please! [Then to MIEP] You see what a little sugar cake does to us? It goes right to our heads!

MR. VAN DAAN: [Handing MRS. FRANK the knife] Here you are, Mrs. Frank.

MRS. FRANK: Thank you. [*Then to* MIEP *as she goes to the table to cut the cake*] Are you sure you won't have some?

MIEP: [*Drinking her tea*] No, really, I have to go in a minute.

[*The sound of the band fades out in the distance*]

PETER: [*To* MIEP] Maybe Mouschi went back to our house . . . they say that cats . . . Do you ever get over there . . . ? I mean . . . do you suppose you could . . . ?

MIEP: I'll try, Peter. The first minute I get I'll try. But I'm afraid, with him gone a week . . .

DUSSEL: Make up your mind, already someone has had a nice big dinner from that cat!

[PETER *is furious, inarticulate. He starts toward* DUSSEL *as if to hit him.* MR. FRANK *stops him.* MRS. FRANK *speaks quickly to ease the situation*]

MRS. FRANK: [*To* MIEP] This is delicious, Miep!

MRS. VAN DAAN: [*Eating hers*] Delicious!

MR. VAN DAAN: [*Finishing it in one gulp*] Dirk's in luck to get a girl who can bake like this!

MIEP: [*Putting down her empty teacup*] I have to run. Dirk's taking me to a party tonight.

ANNE: How heavenly! Remember now what everyone is wearing, and what you have to eat and everything, so you can tell us tomorrow.

MIEP: I'll give you a full report! Good-bye, everyone!

MR. VAN DAAN: [*To* MIEP] Just a minute. There's something I'd like you to do for me.

[*He hurries off up the stairs to his room*]

MRS. VAN DAAN: [*Sharply*] Putti, where are you going? [*She rushes up the stairs after him, calling hysterically*] What do you want? Putti, what are you going to do?

MIEP: [*To* PETER] What's wrong?

PETER: [*His sympathy is with his mother*] Father says he's going to sell her fur coat. She's crazy about that old fur coat.

DUSSEL: Is it possible? Is it possible that anyone is so silly as to worry about a fur coat in times like this?

PETER: It's none of your darn business . . . and if you say one more thing . . . I'll, I'll take you and I'll . . . I mean it . . . I'll . . .

[*There is a piercing scream from* MRS. VAN DAAN *above. She grabs at the fur coat as* MR. VAN DAAN *is starting downstairs with it*]

MRS. VAN DAAN: No! No! No! Don't you dare take that! You hear? It's mine! [*Downstairs* PETER *turns away, embarrassed, miserable*] My father gave me that! You didn't give it to me. You have no right. Let go of it . . . you hear?

[MR. VAN DAAN *pulls the coat from her hands and hurries downstairs.* MRS. VAN DAAN *sinks to the floor, sobbing. As* MR. VAN DAAN *comes into the main room the others look away, embarrassed for him*]

MR. VAN DAAN: [*To* MR. KRALER] Just a little—discussion over the advisability of selling this coat. As I have often reminded Mrs. Van Daan, it's very selfish of her to keep it when people outside are in such desperate need of clothing . . . [*He gives the coat to* MIEP] So if you will please to sell it for us? It should fetch a good price. And by the way, will you get me cigarettes. I don't care what kind they are . . . get all you can.

MIEP: It's terribly difficult to get them, Mr. Van Daan. But I'll try. Good-bye.

[*She goes.* MR. FRANK *follows her down the steps to bolt the door after her.* MRS. FRANK *gives* MR. KRALER *a cup of tea*]

MRS. FRANK: Are you sure you won't have some cake, Mr. Kraler?

MR. KRALER: I'd better not.

MR. VAN DAAN: You're still feeling badly? What does your doctor say?

MR. KRALER: I haven't been to him.

MRS. FRANK: Now, Mr. Kraler! . . .

MR. KRALER: [*Sitting at the table*] Oh, I tried. But you can't get near a doctor these days . . . they're so busy. After weeks I finally managed to get one on the telephone. I told him I'd like an appointment . . . I wasn't feeling very well. You know what he answers . . . over the telephone . . . Stick out your tongue! [*They laugh. He turns to* MR. FRANK *as* MR. FRANK *comes back*] I have some contracts here . . . I wonder if you'd look over them with me . . .

MR. FRANK: [*Putting out his hand*] Of course.

MR. KRALER: [*He rises*] If we could go downstairs . . . [MR. FRANK *starts ahead,* MR. KRALER *speaks to the others*] Will you forgive us? I won't keep him but a minute.

[*He starts to follow* MR. FRANK *down the steps*]

MARGOT: [*With sudden foreboding*] What's happened? Something's happened! Hasn't it, Mr. Kraler?

[MR. KRALER *stops and comes back, trying to reassure* MARGOT *with a pretense of casualness*]

MR. KRALER: No, really. I want your father's advice . . .

MARGOT: Something's gone wrong! I know it!

MR. FRANK: [*Coming back, to* MR. KRALER] If it's something that concerns us here, it's better that we all hear it.

MR. KRALER: [*Turning to him, quietly*] But . . . the children . . . ?

MR. FRANK: What they'd imagine would be worse than any reality.

[*As* MR. KRALER *speaks, they all listen with intense apprehension.* MRS. VAN DAAN *comes down the stairs and sits on the bottom step*]

MR. KRALER: It's a man in the storeroom . . . I don't know whether or not you remember him . . . Carl, about fifty, heavy-set, near-sighted . . . He came with us just before you left.

MR. FRANK: He was from Utrecht?

MR. KRALER: That's the man. A couple of weeks ago, when I was in the storeroom, he closed the door and asked me . . . how's Mr.

Frank? What do you hear from Mr. Frank? I told him I only knew there was a rumor that you were in Switzerland. He said he'd heard that rumor too, but he thought I might know something more. I didn't pay any attention to it . . . but then a thing happened yesterday . . . He'd brought some invoices to the office for me to sign. As I was going through them, I looked up. He was standing staring at the bookcase . . . your bookcase. He said he thought he remembered a door there . . . Wasn't there a door there that used to go up to the loft? Then he told me he wanted more money. Twenty guilders more a week.

MR. VAN DAAN: Blackmail!

MR. FRANK: Twenty guilders? Very modest blackmail.

MR. VAN DAAN: That's just the beginning.

DUSSEL: [Coming to MR. FRANK] You know what I think? He was the thief who was down there that night. That's how he knows we're here.

MR. FRANK: [To MR. KRALER] How was it left? What did you tell him?

MR. KRALER: I said I had to think about it. What shall I do? Pay him the money? . . . Take a chance on firing him . . . or what? I don't know.

DUSSEL: [Frantic] For God's sake don't fire him! Pay him what he asks . . . keep him here where you can have your eye on him.

MR. FRANK: Is it so much that he's asking? What are they paying nowadays?

MR. KRALER: He could get it in a war plant. But this isn't a war plant. Mind you, I don't know if he really knows . . . or if he doesn't know.

MR. FRANK: Offer him half. Then we'll soon find out if it's blackmail or not.

DUSSEL: And if it is? We've got to pay it, haven't we? Anything he asks we've got to pay!

MR. FRANK: Let's decide that when the time comes.

MR. KRALER: This may be all my imagination. You get to a point, these days, where you suspect everyone and everything. Again and again . . . on some simple look or word, I've found myself . . .

[*The telephone rings in the office below*]

MRS. VAN DAAN: [*Hurrying to* MR. KRALER] There's the telephone! What does that mean, the telephone ringing on a holiday?

MR. KRALER: That's my wife. I told her I had to go over some papers in my office . . . to call me there when she got out of church. [*He starts out*] I'll offer him half then. Good-bye . . . we'll hope for the best!

[*The group call their good-byes half-heartedly.* MR. FRANK *follows* MR. KRALER, *to bolt the door below. During the following scene,* MR. FRANK *comes back up and stands listening, disturbed*]

DUSSEL: [*To* MR. VAN DAAN] You can thank your son for this . . . smashing the light! I tell you, it's just a question of time now.

[*He goes to the window at the back and stands looking out*]

MARGOT: Sometimes I wish the end would come . . . whatever it is.

MRS. FRANK: [*Shocked*] Margot!

[ANNE *goes to* MARGOT, *sitting beside her on the couch with her arms around her*]

MARGOT: Then at least we'd know where we were.

MRS. FRANK: You should be ashamed of yourself! Talking that way! Think how lucky we are! Think of the thousands dying in the war, every day. Think of the people in concentration camps.

ANNE: [*Interrupting*] What's the good of that? What's the good of thinking of misery when you're already miserable? That's stupid!

MRS. FRANK: Anne!

[*As* ANNE *goes on raging at her mother,* MRS. FRANK *tries to break in, in an effort to quiet her*]

ANNE: We're young, Margot and Peter and I! You grownups have had your chance! But look at us . . . If we begin thinking of all the horror in the world, we're lost! We're trying to hold onto some kind of ideals . . . when everything . . . ideals, hopes . . . everything, are being destroyed! It isn't our fault that the world is in such a mess! We weren't around when all this started! So don't try to take it out on us!

[*She rushes off to her room, slamming the door after her. She picks up a brush from the chest and hurls it to the floor. Then she sits on the settee, trying to control her anger*]

MR. VAN DAAN: She talks as if we started the war! Did we start the war?

[*He spots* ANNE's *cake. As he starts to take it,* PETER *anticipates him*]

PETER: She left her cake. [*He starts for* ANNE's *room with the cake. There is silence in the main room.* MRS. VAN DAAN *goes up to her room, followed by* VAN DAAN. DUSSEL *stays looking out the window.* MR. FRANK *brings* MRS. FRANK *her cake. She eats it slowly, without relish.* MR. FRANK *takes his cake to* MARGOT *and sits quietly on the sofa beside her.* PETER *stands in the doorway of* ANNE's *darkened room, looking at her, then makes a little movement to let her know he is there.* ANNE *sits up, quickly, trying to hide the signs of her tears.* PETER *holds out the cake to her*] You left this.

ANNE: [*Dully*] Thanks.

[PETER *starts to go out, then comes back*]

PETER: I thought you were fine just now. You know just how to talk to them. You know just how to say it. I'm no good . . . I never can think . . . especially when I'm mad . . . That Dussel . . . when he said that about Mouschi . . . someone eating him . . . all I could think is . . . I wanted to hit him. I wanted to give him such a . . . a . . . that he'd . . . That's what I used to do when there was an argument in school . . . That's the way . . . but here . . . And an old man like that . . . it wouldn't be so good.

ANNE: You're making a big mistake about me. I do it all wrong. I say too much. I go too far. I hurt people's feelings . . .

[DUSSEL *leaves the window, going to his room*]

PETER: I think you're just fine . . . What I want to say . . . if it wasn't for you around here, I don't know. What I mean . . .

[PETER *is interrupted by* DUSSEL'S *turning on the light.* DUSSEL *stands in the doorway, startled to see* PETER. PETER *advances toward him forbiddingly.* DUSSEL *backs out of the room.* PETER *closes the door on him*]

ANNE: Do you mean it, Peter? Do you really mean it?

PETER: I said it, didn't I?

ANNE: Thank you, Peter!

[*In the main room* MR. *and* MRS. FRANK *collect the dishes and take them to the sink, washing them.* MARGOT *lies down again on the couch.* DUSSEL, *lost, wanders into* PETER'S *room and takes up a book, starting to read*]

PETER: [*Looking at the photographs on the wall*] You've got quite a collection.

ANNE: Wouldn't you like some in your room? I could give you some. Heaven knows you spend enough time in there . . . doing heaven knows what . . .

PETER: It's easier. A fight starts, or an argument . . . I duck in there.

ANNE: You're lucky, having a room to go to. His lordship is always here . . . I hardly ever get a minute alone. When they start in on me, I can't duck away. I have to stand there and take it.

PETER: You gave some of it back just now.

ANNE: I get so mad. They've formed their opinions . . . about everything . . . but we . . . we're still trying to find out . . . We have problems here that no other people our age have ever had. And just as you think you've solved them, something comes along and bang! You have to start all over again.

PETER: At least you've got someone you can talk to.

ANNE: Not really. Mother . . . I never discuss anything serious with her. She doesn't understand. Father's all right. We can talk about everything . . . everything but one thing. Mother. He simply won't talk about her. I don't think you can be really intimate with anyone if he holds something back, do you?

PETER: I think your father's fine.

ANNE: Oh, he is, Peter! He is! He's the only one who's ever given me the feeling that I have any sense. But anyway, nothing can take the place of school and play and friends of your own age . . . or near your age? . . . can it?

PETER: I suppose you miss your friends and all.

ANNE: It isn't just . . . [*She breaks off, staring up at him for a second*] Isn't it funny, you and I? Here we've been seeing each other every minute for almost a year and a half, and this is the first time we've ever really talked. It helps a lot to have someone to talk to, don't you think? It helps you to let off steam.

PETER: [*Going to door*] Well, any time you want to let off steam, you can come into my room.

ANNE: [*Following him*] I can get up an awful lot of steam. You'll have to be careful how you say that.

PETER: It's all right with me.

ANNE: Do you mean it?

PETER: I said it, didn't I?

[*He goes out. ANNE stands in her doorway looking after him. As PETER gets to his door he stands for a minute looking back at her. Then he goes into his room. DUSSEL rises as he comes in, and quickly passes him, going out. He starts across for his room. ANNE sees him coming, and pulls her door shut. DUSSEL turns back toward PETER's room. PETER pulls his door shut. DUSSEL stands there, bewildered, forlorn.*
The scene slowly dims out. The curtain falls on the scene. ANNE's VOICE comes over in the darkness . . . faintly at first, and then with growing strength]

ANNE'S VOICE: We've had bad news. The people from whom Miep got our ration books have been arrested. So we have had to cut down on our food. Our stomachs are so empty that they rumble and make strange noises, all in different keys. Mr Van Daan's is deep and low, like a bass fiddle. Mine is high, whistling like a flute. As we all sit around waiting for supper, it's like an orchestra tuning up. It only needs Toscanini to raise his baton and we'd be off in the Ride of the Valkyries. Monday, the sixth of March, nineteen forty-four. Mr. Kraler is in the hospital. It seems he has ulcers. Pim says we are his ulcers. Miep has to run the business and us, too. The Americans have landed on the southern tip of Italy. Father looks for a quick finish to the war. Mr. Dussel is waiting every day for the warehouse man to demand more money. Have I been skipping too much from one subject to another? I can't help it. I feel that spring is coming. I feel it in my whole body and soul. I feel utterly confused. I am longing . . . so longing . . . for everything . . . for friends . . . for someone to talk to . . . someone who understands . . . someone young, who feels as I do . . .

[As *these last lines are being said, the curtain rises on the scene. The lights dim on.* ANNE'S VOICE *fades out*]

SCENE TWO

It is evening, after supper. From outside we hear the sound of children playing. The "grownups," with the exception of MR. VAN DAAN, *are all in the main room.* MRS. FRANK *is doing some mending,* MRS. VAN DAAN *is reading a fashion magazine.* MR. FRANK *is going over business accounts.* DUSSEL, *in his dentist's jacket, is pacing up and down, impatient to get into his bedroom.* MR. VAN DAAN *is upstairs working on a piece of embroidery in an embroidery frame.*

In his room PETER *is sitting before the mirror, smoothing his hair. As the scene goes on, he puts on his tie, brushes his coat and puts it on, preparing himself meticulously for a visit from* ANNE. *On his wall are now hung some of* ANNE's *motion picture stars.*

In her room ANNE *too is getting dressed. She stands before the mirror in her slip, trying various ways of dressing her hair.* MARGOT *is seated on the sofa, hemming a skirt for* ANNE *to wear.*

In the main room DUSSEL *can stand it no longer. He comes over, rapping sharply on the door of his and* ANNE's *bedroom.*

ANNE: [*Calling to him*] No, no, Mr. Dussel! I am not dressed yet. [DUSSEL *walks away, furious, sitting down and burying his head in his hands.* ANNE *turns to* MARGOT] How is that? How does that look?

MARGOT: [*Glancing at her briefly*] Fine.

ANNE: You didn't even look.

MARGOT: Of course I did. It's fine.

ANNE: Margot, tell me, am I terribly ugly?

MARGOT: Oh, stop fishing.

ANNE: No. No. Tell me.

MARGOT: Of course you're not. You've got nice eyes . . . and a lot of animation, and . . .

ANNE: A little vague, aren't you?

[*She reaches over and takes a brassière out of* MARGOT's *sewing basket. She holds it up to herself, studying the effect in the mirror. Outside,* MRS. FRANK, *feeling sorry for* DUSSEL, *comes over, knocking at the girls' door*]

MRS. FRANK: [*Outside*] May I come in?

MARGOT: Come in, Mother.

MRS. FRANK: [*Shutting the door behind her*] Mr. Dussel's impatient to get in here.

ANNE: [*Still with the brassière*] Heavens, he takes the room for himself the entire day.

MRS. FRANK: [*Gently*] Anne, dear, you're not going in again to see Peter?

ANNE: [*Dignified*] That is my intention.

MRS. FRANK: But you've already spent a great deal of time in there today.

ANNE: I was in there exactly twice. Once to get the dictionary, and then three-quarters of an hour before supper.

MRS. FRANK: Aren't you afraid you're disturbing him?

ANNE: Mother, I have some intuition.

MRS. FRANK: Then may I ask you this much, Anne. Please don't shut the door when you go in.

ANNE: You sound like Mrs. Van Daan!

[*She throws the brassière back in* MARGOT's *sewing basket and picks up her blouse, putting it on*]

MRS. FRANK: No. No. I don't mean to suggest anything wrong. I only wish that you wouldn't expose yourself to criticism . . . that you wouldn't give Mrs. Van Daan the opportunity to be unpleasant.

ANNE: Mrs. Van Daan doesn't need an opportunity to be unpleasant!

MRS. FRANK: Everyone's on edge, worried about Mr. Kraler. This is one more thing . . .

ANNE: I'm sorry, Mother. I'm going to Peter's room. I'm not going to let Petronella Van Daan spoil our friendship.

[MRS. FRANK *hesitates for a second, then goes out, closing the door after her. She gets a pack of playing cards and sits at the center table, playing solitaire. In* ANNE's *room* MARGOT *hands the finished skirt to* ANNE. *As* ANNE *is putting it on,* MARGOT *takes off her high-heeled shoes and stuffs paper in the toes so that* ANNE *can wear them*]

MARGOT: [*To* ANNE] Why don't you two talk in the main room? It'd save a lot of trouble. It's hard on Mother, having to listen to those remarks from Mrs. Van Daan and not say a word.

ANNE: Why doesn't she say a word? I think it's ridiculous to take it and take it.

MARGOT: You don't understand Mother at all, do you? She can't talk back. She's not like you. It's just not in her nature to fight back.

ANNE: Anyway . . . the only one I worry about is you. I feel awfully guilty about you.

[*She sits on the stool near* MARGOT, *putting on* MARGOT's *high-heeled shoes*]

MARGOT: What about?

ANNE: I mean, every time I go into Peter's room, I have a feeling I may be hurting you. [MARGOT *shakes her head*] I know if it were me, I'd be wild. I'd be desperately jealous, if it were me.

MARGOT: Well, I'm not.

ANNE: You don't feel badly? Really? Truly? You're not jealous?

MARGOT: Of course I'm jealous . . . jealous that you've got something to get up in the morning for . . . But jealous of you and Peter? No.

[ANNE *goes back to the mirror*]

ANNE: Maybe there's nothing to be jealous of. Maybe he doesn't really like me. Maybe I'm just taking the place of his cat . . . [*She picks up a pair of short white gloves, putting them on*] Wouldn't you like to come in with us?

MARGOT: I have a book.

[*The sound of the children playing outside fades out. In the main room* DUSSEL *can stand it no longer. He jumps up, going to the bedroom door and knocking sharply*]

DUSSEL: Will you please let me in my room!

ANNE: Just a minute, dear, dear Mr. Dussel. [*She picks up her Mother's pink stole and adjusts it elegantly over her shoulders, then gives a last look in the mirror*] Well, here I go . . . to run the gauntlet.

[*She starts out, followed by* MARGOT]

DUSSEL: [*As she appears—sarcastic*] Thank you so much.

[DUSSEL *goes into his room.* ANNE *goes toward* PETER's *room, passing* MRS. VAN DAAN *and her parents at the center table*]

MRS. VAN DAAN: My God, look at her! [ANNE *pays no attention. She knocks at* PETER's *door*] I don't know what good it is to have a son. I never see him. He wouldn't care if I killed myself. [PETER *opens the door and stands aside for* ANNE *to come in*] Just a minute, Anne. [*She goes to them at the door*] I'd like to say a few words to my son. Do you mind? [PETER *and* ANNE *stand waiting*]

Peter, I don't want you staying up till all hours tonight. You've got to have your sleep. You're a growing boy. You hear?

MRS. FRANK: Anne won't stay late. She's going to bed promptly at nine. Aren't you, Anne?

ANNE: Yes, Mother . . .[To MRS. VAN DAAN] May we go now?

MRS. VAN DAAN: Are you asking me? I didn't know I had anything to say about it.

MRS. FRANK: Listen for the chimes, Anne dear.

[The two young people go off into PETER's room, shutting the door after them]

MRS. VAN DAAN: [To MRS. FRANK] In my day it was the boys who called on the girls. Not the girls on the boys.

MRS. FRANK: You know how young people like to feel that they have secrets. Peter's room is the only place where they can talk.

MRS. VAN DAAN: Talk! That's not what they called it when I was young.

[MRS. VAN DAAN goes off to the bathroom. MARGOT settles down to read her book. MR. FRANK puts his papers away and brings a chess game to the center table. He and MRS. FRANK start to play. In PETER's room, ANNE speaks to PETER, indignant, humiliated]

ANNE: Aren't they awful? Aren't they impossible. Treating us as if we were still in the nursery.

[She sits on the cot. PETER gets a bottle of pop and two glasses]

PETER: Don't let it bother you. It doesn't bother me.

ANNE: I suppose you can't really blame them . . . they think back to what they were like at our age. They don't realize how much more advanced we are . . . When you think what wonderful discussions we've had! . . . Oh, I forgot. I was going to bring you some more pictures.

PETER: Oh, these are fine, thanks.

MISTER ROBERTS

Mister Roberts (Henry Fonda) aboard the U. S. Navy Cargo Ship AK 601. Beneath his foot, the captain's precious palm tree.

THE ROSE TATTOO

Maureen Stapleton and Eli Wallach.

THE TEAHOUSE OF THE AUGUST MOON

Lotus Blossom (Mariko Niki) is being introduced to Captain Fisby (John For-
sythe) by Sakini (David Wayne).

LUTHER

Luther (Albert Finney), kneeling, as he is being received into the Order in the Cloister Chapel of the Eremites of St. Augustine.

THE SUBJECT WAS ROSES

The Cleary family enjoy a moment of camaraderie: Martin Sheen, Irene Dailey, Jack Albertson.

THE FOURPOSTER

Michael (Hume Cronyn) carries his bride Agnes (Jessica Tandy) over the thresh
old on their wedding night.

THE DIARY OF ANNE FRANK

A tender moment between Anne Frank (Susan Strasberg) and her father (Joseph
Schildkraut).

The homecoming of David, the blind soldier. Left to right: Cliff DeYoung, Hector Elias, Elizabeth Wilson, Tom

PHOTO: JOSEPH ABELES STUDIO

THE RIVER NIGER

Johnny Williams (Douglas Turner Ward), center, is being comforted by friends and family: Graham Brown, Roxie Roker, Grenna Whitaker, Frances Foster, Les Roberts.

BORSTAL BOY
Niall Toibin and Frank Grimes as, respectively, the older and younger Brendan
Behan.

ANNE: Don't you want some more? Miep just brought me some new ones.

PETER: Maybe later.

[*He gives her a glass of pop and, taking some for himself, sits down facing her*]

ANNE: [*Looking up at one of the photographs*] I remember when I got that . . . I won it. I bet Jopie that I could eat five ice-cream cones. We'd all been playing ping-pong . . . We used to have heavenly times . . . we'd finish up with ice cream at the Delphi, or the Oasis, where Jews were allowed . . . there'd always be a lot of boys . . . we'd laugh and joke . . . I'd like to go back to it for a few days or a week. But after that I know I'd be bored to death. I think more seriously about life now. I want to be a journalist . . . or something. I love to write. What do you want to do?

PETER: I thought I might go off some place . . . work on a farm or something . . . some job that doesn't take much brains.

ANNE: You shouldn't talk that way. You've got the most awful inferiority complex.

PETER: I know I'm not smart.

ANNE: That isn't true. You're much better than I am in dozens of things . . . arithmetic and algebra and . . . well, you're a million times better than I am in algebra. [*With sudden directness*] You like Margot, don't you? Right from the start you liked her, liked her much better than me.

PETER: [*Uncomfortably*] Oh, I don't know.

[*In the main room* MRS. VAN DAAN *comes from the bathroom and goes over to the sink, polishing a coffee pot*]

ANNE: It's all right. Everyone feels that way. Margot's so good. She's sweet and bright and beautiful and I'm not.

PETER: I wouldn't say that.

ANNE: Oh, no, I'm not. I know that. I know quite well that I'm not a beauty. I never have been and never shall be.

PETER: I don't agree at all. I think you're pretty.

ANNE: That's not true!

PETER: And another thing. You've changed . . . from at first, I mean.

ANNE: I have?

PETER: I used to think you were awful noisy.

ANNE: And what do you think now, Peter? How have I changed?

PETER: Well . . . er . . . you're . . . quieter.

[*In his room* DUSSEL *takes his pajamas and toilet articles and goes into the bathroom to change*]

ANNE: I'm glad you don't just hate me.

PETER: I never said that.

ANNE: I bet when you get out of here you'll never think of me again.

PETER: That's crazy.

ANNE: When you get back with all of your friends, you're going to say . . . now what did I ever see in that Mrs. Quack Quack.

PETER: I haven't got any friends.

ANNE: Oh, Peter, of course you have. Everyone has friends.

PETER: Not me. I don't want any. I get along all right without them.

ANNE: Does that mean you can get along without me? I think of myself as your friend.

PETER: No. If they were all like you, it'd be different.

[*He takes the glasses and the bottle and puts them away. There is a second's silence and then* ANNE *speaks, hesitantly, shyly*]

ANNE: Peter, did you ever kiss a girl?

PETER: Yes. Once.

ANNE: [*To cover her feelings*] That picture's crooked. [PETER *goes over, straightening the photograph*] Was she pretty?

PETER: Huh?

ANNE: The girl that you kissed.

PETER: I don't know. I was blindfolded. [*He comes back and sits down again*] It was at a party. One of those kissing games.

ANNE: [*Relieved*] Oh. I don't suppose that really counts, does it?

PETER: It didn't with me.

ANNE: I've been kissed twice. Once a man I'd never seen before kissed me on the cheek when he picked me up off the ice and I was crying. And the other was Mr. Koophuis, a friend of Father's who kissed my hand. You wouldn't say those counted, would you?

PETER: I wouldn't say so.

ANNE: I know almost for certain that Margot would never kiss anyone unless she was engaged to them. And I'm sure too that Mother never touched a man before Pim. But I don't know . . . things are so different now . . . What do you think? Do you think a girl shouldn't kiss anyone except if she's engaged or something? It's so hard to try to think what to do, when here we are with the whole world falling around our ears and you think . . . well . . . you don't know what's going to happen tomorrow and . . . What do you think?

PETER: I suppose it'd depend on the girl. Some girls, anything they do's wrong. But others . . . well . . . it wouldn't necessarily be wrong with them. [*The carillon starts to strike nine o'clock*] I've always thought that when two people . . .

ANNE: Nine o'clock. I have to go.

PETER: That's right.

ANNE: [*Without moving*] Good night.

[*There is a second's pause, then* PETER *gets up and moves toward the door*]

PETER: You won't let them stop you coming?

ANNE: No. [*She rises and starts for the door*] Sometime I might bring my diary. There are so many things in it that I want to talk over with you. There's a lot about you.

PETER: What kind of thing?

ANNE: I wouldn't want you to see some of it. I thought you were a nothing, just the way you thought about me.

PETER: Did you change your mind, the way I changed my mind about you?

ANNE: Well . . . You'll see . . .

[*For a second* ANNE *stands looking up at* PETER, *longing for him to kiss her. As he makes no move she turns away. Then suddenly* PETER *grabs her awkwardly in his arms, kissing her on the cheek.* ANNE *walks out dazed. She stands for a minute, her back to the people in the main room. As she regains her poise she goes to her mother and father and* MARGOT, *silently kissing them. They murmur their good nights to her. As she is about to open her bedroom door, she catches sight of* MRS. VAN DAAN. *She goes quickly to her, taking her face in her hands and kissing her first on one cheek and then on the other. Then she hurries off into her room.* MRS. VAN DAAN *looks after her, and then looks over at* PETER'S *room. Her suspicions are confirmed*]

MRS. VAN DAAN: [*She knows*] Ah hah!

[*The lights dim out. The curtain falls on the scene. In the darkness* ANNE'S VOICE *comes faintly at first and then with growing strength*]

ANNE'S VOICE: By this time we all know each other so well that if anyone starts to tell a story, the rest can finish it for him. We're having to cut down still further on our meals. What makes it worse, the rats have been at work again. They've carried off some of our precious food. Even Mr. Dussel wishes now that Mouschi was here. Thursday, the twentieth of April, nineteen forty-four. Invasion fever is mounting every day. Miep tells us that people outside talk of nothing else. For myself, life has become much more pleasant. I often go to Peter's room after supper. Oh, don't think I'm in love, because I'm not. But it does make life more bearable to have someone with whom you can exchange views. No more tonight. P.S. . . . I must be honest. I must confess that I actually live for the next meeting. Is there anything lovelier than to sit under the skylight and feel the sun on your cheeks and have a darling boy in your arms? I admit now that I'm glad the Van Daans had a son and not a daughter. I've outgrown another dress. That's the third. I'm having to wear Margot's clothes after all. I'm working hard on my French and am now reading *La Belle Nivernaise*.

[*As she is saying the last lines—the curtain rises on the scene. The lights dim on, as* ANNE'S VOICE *fades out*]

SCENE THREE

It is night, a few weeks later. Everyone is in bed. There is complete quiet. In the VAN DAAN'S *room a match flares up for a moment and then is quickly put out.* MR. VAN DAAN, *in bare feet, dressed in underwear and trousers, is dimly seen coming stealthily down the stairs and into the main room, where* MR. *and* MRS. FRANK *and* MARGOT *are sleeping. He goes to the food safe and again lights a match. Then he cautiously opens the safe, taking out a half-loaf of bread. As he closes the safe, it creaks. He stands rigid.* MRS. FRANK *sits up in bed. She sees him.*

MRS. FRANK: [*Screaming*] Otto! Otto! *Komme schnell!*

[*The rest of the people wake, hurriedly getting up*]

MR. FRANK: *Was ist los? Was ist passiert?*

[DUSSEL, *followed by* ANNE, *comes from his room*]

MRS. FRANK: [*As she rushes over to* MR. VAN DAAN] *Er stiehlt das Essen!*

DUSSEL: [*Grabbing* MR. VAN DAAN] You! You! Give me that.

MRS. VAN DAAN: [*Coming down the stairs*] Putti . . . Putti . . . what is it?

DUSSEL: [*His hands on* VAN DAAN'S *neck*] You dirty thief . . . stealing food . . . you good-for-nothing . . .

MR. FRANK: Mr. Dussel! For God's sake! Help me, Peter!

[PETER *comes over, trying, with* MR. FRANK, *to separate the two struggling men*]

PETER: Let him go! Let go!

[DUSSEL *drops* MR. VAN DAAN, *pushing him away. He shows them the end of a loaf of bread that he has taken from* VAN DAAN]

DUSSEL: You greedy, selfish . . . !

[MARGOT *turns on the lights*]

MRS. VAN DAAN: Putti . . . what is it?

[*All of* MRS. FRANK's *gentleness, her self-control, is gone. She is outraged, in a frenzy of indignation*]

MRS. FRANK: The bread! He was stealing the bread!

DUSSEL: It was you, and all the time we thought it was the rats!

MR. FRANK: Mr. Van Daan, how could you!

MR. VAN DAAN: I'm hungry.

MRS. FRANK: We're all of us hungry! I see the children getting thinner and thinner. Your own son Peter . . . I've heard him moan in his sleep, he's so hungry. And you come in the night and steal food that should go to them . . . to the children!

MRS. VAN DAAN: [*Going to* MR. VAN DAAN *protectively*] He needs more food than the rest of us. He's used to more. He's a big man.

[MR. VAN DAAN *breaks away, going over and sitting on the couch*]

MRS. FRANK: [*Turning on* MRS. VAN DAAN] And you . . . you're worse than he is! You're a mother, and yet you sacrifice your child to this man . . . this . . . this . . .

MR. FRANK: Edith! Edith!

[MARGOT *picks up the pink woolen stole, putting it over her mother's shoulders*]

MRS. FRANK: [*Paying no attention, going on to* MRS. VAN DAAN] Don't think I haven't seen you! Always saving the choicest bits for him! I've watched you day after day and I've held my tongue. But not any longer! Not after this! Now I want him to go! I want him to get out of here!

MR. FRANK:	MR. VAN DAAN:	MRS. VAN DAAN:
Edith!	Get out of here?	What do you mean?

MRS. FRANK: Just that! Take your things and get out!

MR. FRANK: [*To* MRS. FRANK] You're speaking in anger. You cannot mean what you are saying.

MRS. FRANK: I mean exactly that!

[MRS. VAN DAAN *takes a cover from the* FRANKS' *bed, pulling it about her*]

MR. FRANK: For two long years we have lived here, side by side. We have respected each other's rights . . . we have managed to live in peace. Are we now going to throw it all away? I know this will never happen again, will it, Mr. Van Daan?

MR. VAN DAAN: No. No.

MRS. FRANK: He steals once! He'll steal again!

[MR. VAN DAAN, *holding his stomach, starts for the bathroom.* ANNE *puts her arms around him, helping him up the step*]

MR. FRANK: Edith, please. Let us be calm. We'll all go to our rooms . . . and afterwards we'll sit down quietly and talk this out . . . we'll find some way . . .

MRS. FRANK: No! No! No more talk! I want them to leave!

MRS. VAN DAAN: You'd put us out, on the streets?

MRS. FRANK: There are other hiding places.

MRS. VAN DAAN: A cellar . . . a closet. I know. And we have no money left even to pay for that.

MRS. FRANK: I'll give you money. Out of my own pocket I'll give it gladly.

[*She gets her purse from a shelf and comes back with it*]

MRS. VAN DAAN: Mr. Frank, you told Putti you'd never forget what he'd done for you when you came to Amsterdam. You said you could never repay him, that you . . .

MRS. FRANK: [*Counting out money*] If my husband had any obligation to you, he's paid it, over and over.

MR. FRANK: Edith, I've never seen you like this before. I don't know you.

MRS. FRANK: I should have spoken out long ago.

DUSSEL: You can't be nice to some people.

MRS. VAN DAAN: [*Turning on* DUSSEL] There would have been plenty for all of us, if *you* hadn't come in here!

MR. FRANK: We don't need the Nazis to destroy us. We're destroying ourselves.

[*He sits down, with his head in his hands.* MRS. FRANK *goes to* MRS. VAN DAAN]

MRS. FRANK: [*Giving* MRS. VAN DAAN *some money*] Give this to Miep. She'll find you a place.

ANNE: Mother, you're not putting *Peter* out. Peter hasn't done anything.

MRS. FRANK: He'll stay, of course. When I say I must protect the children, I mean Peter too.

[PETER *rises from the steps where he has been sitting*]

PETER: I'd have to go if Father goes.

[MR. VAN DAAN *comes from the bathroom.* MRS. VAN DAAN *hurries to him and takes him to the couch. Then she gets water from the sink to bathe his face*]

MRS. FRANK: [*While this is going on*] He's no father to you . . . that man! He doesn't know what it is to be a father!

PETER: [*Starting for his room*] I wouldn't feel right. I couldn't stay.

MRS. FRANK: Very well, then. I'm sorry.

ANNE: [*Rushing over to* PETER] No, Peter! No! (PETER *goes into his room, closing the door after him.* ANNE *turns back to her mother, crying*] I don't care about the food. They can have mine! I don't want it! Only don't send them away. It'll be daylight soon. They'll be caught . . .

MARGOT: [*Putting her arms comfortingly around* ANNE] Please, Mother!

MRS. FRANK: They're not going now. They'll stay here until Miep finds them a place. [*To* MRS. VAN DAAN] But one thing I insist on! He must never come down here again! He must never come to this room where the food is stored! We'll divide what we have . . . an equal share for each! [DUSSEL *hurries over to get a sack of potatoes from the food safe.* MRS. FRANK *goes on, to* MRS. VAN DAAN] You can cook it here and take it up to him.

[DUSSEL *brings the sack of potatoes back to the center table*]

MARGOT: Oh, no. No. We haven't sunk so far that we're going to fight over a handful of rotten potatoes.

DUSSEL: [*Dividing the potatoes into piles*] Mrs. Frank, Mr. Frank, Margot, Anne, Peter, Mrs. Van Daan. Mr. Van Daan, myself . . . Mrs. Frank . . .

[*The buzzer sounds in* MIEP's *signal*]

MR. FRANK: It's Miep!

[*He hurries over, getting his overcoat and putting it on*]

MARGOT: At this hour?

MRS. FRANK: It is trouble.

MR. FRANK: [*As he starts down to unbolt the door*] I beg you, don't let her see a thing like this!

MR. DUSSEL: [*Counting without stopping*] . . . Anne, Peter, Mrs. Van Daan, Mr. Van Daan, myself . . .

MARGOT: [*To* DUSSEL] Stop it! Stop it!

DUSSEL: . . . Mr. Frank, Margot, Anne, Peter, Mrs. Van Daan, Mr. Van Daan, myself, Mrs. Frank . . .

MRS. VAN DAAN: You're keeping the big ones for yourself! All the big ones . . . Look at the size of that! . . . And that! . . .

[DUSSEL *continues on with his dividing.* PETER, *with his shirt and trousers on, comes from his room*]

MARGOT: Stop it! Stop it!

[*We hear* MIEP's *excited voice speaking to* MR. FRANK *below*]

MIEP: Mr. Frank . . . the most wonderful news! . . . The invasion has begun!

MR. FRANK: Go on, tell them! Tell them!

[MIEP *comes running up the steps, ahead of* MR. FRANK. *She has a man's raincoat on over her nightclothes and a bunch of orange-colored flowers in her hand.*]

MIEP: Did you hear that, everybody? Did you hear what I said? The invasion has begun! The invasion!

[*They all stare at* MIEP, *unable to grasp what she is telling them.* PETER *is the first to recover his wits*]

PETER: Where?

MRS. VAN DAAN: When? When, Miep?

MIEP: It began early this morning . . .

[*As she talks on, the realization of what she has said begins to dawn on them. Everyone goes crazy. A wild demonstration takes place.* MRS. FRANK *hugs* MR. VAN DAAN]

MRS. FRANK: Oh, Mr. Van Daan, did you hear that?

[DUSSEL *embraces* MRS. VAN DAAN. PETER *grabs a frying pan and parades around the room, beating on it, singing the Dutch National Anthem.* ANNE *and* MARGOT *follow him, singing, weaving in and out among the excited grownups.* MARGOT *breaks away to take the flowers from* MIEP *and distribute them to everyone. While this pandemonium is going on* MRS. FRANK *tries to make herself heard above the excitement*]

MRS. FRANK: [*To* MIEP] How do you know?

MIEP: The radio . . . The B.B.C.! They said they landed on the coast of Normandy!

PETER: The British?

MIEP: British, Americans, French, Dutch, Poles, Norwegians . . . all of them! More than four thousand ships! Churchill spoke, and General Eisenhower! D-Day they call it!

MR. FRANK: Thank God, it's come!

MRS. VAN DAAN: At last!

MIEP: [*Starting out*] I'm going to tell Mr. Kraler. This'll be better than any blood transfusion.

MR. FRANK: [*Stopping her*] What part of Normandy did they land, did they say?

MIEP: Normandy . . . that's all I know now . . . I'll be up the minute I hear some more!

[*She goes hurriedly out*]

MR. FRANK: [*To* MRS. FRANK] What did I tell you? What did I tell you?

[MRS. FRANK *indicates that he has forgotten to bolt the door after* MIEP. *He hurries down the steps.* MR. VAN DAAN, *sitting on the couch, suddenly breaks into a convulsive sob. Everybody looks at him, bewildered*]

MRS. VAN DAAN: [*Hurrying to him*] Putti! Putti! What is it? What happened?

MR. VAN DAAN: Please. I'm so ashamed.

[MR. FRANK *comes back up the steps*]

DUSSEL: Oh, for God's sake!

MRS. VAN DAAN: Don't, Putti.

MARGOT: It doesn't matter now!

MR. FRANK: [*Going to* MR. VAN DAAN] Didn't you hear what Miep said? The invasion has come! We're going to be liberated! This is a time to celebrate!

[*He embraces* MRS. FRANK *and then hurries to the cupboard and gets the cognac and a glass*]

MR. VAN DAAN: To steal bread from children!

MRS. FRANK: We've all done things that we're ashamed of.

ANNE: Look at me, the way I've treated Mother . . . so mean and horrid to her.

MRS. FRANK: No, Anneke, no.

[ANNE *runs to her mother, putting her arms around her*]

ANNE: Oh, Mother, I was. I was awful.

MR. VAN DAAN: Not like me. No one is as bad as me!

DUSSEL: [*To* MR. VAN DAAN] Stop it now! Let's be happy!

MR. FRANK: [*Giving* MR. VAN DAAN *a glass of cognac*] Here! Here! Schnapps! Locheim!

[VAN DAAN *takes the cognac. They all watch him. He gives them a feeble smile.* ANNE *puts up her fingers in a V-for-Victory sign. As* VAN DAAN *gives an answering V-sign, they are startled to hear a loud sob from behind them. It is* MRS. FRANK, *stricken with remorse. She is sitting on the other side of the room*]

MRS. FRANK: [*Through her sobs*] When I think of the terrible things I said . . .

[MR. FRANK, ANNE *and* MARGOT *hurry to her, trying to comfort her.* MR. VAN DAAN *brings her his glass of cognac*]

MR. VAN DAAN: No! No! You were right!

MRS. FRANK: That I should speak that way to you! . . . Our friends! . . . Our guests!

[*She starts to cry again*]

DUSSEL: Stop it, you're spoiling the whole invasion!

[*As they are comforting her, the lights dim out. The curtain falls*]

ANNE'S VOICE: [*Faintly at first and then with growing strength*] We're all in much better spirits these days. There's still excellent news of the invasion. The best part about it is that I have a feeling that friends are coming. Who knows? Maybe I'll be back in school by fall. Ha, ha! The joke is on us! The warehouse man doesn't know a thing and we are paying him all that money! . . . Wednesday, the second of July, nineteen forty-four. The invasion seems temporarily to be bogged down. Mr. Kraler has to have an operation, which looks bad. The Gestapo have found the radio that was stolen. Mr. Dussel says they'll trace it back and back to the thief, and then, it's just a matter of time till they get to us. Everyone is low. Even poor Pim can't raise their spirits. I have often been downcast myself . . . but never in despair. I can shake off everything if I write. But . . . and that is the great question . . . will I ever be able to write well? I want to so much. I want to go on living even after my death. Another birthday has gone by, so now I am fifteen. Already I know what I want. I have a goal, an opinion.

[*As this is being said—the curtain rises on the scene, the lights dim on, and* ANNE'S VOICE *fades out*]

SCENE FOUR

It is an afternoon a few weeks later . . . Everyone but MARGOT *is in the main room. There is a sense of great tension.*

Both MRS. FRANK *and* MR. VAN DAAN *are nervously pacing back and forth,* DUSSEL *is standing at the window, looking down fixedly at the street below.* PETER *is at the center table, trying to do his lessons.* ANNE *sits opposite him, writing in her diary.* MRS. VAN DAAN *is seated on the couch, her eyes on* MR. FRANK *as he sits reading.*

The sound of a telephone ringing comes from the office below. They all are rigid, listening tensely. MR. DUSSEL *rushes down to* MR. FRANK.

DUSSEL: There it goes again, the telephone! Mr. Frank, do you hear?

MR. FRANK: [*Quietly*] Yes. I hear.

DUSSEL: [*Pleading, insistent*] But this is the third time, Mr. Frank! The third time in quick succession! It's a signal! I tell you it's Miep, trying to get us! For some reason she can't come to us and she's trying to warn us of something!

MR. FRANK: Please. Please.

MR. VAN DAAN: [*To* DUSSEL] You're wasting your breath.

DUSSEL: Something has happened, Mr. Frank. For three days now Miep hasn't been to see us! And today not a man has come to work. There hasn't been a sound in the building!

MRS. FRANK: Perhaps it's Sunday. We may have lost track of the days.

MR. VAN DAAN: [*To* ANNE] You with the diary there. What day is it?

DUSSEL: [*Going to* MRS. FRANK] I don't lose track of the days! I know exactly what day it is! It's Friday, the fourth of August. Friday, and not a man at work. [*He rushes back to* MR. FRANK, *pleading with him, almost in tears*] I tell you Mr. Kraler's dead. That's the only explanation. He's dead and they've closed down the building, and Miep's trying to tell us!

MR. FRANK: She'd never telephone us.

DUSSEL: [*Frantic*] Mr. Frank, answer that! I beg you, answer it!

MR. FRANK: No.

MR. VAN DAAN: Just pick it up and listen. You don't have to speak. Just listen and see if it's Miep.

DUSSEL: [*Speaking at the same time*] For God's sake . . . I ask you.

MR. FRANK: No. I've told you, no. I'll do nothing that might let anyone know we're in the building.

PETER: Mr. Frank's right.

MR. VAN DAAN: There's no need to tell us what side you're on.

MR. FRANK: If we wait patiently, quietly, I believe that help will come.

[*There is silence for a minute as they all listen to the telephone ringing*]

DUSSEL: I'm going down. [*He rushes down the steps.* MR. FRANK *tries ineffectually to hold him.* DUSSEL *runs to the lower door, unbolting it. The telephone stops ringing.* DUSSEL *bolts the door and comes slowly back up the steps*] Too late.

[MR. FRANK *goes to* MARGOT *in* ANNE's *bedroom*]

MR. VAN DAAN: So we just wait here until we die.

MRS. VAN DAAN: [*Hysterically*] I can't stand it! I'll kill myself! I'll kill myself!

MR. VAN DAAN: For God's sake, stop it!

[*In the distance, a German military band is heard playing a Viennese waltz*]

MRS. VAN DAAN: I think you'd be glad if I did! I think you want me to die!

MR. VAN DAAN: Whose fault is it we're here? [MRS. VAN DAAN *starts for her room. He follows, talking at her*] We could've been safe somewhere . . . in America or Switzerland. But no! No! You wouldn't leave when I wanted to. You couldn't leave your things. You couldn't leave your precious furniture.

MRS. VAN DAAN: Don't touch me!

[*She hurries up the stairs, followed by* MR. VAN DAAN. PETER, *unable to bear it, goes to his room.* ANNE *looks after him, deeply concerned.* DUSSEL *returns to his post at the window.* MR. FRANK *comes back into the main room and takes a book, trying to read.* MRS. FRANK *sits near the sink, starting to peel some potatoes.* ANNE *quietly goes to* PETER's *room, closing the door after her.* PETER *is lying face down on the cot.* ANNE *leans over him, holding him in her arms, trying to bring him out of his despair*]

ANNE: Look, Peter, the sky. [*She looks up through the skylight*] What a lovely, lovely day! Aren't the clouds beautiful? You know what I do when it seems as if I couldn't stand being cooped up for one more minute? I *think* myself out. I think myself on a walk in the park where I used to go with Pim. Where the jonquils and the crocus and the violets grow down the slopes. You know the most wonderful part about *thinking* yourself out? You can have it any way you like. You can have roses and violets and chrysanthemums all blooming at the same time . . . It's funny . . . I used to take it all for granted . . . and now I've gone crazy about everything to do with nature. Haven't you?

PETER: I've just gone crazy. I think if something doesn't happen soon . . . if we don't get out of here . . . I can't stand much more of it!

ANNE: [*Softly*] I wish you had a religion, Peter.

PETER: No, thanks! Not me!

ANNE: Oh, I don't mean you have to be Orthodox . . . or believe in heaven and hell and purgatory and things . . . I just mean some religion . . . it doesn't matter what. Just to believe in something! When I think of all that's out there . . . the trees . . . and flowers . . . and seagulls . . . when I think of the dearness of you, Peter . . . and the goodness of the people we know . . . Mr. Kraler, Miep, Dirk, the vegetable man, all risking their lives for us every day . . . When I think of these good things, I'm not afraid any more . . . I find myself, and God, and I . . .

[PETER *interrupts, getting up and walking away*]

PETER: That's fine! But when I begin to think, I get mad! Look at us, hiding out for two years. Not able to move! Caught here like . . . waiting for them to come and get us . . . and all for what?

ANNE: We're not the only people that've had to suffer. There've always been people that've had to . . . sometimes one race . . . sometimes another . . . and yet . . .

PETER: That doesn't make me feel any better!

ANNE: [*Going to him*] I know it's terrible, trying to have any faith . . . when people are doing such horrible . . . But you know what I sometimes think? I think the world may be going through a phase, the way I was with Mother. It'll pass, maybe not for hundreds of years, but some day . . . I still believe, in spite of everything, that people are really good at heart.

PETER: I want to see something now . . . Not a thousand years from now!

[*He goes over, sitting down again on the cot*]

ANNE: But, Peter, if you'd only look at it as part of a great pattern . . . that we're just a little minute in the life . . . [*She breaks off*] Listen to us, going at each other like a couple of stupid grownups! Look at the sky now. Isn't it lovely? [*She holds out her hand to him.* PETER *takes it and rises, standing with her at the window looking out, his arms around her*] Some day, when we're outside again, I'm going to . . .

> [*She breaks off as she hears the sound of a car, its brakes squealing as it comes to a sudden stop. The people in the other rooms also become aware of the sound. They listen tensely. Another car roars up to a screeching stop.* ANNE *and* PETER *come from* PETER'S *room.* MR. *and* MRS. VAN DAAN *creep down the stairs.* DUSSEL *comes out from his room. Everyone is listening, hardly breathing. A doorbell clangs again and again in the building below.* MR. FRANK *starts quietly down the steps to the door.* DUSSEL *and* PETER *follow him. The others stand rigid, waiting, terrified.*
> *In a few seconds* DUSSEL *comes stumbling back up the steps. He shakes off* PETER'S *help and goes to his room.* MR. FRANK *bolts the door below, and comes slowly back up the steps. Their eyes are all on him as he stands there for a minute. They realize that what they feared has happened.* MRS. VAN DAAN *starts to whimper.* MR. VAN DAAN *puts her gently in a chair, and then hurries off up the stairs to their room to collect their things.* PETER *goes to comfort his mother. There is a sound of violent pounding on a door below*]

MR. FRANK: [*Quietly*] For the past two years we have lived in fear. Now we can live in hope.

> [*The pounding below becomes more insistent. There are muffled sounds of voices, shouting commands*]

MEN'S VOICES: *Auf machen! Da drinnen! Auf machen! Schnell! Schnell! Schnell! etc., etc.*

> [*The street door below is forced open. We hear the heavy tread of footsteps coming up.* MR. FRANK *gets two school bags from the shelves, and gives one to* ANNE *and the other to* MARGOT. *He goes to get a bag for* MRS. FRANK. *The sound of feet coming up grows louder.* PETER *comes to* ANNE, *kissing her good-bye, then he goes to his room to collect his things. The*

buzzer of their door starts to ring. MR. FRANK *brings* MRS. FRANK *a bag. They stand together, waiting. We hear the thud of gun butts on the door, trying to break it down.*

ANNE *stands, holding her school satchel, looking over at her father and mother with a soft, reassuring smile. She is no longer a child, but a woman with courage to meet whatever lies ahead.*

The lights dim out. The curtain falls on the scene. We hear a mighty crash as the door is shattered. After a second ANNE'S *voice is heard*]

ANNE'S VOICE: And so it seems our stay here is over. They are waiting for us now. They've allowed us five minutes to get our things. We can each take a bag and whatever it will hold of clothing. Nothing else. So, dear Diary, that means I must leave you behind. Good-bye for a while. P.S. Please, please, Miep, or Mr. Kraler, or anyone else. If you should find this diary, will you please keep it safe for me, because some day I hope . . .

[*Her voice stops abruptly. There is silence. After a second the curtain rises*]

SCENE FIVE

It is again the afternoon in November, 1945. The rooms are as we saw them in the first scene. MR. KRALER *has joined* MIEP *and* MR. FRANK. *There are coffee cups on the table. We see a great change in* MR. FRANK. *He is calm now. His bitterness is gone. He slowly turns a few pages of the diary. They are blank.*

MR. FRANK: No more.

[*He closes the diary and puts it down on the couch beside him*]

MIEP: I'd gone to the country to find food. When I got back the block was surrounded by police . . .

MR. KRALER: We made it our business to learn how they knew. It was the thief . . . the thief who told them.

[MIEP *goes up to the gas burner, bringing back a pot of coffee*]

MR. FRANK: [*After a pause*] It seems strange to say this, that anyone could be happy in a concentration camp. But Anne was happy in the camp in Holland where they first took us. After two years of being shut up in these rooms, she could be out . . . out in the sunshine and the fresh air that she loved.

MIEP: [*Offering the coffee to* MR. FRANK] A little more?

MR. FRANK: [*Holding out his cup to her*] The news of the war was good. The British and Americans were sweeping through France. We felt sure that they would get to us in time. In September we were told that we were to be shipped to Poland . . . The men to one camp. The women to another. I was sent to Auschwitz. They went to Belsen. In January we were freed, the few of us who were left. The war wasn't yet over, so it took us a long time to get home. We'd be sent here and there behind the lines where we'd be safe. Each time our train would stop . . . at a siding, or a crossing . . . we'd all get out and go from group to group . . . Where were you? Were you at Belsen? At Buchenwald? At Mauthausen? Is it possible that you knew my wife? Did you ever see my husband? My son? My daughter? That's how I found out about my wife's death . . . of Margot, the Van Daans . . . Dussel. But Anne . . . I still hoped . . . Yesterday I went to Rotterdam. I'd heard of a woman there . . . She'd been in Belsen with Anne . . . I know now.

[*He picks up the diary again, and turns the pages back to find a certain passage. As he finds it we hear* ANNE'S VOICE]

ANNE'S VOICE: In spite of everything, I still believe that people are really good at heart.

[MR. FRANK *slowly closes the diary*]

MR. FRANK: She puts me to shame.

[*They are silent*]

THE CURTAIN FALLS

LUTHER

John Osborne

John Osborne

Luther represented one of those felicitous occasions in the theatre when all creative elements were perfectly fused. Winner of the 1964 Tony Award, John Osborne's towering drama about the German religious rebel and reformer, Martin Luther, was magnificently staged by Tony Richardson, designed by Jocelyn Herbert, and, above all, had Albert Finney repeating his blazing performance that was a sensation in London two years previously.

The play originated at the Royal Court Theatre in 1961, leading Kenneth Tynan to comment in *The Observer*: ". . . the language is urgent and sinewy, packed with images that derive from bone, blood and marrow . . . I count it the most eloquent piece of dramatic writing to have dignified our theatre since *Look Back in Anger*."

As anticipated, *Luther* did not emerge from Osborne's pen as a conventional historical epic of sixteenth-century Europe and the Reformation. Instead, he illuminated the character and motivations of the man who tore Christendom apart, and himself in the process, with his own fears, loneliness, and personal torment.

The New York opening on September 25, 1963, was no less rousing than it was in London, and once again the majority of local reviewers trotted out their most laudatory adjectives.

Howard Taubman of the New York *Times* wrote: "With *Luther*, John Osborne has ventured on a big theme in a big way" and "he has carried it off with dramatic fervor and passionate eloquence . . . Whatever your allegiance of faith may be, you owe it to yourself to rediscover the excitement that a vital play can generate . . . As drama it has size and distinction. It is about matters worth talking and thinking about. It makes the theatre ten feet tall."

Critic Martin Gottfried stated: "High theatre was brought back to New York last night with the opening of John Osborne's new play *Luther*. It is theatre that is noble in purpose, eloquent in language and universal in conception . . . Mr. Osborne has managed to stick

closely to history while making grand theatre of Martin Luther . . .
It is enobling theatre."

Variety's correspondent Hobe Morrison declared: "There's no
need to worry about whether the theatre will survive as long as there
are plays like Luther. This John Osborne play brings the stage to
pulsating life . . . a stunning work of theatrical importance."

Other journalists shared the enthusiasm of the foregoing, hailing
the play as one that "plunges beneath the surface of facts and becomes a work of power and integrity that embodies dignity, history
and drama . . . It is a massive play of ringing authority—bold, in-
solent, and challenging" and "emerges as a power in the theatre."

In addition to Tony Awards for both play and author, Luther received the New York Drama Critics' Circle Award for the best play
of the 1963–64 season. It ran for 211 performances.

To theatre historians, May 8, 1956, forever will remain a decisive
date in twentieth-century theatrical history, for on that now memorable evening, John Osborne's Look Back in Anger explosively took
hold of the stage at the Royal Court, London, and as it ruthlessly
swept away the cobwebs of the past, it detonated a new awareness
and a strong, angered sense of protest in drama. Reflecting the non-
conformity and the contradictory attitudes of the post-World War II
generation, the play instantaneously established Osborne, at the time
an actor, as a powerful and compelling new dramatist, and also trig-
gered the extraordinary theatrical renaissance that followed in Brit-
ain and, subsequently, spread to other parts of the world. Through
the fire and fury of his central character, Jimmy Porter, Osborne immediately became identified as spokesman for his complex and troubled generation, eager to grasp the hand of "one who speaks out of
the real despairs, frustrations and sufferings of the age we are living
in, now, at this moment."

Look Back in Anger opened in New York in 1957 and won the
New York Drama Critics' Circle Award for Best Foreign Play of the
season.

Born in London on December 12, 1929, and educated at Belmont
College in Devon, Mr. Osborne came to the theatre as an actor after
a brief tenure as a journalist. He made his first stage appearance in
1948, and later joined the English Stage Company, at the Royal
Court, where he remained until 1957.

In that same year, Mr. Osborne's The Entertainer commanded
the West End season with its negative and tragic hero, a third-rate

music hall artist, brilliantly limned by Laurence Olivier. More experimental in nature than its immediate predecessor, the play juxtaposed the music hall conventions with domesticity in order to eliminate the restrictions of the naturalistic theatre.

Among the author's other works for the stage are: *Epitaph for George Dillon*, co-authored with Anthony Creighton (1958); *The World of Paul Slickey* (1959); *Blood of the Bambergs* and *Under Plain Cover* (1962); *A Subject of Scandal and Concern* (1962); *Inadmissible Evidence* (1964); *A Patriot for Me* (1965); *A Bond Honoured, Time Present, The Hotel in Amsterdam* (1968); and *West of Suez* (1971).

Unquestionably one of the world's most influential and popular dramatists, he also has written for television and films; notably, the screenplay for *Tom Jones,* which brought him an Academy Award in 1963.

The first performance of LUTHER was given at the Theatre Royal, Nottingham, on June 26th, 1961, by the English Stage Company. It was directed by Tony Richardson and the décor was by Jocelyn Herbert. The part of Luther was played by Albert Finney.

Luther had its New York première on September 25, 1963, at the St. James Theatre, under the auspices of David Merrick, by arrangement with the English Stage Company and Oscar Lewenstein. The cast was as follows:

KNIGHT	*Glyn Owen*
PRIOR	*Ted Thurston*
MARTIN	*Albert Finney*
HANS	*Kenneth J. Warren*
LUCAS	*Luis Van Rooten*
READER	*Alfred Sandor*
WEINAND	*John Heffernan*
TETZEL	*Peter Bull*
STAUPITZ	*Frank Shelley*
CAJETAN	*John Moffatt*
MILTITZ	*Robert Burr*
LEO	*Michael Egan*
ECK	*Martin Rudy*
KATHERINE	*Lorna Lewis*

MONKS, LORDS, PEASANTS, ETC.: *Thor Arngrim, Harry Carlson, Stan Dworkin, Roger Hamilton, Konrad Matthaei, Alfred Sandor*
SINGERS: *Paul Flores, Dan Goggin, Robert L. Hultman, Marvin Solley* (Soloist)
CHILDREN: *Perry Golkin, Joseph Lamberta*

Directed by Tony Richardson
Scenery and Costumes by Jocelyn Herbert
Supervised by Thea Neu
Music Composed and Arranged by John Addison
Choral Director: Max Walmer

ACT ONE

Scene 1: *The Convent of the Augustinian Order of Eremites at Erfurt. 1506.*

Scene 2: *The same. A year later.*

Scene 3: *Two hours later.*

ACT TWO

Scene 1: *The Market Place, Juterbög. 1517.*

Scene 2: *The Eremite Cloister. Wittenberg. 1517.*

Scene 3: *The steps of the Castle Church. Wittenberg. Eve of All Saints. 1517.*

Scene 4: *The Fugger Palace. Augsburg. October 1518.*

Scene 5: *A hunting lodge. Magliana, Italy. 1519.*

Scene 6: *The Elster Gate. Wittenberg. 1520.*

ACT THREE

Scene 1: *The Diet of Worms. 1521.*

Scene 2: *Wittenberg. 1525.*

Scene 3: *The Eremite Cloister. Wittenberg. 1530.*

NOTE: *At the opening of each act,* THE KNIGHT *appears. He grasps a banner and briefly barks the time and place of the scene following at the audience, and then retires.*

ACT ONE

SCENE ONE

The Cloister Chapel of the Eremites of St. Augustine. Erfurt, Thuringia, 1506. MARTIN *is being received into the Order. He is kneeling in front of the* PRIOR *in the presence of the assembled convent.*

PRIOR: Now you must choose one of two ways: either to leave us now, or give up this world, and consecrate and devote yourself entirely to God and our Order. But I must add this: once you have committed yourself, you are not free, for whatever reason, to throw off the yoke of obedience, for you will have accepted it freely, while you were still able to discard it.

[*The habit and hood of the Order are brought in and blessed by the* PRIOR]

PRIOR: He whom it was your will to dress in the garb of the Order, oh Lord, invest him also with eternal life.

[*He undresses* MARTIN]

PRIOR: The Lord divest you of the former man and of all his works. The Lord invest you with the new man.

[*The* CHOIR *sings as* MARTIN *is robed in the habit and hood. The long white scapular is thrown over his head and hung down, before and behind; then he kneels again before the* PRIOR, *and, with his hand on the statutes of the Order, swears the oath*]

MARTIN: I, brother Martin, do make profession and promise obedience to Almighty God, to Mary the Sacred Virgin, and to you, my brother Prior of this cloister, in the name of the Vicar General of the order of Eremites of the holy Bishop of St. Augustine and his successors, to live without property and in chastity according to the Rule of our Venerable Father Augustine until death.

[*The* PRIOR *wishes a prayer over him, and* MARTIN *prostrates himself with arms extended in the form of a cross*]

PRIOR: Lord Jesus Christ, our leader and our strength, by the fire of humility you have set aside this servant, Martin, from the rest of Mankind. We humbly pray that this fire will also cut him off from carnal intercourse and from the community of those things done on earth by men, through the sanctity shed from heaven upon him, and that you will bestow on him grace to remain yours, and merit eternal life. For it is not he who begins, but he who endures will be saved. Amen.

[*The* CHOIR *sings* Veni Creator Spiritus—*or perhaps* Great Father Augustine. *A newly lighted taper is put into* MARTIN'S *hands, and he is led up the altar steps to be welcomed by the monks with the kiss of peace. Then, in their midst, he marches slowly with them behind the screen and is lost to sight.*
The procession disappears, and, as the sound of voices dies away, two men are left alone in the congregation. One of them, HANS, *gets up impatiently and moves downstage. It is* MARTIN'S FATHER, *a stocky man wired throughout with a miner's muscle, lower-middle class, on his way to become a small, primitive capitalist; bewildered, full of pride and resentment. His companion,* LUCAS, *finishes a respectful prayer and joins him*]

HANS: Well?

LUCAS: Well?

HANS: Don't 'well' me, you feeble old ninny, what do you think?

LUCAS: Think? Of what?

HANS: Yes, think man, think, what do you think, pen and ink, think of all that?

LUCAS: Oh—

HANS: Oh! Of all these monks, of Martin and all the rest of it, what do you think? You've been sitting in this arse-aching congregation all this time, you've been watching, haven't you? What about it?

LUCAS: Yes, well, I must say it's all very impressive.

HANS: Oh, yes?

LUCAS: No getting away from it.

HANS: Impressive?

LUCAS: Deeply. It was moving and oh——

HANS: What?

LUCAS: You must have felt it, surely. You couldn't fail to.

HANS: Impressive! I don't know what impresses me any longer.

LUCAS: Oh, come on——

HANS: Impressive!

LUCAS: Of course it is, and you know it.

HANS: Oh, you—you can afford to be impressed.

LUCAS: It's surely too late for any regrets, or bitterness, Hans. It obviously must be God's will, and there's an end of it.

HANS: That's exactly what it is—an end of it! Very fine for you, my friend, very fine indeed. You're just losing a son-in-law, and you can take your pick of plenty more of those where he comes from. But what am I losing? I'm losing a son; mark: a son.

LUCAS: How can you say that?

HANS: How can I say it? I do say it, that's how. Two sons to the plague, and now another. God's eyes! Did you see that haircut? Brother Martin!

LUCAS: There isn't a finer order than these people, not the Dominicans or Franciscans——

HANS: Like an egg with a beard.

LUCAS: You said that yourself.

HANS: Oh, I suppose they're Christians under their damned cowls.

LUCAS: There are good distinguished men in this place, and well you know it.

HANS: Yes—good, distinguished men——

LUCAS: Pious, learned men, men from the University like Martin.

HANS: Learned men! Some of them can't read their own names.

LUCAS: So?

HANS: So! I—I'm a miner. I don't need books. You can't see to read books under the ground. But Martin's a scholar.

LUCAS: He most certainly is.

HANS: A Master of Arts! What's he master of now? Eh? Tell me.

LUCAS: Well, there it is. God's gain is your loss.

HANS: Half these monks do nothing but wash dishes and beg in the streets.

LUCAS: We should be going, I suppose.

HANS: He could have been a man of stature.

LUCAS: And he will, with God's help.

HANS: Don't tell me. He could have been a lawyer.

LUCAS: Well, he won't now.

HANS: No, you're damn right he won't. Of stature. To the Archbishop, or the Duke, or——

LUCAS: Yes.

HANS: Anyone.

LUCAS: Come on.

HANS: Anyone you can think of.

LUCAS: Well, I'm going.

HANS: Brother Martin!

LUCAS: Hans.

HANS: Do you know why? Lucas: Why? What made him do it?

[*He has ceased to play a role by this time and he asks the
question simply as if he expected a short, direct answer*]

HANS: What made him do it?

[LUCAS *grasps his forearm*]

LUCAS: Let's go home.

HANS: Why? That's what I can't understand. Why? Why?

LUCAS: Home. Let's go home.

[*They go off. The convent bell rings. Some* MONKS *are standing at a refectory table. After their prayers, they sit down,
and, as they eat in silence, one of the* BROTHERS *reads from a
lectern. During this short scene,* MARTIN, *wearing a rough
apron over his habit, waits on the others*]

READER:
What are the tools of Good Works?
First, to love Lord God with all one's heart,
all one's soul, and all one's strength. Then,
one's neighbour as oneself. Then, not to kill.
Not to commit adultery
Not to steal
Not to covet
Not to bear false witness
To honour all men
To deny yourself, in order to follow Christ
To chastise the body
Not to seek soft living
To love fasting
To clothe the naked
To visit the sick
To bury the dead
To help the afflicted
To console the sorrowing
To prefer nothing to the love of Christ

Not to yield to anger
Not to nurse a grudge
Not to hold guile in your heart

Not to make a feigned peace
To fear the Day of Judgment
To dread Hell
To desire eternal life with all your spiritual longing
To keep death daily before your eyes
To keep constant vigilance over the actions of your life
To know for certain that God sees you everywhere
When evil thoughts come into your heart, to dash them
at once on the love of Christ and to manifest them to your
spiritual father
To keep your mouth from evil and depraved talk
Not to love much speaking
Not to speak vain words or such as produce laughter
To listen gladly to holy readings
To apply yourself frequently to prayer
Daily in your prayer, with tears and sighs to
confess your past sins to God
Not to fulfill the desires of the flesh
To hate your own will

Behold, these are the tools of the spiritual craft.
If we employ these unceasingly day and night,
and render account of them on the Day of
Judgment, then we shall receive from the Lord
in return that reward that He Himself has
promised: Eye hath not seen nor ear heard
what God hath prepared for those that love
Him. Now this is the workshop in which we
shall diligently execute all these tasks. May God
grant that you observe all these rules cheerfully
as lovers of spiritual beauty, spreading around
you by the piety of your deportment the sweet
odour of Christ.

[*The convent bell rings. The* MONKS *rise, bow their heads in prayer, and then move upstage to the steps where they kneel.* MARTIN, *assisted by another* BROTHER, *stacks the table and clears it. Presently, they all prostrate themselves, and, beneath flaming candles, a communal confession begins.* MARTIN *returns and prostrates himself downstage behind the rest. This scene throughout is urgent, muted, almost whispered, confidential, secret, like a prayer*]

BROTHER: I confess to God, to Blessed Mary and our holy Father Augustine, to all the saints, and to all present that I have sinned exceedingly in thought, word and deed by my own fault. Wherefore I pray Holy Mary, all the saints of God and you all assembled here to pray for me. I confess I did leave my cell for the Night Office without the Scapular and had to return for it. Which is a deadly infringement of the first degree of humility, that of obedience without delay. For this failure to Christ I abjectly seek forgiveness and whatever punishment the Prior and community is pleased to impose on me.

MARTIN: I am a worm and no man, a byword and a laughing stock. Crush out the worminess in me, stamp on me.

BROTHER: I confess I have three times made mistakes in the Oratory, in psalm singing and Antiphon.

MARTIN: I was fighting a bear in a garden without flowers, leading into a desert. His claws kept making my arms bleed as I tried to open a gate which would take me out. But the gate was no gate at all. It was simply an open frame, and I could have walked through it, but I was covered in my own blood, and I saw a naked woman riding on a goat, and the goat began to drink my blood, and I thought I should faint with the pain and I awoke in my cell, all soaking in the devil's bath.

BROTHER: Let Brother Norbert remember also his breakage while working in the kitchen.

BROTHER: I remember it, and confess humbly.

BROTHER: Let him remember also his greater transgression in not coming at once to the Prior and community to do penance for it, and so increasing his offence.

MARTIN: I am alone. I am alone, and against myself.

BROTHER: I confess it. I confess it, and beg your prayers that I may undergo the greater punishment for it.

MARTIN: How can I justify myself?

BROTHER: Take heart, you shall be punished, and severely.

MARTIN: How can I be justified?

BROTHER: I confess I have failed to rise from my bed speedily enough. I arrived at the Night Office after the Gloria of the 94th Psalm, and though I seemed to amend the shame by not standing in my proper place in the choir, and standing in the place appointed by the Prior for such careless sinners so that they may be seen by all, my fault is too great and I seek punishment.

MARTIN: I was among a group of people, men and women, fully clothed. We lay on top of each other in neat rows about seven or eight across. Eventually, the pile was many people deep. Suddenly, I panicked—although I was on top of the pile—and I cried: what about those underneath? Those at the very bottom, and those in between? We all got up in an orderly way, without haste, and when we looked, those at the bottom were not simply flattened by the weight, they were just their clothes, they were just their clothes, neatly pressed and folded on the ground. They were their clothes, neatly pressed and folded on the ground.

BROTHER: I did omit to have a candle ready at the Mass.

BROTHER: Twice in my sloth, I have omitted to shave, and even excused myself, pretending to believe my skin to be fairer than that of my Brothers, and my beard lighter and my burden also. I have been vain and slothful, and I beg forgiveness and ask penance.

MARTIN: If my flesh would leak and dissolve, and I could live as bone, if I were forged bone, plucked bone and brain, warm hair and a bony heart, if I were all bone, I could brandish myself without terror, without any terror at all—I could be indestructible.

BROTHER: I did ask for a bath, pretending to myself that it was necessary for my health, but as I lowered my body into the tub, it came to me that it was inordinate desire and that it was my soul that was soiled.

MARTIN: My bones fail. My bones fail, my bones are shattered and fall away, my bones fail and all that's left of me is a scraped marrow and a dying jelly.

BROTHER: Let Brother Paulinus remember our visit to our near sister house, and lifting his eyes repeatedly at a woman in the town who dropped alms into his bag.

BROTHER: I remember, and I beg forgiveness.

BROTHER: Then let him remember also that though our dear Father Augustine does not forbid us to see women, he blames us if we should desire them or wish to be the object of their desire. For it is not only by touch and by being affectionate that a man excites disorderly affection in a woman. This can be done also even by looks. You cannot maintain that your mind is pure if you have *wanton* eyes. For a wanton eye is a wanton heart. When people with impure hearts manifest their inclination towards each other through the medium of looks, even though no word is spoken, and when they take pleasure in their desire for each other, the purity of their character has gone even though they may be undefiled by any unchaste act. He who fixes his eyes on a woman and takes pleasure in her glance, must not think that he goes unobserved by his brothers.

MARTIN: I confess that I have offended grievously against humility, being sometimes discontented with the meanest and worst of everything, I have not only failed to declare myself to myself lower and lower and of less account than all other men, but I have failed in my most inmost heart to believe it. For many weeks, many weeks it seemed to me, I was put to cleaning the latrines. I did it, and I did it vigorously, not tepidly, with all my poor strength, without whispering or objections to anyone. But although I fulfilled my task, and I did it well, sometimes there were murmurings in my heart. I prayed that it would cease, knowing that God, seeing my murmuring heart, must reject my work, and it was as good as not done. I sought out my master, and he punished me, telling me to fast for two days. I have fasted for three, but, even so, I can't tell if the murmurings are really gone, and I ask for your prayers, and I ask for your prayers that I may be able to go on fulfilling the same task.

BROTHER: Let Brother Martin remember all the degrees of humility; and let him go on cleaning the latrines.

[*The convent bell rings. After lying prostrate for a few moments, all the* BROTHERS, *including* MARTIN, *rise and move to the* CHOIR. *The Office begins, versicle, antiphon and psalm, and* MARTIN *is lost to sight in the ranks of his fellow* MONKS. *Presently, there is a quiet, violent moaning, just distinguishable amongst the voices. It becomes louder and wilder, the cries more violent, and there is some confusion in* MARTIN'S *section of the* CHOIR. *The singing goes on with only a few heads turned. It seems as though the disturbance has subsided.* MARTIN *appears, and staggers between the stalls. Outstretched hands fail to restrain him, and he is visible to all, muscles rigid, breath suspended, then jerking uncontrollably as he is seized in a raging fit. Two* BROTHERS *go to him, but* MARTIN *writhes with such ferocity, that they can scarcely hold him down. He tries to speak, the effort is frantic, and eventually, he is able to roar out a word at a time]*

MARTIN: Not! Me! I am *not!*

[*The attack reaches its height, and he recoils as if he had bitten his tongue and his mouth were full of blood and saliva. Two more* MONKS *come to help, and he almost breaks away from them, but the effort collapses, and they are able to drag him away, as he is about to vomit. The Office continues as if nothing had taken place*]

SCENE TWO

A knife, like a butcher's, hanging aloft, the size of a garden fence. The cutting edge of the blade points upwards. Across it hangs the torso of a naked man, his head hanging down. Below it, an enormous round cone, like the inside of a vast barrel, surrounded by darkness. From the upstage entrance, seemingly far, far away, a dark figure appears against the blinding light inside, as it grows brighter. The figure approaches slowly along the floor of the vast cone, and stops as it reaches the downstage opening. It is MARTIN, *haggard and streaming with sweat.*

MARTIN: I lost the body of a child, a child's body, the eyes of a child; and at the first sound of my own childish voice. I lost the body of a child; and I was afraid, and I went back to find it. But I'm still afraid. I'm afraid, and there's an end of it! But *I* mean . . . [*Shouts*] . . . Continually! For instance of the noise the Prior's dog makes on a still evening when he rolls over on his side and licks his teeth. I'm afraid of the darkness, and the hole in it; and I see it sometime of every day! And some days more than once even, and there's no bottom to it, no bottom to my breath, and I can't reach it. Why? Why do you think? There's a bare fist clenched to my bowels and they can't move, and I have to sit sweating in my little monk's house to open them. The lost body of a child, hanging on a mother's tit, and close to the warm, big body of a man, and I can't find it.

[*He steps down, out of the blazing light within the cone, and goes to his cell down left. Kneeling by his bed, he starts to try and pray but he soon collapses. From down right appear a procession of* MONKS, *carrying various priest's vestments, candles and articles for the altar, for* MARTIN *is about to perform his very first Mass. Heading them is* BROTHER WEINAND. *They pass* MARTIN's *cell, and, after a few words, they go on, leaving* BROTHER WEINAND *with* MARTIN, *and disappear into what is almost like a small house on the upstage left of the stage: a bagpipe of the period, fat, soft, foolish and obscene looking*]

BRO. WEINAND: Brother Martin! Brother Martin!

MARTIN: Yes.

BRO. WEINAND: Your father's here.

MARTIN: My father?

BRO. WEINAND: He asked to see you, but I told him it'd be better to wait until afterwards.

MARTIN: Where is he?

BRO. WEINAND: He's having breakfast with the Prior.

MARTIN: Is he alone?

BRO. WEINAND: No, he's got a couple of dozen friends at least, I should say.

MARTIN: Is my mother with him?

BRO. WEINAND: No.

MARTIN: What did he have to come for? I should have told him not to come.

BRO. WEINAND: It'd be a strange father who didn't want to be present when his son celebrated his first Mass.

MARTIN: I never thought he'd come. Why didn't he tell me?

BRO. WEINAND: Well, he's here now, anyway. He's also given twenty guilden to the chapter as a present, so he can't be too displeased with you.

MARTIN: Twenty guilden.

BRO. WEINAND: Well, are you all prepared?

MARTIN: That's three times what it cost him to send me to the University for a year.

BRO. WEINAND: You don't look it. Why, you're running all over with sweat again. Are you sick? Are you?

MARTIN: No.

BRO. WEINAND: Here, let me wipe your face. You haven't much time. You're sure you're not sick?

MARTIN: My bowels won't move, that's all. But that's nothing out of the way.

BRO. WEINAND: Have you shaved?

MARTIN: Yes. Before I went to confession. Why, do you think I should shave again?

BRO. WEINAND: No. I don't. A few overlooked little bristles couldn't make much difference, any more than a few imaginary sins. There, that's better.

MARTIN: What do you mean?

BRO. WEINAND: You were sweating like a pig in a butcher's shop. You know what they say, don't you? Whenever you find a melancholy person, there you'll find a bath running for the devil.

MARTIN: No, no, what did you mean about leaving a few imaginary sins?

BRO. WEINAND: I mean there are plenty of priests with dirty ears administering the sacraments, but this isn't the time to talk about that. Come on, Martin, you've got nothing to be afraid of.

MARTIN: How do you know?

BRO. WEINAND: You always talk as if lightning were just about to strike behind you.

MARTIN: Tell me what you meant.

BRO. WEINAND: I only meant the whole convent knows you're always making up sins you've never committed. That's right—well, isn't it? No sensible confessor will have anything to do with you.

MARTIN: What's the use of all this talk of penitence if I can't feel it.

BRO. WEINAND: Father Nathin told me he had to punish you only the day before yesterday because you were in some ridiculous state of hysteria, all over some verse in Proverbs or something.

MARTIN: "Know thou the state of thy flocks."

BRO. WEINAND: And all over the interpretation of one word apparently. When will you ever learn? You must know what you're doing. Some of the brothers laugh quite openly at you, you and your over-stimulated conscience. Which is wrong of them, I know, but you must be able to see why.

MARTIN: It's the single words that trouble me.

BRO. WEINAND: The moment you've confessed and turned to the altar, you're beckoning for a priest again. Why, every time you break wind they say you rush to a confessor.

MARTIN: Do they say that?

BRO. WEINAND: It's their favourite joke.

MARTIN: They say that, do they?

BRO. WEINAND: Martin! You're protected from many of the world's evils in here. You're expected to master them, not be obsessed by them. God bids us hope in His everlasting mercy. Try to remember that.

MARTIN: And you tell me this! What have I gained from coming into this sacred Order? Aren't I still the same? I'm still envious, I'm still impatient, I'm still passionate?

BRO. WEINAND: How can you ask a question like that?

MARTIN: I do ask it. I'm asking you! What have I gained?

BRO. WEINAND: In any of this, all we can ever learn is how to die.

MARTIN: That's no answer.

BRO. WEINAND: It's the only one I can think of at this moment. Come on.

MARTIN: All you teach me in this sacred place is how to doubt——

BRO. WEINAND: Give you a little praise, and you're pleased for a while, but let a little trial of sin and death come into your day and you crumble, don't you?

MARTIN: But that's all you've taught me, that's really all you've taught me, and all the while I'm living in the Devil's worm-bag.

BRO. WEINAND: It hurts me to watch you like this, sucking up cares like a leech.

MARTIN: You *will* be there beside me, won't you?

BRO. WEINAND: Of course, and, if anything at all goes wrong, or if you forget anything, we'll see to it. You'll be all right. But nothing will—you won't make any mistakes.

MARTIN: But what if I do, just one mistake. Just a word, one word —one sin.

BRO. WEINAND: Martin, kneel down.

MARTIN: Forgive me, Brother Weinand, but the truth is this——

BRO. WEINAND: Kneel.

[MARTIN *kneels*]

MARTIN: It's this, just this. All I can feel, all I can feel is God's hatred.

BRO. WEINAND: Repeat the Apostles' Creed.

MARTIN: He's like a glutton, the way he gorges me, he's a glutton. He gorges me, and then spits me out in lumps.

BRO. WEINAND: After me. "I believe in God the Father Almighty, maker of Heaven and Earth . . .

MARTIN: I'm a trough, I tell you, and he's swilling about in me. All the time.

BRO. WEINAND: "And in Jesus Christ, His only Son Our Lord . . .

MARTIN: "And in Jesus Christ, His only Son Our Lord . . .

BRO. WEINAND: "Who was conceived by the Holy Ghost, born of the Virgin Mary, suffered under Pontius Pilate . . .

MARTIN: [*Almost unintelligibly*] "Was crucified, died and was buried; He descended into Hell; the third day He rose from the dead, He ascended into Heaven, and sitteth on the right hand of God the Father Almighty; from thence He shall come to judge the quick and the dead." And every sunrise sings a song for death.

BRO. WEINAND: "I believe——

MARTIN: "I believe——

BRO. WEINAND: Go on.

MARTIN: "I believe in the Holy Ghost; the holy Catholic Church; the Communion of Saints; the forgiveness of sins;

BRO. WEINAND: Again!

MARTIN: "The forgiveness of sins.

BRO. WEINAND: What was that again?

MARTIN: "I believe in the forgiveness of sins."

BRO. WEINAND: Do you? Then remember this: St. Bernard says that when we say in the Apostles' Creed "I believe in the forgiveness of sins" each one must believe that *his* sins are forgiven. Well?——

MARTIN: I wish my bowels would open. I'm blocked up like an old crypt.

BRO. WEINAND: Try to remember, Martin?

MARTIN: Yes, I'll try.

BRO. WEINAND: Good. Now, you must get yourself ready. Come on, we'd better help you.

[*Some* BROTHERS *appear from out of the bagpipe with the vestments, etc. and help* MARTIN *put them on*]

MARTIN: How much did you say my father gave to the chapter?

BRO. WEINAND: Twenty guilden.

MARTIN: That's a lot of money to my father. He's a miner, you know.

BRO. WEINAND: Yes, he told me.

MARTIN: As tough as you can think of. Where's he sitting?

BRO. WEINAND: Near the front, I should think. Are you nearly ready?

[*The Convent bell rings. A procession leads out from the bagpipe*]

MARTIN: Thank you, Brother Weinand.

BRO. WEINAND: For what? Today would be an ordeal for any kind of a man. In a short while, you will be handling, for the first time, the body and blood of Christ. God bless you, my son.

[*He makes the sign of the cross, and the other* BROTHERS *leave*]

MARTIN: Somewhere, in the body of a child, Satan foresaw in me what I'm suffering now. That's why he prepares open pits for me, and all kinds of tricks to bring me down, so that I keep wondering if I'm the only man living who's baited, and surrounded by dreams, and afraid to move.

BRO. WEINAND: [*Really angry by now*] You're a fool. You're really a fool. God isn't angry with you. It's you who are angry with Him.

[*He goes out. The* BROTHERS *wait for* MARTIN, *who kneels*]

MARTIN: Oh, Mary, dear Mary, all I see of Christ is a flame and raging on a rainbow. Pray to your Son, and ask Him to still His anger, for I can't raise my eyes to look at Him. Am I the only one to see all this, and suffer?

[*He rises, joins the procession and disappears off with it. As the Mass is heard to begin offstage, the stage is empty. Then the light within the cone grows increasingly brilliant, and, presently* MARTIN *appears again. He enters through the far entrance of the cone, and advances towards the audience. He is carrying a naked* CHILD. *Presently, he steps down from the cone, comes downstage, and stands still*]

MARTIN: And so, the praising ended—and the blasphemy began.

[*He returns, back into the cone, the light fades as the Mass comes to its end*]

SCENE THREE

The Convent refectory. Some MONKS *are sitting at table with* HANS *and* LUCAS. LUCAS *is chatting with the* BROTHERS *eagerly, but* HANS *is brooding. He has drunk a lot of wine in a short time, and his brain is beginning to heat.*

HANS: What about some more of this, eh? Don't think you can get away with it, you know, you old cockchafer. I'm getting me twenty guilden's worth before the day's out. After all, it's a proud day for all of us. That's right, isn't it?

LUCAS: It certainly is.

BRO. WEINAND: Forgive me, I wasn't looking. Here——

[*He fills* HAN'S *glass*]

HANS: [*Trying to be friendly*] Don't give me that. You monks don't miss much. Got eyes like gimlets and ears like open drains. Tell me—Come on, then, what's your opinion of Brother Martin?

BRO. WEINAND: He's a good, devout monk.

HANS: Yes. Yes, well, I suppose you can't say much about each other, can you? You're more like a team, in a way. Tell me, Brother—would you say that in this monastery—or, any monastery you like—you were as strong as the weakest member of the team?

BRO. WEINAND: No, I don't think that's so.

HANS: But wouldn't you say then—I'm not saying this in any criticism, mind, but because I'm just interested, naturally, in the circumstances—but wouldn't you say that one bad monk, say for instance, one really monster sized, roaring great bitch of a monk, if he really got going, really going, couldn't he get his order such a reputation that eventually, it might even have to go into—what do they call it now—liquidation. That's it. Liquidation. Now, you're an educated man, you understand Latin and Greek and Hebrew——

BRO. WEINAND: Only Latin, I'm afraid, and a very little Greek.

HANS: [*Having planted his cue for a quick, innocent boast*] Oh, really. Martin knows Latin and Greek, and now he's half-way through Hebrew too, they tell me.

BRO. WEINAND: Martin is a brilliant man. We are not all as gifted as he is.

HANS: No, well, anyway what would be your opinion about this?

BRO. WEINAND: I think my opinion would be that the Church is bigger than those who are in her.

HANS: Yes, yes, but don't you think it could be discredited by, say, just a few men?

BRO. WEINAND: Plenty of people have tried, but the Church is still there. Besides, a human voice is small and the world's very large. But the Church reaches out and is heard everywhere.

HANS: Well, what about this chap Erasmus, for instance?

BRO. WEINAND: [*Politely. He knows* HANS *knows nothing about him*] Yes?

HANS: Erasmus. [*Trying to pass the ball*] Well, what about *him*, for instance? What do you think of him?

BRO. WEINAND: Erasmus is apparently a great scholar, and respected throughout Europe.

HANS: [*Resenting being lectured*] Yes, of course, *I* know who he is, I don't need you to tell me that, what I said was: what do you think about him?

BRO. WEINAND: Think about him?

HANS: Good God, you won't stand still a minute and let yourself be saddled, will you? Doesn't he criticize the Church or something?

BRO. WEINAND: He's a scholar, and, I should say, his criticisms could only be profitably argued about by other scholars.

LUCAS: Don't let him get you into an argument. He'll argue about anything, especially if he doesn't know what he's talking about.

HANS: I know what I'm talking about, I was merely asking a question——

LUCAS: Well, you shouldn't be asking questions on a day like today. Just think of it, for a minute, Hans——

HANS: What do you think I'm doing? You soppy old woman!

LUCAS: It's a really 'once only' occasion, like a wedding, if you like.

HANS: Or a funeral. By the way, what's happened to the corpse? Eh? Where's Brother Martin?

BRO. WEINAND: I expect he's still in his cell.

HANS: Well, what's he doing in there?

BRO. WEINAND: He's perfectly all right, he's a little—disturbed.

HANS: [*Pouncing delightedly*] Disturbed! Disturbed! What's he disturbed about?

BRO. WEINAND: Celebrating one's first Mass can be a great ordeal for a sensitive spirit.

HANS: Oh, the bread and the wine and all that?

BRO. WEINAND: Of course; there are a great many things to memorize as well.

LUCAS: Heavens, yes. I don't know how they think of it all.

HANS: I didn't think he made it up as he went along! But doesn't he know we're still here? Hasn't anybody told him we're all waiting for him?

BRO. WEINAND: He won't be much longer—you'll see. Here, have some more of our wine. He simply wanted to be on his own for a little while before he saw anyone.

HANS: I should have thought he had enough of being on his own by now.

LUCAS: The boy's probably a bit—well, you know, anxious about seeing you again, too.

HANS: What's he got to be anxious about?

LUCAS: Well, apart from everything else, it's nearly three years since he last saw you.

HANS: I saw *him*. He didn't see me.

[*Enter* MARTIN]

LUCAS: There you are, my boy. We were wondering what had happened to you. Come and sit down, there's a good lad. Your father and I have been punishing the convent wine cellar, I'm afraid. Bit early in the day for me, too.

HANS: Speak for yourself, you swirly-eyed old gander. We're not *started* yet, are we?

LUCAS: My dear boy, are you all right? You're so pale.

HANS: He's right though. Brother Martin! Brother Lazarus they ought to call you!

[*He laughs and* MARTIN *smiles at the joke with him.* MARTIN *is cautious,* HANS *too, but manœuvring for position*]

MARTIN: I'm all right, thank you, Lucas.

HANS: Been sick, have you?

MARTIN: I'm much better now, thank you, father.

HANS: [*Relentless*] Upset tummy, is it? That what it is? Too much fasting I expect. [*Concealing concern*] You look like death warmed up, all right.

LUCAS: Come and have a little wine. You're allowed that, aren't you? It'll make you feel better.

HANS: I know that milky look. I've seen it too many times. Been sick have you?

LUCAS: Oh, he's looking better already. Drop of wine'll put the colour back in there. You're all right, aren't you, lad?

MARTIN: Yes, what about you——

LUCAS: That's right. Of course he is. He's all right.

HANS: Vomit all over your cell, I expect. [*To* BROTHER WEINAND] But he'll have to clear that up himself, won't he?

LUCAS: [*To* MARTIN] Oh, you weren't were you? Poor old lad, well, never mind, no wonder you kept us waiting.

HANS: Can't have his mother coming in and getting down on her knees to mop it all up.

MARTIN: I managed to clean it up all right. How are *you*, father?

HANS: [*Feeling an attack, but determined not to lose the initiative*] Me? Oh, I'm all right. I'm all right, aren't I, Lucas? Nothing ever wrong with me. Your old man's strong enough. But then that's because we've got to be, people like Lucas and me. Because if *we* aren't strong, it won't take any time at all before we're knocked flat on our backs, or flat on our knees, or flat on something or other. Flat on our backs and finished, and we can't afford to be finished because if we're finished, that's it, that's the end, so we just have to stand up to it as best we can. But that's life, isn't it?

MARTIN: I'm never sure what people mean when they say that.

LUCAS: Your father's doing very well indeed, Martin. He's got his own investment in the mine now, so he's beginning to work for himself if you see what I mean. That's the way things are going everywhere now.

MARTIN: [*To* HANS] You must be pleased.

HANS: I'm pleased to make money. I'm not pleased to break my back doing it.

MARTIN: How's mother?

HANS: Nothing wrong there either. Too much work and too many kids for too long, that's all. [*Hiding embarrassment*] I'm sorry she couldn't come, but it's a rotten journey as you know, and all that, so she sent her love to you. Oh, yes, and there was a pie, too. But I was told [*At* BROTHER WEINAND] I couldn't give it to you, but I'd have to give it to the Prior.

MARTIN: That's the rule about gifts, father. You must have forgotten?

HANS: Well, I hope you get a piece of it anyway. She took a lot of care over it. Oh, yes, and then there was Lucas's girl, she asked to be remembered to you.

MARTIN: Oh, good. How is she?

HANS: Didn't she, Lucas? She asked specially to be remembered to Martin, didn't she?

LUCAS: Oh, she often talks about you, Martin. Even now. She's married, you know.

MARTIN: No, I didn't know.

LUCAS: Oh, yes, got two children, one boy and a girl.

HANS: That's it—two on show on the stall, and now another one coming out from under the counter again—right, Lucas?

LUCAS: Yes, oh, she makes a fine mother.

HANS: And what's better than that? There's only one way of going 'up you' to Old Nick when he does come for you and that's when you show him your kids. It's the one thing—that is, if you've been lucky, and the plagues kept away from you—you can spring it out from under the counter at him. *That* to you! Then you've done something for yourself forever—forever and ever. Amen. [*Pause*] Come along, Brother Martin, don't let your guests go without. Poor old Lucas is sitting there with a glass as empty as a nun's womb, aren't you, you thirsty little goosey?

MARTIN: Oh, please, I'm sorry.

HANS: That's right, and don't forget your old dad. [*Pause*] Yes, well, as I say, I'm sorry your mother couldn't come, but I don't suppose she'd have enjoyed it much, although I dare say she'd like to have watched her son perform the Holy Office. Isn't a mother supposed to dance with her son after the ceremony? Like Christ danced with *his* mother? Well, I can't see her doing that. I suppose you think *I'm* going to dance with you instead.

MARTIN: You're not obliged to, father.

HANS: It's like giving a bride away, isn't it?

MARTIN: Not unlike.

[*They have been avoiding any direct contact until now, but now they look at each other, and both relax a little*]

HANS: [*Encouraged*] God's eyes! Come to think of it, you look like a woman, in all that!

MARTIN: [*With affection*] Not any woman you'd want, father.

HANS: What do *you* know about it, eh? Eh? What do you know about it? [*He laughs but not long*] Well, Brother Martin.

MARTIN: Well? [*Pause*] Have you had some fish? Or a roast, how about that, that's what you'd like, isn't it?

HANS: Brother Martin, old Brother Martin. Well, Brother Martin, you had a right old time up there by that altar for a bit, didn't you? I wouldn't have been in your shoes, I'll tell you. All those people listening to you, every word you're saying, watching every little tiny movement, watching for one little lousy mistake. I couldn't keep my eyes off it. We all thought you were going to flunk it for one minute there, didn't we, Lucas?

LUCAS: Well, we had a couple of anxious moments——

HANS: Anxious moments! I'll say there were. I thought to myself, "he's going to flunk it, he can't get through it, he's going to flunk it." What was that bit, you know, the worst bit where you stopped and Brother——

MARTIN: Weinand.

HANS: Weinand, yes, and he very kindly helped you up. He was actually holding you up at one point, wasn't he?

MARTIN: Yes.

BRO. WEINAND: It happens often enough when a young priest celebrates Mass for the first time.

HANS: Looked as though he didn't know if it was Christmas or Wednesday. We thought the whole thing had come to a standstill for a bit, didn't we? Everyone waiting and nothing happening. What was that bit, Martin, what was it?

MARTIN: I don't remember.

HANS: Yes, you know, the bit you really flunked.

MARTIN: [*Rattling it off*] Receive, oh Holy Father, almighty and eternal God, this spotless host, which I, thine unworthy servant, offer unto thee for my own innumerable sins of commission and omission, and for all here present and all faithful Christians, living and dead, so that it may avail for their salvation and everlasting life. When I entered the monastery, I wanted to speak to God directly, you see. Without any embarrassment, I wanted to speak to Him myself, but when it came to it, I dried up—as I always have.

LUCAS: No, you didn't, Martin, it was only for a few moments, besides——

MARTIN: Thanks to Brother Weinand. Father, why do you hate me being here?

[HANS *is outraged at a direct question*]

HANS: Eh? What do you mean? I don't hate you being here.

MARTIN: Try to give me a straight answer if you can, father. I should like you to tell me.

HANS: What are you talking about, Brother Martin, you don't know what you're talking about. You've not had enough wine, that's your trouble.

MARTIN: And don't say I could have been a lawyer.

HANS: Well, so you could have been. You could have been better than that. You could have been a burgomaster, you could have been a magistrate, you could have been a chancellor, you could have been anything! So what! I don't want to talk about it. What's the matter with you! Anyway, I certainly don't want to talk about it in front of complete strangers.

MARTIN: You make me sick.

HANS: Oh, do I? Well, thank you for that, Brother Martin! Thank you for the truth, anyway.

MARTIN: No, it isn't the truth. It isn't the truth at all. You're drinking too much wine—and I'm . . .

HANS: Drinking too much wine! I could drink this convent piss from here till Gabriel's horn—and from all accounts, that'll blow about next Thursday—so what's the difference? [*Pause.* HANS *drinks*] Is this the wine you use? Is it? Well? I'm asking a straight question myself now. Is this the wine you use? [*To* MARTIN] Here, have some. [MARTIN *takes it and drinks*] You know what they say?

MARTIN: No, what do they say?

HANS: I'll tell you:
Bread thou art and wine thou art
And always shall remain so.

   [*Pause*]

MARTIN: My father didn't mean that. He's a very devout man, I know.

   [*Some of the* BROTHERS *have got up to leave*]

MARTIN: [*To* LUCAS] Brother Weinand will show you over the convent. If you've finished, that is.

LUCAS: Yes, oh yes, I'd like that. Yes, I've had more than enough, thank you. Right, well, let's go, shall we, Brother Weinand? I'll come back for you, shall I? Hans, you'll stay here?

HANS: Just as you like.

LUCAS: [*To* MARTIN] You're looking a bit better now, lad. Good-bye, my boy, but I'll see you before I go, won't I?

MARTIN: Of course.

> [*They all go, leaving* MARTIN *and* HANS *alone together. Pause*]

HANS: Martin, I didn't mean to embarrass you.

MARTIN: No, it was my fault.

HANS: Not in front of everyone.

MARTIN: I shouldn't have asked you a question like that. It was a shock to see you suddenly, after such a long time. Most of my day's spent in silence you see, except for the Offices; and I enjoy the singing, as you know, but there's not much speaking, except to one's confessor. I'd almost forgotten what your voice sounded like.

HANS: Tell me, son—what made you get all snarled up like that in the Mass?

MARTIN: You're disappointed, aren't you?

HANS: I want to know, that's all. I'm a simple man, Martin, I'm no scholar, but I can understand all right. But you're a learned man, you speak Latin and Greek and Hebrew. You've been trained to remember ever since you were a tiny boy. Men like you don't just forget their words!

MARTIN: I don't understand what happened. I lifted up my head at the host, and, as I was speaking the words, I heard them as if it were the first time, and suddenly—[*Pause*] they struck at my life.

HANS: I don't know, I really don't. Perhaps your father and mother are wrong, and God's right, after all. Perhaps. Whatever it is you've got to find, you could only find out by becoming a monk; maybe that's the answer.

MARTIN: But you don't believe that. Do you?

HANS: No; no I don't.

MARTIN: Then say what you mean.

HANS: All right, if that's what you want, I'll say just what I mean. I think a man murders himself in these places.

MARTIN: [*Retreating at once*] I am holy. I kill no one but myself.

HANS: I don't care. I tell you it gives me the creeps. And that's why I couldn't bring your mother, if you want to know.

MARTIN: The Gospels are the only mother I've ever had.

HANS: [*Triumphantly*] And haven't you ever read in the Gospels, don't you know what's written in there? "Thou shalt honour thy father and thy mother."

MARTIN: You're not understanding me, because you don't want to.

HANS: That's fine talk, oh yes, fine, holy talk, but it won't wash, Martin. It won't wash because you can't ever, however you try, you can't ever get away from your body because that's what you live in, and it's all you've got to die in, and you can't get away from the body of your father and your mother! We're bodies, Martin, and so are you, and we're bound together for always. But you're like every man who was ever born into this world, Martin. You'd like to pretend that you made yourself, that it was *you* who made you—and not the body of a woman and another man.

MARTIN: Churches, kings, and fathers—why do they ask so much, and why do they all of them get so much more than they deserve?

HANS: You think so. Well, I think I deserve a little more than you've given me——

MARTIN: I've given you! I don't have to give you! I *am*—that's all I need to give to you. That's your big reward, and that's all you're ever going to get, and it's more than any father's got a right to. You wanted me to learn Latin, to be a Master of Arts, be a lawyer. All you want is me to justify *you!* Well, I can't, and, what's more, I won't. I can't even justify myself. So just stop asking me what have I accomplished, and what have I done for you. I've done all for you I'll ever do, and that's live and wait to die.

HANS: Why do you blame *me* for everything?

MARTIN: I don't blame you. I'm just not grateful, that's all.

HANS: Listen, I'm not a specially good man, I know, but I believe in God and in Jesus Christ, His Son, and the Church will look after me, and I can make some sort of life for myself that has a little joy in it somewhere. But where is your joy? You wrote to me once, when you were at the University, that only Christ could light up the place you live in, but what's the point? What's the point if it turns out the place you're living in is just a hovel? Don't you think it mightn't be better not to see at all?

MARTIN: I'd rather be able to see.

HANS: You'd rather see!

MARTIN: You really are disappointed, aren't you? Go on.

HANS: And why? I see a young man, learned and full of life, my son, abusing his youth with fear and humiliation. You think you're facing up to it in here, but you're not; you're running away, you're running away and you can't help it.

MARTIN: If it's so easy in here, why do you think the rest of the world isn't knocking the gates down to get in?

HANS: Because they haven't given up, that's why.

MARTIN: Well, there it is: you think I've given up.

HANS: Yes, there it is. That damned monk's piss has given me a headache.

MARTIN: I'm sorry.

HANS: Yes, we're all sorry, and a lot of good it does any of us.

MARTIN: I suppose fathers and sons always disappoint each other.

HANS: I worked for you, I went without for you.

MARTIN: Well?

HANS: Well! [*Almost anxiously*] And if I beat you fairly often, and pretty hard sometimes I suppose, it wasn't any more than any other boy, was it?

MARTIN: No.

HANS: What do you think it is makes you different? Other men are all right, aren't they? You were stubborn, you were always stubborn, you've always had to resist, haven't you?

MARTIN: You disappointed me too, and not just a few times, but at some time of every day I ever remember hearing or seeing you, but, as you say, maybe that was also no different from any other boy. But I loved you the best. It was always *you* I wanted. I wanted your love more than anyone's, and if anyone was to hold me, I wanted it to be you. Funnily enough, my mother disappointed me the most, and I loved her less, much less. She made a gap which no one else could have filled, but all she could do was make it bigger, bigger and more unbearable.

HANS: I don't know what any of that means; I really don't. I'd better be going, Martin. I think it's best; and I dare say you've got your various duties to perform.

MARTIN: She beat me once for stealing a nut, your wife. I remember it so well, she beat me until the blood came, I was so surprised to see it on my finger-tips; yes, stealing a nut, that's right. But that's not the point. I had corns on my backside already. Always before, when I was beaten for something, the pain seemed outside of me in some way, as if it belonged to the rest of the world, and not only me. But, on that day, for the first time, the pain belonged to me and no one else, it went no further than *my* body, bent between *my* knees and *my* chin.

HANS: You know what, Martin, I think you've always been scared —ever since you could get up off your knees and walk. You've been scared for the good reason that that's what you most like to be. Yes, I'll tell you. I'll tell you what! Like that day, that day when you were coming home from Erfurt, and the thunderstorm broke, and you were so piss-scared, you lay on the ground and cried out to St. Anne because you saw a bit of lightning and thought you'd seen a vision.

MARTIN: I saw it all right.

HANS: And you went and asked her to save you—on condition that you became a monk.

MARTIN: I saw it.

HANS: Did you? So it's still St. Anne is it? I thought you were blaming your mother and me for your damned monkery!

MARTIN: Perhaps I should.

HANS: And perhaps sometime you should have another little think about that heavenly vision that wangled you away into the cloister.

MARTIN: What's that?

HANS: I mean: I hope it really was a vision. I hope it wasn't a delusion and some trick of the devil's. I really hope so, because I can't bear to think of it otherwise. [*Pause*] Good-bye, son. I'm sorry we had to quarrel. It shouldn't have turned out like this at all today.

[*Pause*]

MARTIN: Father—why did you give your consent?

HANS: What, to your monkery, you mean?

MARTIN: Yes. You could have refused, but why didn't you?

HANS: Well, when your two brothers died with the plague . . .

MARTIN: You gave me up for dead, didn't you?

HANS: Good-bye, son. Here—have a glass of holy wine.

[*He goes out.* MARTIN *stands, with the glass in his hand and looks into it. Then he drinks from it slowly, as if for the first time. He sits down at the table and sets the glass before him*]

MARTIN: But—but what if it isn't true?

CURTAIN

DÉCOR NOTE: *After the intense private interior of Act One, with its outer darkness and rich, personal objects, the physical effect from now on should be more intricate, general, less personal; sweeping, concerned with men in time rather than particular man in the unconscious; caricature not portraiture, like the popular woodcuts of the period, like Dürer. Down by the apron in one corner there is now a heavily carved pulpit.*

ACT TWO

*The market place, Juterbög, 1517. The sound of loud music,
bells as a procession approaches the centre of the market
place, which is covered in the banners of welcoming trade
guilds. At the head of the slow-moving procession, with its
lighted tapers and to the accompaniment of singing, prayers
and the smoke of incense, is carried the Pontiff's bull of grace
on a cushion and cloth of gold. Behind this the arms of the
Pope and the Medici. After this, carrying a large red wooden
cross, comes the focus of the procession,* JOHN TETZEL, *Dominican, inquisitor and most famed and successful indulgence
vendor of his day. He is splendidly equipped to be an ecclesi-
astical huckster, with alive, silver hair, the powerfully calcu-
lating voice, range and technique of a trained orator, the terrible, riveting charm of a dedicated professional able to winkle
coppers out of the pockets of the poor and desperate.*
The red cross is taken from TETZEL *and established promi-
nently behind him, and, from it are suspended the arms of
the Pope.*

TETZEL: Are you wondering who I am, or what I am? Is there anyone here among you, any small child, any cripple, or any sick idiot
who hasn't heard of me, and doesn't know why I am here? No?
No? Well, speak up then if there is? What, no one? Do you all
know me then? Do you all know who I am? If it's true, it's very
good, and just as it should be. Just as it should be, and no more
than that! However, however—just in case—just in case, mind,
there is one blind, maimed midget among you today who can't
hear, I will open his ears and wash them out with sacred soap for

him! And, as for the rest of you. I know I can rely on you all to listen patiently while I instruct him. Is that right? Can I go on? I'm asking you, is that right, can I go on? I say "can I go on"?

[*Pause*]

Thank you. And what is there to tell this blind, maimed midget who's down there somewhere among you? No, don't look round for him, you'll only scare him and then he'll lose his one great chance, and it's not likely to come again, or if it does come, maybe it'll be too late. Well, what's the good news on this bright day? What's the information you want? It's this! Who is this friar with his red cross? Who sent him, and what's he here for? Don't try to work it out for yourself because I'm going to tell you now, this very minute. I am John Tetzel, Dominican, inquisitor, subcommissioner to the Archbishop of Mainz, and what I bring you is indulgences. Indulgences made possible by the red blood of Jesus Christ, and the red cross you see standing up here behind me is the standard of those who carry them. Look at it! Go on, look at it! What else do you see hanging from the red cross? Well, what do they look like? Why, it's the arms of his holiness, because why? Because it's him who sent me here. Yes, my friend, the Pope himself has sent me with indulgences for you! Fine, you say, but what are indulgences? And what are they to me? What are indulgences? They're only the most precious and noble of God's gifts to men, that's all they are! Before God, I tell you I wouldn't swap my privilege at this moment with that of St. Peter in Heaven because I've already saved more souls with my indulgences than he could ever have done with all his sermons. You think that's bragging, do you? Well, listen a little more carefully, my friend, because this concerns *you!* Just look at it this way. For every mortal sin you commit, the Church says that after confession and contrition, you've got to do penance—either in this life or in purgatory—for seven years. Seven years! Right? Are you with me? Good. Now then, how many mortal sins are committed by you—by you—in a single day? Just think for one moment: in one single day of your life. Do you know the answer? Oh, not so much as one a day. Very well then, how many in a month? How many in six months? How many in a year? And how many in a whole lifetime? Yes, you needn't shuffle your feet—it doesn't bear thinking about, does it? You couldn't even add up all those years without a merchant's clerk to do it for you! Try and add up all the years of torment piling up! What about it? And isn't there anything you can do about this terrible situation you're in? Do you really want to know? Yes! There is something, and that something I have here with me now up here, letters, letters of indulgence. Hold up the letters so that everyone can see them. Is there anyone so small he can't see? Look at them, all properly sealed, an indulgence in every envelope, and one of them can be yours today, now, before it's too late! Come on, come up as close as you like, you won't squash me so easily. Take a good look. There isn't any one sin so big that one of these letters can't remit it. I challenge any one here, any member of this audience, to present me with a sin, anything, any kind of a sin, I don't care what it is, that I can't settle for him with one of these precious little envelopes. Why, if any one had ever offered violence to the blessed Virgin Mary, Mother of God, if he'd only pay up—as long as he paid up all he could— he'd find himself forgiven. You think I'm exaggerating? You do, do you? Well, I'm authorized to go even further than that. Not only am I empowered to give you these letters of pardon for the sins you've already committed, I can give you pardon for those sins you haven't even committed [Pause . . . then slowly] but, which, however you *intend* to commit! But, you ask—and it's a fair question—but, you ask, why is our Holy Lord prepared to distribute such a rich grace to me? The answer, my friends, is all too simple. It's so that we can restore the ruined church of St. Peter and St. Paul in Rome! So that it won't have its equal anywhere in the world. This great church contains the bodies not only of the holy apostles Peter and Paul, but of a hundred thousand martyrs and no less than forty-six popes! To say nothing of the relics like St. Veronica's handkerchief, the burning bush of Moses and the very rope with which Judas Iscariot hanged himself! But, alas, this fine old building is threatened with destruction, and all these things with it, if a sufficient restoration fund isn't raised, and raised soon. [With passionate irony] . . . Will anyone dare to say that the cause is not a good one? [Pause] . . . Very well, and won't you, for as little as one quarter of a florin, my friend, buy yourself one of these letters, so that in the house of death, the gate through which sinners enter the world of torment shall be closed against you, and the gate leading to the joy of paradise be flung open for you? And, remember this, these letters aren't just for the living but for the dead, too. There can't be one amongst you who hasn't at least one dear one who has departed—and to who knows what? Why, these letters are for them, too. It isn't even necessary to repent. So don't hold back, come forward, think of your dear ones, think of yourselves! For twelve groats, or whatever it is we think you can afford, you can rescue your father from agony and yourself from certain disaster. And if you only have the coat on your back to call your own, then strip it off, strip it off now so that you too can obtain grace. For remember: As soon as your money rattles in the box and the cash bell rings, the soul flies out of purgatory and sings! So, come on then. Get your money out! What is it then, have your wits flown away with your faith? Listen then, soon, I shall take down the cross, shut the gates of heaven, and put out the brightness of this sun of grace that shines on you here today. [*He flings a large coin into the open strong box, where it rattles furiously*] The Lord our God reigns no longer. He has resigned all power to the Pope. In the name of the Father, and of the Son and of the Holy Ghost. Amen.

[*The sound of coins clattering like rain into a great coffer as the light fades*]

SCENE TWO

The Eremite Cloister, Wittenberg. 1517. Seated beneath a single pear tree is JOHANN VON STAUPITZ, *Vicar General of the Augustinian Order. He is a quiet, gentle-voiced man in late middle age, almost stolidly contemplative. He has profound respect for* MARTIN, *recognizing in him the powerful potential of insight, sensitivity, courage and, also, heroics that is quite outside the range of his own endeavour. However, he also understands that a man of his own limitations can offer a great deal to such a young man at this point in his development, and his treatment of* MARTIN *is a successful astringent mixture of sympathy and ridicule. Birds sing as he reads in the shade, and* MARTIN *approaches, prostrating himself.* STAUPITZ *motions him to his feet.*

MARTIN: [*Looking up*] The birds always seem to fly away the moment I come out here.

STAUPITZ: Birds, unfortunately, have no faith.

MARTIN: Perhaps it's simply that they don't like me.

STAUPITZ: They haven't learned yet that you mean them no harm, that's all.

MARTIN: Are you treating me to one of your allegories?

STAUPITZ: Well, you recognized it, anyway.

MARTIN: I ought to. Ever since I came into the cloister, I've become a craftsman allegory maker myself. Only last week I was lecturing on Galatians Three, verse three, and I allegorized going to the lavatory.

STAUPITZ: [*Quoting the verse*] "Are ye so foolish, that ye have begun in the spirit, you would now end in the flesh."

MARTIN: That's right. But allegories aren't much help in theology —except to decorate a house that's been already built by argument.

STAUPITZ: Well, it's a house you've been able to unlock for a great many of us. I never dreamed when I first came here that the University's reputation would ever become what it has, and in such a short time, and it's mostly due to you.

MARTIN: [*Very deliberately turning the compliment*] If ever a man could get to heaven through monkery, that man would be me.

STAUPITZ: I don't mean that. You know quite well what I mean. I'm talking about your scholarship, and what you manage to do with it, not your monkishness as you call it. I've never had any patience with all your mortifications. The only wonder is that you haven't killed yourself with your prayers, and watchings, yes and even your reading, too. All these trials and temptations you go through, they're meat and drink to you.

MARTIN: [*Patient*] Will you ever stop lecturing me about this?

STAUPITZ: Of course not, why do you think you come here—to see me in the garden when you could be inside working?

MARTIN: Well, if it'll please you, I've so little time, what with my lectures and study, I'm scarcely able to carry out even the basic requirements of the Rule.

STAUPTIZ: I'm delighted to hear it. Why do you think you've always been obsessed with the Rule? No, I don't want to hear all your troubles again. I'll tell you why: you're obsessed with the Rule because it serves very nicely as a protection for you.

MARTIN: What protection?

STAUPITZ: You know perfectly well what I mean, Brother Martin, so don't pretend to look innocent. Protection against the demands of your own instincts, that's what. You see, you think you admire authority, and so you do, but unfortunately, you can't submit to it. So, what you do, by your exaggerated attention to the Rule, you make the authority ridiculous. And the reason you do that is because you're determined to substitute that authority with something else—yourself. Oh, come along, Martin, I've been Vicar General too long not to have made that little discovery. Anyway, you shouldn't be too concerned with a failing like that. It also provides the strongest kind of security.

MARTIN: Security? I don't feel *that*.

STAUPITZ: I dare say, but you've got it all the same, which is more than most of us have.

MARTIN: And how have I managed to come by this strange security?

STAUPITZ: Quite simply: by demanding an impossible standard of perfection.

MARTIN: I don't see what work or merit can come from a heart like mine.

STAUPITZ: Oh, my dear, dear friend, I've sworn a thousand times to our holy God to live piously, and have I been able to keep my vows? No, of course I haven't. Now I've given up making solemn promises because I know I'm not able to keep them. If God won't be merciful to me for the love of Christ when I leave this world, then I shan't stand before Him on account of all my vows and good works, I shall perish, that's all.

MARTIN: You think I lavish too much attention on my own pain, don't you?

STAUPITZ: Well, that's difficult for me to say, Martin. We're very different kinds of men, you and I. Yes, you do lavish attention on yourself, but then a large man is worth the pains he takes. Like St. Paul, some men must say "I die daily."

MARTIN: Tell me, Father, have you never felt humiliated to find that you belong to a world that's dying?

STAUPITZ: No, I don't think I have.

MARTIN: Surely, this must be the last age of time we're living in. There can't be any more left but the black bottom of the bucket.

STAUPITZ: Do you mean the Last Judgment?

MARTIN: No. I don't mean that. The Last Judgment isn't to come. It's here and now.

STAUPITZ: Good. That's a little better, anyway.

MARTIN: I'm like a ripe stool in the world's straining anus, and at any moment we're about to let each other go.

STAUPITZ: There's nothing new in the world being damned, dying or without hope. It's always been like that, and it'll stay like it. What's the matter with you? What are you making funny faces for?

MARTIN: It's nothing, Father, just a—a slight discomfort.

STAUPITZ: Slight discomfort? What are you holding your stomach for? Are you in pain?

MARTIN: It's all right. It's gone now.

STAUPITZ: I don't understand you. What's gone now? I've seen you grabbing at yourself like that before. What is it?

MARTIN: I'm—constipated.

STAUPTIZ: Constipated? There's always something the matter with you, Brother Martin. If it's not the gripes, insomnia, or faith and works, it's boils or indigestion or some kind of bellyache you've got. All these severe fasts——

MARTIN: That's what my father says.

STAUPITZ: Your father sounds pretty sensible to me.

MARTIN: He is, and you know, he's a theologian too, I've discovered lately.

STAUPITZ: I thought he was a miner.

MARTIN: So he is, but he made a discovery years and years ago that took me sweat and labour to dig out of the earth for myself.

STAUPITZ: Well, that's no surprise. There's always some chunk of truth buried down away somewhere which lesser men will always reach with less effort.

MARTIN: Anyway, he always knew that works alone don't save any man. Mind you, he never said anything about faith coming first.

STAUPITZ: [*Quoting*] "Oh, well, that's life, and nothing you can do's going to change it."

MARTIN: The same speech.

STAUPITZ: You can't change human nature.

MARTIN: Nor can you.

STAUPITZ: That's right, Martin, and you've demonstrated it only too well in your commentaries on the Gospels and St. Paul. But don't overlook the fact that your father's taken a vow of poverty too, even though it's very different from your own. And he took it the day he told himself, and told *you*, that he was a complete man, or at least, a contented man.

MARTIN: A hog waffling in its own crap is contented.

STAUPITZ: Exactly.

MARTIN: My father, faced with an unfamiliar notion is like a cow staring at a new barn door. Like those who look on the cross and see nothing. All they hear is the priest's forgiveness.

STAUPITZ: One thing I promise you, Martin. You'll never be a spectator. You'll always take part.

MARTIN: How is it you always manage somehow to comfort me?

STAUPITZ: I think some of us are not much more than pretty modest sponges, but we're probably best at quenching big thirsts. How's your tummy?

MARTIN: Better.

STAUPITZ: One mustn't be truly penitent because one anticipates God's forgiveness, but because one already possesses it. You have to sink to the bottom of your black bucket because that's where God judges you, and then look to the wounds of Jesus Christ. You told me once that when you entered the cloister, your father said it was like giving away a bride, and again your father was right. You are a bride and you should hold yourself ready like a woman at conception. And when grace comes and your soul is penetrated by the spirit, you shouldn't pray or exert yourself, but remain passive.

MARTIN: [*Smiles*] That's a hard role.

STAUPITZ: [*Smiles too*] Too hard for you, I dare say. Did you know the Duke's been complaining to me about you?

MARTIN: Why, what have I done?

STAUPITZ: Preaching against indulgences again.

MARTIN: Oh, that—I was very mild.

STAUPITZ: Yes, well I've heard your mildness in the pulpit. When I think sometimes of the terror it used to be for you, you used to fall up the steps with fright. Sheer fright! You were too frightened to become a Doctor of Theology, and you wouldn't be now if I hadn't forced you. "I'm too weak, I'm not strong enough. I shan't live long enough!" Do you remember what I said to you?

MARTIN: "Never mind, the Lord still has work in heaven, and there are always vacancies."

STAUPITZ: Yes, and the Duke paid all the expenses of your promotion for you. He was very cross when he spoke to me, I may say. He said you even made some reference to the collection of holy relics in the Castle Church, and most of those were paid for by the sale of indulgences, as you know. Did you say anything about them?

MARTIN: Well, yes, but not about those in the Castle Church. I did make some point in passing about someone who claimed to have a feather from the wing of the angel Gabriel.

STAUPITZ: Oh yes, I heard about him.

MARTIN: And the Archbishop of Mainz, who is supposed to have a flame from Moses' burning bush.

STAUPITZ: Oh dear, you shouldn't have mentioned that.

MARTIN: And I just finished off by saying how does it happen that Christ had twelve apostles and eighteen of them are buried in Germany?

STAUPITZ: Well, the Duke says he's coming to your next sermon to hear for himself, so try to keep off the subject, if you possibly can. It's All Saints' Day soon, remember, and all those relics will be out on show for everyone to gawp at. The Duke's a good chap, and he's very proud of his collection, and it doesn't help to be rude about it.

MARTIN: I've tried to keep off the subject because I haven't been by any means sure about it. Then I did make a few mild protests in a couple of sermons, as I say.

STAUPITZ: Yes, yes, but what did you actually say?

MARTIN: That you can't strike bargains with God. There's a Jewish, Turkish, Pelagian heresy if you like.

STAUPITZ: Yes, more mildness. Go on.

MARTIN: I said, oh it was an evil sanction because only *you* could live *your* life, and only you can die your death. It can't be taken over for you. Am I right?

STAUPITZ: [*Doubtfully*] Yes, what's difficult to understand is why your sermons are so popular.

MARTIN: Well, there are plenty who sit out there stiff with hatred, I can tell you. I can see their faces, and there's no mistaking them. But I wanted to tell you something—

STAUPITZ: Yes?

MARTIN: About all this. The other day a man was brought to me, a shoemaker. His wife had just died, and I said to him, "What've you done for her?" so he said, "I've buried her and commended her soul to God." "But haven't you had a Mass said for the repose of her soul?" "No," he said, "what's the point? She entered heaven the moment she died." So I asked him, "How do you know that?" And he said, "Well, I've got proof, that's why." And out of his pocket he took a letter of indulgence.

STAUPITZ: Ah.

MARTIN: He threw it at me, and said, "And if you still maintain that a Mass is necessary, then my wife's been swindled by our most holy father the Pope. Or, if not by him, then by the priest who sold it to me."

STAUPITZ: Tetzel.

MARTIN: Who else?

STAUPITZ: That old tout!

MARTIN: There's another story going around about him which is obviously true because I've checked it at several sources. It seems that a certain Saxon nobleman had heard Tetzel in Juterbög. After Tetzel had finished his usual performance, he asked him if he'd repeat what he'd said at one stage, that he—Tetzel I mean—had the power of pardoning sins that men intended to commit. Tetzel was very high and mighty, you know what he's like, and said, "What's the matter, weren't you listening? Of course I can give pardon not only for sins already committed but for sins that men *intend* to commit." "Well, then, that's fine," says this nobleman, "because I'd like to take revenge on one of my enemies. You know, nothing much, I don't want to kill him or anything like that. Just a little slight revenge. Now, if I give you ten guilden, will you give me a letter of indulgence that will justify me—justify me freely and completely?" Well, it seems Tetzel made a few stock objections, but eventually agreed on thirty guilden, and they made a deal. The man went away with his letter of indulgence, and Tetzel set out for the next job, which was Leipzig. Well, half-way between Leipzig and Treblen, in the middle of a wood, he was set on by a band of thugs, and beaten up. While he's lying there on the grass in a pool of his own blood, he looks up and sees that one of them is the Saxon nobleman and that they're making off with his great trunk full of money. So, the moment he's recovered enough, he rushes back to Juterbög, and takes the nobleman to court. And what does the nobleman do? Takes out the letter of indulgence and shows it to Duke George himself—case dismissed!

STAUPITZ: [*Laughing*] Well, I leave you to handle it. But try and be careful. Remember, *I* agree with all you say, but the moment someone disagrees or objects to what you're saying, *that* will be the moment when you'll suddenly recognize the strength of your belief!

MARTIN: Father, I'm never sure of the words till I hear them out loud.

STAUPITZ: Well, that's probably the meaning of the Word. The Word is me, and I am the Word. Anyway, try and be a little prudent. Look at Erasmus: he never really gets into any serious trouble, but he still manages to make his point.

MARTIN: People like Erasmus get upset because I talk of pigs and Christ in the same breath. I must go.

[*Clutches himself unobtrusively*]

STAUPITZ: Well, you might be right. Erasmus is a fine scholar, but there are too many scholars who think they're better simply because they insinuate in Latin what you'll say in plain German. What's the matter, are you having that trouble again? Good heavens! Martin—just before you go: a man with a strong sword will draw it at some time, even if it's only to turn it on himself. But whatever happens, he can't just let it dangle from his belt. And, another thing, don't forget—you began this affair in the name of Our Lord Jesus Christ. You must do as God commands you, of course, but remember, St. Jerome once wrote about a philosopher who destroyed his own eyes so that it would give him more freedom to study. Take care of your eyes, my son, and do something about those damned bowels!

MARTIN: I will. Who knows? If I break wind in Wittenberg, they might smell it in Rome.

[*Exit. Church bells*]

SCENE THREE

*The steps of the Castle Church, Wittenberg, October 31st,
1517. From inside the Church comes the sound of Matins
being sung. Sitting on the steps is a* CHILD, *dirty, half-naked
and playing intently by himself.* MARTIN *enters with a long
roll of paper. It is his ninety-five theses for disputation against
indulgences. As he goes up the steps, he stops and watches
the* CHILD, *absorbed in his private fantasy. He is absorbed by
the* CHILD, *who doesn't notice him at first, but, presently, as
soon as the boy becomes aware of an intruder, he immediately
stops playing and looks away distractedly in an attempt to ex-
clude outside attention.* MARTIN *hesitates briefly, then puts
out his hand to the* CHILD, *who looks at it gravely and deliberately, then slowly, not rudely, but naturally, gets up and skips
away sadly out of sight.* MARTIN *watches him, then walks
swiftly back down the steps to the pulpit and ascends it.*

MARTIN: My text is from the Epistle of Paul the Apostle to the
Romans, chapter one, verse seventeen: "For therein is the righteousness of God revealed from faith to faith." [*Pause*] We are
living in a dangerous time. You may not think so, but it could be
that this is the most dangerous time since the light first broke
upon the earth. It may not be true, but it's very probably true—
but, what's most important is that it's an assumption we are
obliged to make. We Christians seem to be wise outwardly and
mad inwardly, and in this Jerusalem we have built there are
blasphemies flourishing that make the Jews no worse than giggling
children. A man is not a good Christian because he understands
Greek and Hebrew. Jerome knew five languages, but he's inferior
to Augustine, who knew only one. Of course, Erasmus wouldn't
agree with me, but perhaps one day the Lord will open his eyes for
him. But listen! A man without Christ becomes his own shell. We
are content with shells. Some shells are whole men and some are
small trinkets. And, what are the trinkets? Today is the eve of All

Saints, and the holy relics will be on show to you all; to the hungry ones whose lives are made satisfied by trinkets, by an imposing procession and the dressings up of all kinds of dismal things. You'll mumble for magic with lighted candles to St. Anthony for your erysipelas; to St. Valentine for your epilepsy; to St. Sebastian for the pestilence; to St. Laurentis to protect you from fire, to St. Appolonia if you've got the toothache, and to St. Louis to stop your beer from going sour. And tomorrow you'll queue for hours outside the Castle Church so that you can get a cheap-rate glimpse of St. Jerome's tooth, or four pieces each of St. Chrysostom and St. Augustine, and six of St. Bernard. The deacons will have to link hands to hold you back while you struggle to gawp at four hairs from Our Lady's head, at the pieces of her girdle and her veil stained with her Son's blood. You'll sleep outside with the garbage in the streets all night so that you can stuff your eyes like roasting birds on a scrap of swaddling clothes, eleven pieces from the original crib, one wisp of straw from the manger and a gold piece specially minted by three wise men for the occasion. Your emptiness will be frothing over at the sight of a strand of Jesus' beard, at one of the nails driven into His hands, and at the remains of the loaf at the Last Supper. Shells for shells, empty things for empty men. There are some who complain of these things, but they write in Latin for scholars. Who'll speak out in rough German? Someone's got to bell the cat! For you must be made to know that there's no security, there's no security at all, either in indulgences, holy busywork or anywhere in this world. It came to me while I was in my tower, what they call the monk's sweathouse, the jakes, the john or whatever you're pleased to call it. I was struggling with the text I've given you: "For therein is the righteousness of God revealed, from faith to faith; as it is written, the just shall live by faith." And seated there, my head down, on that privy just as when I was a little boy, I couldn't reach down to my breath for the sickness in my bowels, as I seemed to sense beneath me a large rat, a heavy, wet, plague rat, slashing at my privates with its death's teeth. [*He kneads his knuckles into his abdomen, as if he were suppressing pain. His face runs with sweat*] I thought of the righteousness of God, and wished his gospel had never been put to paper for men to read; who demanded my love and made it impossible to return it. And I sat in my heap of pain until the words emerged and opened out. "The just shall live by faith." My pain vanished, my bowels flushed and I could get up. I could see the life I'd lost. No man is just because he does just works. The works are just if the man is just. If a man doesn't believe in Christ, not only are his sins mortal, but his good works. This I know; reason is the devil's whore, born of one stinking goat called Aristotle, which believes that good works make a good man. But the truth is that the just shall live by faith alone. I need no more than my sweet redeemer and mediator, Jesus Christ, and I shall praise Him as long as I have voice to sing; and if anyone doesn't care to sing with me, then he can howl on his own. If we are going to be deserted, let's follow the deserted Christ.

[*He murmurs a prayer, descends from the pulpit, then walks up the steps to the Church door, and nails his theses to it. The singing from within grows louder as he walks away*]

SCENE FOUR

The Fugger Palace, Augsburg. October 1518. As a backcloth a satirical contemporary woodcut, showing, for example, the Pope portrayed as an ass playing the bagpipes, or a cardinal dressed up as a court fool. Or perhaps Holbein's cartoon of Luther with the Pope suspended from his nose. However, there is a large area for the director and designer to choose from.
Seated at a table is THOMAS DE VIO, *known as* CAJETAN, *Cardinal of San Sisto, General of the Dominican Order, as well as its most distinguished theologian, papal legate, Rome's highest representative in Germany. He is about fifty, but youthful, with a shrewd, broad, outlook, quite the opposite of the vulgar bigotry of* TETZEL, *who enters.*

TETZEL: He's here.

CAJETAN: So I see.

TETZEL: What do you mean?

CAJETAN: You look so cross. Is Staupitz with him?

TETZEL: Yes. At least *he's* polite.

CAJETAN: I know Staupitz. He's a straightforward, four-square kind of a man, and probably very unhappy at this moment. From all accounts, he has a deep regard for this monk—which is all to the good from our point of view.

TETZEL: He's worried all right, you can see that. These Augustinians, they don't have much fibre.

CAJETAN: What about Dr. Luther? What's he got to say for himself?

TETZEL: Too much. I said to him if our Lord the Pope were to offer you a good Bishopric and a plenary indulgence for repairing your church, you'd soon start singing a different song.

CAJETAN: Dear, oh, dear, and what did he say to that?

TETZEL: He asked me——

CAJETAN: Well?

TETZEL: He asked me how was my mother's syphilis.

CAJETAN: It's a fair question in the circumstances. You Germans, you're a crude lot.

TETZEL: He's a pig.

CAJETAN: I've no doubt. After all, it's what your country's most famous for.

TETZEL: That's what I said to him—you're not on your own ground here, you know. These Italians they're different. They're not just learned, they're subtle, experienced antagonists. You'll get slung in the fire after five minutes.

CAJETAN: And?

TETZEL: He said, "I've only been to Italy once, and they didn't look very subtle to me. They were lifting their legs on street corners like dogs."

CAJETAN: I hope he didn't see any cardinals at it. Knowing some of them as I do, it's not impossible. Well, let's have a look at this foul-mouthed monk of yours.

TETZEL: What about Staupitz?

CAJETAN: Let him wait in the corridor. It'll help him to worry.

TETZEL: Very well, your eminence. I hope he behaves properly. I've spoken to him.

[TETZEL *goes out and returns presently with* MARTIN, *who advances, prostrates himself, his face to the ground before* CAJETAN. CAJETAN *makes a motion and* MARTIN *rises to a kneeling position, where* CAJETAN *studies him*]

CAJETAN: [*Courteous*] Please stand up, Dr. Luther. So you're the one they call the excessive doctor. You don't look excessive to me. Do you feel very excessive?

MARTIN: [*Conscious of being patronized*] It's one of those words which can be used like a harness on a man.

CAJETAN: How do you mean?

MARTIN: I mean it has very little meaning beyond traducing him.

CAJETAN: Quite. There's never been any doubt in my mind that you've been misinterpreted all round, and, as you say, traduced. Well, what a surprise you are! Here was I expecting to see some doddering old theologian with dust in his ears who could be bullied into a heart attack by Tetzel here in half an hour. And here you are, as gay and sprightly as a young bull. How old are you, my son?

MARTIN: Thirty-four, most worthy father.

CAJETAN: Tetzel, he's a boy—you didn't tell me! And how long have you been wearing your doctor's ring?

MARTIN: Five years——

CAJETAN: So you were only twenty-nine! Well, obviously, everything I've heard about you is true—you must be a very remarkable young man. I wouldn't have believed there was one doctor in the whole of Germany under fifty. Would you, Brother John?

TETZEL: Not as far as I know.

CAJETAN: I'm certain there isn't. What is surprising, frankly, is that they allowed such an honour to be conferred on anyone so young and inexperienced as a man must inevitably be at twenty-nine. [*He smiles to let his point get home*] Your father must be a proud man.

MARTIN: [*Irritated*] Not at all, I should say he was disappointed and constantly apprehensive.

CAJETAN: Really? Well, that's surely one of the legacies of parenthood to offset the incidental pleasures. Now then, to business. I was saying to Tetzel, I don't think this matter need take up very much of our time. But, before we do start, there's just one thing I would like to say, and that is I was sorry you should have decided to ask the Emperor for safe conduct. That was hardly necessary, my son, and it's a little—well, distressing to feel you have such an opinion of us, such a lack of trust in your mother church, and in those who have, I can assure you, your dearest interests at heart.

MARTIN: [*Out-manœuvred*] I——

CAJETAN: [*Kindly*] But never mind all that now, that's behind us, and, in the long run, it's unimportant, after all, isn't it? Your Vicar General has come with you, hasn't he?

MARTIN: He's outside.

CAJETAN: I've known Staupitz for years. You have a wonderful friend there.

MARTIN: I know. I—have great love for him.

CAJETAN: And he certainly has for you, I know. Oh, my dear, dear son, this is such a ridiculous, unnecessary business for us all to be mixed up in. It's such a tedious, upsetting affair, and what purpose is there in it? Your entire order in Germany has been brought into disgrace. Staupitz is an old man, and he can't honestly be expected to cope. Not now. I have my job to do, and, make no mistake, it isn't all honey for an Italian legate in your country. You know how it is, people are inclined to resent you. Nationalist feeling and all that—which I respect—but it does complicate one's task to the point where this kind of issue thrown in for good measure simply makes the whole operation impossible. You know what I mean? I mean, there's your Duke Frederick, an absolutely fair, honest man, if ever there was one, and one his holiness values and esteems particularly. Well, he instructed me to present him with the Golden

Rose of Virtue, so you can see . . . As well as even more indulgences for his Castle Church. But what happens now? Because of all this unpleasantness and the uproar it's caused throughout Germany, the Duke's put in an extremely difficult position about accepting it. Naturally, he wants to do the right thing by everyone. But he's not going to betray you or anything like that, however much he's set his heart on that Golden Rose, even after all these years. And, of course he's perfectly right. I know he has the greatest regard for you and for some of your ideas—even though, as he's told me—he doesn't agree with a lot of them. No, I can only respect him for all that. So, you see, my dear son, what a mess we are in. Now, what are we going to do? Um? The Duke is unhappy. I am unhappy, his holiness is unhappy, and, you, my son, you are unhappy.

MARTIN: [*Formal, as if it were a prepared speech*] Most worthy father, in obedience to the summons of his papal holiness, and in obedience to the orders of my gracious lord, the Elector of Saxony, I have come before you as a submissive and dutiful son of the holy Christian church, and acknowledge that I have published the proposition and theses ascribed to me. I am ready now to listen most obediently to my indictment, and if I have been wrong, to submit to your instruction in the truth.

CAJETAN: [*Impatient*] My son, you have upset all Germany with your dispute about indulgences. I know you're a very learned doctor of the Holy Scriptures, and that you've already aroused some supporters. However, if you wish to remain a member of the Church, and to find a gracious father in the Pope, you'd better listen. I have here, in front of me, three propositions which, by the command of our holy father, Pope Leo the Tenth, I shall put to you now. First, you must admit your faults, and retract all your errors and sermons. Secondly, you must promise to abstain from propagating your opinions at any time in the future. And, thirdly, you must behave generally with greater moderation, and avoid anything which might cause offence or grieve and disturb the Church.

MARTIN: May I be allowed to see the Pope's instruction?

CAJETAN: No, my dear son, you may not. All you are required to do is confess your errors, keep a strict watch on your words, and not go back like a dog to his vomit. Then, once you have done that, I have been authorized by our most holy father to put everything to rights again.

MARTIN: I understand all that. But I'm asking you to tell me where I have erred.

CAJETAN: If you insist. [*Rattling off, very fast*] Just to begin with, here are two propositions you have advanced, and which you will have to retract before anything else. First, the treasure of indulgences does not consist of the sufferings and torments of our Lord Jesus Christ. Second, the man who received the holy sacrament must have faith in the grace that is presented to him. Enough?

MARTIN: I rest my case entirely on Holy Scriptures.

CAJETAN: The Pope alone has power and authority over all those things.

MARTIN: Except Scripture.

CAJETAN: Including Scripture. What do you mean?

TETZEL: Only the Pope has the right of deciding in matters of Christian faith. He alone and no one else has the power to interpret the meaning of Scripture, and to approve or condemn the views of other men, whoever they are—scholars, councils or the ancient fathers. The Pope's judgement cannot err, whether it concerns the Christian faith or anything that has to do with the salvation of the human race.

MARTIN: That sounds like your theses.

TETZEL: Burned in the market place by your students in Wittenberg—thank you very much——

MARTIN: I assure you, I had nothing to do with that.

CAJETAN: Of course. Brother John wasn't suggesting you had.

MARTIN: I can't stop the mouth of the whole world.

TETZEL: Why, your heresy isn't even original. It's no different from Wyclif or Hus.

CAJETAN: True enough, but we mustn't try to deprive the learned doctor of his originality. An original heresy may have been thought of by someone else before you. In fact, I shouldn't think such a thing as an original heresy exists. But it is original so long as it originated in *you*, the virgin heretic.

TETZEL: The time'll come when you'll have to defend yourself before the world, and then every man can judge for himself who's the heretic and schismatic. It'll be clear to everyone, even those drowsy snoring Christians who've never smelled a Bible. They'll find out for themselves that those who scribble books and waste so much paper just for their own pleasure, and are contemptuous and shameless, end up by condemning themselves. People like you always go too far, thank heaven. You play into our hands. I give you a month, Brother Martin, to roast yourself.

MARTIN: You've had your thirty pieces of silver. For the sake of Christ, why don't you betray someone?

CAJETAN: [*To* TETZEL] Perhaps you should join Staupitz.

TETZEL: Very well, your eminence.

[*He bows and goes out*]

CAJETAN: In point of fact, he gets eighty guilden a month plus expenses.

MARTIN: What about his vow of poverty?

CAJETAN: Like most brilliant men, my son, you have an innocent spirit. I've also just discovered that he has managed to father two children. So there goes another vow. Bang! But it'll do him no good, I promise you. You've made a hole in that drum for him. I may say there's a lot of bad feelings among the Dominicans about you. I should know—because I'm their General. It's only natural, they're accustomed to having everything their own way. The Franciscans are a grubby, sentimental lot, on the whole, and mercifully ignorant as well. But your people seem to be running alive with scholars and would-be politicians.

MARTIN: I'd no idea that my theses would ever get such publicity.

CAJETAN: Really now!

MARTIN: But it seems they've been printed over and over again, and circulated well, to an extent I'd never dreamed of.

CAJETAN: Oh yes, they've been circulated and talked about wherever men kneel to Christ.

MARTIN: Most holy father, I honour the Holy Roman Church, and I shall go on doing so. I have sought after the truth, and everything I have said I still believe to be right and true and Christian. But I am a man, and I may be deceived, so I am willing to receive instruction where I have been mistaken——

CAJETAN: [*Angrily*] Save your arrogance, my son, there'll be a better place to use it. I can have you sent to Rome and let any of your German princes try to stop me! He'll find himself standing outside the gates of heaven like a leper.

MARTIN: [*Stung*] I repeat, I am here to reply to all the charges you may bring against me——

CAJETAN: No, you're not——

MARTIN: I am ready to submit my theses to the universities of Basle, Freibourg, Louvain or Paris——

CAJETAN: I'm afraid you've not grasped the position. I'm not here to enter into a disputation with you, now or at any other time. The Roman Church is the apex of the world, secular and temporal, and it may constrain with its secular arm any who have once received the faith and gone astray. Surely I don't have to remind you that it is not bound to use reason to fight and destroy rebels. [*He sighs*] My son, it's getting late. You must retract. Believe me, I simply want to see this business ended as quickly as possible.

MARTIN: Some interests are furthered by finding truth, others by destroying it. I don't care—what pleases or displeases the Pope. He is a man.

CAJETAN: [*Wearily*] Is that all?

MARTIN: He seems a good man, as Popes go. But it's not much for a world that sings out for reformation. I'd say that's a hymn for everyone.

CAJETAN: My dear friend, think, think carefully, and see if you can't see some way out of all this. I am more than prepared to reconcile you with the Church, and the sovereign bishop. Retract, my son, the holy father prays for it——

MARTIN: But won't you discuss——

CAJETAN: Discuss! I've not *discussed* with you, and I don't intend to. If you want a disputation, I dare say Eck will take care of you——

MARTIN: John Eck? The Chancellor of Ingolstadt?

CAJETAN: I suppose you don't think much of him?

MARTIN: He knows theology.

CAJETAN: He has a universal reputation in debate.

MARTIN: It's understandable. He has a pedestrian style and a judicial restraint and that'll always pass off as wisdom to most men.

CAJETAN: You mean he's not original, like you——

MARTIN: I'm not an original man, why I'm not even a teacher, and I'm scarcely even a priest. I know Jesus Christ doesn't need my labour or my services.

CAJETAN: All right, Martin, I *will* argue with you if you want me to, or, at least, I'll put something to you, because there is something more than your safety or your life involved, something bigger than you and I talking together in this room at this time. Oh, it's fine for someone like you to criticize and start tearing down Christendom, but tell me this, just tell me this: what will you build in its place?

MARTIN: A withered arm is best amputated, an infected place is best scoured out, and so you pray for healthy tissue and something sturdy and clean that was crumbling and full of filth.

CAJETAN: Can't you see? My son, you'll destroy the perfect unity of the world.

MARTIN: Someone always prefers what's withered and infected. But it should be cauterized as honestly as one knows how.

CAJETAN: And how honest is that? There's something I'd like to know: suppose you *did* destroy the Pope. What do you think would become of you?

MARTIN: I don't know.

CAJETAN: Exactly, you wouldn't know what to do because you need him, Martin, you need to hunt him more than he needs his silly wild boar. Well? There have always been Popes, and there always will be, even if they're called something else. They'll have them for people like *you*. You're not a good old revolutionary, my son, you're just a common rebel, a very different animal. You don't fight the Pope because he's too big, but because for your needs he's not big enough.

MARTIN: My General's been gossiping——

CAJETAN: [*Contemptuous*] I don't need Staupitz to explain you to me. Why, some deluded creature might even come to you as a leader of their revolution, but you don't want to break rules, you want to make them. You'd be a master breaker and maker and no one would be able to stand up to you, you'd hope, or ever sufficiently repair the damage you did. I've read some of your sermons on faith. Do you know all they say to me?

MARTIN: No.

CAJETAN: They say: I am a man struggling for certainty, struggling insanely like a man in a fit, an animal trapped to the bone with doubt.

[MARTIN *seems about to have a physical struggle with himself*]

CAJETAN: Don't you see what could happen out of all this? Men could be cast out and left to themselves for ever, helpless and frightened!

MARTIN: Your eminence, forgive me. I'm tired after my journey—I think I might faint soon——

CAJETAN: That's what would become of them without their Mother Church—with all its imperfections, Peter's rock, without it they'd be helpless and unprotected. Allow them their sins, their petty indulgences, my son, they're unimportant to the comfort we receive——

MARTIN: [*Somewhat hysterical*] Comfort! It—doesn't concern me!

CAJETAN: We live in thick darkness, and it grows thicker. How will men find God if they are left to themselves each man abandoned and only known to himself?

MARTIN: They'll have to try.

CAJETAN: I beg of you, my son, I beg of you. Retract.

[*Pause*]

MARTIN: Most holy father, I cannot.

[*Pause*]

CAJETAN: You look ill. You had better go and rest. [*Pause*] Naturally, you will be released from your order.

MARTIN: I——

CAJETAN: Yes?

MARTIN: As you say, your eminence. Will you refer this matter to the Pope for his decision?

CAJETAN: Assuredly. Send in Tetzel. [MARTIN *prostrates himself, and then kneels.* CAJETAN *is distressed but in control*] You know, a time will come when a man will no longer be able to say, "I speak Latin and am a Christian" and go his way in peace. There will come frontiers, frontiers of all kinds—between men—and there'll be no end to them.

[MARTIN *rises and goes out.* TETZEL *returns*]

TETZEL: Yes?

CAJETAN: No, of course he didn't—that man hates himself. And if he goes to the stake, Tetzel, you can have the pleasure of inscribing it: he could only love others.

SCENE FIVE

A hunting lodge at Magliana in Northern Italy, 1519. Suspended the arms, the brass balls, of the Medici. KARL VON MILTITZ, *a young Chamberlain of the Pope's household is waiting. There are cries off, and sounds of excitement,* POPE

LEO THE TENTH *enters with a* HUNTSMAN, *dogs and* DOMINICANS. *He is richly dressed in hunting clothes and long boots. He is indolent, cultured, intelligent, extremely restless, and well able to assimilate the essence of anything before anyone else. While he is listening, he is able to play with a live bird with apparent distraction. Or shoot at a board with a crossbow. Or generally fidget.* MILTITZ *kneels to kiss his toe.*

LEO: I should forget it. I've got my boots on. Well? Get on with it. We're missing the good weather.

[*He sits and becomes immediately absorbed in his own play, as it seems.* MILTITZ *has a letter, which he reads*]

MILTITZ: "To the most blessed father Leo the tenth, sovereign bishop, Martin Luther, Augustine Friar, wishes eternal salvation. I am told that there are vicious reports circulating about me, and that my name is in bad odour with your holiness. I am called a heretic, apostate, traitor and many other insulting names. I cannot understand all this hostility, and I am alarmed by it. But the only basis of my tranquility remains, as always, a pure and peaceful conscience. Deign to listen to me, most holy father, to me who is like a child. [LEO *snorts abstractedly*] There have always been, as long as I can remember, complaints and grumbling in the taverns about the avarice of the priests and attacks on the power of the keys. And this has been happening throughout Germany. When I listened to these things my zeal was aroused for the glory of Christ, so I warned not one, but several princes of the Church. But, either they laughed in my face or ignored me. The terror of your name was too much for everyone. It was then I published my disputation, nailing it on the door of the Castle Church here in Wittenberg. And now, most holy father, the whole world has gone up in flames. Tell me what I should do? I cannot retract; but this thing has drawn down hatred on me from all sides, and I don't know where to turn to but to you. I am far too insignificant to appear before the world in a matter as great as this. [LEO *snaps his fingers to glance at this passage in the letter. He does so and returns it to* MILTITZ *who continues reading*] But in order to quieten my enemies and satisfy my friends I am now addressing myself to you most holy father and speak my mind in the greater safety of the shadow of your wings. All this respect I show to the power of the keys. If I had not behaved properly it would have been impossible for the most serene Lord Frederick, Duke and Elector of Saxony, who shines in your apostolic favour, to have endured me in his University of Wittenberg. Not if I am as dangerous as is made out by my enemies. For this reason, most holy father, I fall at the feet of your holiness, and submit myself to you, with all I have and all that I am. Declare me right or wrong. Take my life, or give it back to me, as you please. I shall acknowledge your voice as the voice of Jesus Christ. If I deserve death, I shall not refuse to die. The earth is God's and all within it. May He be praised through all eternity, and may He uphold you for ever. Amen. Written the day of the Holy Trinity in the year 1518, Martin Luther, Augustine Friar."

[*They wait for* LEO *to finish his playing and give them his full attention. Presently, he gets up and takes the letter from* MILTITZ. *He thinks*]

LEO: Double faced German bastard! Why can't he say what he means? What else?

MILTITZ: He's said he's willing to be judged by any of the universities of Germany, with the exception of Leipzig, Erfurt and Frankfurt, which he says are not impartial. He says it's impossible for him to appear in Rome in person.

LEO: I'm sure.

MILTITZ: Because his health wouldn't stand up to the rigours of the journey.

LEO: Cunning! Cunning German bastard! What does Staupitz say for him?

MILTITZ: [*Reading hastily from another letter*] "The reverend father, Martin Luther, is the noblest and most distinguished member of our university. For many years, we have watched his talents——"

LEO: Yes, well we know all about that. Write to Cajetan. Take this down. We charge you to summon before you Martin Luther. Invoke for this purpose, the aid of our very dear son in Christ, Maximilian, and all the other princes in Germany, together with all communities, universities, potentates ecclesiastic and secular. And, once you get possession of him, keep him in safe custody, so that he can be brought before us. If, however, he should return to his duty of his own accord and begs forgiveness, we give you the power to receive him into the perfect unity of our Holy Mother the Church. But, should he persist in his obstinacy and you cannot secure him, we authorize you to outlaw him in every part of Germany. To banish and excommunicate him. As well as all prelates, religious orders, universities, counts, and dukes who do not assist in apprehending him. As for the laymen, if they do not immediately obey your orders, declare them infamous, deprived of Christian burial and stripped of anything they may hold either from the apostolic see or from any lord whatsoever. There's a wild pig in our vineyard, and it must be hunted down and shot. Given under the seal of the Fisherman's Ring, etcetera. That's all.

[*He turns quickly and goes out*]

SCENE SIX

The Elster Gate, Wittenberg. 1520. Evening. A single bell. As a backcloth the bull issued against LUTHER. *Above it a fishhead and bones. The bull is slashed with the reflection of the flames rising round the Elster Gate where the books of canon law, the papal decretals, are burning furiously.* MONKS *come to and fro with more books and documents, and hurl them on the fire.* MARTIN *enters and ascends the pulpit.*

MARTIN: I have been served with a piece of paper. Let me tell you about it. It has come to me from a latrine called Rome, that capital of the devil's own sweet empire. It is called the papal bull and it claims to excommunicate me, Dr. Martin Luther. These lies they rise up from paper like fumes from the bog of Europe; because papal decretals are the devil's excretals. I'll hold it up for you to see properly. You see the signature? Signed beneath the seal of the Fisherman's Ring by one certain midden cock called Leo, an over-indulged jakes' attendant to Satan himself, a glittering worm in excrement, known to you as his holiness the Pope. You may know him as the head of the Church. Which he may still be: like a fish is the head of a cat's dinner; eyes without sight clutched to a stick of sucked bones. God has told me: there can be no dealings between this cat's dinner and me. And, as for this bull, it's going to roast, it's going to roast and so are the balls of the Medici! [*He descends and casts the bull into the flames. He begins to shake, as if he were unable to breathe; as if he were about to have another fit. Shaking, he kneels*] Oh, God! Oh, God! Oh, thou my God, my God, help me against the reason and wisdom of the world. You must—there's only you—to do it. Breathe into me. Breathe into me, like a lion into the mouth of a stillborn cub. This cause is not mine but yours. For myself, I've no business to be dealing with the great lords of this world. I want to be still, in peace, and alone. Breathe into me, Jesus. I rely on no man, only on you. My God, my God do you hear me? Are you dead? Are you dead? No, you can't die, you can only hide yourself, can't you? Lord, I'm afraid. I am a child, the lost body of a child. I am stillborn. Breathe into me, in the name of Thy Son, Jesus Christ, who shall be my protector and defender, yes, my mighty fortress, breathe into me. Give me life, oh Lord. Give me life.

[MARTIN *prays as the deep red light of the flames flood the darkness around him*]

ACT THREE

SCENE ONE

The Diet of Worms, April 18th, 1521. A gold front-cloth, and on it, in the brightest sunshine of colour, a bold, joyful representation of this unique gathering of princes, electors, dukes, ambassadors, bishops, counts, barons, etc. Perhaps LUTHER'S *two-wheeled wagon which brought him to Worms. The mediaeval world dressed up for the Renaissance.*

Devoid of depth, such scenes are stamped on a brilliant ground of gold. Movement is frozen, recession in space ignored and perspective served by the arrangement of figures, or scenes, one above the other. In this way, landscape is dramatically substituted by objects in layers. The alternative is to do the opposite, in the manner of, say, Altdorfer. Well in front of the cloth is a small rostrum with brass rails sufficient to support one man. If possible, it would be preferable to have this part of the apron projected a little into the audience. Anyway, the aim is to achieve the maximum in physical enlargement of the action, in the sense of physical participation in the theatre, as if everyone watching had their chins resting on the sides of a boxing-ring. Also on the apron, well to the front are several chairs. On one side is a table with about twenty books on it. The table and books may also be represented on the gold cloth. The rostrum has a small crescent of chairs around it. From all corners of the auditorium comes a fanfare of massed trumpets, and, approaching preferably from the auditorium up steps to the apron, come a few members of the Diet audience (who may also be represented on the gold cloth). Preceded by a HERALD, *and seating themselves on the chairs, they should include* THE EMPEROR CHARLES THE FIFTH (*in front of the rostrum*), ALEANDER, THE PAPAL NUNCIO; ULRICH VON HUTTEN, KNIGHT; THE ARCHBISHOP OF

TRIER *and* HIS SECRETARY, JOHAN VON ECK, *who sit at the table with the books. The trumpets cease, and they wait.* MARTIN *appears from the stage, and ascends the rostrum centre.*

ECK: [*Rising*] Martin Luther, you have been brought here by His Imperial Majesty so that you may answer two questions. Do you publicly acknowledge being the author of the books you see here? When I asked you this question yesterday, you agreed immediately that the books were indeed your own. Is that right? [MARTIN *nods in agreement*] When I asked you the second question, you asked if you might be allowed time in which to consider it. Although such time should have been quite unnecessary for an experienced debater and distinguished doctor of theology like yourself, His Imperial Majesty was graciously pleased to grant your request. Well, you have had your time now, a whole day and a night, and so I will repeat the question to you. You have admitted being the author of these books. Do you mean to defend all these books, or will you retract any of them?

[ECK *sits.* MARTIN *speaks quietly, conversationally, hardly raising his voice throughout, and with simplicity*]

MARTIN: Your serene highness, most illustrious princes and gracious lords, I appear before you by God's mercy, and I beg that you will listen patiently. If, through any ignorance, I have not given anyone his proper title or offended in any way against the etiquette of such a place as this, I ask your pardon in advance for a man who finds it hard to know his way outside the few steps from wall to wall of a monk's cell. We have agreed these books are all mine, and they have all been published rightly in my name. I will reply to your second question. I ask your serene majesty and your gracious lordships to take note that not all my books are of the same kind. For instance, in the first group, I have dealt quite simply with the values of faith and morality, and even my enemies have agreed that all this is quite harmless, and can be read without damaging the most fragile Christian. Even the bull against me, harsh and cruel as it is, admits that some of my books are offensive to no one. Perhaps it's the strange nature of such a questionable compliment, that the bull goes on to condemn these with the rest, which it considers offensive. If I'm to begin withdrawing these books, what should I be doing? I should be condemning those very things my friends and enemies are agreed on. There is a second group of books I have written, and these all attack the power of the keys, which has ravaged Christendom. No one can deny this, the evidence is everywhere and everyone complains of it. And no one has suffered more from this tyranny than the Germans. They have been plundered without mercy. If I were to retract those books now, I should be issuing a licence for more tyranny, and it is too much to ask of me.

I have also written a third kind of book against certain, private, distinguished, and, apparently—highly established—individuals. They are all defenders of Rome and enemies of my religion. In these books, it's possible that I have been more violent than may seem necessary, or, shall I say, tasteful in one who is, after all, a monk. But then, I have never set out to be a saint and I've not been defending my own life, but the teaching of Christ. So you see, again I'm not free to retract, for if I did, the present situation would certainly go on just as before. However, because I am a man and not God, the only way for me to defend what I have written is to employ the same method used by my Saviour. When He was being questioned by Annas, the high priest, about His teaching, and He had been struck in the face by one of the servants, He replied: "If I have spoken lies tell me what the lie is." If the Lord Jesus Himself, who could not err, was willing to listen to the arguments of a servant, how can I refuse to do the same? Therefore, what I ask, by the Mercy of God, is let someone expose my errors in the light of the Gospels. The moment you have done this, I shall ask you to let me be the first to pick up my books and hurl them in the fire.

I think this is a clear answer to your question. I think I understand the danger of my position well enough. You have made it very clear to me. But I can still think of nothing better than the Word of God being the cause of all the dissension among us. For Christ said, "I have not come to bring peace, but a sword. I have come to set a man against his father." We also have to be sure that the reign of this noble, young Prince Charles, so full of promise, should not end in the misery of Europe. We must fear God alone. I commend myself to your most serene majesty and to your lordships, and humbly pray that you will not condemn me as your enemy. That is all.

ECK: [*Rising*] Martin, you have not answered the question put to you. Even if it were true that some of your books are innocuous— a point which, incidentally, we don't concede—we still ask that you cut out these passages which are blasphemous; that you cut out the heresies or whatever could be construed as heresy, and, in fact, that you delete any passage which might be considered hurtful to the Catholic faith. His sacred and imperial majesty is more than prepared to be lenient, and, if you will do these things, he will use his influence with the supreme pontiff to see that the good things in your work are not thrown out with the bad. If, however, you persist in your attitude, there can be no question that all memory of you will be blotted out, and everything you have written, right or wrong, will be forgotten.

You see, Martin, you return to the same place as all other heretics—to Holy Scripture. You demand to be contradicted from Scripture. We can only believe that you must be ill or mad. Do reasons have to be given to anyone who cares to ask a question? Any question? Why, if anyone who questioned the common understanding of the Church on any matter he liked to raise, and had to be answered irrefutably from the Scriptures, there would be nothing certain or decided in Christendom. What would the Jews and Turks and Saracens say if they heard us *debating* whether what we have always believed is true or not? I beg you, Martin, not to believe that you, and you alone, understand the meaning of the Gospels. Don't rate your own opinion so highly, so far beyond that of many other sincere and eminent men. I ask you: don't throw doubt on the most holy, orthodox faith, the faith founded by the most perfect legislator known to us, and spread by His apostles throughout the world, with their blood and miracles. This faith has been defined by sacred councils, and confirmed by the Church. It is your heritage, and we are forbidden to dispute it by the laws of the emperor and the pontiff. Since no amount of argument can lead to a final conclusion, they can only condemn those who refuse to submit to them. The penalties are provided and will be executed. I must, therefore, ask again, I must demand that you answer sincerely, frankly and unambiguously, yes or no: will you or will you not retract your books and the errors contained in them.

MARTIN: Since your serene majesty and your lordships demand a simple answer, you shall have it, without horns and without teeth. Unless I am shown by the testimony of the Scriptures—for I don't believe in popes or councils—unless I am refuted by Scripture and my conscience is captured by God's own word, I cannot and will not recant, since to act against one's conscience is neither safe nor honest. Here I stand; God help me; I can do no more. Amen.

SCENE TWO

Wittenberg. 1525. A marching hymn, the sound of cannon and shouts of mutilated men. Smoke, a shattered banner bearing the cross and wooden shoe of the Bundschuh, emblem of the Peasants' Movement. A small chapel altar at one side of the stage opposite the pulpit. Centre is a small handcart, and beside it lies the bloody bulk of a PEASANT'S CORPSE. *Downstage stands* THE KNIGHT, *fatigued, despondent, stained and dirty.*

KNIGHT: There was excitement that day. In Worms—that day I mean. Oh, I don't mean now, not now. A lot's happened since then. There's no excitement like that any more. Not unless murder's your idea of excitement. I tell you, you can't have ever known the kind of thrill that monk set off amongst that collection of all kinds of men gathered together there—those few years ago. We all felt it, every one of us, just without any exception, you couldn't help it, even if you didn't want to, and, believe me, most of those people didn't want to. His scalp looked blotchy and itchy, and you felt sure, just looking at him, his body must be permanently sour and white all over, even whiter than his face and like a millstone to touch. He'd sweated so much by the time he'd finished, I could smell every inch of him even from where I was. But he fizzed like a hot spark in a trail of gunpowder going off in us, that dowdy monk, he went off in us, and nothing could stop it, and it blew up and there was nothing we could do, any of us, that was it. I just felt quite sure, quite certain in my own mind nothing could ever be the same again, just simply that. Something had taken place, something had changed and become something else, an event had occurred in the flesh, in the flesh and the breath—like, even like when the weight of that body slumped on its wooded crotch-piece and the earth grew dark. That's the kind of thing I mean by happen, and this also happened in very likely the same manner to all those of us who stood there, friends and enemies alike. I don't think, no I don't think even if I could speak and write like him, I could begin to give you an idea of what we thought, or what some of us thought, of what we might come to. Obviously, we couldn't have all felt quite the same way, but I wanted to burst my ears with shouting and draw my sword, no, not draw it, I wanted to pluck it as if it were a flower in my blood and plunge it into whatever he would have told me to. [THE KNIGHT *is lost in his own thoughts, then his eyes catch the body of the* PEASANT. *He takes a swipe at the cart*] If one could only understand him. He baffles me, I just can't make him out. Anyway, it never worked out. [*To* CORPSE] Did it, my friend? Not the way we expected anyway, certainly not the way *you* expected, but who'd have ever thought we might end up on different sides, him on one and us on the other. That when the war came between you and them, he'd be there beating the drum for *them* outside the slaughter house, and beating it louder and better than anyone, hollering for *your* blood, cutting you up in your thousands, and hanging you up to drip away into the fire for good. Oh well, I suppose all those various groups were out for their different things, or the same thing really, all out for what we could get, and more than any of us had the right to expect. They were all the same, all those big princes and archbishops, the cut rate nobility and rich layabouts, honourable this and thats scrabbling like boars round a swill bucket for every penny those poor peasants never had. All those great abbots with their dewlaps dropped and hanging on their necks like goose's eggs, and then those left-over knights, like me for instance, I suppose, left-over men, impoverished, who'd seen better days and were scared and'd stick at nothing to try and make sure they couldn't get any worse. Yes. . . . Not one of them could read the words WAY OUT when it was written up for them, marked out clearly and unmistakably in the pain of too many men. Yes. They say, you know, that the profit motive—and I'm sure you know all about that one—they say that the profit motive was born with the invention of double entry bookkeeping in the monasteries. Bookkeeping! In the monasteries, and ages before any of us had ever got round to burning them down. But, you know, for men with such a motive, there is only really one entry. The profit is theirs, the loss is someone else's, and usually they don't even bother to write it up. [*He nudges the* CORPSE *with his toe*] Well, it was your old loss wasn't it, dead loss, in fact, my friend, and you could say his life was more or less a write-off right from the day he was born. Wasn't it? Um? And all the others like him, everywhere, now and after him. [THE KNIGHT *starts rather weakly to load the body on to the cart.* MARTIN *enters, a book in his hands. They look at each other then* MARTIN *at the* PEASANT. THE KNIGHT *takes his book and glances at it, but he doesn't miss* MARTIN *shrink slightly from the* PEASANT] Another of yours? [*He hands it back*] Do you think it'll sell as well as the others? [*Pause*] I dare say it will. Someone's always going to listen to you. No? [MARTIN *moves to go, but* THE KNIGHT *stops him*] Martin. Just a minute. [*He turns and places his hand carefully, ritually, on the body in the cart. He smears the blood from it over* MARTIN] There we are. That's better. [MARTIN *makes to move again, but again* THE KNIGHT *stops him*] You're all ready now. You even look like a butcher——

MARTIN: God is the butcher——

KNIGHT: Don't you?

MARTIN: Why don't you address your abuse to Him?

KNIGHT: Never mind—you're wearing His apron. [MARTIN *moves to the stairs of the pulpit*] It suits you. [*Pause*] Doesn't it? [*Pause*] That day in Worms [*Pause*] you were like a pig under glass weren't you? Do you remember it? I could smell every inch of you even where I was standing. All you've ever managed to do is convert everything into stench and dying and peril, but you could have done it, Martin, and you were the only one who could have ever done it. You could even have brought freedom and order in at one and the same time.

MARTIN: There's no such thing as an orderly revolution. Anyway, Christians are called to suffer, not fight.

KNIGHT: But weren't we all of us, all of us, without any exceptions to please any old interested parties, weren't we all redeemed by Christ's blood? [*Pointing to the* PEASANT] Wasn't he included when the scriptures were being dictated? Or was it just you who was made free, you and the princes you've taken up with, and the rich burghers and——

MARTIN: Free? [*Ascends the pulpit steps*] The princes blame me, you blame me and the peasants blame me——

KNIGHT: [*Following up the steps*] You put the water in the wine didn't you?

MARTIN: When I see chaos, then I see the devil's organ and then I'm afraid. Now, that's enough——

KNIGHT: You're breaking out again——

MARTIN: Go away——

KNIGHT: Aren't you?

[MARTIN *makes a sudden effort to push him back down the steps, but* THE KNIGHT *hangs on firmly*]

MARTIN: Get back!

KNIGHT: Aren't you, you're breaking out again, you canting pig, I can smell you from here!

MARTIN: He heard the children of Israel, didn't He?

KNIGHT: Up to the ears in revelation, aren't you?

MARTIN: And didn't He deliver them out of the Land of Pharaoh?

KNIGHT: You canting pig, aren't you?

MARTIN: Well? Didn't He?

KNIGHT: Cock's wounds! Don't hold your Bible to my head, piggy, there's enough revelation of my own in there for me, in what I see for myself from here! [*Taps his forehead*] Hold your gospel against that!

[THE KNIGHT *grabs* MARTIN's *hand and clamps it to his head*]

KNIGHT: You're killing the spirit, and you're killing it with the letter. You've been swilling about in the wrong place, Martin, in your own stink and ordure. Go on! You've got your hand on it, that's all the holy spirit there is, and it's all you'll ever get so feel it!

[*They struggle, but* THE KNIGHT *is very weak by now, and* MARTIN *is able to wrench himself away and up into the pulpit*]

MARTIN: The world was conquered by the Word, the Church is maintained by the Word——

KNIGHT: Word? What Word? Word? That word, whatever that means, is probably just another old relic or indulgence, and you know what you did to those! Why, none of it might be any more than poetry, have you thought of that, Martin. Poetry! Martin, you're a poet, there's no doubt about that in anybody's mind, you're a poet, but do you know what most men believe in, in their hearts—because they don't see in images like you do—they believe in their hearts that Christ was a man as we are, and that He was a prophet and a teacher, and they also believe in their hearts that His supper is a plain meal like their own—if they're lucky enough to get it—a plain meal of bread and wine! A plain meal with no garnish and no word. And *you* helped them to begin to believe it!

MARTIN: [*Pause*] Leave me.

KNIGHT: Yes. What's there to stay for? I've been close enough to you for too long. I even smell like you.

MARTIN: [*Roaring with pain*] I smell because of my own argument, I smell because I never stop disputing with Him, and because I expect Him to keep His Word. Now then! If your peasant rebelled against that Word, that was worse than murder because it laid the whole country waste, and who knows now what God will make of us Germans!

KNIGHT: Don't blame God for the Germans, Martin! [*Laughs*] Don't do that! You thrashed about more than anyone on the night they were conceived!

MARTIN: Christ! Hear me! My words pour from Your Body! They deserved their death, these swarming peasants! They kicked against authority, they plundered and bargained and all in Your name! Christ, believe me! [*To* THE KNIGHT] I demanded it, I prayed for it, and I got it! Take that lump away! Now, drag it away with you!

[THE KNIGHT *prepares to trundle off the cart and* CORPSE]

KNIGHT: All right, my friend. Stay with your nun then. Marry and stew with your nun. Most of the others have. Stew with her, like a shuddering infant in *her* bed. You think you'll manage?

MARTIN: [*Lightly*] At least my father'll praise me for *that*.

KNIGHT: Your father?

[THE KNIGHT *shrugs, pushes the cart wearily, and goes off.* MARTIN's *head hangs over the edge of the pulpit*]

MARTIN: I [*Whispering*] trust you . . . I trust you . . . You've overcome the world . . . I trust you . . . You're all I wish to have . . . ever . . . [*Slumped over the pulpit, he seems to be unconscious. Then he makes an effort to recover, as if he had collapsed in the middle of a sermon*] I expect you must . . . I'm sure you must remember—Abraham. Abraham was—he was an old man . . . a . . . very old man indeed, in fact, he was a hundred years old, when what was surely, what must have been a miracle happened, to a man of his years—a son was born to him. A son. Isaac he called him. And he loved Isaac. Well, he loved him with such intensity, one can only diminish it by description. But to Abraham his little son was a miraculous thing, a small, incessant . . . animal . . . astonishment. And in the child he sought the father. But, one day, God said to Abraham: Take your little son whom you love so much, kill him, and make a sacrifice of him. And in that moment everything inside Abraham seemed to shrivel once and for all. Because it had seemed to him that God had promised him life through his son. So then he took the boy and prepared to kill him, strapping him down to the wood of the burnt offering just as he had been told to do. And he spoke softly to the boy, and raised the knife over his little naked body, the boy struggling not to flinch or blink his eyes. Never, save in Christ, was there such obedience as in that moment, and, if God had blinked, the boy would have died then, but the Angel intervened, and the boy was released, and Abraham took him up in his arms again. In the teeth of life we seem to die, but God says no—in the teeth of death we live. If He butchers us, He makes us live. [*Enter* THE KNIGHT, *who stands watching him, the Bundschuh banner in his hands*] Heart of my Jesus save me; Heart of my Saviour deliver me; Heart of my Shepherd guard me; Heart of my Master teach me; Heart of my King govern me; Heart of my Friend stay with me.

[*Enter* KATHERINE VON BORA, *his bride, accompanied by two* MONKS. MARTIN *rises from the pulpit and goes towards her. A simple tune is played on a simple instrument. She takes his hand, and they kneel together centre.* THE KNIGHT *watches. Then he smashes the banner he has been holding, and tosses the remains on to the altar*]

SCENE THREE

A hymn. The Eremite Cloister. Wittenberg. 1530. The refectory table, and on it two places set, and the remains of two meals. MARTIN *is seated alone. The vigour of a man in his late thirties, and at the height of his powers, has settled into the tired pain of a middle age struggling to rediscover strength.* KATHERINE *enters with a jug of wine. She is a big, pleasant-looking girl, almost thirty.*

MARTIN: How is he?

KATHERINE: He's all right. He's just coming. Wouldn't let me help him. I think he's been sick.

MARTIN: Poor old chap. After living all your life in a monastery, one's stomach doesn't take too easily to your kind of cooking.

KATHERINE: Wasn't it all right?

MARTIN: Oh, it was fine, just too much for an old monk's shrivelled digestion to chew on, that's all.

KATHERINE: Oh, I see. *You're* all right, aren't you?

MARTIN: Yes, I'm all right, thank you, my dear. [*Smile*] I expect I'll suffer later though.

KATHERINE: You like your food, so don't make out you don't.

MARTIN: Well, I prefer it to fasting. Did you never hear the story of the soldier who was fighting in the Holy Crusades? No? Well, he was told by his officer that if he died in battle, he would dine in Paradise with Christ; and the soldier ran away. When he came back after the battle, they asked him why he'd run away. "Didn't you want to dine with Christ?" they said. And he replied, "No, I'm fasting today."

KATHERINE: I've brought you some more wine.

MARTIN: Thank you.

KATHERINE: Should help you to sleep.

[STAUPITZ *enters, supporting himself with a stick*]

MARTIN: There you are! I thought you'd fallen down the jakes— right into the devil's loving arms.

STAUPITZ: I'm so sorry. I was—I was wandering about a bit.

MARTIN: Well, come and sit down. Katie's brought us some more wine.

STAUPITZ: I can't get over being here again. It's so odd. This place was full of men. And now, now there's only you, you and Katie. It's very, very strange.

KATHERINE: I shouldn't stay up too long, Martin. You didn't sleep well again last night. I could hear you—hardly breathing all night.

MARTIN: [*Amused*] You could hear me hardly breathing?

KATHERINE: You know what I mean. When you don't sleep, it keeps me awake, too. Good night, Dr. Staupitz.

STAUPITZ: Good night, my dear. Thank you for the dinner. It was excellent. I'm so sorry I wasn't able to do justice to it.

KATHERINE: That's all right. Martin's always having the same kind of trouble.

STAUPITZ: Yes? Well, he's not changed much then.

MARTIN: Not a bit. Even Katie hasn't managed to shift my bowels for me, have you?

KATHERINE: And if it's not that, he can't sleep.

MARTIN: Yes, Katie, you've said that already. I've also got gout, piles and bells in my ears. Dr. Staupitz has had to put up with all my complaints for longer than you have, isn't that right?

KATHERINE: Well, try not to forget what I said.

[She kisses MARTIN's cheeks]

MARTIN: Good night, Katie.

[She goes out]

STAUPITZ: Well, you've never been so well looked after.

MARTIN: It's a shame everyone can't marry a nun. They're fine cooks, thrifty housekeepers, and splendid mothers. Seems to me there are three ways out of despair. One is faith in Christ, the second is to become enraged by the world and make its nose bleed for it, and the third is the love of a woman. Mind you, they don't all necessarily work—at least, only part of the time. Sometimes, I'm lying awake in the devil's own sweat, and I turn to Katie and touch her. And I say: get me out, Katie, please, Katie, please try and get me out. And sometimes, sometimes she actually drags me out. Poor old Katie, fishing about there in bed with her great, hefty arms, trying to haul me out.

STAUPITZ: She's good.

MARTIN: Wine?

STAUPITZ: Not much. I must go to bed myself.

MARTIN: Help you sleep. You're looking tired.

STAUPITZ: Old. Our old pear tree's in blossom, I see. You've looked after it.

MARTIN: I like to get in a bit in the garden, if I can. I like to think it heals my bones somehow. Anyway, I always feel a bit more pleased with myself afterwards.

STAUPITZ: We'd a few talks under that tree.

MARTIN: Yes.

STAUPITZ: Martin, it's so still. I don't think I'd ever realized how eloquent a monk's silence really was. It was a voice. [*Pause*] It's gone. [*He shakes his head, pause*] How's your father these days?

MARTIN: Getting old, too, but he's well enough.

STAUPITZ: Is he—is he pleased with you?

MARTIN: He was never pleased about anything I ever did. Not when I took my master's degree or when I got to be Dr. Luther. Only when Katie and I were married and she got pregnant. Then he was pleased.

STAUPITZ: Do you remember Brother Weinand?

MARTIN: I ought to. He used to hold my head between my knees when I felt faint in the choir.

STAUPITZ: I wonder what happened to him. [*Pause*] He had the most beautiful singing voice.

MARTIN: My old friend, you're unhappy. I'm sorry. [*Pause*] We monks were really no good to anyone, least of all to ourselves, every one of us rolled up like a louse in the Almighty's overcoat.

STAUPITZ: Yes. Well, you always have a way of putting it. I was always having to give you little lectures about the fanatic way you'd observe the Rule all the time.

MARTIN: Yes, and you talked me out of it, remember? [*Pause*] Father, are *you* pleased with me?

STAUPITZ: Pleased with you? My dear son, I'm not anyone or anything to be pleased with you any more. When we used to talk together underneath that tree you were like a child.

MARTIN: A child.

STAUPITZ: Manhood was something you had to be flung into, my son. You dangled your toe in it longer than most of us could ever bear. But you're not a frightened little monk any more who's come to his prior for praise or blame. Every time you belch now, the world stops what it's doing and listens. Do you know, when I first came to take over this convent, there weren't thirty books published every year. And now, last year it was more like six or seven hundred, and most of those published in Wittenberg, too.

MARTIN: The best turn God ever did Himself was giving us a printing press. Sometimes I wonder what He'd have done without it.

STAUPITZ: I heard the other day they're saying the world's going to end in 1532.

MARTIN: It sounds as good a date as any other. Yes—1532. That could easily be the end of the world. You could write a book about it, and just call it that—1532.

STAUPITZ: I'm sorry, Martin. I didn't mean to come and see you after all this time and start criticizing. Forgive me, I'm getting old and a bit silly and frightened, that meal was just too much for me. It wasn't that I didn't——

MARTIN: Please—I'm sorry, too. Don't upset yourself. I'm used to critics, John. They just help you to keep your muscles from getting slack. All those hollow cavillers, that subtle clown Erasmus, for instance. He ought to know better, but all he wants to do is to be able to walk on eggs without breaking any. As for that mandrill-arsed English baboon Henry, that leprous son of a bitch never had an idea of his own to jangle on a tombstone, let alone call himself Defender of the Faith. [*Pause.* STAUPITZ *hasn't responded to his attempt at lightness*] Still, one thing for Erasmus, he didn't fool about with all the usual cant and rubbish about indulgences and the Pope and Purgatory. No, he went right to the core of it. He's still up to his ears with stuff about morality, and men being able to save themselves. No one does good, not anyone. God is true and one. But, and this is what he can't grasp, He's utterly incomprehensible and beyond the reach of minds. A man's will is like a horse standing between two riders. If God jumps on its back, it'll go where God wants it to. But if Satan gets up there, it'll go where he leads it. And not only that, the horse can't choose its rider. That's left up to them, to those two. [*Pause*] Why are you accusing me? What have I done?

STAUPITZ: I'm not accusing you, Martin. You know that. A just man is his own accuser. Because a just man judges as he is.

MARTIN: What's that mean? I'm not just?

STAUPITZ: You try. What else can you do?

MARTIN: You mean those damned peasants, don't you? You think I should have encouraged them!

STAUPITZ: I don't say that.

MARTIN: Well, what do you say?

STAUPITZ: You needn't have encouraged the princes. They were butchered and *you* got them to do it. And they had just cause, Martin. They did, didn't they?

MARTIN: I didn't say they hadn't.

STAUPITZ: Well, then?

MARTIN: Do you remember saying to me, "Remember, brother, you started this in the name of the Lord Jesus Christ?

STAUPITZ: Well?

MARTIN: Father, the world can't be ruled with a rosary. They were a mob, a mob, and if they hadn't been held down and slaughtered, there'd have been a thousand more tyrants instead of half a dozen. It was a mob, and because it was a mob it was against Christ. No man can die for another, or believe for another or answer for another. The moment they try they become a mob. If we're lucky we can be persuaded in our own mind, and the most we can hope for is to die each one for himself. Do I have to tell you what Paul says? You read! "Let every soul be subject unto the highest powers. For there is no power but of God: the powers that be are ordained of God. Whosoever therefore resisteth that power, resisteth the ordinance of God": that's Paul, Father, and that's Scripture! "And they that resist shall receive to themselves damnation."

STAUPITZ: Yes, you're probably right.

MARTIN: "Love worketh no ill to his neighbour: therefore love is the fulfilling of the law."

STAUPITZ: Yes, well it seems to be all worked out. I must be tired.

MARTIN: It was worked out for me.

STAUPITZ: I'd better get off to bed.

MARTIN: They're trying to turn me into a fixed star, Father, but I'm a shifting planet. You're leaving me.

STAUPITZ: I'm not leaving you, Martin. I love you. I love you as much as any man has ever loved most women. But we're not two protected monks chattering under a pear tree in a garden any longer. The world's changed. For one thing, you've made a thing called Germany; you've unlaced a language and taught it to the Germans, and the rest of the world will just have to get used to the sound of it. As we once made the body of Christ from bread, you've made the body of Europe, and whatever our pains turn out to be, they'll attack the rest of the world, too. You've taken Christ away from the low mumblings and soft voices and jewelled gowns and the tiaras and put Him back where He belongs. In each man's soul. We owe so much to you. All I beg of you is not to be too violent. In spite of everything, of everything you've said and shown us, there *were* men, *some* men who did live holy lives here once. Don't—don't believe you, only you are right.

[STAUPITZ *is close to tears, and* MARTIN *doesn't know what to do*]

MARTIN: What else can I do? What can I do?

[*He clutches at his abdomen*]

STAUPITZ: What is it?

MARTIN: Oh, the old trouble, that's all. That's all.

STAUPITZ: Something that's puzzled me, and I've always meant to ask you.

MARTIN: Well?

STAUPITZ: When you were before the Diet in Worms, and they asked you those two questions—why did you ask for that extra day to think over your reply?

MARTIN: Why?

STAUPITZ: You'd known what your answer was going to be for months. Heaven knows, you told me enough times. Why did you wait?

[*Pause*]

MARTIN: I wasn't certain.

STAUPITZ: And were you? Afterwards?

MARTIN: I listened for God's voice, but all I could hear was my own.

STAUPITZ: Are you sure?

[*Pause*]

MARTIN: No.

[STAUPITZ *kisses him*]

STAUPITZ: Thank you, my son. May God bless you. I hope you sleep better. Goodnight.

MARTIN: Goodnight, Father.

[STAUPITZ *goes out, and* MARTIN *is left alone. He drinks his wine*]

MARTIN: Oh, Lord, I believe. I believe. I do believe. Only help my unbelief.

[*He sits slumped in his chair.* KATHERINE *enters. She is wearing a nightdress, and carries in her arms* HANS, *their young son*]

KATHERINE: He was crying out in his sleep. Must have been dreaming again. Aren't you coming to bed?

MARTIN: Shan't be long, Katie. Shan't be long.

KATHERINE: All right, but try not to be too long. You look—well, you don't look as well as you should.

[*She turns to go*]

MARTIN: Give him to me.

KATHERINE: What?

MARTIN: Give him to me.

KATHERINE: What do you mean, what for? He'll get cold down here.

MARTIN: No, he won't. Please, Katie. Let me have him.

KATHERINE: You're a funny man. All right, but only for five minutes. Don't just sit there all night. He's gone back to sleep now. He'll be having another dream if you keep him down here.

MARTIN: Thank you, Katie.

KATHERINE: There! Keep him warm now! He's *your* son.

MARTIN: I will. Don't worry.

KATHERINE: Well, make sure you do. [*Pausing on way out*] Don't be long now, Martin.

MARTIN: Good night, Kate.

[*She goes out, leaving* MARTIN *with the sleeping child in his arms*]

MARTIN: [*Softly*] What was the matter? Was it the devil bothering you? Um? Was he? Old Nick? Up you, old Nick. Well, don't worry. One day you might even be glad of him. So long as you can show him your little backside. That's right, show him your backside and let him have it. So try not to be afraid. The dark isn't quite as thick as all that. You know, my father had a son, and he'd to learn a hard lesson, which is a human being is a helpless little animal, but he's not created by his father, but by God. It's hard to accept you're anyone's son, and you're not the father of yourself. So, don't have dreams so soon, my son. *They'll* be having *you* soon enough. [*He gets up*] You should have seen me at Worms. I was almost like you that day, as if I'd learned to play again, to play, to play out in the world, like a naked child. "I have come to set a man against his father," I said, and they listened to me. Just like a child. Sh! We must go to bed, musn't we? A little while, and you *shall* see me. Christ said that, my son. I hope that'll be the way of it again. I hope so. Let's just hope so, eh? Eh? Let's just hope so.

[MARTIN *holds the child in his arms, and then walks off slowly*]

CURTAIN

THE SUBJECT WAS ROSES

Frank D. Gilroy

From About Those Roses *and* The Subject Was Roses *by Frank D. Gilroy*

Frank D. Gilroy

Winner of the theatre's triple crown, the 1965 Tony Award, the Pulitzer Prize, and New York Drama Critics' Circle Award for the 1964-65 season, *The Subject Was Roses* started life rather inauspiciously. As Frank D. Gilroy himself has related in his meticulously kept log *About Those Roses or How Not To Do a Play and Succeed* which appears with the original publication of the play, the setbacks, frustrations, and disappointments before the play finally went into production and during rehearsals were enough to discourage or stagger any dramatist.

According to the author: "On May 25, 1964, *The Subject Was Roses* opened on Broadway with a producer who had never produced a Broadway play; a director who had never directed one; a scenic artist who had never designed one; a general manager who had never managed one; and three actors who were virtually unknown . . . We opened with a $165 advance sale; registered substantial losses until our fourth week; borrowed some $10,000; received invaluable aid and encouragement from many people (too many to name) who made a cause of our survival . . . We did not have a sold-out house until our 136th performance . . . We moved to the Winthrop Ames Theatre on September 7, 1964, and intend to run (as Jack Albertson puts it) 'until we do it right.' "

And what they did turned out to be not only right, but one of those show business miracles. In addition to winning all the major prizes in sight, the play went on to run for 832 performances.

Most of the press was enamored of the play from the very beginning.

Howard Taubman of the New York *Times* declared: "Frank D. Gilroy has made good on the promise of *Who'll Save the Plowboy?* (1962). His new play, *The Subject Was Roses* is not only an impressive stride forward but also an honest and touching work in its own right. Mr. Gilroy has not resorted to gimmicks, razzle-dazzle or advanced techniques to be in fashion. He has written a straightforward, realistic play that wears no airs. With simplicity, humor and integrity he has looked into the hearts of three decent people and discovered, by letting them discover, the feelings that divide and join them . . . It never loses a beat in its building of mood and conflict. It knows where it's going. It makes every line and gesture work and convey meaning."

Walter Kerr stated in the New York *Herald Tribune*: "*The Subject Was Roses* is quite the most interesting new American play to be offered on Broadway this season . . . In the writing and in the staging there is an economy of effect, a directness of tongue, together with a simplicity of gesture, that very nearly opens the door to an unexpected—but most plausible—poetry."

Norman Nadel lauded the work in the New York *World-Telegram*: "From this day forth, Frank D. Gilroy is a major playwright. The American theatre needs Gilroy. Last night he gave us more than a fine and beautiful play; he also gave us the prospect of others to come . . . To the most profound depths of the human heart; that's how far Gilroy takes us. Along the way he blends the humor and poignancy of family relationship into a play as beguiling as it is honest."

In his coverage for the New York *Post*, Richard Watts, Jr., noted: "The skill of Mr. Gilroy is striking . . . He has remarkable efficiency, never wasting a word and concentrating on what he has to say without a lost moment. He has an unfailing ear for dialogue, and every speech is unerring in its sound of actuality. And all three of his characters, a father, mother and war-veteran son, are observed with a ruthless credibility that is at the same time merciless and compassionate through understanding . . . it is realism of a high order."

A Tony Award also was presented to Jack Albertson for his brilliant portrayal of the baffled and cantankerous husband and father. Later, he re-created his role (opposite Patricial Neal) in the film version and it brought him an Academy Award in 1968.

Frank D. Gilroy was born in New York City on October 13, 1925. He attended DeWitt Clinton High School in the Bronx and soon after graduating went into the U. S. Army. While in service he managed to do some writing and contributed two stories to the divisional paper. Coming out of the army with "a burning desire and determination to write," he enrolled in Dartmouth College, and although he had been writing poems and stories for some time, a playwriting course taken in his junior year made him realize that drama was his proper genre. During his tenure at Dartmouth, he wrote two full-length and six short plays that were produced at the college. He also served as editor of the college newspaper. Graduating from Dartmouth in 1950 with a B.A. degree *magna cum laud,* he won a year's post-graduate study at the Yale School of Drama.

After Yale, Mr. Gilroy held a succession of odd jobs, all the while continuing to write. Television drama was coming into its own at the time, and he decided to make "an all-out total assault" on the medium. The breakthrough came in 1952 when he sold a sketch for Kate Smith. This soon was followed by other scripts performed on almost all of the major dramatic shows during television's Golden Age. He also started to write for films, notably the screenplays for *The Fastest Gun Alive* with Glenn Ford, and *The Gallant Hours* with James Cagney.

He next invaded the theatre with *Who'll Save the Plowboy?,* presented Off-Broadway at the Phoenix Theatre in 1962. The play and author were hailed by most reviewers and it brought him his first theatre award, an "Obie" for the best new American play of the year.

In 1967, Mr. Gilroy was represented again on Broadway with *That Summer—That Fall,* with Jon Voight and Irene Pappas. This was followed in 1968 by *The Only Game in Town,* a three-character vehicle that costarred Tammy Grimes, Barry Nelson and Leo Genn. It later was filmed with Elizabeth Taylor.

Present Tense, a bill of four short plays by the author was presented in 1972 at the Off-Broadway Sheridan Square Playhouse, prompting drama critic Emory Lewis to report: "It's good to know that Frank D. Gilroy is alive and well and still a leading playwright!"

Mr. Gilroy made his directorial debut with the 1971 film, *Desperate Characters* starring Shirley MacLaine, and he also is the author of two novels, *Private* and *From Noon Till Three.*

The Subject Was Roses was first presented by Edgar Lansbury on May 25, 1964, at the Royale Theatre, New York. The cast was as follows:

JOHN CLEARY   Jack Albertson
NETTIE CLEARY   Irene Dailey
TIMMY CLEARY   Martin Sheen

Directed by Ulu Grosbard
Scenery designed by Edgar Lansbury
Lighting by Jules Fisher
Costumes by Donald Foote

ACT ONE

A middle-class apartment.
May 1946.

Scene 1:   Saturday morning.
Scene 2:   Saturday afternoon.
Scene 3:   Two A.M. Sunday morning

ACT TWO

The same place

Scene 1:   Sunday morning.
Scene 2:   Sunday evening.
Scene 3:   Two A.M. Monday morning.
Scene 4:   Nine A.M. Monday morning.

ACT ONE

SCENE ONE

SCENE: *The kitchen and living room of a middle-class apart-ment in the West Bronx. A doorway links the two rooms; an invisible wall divides them. The living room is furnished with the heavy upholstered pieces [replete with antimacassars] considered fashionable in the late twenties and early thirties. There is evidence of a party given the night before: a beer keg, a stack of camp chairs, a sagging banner that is hand let-tered—"Welcome Home, Timmy."*

TIME: *A Saturday morning in May of 1946.*

... ...n stands alone in the kitchen, lost in contem-
...rmy jacket hanging from the door. The man,
...fifty. The army jacket bears an infantry divi-
...poral chevrons, service ribbons [including the
...battle stars, and a presidential unit citation],
...Bars" marking two years of overseas duty, and
...l Duck" signifying recent discharge. JOHN
...sion as he regards the jacket is one of almost
...ty. He touches the jacket, feels the material,
...e of the chevrons inquiringly. Now, on an im-
...the jacket from the hanger, dons it furtively, is
...s obviously a secret moment when he hears a
...front door. Quickly returning the jacket to the
...es a seat at the kitchen table and appears
...newspaper as the door opens and his wife,
...e, enters with a bundle of groceries.

...lay . . . Timmy still asleep?

...him . . . Better give me mine.

NETTIE: I thought we'd all have breakfast together.

JOHN: I have to go downtown.

NETTIE: Today?

JOHN: Ruskin wants to see me. [*She regards him a moment, then begins to set the food before him*] I'm going to stop at St. Francis on the way . . . to offer a prayer of thanks.

NETTIE: Toast?

JOHN: Yes . . . All those casualties and he never got a scratch. We're very lucky.

NETTIE: What do you want on it?

JOHN: Marmalade . . . The Freeman boy dead. The Mullin boy crippled for life . . . Makes you wonder . . . Think he enjoyed the party?

NETTIE: He seemed to.

JOHN: First time I ever saw him take a drink.

NETTIE: He drank too much.

JOHN: You don't get out of the army every day.

NETTIE: He was sick during the night.

JOHN: Probably the excitement.

NETTIE: It was the whiskey. You should have stopped him.

JOHN: For three years he's gotten along fine without anyone telling him what to do.

NETTIE: I had to hold his head.

JOHN: No one held his head in the army.

NETTIE: That's what *he* said.

JOHN: But that didn't stop *you*.

NETTIE: He's not in the army any more.

JOHN: It was a boy that walked out of this house three years ago. It's a man that's come back in.

NETTIE: You sound like a recruiting poster.

JOHN: *You* sound ready to repeat the old mistakes.

NETTIE: Mistakes?

JOHN: Pardon me.

NETTIE: You said mistakes.

JOHN: Slip of the tongue.

NETTIE: I'd like to know what mistakes you're referring to.

JOHN: The coffee's excellent.

NETTIE: I'd really like to know.

JOHN: He was eighteen when he went away. Until that time, he showed no special skill at anything, but you treated him like he was a protégé.

NETTIE: I think you mean prodigy.

JOHN: What I really mean is baby.

NETTIE: For a baby he certainly did well in the army.

JOHN: I didn't say he was a baby. I said you treated him like one.

NETTIE: You were surprised he did well. You didn't think he'd last a week.

JOHN: Bless us and save us, said Mrs. O'Davis.

NETTIE: Do you know why you were surprised?

JOHN: Joy, joy, said Mrs. Malloy.

NETTIE: Because you never understood him.

JOHN: Mercy, mercy, said old Mrs. Percy.

NETTIE: I never doubted that he'd do as well as anyone else.

JOHN: Where he's concerned you never doubted, period. If he came in here right now and said he could fly, you'd help him out the window.

NETTIE: If you're saying I have confidence in him, you're right. And why not? Who knows him better?

JOHN: Is there more coffee?

NETTIE: He's exceptional.

JOHN: Here we go again.

NETTIE: Yes—exceptional!

JOHN: In what way?

NETTIE: I refuse to discuss it.

JOHN: A person who's going to be famous usually drops a *few* clues by the time they're twenty-one.

NETTIE: I didn't say famous—I said exceptional.

JOHN: What's the difference?

NETTIE: You wouldn't understand.

JOHN: Here's something you better understand—you can't treat him as though he'd never been away. He's not a kid.

NETTIE: If you had stopped him from drinking too much that would have been treating him like a kid?

JOHN: This is where I came in.

NETTIE: He was trying to keep up with you and you knew it.

JOHN: You sound like you're jealous.

NETTIE: The two of you so busy drinking you hardly paid attention to anyone else.

JOHN: You *are* jealous!

NETTIE: Don't be absurd.

JOHN: He and I got along better yesterday than we ever did before and you're jealous. [*She turns away*] Well, well, well.

[*He finishes the last of his coffee. Rises to leave*]

NETTIE: Can't Ruskin wait till Monday?

JOHN: No. And don't pretend you're disappointed. What a charming little breakfast you and he will have together.

NETTIE: You're welcome to stay.

JOHN: My ears are burning already.

NETTIE: I've never said a word against you and you know it.

JOHN: Don't forget my excursion to Montreal.

NETTIE: It was always your own actions that turned him against you.

JOHN: And the convention—don't leave that out.

[*He starts from the room*]

NETTIE: The curtains. [*He regards her*] The curtains for Timmy's room. They're coming today.

JOHN: I don't know anything about curtains.

NETTIE: Yes, you do.

JOHN: I do not.

NETTIE: They'll be ten dollars.

JOHN: What's the matter with the old ones?

[TIMMY CLEARY, *twenty-one, wearing army suntans, open at the neck, emerges from his room, starts toward the kitchen, is arrested by their voices. He stops, listens*]

NETTIE: They're worn out.

JOHN: They look all right to me.

NETTIE: They aren't all right.

JOHN: Ten dollars for curtains.

NETTIE: Timmy will want to bring friends home.

JOHN: The old squeeze play.

[TIMMY *puts his hands over his ears*]

NETTIE: Are you going to give me the money?

[JOHN *extracts a bill from his wallet, slaps it on the table*]

JOHN: Here!

NETTIE: I need five dollars for the house.

JOHN: I gave you fifteen yesterday.

NETTIE: That went for the party.

JOHN: That party cost close to a hundred dollars.

NETTIE: It was worth it.

JOHN: Did I say it wasn't? [*He takes another bill from his wallet and puts it down*] There.

[TIMMY *goes back, slams the door of his room to alert them, then approaches the kitchen.* NETTIE *and* JOHN *compose themselves cheerfully as* TIMMY, *equally cheerful, enters*]

TIMMY: Good morning.

JOHN: Champ.

NETTIE: Morning, son.

[TIMMY *shakes hands with his father; kisses his mother on the cheek*]

JOHN: We thought you were going to sleep all day.

TIMMY: I smelled the coffee.

JOHN: Mother said you were sick during the night.

TIMMY: I'm fine now.

JOHN: I was a little rocky myself.

TIMMY: I wonder why.

[*They both laugh*]

NETTIE: [*To* JOHN] What time is your appointment?

JOHN: Eleven-fifteen.

NETTIE: It's twenty-five of.

JOHN: [*To* TIMMY] Mr. Ruskin wants to see me.

TIMMY: That's too bad.

JOHN: Why?

TIMMY: Thought we might take in the Giant game.

NETTIE: [*To* JOHN] Why don't you?

JOHN: You know I can't. [*To* TIMMY] This thing with Ruskin means a sure sale.

TIMMY: I understand.

JOHN: We'll go tomorrow.

NETTIE: My mother expects us for dinner tomorrow.

   [JOHN *looks at* NETTIE *as though he might say something, thinks better of it, turns to* TIMMY]

JOHN: How about *next* Saturday?

TIMMY: All right.

JOHN: We'll get box seats—the works.

TIMMY: Sounds fine.

JOHN: Swell.

NETTIE: What time will you be home?

JOHN: I'll call you.

NETTIE: I'll be at my mother's.

JOHN: [*Appraising* TIMMY] I understand none of your old clothes fit.

TIMMY: That's right.

JOHN: Meet me downtown on Monday and we'll get you some new ones.

TIMMY: Okay.

   [JOHN *feints a jab.* TIMMY *covers up. They spar good-naturedly until* TIMMY *drops his hands*]

JOHN: I still think I can take you.

TIMMY: I wouldn't be surprised.

JOHN: See you later.

TIMMY: Right.

[JOHN *moves toward the door, stops before the army jacket, indicates one of the ribbons*]

JOHN: What did you say this one was for?

TIMMY: It's a combat infantry badge.

JOHN: How about that?

TIMMY: It's not as important as it sounds.

JOHN: We'll have to sit down and have a real talk. I want to hear all about it.

TIMMY: All right.

JOHN: It's great to have you home.

TIMMY: It's great to be home.

JOHN: The Mullin boy crippled. The Freeman boy dead. We're very lucky.

TIMMY: I know.

JOHN: I'm stopping off at St. Francis this morning to offer a prayer of thanks . . . See you later.

TIMMY: Right.

[JOHN *exits from the apartment.* TIMMY *looks after him.*]

NETTIE: How did you sleep?

TIMMY: Fine . . . How's he feeling?

NETTIE: All right.

TIMMY: He looks a lot older.

NETTIE: It's been two years . . . It must have seemed strange. [*He glances at her*] Sleeping in your own bed.

TIMMY: [*Turning away again*] Yes . . . How's his business?

NETTIE: Who knows?

TIMMY: The coffee market's off.

NETTIE: I hope you're hungry.

TIMMY: I can't get over the change in him.

NETTIE: Guess what we're having for breakfast.

TIMMY: It's not just the way he looks.

NETTIE: *Guess what we're having for breakfast.* [*He turns to her*] Guess what we're having.

TIMMY: What?

NETTIE: Guess.

TIMMY: I don't know.

NETTIE: Yes, you do.

TIMMY: No.

NETTIE: Sure you do.

TIMMY: What is it?

NETTIE: You're fooling.

TIMMY: What is it?

NETTIE: What's your favorite?

TIMMY: Bacon and eggs?

NETTIE: Now I know you're fooling.

TIMMY: No.

NETTIE: I forgot what a tease you were.

TIMMY: I'm not teasing.

NETTIE: Waffles. We're having waffles.

TIMMY: Fine.

NETTIE: You used to be crazy about waffles.

TIMMY: I still am.

NETTIE: I've got the waffle batter ready.

TIMMY: Swell.

NETTIE: Your first morning home, you're entitled to whatever you want.

TIMMY: I want waffles.

NETTIE: I used the last egg in the batter.

TIMMY: *I want waffles.*

NETTIE: Really?

TIMMY: Cross my heart.

NETTIE: All right.

[*While she prepares things, he goes to a window, gazes out*]

TIMMY: I see a new butcher.

NETTIE: Quite a few new stores.

TIMMY: Pop said the Bremens moved.

NETTIE: And the Costellos . . . Remember old Zimmer the tailor?

TIMMY: Sure.

NETTIE: A few weeks ago a woman brought him a coat she wanted altered. Zimmer started to fix it, then very politely excused himself, went up to the roof and jumped. No one knows why.

TIMMY: Who was the woman?

NETTIE: Mrs. Levin.

TIMMY: That explains it.

NETTIE: That's not funny.

TIMMY: Sorry.

NETTIE: What a thing to say.

TIMMY: I said I'm sorry.

NETTIE: I'm surprised at you.

TIMMY: Bless us and save us.

NETTIE: *What?*

TIMMY: Bless us and save us. As in "Bless us and save us, said Mrs. O'Davis; Joy, joy, said Mrs. Malloy . . ." [*She regards him incredulously*] What's the matter?

NETTIE: I never expected to hear that nonsense from *you!*

TIMMY: It beats swearing.

NETTIE: You used to cover your ears when your father said it.

TIMMY: [*With mock solemnity*] I'll never say it again.

NETTIE: *Don't talk to me like that! . . .* I'm sorry. I don't know what's wrong with me this morning. I don't think I slept well . . . Too much excitement—the party and all. [*She resumes the preparation of breakfast: pours batter on the waffle iron while he, still not recovered from her outburst, studies her*] Will you have bacon with it?

TIMMY: Just the waffles will be fine.

NETTIE: Did you like the party?

TIMMY: Yes.

NETTIE: I wish the house had looked better.

TIMMY: What's wrong with it?

NETTIE: It needs painting. The sofa's on its last legs. And the rugs . . . Well, now that you're here I'll get it all fixed up.

TIMMY: It looks fine to me.

NETTIE: I still can't believe you're here.

TIMMY: I find it a little hard to believe myself.

NETTIE: You *are* here?

TIMMY: Want to pinch me? . . . Go ahead. [*She hesitates. He holds out his hand*] Go on. [*She takes his hand*] Believe it now? [*She continues to hold his hand. He becomes uneasy*] Hey. [*Oblivious to his resistance, she still clings to his hand*] What are you doing? [*She persists. His agitation mounts*] Cut it out . . . *Cut it out!* [*He jerks free of her; immediately tries to make light of it*] One pinch to a customer . . . House rule. [*She regards him mutely*] The waffles must be ready; the light on the iron went out. [*She just looks at him*] Isn't that what it means when that little light goes out? [*She looks at him a moment more, then goes to the waffle iron, lifts the cover, starts to remove the waffles, stops, moves to a chair, sits, folds her hands in her lap and begins to cry*] What's the matter? . . . What's wrong? . . . What is it? . . . *What is it?*

NETTIE: [*Continuing to cry*] They stuck.

TIMMY: What?

NETTIE: Why did they have to stick today?

TIMMY: The waffles?

NETTIE: I can't remember the last time they stuck.

TIMMY: What's that to cry about?

NETTIE: I've looked forward to this morning for three years and nothing's right.

TIMMY: Why do you say that?

NETTIE: Not one thing.

TIMMY: What isn't right?

NETTIE: Not one single thing.

TIMMY: Will you please stop?

NETTIE: The things you've been saying—your attitude.

TIMMY: What things? What attitude?

NETTIE: You haven't even asked about Willis.

TIMMY: . . . How is he?

NETTIE: Every time I look at you, you avoid me.

TIMMY: [*Turning away*] That's ridiculous.

NETTIE: You're doing it now.

TIMMY: I am not!

NETTIE: How could you forget waffles were your favorite?

TIMMY: I just forgot.

NETTIE: Then you must have forgotten a lot of things.

TIMMY: *I'll tell you one thing I didn't forget.* [*She looks at him*] The dance. [*No reaction from her*] The one we were going to have the first morning I was home.

NETTIE: What made you think of that?

TIMMY: It's been on my mind all along.

NETTIE: I'll bet.

TIMMY: I was about to turn the radio on when you started crying.

NETTIE: I'll bet.

TIMMY: If you're through, I'll do it now. Are you through?

NETTIE: I haven't danced in so long I've probably forgotten how.

[He goes to the living room, snaps on the radio, dials to a band playing a slow fox trot, returns to the kitchen]

TIMMY: Shall we have a go at it?

NETTIE: I can't remember the last time I danced.

TIMMY: Come on.

NETTIE: You really want to?

TIMMY: Yes.

NETTIE: [Rising] You asked for it.

TIMMY: That-a-girl. [He puts his arms about her] Here we go. [They move smoothly, gracefully] Forgot how to dance—who you kidding?

NETTIE: I guess it's one of those things you never forget.

TIMMY: Remember this? [He goes into a maneuver that she follows perfectly] You've been taking lessons.

NETTIE: Of course.

[They dance from the kitchen into the living room]

TIMMY: Come here off-ten?

NETTIE: Foist time.

TIMMY: Me likewise . . . By yuhself?

NETTIE: Widda goil friend.

[The song ends]

ANNOUNCER'S VOICE: That's all the time we have on Dance Parade this morning. I hope—

[TIMMY *goes to the radio, dials, picks up a polka band going full blast*]

TIMMY: What do you say?

NETTIE: The spirit's willing.

TIMMY: Let's go! [*They take off*] Not bad . . . not bad.

NETTIE: What will the neighbors think?

TIMMY: The worst. [*The rhythm begins to accelerate*] We're coming into the home stretch. Hang on.

[*They move faster and faster*]

NETTIE: I'm getting dizzy.

[*As they whirl about the room they begin to laugh*]

TIMMY: Hang on.

NETTIE: I can't do any more.

[*The laughter grows*]

TIMMY: Hang on!

NETTIE: I can't!

[*The laughter becomes hysterical*]

TIMMY: Hang on! Hang on!

NETTIE: I can't! I . . .

[*They trip, collapse to the floor*]

TIMMY: You all right?

NETTIE: I think so.

[*Both breathe laboredly. The laughter subsides. He snaps the radio off, then sits on the floor facing her*]

TIMMY: I'm dead . . . absolutely dead.

NETTIE: So am I.

TIMMY: I can't remember the last time I laughed like that.

NETTIE: I can . . . We were driving to the lake and stopped at that dinky carnival.

TIMMY: The time I got you to go on that ride.

NETTIE: Your father thought we'd lost our minds. He kept begging the man to stop the engine.

TIMMY: Which made us laugh all the harder.

NETTIE: Know something?

TIMMY: What?

NETTIE: I really believe you're here now.

TIMMY: So do I.

NETTIE: What are you going to do today?

TIMMY: I don't know.

NETTIE: Why don't you come to Mama's with me?

TIMMY: We're going there for dinner tomorrow.

NETTIE: Willis would love to see you.

TIMMY: I'll see him tomorrow.

NETTIE: When we told him you were coming home he began to sing. It's the first time he's done that in months.

TIMMY: All right, I'll go.

NETTIE: We won't stay long.

TIMMY: All right.

[*The door opens and* JOHN *enters, sees them on the floor*]

JOHN: Well, hello. [TIMMY *rises*] Don't get up on my account.

TIMMY: We were dancing and fell down.

NETTIE: [*To* JOHN] What did you forget?

JOHN: Nothing.

NETTIE: [*Rising*] Why did you come back?

JOHN: I changed my mind. [*To* TIMMY] If you still want to go to the ball game, it's a date.

NETTIE: What about Ruskin?

JOHN: To hell with him. [*To* TIMMY] Still want to go?

TIMMY: Yes.

NETTIE: What about Willis?

JOHN: What *about* Willis?

NETTIE: Timmy was going to see him this afternoon.

TIMMY: I'll see him tomorrow.

NETTIE: I told him you'd be over today.

TIMMY: Before you even asked me?

NETTIE: I thought sure you'd want to.

TIMMY: You had no right to do that.

NETTIE: What will I tell him?

TIMMY: Tell him I'll be there tomorrow.

NETTIE: He'll be disappointed.

TIMMY: That's not my fault.

JOHN: The game starts at twelve.

TIMMY: Just have to get my tie.

NETTIE: You haven't eaten.

TIMMY: We'll grab something on the way.

[*He exits*]

JOHN: I came out of St. Francis and started for the subway. Was halfway there when I thought of Mr. Freeman: What wouldn't *he* give to be able to spend a day with his son? . . . It made me turn around and come back. [*She just looks at him*] You're mad. [*No reply*] You told me to take him to the game.

NETTIE: And you always do what I tell you.

JOHN: Bless us and save us.

[TIMMY, *knotting his tie, reappears, puts on his jacket, snaps to attention*]

TIMMY: Corporal Cleary reporting for duty.

JOHN: Kiss your mother good-bye.

TIMMY: That's not a duty. [*He kisses* NETTIE *on the cheek. She receives the kiss impassively*] So long, Mom.

JOHN: We won't be late.

[*He and* TIMMY *exit. She stands as she is*]

CURTAIN

SCENE TWO

TIME: *Late afternoon—the same day.*
AT RISE: JOHN *and* TIMMY *enter the apartment.* TIMMY *carries a bouquet of red roses.* JOHN *has just concluded a joke and they are both laughing.*

JOHN: I haven't told that one in years.

TIMMY: I was considered a very funny fellow. Thanks to you.

JOHN: Hello? . . . Anybody home? [*No answer*] Still at her mother's.

TIMMY: [*Indicating the roses*] I better put these in water.

[*They move into the kitchen*]

JOHN: Stand another beer?

TIMMY: Sure.

[*While* TIMMY *puts the roses in a vase,* JOHN *gets two cans of beer from the refrigerator*]

JOHN: [*Opening the beers*] How did you remember all those jokes of mine?

TIMMY: Just came to me.

JOHN: I don't remember most of them myself . . . [*Hands* TIMMY *a beer*] Here you go.

TIMMY: Thanks.

JOHN: What'll we drink to?

TIMMY: The Chicago Cubs.

JOHN: Think it'll help them?

TIMMY: Can it hurt?

JOHN: [*Raising the can*] To the Cubs.

TIMMY: To the Cubs.

[*They both drink*]

JOHN: Sixteen to three.

TIMMY: I'm still glad we went.

JOHN: So am I. [*Drinks*] That was a beautiful catch Ott made.

TIMMY: Yes.

JOHN: For a moment I thought he lost it in the sun. [TIMMY *says nothing.* JOHN *drinks*] So they really went for the old man's jokes?

TIMMY: Especially the ones about Uncle Mike.

JOHN: Such as?

TIMMY: The Pennsylvania Hotel gag.

JOHN: Columbus told that one to the Indians.

TIMMY: Uncle Mike was a famous man in our outfit.

JOHN: Joking aside, he was quite a good guy. Stood six three. Weighed close to two fifty.

TIMMY: I remember his picture.

JOHN: He was in the Spanish American War.

TIMMY: I know.

JOHN: Got hit by a bullet once that knocked him out. When he came to, he was lying in a field full of wounded men. The ones that were sure goners were marked with yellow tags so no one would waste time on them. The others had blue tags. Mike found a yellow tag around his waist. The fellow next to him who was unconscious had a blue one. Quick as a wink Mike switched the tags and . . . How about that? I'm telling *you* war stories. Go on—you do the talking.

TIMMY: About what?

JOHN: You must have seen some pretty bad things.

TIMMY: Not as much as a lot of others.

JOHN: Maybe you'd rather not talk about it.

TIMMY: I don't mind.

JOHN: I'd like to hear what you have to say.

TIMMY: I don't know how to begin.

JOHN: Anything that comes to mind.

TIMMY: Want to hear the bravest thing I ever did?

JOHN: Yes.

TIMMY: The first night we were in combat I slept with my boots off.

JOHN: Go on.

TIMMY: That's it.

JOHN: You slept with your boots off?

TIMMY: Doesn't sound like much, does it?

JOHN: Not offhand.

TIMMY: The fellows who eventually cracked up were all guys who couldn't sleep. If I hadn't decided to take my boots off I'd have ended up being one of them.

JOHN: I see.

TIMMY: Want to know the smartest thing I did?

JOHN: Sure.

TIMMY: I never volunteered. One day the lieutenant bawled me out for it. I said, "Sir, if there's anything you want me to do, you tell me and I'll do it. But if you wait for me to volunteer you'll wait forever."

JOHN: What did he say to that?

TIMMY: Nothing printable. The fact is I wasn't a very good soldier, Pop.

JOHN: You did everything they asked you.

TIMMY: The good ones do more. You'd have been a good one.

JOHN: What makes you say that?

TIMMY: I can tell.

JOHN: Well, thanks.

TIMMY: You're welcome.

JOHN: It's one of the big regrets of my life that I was never in the service.

TIMMY: I know.

JOHN: The day World War One was declared I went to the recruiting office. When they learned I was the sole support of the family, they turned me down.

TIMMY: I know.

JOHN: A lot of people made cracks. Especially guys like Clayton and Harper who waited to be drafted and then wangled safe jobs at Governor's Island and the Navy Yard . . . I fixed their wagons one night—sent the army flying one way and the navy the other. That was the last about slacking I heard from *them* . . . Still it bothers me—missing out on the whole thing . . . I keep wondering what difference it might have made in my life . . . And then I wonder how I'd have made out . . . I wouldn't have settled for a desk job. I'd have gotten to the front.

TIMMY: I'm sure of that.

JOHN: But once there, how would I have done?

TIMMY: Fine.

JOHN: How do you know?

TIMMY: You're a born fighter.

JOHN: They say a lot of fellows who were terrors as civilians turned to jelly when they heard those bullets.

TIMMY: Not you.

JOHN: It doesn't seem so. But you can't be sure . . . That's always bothered me. [*Drinks the last of his beer*] How about another?

TIMMY: Fine.

JOHN: Maybe we shouldn't.

TIMMY: Why?

JOHN: Your mother blames me for your getting sick last night; says I encouraged you to drink too much.

TIMMY: It wasn't what I drank. It was the excitement.

JOHN: That's what I told her.

TIMMY: *I'll* open two more.

JOHN: All right. [*While* TIMMY *gets the beers,* JOHN *regards the roses*] Her father used to send her roses every birthday . . . A dozen red ones . . . Never missed . . . Even at the end.

TIMMY: Tell her they were your idea.

JOHN: What?

TIMMY: Tell her the roses were your idea.

JOHN: Why?

TIMMY: She'll get a kick out of it . . . All right?

JOHN: If you like.

TIMMY: [*Handing him a beer*] Here you go.

JOHN: Thanks.

TIMMY: You call it this time.

JOHN: [*Raising his beer*] To the two nicest fellows in the house.

TIMMY: I'll buy that. [*They drink.* TIMMY *regards the can*] Funny how you acquire a taste for things.

JOHN: Yes.

TIMMY: When I was a kid I couldn't even stand the smell of beer.

JOHN: Believe it or not I was the same.

TIMMY: We seem to have gotten over it.

JOHN: Yes . . . Can I say something to you?

TIMMY: Sure.

JOHN: You won't take it the wrong way?

TIMMY: No.

JOHN: I owe you an apology.

TIMMY: For what?

JOHN: You were always sick; always home from school with one thing or another. I never thought you'd last in the army.

TIMMY: Neither did I.

JOHN: Really?

TIMMY: Really.

JOHN: When Dr. Goldman heard they took you he said it was ridiculous. When they put you in the infantry he said it was inhuman.

TIMMY: And when I survived?

JOHN: He said it was a miracle. [*They both laugh*] I don't think it was a miracle. I think we just underestimated you . . . Especially me . . . That's what I wanted to apologize for.

TIMMY: Remember that corny thing you used to recite—about how a boy thinks his father is the greatest guy in the world until he's fifteen. Then the doubts start. By the time he's eighteen he's convinced his father is the worst guy in the world. At twenty-five the doubts start again. At thirty it occurs to him that the old man wasn't so bad after all. At forty—

JOHN: What about it?

TIMMY: There's some truth to it.

JOHN: I think you've had too much to drink.

TIMMY: I'm not saying you're a saint.

JOHN: That's a relief.

TIMMY: But taking into account where you started from, and the obstacles you had to overcome, what you've done is something to be proud of.

JOHN: Well, thank you.

TIMMY: How many guys that you grew up with even turned out legitimate?

JOHN: Not many.

TIMMY: And most of *them* are still scraping along where they started.

JOHN: That's true.

TIMMY: How many years of school did you have?

JOHN: I had to quit after the fourth grade.

TIMMY: I've met college graduates who don't know nearly as much as you about the things that really count.

JOHN: Must have been Yale men.

TIMMY: I'm serious.

JOHN: Speaking of college . . . If you get into one of those big ones and it's more than the G.I. Bill pays for, I'll help you out.

TIMMY: Thanks.

JOHN: That's just between you and me.

TIMMY: Why?

JOHN: I don't want people getting wrong notions.

TIMMY: About what?

JOHN: That I'm loaded.

TIMMY: *Are* you loaded?

JOHN: Don't be ridiculous.

TIMMY: That doesn't answer my question.

JOHN: The question's ridiculous.

TIMMY: That's still no answer.

JOHN: No, I'm not loaded.

TIMMY: How much do you have?

JOHN: What?

TIMMY: How much money do you have?

JOHN: Is this your idea of a joke?

TIMMY: *No.*

JOHN: Then why are you doing it?

TIMMY: I don't want to take money from you if you can't afford it.

JOHN: I can afford it.

TIMMY: Some of the places I applied at are pretty expensive.

JOHN: I can afford it!

TIMMY: Then you must be loaded.

JOHN: *I am not loaded!*

TIMMY: We have a summer place, a car. Now you tell me you can afford any school in the country. You must be fairly loaded.

JOHN: *If I hear that word once more, I'm marching right out the door!*

[TIMMY *is unable to suppress his laughter any longer*]

TIMMY: You haven't changed a bit. [JOHN *regards him uncertainly*] You look as though I'd asked you to betray your country.

[JOHN, *against his will, smiles*]

JOHN: You son of a gun.

TIMMY: I really had you going.

JOHN: Some joke.

TIMMY: Oh, say, Pop.

JOHN: What?

TIMMY: How much *do* you have?

JOHN: *Enough's enough!* [TIMMY *laughs anew*] I think we better change the subject.

TIMMY: How did you meet Mother? [JOHN *regards him*] You said change the subject.

JOHN: You know all about that.

TIMMY: Just that you picked her up on the subway.

JOHN: It wasn't like that at all.

TIMMY: Then I don't know all about it.

JOHN: "Picked her up" makes it sound cheap.

TIMMY: Sorry.

JOHN: The first time I spoke to her was on the subway but there's more to it.

TIMMY: Tell me.

JOHN: Why?

TIMMY: I might become a writer and want to do a story about it someday.

JOHN: A writer?

TIMMY: Maybe.

JOHN: Well, that's the first I heard about that.

TIMMY: Me, too. Must be the beer . . . What year was it you met her?

JOHN: Nineteen twenty-one . . . A writer?

TIMMY: A writer . . . Where were you working then?

JOHN: At Emerson's . . .

TIMMY: And?

JOHN: One morning I saw her walk by. That afternoon she passed again. Same the next day. Turned out she worked around the corner. I . . . You sure you want to hear this?

TIMMY: Uh-huh.

JOHN: One evening I happened to be leaving at the same time she did. Turned out we took the same subway. She got off at Seventy-second Street . . . To make a long story short, I got a seat next to her one day and we started talking.

TIMMY: That's it?

JOHN: Yes.

TIMMY: Sounds like an ordinary pickup to me.

JOHN: *Well, it wasn't* . . . I left some things out.

TIMMY: Such as?

JOHN: I don't remember . . . It was twenty-five years ago.

TIMMY: The way I heard it, you followed her for a month before you finally got the nerve to speak.

JOHN: I thought you didn't know the story.

TIMMY: To convince her your intentions were honorable, you asked if you might call at her home? True or false? . . . Well?

JOHN: True. [*Chuckles*] You wouldn't believe how nervous I was. And she didn't make it any easier . . . Pretended the whole thing was a complete surprise. Bernhardt couldn't have done it nicer . . . Or looked nicer . . . All in blue . . . Blue dress, blue hat, blue shoes . . . Everything blue . . . Light blue . . . And dignified . . . One look at her, you knew she was a lady . . . My family *called* her The Lady. To their minds it was an insult. [*Regards* TIMMY] How did we get on this?

TIMMY: You were—

[*He is interrupted by the opening of the outside door.* NETTIE *enters*]

JOHN: Join the party.

[*She enters the kitchen*]

TIMMY: We're having a little hair of the dog.

NETTIE: How was the game?

JOHN: One-sided.

TIMMY: Pop was just telling me how you and he met.

[NETTIE *turns to* JOHN *questioningly*]

JOHN: He asked me.

TIMMY: [*To his mother, indicating his father*] His version is a little different from yours.

NETTIE: What do you mean?

TIMMY: He says *you* chased *him.*

NETTIE: That'll be the day.

TIMMY: Says you did everything but stand on your head to attract his attention. [NETTIE *is not sure now whether he's kidding or not*] That's what he said.

[NETTIE *looks uncertainly from* TIMMY *to* JOHN. *They break up simultaneously*]

NETTIE: You two!

JOHN: How about a beer?

NETTIE: No, thanks.

JOHN: Come on—

TIMMY: Be a sport.

NETTIE: All right.

JOHN: That-a-girl.

NETTIE: Just a glass. [*To* TIMMY, *while* JOHN *gets the beer*] What *did* he tell you?

TIMMY: He said you were dressed in blue and nobody ever looked nicer.

NETTIE: I'll bet.

TIMMY: [*To* JOHN] Didn't you say that?

JOHN: I'm a stranger here.

NETTIE: Did he tell you how he used his friend Eddie Barnes?

JOHN: Bless us and save us.

NETTIE: Every night they'd get on the subway, stand right in front of me, and have a loud conversation about how well they were doing in business.

JOHN: It wasn't every night.

NETTIE: Poor Eddie had to go an hour out of his way.

TIMMY: That's what I call a friend.

JOHN: The best I ever had. [*Extends a glass of beer to* NETTIE] Here you go. [*She stares past him*] Here's your beer.

[*She continues looking off. He follows her gaze to the roses*]

NETTIE: Where did they come from?

TIMMY: Pop got them . . . for you.

NETTIE: [*To* JOHN] You did?

JOHN: Yes.

[*She goes to the roses*]

NETTIE: They're beautiful . . . Thank you.

JOHN: You're welcome.

NETTIE: What made you do it?

JOHN: We happened to pass a place and I know you like them.

NETTIE: I haven't had red roses since Papa died. [*To* TIMMY] He used to send me a dozen on my birthday. Never missed.

TIMMY: I remember.

NETTIE: [*To* JOHN] Thank you.

JOHN: You're welcome.

NETTIE: I'm going to cry.

   [*She does*]

JOHN: You don't bring flowers—they cry. You do—they cry.

NETTIE: I'm sorry.

TIMMY: What's to be sorry?

NETTIE: He was the kindest, gentlest man that ever lived.

TIMMY: I know.

NETTIE: I'm all right now.

JOHN: [*Handing her the glass of beer*] Here's what you need.

NETTIE: Maybe so.

TIMMY: [*Raising his beer*] To happy days.

JOHN AND NETTIE: To happy days.

   [*They all drink*]

NETTIE: [*Regarding the roses*] They're just beautiful.

JOHN: [*Anxious to change the subject*] Talking of Eddie Barnes before, God rest his soul, reminds me of the time old Emerson put up a second-hand car for the man who sold the most coffee over a three-month period. I won it, but couldn't drive. Eddie said he'd teach me. We didn't get two blocks from the office when he ran broadside into an ice truck.

NETTIE: How about that ride to Connecticut? He practically killed us all.

JOHN: What was the name of the place we stayed at?

NETTIE: The Rainbow Grove.

JOHN: That's right. Big fat red-haired dame ran it.

NETTIE: Mrs. Hanlon.

JOHN: [*Mimicking Mrs. Hanlon à la Mae West*] "My friends all call me Daisy." [*He and* NETTIE *laugh*] I dubbed her the Will Rogers of Connecticut—she never met a man she didn't like.

[*They all laugh*]

NETTIE: Remember the night you, Eddie, and a couple of others picked her up, bed and all, and left her sleeping in the middle of the baseball field?

JOHN: In the morning when we went out to play, she was still there.

TIMMY: What did you do?

JOHN: We ruled that any ball hitting her on the fly was a ground rule double. [*They all laugh*] We had a lot of fun at that place.

NETTIE: Yes.

JOHN: I wonder if it's still there.

NETTIE: I wonder.

JOHN: Let's take a ride someday and see.

NETTIE: All right.

[*She starts to rise*]

JOHN: Where are you going?

NETTIE: Have to start supper.

JOHN: Forget it—we're eating out!

NETTIE: I bought a steak.

JOHN: It'll keep. [*To* TIMMY] Where would you like to go, Champ?

NETTIE: Maybe he has a date.

JOHN: Bring her along.

TIMMY: I don't have a date.

NETTIE: I thought you'd be seeing that Davis girl?

TIMMY: That's finished.

NETTIE: She was a nice girl.

JOHN: She was a dunce.

NETTIE: John!

TIMMY: Pop's right.

NETTIE: You men are terrible.

TIMMY: You're too kind.

JOHN: Well, where are we going?

TIMMY: You two settle it while I see a man about a dog.

[*He exits*]

JOHN: How about the Concourse Plaza?

NETTIE: All right.

JOHN: I had a nice day today.

NETTIE: I'm glad.

JOHN: He's quite a boy.

NETTIE: That's what I've been telling you for years.

JOHN: We talked about things. Really talked. The way Eddie and I used to . . . The hell with the Concourse Plaza! Let's go downtown! Let's go to the New Yorker!

NETTIE: You *are* in a good mood.

JOHN: Because I want to go downtown?

NETTIE: That and the roses.

JOHN: Are you going to talk about those roses all night?

NETTIE: I just wanted to thank you for them.

JOHN: You already have.

NETTIE: You sound as though you're sorry you got them.

JOHN: Don't be ridiculous.

NETTIE: Then what are you angry about?

JOHN: I'm just tired of hearing about them. A guy gets some roses —big deal.

NETTIE: You're embarrassed.

JOHN: I am not.

NETTIE: You did something nice and you're embarrassed.

JOHN: You don't know what you're talking about.

NETTIE: Don't worry, I won't tell anyone.

JOHN: *Nettie, please.*

NETTIE: All right, but I want to let you know how much I appreciate it.

JOHN: Good. I'm glad.

NETTIE: I do . . . I really do. [*On an impulse she touches his shoulder. The contact is mutually startling. Flustered, she turns away*] We haven't been to the New Yorker in years . . . I wonder if they still have the ice show? . . . Do you suppose we'll have any trouble getting in on a Saturday night?

[TIMMY *enters*]

TIMMY: What did you decide?

JOHN: We're going to the Hotel New Yorker.

TIMMY: Well, digga digga doo.

JOHN: After that we're going to the Diamond Horseshoe. And then the Sawdust Trail.

TIMMY: Sounds like our night to howl.

JOHN: That's what it is.

[*He howls*]

TIMMY: You call that a howl?

[*He howls louder. Now* JOHN *howls. Now* TIMMY. *Now* JOHN. *Now* TIMMY. *Each howl is louder than the last*]

CURTAIN

SCENE THREE

TIME: *Two A.M. Sunday morning.*
AT RISE: *The apartment is in darkness. From the hallway outside the apartment, we hear* TIMMY *and* JOHN *in loud but dubious harmony.*

TIMMY *and* JOHN: [*Offstage*] "Farewell, Piccadilly . . . Hello, Leicester Square . . . It's a long, long way to Tipperary . . . But my heart's right there."

NETTIE: [*Offstage*] You'll wake the Feldmans.

JOHN: [*Offstage*] Nothing could wake the Feldmans.

[TIMMY *and* JOHN *laugh*]

NETTIE: [*Offstage*] Open the door.

JOHN: [*Offstage*] Can't find my keys.

TIMMY: [*Offstage—giggling*] I can't find the door.

NETTIE: [*Offstage*] Honestly.

JOHN: [*Offstage*] Where would you be if you were my keys?

NETTIE: [*Offstage*] Here—I'll do it.

JOHN: [*Offstage*] Did you ever see such pretty hair?

NETTIE: [*Offstage*] Stop.

TIMMY: [*Offstage*] Beautiful hair.

NETTIE: [*Offstage*] Will you please let me open this door?

[*A key turns. The door opens.* NETTIE, *followed by* JOHN *and* TIMMY, *enters. She turns on the lights*]

JOHN: Home to wife and mother.

NETTIE: [*To* JOHN] Someday we'll break our necks because you refuse to leave a light.

TIMMY: [*Sings*] "By the light . . . [JOHN *joins in*] Of the silvery moon—"

NETTIE: That's just enough.

JOHN: Whatever you say, Antoinette.

NETTIE: I say to bed.

JOHN: Shank of the evening. [*He grabs her around the waist and manages a squeeze before she breaks away. Ignoring the look of censure she directs at him, he turns to* TIMMY] No sir, you can't beat a law degree. Springboard for anything.

TIMMY: So they say.

NETTIE: [*To* JOHN] Anyone can be a lawyer. How many people become writers?

JOHN: That's my point.

NETTIE: You should be proud to have a son who wants to try something different.

JOHN: Did I say I wasn't proud of him?

TIMMY: Abra ka dabra ka deedra slatter-in. [*They regard him*] The fellow in the red jacket who leads the horses to the post at Jamaica always says that when they reach the starting gate. Abra ka dabra ka deedra slatter-in. And here are your horses for the fifth race . . . Long as you can say it, you're not drunk . . . *Abra ka dabra ka deedra slatter-in.*

JOHN: Abra ka dabra . . .

TIMMY: Ka deedra slatter-in.

NETTIE: Honestly.

JOHN: Ka zebra—

TIMMY: Not zebra. Deedra . . . Ka deedra slatter-in . . . Abra ka dabra ka deedra slatter-in.

JOHN: Abra . . . ka dabra . . . ka deedra . . . slatter-in.

TIMMY: Faster.

JOHN: Abra, ka dabra, ka deedra, slatter-in.

TIMMY: Faster.

JOHN: Abra ka dabra ka deedra slatter-in.

NETTIE: Have you both lost your minds?

JOHN: Nothing wrong with us that a little nightcap wouldn't cure.

[*He enters the kitchen*]

NETTIE: [*Following him*] I'll nightcap you.

TIMMY: I can't bear to hear married people fight.

JOHN: [*To* NETTIE] We ought to go dancing more.

NETTIE: Now I know you're drunk.

TIMMY: [*Calling from the living room*] Who was it that used to call us The Four Mortons?

JOHN: [*Calling back*] Harold Bowen.

TIMMY: [*Staring at the audience*] I wish we were.

JOHN: [*To* NETTIE] Remember the first dance I took you to?

NETTIE: Of course.

JOHN: I'll bet you don't.

NETTIE: Of course I do.

TIMMY: [*Lost in contemplation of the audience*] I have this magical feeling about vaudeville.

JOHN: [*To* NETTIE] Where was it, then?

NETTIE: The Crystal Terrace.

JOHN: And what was the first song?

NETTIE: It's too late for quiz games.

TIMMY: It doesn't matter how cheap and tinny the show is . . . Soon as the house lights go down and the band starts up, I could cry.

JOHN: [*To* NETTIE] The first song we ever danced to was "Pretty Baby." A blond guy crooned it.

NETTIE: Through a gold megaphone.

JOHN: You *do* remember.

NETTIE: Of course.

[JOHN *moves to touch* NETTIE. *To elude him, she re-enters the living room. He follows*]

TIMMY: [*To the audience—á la Smith and Dale*] "I've got snew in my blood" . . . "What's snew?" . . . "Nothing. What's snew with you?"

NETTIE: [*To* JOHN—*indicating* TIMMY] What's he doing?

JOHN: Playing the Palace.

TIMMY: [*To the audience*] "Take off the coat, my boy . . . Take . . . off . . . the . . . coat . . . Tay-ake . . . o-f-f-f-f . . . the coat-t-t-t-t."

JOHN *and* TIMMY: "The coat is off."

NETTIE: [*To* TIMMY] Will you please go to bed?

TIMMY: [*To the audience*] In closing I would like to do a dance made famous by the inimitable Pat Rooney. [*Nods to* JOHN] Maestro, if you please.

[JOHN *begins to hum "The Daughter of Rosie O'Grady" as both he and* TIMMY *dance in the manner of Pat Rooney*]

NETTIE: John! Timmy! [*They stop dancing*] Mama expects us at twelve.

TIMMY: [*To the audience*] We're running a bit long, folks: No dance tonight. My mother thanks you. My father thanks you. My sister thanks you. And the Feldmans thank you. [*He goes into Jimmy Durante's closing song*] "Good night . . . Good night . . . Good night—"

NETTIE: *Good night.*

TIMMY: [*Kisses* NETTIE] Good night, Mrs. Cleary—whoever you are.

NETTIE: Good night, dear.

TIMMY: [*To* JOHN—*indicating the audience*] Tough house, but I warmed them up for you.

JOHN: Thanks.

TIMMY: Don't look now, but your leg's broken.

JOHN: The show must go on.

TIMMY: [*To* NETTIE—*indicating* JOHN] Plucky lad. [*Extends his hand to* JOHN] Honor to share the bill with you.

JOHN: [*Shaking with him*] Likewise.

TIMMY: Sleep well, chaps.

JOHN: Night, Champ.

NETTIE: Sure you don't want an Alka Seltzer?

TIMMY: Abra ka dabra ka deedra slatter-in . . . see you in the morning.

JOHN: With the help of God.

TIMMY: [*Moving toward his room*] Abra ka dabra ka deedra slatter-in . . . Abra ka dabra ka deedra slatter-in . . . And here are your horses for . . .

[*He enters his room, closes the door*]

NETTIE: Home two days and both nights to bed like that.

JOHN: He's entitled. You should hear some of the things he's been through. They overran one of those concentration camps—

NETTIE: I don't want to hear about it now.

JOHN: You're right. It's no way to end a happy evening.

NETTIE: I think we have some aspirin in the kitchen.

[*She moves into the kitchen. He follows, watches her take a bottle of aspirin from a cabinet*]

JOHN: You didn't say anything before about a headache.

NETTIE: I don't have a headache.

JOHN: Then what—

NETTIE: I read that if you put an aspirin in cut flowers they keep longer. [*She drops an aspirin in the vase, regards the roses*] I wonder what made you get them?

JOHN: I don't know.

NETTIE: There must have been some reason.

JOHN: I just thought it would be nice to do.

   [*She turns to him*]

NETTIE: It was.

   [*They regard each other a moment*]

JOHN: I like your dress.

NETTIE: You've seen it before.

JOHN: It looks different . . . Everything about you looks different.

NETTIE: What Mass are you going to?

JOHN: Ten o'clock.

NETTIE: [*Picking up the vase of roses and starting toward the living room*] I better set the alarm.

JOHN: Nettie? [*She turns to him*] I had a good time tonight.

NETTIE: So did I.

   [NETTIE *enters the living room and places the roses on a table*]

JOHN: [*Following her into the living room*] Did you really? Or were you putting it on for his sake?

NETTIE: I really did.

JOHN: So did I.

NETTIE: I'll set the alarm for nine-fifteen.

   [*She starts away again*]

JOHN: Now that he's back we'll have lots of good times.

   [*She stops*]

NETTIE: What's wrong between you and I has nothing to do with him.

JOHN: I didn't say it did.

NETTIE: We have to solve our own problems.

JOHN: [*Coming up behind her*] Of course.

NETTIE: They can't be solved in one night.

JOHN: [*Touching her*] I know.

NETTIE: One nice evening doesn't make everything different.

JOHN: Did I say it did?

    [*His lips brush the nape of her neck*]

NETTIE: I guess you don't understand.

JOHN: I forgot how nice you smelled.

NETTIE: You'll spoil everything.

JOHN: I want things right between us.

NETTIE: You think this is going to make them right?

JOHN: [*His hand moving to her breasts*] We have to start some place.

NETTIE: [*Breaking away*] Start?

JOHN: Bless us and save us.

NETTIE: *That's not my idea of a start.*

JOHN: Nettie, I want you . . . I want you like I never wanted anything in my life.

NETTIE: [*Covering her ears*] Stop.

JOHN: *Please?*

NETTIE: You're drunk.

JOHN: *Do you think I could ask again if I wasn't?*

NETTIE: I'm not one of your hotel lobby whores.

JOHN: If you were I wouldn't have to ask.

NETTIE: A couple of drinks, a couple of jokes, and let's jump in bed.

JOHN: Maybe that's my mistake.

NETTIE: How do you suppose Ruskin managed without you today?

JOHN: Maybe you don't want to be asked!

[*He seizes her*]

NETTIE: Let me alone.

JOHN: [*As they struggle*] *You've had the drinks! You've had the jokes!*

NETTIE: *Stop!*

[*She breaks free of him; regards him for a moment, then picks up the vase of roses and hurls them against the floor. The impact is shattering. They both freeze. For a moment there is silence. Now* TIMMY's *door opens*]

TIMMY: [*Entering*] What happened?

NETTIE: The roses . . . I knocked them over.

TIMMY: Sounded like a bomb.

NETTIE: I'm sorry I woke you. [TIMMY *bends to pick up a piece of the vase*] Don't . . . I'll clean up. You go back to bed. [*He hesitates*] Please.

TIMMY: All right . . . Good night.

NETTIE: Good night.

TIMMY: Good night, Pop.

[JOHN, *his back to* TIMMY, *remains silent.* TIMMY *hesitates a moment, then goes off to his room and closes his door*]

NETTIE: [*To* JOHN] You moved me this afternoon . . . When you brought the roses, I felt something stir I thought was dead forever. [*Regards the roses on the floor*] And now this . . . I don't understand.

JOHN: [*Without turning*] I had nothing to do with the roses . . . They were *his* idea.

[*She bends and starts to pick up the roses*]

CURTAIN

ACT TWO

SCENE ONE

TIME: *Nine-fifteen* A.M. *Sunday morning.*
AT RISE: JOHN *and* NETTIE *are at the breakfast table.*

JOHN: Coffee's weak.

NETTIE: Add water.

JOHN: I said *weak* . . . Waste of time bringing good coffee into this house . . . [*He looks for a reaction. She offers none*] I'm thinking about renting the lake house this summer . . . [*Still no reaction from her*] Business is off . . . [*Still no reaction*] Well, what do you say?

NETTIE: About what?

JOHN: Renting the lake house.

NETTIE: Timmy will be disappointed.

JOHN: How about you?

NETTIE: I'm in favor of it.

JOHN: Of course you are.

NETTIE: I wonder why.

[TIMMY *enters*]

TIMMY: Morning.

NETTIE: Good morning.

[TIMMY *kisses her*]

TIMMY: [*To* JOHN] Morning.

JOHN: Nice of you to join us.

TIMMY: My pleasure.

JOHN: This isn't a hotel. We have our meals at certain times.

[TIMMY *now senses his father's irritation*]

TIMMY: You should have woke me.

NETTIE: [*To* TIMMY] It's all right.

JOHN: Of course it is.

NETTIE: [*To* TIMMY, *who regards his father puzzledly*] Sit down.
[TIMMY *sits*] What do you want?

TIMMY: Coffee.

NETTIE: Just coffee?

TIMMY: Stomach's a bit shaky.

NETTIE: You should have taken that Alka Seltzer.

TIMMY: I'll be all right.

JOHN: Two days—two hangovers. Is that what they taught you in
the army?

TIMMY: [*To* JOHN] Cream, please? [JOHN *passes the cream*] Thank
you.

JOHN: I'm thinking of renting the lake house.

TIMMY: How come?

JOHN: I can use the money.

TIMMY: Oh . . .

JOHN: That all you're going to say?

TIMMY: What do you expect me to say?

JOHN: I thought that house meant something to you.

TIMMY: It does. But if you need the money—

JOHN: A bunch of strangers sleeping in our beds, using our things —doesn't bother you at all?

TIMMY: If it has to be it has to be.

JOHN: Of course! I forgot! What's a little summer cottage, after the earth-shattering things you've been through?

TIMMY: [*To* NETTIE—*holding up the cream pitcher*] Do you have more cream?

NETTIE: [*Taking the pitcher*] Yes.

JOHN: What do you want more cream for?

TIMMY: Coffee's strong.

JOHN: It's weak.

TIMMY: It's too strong for me. [NETTIE *returns the refilled pitcher to him*] Thanks.

   [*He adds cream to his coffee*]

JOHN: A few months in the army and they're experts on everything. Even coffee.

TIMMY: Who said that?

JOHN: By the time I was your age I was in the coffee business nine years . . . Nine years . . . When I was seventeen they sent me to Brazil for three months.

TIMMY: I know.

JOHN: I'd never even been out of New York before but I went down there on my own and did my job.

TIMMY: For Emerson, wasn't it?

JOHN: No uniform. No buddies. No Uncle Sam to lean on. Just myself . . . All alone in that strange place.

TIMMY: That's the time you grew the mustache to look older.

JOHN: Who's telling the story?

TIMMY: Sorry.

JOHN: Thirty-five years in the business and *he's* going to tell me about coffee.

TIMMY: I wasn't telling you anything about anything. I just said that for me, the coffee was too strong.

JOHN: It isn't strong!

TIMMY: [*To* NETTIE] What time's dinner?

NETTIE: Mama expects us at twelve.

JOHN: I suppose you'll wear your uniform.

TIMMY: It's the only thing I have that fits.

JOHN: Are you sure? I mean maybe you haven't grown as much as you think.

[TIMMY, *studiously trying to avoid a fight, turns to* NETTIE]

TIMMY: Ravioli?

NETTIE: And meat balls.

JOHN: G.I. Bill, home loans, discharge bonus, unemployment insurance—you boys did pretty well for yourselves.

NETTIE: They did pretty well for us, too.

JOHN: [*Sings*] "Oh, say can you see."

TIMMY: What's your point, Pop?

JOHN: The war's over.

TIMMY: I'll buy that.

JOHN: The world doesn't owe anyone a living—including veterans.

TIMMY: I'll buy that, too.

JOHN: Let the Jews support you.

TIMMY: Come again?

JOHN: Wasn't for them we wouldn't have gotten in it in the first place.

TIMMY: I thought you broke that record.

JOHN: Lousy kikes.

NETTIE: John!

TIMMY: [*To* NETTIE] I changed my mind—I'll have some toast.

JOHN: [*To* TIMMY] Don't tell me you've lost your great love for the Jews?

NETTIE: *Stop it!*

TIMMY: [*To* NETTIE] It's all right.

JOHN: How nice of you to let me talk in my own house. And me not even a veteran.

TIMMY: Would you mind telling me what you're mad about?

JOHN: Who's mad?

NETTIE: [*To* TIMMY] Anything on the toast?

TIMMY: Honey, if you've got it.

JOHN: A man states a few facts and right away he's mad.

NETTIE: [*At the cupboard*] How about strawberry jam?

TIMMY: No.

JOHN: If I get a halfway decent offer I might sell the lake house.

NETTIE: Peach?

TIMMY: All right.

JOHN: Hurry up with your breakfast.

TIMMY: What for?

JOHN: Mass starts in twenty minutes and you're not even dressed.

TIMMY: Mass?

JOHN: Mass.

TIMMY: I haven't been to Mass in over two years. You know that.

JOHN: Lots of bad habits you boys picked up that you'll have to get over.

TIMMY: Not going to Mass isn't a habit I picked up. It's a decision I came to after a lot of thought.

JOHN: What way is that for a Catholic to talk?

TIMMY: I haven't considered myself a Catholic for quite a while.

JOHN: Must be something wrong with my ears.

NETTIE: [To JOHN] You knew this was coming. Why pretend it's such a shock?

JOHN: Now there's a familiar alliance. [To TIMMY] So you've outgrown the Faith?

TIMMY: It doesn't answer my needs.

JOHN: Outgrown your old clothes and outgrown the Faith.

TIMMY: Pop, will you listen to me—

JOHN: Billions of people have believed in it since the beginning of time but it's not good enough for you.

TIMMY: It's not a question of good enough.

JOHN: What do you say when people ask what religion you are?

TIMMY: Nothing.

JOHN: You say you're nothing?

TIMMY: Yes.

JOHN: The Clearys have been Catholics since . . . since the beginning of time. And now you, a Cleary, are going to tell people that you're nothing?

TIMMY: Yes.

JOHN: *You're an atheist!*

NETTIE: John!

JOHN: When you come to the blank after religion on those college applications, put down atheist. Make a big hit in those Ivy League places, from what I hear.

TIMMY: I'm not an atheist.

JOHN: Then what are you?

TIMMY: I don't know . . . But I'd like a chance to find out.

JOHN: You don't know what you believe in?

TIMMY: Do *you?*

JOHN: Yes.

TIMMY: Tell me . . . Well, go on!

JOHN: I believe in the Father, the Son and the Holy Ghost . . . I believe that God created man in his own image . . . I—

TIMMY: Pop, look . . . if your faith works for you, I'm glad. I'm very glad. I wish it worked for me . . . But it doesn't.

JOHN: Do you believe in God—yes or no?

TIMMY: I don't believe in Heaven, or Hell, or Purgatory, or—

JOHN: *Yes or no?*

TIMMY: I believe there's something bigger than myself. What you call it or what it is I don't know.

JOHN: Well, this is a fine how-do-you-do.

NETTIE: [*To* JOHN] Yesterday you said he was a man. A man has a right to decide such things for himself.

JOHN: "Good morning, Father Riley." "Good morning, Mr. Cleary. I understand your boy's out of service." "Yes, Father." "Where is he this fine Sunday morning, Mr. Cleary?" "Home, Father." "Is he sick, Mr. Cleary?" "No, Father." "Then why isn't he here in church, Mr. Cleary?" "He's become an atheist, Father."

TIMMY: I'm not an atheist!

JOHN: Whatever you are, I won't have it! I'm the boss of this house. If you want to go on living here you'll do as I say. And I say you're going to church with me this morning.

NETTIE: [*To* JOHN] *Do you know what you're doing?*

JOHN: [*To* NETTIE] Keep out! [*To* TIMMY] Well?

NETTIE: [*To* TIMMY] Don't pay any attention to him.

TIMMY: [*To* NETTIE] It's all right. [*To* JOHN] I'll go to church with you. [*Rises*] Be out in a minute.

[*He starts from the room*]

JOHN: Forget it!

TIMMY: What?

JOHN: I said forget it. The Lord doesn't want anybody in His house who has to be dragged there. [*To* NETTIE *as he puts on his jacket*] Score another one for your side.

TIMMY: It has nothing to do with her.

JOHN: [*To* TIMMY] Wait till you're down on all fours someday— you'll be glad to see a priest then.

[*He starts out*]

NETTIE: We'll meet you at Mama's.

JOHN: I won't be there.

NETTIE: She expects us.

JOHN: We all have our disappointments.

TIMMY: I said I'd go with you.

[JOHN *exits, slamming the door*]

NETTIE: Now what was that all about?

TIMMY: [*Furious with himself*] I should have gone with him.

NETTIE: I'll never understand that man.

TIMMY: Why didn't I just go? Why did I have to make an issue?

NETTIE: It wasn't your fault.

TIMMY: It never *is*.

NETTIE: When he's in one of those moods there's nothing anyone can do.

TIMMY: The alliance, he called us.

NETTIE: Everyone's entitled to their own beliefs.

TIMMY: That's what we must seem like to him—an alliance. Always two against one. Always us against him . . . Why?

NETTIE: If you're through eating, I'll clear the table.

TIMMY: Didn't you hear me?

NETTIE: Evidently your father's not the only one who got up on the wrong side of the bed this morning.

TIMMY: *I'm not talking about this morning.*

NETTIE: There's no need to shout.

TIMMY: You, and him, and me, and what's been going on here for twenty years . . . It's got to stop.

NETTIE: What's got to stop?

TIMMY: *We've* got to stop ganging up on him.

NETTIE: Is that what we've been doing?

TIMMY: You said you've never understood him.

NETTIE: And never will.

TIMMY: Have you ever really tried? . . .

NETTIE: Go on.

TIMMY: Have you ever tried to see things from his point of view?

NETTIE: What things?

TIMMY: The lake house, for instance.

NETTIE: The lake house?

TIMMY: It's the pride and joy of his life and you're always knocking it.

NETTIE: Do you know why?

TIMMY: Because he bought it without consulting you.

NETTIE: Drove me out to this Godforsaken lake. Pointed to a bungalow with no heat or hot water and said, "That's where we'll be spending our summers from now on."

TIMMY: An hour's ride from New York City isn't exactly God-forsaken.

NETTIE: It wasn't an hour's ride twenty years ago.

TIMMY: The point is, would he have gotten it any other way? If he had come to you and said he wanted to buy a cottage on a lake in New Jersey, would you have said yes?

NETTIE: I might have.

TIMMY: No. Not if it had been a palace with fifty servants.

NETTIE: I don't like the country.

TIMMY: We'd have spent every summer right here.

NETTIE: My idea of a vacation is to travel—see something new.

TIMMY: You had a chance to see Brazil.

NETTIE: That was different.

TIMMY: The fellow who took that job is a millionaire today.

NETTIE: And still living in Brazil.

TIMMY: Which is not to be compared with the Bronx.

NETTIE: So it's my fault we're not millionaires.

TIMMY: Who knows—your mother might have loved Brazil! [*This causes her to turn from him*] You violently objected to moving from Yorkville to the Bronx . . . Why?

NETTIE: [*Clearing the table in an effort to avoid him*] I hate the Bronx.

TIMMY: [*Pursuing her*] But you insisted that your mother move up here.

NETTIE: They tore down her building. She had to move somewhere.

TIMMY: Except for summers at the lake, have you ever gone two days without seeing her?

NETTIE: Only because of Willis. [*He starts from the room*] Where are you going?

TIMMY: To get dressed. Then I'm going to church and apologize to him for acting like a fool.

NETTIE: You'll be at Mama's for dinner?

TIMMY: Only if he'll come with me.

NETTIE: You disappointed Willis yesterday. You can't do it again.

TIMMY: Oh yes I can!

NETTIE: How cruel.

TIMMY: Not as cruel as your dragging me over there every day when I was little. And when I was bigger, and couldn't go every day, concentrating on Sunday. "Is it too much to give your crippled cousin one day a week?" And when I didn't go there on Sunday, I felt so guilty that I couldn't enjoy myself anyway . . . I hate Sunday, and I don't think I'll ever get over it. But I'm going to try.

NETTIE: How fortunate for the cripples in this world that everyone isn't as selfish as you.

TIMMY: Why do you keep calling him a cripple? That's not the worst thing wrong with Willis. It's his mind. He's like a four-year-old.

NETTIE: Can a four-year-old read a book?

TIMMY: [*Pressing his attack relentlessly*] Yes, he reads. After you drilling him every day for twenty years. But does he have any idea what he's reading about? . . . If you and the rest of them over there want to throw your lives away on him, you go ahead and do it! But don't try and sacrifice me to the cause! [NETTIE, *stunned by* TIMMY's *assault, exits from the kitchen, disappears into the bedroom. Immediately regretful at having vented his feelings so strongly,* TIMMY *moves into the living room; is pondering the best way to apologize, when* NETTIE, *carrying a pocketbook, appears, takes a coat from the hall closet, puts it on*] Where are you going? [*No answer*] Your mother doesn't expect us till twelve. [*No answer*] Give me a minute to dress and I'll go with you. [*As* NETTIE *reaches for her pocketbook,* TIMMY *also reaches for it in an effort to prevent her departure. He wrests it from her. As he does so, his face registers surprise*] This is like lead. [*He opens the bag, regards the contents, looks at her puzzledly]* You've got all your coins in here . . . You're taking your coins . . . What for? *[She extends her hand for the bag. He surrenders it. She moves toward the door] Will you please say something?*

NETTIE: Thank you for the roses.

[*She exits*]

CURTAIN

SCENE TWO

TIME: *Ten P.M. Sunday.*
AT RISE: TIMMY, *highball glass in hand, whiskey bottle on the coffee table before him, sits on the sofa in the living room. It is plain that he has been drinking for some time.* JOHN, *cold sober, moves about the room nervously.*

TIMMY: I remember sitting here like this the night she went to have John.

JOHN: Why would she just walk out and not tell anyone where she was going?

TIMMY: I was six.

JOHN: Without any reason.

TIMMY: Dr. Goldman came at midnight and took her to the hospital.

JOHN: It doesn't make sense.

TIMMY: After they left, I started to cry. You did, too.

JOHN: It's not like her.

TIMMY: I asked you if you loved her. You nodded. I asked you to say it. You hesitated. I got hysterical. To quiet me you finally said, "I love her."

JOHN: Maybe she's at Sophie's.

TIMMY: No. [JOHN *regards him questioningly*] I called Sophie.

JOHN: [*Looking at a pocket watch*] It's after ten.

TIMMY: I called everybody.

JOHN: She's been gone twelve hours.

TIMMY: They all said they'd call back if they heard from her.

JOHN: If she's not here by eleven o'clock I'm calling the police.

TIMMY: I wonder what difference it would have made if John lived.

JOHN: I wonder what department you call.

TIMMY: I remember you and I going to visit her at the hospital on a Sunday afternoon. I had to wait downstairs. First time I ever heard the word incubator . . . In-cubator.

JOHN: I guess you call Missing Persons.

TIMMY: As we left the hospital and started down the Concourse, we ran into an exotic Spanish-looking woman whom you'd met on one of your trips to Brazil. She was a dancer. Very beautiful. You and she spoke awhile and then you and I went to a movie. Fred Astaire and Ginger Rogers in *Flying Down to Rio*.

JOHN: What are you talking about?

TIMMY: I always thought that was a coincidence—meeting a South American woman and then seeing a picture about Rio . . . *Was* it a coincidence?

JOHN: What?

TIMMY: [*Sings*] "Hey Rio, Rio by the sea-o. Got to get to Rio and I've got to make time."

JOHN: You're drunk.

TIMMY: Abra ka dabra ka deedra slatter-in.

JOHN: Fine time you picked for it.

TIMMY: A bunch of chorus girls stood on the wings of a silver plane singing that song—"Hey Rio. Flying down to Rio—"

JOHN: You're the last one who saw her. The police will want to question you.

TIMMY: She left the house at ten A.M., your Honor. Didn't say boo but I assumed she was going to her mother's. Brown coat. Brown hat. When I got to her mother's, she wasn't there. They hadn't seen her—hadn't heard from her. I had two helpings of ravioli and meat balls. Came back here to wait. When she didn't call by three o'clock I started to worry—

JOHN: And drink.

TIMMY: *When she didn't call by three o'clock I started to worry* . . . I tried to get in touch with my father. Called all the bars I could think of—"Is Mr. Cleary there?" . . . "If he comes in would you please tell him to call his house?" . . . It was like old times.

JOHN: I told you—I had dinner and went to a movie.

TIMMY: "*Is* Mr. Cleary there?"—Shows how long I've been away. You never say, "*Is* Mr. Cleary there?" You say, "Let me speak to Mr. Cleary." As though you *knew* he was there.

JOHN: I was at a movie.

TIMMY: Did it have a happy ending?

JOHN: *Gilda*, with Rita Hayworth and Glenn Ford.

TIMMY: I didn't ask you what it was.

JOHN: At the Loew's Paradise.

TIMMY: *I didn't ask you what it was!*

JOHN: What's the matter with you?

TIMMY: [*About to pour another drink*] Join me?

JOHN: No, and I think you've had enough.

TIMMY: First time I ever saw you refuse a drink.

JOHN: I want you to stop.

TIMMY: But you're powerless to stop me. It's a lousy position to be in, *I* know.

JOHN: That's your last one.

[*He starts to remove the bottle*]

TIMMY: Take it and I leave!

[JOHN *hesitates, puts the bottle down*]

JOHN: Joy, joy, said Mrs. Malloy.

TIMMY: Louder louder, said Mrs. . . . What rhymes with louder?

JOHN: You were sick Friday night. Sick last night.

[*The phone rings. By the time* TIMMY *gets to his feet* JOHN *is picking up the receiver*]

JOHN: [*On the phone*] Hello? . . . Oh . . . [*The abrupt disinterest in his voice causes* TIMMY *to sit down*] Nothing . . . I said we haven't heard anything . . . I know how long she's been gone . . . Of course I'm concerned . . . *I don't care how I sound—I'm concerned* . . . If she's not here by eleven, that's what I'm going to do . . . That's a comforting bit of information. [*He hangs up, returns to the living room*] Her mother again. Wanted to let me know how many muggings there's been lately.

TIMMY: I've got it! Earl Browder.

JOHN: What?

TIMMY: Louder, louder, said Mrs. Earl Browder.

JOHN: I'm glad you can take the whole thing so calmly.

TIMMY: To quote a famous authority: "I don't care how I sound—I'm concerned."

JOHN: [*Regards his watch*] Ten after ten.

TIMMY: Trouble with you is you haven't had enough experience in these matters.

JOHN: Where the devil can she be?

TIMMY: I'm an old hand.

JOHN: Never done anything like this before in her life.

TIMMY: All those nights I lay in bed waiting for your key to turn in the door. Part of me praying you'd come home safe, part of me dreading the sound of that key because I knew there'd be a fight.

JOHN: I'll give her a few minutes more.

TIMMY: All those mornings I woke up sick. Had to miss school. The boy's delicate, everyone said, has a weak constitution.

JOHN: I'll give her till half-past.

TIMMY: From the day I left this house I was never sick. Not once. Took me a long time to see the connection.

JOHN: Where can she go? She has no money.

TIMMY: Wrong.

JOHN: What?

TIMMY: Nothing.

JOHN: You said wrong.

TIMMY: [*Sings*] "Hey Rio. Rio by the—"

JOHN: I want to know what you meant.

TIMMY: She took her coins.

[JOHN *goes into the bedroom*]

TIMMY: [*Quietly*] "Hey Rio. Rio by the sea-o."

[JOHN *reappears*]

JOHN: Why didn't you mention it before?

TIMMY: Slipped my mind.

JOHN: Over fifty dollars in dimes and quarters, and she took them all.

TIMMY: Person could go quite a ways with fifty dollars.

JOHN: You saw her take them?

TIMMY: Yes.

JOHN: Didn't it strike you as peculiar?

TIMMY: Everything strikes me as peculiar.

JOHN: There's something you're not telling me.

TIMMY: We all have our little secrets.

JOHN: There *is* something!

TIMMY: Take you and your money for instance.

JOHN: I want to know what it is.

TIMMY: For all I know, we're millionaires.

JOHN: I want to know why she walked out.

TIMMY: Just between us chickens, how much do you have?

[TIMMY *reaches for the bottle to pour another drink, but* JOHN *snatches it out of his reach*]

JOHN: Answer me.

TIMMY: If you don't put that bottle down, I'm leaving.

JOHN: I want an answer!

TIMMY: [*Rising*] See you around the pool hall.

JOHN: [*Shoving him down hard on the sofa*] *I want an answer!*

TIMMY: Hell of a way to treat a veteran.

JOHN: I've taken all the crap from you I'm going to.

TIMMY: You want an answer. I want a drink. It's a deal.

[*He reaches for the bottle but* JOHN *keeps it from him*]

JOHN: First the answer.

TIMMY: I forget the question.

JOHN: Why did your mother leave this house? . . . Well?

TIMMY: We had an argument.

JOHN: About what?

TIMMY: I don't remember.

JOHN: Probably something to do with your drinking.

TIMMY: Yes, that's what it was. She said I drank too much.

JOHN: She's right.

TIMMY: Yes.

JOHN: I never thought I'd see the day when you and she would argue.

TIMMY: Neither did I.

JOHN: She didn't say where she was going? Just took the coins and left?

TIMMY: That's right.

JOHN: Beats me.

[*He starts toward the kitchen*]

TIMMY: Where you going?

JOHN: To get something to eat.

TIMMY: *Eat?*

JOHN: I didn't have any supper.

TIMMY: A minute ago you were so worried you couldn't even sit down.

JOHN: I'm just going to have a sandwich.

TIMMY: Have a banquet!

JOHN: What are you getting mad at *me* for? You're the one who argued with her.

TIMMY: Which absolves you completely! She might jump off a bridge but *your* conscience is clear!

JOHN: A person doesn't take a bunch of change along if they're planning to do something like that.

TIMMY: *She thanked me for the roses!* [JOHN *just looks at him*] Don't you have any consideration for other people's feelings?

JOHN: Consideration?

TIMMY: Don't you know how much it pleased her to think they were from you?

JOHN: *You* talk about consideration?

TIMMY: How could you do it?

JOHN: Do you have any idea how I looked forward to this morning? To Mass, and dropping in at Rafferty's afterwards with you in your uniform?

TIMMY: Always the injured party.

JOHN: You'll be the injured party in about two minutes.

TIMMY: I already am.

JOHN: Real rough you had it. Good food. Good clothes. Always a roof over your head.

TIMMY: Heigh-ho, everybody, it's count-your-blessings time.

JOHN: I'll tell you what rough is—being so hungry you begged. Being thrown out in the street with your few sticks of furniture for all the neighbors to enjoy. Never sleeping in a bed with less than two other people. Always hiding from collectors. Having to leave school at the age of ten because your father was crippled for life and it was your job to support the house . . . You had it rough, all right.

TIMMY: The subject was roses.

JOHN: Where I couldn't have gone with your advantages . . . What I couldn't have been.

TIMMY: I still want to know why you told her about the roses.

JOHN: We were having words and it slipped out.

TIMMY: Words about what? . . . Well?

JOHN: Stop pushing or I'll tell you.

TIMMY: Go on! Go on!

JOHN: *The humping I'm getting is not worth the humping I'm getting.*

TIMMY: [*Rising*] You pig!

JOHN: I'm warning you!

TIMMY: *You pig!* [JOHN's *right hand shoots out, catches* TIMMY *hard across the side of his face.* NETTIE *enters*] Bon soir. [NETTIE *regards them with an air of detached curiosity*] Had one too many . . . Lost my ka deedra slatter-in.

[NETTIE *removes her hat and coat*]

JOHN: Where have you been? [NETTIE *lays her hat, coat and pocketbook on a chair in the foyer*] I was about to call the police. [NETTIE *gives no indication that she even hears him*] I want to know where you've been. [NETTIE *moves through the living room, stops in front of* TIMMY, *who has just poured himself another drink*] Are you going to tell me where you've been?

NETTIE: You wouldn't believe me.

JOHN: Of course I'd believe you.

NETTIE: [*To* TIMMY] You don't look well.

TIMMY: Appearances are deceiving—I feel terrible.

JOHN: Why wouldn't I believe you?

NETTIE: You just wouldn't.

JOHN: Tell me and see.

NETTIE: I went to the movies.

JOHN: Go on.

NETTIE: That's it.

JOHN: You just went to the movies?

NETTIE: That's right.

JOHN: You've been gone over twelve hours.

NETTIE: I stayed for several shows.

JOHN: Are you trying to tell me you were at a movie for twelve hours?

NETTIE: I knew you wouldn't believe me.

TIMMY: *I* believe you.

NETTIE: Thank you.

TIMMY: What did you see?

NETTIE: That means you *don't* believe me.

TIMMY: No, I guess not.

JOHN: I demand to know where you were.

NETTIE: I went to the Hotel Astor, picked up a man, had a few drinks, a few jokes, went to his room and—

JOHN: Stop it!

NETTIE: I was just getting to the best part.

JOHN: You're making a fool of yourself.

NETTIE: Is there anything I could say that you *would* believe?

TIMMY: Say you took a bus downtown, walked around, visited a museum, had dinner, went to Radio City, and came home.

NETTIE: I took a bus downtown, walked around, visited a museum, had dinner . . .

TIMMY: Went to Radio City and came home.

NETTIE: Went to Radio City and came home.

TIMMY: I'll buy that. [*To* JOHN] If you had any sense you'd buy it, too.

JOHN: I don't have any sense. I'm just a poor, ignorant slob whose wife's been missing twelve hours—and I want to know where she was.

TIMMY: What difference does it make?

JOHN: Stay out of this!

TIMMY: How?

JOHN: [*To* NETTIE] What are you going to tell your mother?

NETTIE: Nothing.

JOHN: The poor woman's almost out of her mind.

TIMMY: There's a joke there some place.

JOHN: At least call her and say you're home.

NETTIE: She'll want an explanation. When I tell her, she won't believe me any more than you did.

JOHN: I'll believe you when you tell the truth.

TIMMY: What *is* truth? [JOHN *shoots him a furious glance*] Sorry.

NETTIE: I'll tell you this . . . In all my life, the past twelve hours are the only real freedom I've ever known.

TIMMY: Did you enjoy it?

NETTIE: Every moment.

TIMMY: Why did you come back?

NETTIE: I'm a coward.

JOHN: *Will somebody tell me what's going on?*

TIMMY: [*To the audience*] You heard the question. [*He peers out into the theatre, points*] Up there in the balcony. The bearded gentleman with the . . . [*He stops abruptly, rubs his stomach, regards the audience wanly*] Sorry, folks, but I'm about to be ill.

     [*He hastens offstage.* NETTIE *follows him.* JOHN *takes advantage of her absence to examine her pocketbook, is going through it when she returns*]

NETTIE: He wouldn't let me hold his head, ordered me out of the bathroom, locked the door.

JOHN: What happened to your coins?

NETTIE: I spent them.

JOHN: How?

NETTIE: I took a bus downtown, walked around, visited a museum—

     [JOHN *interrupts her by slamming the pocketbook to the table*]

JOHN: Wasn't for his drinking, none of this would have happened.

NETTIE: Why do you say that?

JOHN: If he didn't drink, you and he wouldn't have argued. [*She regards him uncomprehendingly*] Isn't that why you left? Because you had an argument about his drinking?

NETTIE: We had an argument, but it wasn't about drinking.

JOHN: What was it about?

NETTIE: You, mostly.

JOHN: Go on.

NETTIE: He thinks I don't give you enough credit . . . Feels you're quite a guy . . . Said we had to stop ganging up on you.

[JOHN *turns away*]

CURTAIN

SCENE THREE

TIME: *Two* A.M. *Monday.*
AT RISE: *The apartment is in darkness. Now a crack of light appears beneath the door to* TIMMY's *room. The door opens.* TIMMY, *in pajamas, emerges, goes to the living room, turns on a lamp which reveals* NETTIE, *in nightgown and robe, sitting on the sofa.*

NETTIE: I couldn't sleep.

TIMMY: Neither could I. Came out to get a magazine.

NETTIE: You feel all right?

TIMMY: Yes.

[*He looks through a pile of magazines, selects one*]

NETTIE: What time is it?

TIMMY: Almost two . . . Are *you* all right?

NETTIE: Yes.

TIMMY: Well, I guess I'll turn in. [*She offers no comment*] Good night.

[*Again, no response. He starts away*]

NETTIE: Isn't there something you want to tell me?

TIMMY: As a matter of fact there is . . . but it'll keep till morning.

NETTIE: You've decided to leave.

TIMMY: Yes.

NETTIE: When?

TIMMY: It's not a sudden decision.

NETTIE: When are you leaving?

TIMMY: In the morning. [*He looks for a comment from her, but she remains silent*] This fellow I went to high school with has a flat on Twenty-second Street. His roommate just got married and he's looking for a replacement. I figured . . . [*He becomes aware that she isn't listening*] Hey . . . [*Still no reaction*] Hey. [*She regards him absently*] Give you a penny for them.

NETTIE: An apple core.

TIMMY: What?

NETTIE: An apple core . . . I was due to start working for a law firm. Passed all the interviews and had been notified to report for work the following Monday . . . On Sunday, my sister and I were walking in the park when a blond boy who had a crush on me but was too bashful to speak, demonstrated his affection by throwing an apple core which struck me here. [*She indicates the area beneath her left eye*] When I woke up Monday morning, I had the most beautiful black eye you ever saw. Too embarrassed to start a new job looking like that, I called in sick. They called back to say the position had been filled by someone else . . . The next job I found was the one that brought your father and I together . . . I often think of that apple core and wonder what my life would be like if it had never been thrown.

TIMMY: Everyone wonders about things like that.

NETTIE: I was going in early to type up some dictation I'd taken the night before . . . Front Street was deserted . . . As I walked, I had the sensation of being watched . . . I glanced up at the office I was passing and saw this young man, your father, staring down . . . He regarded me intensely, almost angrily, for a moment, then

suddenly realized I was looking back at him and turned away . . .
In that moment, I knew that that young man and I were not
suited to each other . . . And at the same time I knew we would
become involved . . . that it was inevitable.

TIMMY: Why? You had others to choose from.

NETTIE: Oh yes . . . All gentle, considerate men. All very much like
my father . . . One of them was the baker from Paterson, New
Jersey, that we always joke about.

TIMMY: The fellow who brought a hatbox full of pastries whenever
he called on you.

NETTIE: Yes . . . What a sweet man . . . How he begged me to
marry.

TIMMY: What was it that drew you to Pop?

NETTIE: I think it was his energy . . . a certain wildness. He was
not like my father at all . . . I was attracted . . . and I was afraid.
I've always been a little afraid of him . . . And then he was clearly
a young man who was going places. Twenty-four when I met him
and making well over a hundred a week. Great money in those
days and his prospects were unlimited . . . Money was never plen-
tiful in our house. We weren't poor like his people, you understand. Never without rent, or food, or tickets to the opera, or nice
clothes. But still we weren't well-to-do . . . My father brought
home stories from the hotel about the various bigwigs who came
in and what they wore and how they talked and acted. And we
went to the opera. And we had friends who were cultured.
Musical Sunday afternoons. Those were Papa's happiest moments
. . . Yes, I liked good things. Things that the baker from Paterson
and the others could never give me . . . But your father surely
would. The way he was going he would be a millionaire . . . That
was his dream, you know—to be a millionaire by the time he was
forty . . . Nineteen twenty-nine took care of that. He was never
quite the same afterwards . . . But when I met him he was cock
of the walk. Good-looking, witty young Irishman. Everyone liked
him and those who didn't at least feared him because he was a
fierce fellow. Everyone wanted to go into business with him. Everyone wanted to be social with him . . . He was immediately at
home on a ship, a train . . . in any bar. Strangers thought he was

magnificent. And he *was* . . . as long as the situation was impersonal . . . At his best in an impersonal situation . . . But that doesn't include the home, the family . . . The baker from Paterson was all tongue-tied outside, but in the home he would have been beautiful . . . Go to bed now.

[*He kisses her on the forehead*]

TIMMY: Want the light off?

NETTIE: Please.

[*He moves to the lamp, is about to turn it off, hesitates*]

TIMMY: When I left this house three years ago, I blamed *him* for everything that was wrong here . . . When I came home, I blamed *you* . . . Now I suspect that no one's to blame . . . Not even me. [*He turns the light off*] Good night.

NETTIE: Good night.

[TIMMY *exits into his room, closes the door. For a moment there is silence. Then . . .*]

NETTIE: "Who loves you, Nettie?" . . . "You do, Papa." . . . "Why, Nettie?" . . . "Because I'm a nice girl, Papa."

CURTAIN

SCENE FOUR

TIME: *Nine* A.M. *Monday.*
AT RISE: JOHN *and* NETTIE *are in the kitchen.*

JOHN: One word from you . . . That's all it would take.

NETTIE: I'm not so sure.

JOHN: Try.

NETTIE: No.

JOHN: Do you want him to go?

NETTIE: No.

JOHN: Then say something before it's too late.

NETTIE: What do you want for breakfast?

JOHN: Who cares about breakfast?

NETTIE: Timmy's having scrambled eggs.

JOHN: *Am I the only one who's upset by what's going on here?*

NETTIE: No.

JOHN: Then how can you just stand there?

NETTIE: Would you feel better if I wept?

JOHN: You'll weep when he's gone.

NETTIE: But not now.

JOHN: All I want you to do is tell him how you feel.

NETTIE: He knows that.

JOHN: You won't speak to him.

NETTIE: I can't.

JOHN: You're the one who'll miss him most . . . With me it's different. I've got my business.

NETTIE: I envy you.

JOHN: Just ask him to wait a couple of days and think it over.

NETTIE: After a couple of days, we'd be used to having him around. It would be that much harder to see him leave.

JOHN: He might change his mind. Might not want to leave.

NETTIE: He has to leave sometime.

JOHN: But not now. Not like this.

NETTIE: Twenty-second Street isn't the end of the world.

JOHN: If he leaves this house today I don't want to see him ever again!

NETTIE: If you say that to him, make it clear that you're speaking for yourself.

JOHN: Who's this fellow he's moving in with?

NETTIE: A boy he knew at high school.

JOHN: Everything he wants right here—food, clothing, a room of his own. And he has to move into a dirty cold-water flat.

NETTIE: I think I understand his feeling.

JOHN: Home two days and gone again. The neighbors will have a field day.

NETTIE: I'm going in to call him now.

JOHN: I want to see him alone.

NETTIE: If you're wise you won't start a row.

JOHN: *I want to see him alone.*

NETTIE: All right.

[*She goes inside, knocks at* TIMMY's *door*]

TIMMY's VOICE: Come in.

[*She enters the room, closes the door after her*]

JOHN: [*Addresses* TIMMY's *place at the table*] I understand you've decided to leave us . . . [*Not satisfied with this opening, he tries another*] What's this nonsense about your leaving? . . . [*And another*] Your mother tells me you're moving out. I would like to know why. [*The first part of this opening pleases him, the last part doesn't. He tries variations on it:*] I *demand* to know why . . . Would you be so good as to tell me why? . . . Why, God-damn it?

[*He is puzzling over these various approaches when* TIMMY *enters the kitchen*]

TIMMY: Good morning.

JOHN: Morning.

TIMMY: Mother said you wanted to see me.

JOHN: Sleep well?

TIMMY: Yes.

JOHN: Good . . .

TIMMY: You wanted to see me?

JOHN: Mother says you're leaving.

TIMMY: Yes.

JOHN: Rather sudden, isn't it?

TIMMY: Not really.

JOHN: Mind telling me why?

TIMMY: I just think it's best.

JOHN: For who?

TIMMY: Everyone.

JOHN: Crap! [TIMMY *starts from the room*] Wait. [*The note of entreaty in his voice causes* TIMMY *to halt*] I didn't mean that . . . The fact is I don't blame you for wanting to leave. I had no business hitting you.

TIMMY: That's not why I'm going.

JOHN: If there was any way I could undo last night, I would.

TIMMY: It's not a question of last night.

JOHN: If I had to do it over again I'd cut my arm off.

TIMMY: Pop, listen—

JOHN: I don't know what gets into me sometimes.

TIMMY: Pop! [JOHN *looks at him*] I'm not leaving because of anything that happened last night . . . I always intended to leave.

JOHN: You never mentioned it.

TIMMY: I planned to stay a couple of weeks and then go.

JOHN: A couple of days isn't a couple of weeks.

TIMMY: It's not like I'm going to China.

JOHN: Why two days instead of two weeks?

TIMMY: Because I know that if I stay two weeks I'll *never* leave.

JOHN: If it's what I said yesterday, about me being the boss and you'd have to do what I said—forget it.

TIMMY: It's not that.

JOHN: I was just letting off steam.

TIMMY: *It's not that.*

JOHN: As far as I'm concerned you're a man—you can come and go as you please, do as you please. That goes for religion, drinking, anything.

TIMMY: How can I make you understand?

JOHN: Even girls. I know how it is to be your age. Give me a little advance notice and I'll see that you have the house to yourself whenever you want.

TIMMY: Pop, for Chrisake.

JOHN: [*Flares momentarily*] *What kind of language is that?* [*Then hastily*] I'm sorry. I didn't mean that. Talk any way you want.

TIMMY: I don't know what to say to you.

JOHN: What I said yesterday about the Jews, I was just trying to get a rise out of you.

TIMMY: I know.

JOHN: The time those bums from St. Matthew's jumped the I-cash-clothes man. I was the one who saved him.

TIMMY: I know.

JOHN: Whole crowd of people watching but I was the only one who did anything.

TIMMY: Do you think I could forget that?

JOHN: Stay another week. Just a week.

TIMMY: I can't.

JOHN: Stay till Wednesday.

TIMMY: No.

JOHN: Do you have any idea how your mother looked forward to your coming home?

TIMMY: Yes.

JOHN: Then how can you do it?

TIMMY: We're just going around in circles.

JOHN: What happens to the lake house?

TIMMY: What do you mean?

JOHN: Without you, what's the good of it?

TIMMY: I'll be spending time there.

JOHN: I thought we'd have a real summer together like before the war.

TIMMY: You're making this a lot tougher than it has to be.

JOHN: *Did you expect me to say nothing? Like her?* . . .

TIMMY: Are you through?

JOHN: [*Trying a new tack*] I know what the trouble is. You know what the trouble is? You're like me . . . Stubborn . . . All the Clearys are stubborn . . . Would rather die than admit a mistake . . . Is that a fact? Yes or no?

TIMMY: I don't know.

JOHN: [*Points to himself*] Well, here's one donkey who's seen the light. I've been wrong in my dealings with you and I admit it.

TIMMY: Pop—

JOHN: Not just wrong last night, but all along. Well, those days are gone forever, and I'll prove it . . . You know how much money I have?

TIMMY: I don't want to know.

JOHN: Fourteen thousand three hundred and fifty-seven dollars.

TIMMY: Pop!

JOHN: Plus a bit more in stocks . . . Now *you* admit that *you* made a mistake—admit you don't really want to leave and we'll forget the whole thing.

TIMMY: I *don't* want to leave.

JOHN: See—

TIMMY: But I'm leaving.

JOHN: [*Turning away*] *Then go and good riddance!*

TIMMY: Listen to me.

JOHN: The sooner the better.

TIMMY: *Listen to me!* [*Pauses—then goes on quietly, intensely*] There was a dream I used to have about you and I . . . It was always the same . . . I'd be told that you were dead and I'd run crying into the street . . . Someone would stop me and ask why I was crying and I'd say, "My father's dead and he never said he loved me."

JOHN: [*Trying unsuccessfully to shut out* TIMMY's *words*] I only tried to make you stay for her sake.

TIMMY: I had that dream again last night . . . Was thinking about it this morning when something occurred to me that I'd never thought of before.

JOHN: She's the one who'll miss you.

TIMMY: It's true you've never said you love me. But it's also true that I've never said those words to you.

JOHN: I don't know what you're talking about.

TIMMY: I say them now—

JOHN: *I don't know what you're talking about.*

TIMMY: I love you, Pop. [JOHN's *eyes squeeze shut, his entire body stiffens, as he fights to repress what he feels*] I love you. [*For another moment,* JOHN *continues his losing battle, then, overwhelmed, turns, extends his arms.* TIMMY *goes to him. Both in tears, they embrace.* NETTIE *emerges from* TIMMY's *room, closes the door with emphasis to alert them to her approach.* TIMMY *and* JOHN *separate hastily*]

JOHN: What I said about the money—that's strictly between us.

TIMMY: I understand.

[NETTIE *enters the kitchen. If she is aware of anything unusual in their appearance or manner, she doesn't show it*]

NETTIE: Ready for breakfast? [*They nod*] Sit down. [*They sit. She pours the coffee*]

NETTIE: [*To* TIMMY] Your bag is packed and ready to go.

TIMMY: I've changed my mind.

NETTIE: What?

TIMMY: I've changed my mind. I'm going to stay a few more days.

JOHN: I'm afraid that's out of the question. [TIMMY *and* NETTIE *regard him incredulously*] When you said you were going, I called the painters. They're coming in to do your room tomorrow . . . You know how hard it is to get the painters. If we don't take them now, it'll be months before they're free again.

TIMMY: Then I guess I better leave as scheduled.

JOHN: I think so. [*To* NETTIE] Don't you?

NETTIE: . . . Yes.

[JOHN *tastes the coffee—scowls*]

JOHN: I don't know why I bother to bring good coffee into this house. If it isn't too weak, it's too strong. If it isn't too strong, it's too hot. If it isn't . . .

CURTAIN

Brendan Behan's

BORSTAL BOY

Adapted for the Stage by Frank McMahon

Mrs. Brendan Behan, in her kindness, gave permission for this adaptation. Tomás Mac Anna, artistic director of the Abbey Theatre, endowed it with magic. The Abbey Theatre, Dublin, gave birth to it.

Brendan Behan and Frank McMahon

At the age of fourteen, Brendan Behan—one of the most colorful and controversial of modern Irish writers—became a messenger for the Irish Republican Army. When he was sixteen, he was sent by the I.R.A. to blow up the shipyards at Liverpool. Arrested there, he was jailed and then sentenced to three years at a Borstal (reformatory for boys). It is these years that he vividly recorded in an autobiography of his late teens, *Borstal Boy*—published in 1958—on which Frank McMahon's play is based.

Originating at the Abbey Theatre, Dublin, in 1967, the play was acclaimed by the Irish press with such statements as: "The dramatization has all the pulsating life of the Behan original . . . One of the most inventive, original and dashing productions to appear on the Dublin stage for some time . . . Three hours of brilliant theatre . . . The Abbey, of a certainty, has a world winner on its hands."

Borstal Boy enjoyed the longest consecutive run in the seventy-two-year history of the celebrated theatre and, subsequently, was presented for a guest engagement at the Theatre of Nations Festival in Paris.

With a number of members of the original cast (including Niall Toibin and Frank Grimes who, respectively, played the older and younger Brendan Behan) the play opened in New York on March 31, 1970, and once again it was warmly welcomed by most critics. *Time* magazine's correspondent reported that *"Borstal Boy* is full of the warm stuff of life, brave and craven, joyous and sorrowing, abased one moment and noble the next. You don't have to be Irish to laugh and cry with it."

John Chapman of the New York *Daily News* voted it "a lovely piece for the stage, filled with song and sorrow, profane at times and tender at others . . . and, of course, thoroughly Irish."

Hobe Morrison reported in *Variety:* "The late Brendan Behan's book of autobiographical sketches, *Borstal Boy*, artfully dramatized by Frank McMahon and eloquently played by an international cast, is one of the most enthralling and moving plays of recent seasons."

The New Yorker's Brendan Gill described it as: "An exceedingly skillful adaptation of the Behan book . . . It has been Mr. McMahon's brilliant notion to give us not one Behan but two—the idealistic, teen-age Behan bungling his first bombing assignment in Liverpool and suffering torture and imprisonment as a result, and the Behan of thirty-odd years, fat, satiric, tenderhearted . . ."

Their colleagues echoed the sentiment that here was "a warm and wonderful show" that had both "point and diversion," all adding up to "a touching and entertaining piece of theatre" making it "a distinguished addition to the Broadway season.

The play won the 1970 Tony Award as well as the New York Drama Critics' Circle Award for best play of the 1969–70 season.

Brendan Behan was born in Dublin on February 9, 1923. The son of a housepainter, he had little formal education and was a nonconformist most of his life.

His first play, *The Quare Fellow*, a powerful tragi-comedy set in a Northern Irish prison, was an immediate success, leading critics to hail the author as "Ireland's most exciting new playwright since Sean O'Casey." The drama had its American première at the Circle in the Square, New York, in 1958.

His second play, *The Hostage*, stirred even more acclaim. Opening in London in 1959, it ran for a total of 452 performances. The Broadway production opened in 1960, and a subsequent Off-Broadway revival (1961) was given for 545 performances.

In addition to *Borstal Boy*, the author's other published works include: a novel, *The Scarperers*; a second autobiography, *Confessions of an Irish Rebel*; and *Hold Your Hour and Have Another*.

Brendan Behan died in Dublin in 1964 at the age of forty-one.

Frank McMahon is a native New Yorker who now makes his home in Ireland. After graduating from Fordham University, he served in the United States Navy in World War II. He has been an executive with NBC, and most recently, with Irish Television. At present, he runs his own publishing house in Dublin.

Borstal Boy represents Mr. McMahon's first play for the legitimate theatre.

Borstal Boy was first presented on October 10, 1967, at the Abbey Theatre in Dublin. It was first presented in New York City on March 31, 1970, by Michael McAloney and Burton C. Kaiser, in association with the Abbey Theatre of Dublin, at the Lyceum Theatre. The cast was as follows:

BEHAN (*Brendan Behan as an older man*)	*Niall Toibin*
BRENDAN (*Brendan Behan in his youth*)	*Frank Grimes*
SHEILA	*Patricia McAneny*
MRS. GILDEA	*Mairin D. O'Sullivan*
I.R.A. MEN	*Brendan Fay*
	Liam Gannon
	Don Billet
	Michael Cahill
LIVERPOOL LANDLADY	*Phyllis Craig*
INSPECTOR	*John MacKay*
DETECTIVE VEREKER	*Dean Santoro*
SERGEANT	*Joseph Warren*
CHARLIE MILLWALL	*Bruce Heighley*
FIRST WARDER, MR. WHITBREAD	*Francis Bethencourt*
SECOND WARDER, MR. HOLMES	*Arthur Roberts*
CALLAN	*Liam Gannon*
TUBBY	*Kenneth McMillan*
PRISON CHAPLAIN	*Stephen Scott*
LIBRARY WARDER	*Brendan Fay*
BROWNY	*Terry Lomax*
DALE	*James Woods*
JAMES	*Drout Miller*
PRISON GOVERNOR	*John MacKay*
VOICE OF JUDGE	*Brendan Fay*
WELSH WARDER, MR. HACKNELL	*Arthur Roberts*
GOVERNOR OF THE BORSTAL	*Stephen Scott*
WARDER O'SHEA	*Joseph Warren*
PRIEST	*Don Perkins*
COOK	*Kenneth McMillan*
IMMIGRATION MAN	*Brendan Fay*
WARDER'S WIFE	*Amy Burke*

HARTY	*Norman Allen*
JOE	*Drout Miller*
JOCK	*Don Billet*
RIVERS	*Liam Gannon*
SHAGGY	*Terry Lomax*
CRAGG	*Dean Santoro*
CHEWLIPS	*Michael Cahill*
TOM MEADOWS	*James Woods*
KEN JONES	*George Connolly*

CROWDS, NEWSBOYS, POLICEMEN, OTHER WARDERS, ETC.: *Tom Signorelli, Richard Yesso, Marilyn Crawley, Richard Yanko, Roslyn Dickens, Peter Hock*

Production Directed and Designed by Tomás Mac Anna
Associate Producer: Joyce Sloane
Set Supervision and Lighting by Neil Peter Jampolis
Costume Supervision by Robert Fletcher

ACT ONE

The many scenes begin in the streets of Liverpool in the summer of 1939, when the Irish Republican Army was engaged in its bombing campaign to free Northern Ireland; then to Dublin, and back to Liverpool—to a boarding house, Walton Jail, and the Liverpool court.

ACT TWO

Most of the action takes place at Hollesley Bay, a boys' Borstal (detention home for juvenile delinquents) in England. The final scenes take place aboard a ship headed for Ireland and on the Dublin quayside.

ACT ONE

As the curtain rises, a portrait of BRENDAN BEHAN *and a solitary cell and bed without mattress come into view. Then the stage goes dark, and the props and scenery are removed.*

BEHAN: [*Offstage, singing*]
Oh, listen to me story,
'Tis about a stout young lad
Who up and joined the I.R.A.
Just like his fighting dad,
But all the rebels taught him
With their patriotic talk,
Was to fix a stick o' gelignite
On an oul' alarm clock

[*A clock is heard ticking ominously offstage. Suddenly there is an explosion. People are running, screaming and shouting. Police whistles are heard. A crowd gathers.* NEWSBOYS *run in*]

NEWSBOYS: I.R.A. outrage! Bomb explosion Liverpool! I.R.A. terrorist captured! Another I.R.A outrage in Liverpool! I.R.A. terrorist injured by his own bomb!

[*From the outskirts of the crowd, a familiar figure comes forward to address the audience. It is the elder* BRENDAN BEHAN. *The crowd clears the stage*]

BEHAN: That poor fellow was a Dubliner called Jerry Gildea, a clerk in Guinness' Brewery. He volunteered to go active in England for the period of his summer holidays—a fast whip over via the boat, a time bomb planted in a railway or a dock warehouse and back to the office. Begod there's many a man became a Senator for less. But the inscrutable ways of the Lord being what they are, the first day he was in Liverpool an incendiary primer ex-

ploded in his pocket, and with half his face burned off he was
savaged and nearly lynched by the populace, who apparently disapproved of having the dump burned about their ears. (*Young*
BRENDAN BEHAN *enters and is caught in an early morning shaft of
sunlight*] At that time I was being trained in an old castle the
I.R.A. had taken over at Killiney, near Bernard Shaw's cottage,
looking away over the Irish Sea. Shaw said that no man was ever
the same after seeing it at dawn or sunset. You could sing that if
you had an air to it. I know a good many besides meself that are
not the same after seeing it, some of them being hung or shot or
gone mad, or otherwise unable to tell the difference. Anyway, I
was detailed to break the news to Gildea's mother . . . His cousin
escorted me to the house. A lovely girl—just my weight, in fact, if
I could screw up the courage to try.

[SHEILA, *a young Dublin girl of eighteen, comes in.* BRENDAN
goes to meet her]

BRENDAN: Hello, Sheila.

SHEILA: Hello. [*After a silence*] Well, come on. [*They walk around*]
He got fifteen years.

BRENDAN: There'll be a vacant stool in Guinness' for a while to
come.

SHEILA: That's a rotten thing to say. Maybe it'll happen to yourself
some day.

BRENDAN: M-m-maybe.

BEHAN: And all the people at home will say, "Ah, sure, God help
poor Brendan. Wasn't I only talking to him a week ago. Bejaysus
wasn't he a great lad all the same—and he only sixteen!"

SHEILA: [*After another pause*] It's not in the paper. About Jerry,
I mean.

BRENDAN: It's in the paper all right. [*Shows her*] There. Look.

SHEILA: But it says Clarence Rossiter.

BRENDAN: Yeh. All the I.R.A. use mostly Norman names. Could be
Irish or English. Like D'Arcy or Dillon.

BEHAN: I knew a Connemara man who christened himself Thomas de Quincey. He could hardly speak English.

[BRENDAN *and* SHEILA *walk on a little more*]

BRENDAN: We . . . We don't have to rush, do we? I mean, why all the hurry? Such a nice evening.

SHEILA: She was expecting him home today.

BRENDAN: I know.

SHEILA: She doesn't even know Jerry was in the Movement.

BRENDAN: I know. It's going to be v-v-v-very h-h-h-hard.

BEHAN: A man needs to keep his heart up in a moment like this. Go on.

[BRENDAN *kisses her on the cheek*]

SHEILA: That's enough, now. [BRENDAN *grabs her to kiss her again. She breaks away*] You should be ashamed of yourself, and you an I.R.A. man. Especially at a time like this.

BRENDAN: Aw, come on, Sheila. Just one.

SHEILA: No.

BRENDAN: I'll make an awful eejit of meself now, telling his mother . . . You should have let me.

SHEILA: What do you take me for? Come on! (*They reach* MRS. GILDEA'S *house.* SHEILA *knocks*] She's coming.

MRS. GILDEA: [*Comes out*] Sheila. It's nice to see you.

SHEILA: Aunty, this is an . . . er . . . friend of mine, Brendan Behan.

MRS. GILDEA: You're welcome, Brendan. Come in, both of you, and I'll make you a cup of tea.

BRENDAN: Er . . . no . . . n-n-no, ma'am . . . I . . . er . . . never drink tea.

SHEILA: Brendan has a message for you, Aunty.

BRENDAN: Well . . . no . . . n-n-not exactly . . . er . . .

SHEILA: It's about Jerry. Go on, Brendan. [*Pauses*] Well, go on. Tell her.

BRENDAN: M-m-m-Mrs. Gildea, y-y-your son, J-j-j-Jerry, w-w-was—

MRS. GILDEA: [*Easily*] Yes, lad?

BRENDAN: Y-y-your s-s-son, J-j-j-Jerry—

MRS. GILDEA: [*Proceeding to help out*] Ah, sure, God help us, take your time, son. My son, Jerry, was—?

BRENDAN: H-h-h-he was—

MRS. GILDEA: He was delayed by the boat, was he? Ah, sure, you could expect that this time of year. I'm told the crowds of the world does be in the Isle of Man.

BRENDAN: H-h-h-he w-was—

MRS. GILDEA: Nice place, too, and a nice class of people, be all accounts. Talk Irish, and all, some of them. More nor I could do. Though the cats doesn't have any tails.

BRENDAN: [*Desperate*] He was s-s-s-sen—

MRS. GILDEA: God knows, they must be the queer-looking beasts. Still, everyone to their fancy, as the old one said when she kissed the ass.

BRENDAN: [*Catching her by the sleeve*] H-h-he w-w-was s-s-sent—

MRS. GILDEA: God help you, and such a nice boy, too. Maybe, it'd be God's Holy Will that you'd grow out of it. Sure, you're not finished growing yet.

BRENDAN: He was s-s-sentenced—

MRS. GILDEA: Sentenced?

BRENDAN: [*In a rush*] To f-fifteen years in Liverpool today.

MRS. GILDEA: Jerry . . . sentenced in Liverpool? . . . But . . .

BRENDAN: He . . . he was . . . in . . . in . . . t-t-t-the I.R.A., Mrs. Gildea. He . . . he had an accident—

MRS. GILDEA: Mother of God!

BRENDAN: H-he w-w-w-was caught, Mrs. Gildea.

MRS. GILDEA: Sweet mother of Jesus, comfort me this night!

[*She goes off, weeping, supported by* SHEILA]

SHEILA: You could have broken it easier to her, couldn't you?

BRENDAN: Jaysus!

[BRENDAN *stands alone. Four* I.R.A. MEN *in trench coats come to him, one with a suitcase. He opens it*]

I.R.A. MAN: It's all there. Gelignite, detonators, potassium chloride, sulphuric acid. And a brand new alarm clock. Make sure you get rid of them first if there's trouble. Understand?

BRENDAN: Yes.

SECOND I.R.A MAN: Travel permit and instructions—in Gaelic. Good luck.

I.R.A. MEN: Up the Republic!

BRENDAN: Up the Republic!

[*They shake hands with him and leave*]

I.R.A. MAN: Oh, I nearly forgot. Your ticket.

BRENDAN: [*Alone, looking at ticket*] Dublin-Liverpool, third class. One way! Jaysus!

[BEHAN *sings the song "Old Alarm Clock" as young* BRENDAN *makes his way through crowds of people, as if on the streets of Liverpool. A* POLICEMAN *sees him with his suitcase, and starts to follow him*]

BEHAN: [*Sings*]

When first I came to Liverpool
In the year of thirty-nine,
The city looked so wonderful
And the girls were so divine,
I walked on air among them
And of me they did take stock,
But they didn't see me gelignite
And me oul' alarm clock.

NEWSBOYS: Great victory for Royal Navy! German battleship scuttled! *Graf Spee* sunk off Argentine! Great British sea victory!

[*The crowds are clearing away, and suddenly* BRENDAN *is
alone in the center of the stage. The lighting changes to show
a room with a bed and a rickety chair. The* LANDLADY, *a middle-aged, sharp-featured woman, is making the bed*]

BEHAN: [*Singing*]
*Tomorrow down be Cammell Lairds
If I only get the chance,
I'll show you how me small machine
Can make the coppers dance:
It ticks away politely
Till you get an awful shock,
And it ticks away the gelignite
In me oul' alarm clock.*

[BRENDAN *knocks on the door; the* LANDLADY *opens it*]

BRENDAN: My name is Brendan Behan, ma'am!

LANDLADY: Oh, come in, Mr. Behan. You'll be more than comfortable here, Mr. Behan. But you must remember one thing: one
thing all my lodgers must remember. I shut the hall door every
night regularly at half past ten of the clock, and then we all kneel
down and say the rosary. Being from Ireland, of course you'll join
us. The other lodger always does—wouldn't miss a night.

BRENDAN: Yes, ma'am.

LANDLADY: Especially the three Hail Marys I always add for holy
purity.

BEHAN: Three Hail Marys for holy purity and the protection of her
person and modesty! You'd think half the men in Liverpool were
running after her, panting for a lick of her big buck teeth! [*The*
INSPECTOR, DETECTIVE VEREKER *and the* SERGEANT *appear and knock
on the door*] Get rid of the stuff!

LANDLADY: [*Opens the door for the men*] Oh God, oh Jesus, oh Sacred Heart! Boy! There's gentlemen below to see you!

[BRENDAN *frantically grabs the suitcase and starts to run with
it*]

INSPECTOR: Grab him, the bastud! [*The* DETECTIVE *seizes* BRENDAN. *The* INSPECTOR *opens the case and takes out the clock*] Got a gun, Paddy?

BRENDAN: If I'd have had a gun, you wouldn't have come through that door so shagging easy!

INSPECTOR: [*Sighing*] Turn him over. [*The* DETECTIVE *begins to frisk* BRENDAN *violently*] No, not you, Vereker—Sergeant.

[*The* SERGEANT *searches* BRENDAN *efficiently but without fuss, even along the seams of his fly. From an inside pocket, he extracts* BRENDAN's *money, travel permit, cigarettes and a letter. He hands the letter to the* DETECTIVE]

DETECTIVE: Gaelic! [*Infuriated*] You bloody bastud, how would you like to see a woman cut in two by a plate-glass window?

BEHAN: Maybe I should have answered, "What about bloody Sunday, when the Black and Tans machine-gunned a football crowd in our street?" I had it all ready too, but the old stutter let me down.

SERGEANT: Well, Paddy, there are people gathered 'round this house, and I don't think they mean you any good. [*He snorts*] We'll get you to the Assizes all right, safe and sound. Take no heed of them. [*He sits down on the bed with a grunt*] We'll sit here awhile. [*He indicates to* BRENDAN *to sit beside him*] I wish to Christ I was your age, Paddy, I'd have something better to do than throwing bombs around. How old are you?

BRENDAN: I'm sixteen, and I'll be seventeen in February.

SERGEANT: So they sent you over here, you silly little twerp, while the big shots are in America, going around spouting and raking in the dollars and living on the fat of the land.

[*The* INSPECTOR *takes* BRENDAN's *cigarettes and tosses them to him*]

INSPECTOR: Have a fag, Paddy. They'll take them off you soon enough in the Walton Prison.

SERGEANT: [*Pointing his pipe at the suitcase*] You're a silly lot of chaps, going on with this. You don't even know why you're bloody well doing it. It's supposed to be about partition. Northern Ireland, about the six counties. Right? [BRENDAN *nods*] Well, I've interviewed a lot of your fellows and God blind old Reilly if one of them could even name the bloody things. Not all six, they couldn't. Go on, now, you. The whole six, mind.

BRENDAN: You want me to name them now?

SERGEANT: Yeah, go on.

BRENDAN: [*Slowly*] Antrim . . . Armagh . . .

SERGEANT: Right, that's two you've got.

BRENDAN: Down . . . Derry . . . Fermanagh and . . .

SERGEANT: Right, five you got. Come on, the last one—

BRENDAN: Down, Derry and Fermanagh and . . .

SERGEANT: [*Triumphantly*] There you are, Paddy, what did I tell you.

BEHAN: I left out County Tyrone, for he was a nice old fellow.

BRENDAN: I'd like to make a statement.

BEHAN: Propaganda for the cause. It would look well at home, too.

SERGEANT: [*Taking out a notebook*] Go on, Paddy.

BRENDAN: My name's not Paddy. My name is Brendan Behan. I came over here to fight for . . . for . . . for . . .

[*The* SERGEANT *scribbles all this down furiously. The* DETECTIVE *glares at* BRENDAN]

BEHAN: For the Irish Workers' and Small Farmers' Republic.

BRENDAN: For the Irish Workers' and Small Farmers' Republic . . .

BEHAN: For a full and free life, North and South, and for the removal of the baneful influence of British imperialism from Irish affairs!

BRENDAN: For . . . for . . . [*Desperate*] God save Ireland!

SERGEANT: Now, what's all this about small farmers? I never seen a small farmer, Irish or English. They're all bloody big fellows with bull's-'eads on 'em, from eating bloody great feeds and drinking cider.

INSPECTOR: Look here, Paddy, I'm an Irishman, the same as you. I'm from Cork. Ever heard of the O'Sullivans?

BRENDAN: O'Sullivan's a Cork name, sir.

INSPECTOR: So it is—but what kind of name is Behan?

BRENDAN: It's a very Irish name, sir. Literary family once prominent in South Leinster. From "beach," meaning a bee, one who keeps bees.

INSPECTOR: I don't read Irish, Behan, nor do I speak it. A lot of good it would do me if I did.

BEHAN: It might help you to read that frigging document.

INSPECTOR: I suppose you realize you can go to jail for the best part of your life over this business? One of your crowd is lying under sentence of death in Birmingham. For a cowardly murder.

BRENDAN: [*Quietly*] It was no murder.

DETECTIVE: It was no murder? [*With mounting anger*] To put a bomb in a crowded street and kill five innocent people? You bloody little—[*He raises his hand to strike*]—I'll give you murder!

[*The* SERGEANT *and* INSPECTOR *jump forward to restrain him*]

INSPECTOR: All right, Vereker!

DETECTIVE: [*Regaining control*] All right, Inspector, all right. Don't you come that stuff here, Behan. You're not with your murder-gang pals in Dublin or Belfast now.

INSPECTOR: [*Reasonably*] Listen, Behan, you're only a boy, and your leaders are safe home in Ireland, or in America. We don't want to be hard on you, but the only one who can help you is yourself. You need not consider other people. They're not considering you. [*Growing intimate*] But if you tell us where we can lay our hands on more of this stuff in England, we'll go and get it. No questions asked on one side or the other.

BRENDAN: I don't know where there is any other stuff in England, sir.

INSPECTOR: Listen, Behan, if you're afraid of what will happen to you when you go home, I can tell you this. If you help us, we can look after you. You won't be the cause of anyone being arrested, because we can't make arrests in Ireland. But you help us in stopping this business and, as I say, we'll look after you. [*He pauses to let it sink in*] You're a young man, not even that yet. We'll send you to the colonies, Canada maybe, put you on the boat with money in your pocket. [*Pauses*] Well?

BRENDAN: I can't help you, sir.

INSPECTOR: You mean you won't. Well, you've a long time to go till the Assizes.

SERGEANT: I think we can move now, sir. There ain't so many people outside.

INSPECTOR: Right. Open his buttons. That will keep him quiet. No, not you, Vereker. Sergeant.

[*The* SERGEANT *undoes* BRENDAN's *pants buttons*]

SERGEANT: That landlady of yours won't have a window left in her house tonight. They'll probably give the lodgers a kicking and all, too.

INSPECTOR: Come on!

SERGEANT: I shouldn't be surprised if they leave the house a wreck.

[BRENDAN *is led away. Soon he is moving through a Liverpool crowd, such as we saw earlier, shouting at him in fury*]

CROWD: Filthy murderers! . . . Dirty Irish swine! . . . Kill the bastard! . . . String 'im up!

LANDLADY: Oh, God! Oh, Jesus! Oh, Sacred Heart!

[*Policemen move the crowd along*]

CROWD: Hang him, the bastard! . . . Dirty I.R.A. swine! . . . Burn down the house!

[*The crowd starts to clear away, leaving an empty stage.* BRENDAN *is handed over to two* POLICEMEN]

BEHAN: [Sings]
Said the judge, "Now, listen here, me man
And I'll tell you of our plan,
For you and all your countrymen
I do not give a damn."

Said he, "I'm going to charge you
With possession of this machine,
And I'm also going to charge you
With the wearing of the green!"

Says I to him, "Your Honor,
It is surely not a crime,
To try to make oul' Ireland free
And not before its time!"

Said he, "When we have done with you,
You'll be twenty years in dock,
You can count it by the ticking
Of your oul' alarm clock."

[*The light is dim. The scene is now the prison lockup. A* PO-
LICEMAN *and the* DETECTIVE *bring* BRENDAN *in. The* POLICE-
MAN *hands him to the* SECOND WARDER, MR. HOLMES, *who is
waiting*]

POLICEMAN: I.R.A. prisoner, one off to you, sir.

SECOND WARDER: Hope he chokes during the bleeding night. Take
off them bloody shoes.

[*They throw* BRENDAN *in a cell*]

DETECTIVE: You ain't sleeping with the pigs now, you know.

SECOND WARDER: Come on, off with them. Look sharp.

[BRENDAN *eyes the two warily*]

DETECTIVE: Don't keep the officer waiting here all night, you sloppy
Irish pig. You're bloody good soldiers and no mistake. "Up the
Republic" outside a boozer on Saturday night. But you won't be
long cracking up after a few hours in here.

SECOND WARDER: What'll you feel like after twenty years? That's if

you're lucky, and they don't 'ang you. Now, off with the jacket.
Undo your suspenders.

[BRENDAN *bends slowly to untie his shoelaces, not taking his
eyes off the* POLICEMEN]

DETECTIVE: Give them to the officer.

[BRENDAN *obeys*]

SECOND WARDER: You might decide to 'ang yourself in the night.
Not that that would be any loss.

DETECTIVE: Going to put bombs in the new battleships in Cammell
Lairds Shipyards, was you? We didn't do in half enough of you
during the Trouble.

BRENDAN: I wasn't born the time of the Trouble.

DETECTIVE: Well, I got my fill of the I.R.A. and as for you, you
bloody swine, I know what I'd do with you.

BRENDAN: We chased you out of it anyway! You haven't stopped
running yet!

[*The* DETECTIVE *punches him in the stomach*]

SECOND WARDER: Don't 'eed the dirty little bugger. 'E's not worth a
kick in the arse'ole.

DETECTIVE: One peep out of you during the night, and the officers
will come down and they'll bloody murder you.

SECOND WARDER: I 'ope 'e gets twenty years. Fecking little bastard.

[*They go off*]

BRENDAN: I wish I could wake up and find out I'm only dreaming
this.

BEHAN: Yeh. The way you used to wake up at home and say,
"Well, that's how it would be if I was pinched in England!"

BRENDAN: And here I am pinched in England.

BEHAN: And this is the way it would be.

BRENDAN: Would be? Is.

[*He starts to hum*]

BEHAN: That's right. Sing. We never died a winter yet.
    [*Sings*]
Now, this dirty, ugly city
Would put many in the jigs,
The cell it isn't pretty
And it isn't very big,
And I'd long ago have left the place
If only I had got
        [BRENDAN *joins in*]
Me couple o' sticks o' gelignite
And me oul' alarm clock.

[*There is a blackout. Then a different light comes up. A group of* PRISONERS *shuffle in. A title board flies in, saying* WALTON PRISON. *It is the next day. There are iron wash troughs onstage.* BRENDAN *joins* CHARLIE, *a youth of seventeen in sailor's uniform, at a trough. One old lag is smoking*]

CHARLIE: [*Rubbing his chin*] Could do with a rasp, mate. Been here three days now. They won't let you have your bleedin' razor.

BRENDAN: I only came in last night. I'm not so bad.

CHARLIE: You Irish? [BRENDAN *nods and starts to wash up*] Well, there's a lot of blokes 'round our way that are Irish. We all used to sing Irish songs. Confidentially, I don't like these Lancashire blokes, myself. I'm from London. Smashing place and all, it is, London. Not like Liverpool. Bleeding hole.

BRENDAN: Hole is right.

CHARLIE: I was picked up for some screwing jobs. Here and in Manchester—another bloody graveyard. What are you in for, Pad? Boozer battle or something?

BRENDAN: No, I'm in over the I.R.A. Explosives.

CHARLIE: Are you—

BRENDAN: I am, though.

CHARLIE: Straight up?

BRENDAN: Straight up.

CHARLIE: Cor, you won't half cop it for that lot. Maybe you could say someone gave you the stuff to mind and you didn't know what was in it?

BRENDAN: Maybe. Don't the warders mind the smoking?

CHARLIE: It's got bugger all to do with them.

BRENDAN: They took my cigarettes and matches away from me.

CHARLIE: [Seriously] Oh well, Pad, it might be different for you. Being I.R.A., like. It's a sort of 'igh treason, isn't it? But bugger 'em all, china,* you can have some of mine. [BRENDAN turns away from the washbowl, protesting] Yes, you bloody will. I'll give you three snout, a card of matches, and a packet of chewing gum. And 'ave you got anything to read?

BRENDAN: No, I haven't.

CHARLIE: Well, I'll give you last week's News of the World. [Taking it out of his pocket] Though maybe you saw this one?

BRENDAN: News of the World? Oh yes, let's see now . . . [Reads] "Hull magistrate on rape charge. Girls of eleven and thirteen—the magistrate was accustomed to giving them free vegetables from his greengrocer's shop."

CHARLIE: Yes! The price of everything's going up.

BRENDAN: No, I haven't seen that issue. Thanks.

CHARLIE: Your hands are wet, Paddy. I'll shove them in your pocket for you—[He makes a move to put cigarettes into BRENDAN's pants pocket]—that one's got an 'ole in it. [He tries the other side] That's all right. I'll shove the snout, matches and chewing gum in here. [BRENDAN, his wet hands outstretched, smiles] And I'll put the paper inside your shirt, so's that old grass'opper won't tumble it. [Does so] He won't tumble it there, Paddy, under your shirt.

BRENDAN: Thanks, kid.

CHARLIE: That's all right, kid. And, Paddy, my name is Charlie.

BRENDAN: Thanks, Charlie.

*Chum (from cockney rhyming slang: mate—china plate).

CHARLIE: That's all right, kid . . . I know Irish songs . . . [*He begins to sing the first line of "Galway Bay," then stops and smiles*] . . . and I'll sing you one when we get into the cells. You'll hear me, all right.

[MR. WHITBREAD, *the* FIRST WARDER, *and* MR. HOLMES, *the* SECOND WARDER, *come in*]

FIRST WARDER: Answer when your name is called and place your property on the counter. Hartigan!

HARTY: Yes, sir.

[*Goes to the counter and empties his pockets*]

BRENDAN: [*To* CHARLIE] What'll I do with the cigarettes?

CHARLIE: Hold on to what you can. Watch me.

FIRST WARDER: Millwall!

CHARLIE: Here, sir.

[*He moves up to the counter*]

FIRST WARDER: Smith!

JOCK: Here, sir.

[*He goes to the counter*]

FIRST WARDER: Callan! [*Roars*] Callan!

[SECOND WARDER *grabs* CALLAN *and brings him to the counter*]

CALLAN: Here . . . [*The* FIRST WARDER *shoots him a baleful look*] sir.

FIRST WARDER: [*To* SECOND WARDER] Keep an eye on your coat, Mr. 'Olmes. That Irish mick 'as the light touch. Pinched 'Arry Lauder's overcoat from 'is car outside the Alhambra, 'e did. James!

JAMES: Here, sir.

[*He goes to the counter*]

FIRST WARDER: Bee-han!

BRENDAN: Here, sir.

[*He whispers to* CHARLIE]

FIRST WARDER: [*Looking up sharply*] Hey, you, cut out that nattering. You're in prison now, and if you don't want to begin with a dose of bread and water, keep your mouth shut. [BRENDAN *goes to the counter and back. To* SECOND WARDER] Will you turn 'em over, Mr. 'Olmes?

[SECOND WARDER *emerges from behind the counter. The* PRISONERS *are lined up*]

SECOND WARDER: Right, sir. [*He begins with* CHARLIE. *He finds a piece of shoelace and holds it up*] Want to practice sailor's knots or something? [CHARLIE *is sheepish and silent*] Why didn't you 'and it over?

CHARLIE: [*Fumbling*] I didn't know.

SECOND WARDER: You didn't know *what?*

CHARLIE: I didn't know it was any harm.

SECOND WARDER: [*Shouting*] You didn't know it was any 'arm, *what?*

CHARLIE: Oh, I didn't know, sir. Sir, I didn't know, sir, sorry, sir.

[*The* FIRST WARDER *strides up to* CHARLIE *and looks him dead in the eye*]

FIRST WARDER: [*Slowly and deliberately*] Remember, when you speak to Mr. 'Olmes in future, you'll 'ave respect and haddress 'im properly.

SECOND WARDER: Or any other hofficer of the services, as Mr. Whitbread will tell you. [*The two* WARDERS *look at each other with gravity.* SECOND WARDER *searches* CALLAN *and finds a piece of paper in his pocket. He holds it up at arm's length for all to see. Sarcastically*] We give you toilet paper 'ere.

CALLAN: I know all about what you give here.

[*The* SECOND WARDER *passes to* BRENDAN. *He frisks him and discovers the cigarettes, with some excitement*]

SECOND WARDER: What 'ave we got 'ere, eh? [*Tensely*] Mr. Whitbread, sir.

[FIRST WARDER *comes down and stands by* BRENDAN. SECOND WARDER *holds up the pack of cigarettes*]

FIRST WARDER: [*Slightly aghast*] Who 'ad this little lot, then, Mr. 'Olmes?

SECOND WARDER: [*Shaken*] This one 'ere, sir. [*Thrusts his face into* BRENDAN's] Tell Mr. Whitbread your name, you.

BRENDAN: B-b-Behan, sir.

SECOND WARDER: Tell Mr. Whitbread your Christian name.

BRENDAN: Br-br-br-Brendan Behan, sir.

FIRST WARDER: [*With quiet menace*] Yes, Behan, I've got you, all right. I.R.A. man, ain't you? Don't like us much over 'ere, do you, Behan? Pity, you know, seeing as you're going to spend a long, long time with us.

SECOND WARDER: About twenty years.

FIRST WARDER: That's what the last got at Manchester, wasn't it? [*He pushes his face closer*] And you was going to blow us all up, Behan? Weren't you, Behan? Weren't you, Behan? [*Shouting*] Weren't you, Behan? Weren't you?

SECOND WARDER: [*Reproachfully*] Answer Mr. Whitbread, Behan.

FIRST WARDER: Not much of the old rebel in you now, is there? Thought you blokes would 'ave brought your ox-guns over with you. Do you know what an ox-gun is, Behan? It's what they 'ave in Ireland for shooting bullshit out of. [*He looks quickly at the others. They laugh, except* CHARLIE *and* CALLAN. CHARLIE's *face is serious and troubled, but then he too looks away from* BRENDAN *and snickers*] And 'old up your 'ead when I speak to you.

SECOND WARDER: 'Old up your 'ead when Mr. Whitbread speaks to you.

[BRENDAN *looks around at* CHARLIE *for an instant*]

FIRST WARDER: What are you looking 'round at, Behan? Look at me.

[BRENDAN *turns his face slowly toward the* WARDER *and returns the latter's look steadily*]

BRENDAN: [*Quietly*] I am looking at you.

SECOND WARDER: You are looking at Mr. Whitbread, what?

BRENDAN: I am looking at Mr. Whitbread.

[MR. HOLMES *looks gravely at* MR. WHITBREAD, *then punches* BRENDAN *in the middle of his back.* BRENDAN *reels*]

SECOND WARDER: [*Panting*] You are looking at Mr. Whitbread, what, Behan?

BRENDAN: [*Gasping*] I, sir, please sir, I am looking at Mr. Whitbread, sir.

FIRST WARDER: Well, Behan, now you've learned your lesson, remember this: we've only one sort of tobacco 'ere, Three Nuns. None today, none tomorrow, and none the day after. [*The others snicker,* CHARLIE *looking away from* BRENDAN] Understand that, Behan?

[BRENDAN *is still dazed*]

SECOND WARDER: Answer Mr. Whitbread, Behan.

BRENDAN: Yes—sir. Yes, Mr. Whitbread.

FIRST WARDER: Don't you forget it.

BRENDAN: [*Beaten*] No, Mr. Whitbread, no, sir.

SECOND WARDER: All right, you lot—line up for your uniforms. Look smart now.

[*They go off.* TUBBY *comes in. He is a prisoner in charge of the baths. He is carrying Borstal uniforms, which he distributes to the boys as they bathe*]

TUBBY: [*Easy and genial*] Don't you go believing anything a copper tells you. It's their *business*—putting the wind up you when they ain't being sweet to you. Like fecking parsons, they are. [*To* BRENDAN] Okay, Paddy, like me to rub your back?

BRENDAN: [*Smiling*] No, thanks.

TUBBY: You'll all go to Borstal, and you'll 'ave a good time, with football . . . concerts . . . swimming . . . Maybe you'll be sent to Portland, where I was. [*They are all ears*] Drake 'Ouse, I was in. Good old Drake! You might even be sent to one of them open Borstals. You give your word of honor not to scarper, and there's no lock on the dormitory door even.

CHARLIE: What about Sherwood Forest?

TUBBY: That's one place you'd want to stay clear of. First thing when the Sherwood gates shut behind you, you get a poke in the mush from an effing great screw.* 'E'll tell you, "That's for feck all, so just see what you get when you do feck about!" [CHARLIE, *who has finished drying himself, has been donning his uniform.* TUBBY *eyes him admiringly*] He'll probably go to Borstal and all. Want to watch his ring-a-ding-a-do, though. [*To* CHARLIE] Hey, Jack, any old three-badge stoker ever shown you the golden rivet?

CHARLIE: [*Fierce*] I'll show you a knee in your marriage prospects.

TUBBY: [*Laughs*] Don't mind me, kid. There's no 'arm in me. Just a bit of good clean fun.

SECOND WARDER: [*Shouts, offstage*] Ready over there?

TUBBY: [*Shouting back*] Right, sir! Be right along, sir. [*Dropping his voice*] You fecking shit-'ouse. [*To* BRENDAN] Ever 'ear of the screw that married the prostitute? 'E dragged 'er down to 'is own level.

[*He explodes with laughter, then composes his face into becoming gravity*]

SECOND WARDER: [*Offstage*] Hurry up, there!

TUBBY: Right, sir! Just coming, sir! [*Smartly, to the boys*] And now, we're 'aving a mannyquin parade.

[TUBBY *sashays off, getting a venomous look from* SECOND WARDER *as he enters*]

SECOND WARDER: All right, you lot. Stand in line! [*The lights dim to almost total darkness as the boys form up to be marched to*

*Prison warder.

their cells. The WARDER *shouts commands; they are marched left and right; keys jangle; they halt.* BRENDAN *keeps moving. They continue to shuffle around in the dark. The lights come up a bit to reveal cells]* Keep moving! Move along! Stand to the door of your cells.

[*He throws open cell doors, revealing two tiny cells. The boys start in horror*]

BRENDAN: [*Entering one cell*] Jaysus! A dwarf's coffin.

CHARLIE: [*Entering the other cell*] A bloody hole in the wall.

BRENDAN: Smells like a refrigerated lavatory.

SECOND WARDER: Silence! Come on, get your bed made down. Don't keep us 'ere all bloody day.

[*He slams the door and leaves*]

BRENDAN: [*Surveys the cell, which has a table, a chair, and a bunk that is unmade but has a pile of bedclothes on it. A copy of the regulations hangs on the wall*] All the way back to Dickens.

[*He stamps off five paces, wall to wall*]

A VOICE: [*Offstage*] Hey, you up there!

BRENDAN: Yes?

A VOICE: [*Offstage*] You rotten sod, kip in. Get on your bloody bench and lay there, you four-footed bastard!

BRENDAN: [*A whispered ejaculation*] Jaysus! [*He takes the regulations off the wall and begins reading them.* CHARLIE, *from the next cell, knocks on the wall.* BRENDAN *knocks back*]

CHARLIE: Hey, Paddy! That you, china?

BRENDAN: Hello, Charlie.

CHARLIE: Good old Pad. Hey, Pad!

BRENDAN: Here, china.

CHARLIE: What about that song?

BRENDAN: I'll sing you one.

[*He puts the regulations on the floor*]

CHARLIE: Sure. An Irish song. "Mother Machree" or "Galway Bay."

BRENDAN: "Mother Machree" me arse! I'll sing a song I learned at school. [*Grandiloquently*] Ireland weeping for Bonnie Prince Charlie. Not that him or anyone belonging to him ever did anything for us—but it was a good song.

[*He sings*]

Walk, walk, walk, my own,
Not even God can make us one,
Now you have left me here alone,
Is go dtéighidh tú, a mhúirnín, slán.

CHARLIE: Hey, Pad, that last bit's Irish, isn't it?

BRENDAN: Yeah, it's Irish.

CHARLIE: What does it mean?

BRENDAN: What does it mean? It means "May you always be in the palm of God's hand."

CHARLIE: Nick, Pad, nick! They're coming down.

[*Footsteps clump overhead*]

BRENDAN: [*Frantically*] They're coming down to me . . . Charlie, they could easily kill you in this place. Say you cut up rough. Who'd give a fish's tit about you over here? [*A key jangles; the door swings open*] Into Thy hands, I commend my spirit, Lord Jesus.

FIRST WARDER: You all right in here?

BRENDAN: Smashing, mate.

FIRST WARDER: [*Viciously*] What do you mean "*mate?*" Where the bloody 'ell do you think you are, "*mate?*" And what do you think you're on, putting those regulations on the floor?

BRENDAN: I was only having a read of them, sir.

FIRST WARDER: [*Enraged*] Read them where they're supposed to be read—on the wall. Come on, put 'em back.

BRENDAN: Yes, sir.

[*He hastily puts them back*]

FIRST WARDER: And what bloody way 'ave you your kit laid out? [*Pointing at the bunk*] Get that bloody lot into shape, or I'll really get angry, you sloppy Irish mick.

BRENDAN: Yes, sir.

[*Bewildered, makes a hopeless stab at doing the bed*]

FIRST WARDER: [*Shouts*] Millwall! [CHARLIE *comes into* BRENDAN'S *cell.* BRENDAN *looks relieved: he is not to be assaulted. To* CHARLIE] Your cell is not extra good, but it's better than this Irish pig's pigsty—and you know how to make your bed up. Well, show 'im, and try and get some shape on this bloody lot before the R.C. priest gets 'ere.

[*He goes out.* CHARLIE *and* BRENDAN *regard each other happily*]

CHARLIE: This is a bit of all right, Pad, 'n't it?

BRENDAN: Handy enough. That's an awful whore's melt, that screw, Charlie.

CHARLIE: [*Starts to make the bed over*] He is and all, china, there's nothing the matter with your furniture, the way it's laid out. [*Nods toward the regulations*] It's just like it says on the card there—the bedclothes could do with a bit of straightening out. [BRENDAN *helps him arrange the bedding*] But the screws just find fault with everyone. It's like in the Glass'ouse. They give you a toothbrush and an eggcup of soapy water, and tell you to scrub the lawn. It's just to be bastards, that's all. [*Lowers his voice*] The screws don't like Irishmen. According to what he was saying, Pad, they got the dead needle for you, Pad, the screws. [*Worried and embarrassed*] And Pad, some of the blokes don't fancy you, neither.

BRENDAN: They can go hump off, Charlie. I didn't expect anyone to lay down a red carpet for me if I was pinched over here.

CHARLIE: I don't care, Paddy, if you were in the I.R.A. or what you were bleedin' in. You're my china, Paddy.

[BRENDAN *looks into* CHARLIE'S *steadfast, serious eyes, and smiles*]

BRENDAN: I know that, Charlie.

CHARLIE: [*Smiling back*] That's straight-up, Pad.

[SECOND WARDER *comes in; he takes in the situation at a glance*]

SECOND WARDER: [*Stiffly*] You should be finished now.

CHARLIE: Yes, sir, I was just showin' 'im.

SECOND WARDER: Well, go down to the bagroom, you. We've no married quarters 'ere.

CHARLIE: [*Wounded*] Yes, sir.

[*He goes out quickly without looking up*]

SECOND WARDER: You get ready for the R.C. priest.

[*He goes out.* BEHAN *comes in to one side*]

BRENDAN: Yes, sir.

[*He kneels beside the bed*]

BEHAN: The day I made my First Communion—[*He smiles and shakes his head*]—I prayed to God to take me when I would go straight to heaven. Napoleon did the same. I was a daily communicant sometimes—in spasms—especially during Lent. Then I had difficulties, when I was thirteen or so. With myself and—sex. [*Resentfully*] And with the Catholic Church too, because they always seemed to be against the Republicans. But I never gave up the Faith! Even in this smelly nineteenth-century English lavatory, I made up my mind to pray to Our Lady, the Delight of the Gael, the Pride of Poets and Artists—Dante, François Villon—and maybe out of being here I would get back into the state of grace and stop in it . . . well, not stop out of it.

SECOND WARDER: [*Enters; shouts*] Attention!

[*The* CHAPLAIN *appears. He is a stout block of a man, going bald; he is wearing glasses, and when he speaks it is with an English "Haw, old boy" accent.* BRENDAN *takes an eager step toward him*]

BRENDAN: [*Smiling respectfully*] Good evening, Father.

CHAPLAIN: [*Unbending; glares*] When are you going to give up this business? [BRENDAN *is taken aback and stares at him in astonishment*] Haven't you any manners, Behan?

SECOND WARDER: Answer Father Lane, Behan.

BRENDAN: [*Quietly*] I don't know what business you are talking about, Father.

CHAPLAIN: You know perfectly well. Your membership of this murder gang, the I.R.A.

BRENDAN: [*Gripping tightly*] The I.R.A. is not a murder gang, Father.

SECOND WARDER: Don't answer Father Lane back, you f-f-f—

[*He holds back the expletive with difficulty, upraising his clenched fist*]

CHAPLAIN: [*Waving a restraining hand and sighing*] Mr. Holmes. [*They exchange sympathetic nods; he starts up again patiently*] Cardinal Hinsley and the bishops of England have issued pastorals denouncing the I.R.A., and while you're here I can *not* let you come to the altar, unless you tell me once and for all that you will have nothing more to do with this gang.

[*He regards* BRENDAN *with narrow eyes, his lips tight with authority*]

BRENDAN: [*With an effort to keep a steady voice*] Why should the bishops of England have the right to dictate about politics to an Irishman, Father?

CHAPLAIN: The bishops of Ireland have denounced the I.R.A., Behan, time and again, even early this year. The Church has always been Ireland's best friend—in Ireland, here in England, and all over the world. I must inform you that your own clergy and hierarchy have excommunicated the I.R.A. [*At this,* BRENDAN *opens his mouth to reply, but the* CHAPLAIN *restrains him with upraised hand*] You are *automatically* excommunicated unless you repent of your sin in being a member of it, and promise God in confession to sever all connection with it. [*Changing his tone to one of sweet reason*] Surely you can't set yourself up against the bishops? You, an ignorant lad, against educated men who have spent their lifetime studying these matters?

BRENDAN: [*Fiercely*] I didn't spend a lifetime studying theology, but I know that the Church has always been against Ireland and for the British Empire.

BEHAN: You could sing that if you had an air to it.

BRENDAN: With no disrespect for you, Father, a synod of Irish bishops eight hundred years ago decided to excommunicate any Irishman who refused to acknowledge the King of England as his ruler. That was only three years after the Normans landed, and held only a bit of the country. Even after the Reformation, the O'Neills in Ulster had to threaten the Pope that they would burn the Catholic archbishop out of the cathedral if he didn't take Queen Elizabeth's soldiers out of it.

[*He is gathering steam*]

BEHAN: What about 1798?

BRENDAN: In 1798, weren't the rebels excommunicated and wasn't Father John Murphy, that was burned alive by the English yeomen, excommunicated?

SECOND WARDER: Look here, you—

[*The* CHAPLAIN *has dropped his tolerant look for one of surprised anger*]

BRENDAN: And during the famine didn't they tell the people to give up their crops and die of the hunger in the ditches at home, with the grass-juice running green from the dead mouth of a mother clutching a live infant?

CHAPLAIN: [*Roars*] Here, you—!

BRENDAN: Weren't all the Irish patriots excommunicated, and didn't the bishop of Cork excommunicate the I.R.A. and support the Black and Tans? Wasn't—[*The* PRIEST *backs to the door*]— wasn't my own *father* excommunicated? [*Calls after the exiting* CHAPLAIN] So feck off, you fat bastard! And to hell with England, and to hell with Rome! Up the Republic!

SECOND WARDER: [*Shouts*] You swine! [*Hits* BRENDAN *on the back of his neck*] Mr. Whitbread! Mr. Whitbread, sir! [FIRST WARDER *enters, on the run.* SECOND WARDER *is almost gasping with indignation. He has a half-nelson on* BRENDAN] This—Irish swine —insulting—the priest—

FIRST WARDER: [*Through gritted teeth*] You fecking shit-'ouse, we'll teach you how to be'ave. [*He beats* BRENDAN, *who goes down sprawling. They kick him; become breathless with exertion*] Filthy swine. Insulting—the—priest! Irish bastard!

[FIRST WARDER *goes out. The cell is in disorder from the fray —bedclothes scattered, bedboards and furniture overturned.* BRENDAN *cowers in a ball to protect himself*]

SECOND WARDER: Get up, you pig! Clean up this bloody mess. Get this pigsty straightened out!

[*He deliberately overturns the chair, then goes out, slamming the cell door and locking it*]

BEHAN: Maybe this will cure you of the idea that religion of any description has anything to do with mercy or pity or love. And when they come to you with their creeping Jesus gab, you'll say to them, "What about the night in Walton Jail?"

BRENDAN: Me mouth is raw and bleedin' . . . an', God, me kidneys are sore. If that's the things you have on your sides.

[*He lies down on the bed*]

BEHAN: Ah, well! Maybe this bit of a belting I got would be a contributory cause of an early death in the years to come . . . but, sure, what matter of that?

[*He exits. For the first few moments,* BRENDAN *does not stir. He is gasping for breath. A key is heard in the door. He starts in terror. The cell door opens.* BROWNY *comes in, carrying two books. With him is the* LIBRARY WARDER. BRENDAN *gazes at them, dazed and uncomprehending.* BROWNY *sets the two books on the table, after righting it. The* LIBRARY WARDER *has a pencil poised over a pad and glances up at* BROWNY, *who calls out the titles*]

BROWNY: Three-five-oh-one, Behan. Fiction: *Under the Greenwood Tree*, Hardy . . . Nonfiction: *Selfridge's Furniture Catalogue.*

LIBRARY WARDER: [*As he writes, and with an easygoing cockney accent*] Don't go swopping them, now, you—unless you want to 'ave a little trip down to chokey.*

[BROWNY *hastily rights the rest of the furniture, smiling at* BRENDAN]

BRENDAN: [*Fervently*] I will not, sir, and thanks very much.

LIBRARY WARDER: Don't thank me, thank the Lord. You're an Irishman ain't you? Ever 'ear of the great Irish leader, Michael Collins?

BRENDAN: Michael Collins gave my mother a five-pound note on O'Connell Bridge a few months before I was born, when my father was locked up by Michael Collins' Government.

LIBRARY WARDER: [*Looks toward ceiling, searching his memory*] I got a book about Ireland. Remind me about it or ask for it by writing on your slate for me when we come round Tuesday next week. Write on it: "Please leave the Irish book! *The Faerie Queene.*"

BROWNY: P'raps 'e don't like dirty books!

BRENDAN: [*Softly, looking gratefully from the* WARDER *to* BROWNY] Thank you very much, and I'll leave you the note if I don't see you.

LIBRARY WARDER: [*At the cell door*] Right, Paddy.

BROWNY: [*Smiling*] It'll be all right, Paddy. My name's Browny.

[*He goes out. The* LIBRARY WARDER *pauses at the door, turns back to* BRENDAN *with a grin and gives a thumbs-up gesture*]

LIBRARY WARDER: [*Sotto voce*] Up the Republic!

[*He exits, locking the door.* BRENDAN *stands open-mouthed at the mystery of the world. He stares after the warder, wiping his bloody nose on his sleeve*]

*Solitary confinement.

BRENDAN: It's a queer world, God knows, but the best we have to be going on with.

[*He lies down on the bed. The* PRISONERS *troop in, collect their mailbags and commence to stitch, sitting in various places on the stage.* BROWNY *sits at a table, checking a list. Somewhere a* PRISONER *is making a noise of bagpipes*]

FIRST WARDER: [*Through his teeth*] 'Oo's making that bleedin' noise, eh? [*The* PRISONERS *open their mouths so the* WARDER *can see they are not making the noise. He stares intently at each face in turn, in a quiet frenzy, but still the piping goes on. The piping ceases. He starts back to his place. The piping resumes, resolute though quiet. He stares about him, cocks his head to see if he is imagining the noise, then nods slowly. The* WARDER *fixes his eyes on one* PRISONER, *dives through the ranks, collars* JOCK] It's you, you Scotch bastard. Want to play your bleedin' bagpipes, do you? Mr. 'Olmes, sir!

JOCK: W-wait, sir . . . I . . . It wasn't me. I swear it wasn't . . .

FIRST WARDER: Playing the bleedin' bagpipes through 'is bleedin' teeth, 'e was. [SECOND WARDER *enters, takes* JOCK *by the scruff of the neck, drags him off. They hear a new sound; this time it is whistling. The* WARDER *looks down stupidly on them. He goes through the same routine again. He comes to* DALE *and* CALLAN. DALE *indicates* CALLAN] Callan! So it's you—Irish scum!

[*He pounces on* CALLAN]

CALLAN: Up the Republic!

FIRST WARDER: We'll give you "Up the Republic!" You swine!

[*The* WARDERS *drag him off;* DALE *leaps up and darts to the table;* JAMES *follows*]

DALE: Finished work. [*Puts his bag down. He grabs* BROWNY *and throws him to* JAMES] You were down to the loo, wa'nt you?

BROWNY: [*Terrified*] 'Ere, what's eating you, tosh?

DALE: You know bloody well what's eating me. Where's me fagends?

BROWNY: What?

DALE: [*Snarling*] Me fecking fag-ends that you knocked off, 'at's what.

BROWNY: I didn't, tosh—honest to Christ, I didn't. Swear to—

TUBBY: Nick, nick!

[DALE *hears* FIRST WARDER *approaching and runs back with his bag*]

FIRST WARDER: Silence!

DALE: [*Holding his bag aloft*] Finished work.

FIRST WARDER: Right. And remember, four stitches to the inch, all neat and proper-like, or you'll be needing a few stitches yourselves.

[*The* PRISONERS *begin to sew quietly. The* WARDER *saunters away, and as soon as his back is turned, the* PRISONERS *behave like schoolboys, whispering behind their hands, signaling each other, laughing silently.* DALE *nudges* JAMES *again, and then leans toward* BRENDAN *on his other side*]

DALE: [*To* BRENDAN] Irishman, eh, Paddy?

BRENDAN: I am.

DALE: My mum was Irish, Paddy. [BRENDAN *sews on, noncommittal*] But that don't mean I like Paddies. Bleedin' scabs, the Paddies. Come over to Liverpool and work for scab wages.

BRENDAN: [*Offended*] Irishmen are not scabs—

JAMES: Why don't you all stay 'ome in starvin' Ireland?

DALE: With the pigs in the parlor, instead of scabbing on honest blokes.

BRENDAN: [*Flaring up*] Y-y-you're wr-wr-wrong. We m-make good wages in Ireland. We—

[DALE *turns on* BRENDAN *as though* BRENDAN *has done something to him, and as though he is just barely restraining himself from giving him a belt*]

DALE: [*So that the* WARDER *will hear*] Shag off, you Killarney mick, or I'll 'it you.

FIRST WARDER: [*Angrily*] What's to-do down there?

DALE: It's this Irish mick, sir. 'E keeps talking all the time. I just told 'im 'e'd get me in trouble.

BRENDAN: That's a bloody lie. H-h-he . . . s-s-spoke t-t-to m-me f-first!

FIRST WARDER: [*Boring in venomously*] I'm just about browned off with you. Move over there—[BRENDAN *starts to object*]—and shut your hole. Move over there. Get on with it, I shan't warn you again, I shan't. I've warned you before.

BROWNY: Can I go to the loo, sir?

FIRST WARDER: [*Moving away*] What, again? What you want is a bottle of gin for your kidneys. Oh, all right. Dale, you take over from Brown.

[BROWNY *gets up and leaves.* DALE *jumps up*]

DALE: Yes, sir.

[*He glances at* JAMES]

FIRST WARDER: Right, James, you help Dale.

JAMES: Thank you, sir.

[*They go behind the table and begin fussing with the bags and supplies*]

CHARLIE: Finished work, sir.

[*He holds up his bag. The* WARDER *nods assent.* CHARLIE *takes his bag to the table.* DALE *gives it a cursory inspection and hands it to* JAMES. JAMES *gives* CHARLIE *a replacement to work on.* CHARLIE *returns to his seat. The warder paces offstage and back*]

BRENDAN: [*Holding his bag up*] Finished, sir. [*The* WARDER *nods.* BRENDAN *gets up.* DALE *nudges* JAMES *and they smirk as* BRENDAN *goes to the table. To* DALE] Finished work.

[DALE *grabs the bag rudely and makes a thing of inspecting it. He assumes a pained expression*]

DALE: Mr. Whitbread, sir?

[*He holds out the bag for the* WARDER *to see.* FIRST WARDER *looks at it quickly and thrusts it back at* BRENDAN]

FIRST WARDER: You stupid Irish mick. Four to the inch, four to the inch. Now pick it up and do it proper.

[DALE *and* JAMES *laugh.* BRENDAN *looks at* DALE, *then at* JAMES. *He goes back to his chair, sits down and rips some stitches and starts sewing again.* CHARLIE *throws furtive and worried glances at him*]

DALE: [*Not loud enough to carry to the warder*] Stupid Irish mick!

JAMES: 'Ow's the pigs in the parlor, Paddy?

[*They all get convulsed*]

DALE: Leave 'im alone, can't you see 'e's 'omesick? 'E misses the pigs and prayties.

[*There are more snickers*]

HARTY: Finished work.

FIRST WARDER: Right.

[*They all bend over their work.* CHARLIE *nudges* BRENDAN, *and taking* BRENDAN's *bag, gives him his own, nodding toward the table.* BRENDAN *holds it aloft*]

BRENDAN: Finished work. [*He barely waits for the* WARDER's *nod. He fingers the metal palm on his hand, then strides up to the table and stands there till* JAMES *stands up.* BRENDAN *holds out the bag to him*] That's finished work!

JAMES: [*With a thick sneer*] Oh, is it? [*He looks at it in great annoyance—glad, though, to have another diversion at* BRENDAN's *expense. He looks at* BRENDAN *and takes up the bag. All the others watch intently*] What's to do with you? That's another you 'aven't done right. 'Ere, take it back and do it again, cop.

[*He flings the bag at* BRENDAN. DALE *laughs.* BRENDAN *knocks* JAMES *down, and thrashes him with his metal thimble.* FIRST

WARDER *rushes in and breaks up the fight. Blood is pouring from* JAMES' *face*]

FIRST WARDER: Mr. 'Olmes!

[*The* SECOND WARDER *comes on the run*]

SECOND WARDER: What is it, sir?

FIRST WARDER: Been a bit of a bother 'ere. You take James to the hospital while I take Behan before the Governor.

SECOND WARDER: [*To* JAMES] Right, come on, take your 'and off your eyes if you don't want to trip over yourself and do yourself some more damage. You are a bloody mess.

[*He leads the moaning* JAMES *off. The* FIRST WARDER *turns back to* BRENDAN *and takes him by the arm. There is no laughing or grinning or leering or jibing in the* PRISONERS *now. They look at* BRENDAN, *and he, head high, looks down on them in triumph.* CHARLIE *gives him a proud and friendly look. The* PRISONERS *troop off, taking chairs with them. Elderly* PRISON GOVERNOR *comes in and sits behind the table.* BRENDAN *is marched around to face him*]

FIRST WARDER: Stand to the mat and state your full name, number, age, religion and sentence.

BRENDAN: Behan, Brendan, sir. Three-five-oh-one, age sixteen, Roman Catholic, awaiting trial.

PRISONER GOVERNOR: We'll win—er—we'll win all the time. We can make it—er—very bad for you—er—it's all the same to us. And it's up to you—er—whatever way you want it.

BRENDAN: Yes, sir.

[*The* GOVERNOR *reads the papers given to him by the* WARDER. *Now* BEHAN *comes in to one side of the stage*]

BEHAN: Yes, sir, said I, with my hands at the seams of my trousers and looking manly, admitting my fault to this tired old consul, weary from his labors amongst the lesser breeds, administering the King's justice equal and fairly to wild Irish and turbulent Pathan, teaching fair play to the wily Arab and a sense of sportsmanship to the smooth Confucian. In my ballocks, said I, you dull scruffy old creeping Jesus, gone past the Bengal Lancer act now. Any decent horse would drop dead from the shame if you managed to get up on its back.

PRISON GOVERNOR: I must take this opportunity of warning you that if this assault had been carried out on one of my officers, you would most certainly have been flogged. I sentence you to one day's cellular confinement, one day's deprivation of mattress, and one day's Number One diet.

[*He exits, stiff and bowlegged*]

BEHAN: Yoicks! Tallyho!

FIRST WARDER: [*Roars*] Attention! About turn! March! [BRENDAN *is marched around to the door of his cell, which is now stripped of bedclothes, etc.*] Now take off your stockings, your shoes and your jacket, and put them outside here.

[BRENDAN *strips, gathers his clothes in a bundle, starts to hand them to* FIRST WARDER, *then realizes his blunder*]

BRENDAN: It's very cold, isn't it, sir?

FIRST WARDER: Never mind about the weather. I'll give you a kick that will send your ass up to your shoulder blades.

[BRENDAN *puts his clothes outside the cell, and comes back in*]

BRENDAN: [*As the* WARDER *leaves*] Thank you, sir. [*The* WARDER *slams the cell door, locks it and goes off.* BRENDAN *shudders with the cold, blows on his hands to warm them, and takes out a bucket to sit on. A book falls out of it. Looking at the title*] Cranford, by Mrs. Gaskell. Jaysus! [*He puts the book under his arm and begins to whistle softly pacing his cell.* WARDERS *are heard shouting distantly. He stops*] I'd sing out loud, only they might hear me.

BEHAN: Better to be defiant in a quiet sort of way. These sportsmen would be serious men if it came to kicking the shit out of you. A terrible thing for the Germans or the Russians or the Fuzzie-Wuzzies to do as much to one of theirs, and a crime against humanity. [*Shrugs*] Still, you can't blame them. Everyone has his own way of looking at things.

BRENDAN: [*Sniffs*] I can smell the dinner. [*He whistles a few furious bars*] That it may choke you, you shower of bastards!

BEHAN: Think of Terence MacSwiney, lad—longest hunger strike on record: seventy-eight days with no scoff at all.

BRENDAN: And me father, on hunger strike with thousands of others.

BEHAN: Didn't MacSwiney drive the bastards mad with the publicity he was getting? They were up and offering him every conceivable delicacy: chicken, ham, turkey, roast pork, steak—

BRENDAN: Oh, for the love of Jaysus, give over. Mother of Christ, aren't there a thousand places between Belfast and Bantry Bay where a fellow would be stuffed with grub, not to mind dowsed with porter, if he could only be there and here at the same time?

BEHAN: I suppose that would be like trying to get a drink at your own funeral. [DALE *starts across the stage, sees* BROWNY *and* FIRST WARDER *coming from the other side, passes them and goes out.* BEHAN *acts the host*] Make way there, you with the face, and let in the man that's doing jail for Ireland, and suffering hunger and abuse amongst that parcel of white-livered—

BRENDAN: —thin-lipped—

BEHAN: —paper-waving—

BRENDAN: —key-rattling hangmen over—

[*He spins around. The* WARDER *opens up the cell to let* BROWNY *in; goes off*]

BROWNY: 'Ello. 'Ere, Paddy, lad, I 'ave your cob and water. [*Soft and smiling*] It's not much but it'll keep the guts together till teatime.

BRENDAN: [*Taking the can of water and bread*] Do I get more then?

BROWNY: 'Course you do. And more tomorrow. You're out then at dinnertime and all's well again.

BRENDAN: But I thought it was three days—

BROWNY: Nay, you silly feller, 'tis all one day.

BRENDAN: Well, it was worth it, to give that bastard James a trimming.

BROWNY: [*Worried*] Only thing to be afeered of is 'im or 'is china, Dale, coming at you all of a sudden.

BRENDAN: I'll look out for that, Browny.

BROWNY: Bit of snout, Pad?

BRENDAN: Thanks, Browny.

BROWNY: And 'ere's match.

BRENDAN: Your blood should be bottled.

BROWNY: Don't thank me, Pad. Thank Dale. [*He glances over his shoulder to make sure he is unheard, then grins*] Screw, 'e empties buckets of butts down loo. Some float 'round, like. Dale, 'e fishes butts out, puts on sill to dry. I nip in and knock them off.

[BRENDAN *looks down at the butt and then holds it up to* BROWNY]

BRENDAN: Was that down the loo? Big daddy Dale's? Jaysus!

[BROWNY *nods,* BRENDAN *sniffs the butt and they both laugh*]

BROWNY: Lots more where that came from. Be back in a minute.

[*He smiles and winks and goes off.* BRENDAN *protests*]

BEHAN: John Howard, the Quaker, invented solitary, they say. He must have had terrible little to do. These religious maniacs, they have empty minds on account of not going in for sex or sports or drink, or swimming or reading bad books. And Satan will find work for idle hands.

[*He goes out*]

DALE: [*Offstage*] Browny, I've got you, you little bastard.

BROWNY: [*Offstage*] No, no, Dale, I was only kidding . . .

[*Screams are heard.* BROWNY *comes in, lurching crazily, clutching his wounds and trying to hold himself up. He totters and collapses.* BRENDAN *comes out of his cell quickly and runs to* BROWNY]

BRENDAN: Oh, Jaysus!

FIRST WARDER: [*Running in*] You know anything about this, Behan?

BRENDAN: No, sir.

FIRST WARDER: We'll see about that. Better get 'im to 'ospital.

[SECOND WARDER *rushes in*]

SECOND WARDER: What's to do? What happened to Brown?

FIRST WARDER: Got 'imself carved up. 'E's passed out. Get back to your cell, Behan.

[*Both* WARDERS *pick up* BROWNY *and drag him off*]

BRENDAN: Yes, sir.

[CHARLIE *and* CALLAN *have entered, carrying buckets of water and mops*]

CHARLIE: All for a miserable bit of snout. Poor Browny.

CALLAN: The screws know Dale did it, anyway—cut him into ribbons with a razor. I hope they kick 'im 'round a bit, the perishing bastard.

[*The* FIRST WARDER *returns*]

FIRST WARDER: Behan, I told you to get back in your cell! [BRENDAN *goes back and gets locked in. He looks down at the floor*] Christ, what a mess. Millwall—

CHARLIE: Yes, sir.

FIRST WARDER: Bring your bucket over here. Be'aving like a pack of dirty animals. All right, get on with it. It's this sort of thing that turns a good officer wicked.

[*He leaves.* CHARLIE *goes to the cell and hands* BRENDAN *a cigarette through the peephole*]

CHARLIE: Hey, Paddy, it's Charlie. Here's a bit of snout.

BRENDAN: Thanks, china.

CALLAN: [*Comes over to* BRENDAN's *peephole*] Behan!

BRENDAN: Hello, Callan.

CALLAN: Have you heard the news?

BRENDAN: About Browny?

CALLAN: No, not him—the two I.R.A. men in Birmingham. They're going to hang them tomorrow.

BRENDAN: [*Crossing himself*] Tomorrow. Ash Wednesday.

CALLAN: [*Fiercely*] Two innocent men.

BRENDAN: Don't we all know that.

CALLAN: [*First looking up and down the landing*] Here. [*He takes a newspaper from under his shirt and pushes it in to* BRENDAN] Read it yourself.

BRENDAN: "Before he was sentenced to death, one of the I.R.A. prisoners told the court that he would walk out smiling, thinking of all the other men that had died for Ireland. The judge said, 'May the Lord have mercy on your soul' and the condemned replied, 'You too.'" It says here that there are demonstrations by the Irish all over America.

CALLAN: And there'll be one here tonight, too!

BRENDAN: [*Dumbfounded*] Here?

CALLAN: My cell is right above yours. I'll signal on the pipes.

[*He goes off*]

BRENDAN: Callan! I wouldn't try that here . . . [*Getting frantic*] Callan! It's a truce I want, not a bloody demonstration. Do you want to be kicked to death or insanity? [*He paces the cell in agitation*] Yes, because they're even bigger bastards and crueler bastards than I ever took them for. Jaysus, aren't my kidneys still paining me from the beating they gave me. [*He rushes back to the peephole*] Callan, you bloody madman! Not here, not here, for dear Jaysus' sake—*not here!* [*He runs his hands through his hair*] That's it—a read. I'll have a read. [*He takes the book, then looks up with a sudden thought*] Maybe Callan would keep easy till morning. [*Reads*] "For Miss Barker had ordered all sorts of good things for supper—scalloped oysters, potted lobster— [CALLAN *enters far upstage and begins tapping on the floor with a bucket.* BRENDAN *starts nervously, and turns his head slowly and apprehensively in the direction of the tapping. It stops, then starts again, louder. He goes back to his book*]—potted lobster, jelly, a dish called 'Little Cupids'—[*There is more tapping*]—macaroons sopped in brandy, I should have called it, if I had not known its more refined classical name. In short we were to—[CALLAN *taps again*]—to be feasted."

CALLAN: [*Roaring unmercifully*] Uuuuuup the Repuuuublic!

BRENDAN: [*Springs up wildly from the mattress; furious sotto voce*] That the devil may choke you and the Republic!

[*He cocks his head and listens grimly*]

CALLAN: Be-eee-han. Bren-daaaaaan Be-eehaaaaaaan!

BRENDAN: [*Goes mad; still sotto voce*] You louse-bound bastard. Don't drag me into it! You're not much good alone and unarmed, are you? Leave me out of it!

CALLAN: Uuuuuuuup the Rep-uuuuuuub-lic!

BRENDAN: Holy Mother of God! Give the man back his overcoat and leave the Republic to look after itself.

CALLAN: Be-eeeeeee-han Get up and give a shout—a shooooooooo-ooouuuuuuuuut!

BRENDAN: [*Frantically and low*] A kick in the ass is what I'd like to give you. [*He stands for a moment, wondering what to do*] May God direct me!

CALLAN: Uuuuuuuu-uuu-uuup the Rep-uuub-lic, Beee-haaan!

BRENDAN: All right. All right. [*He goes to the vent above the pipes, puts his mouth to it, and shouts discreetly down*] Up the Republic! [*He looks over his shoulder fearfully*]

CALLAN: I caaaaaaaaa-an't heeeear youuuuuuu riiiightly.

BRENDAN: [*Into the vent*] I'm shouting. The walls here are three feet thick.

CALLAN: All right. Goooood maaaaan. Up the Reeeee-puuuub-lic!

BRENDAN: [*Even lower*] Up the Republic. We defy you. To hell with the British Empire.

[*There is a brouhaha of voices; the jangling of keys is heard from below.* BRENDAN *jumps back onto his mattress, and feigns concentration in his book. The* WARDERS *run up to his cell door, and open it*]

SECOND WARDER: What are you doing there, Behan?

[BRENDAN *puts down his book innocently*]

BRENDAN: I'm reading, sir. [*The* WARDERS *close the door and go off. They reenter upstage to where* CALLAN *is, and drag him off as he yells and curses*] They've taken him to chokey! [*Reads*] " 'It's very strong,' said Miss Pole as she put down her empty glass. 'I do believe there's spirit in it. I often feel tipsy myself from eating damson tart,' said Miss Barker." [*He listens*] Up the Republic . . .

[*It is a whisper only. Darkness*]

BEHAN: [*Enters and sings*]
Let cowards mock and tyrants frown,
Ah, little do we care.
A felon's cap is the noblest crown
An Irish head can wear.
And, brothers, say, shall we today
Unmoved, like cowards stand,
While traitors shame and foes defame
The felons of our land.

[*The stage is cleared of the cells. A crowd comes in, as if to court.* BRENDAN *stands in the center, looking out toward the audience*]

VOICE OF CLERK: His Majesty versus Elsie Jankins, Elsie Jankins, Elsie Jankins. His Majesty versus Brendan Behan, Brendan Behan, Brendan Behan.

VOICE OF JUDGE: Is the prisoner represented?

BEHAN: I'll represent him, Your Honor, seein' there's no one else. [*Aside, to* BRENDAN] Refuse to recognize the court.

BRENDAN: As a soldier of the Irish Republican Army, I refuse to recognize the court.

BEHAN: Sure, he's only a foolish boy that never stood a chance, Your Honor. Connected with the I.R.A. since he could walk. Didn't he see his father for the first time through the bars of a prison?

VOICE OF JUDGE: The court—

BEHAN: A-a-a-ah, don't be too hard on him now, and he'll give his word not to attend any more parades, and drop out of the I.R.A., and attend more to his trade, and go out dancing or something and—and—and get married. [To BRENDAN] Won't you, you *amadan*?*

BRENDAN: The young Irish hero, Cuchulainn, with his enemies ringed 'round him, held his back to a tree and called on the gods of death and grandeur to hold him up till his last blood flowed.

BEHAN: Last blood? Sure to God, you'll kill yourself more with the drink than you ever will with the I.R.A.

VOICE OF JUDGE: The court finds the prisoner mute of malice. Enter a plea of "Not Guilty." Has the prisoner anything to say before sentence is passed?

BEHAN: Has he? He's been workin' on the bloody speech for a month. [To BRENDAN] Go on, and mind the oul' stutter!

BRENDAN: My lord and gentlemen, it is my privilege and honor today to stand, as so many of my countrymen have done—

VOICE OF JUDGE: Neither the jury nor this court wish to listen to a political speech.

BRENDAN: —as so many of my countrymen have done, in an English court, to testify to the unyielding determination of the Irish people to regain every inch of our national territory and to give expression to the noble aspirations for which so much Irish blood has been shed, so many brave and manly hearts have been broken, and for which so many of my comrades are now lying in your jails . . .

BEHAN: Go on, now—throw the hammer after the hatchet!

BRENDAN: . . . and this . . . and this to a proud and intelligent

* Stupid person.

people, who had a language, a literature, when the barbarian woad-painted Briton was first learning to walk upright. By plantation, famine, and massacre, you have striven to drive the people of Ireland from off the soil of Ireland, but in seven centuries you have not succeeded, and until the thirty-two-county Republic of Ireland is once more functioning, Ireland unfree shall never be at peace.

BEHAN: No surrender!

VOICE OF JUDGE: [*In a temper*] Prisoner at the bar, you have taken advantage of the mildness of British law in regard to the punishment of persons under eighteen.

BEHAN: I'll tell you what your man the judge is going to say now. He's going to say that in this court, you'll get justice the like of which you'll get nowhere else in the world. Which is what the judge told the two I.R.A. men in Birmingham. And then he sentenced them to be hanged. Which they were.

[BRENDAN *remains silent*]

VOICE OF JUDGE: This court regrets that it cannot sentence you to the fourteen years penal servitude you so richly deserve.

BEHAN: Thanks be to Jaysus!

VOICE OF JUDGE: Though young in age, you are mature in purpose—

BEHAN: Oh, indeed!

VOICE OF JUDGE: —and I deeply regret that the law makes no allowance for persons of your type. I now sentence you to three years' Borstal detention.

BEHAN and BRENDAN: [*Shouting together*] Up the Republic!

[BRENDAN *is led away by a* POLICEMAN *and a* SERGEANT]

BEHAN: [*Sings*]
Some in the convict's dreary cell,
Have found a living tomb,
And some unseen, unfriended, fell
Within the dungeon's gloom,

But what care we, although it be
Trod by a ruffian band,
God bless the clay where rest today
The felons of our land . . .

CURTAIN

ACT TWO

The scene is Hollesley Bay, a boys' Borstal on the eastern coast of England. As the curtain rises, the BORSTAL BOYS *are sitting on stools, as if on a moving bus.* BEHAN *is singing.*

BEHAN:
There was burglars and ponces and forgers,
Rapers and robbers and homicides, too,
There was thieves, pickpockets, shoplifters,
In the Hollesley Bay criminal zoo,
There was murderers there in abundance,
'Twould make old Bluebeard turn pale,
'Twould kill a lad twice, to be travelin' so nice,
On the bus to the Hollesley Bay jail.

WELSH WARDER: [*Enters; blows a whistle*] All out! [*Bellows*] Answer when your name is called! [BEHAN *has now nonchalantly seated himself at the side of the stage, where he comments on the* BOYS] Five-two-nine, Hartigan.

HARTY: 'Ere, sir.

BEHAN: He's in for screwing. Not in the dictionary. Means lifting, fecking, removing or otherwise converting for own use.

HARTY: I been screwing since I was ten. I 'ad to. I wouldn't 'ave eaten if I didn't. [*Plucks his shorts*] This is like the bleedin' Boy Scouts.

WELSH WARDER: Five-three-oh, Da Vinci.

JOE: 'Ere, sir.

BEHAN: Piccadilly pimp.

JOE: I'm out of my natural element. I feel like a fecking whore at a christening.

WELSH WARDER: Five-three-one, Jones.

KEN: Here, sir.

BEHAN: H.M.P. His Majesty's Pleasure. That means murder.

KEN: I've a brother who'll spring me from this place, just wait and see.

WELSH WARDER: Five-three-two, Tonks.

CHEWLIPS: 'Ere, sir.

BEHAN: Chewlips. Yeh, that's what we call him, Chewlips, because he pinched a truckload of tulips.

CHEWLIPS: Fruit and flowers, that's my trade. [*Bawls*] Foh-pance a pahnd—pehhs!*

BORSTAL BOYS: Shut up, can't you.

BEHAN: He's not as green as he looks. Has the stuff stashed away somewhere.

WELSH WARDER: Five-three-three, Smith.

JOCK: Here, sir.

BEHAN: Jock. Rape.

JOCK: It were all a mistake.

BEHAN: The course of true love never runs smooth.

JOCK: Never trust a judy.

BEHAN: [*Winks*] Could happen to a fellow with his own girl.

JOCK: It did.

WELSH WARDER: Five-three-four, Millwall.

CHARLIE: 'Ere, sir.

BEHAN: Good old Charlie.

CHARLES: Up the Hoy Har Hay!

BEHAN: The English are the worst.

WELSH WARDER: Five-three-five, Meadows.

*Four pence a pound—pears!

TOM: 'Ere sir. [*With loathing*] Fine lot! Thieves, pimps, rapists. They're just a dirty, degenerate scum, and no decent lad should have ought to do with them.

BEHAN: Thanks be to God he's not on the bench at the Old Bailey. It'd be a poor day for the prisoners in the dock if he was.

WELSH WARDER: Five-three-six, Rivers.

RIVERS: Here, sir.

BEHAN: Cat burglar. Oxford.

RIVERS: No, no, no—Harrow.

BEHAN: Likes it better here, though.

RIVERS: The grub's much better.

BOYS: Good show!

RIVERS: Bloody good show.

WELSH WARDER: Five-three-seven, Cragg.

CRAGG: Here, sir.

BEHAN: Decent bloke. He thinks the world is flat.

CRAGG: It's not altogether flat. There's bumps here and there for mountains and such like. But mostly it's flat.

BEHAN: Another H.M.P. Domestic problems.

CRAGG: A little difference of opinion with me late father-in-law.

WELSH WARDER: Five-three-eight, Callaghan.

SHAGGY: 'Ere, sir.

BEHAN: Shaggy. Ex-British Army, believe it or not. Caught selling his rifle to the I.R.A.

SHAGGY: I was stationed in Northern Ireland, at Ballykinlar.

BEHAN: The Belfast I.R.A. got so many rifles from Ballykinlar, they used to call it the Stores.

WELSH WARDER: Fire-three-nine, Bee-haun.

BRENDAN: Still here, sir.

WELSH WARDER: Don't you try any smart answers with me, Bee-han, or I shall clip your bloody ear'ole.

BORSTAL BOYS: [*In chorus*] Runnin' round with bleedin' time bombs.

WELSH WARDER: 'Ere, I seem to 'ave one too many. 'Ave you sods been breeding? [*Counts again*] Right. That's it, then. Grub's up!

> [*He blows his whistle. The* BOYS *break up and re-form, as if at a table. The* WARDER *leaves*]

JOE: Smashin' scoff!

CHEWLIPS: [*Happily*] Foh-pance a pahnd—pehhs!

BORSTAL BOYS: Cor! Stuff it, will you?

HARTY: Smashin' scoff? Bloody sickening, I calls it. Can't keep it on me stomach. Too much, all of a sudden.

> [*He tears offstage*]

CRAGG: There's always a certain amount of diarrhea among new blokes.

JOE: 'Course, there's some blokes couldn't be 'appy no matter where they were. If they was in the Ritz 'Otel with a million nicker and Rita 'Ayworth they'd still find some bloody thing to moan about.

RIVERS: [*To* CHEWLIPS] What exactly are you doing?

CHEWLIPS: [*Abashed*] Fixin' me 'air s'all!

JOE: With margarine? 'E's puttin' the margarine on 'is 'air!

> [HARTY *reenters*]

SHAGGY: [*To* BRENDAN] What did they cop you for, Paddy?

CHARLIE: 'E's political.

HARTY: Tried to blow up Cammell Lairds Shipyards, 'e did.

RIVERS: How about the poor blighters working there, and their wives and kids?

JOE: Why didn't you do in some of the big pots?

CHEWLIPS: Like that old Lady Astor.

JOE: Instead of puttin' bombs in railway stations.

HARTY: Bloody lot of murderers. What about—

CHARLIE: 'Ere, let 'im alone. Turn it up, can't you?

SHAGGY: Oh, kip in, you Croydon puff.

CHARLIE: [*Jumping up*] I won't kip in, you little short-arsed bastard.

BEHAN: Compliments pass when the quality meet.

[SHAGGY *takes a fighter stance; goes for* CHARLIE]

BRENDAN: [*Shouts*] Leave him alone, you!

SHAGGY: Oh, so you want to bundle, Paddy?

BORSTAL BOYS: Go on! 'Ave a go! Your muvver won't know!

CRAGG: [*Like a referee*] Now, no knee and nut stuff and no catching by the cobs. And break quickly if we give the nick.

[BRENDAN *and* SHAGGY *circle each other warily*]

BORSTAL BOYS: Give 'im one, Shaggy!

CHARLIE: 'E won't, you know.

CRAGG: Come on, get cracking!

HARTY: Like a pair of old judies.

JOE: Go on, less natter and more batter!

[BRENDAN *makes a determined rush at* SHAGGY, *and goes down before a lightning punch.* SHAGGY *stands over him, laughing*]

JOCK: [*Raising* SHAGGY's *arm*] And still champeen!

SHAGGY: Get up, you silly old sod, I could 'ave booted the 'ead off you. [BRENDAN *picks himself up, dazed*] Come on, you silly old silly.

JOE: Just like when you topped the bill at Lambeth Baths, eh, Shaggy?

[BRENDAN *looks from* JOE *to* SHAGGY, *astonished*]

JOCK: [*Shadowboxing*] You didn't know about Shaggy being fly-weight champion of the Army.

SHAGGY: You, being an Irishman, thought you'd 'ave a go at a professional boxer.

[BRENDAN *nods deprecatingly and smiles.* SHAGGY *gives him a cigarette and they all light up*]

CRAGG: Nothing an Irishman likes better than a bundle.

CHEWLIPS: I 'eard my old man say that the Irish will fight till there's only one left—and 'e'll bleedin' well commit suicide 'cause there's no other fecker left to fight with.

WELSH WARDER: [*Enters; blows his whistle*] The Governor!

[*The* BOYS *duck their cigarettes. The* GOVERNOR *comes in wearing plus fours. He smiles at them all and nods*]

GOVERNOR: [*Very civilly*] You may sit down.

WELSH WARDER: Sit down!

GOVERNOR: You may smoke. [*They are delighted*] While you are here, the first thing I ask of you is courtesy to each other . . .

CHEWLIPS: 'Ear that? You've got to be courteous to me.

CHARLIE: [*To* CHEWLIPS] You all right, love?

WELSH WARDER: Silence!

GOVERNOR: Courtesy to the staff and to myself. And in other matters I must have your cooperation.

BORSTAL BOYS: Yes, sir.

GOVERNOR: We have a great deal to do in the gardens, on the farm, and keeping the sea back—or we won't have either. So don't worry, we'll find jobs for you. [*The* BOYS *groan*] Eh, good morning and good luck to you.

[*He goes off. The* WARDER *exits. The Protestant* MINISTER *comes on*]

MINISTER: Good morning, boys. Welcome to Hollesley Bay.

BORSTAL BOYS: Good morning.

BRENDAN: Good morning, Father.

MINISTER: Good morning! And God bless you, Paddy, whoever you are.

[He goes off]

JOE: You shouldn't 'ave called 'im "Father."

BRENDAN: Well, I couldn't have called him "Mother."

CHARLIE: He's the minister. The Church of England bloke.

JOE: 'E's not the priest.

BRENDAN: I've as good a right to ordain priests as the Cardinal. It's only the difference of the Cardinal getting paid for it.

RIVERS: Marlowe said he had as good a right to mint money as the Queen of England. Did you know that?

BRENDAN: I did. And I'm glad someone else knows it, too.

WELSH WARDER: [Enters; blows his whistle] Garden Party! Turn to! On the double! One, two!

[The BOYS form up and march around. As they do, they collect hoes from the WARDER and sing "The Borstal Song"]

BORSTAL BOYS:
Oh, they say I ain't no good 'cause I'm a Borstal Boy,
But a Borstal Boy is what I'll always be.
I know it is a title, a title I bear with pride,
To Borstal, to Borstal, and the beautiful countryside!
I turned my back upon the 'ole society
And spent me life a-thievin' 'igh and low,
I've got the funniest feelin' for 'alf-inchin' and for stealin'
I should 'ave been in Borstal years ago, cor blimey!
I should 'ave been in Borstal years ago!

[The lighting goes up. The BOYS are now in open fields, bright sunlight. The WARDER blows his whistle. They start to dig]

BEHAN: My old man told me about the land and how our ancestors came from it and how healthy it was. So I asked my grandmother, and she said she was my ancestor and that all our family's land was in window boxes.

BRENDAN: Charlie, I can smell the sea!
    [*He sings*]
The sea, oh, the sea, a ghradh gheal mo chroidhe,
Oh, long may you roll between England and me,
God help the poor Scotchmen, they'll never be free,
But we're entirely surrounded by water.

BORSTAL BOYS: Good old Paddy!

CHEWLIPS: [*Proudly*] 'E's a comical bastard, 'n't 'e?

    [*The* WARDER *blows his whistle. The* BOYS *look at him, puzzled*]

WELSH WARDER: Well, fall out!

    [*The* BOYS *break off work and sit around. They begin to roll cigarettes and light up.* BRENDAN *finds himself beside* KEN JONES]

BRENDAN: [*To* KEN] Have you no snout?

KEN: No, Paddy. Smoked mine all up.

BRENDAN: Have some of mine.

    [*He gives* KEN *a cigarette paper and tobacco*]

CHARLIE: Didn't you get no snout, then?

KEN: I bought ten Woodbines. I don't like them much, but at least they're tailor-made. I don't fancy these things. I'm not a cowboy.

CHARLIE: None of us aren't cowboys. But if we're only getting fivepence or sixpence a week, this 'alf ounce snout lasts longer.

    [*He gets up and leaves them for another group*]

JOE: [*Calling after* CHARLIE *in a public-school voice*] I 'eard my old man say the Woodbine is the dearest smoke there is—and the most expensive tobacco.

KEN: [*Ignoring* JOE] Thanks for the smoke, Paddy.

BRENDAN: You're welcome.

[JOE *moves off in mock disgust*]

KEN: I'll send you in some from the outside, Paddy, when I get out.

BRENDAN: Sure, kid.

KEN: You think I'm geeing you, Paddy, and that it'll be a long time before I'm on discharge. [*He drops his voice*] But I'm not going to wait for that.

BRENDAN: No?

KEN: No. I got it all worked out on a map I got in the library. My brother will come up here and pick me up in his Jaguar. He's a smashing driver, Paddy, and an officer in the Marines.

BRENDAN: Well, of course, if you could do it, if you could get away with it.

KEN: We'll be fifty miles away in the Jag before they even start looking for me. You don't think I'm kidding, do you?

BRENDAN: No, Ken, I don't, of course I don't.

KEN: I've got a pair of overalls planted and I'm going to fall out during this break.

BRENDAN: Maybe, kid, it would be better if you waited till later. You'd have the whole night before you then.

KEN: No, I wouldn't. There's a watchman goes 'round winding a clock every hour. They'll expect me to make for the main road, but I'm way ahead of them there, Paddy, you'll see.

BRENDAN: Here, you'll need some snout. [*He passes* KEN *more tobacco*] And here's some matches.

KEN: Thanks, Paddy. You're a decent fellow. More than I can say for these others. Some people don't like the Irish—I do.

BRENDAN: We're very popular among ourselves.

KEN: You're a funny bloke, Paddy. Well, goodbye.

BRENDAN: Good luck, Ken, and God go with you.

BEHAN: It was sad—like seeing someone off to America.

[KEN *approaches the* WELSH WARDER]

KEN: Fall out, sir?

WELSH WARDER: [*To* KEN] Why don't you blokes put a washer on it? Go on, then. [KEN *exits. The* WARDER *blows his whistle*] Break up—back to work, come on, yew shower, bend those backs like a leetle jackknife.

BEHAN: Ken was dead lonely. More lonely than I, and with good reason. The other lads might give me the rub about Ireland or about the bombing campaign, and that was seldom enough, and I was never short of an answer—historically informed and obscene. But I was nearer to them than they would ever let Ken be.

CHARLIE: What did you give that Kensington puff a bit of snout for?

BRENDAN: Because he hasn't anything to smoke and I was reared that way by me mother, who would never see anyone go without a smoke.

CHARLIE: Bloody college boy.

BRENDAN: Well, sure he has to do his time like anyone else, no matter what he is.

[*They go on working*]

BEHAN: I had the same rearing as most of them—Dublin, Liverpool, Manchester, Glasgow, London. All our mothers had done the pawn—pledging on Monday, releasing on Saturday. But Ken they never would accept. In a way, as the middle class and the upper class in England spend so much money and energy in maintaining the difference between themselves and the working class, Ken was only getting what his people paid for.

[*He goes out*]

CHARLIE: What's happened to your china with the old school tie?

BRENDAN: What about him?

CHARLIE: He hasn't come back from the loo yet. Where's 'e gone?

BRENDAN: I haven't got him in my fecking pocket.

CHARLIE: No need to take the needle for nothing.

BRENDAN: I'm not taking the needle, but you keep on about this bloke.

CHARLIE: [*Shaking his head in temper*] Oh, hump off, you, you just about got me brassed off. A bloke can't ask you a simple question. Sod off your sodding college-boy china, then, and 'ave 'im for a china, and sod you.

BRENDAN: And sod you, too. And your friends in America and double-sod you.

[*The* WARDER *comes down, checking the* PRISONERS *and frowning*]

WELSH WARDER: Where's your mate, Behaun?

BRENDAN: You mean that lad that was working beside me, sir? In the next row, there?

WELSH WARDER: Yes, and don't you come the old soldier, Behaun. You know bloody well who I mean.

BRENDAN: He fell out at break, sir.

WELSH WARDER: "He fell out at break, sir." I know bloody well he fell out at break, but where the hell is he now? [*Shouts*] Jones! Jones! [*Louder still*] Jo-o-ones.

[*He hurries off, blowing his whistle*]

CHEWLIPS: [*Excited*] Scarper, did 'e?

WELSH WARDER: [*Offstage*] Jones! Jo-o-nes! Hey, Jones!

BORSTAL BOYS: Hear that? Jones! Ken Jones! Scarpered! Taken a powder! Blimey! Humped off! Blown!

[*The* BOYS *gather around in great excitement*]

CHARLIE: I'm sorry I was so leery with you, Paddy. You knew he was scarpering, didn't you?

BRENDAN: Of course I knew. But I couldn't tell you that, and the screw only a few yards from us.

CHARLIE: You were dead right. I wouldn't like to grass on a bloke, neither. I suppose he goes to that bleedin' Sherwood Forest if they get him.

CHEWLIPS: With Robin 'Ood and 'is merry men.

JOE: No, not Jones. [*Slowly*] 'E's doing His Majesty's Pleasure.

CHARLIE: That's murder, isn't it?

HARTY: Yeh! [*Nodding*] One of the lucky ones. The judge said 'e'd 'ave 'ad 'im 'anged, but for 'is age.

CHARLIE: Cor!

HARTY: Most brutal murder and all that lot. 'E pushed 'is crippled brother's bath chair over a cliff.

BRENDAN: His brother's bath chair?

HARTY: With the brother in it.

BRENDAN: Jaysus.

JOE: Paralyzed or somethin', 'e was, from birth.

BRENDAN: How many brothers had he?

JOE: Only the one if y'ask me—I didn't know the family. Shouldn't bloody want to, neither.

WELSH WARDER: [*Enters and blows his whistle*] Come on, line up, look sharp. Now, get a move on. Don't be all day about it! Move!

CHEWLIPS: [*Mischievously, to the* WARDER] Fall out, sir?

[*The* WARDER *chases him off*]

BORSTAL BOYS: [*Singing as they march around and exit*]
We're 'ere in Hollesley prison, fine Borstal Boys are we,
We're not down yet for discharge, but we're waiting patiently.
And when it comes upon us, as it comes upon us all,
This chorus we will sing for you in South 'Ouse dining hall.
"Goodbye to dear old Borstal, goodbye to this old shack!
No more we'll see ya, Hollesley, for we're never coming back!"

JOCK: [*Singing, very sad*]
Ken Jones is never coming back!

[*The lights dim. It is now night.* KEN JONES *is brought in by another* WARDER *and a man with a shotgun*]

WELSH WARDER: Doesn't seem such a good idea now, eh? Scarperin', I mean.

OTHER WARDER: It's the Governor and chokey for you, lad.

[*The* BOYS *congregate at the back of the stage, whispering*]

CHEWLIPS: Old Jonesy didn't make out, eh Pad?

BRENDAN: I'd sooner it was him than me, kid.

CHARLIE: Doesn't look so bleedin' 'ot, does he?

BRENDAN: Give us a bit o' snout for him.

CHARLIE: For 'im? For that college puff?

BRENDAN: Come on. He's been out in that rain all night.

HARTY: And 'e'll get chokey till 'is 'air falls out!

[CHARLIE *reluctantly parts with a butt*]

CHARLIE: I'm not in the bloody Salvation Army.

JOE: He's no china of ours.

BRENDAN: We're all chinas when we're in trouble. Come on. [BRENDAN *approaches* KEN. *The* WARDERS *pretend not to notice*] Well, Lamb of God, if it's not yourself.

KEN: [*Almost in tears*] Hello, Paddy.

BRENDAN: The dead arose and appeared to many. Where did you drop out of at all, at all.

KEN: I almost made it, Pad! Just bad luck.

BRENDAN: Sure, kid. Could happen to a bishop!

KEN: Wish to God I'd been caught sooner. [*Sobs*] I thought that with the overalls on me and the big boots the bus conductor would take me for a farm laborer.

BRENDAN: Ah, sure, God give you sense.

JOE: As much chance of 'em takin' me for Anthony Eden.

KEN: Instead, the bastard brought me to the cop shop.

JOE: He had you tumbled all the time. It was on the nine o'clock news.

A WARDER: [*Blows his whistle, enters and calls*] The Governor!

[*The* BOYS *start to run off*]

GOVERNOR: [*Enters*] Boys! Boys! There you are! What did I tell you! Nobody ever succeeds in scarpering. Walk out any time day or night. Who's to stop you? But you saw what happened to Jones. Thank God he didn't steal anything, anyway—or I'd be told off by the people living around the place. You'd almost think I'd done the stealing. So now, look, boys, don't sneak off without telling me.

[*They all go out. The lights dim to almost total darkness. There is a bugle call*]

VOICE ON P.A. SYSTEM: [*Offstage*] Five-three-nine, Behan . . . Five-three-three, Smith . . . Five-three-nine, Behan . . . Five-three-three, Smith. Report to engineers' yard at once . . . Report to engineers' yard at once.

[WARDER O'SHEA *has entered in the dark; the lights come up on him.* BRENDAN *and* JOCK *appear and then run off as he sees them*]

O'SHEA: Behan. I want you. You too, Smith! On the double! [BRENDAN *and* JOCK *come in*] I see you two fellows want to leave the Garden Party.

BRENDAN and JOCK: [*Together*] That's right, sir.

O'SHEA: You don't like it?

JOCK: It's not that, sir. We're more used to building work, sir.

BRENDAN: I was a painter in Dublin. It's not that we don't like working, but—

O'SHEA: The old blarney. Well, fair exchange is no robbery. We're getting two lads that want to be transferred to the gardens. So they'll be coming down to us and you'll be reporting to the engineers' yard.

BRENDAN: Thank you, sir.

O'SHEA: Don't thank me, thank the Lord.

[*He goes*]

BRENDAN: Imagine getting into overalls again.

JOCK: A real building job.

BRENDAN: Just like outside.

JOCK: Well, it's nearly the same as being outside. Old dolls up in the quarters, screws' wives making cups of tea for you, and all that. And there's two young maids in one big house we're going to. [*Digs* BRENDAN *in the ribs*] They'd eat it.

BRENDAN: Would they?

JOCK: Yes, a bloke called Yorky Turner got done over one of them. Six months they gave him.

BRENDAN: They might as well have left him alone. Nature breaks out in the eyes of a cat.

JOCK: It broke out in him, anyway. They let no one near the big house now. Only the plumber or the painter.

BRENDAN: Good openings for willing lads.

[*He sings*]

. . . *Oh, there was the plumber in the servants' hall,*
D'you think, oh me dear, he's going to solder us all?

[JOE, RIVERS *and* HARTY *come in*]

JOE: What about us, then? Why ain't we given a chance to follow our trade in 'ere, eh?

[BRENDAN *and* JOCK *burst out laughing*]

JOCK: Go away, you registered pimp.

JOE: [*Feigning rage*] And a better bloody trade than yours or Paddy's. It's a diabolical liberty. Geezers get no chance to follow their trade. 'Ere's me, I get no chance whatso-bleedin'-ever to keep my 'and in.

BRENDAN: Your hand in what, Joe? [CHARLIE *comes in, carrying his bedding*] Where are you going with that, china?

CHARLIE: [*Indignantly*] You and me ain't chinas. You go and work with Jock, and get Jock to put 'is bleedin' kip next to yours, and all. You go anywhere you bloody like, you and that bleedin' Jock.

[*He totters off*]

BRENDAN: [*Looking after him*] What can't be cured must be endured.

[*The navvy gang, with wheelbarrow and picks and shovels, come on.* CHEWLIPS, TOM, CRAGG *and* SHAGGY *are among them*]

CHEWLIPS and TOM: [*Singing*]

One, two, three, four,
Hitler has only got one ball,
Goering has two, but very small.
Himmler has something similar
And poor old Goebbels has no balls at all.

JOCK: [*To* BRENDAN] We don't go with them. We report to the painter-in-charge and the plumber-in-charge.

BRENDAN: [*Crossing himself*] Thanks be to God we're not going with that bunch.

JOCK: Say, blokes, do you know where we might find the painter-in-charge and the plumber-in-charge?

[*The navvies eye him in silence for a moment*]

CRAGG: What do you want them for?

JOCK: Well, me and Paddy are working with them and we want to get our tools and brushes.

[*A roar of laughter from the navvies. They shriek and splutter, clapping each other on the back.* WARDER O'SHEA *rushes back in*]

O'SHEA: [*Roaring*] Kip in, you shower. [*They fall instantly silent. He rounds on* JOCK *and* BRENDAN] Where the bloody 'ell do you pair think you're wandering to?

BRENDAN: We're—looking for the painter and plumber.

CRAGG: [*Shouting*] Please, sir, the Jock says they're looking for their tools and brushes.

[*The navvies fall into an even louder explosion of laughter than the first*]

O'SHEA: [*Waving his arms*] Sharrap! Sharrap, I'm telling you.

[*They do, for a second*]

SHAGGY: Tell them they can have a loan of mine!

[*They all burst out laughing again. The* WARDER *shouts; he goes unheeded. Now he lunges at them in a real temper*]

O'SHEA: [*Roaring*] For the last time, keep shut, you shower! [*He turns back to* JOCK *and* BRENDAN] You'll get your tools and brushes. You'll get your tools out of the box like anyone else—a pick and shovel and—

SHAGGY: [*Wheeling in a barrow*] A bloody big barrer!

[*They burst into laughter again*]

O'SHEA: I've warned you shower for the last time. You two get in line there, and I'll fix you up with brushes and tools. A wet day in the place and you think you're going to walk into a detached job. Wonder you don't get after the bloody padre's job. You shift enough shite out of that bloody big 'ole we got up 'ere, and throw down enough concrete, and barrow enough earth, and 'ave a bit more manners than this bloody shower—and then we'll see about brushes and tools. In six months time maybe. [*He roars*] Garden Party! [*Gestures to them to go*] And you there, put out that snout. Put it out or I'll put your bloody lights out! Quick march!

[O'SHEA *goes out*]

BORSTAL BOYS: [*March off, singing*]

We are the nite shite shifters, we shift shite by night.
We shift muck, we shift dirt, and sometimes we shift—sweet violets . . .

[*An Italian* PRIEST *has entered, carrying a missal*]

PRIEST: You're the new Irish boy.

BRENDAN: Well, I'm not all that new, Father, but I'll do.

PRIEST: You're a Catholic, then?

BRENDAN: Am I?

PRIEST: [*Surprised*] Aren't you?

BRENDAN: Yes, Father.

PRIEST: Good. And I see you're a singer.

BRENDAN: The divil a one better.

PRIEST: I need a server.

BRENDAN: You mean a Mass server, Father?

PRIEST: Yes. You can serve Mass, can't you?

BRENDAN: Of course I can. But—I'm excommunicated.

PRIEST: Excommunicated? I don't understand. By whom? When?

BRENDAN: The bishops . . . both the Irish and the English sort. I'm in the I.R.A. and the bishop of this diocese won't let me have the sacraments because I question the right of his country to rule mine.

PRIEST: Remember, when you serve Mass, you do not serve me or the bishop. You serve God. Take the missal. You must try not to be bitter.

   [*He goes out*]

BEHAN: [*Has entered*] Bitter? [*He shrugs*] Walton Jail scalded my heart with regard to my religion, but it also lightened it. My sins had fallen from me because I had almost forgotten there were such things. And when I got over it—my expulsion from religion —it was like being pushed outside a prison and told not to come back.

BRENDAN: Look at me now. Serving Mass.

BEHAN: If you're willing to serve Mass, it is in memory of our ancestors standing around a rock, in a lonely glen, for fear of the English landlords and their yeomen.

   [BRENDAN *stands a moment in reflection; then* JOE, JOCK, HARTY *and* SHAGGY *come on*]

JOE: You're going to serve Mass, Pad?

BRENDAN: That's what the man said.

JOE: You got to go out a bit tasty like.

[*The* BOYS *prepare* BRENDAN *for serving Mass.* CRAGG *enters*]

JOE: You should have shaved again like I told you, Pad. [*He inspects* BRENDAN's *chin*] This is one Mass I'm not going to miss.

HARTY: If we missed Mass on Sundays, my dad would beat our mum. She told us Catholics worshiped the devil, but she got on 'er knees to us to go because 'e'd give 'er a kicking if she didn't, so we went because 'e'd kick 'ell out of us, too.

[*There is a moment of sympathetic silence*]

JOCK: Tell you what, Harty, can you run 'im through the Latin?

HARTY: Me? Not bloody likely. I can 'ardly read English.

JOCK: What about you, Cragg?

JOE: 'E shouldn't be 'ere at all. 'E's an atheist, 'e is.

CRAGG: That's years ago, you silly-born bastard, when I was in Durham Prison. The padre wore robes at service, and 'e came into the condemned cell—

HARTY: [*In a whisper*] 'E was in the condemned cell in Durham.

CRAGG: —and 'e asked me if I knew the significance of the different colors. I said I didn't but 'e should keep with the violet ones—they suited 'im. 'E did look well in them, though, that's truth . . . My wife came on a visit once!

JOE: Don't know what she ever saw in that dossy puff. Two nice kids, too. She comes two 'undred miles 'ere every month to see 'im.

CRAGG: Even though I croaked 'er old man.

[*There is silence.* BRENDAN *looks at* CRAGG *in astonishment*]

HARTY: Go on with what you were tellin' Paddy about the padre.

CRAGG: Ah, 'e asks me 'ow I was getting on with my wife, so I said we were getting along champion, and I asks 'im 'ow 'e was getting on with 'is and was 'e keeping 'er off the old rum bottle, and 'e looks at me like I should 'ave been 'ung, too, and maybe I should, and I wouldn't 'ave minded neither, only it's so bloody painful. They used to 'ave religious texts on the wall of the condemned cell in Durham that Chaplain 'ad put there. One of them said, "Today is the morrow you worried about yesterday and nothing's 'appened." It was the last thing a bloke saw as 'e went out to be hanged.

[*He leaves. They are all silent*]

JOCK: Come on and we'll run Paddy through 'is Latin. I'll do it. *In . . . tro . . . ibo . . . ad . . .*

[CHARLIE *enters*]

JOE: Call that Latin? 'Ere, give me that. Come on, Pad. *Introibo ad altare Dei.*

BRENDAN: *Ad Deum qui laetificat juventutem meam.*

CHARLIE: [*Sulking over a cigarette, at being left out*] Muttering there, like a set of bleeding witch doctors.

JOCK: Well, it's one thing in our Church: no matter where you go, the service is the same.

JOE: That's right, you go in a Catholic Church anywhere in the world and it's the same language.

CHARLIE: Well, they're all bleeding foreigners.

JOCK: And at every minute of the day, somewhere in the world a Mass is being said.

CHARLIE: 'Ow about the North Pole? I reckon in the C. of E. at least you know what the bloke is saying.

JOE: Well, seein' as 'e's usually saying feck all, that shouldn't be hard. The C. of E. ain't a religion at all. They allow divorce and every fecking thing. They only got started because they allowed the King to 'ave a divorce when the Pope wouldn't 'ear of it.

BRENDAN:
"Don't speak of the alien minister
Nor of his Church without meaning nor faith,
For the foundation stone of his temple

Is the balls of Henry the Eighth!"
That's what a preacher said in Ireland four hundred years ago.

CHARLIE: 'E must 'ave been a lovely preacher to come out with language like that in church.

[*The Mass bell sounds*]

BRENDAN: There's the bell. See you after Mass, Charlie.

CHARLIE: Maybe.

[*He goes; then* SHAGGY]

BORSTAL BOYS: Good luck, Pad! Don't let us down! Up the High Hor Ay!

[*The lights grow dim.* BRENDAN *advances alone, as if to the altar. We hear the voice of the* PRIEST]

BRENDAN: *Ad Deum qui laetificat juventutem meam.*

BEHAN: To God, Who giveth joy to my youth.

PRIEST: [*Offstage*] To thee, O God, my God, I will give praise upon the harp.

BEHAN: Why art thou sad, O my soul, and why dost thou disquiet me? I know what you're thinking, kneeling there murmuring the responses . . . You're thinking of the mother singing, "In that dread hour when in my bed I'm lying," while she scrubbed hell out of the washboard, and of Grandmother, shaking a pinch of snuff to her nostril during the sermon, and of old Sister Monica, telling us to go asleep with our arms folded so that if we died in the night, we'd have the sign of the cross on us.

[BRENDAN *genuflects and crosses himself. The lights change. There is a sudden commotion and* BRENDAN *is in the middle of the boys.* CHARLIE *and* SHAGGY *enter*]

JOE: Pad was smashing. Nearly better than the priest! There was that young puff of a college boy, and Paddy 'ad 'im down every time. Paddy worked the priest the wine and all—left his college boy with the water.

CHARLIE: You could show a lot of these bastards up—these bleedin' college boys we get 'ere.

HARTY: Will there be another Mass tomorrow?

JOCK: Every morning. And Stations of the Cross on Friday.

JOE: [*Exultantly*] All this arsin' 'round the chapel will be as good as a trip to Switzerland or a cruise in the Mediterranean.

CHARLIE: [*Resentfully*] You lucky bastards. You'll be going down every afternoon from the mailbag room. You and Joe and Jock and Harty.

JOE: That's right. You blokes can stop in the mailbag room and carry on with the seaming and bottoming and siding and roping while we'll be going down to the R.C. chapel and back. It's your own fault you're not coming. It's because you're a bloody 'eathen.

CHARLIE: [*Indignantly*] I'm not a bloody 'eathen. I'm Church of England.

BRENDAN: Don't mind Joe, he's only taking the piss.

CHARLIE: 'E's got no call to go calling me a bloody 'eathen, even if he is only taking the piss.

SHAGGY: [*Generously*] I don't see why he can't come.

HARTY: No, I don't see why he can't come.

CHARLIE: It's because I'm not a Roman Catholic. The screw will fall in only the R.C.'s.

JOE: The screw won't know what number 'e's to get the first day, and after that, once 'e gets the same number, 'e won't care.

CHEWLIPS: [*Enter. Shyly*] Can I—can I come, too, Paddy?

[*They all turn to* CHEWLIPS *with surprise, and study him*]

BRENDAN: You want to come to the R.C. services every day?

CHEWLIPS: [*Anxiously*] It'd be smashin', Paddy.

JOE: [*To* CHEWLIPS] You don't want to ask 'im. What do you think 'e is, the bleedin' Pope?

CHEWLIPS: Well, I'd just like to . . . matter of fact, I think I was inside a church only once. It's very interesting.

JOE: [*Proudly*] And this is different to the one you go to on Sunday. It's got candles, and . . . and incense, and . . . the lot.

CHEWLIPS: What's incense?

BRENDAN: It's a kind of smoke with perfume in it.

CHEWLIPS: Cor, smashing. Like the Jews.

CHARLIE: What's on this evening?

JOCK: Stations of the Cross.

[*The chapel bell rings. The lights grow dim, and the* BOYS *arrange themselves uncertainly, genuflect awkwardly, and grow confused when making the sign of the cross.* CHEWLIPS *kneels, facing the wrong way.* BRENDAN *set him right.* CHEWLIPS *faces the altar. He reaches out for it and gasps, "Cor, Chewlips!"* BRENDAN *pulls him back. The organ begins to play "Stabat Mater." The* WELSH WARDER *is looking on*]

BEHAN: 'Round the Stations we went, and the little Italian priest gave us a long and sorrowful account of the agony in the garden and of Our Lord's betrayal by Judas. Chewlips followed this with breathless attention and muttered some comments about Judas.

CHEWLIPS: Bleedin' grass'opper!

PRIEST: [*Offstage*] And Jesus said to him, "Judas, dost thou betray the Son of Man with a kiss?

CHEWLIPS: [*Greatly agitated, to* BRENDAN] Just like me, bleedin' bastard. We're going 'round into Russell Street and—

CHARLIE: [*In a fierce whisper*] Kip in, you'll get us done.

[*The* WARDER *is giving them very hard looks*]

PRIEST: [*Offstage*] And they that were about Him, seeing what would follow, said to Him, "Lord, shall we strike with the sword?"

CHEWLIPS: [*Jumping up*] That's it—carve the bastard up!

[*The others pull him back*]

CHARLIE: Shahrrrapp! That screw has you copped.

[*The others now mime what* BEHAN *is describing*]

BEHAN: The padre was most upset about Our Lord's Holy Passion and how he was taken in the Garden of Olives by the other crowd on information received, having been shopped by Judas and then taken off and most cruelly flogged. Joe was there in the middle, shouting the "Stabat Mater" and "Whose sorrow is like unto mine?"—and his hands deep in Shaggy's pocket and he comes up with a whole cigarette and big dog-end. And there is old Cragg, exploring a bag he's just taken out of someone's pocket, and he hands me a piece of jelly from it, which I stick into my mouth and swallow in one delicious gulp. Joe gets a light for his butt off Jock, and there are plenty of lads in the middle of the congregation smoking, but the screws can't tell cigarette smoke from incense. There is Harty leaning against a statue of St. Jude, the Patron of Hopeless Cases, reading a *News of the World*, and two of the chokey blokes savaging sandwiches, and Shaggy for dessert eating a Mars bar and looking over at the priest and the crowd 'round the picture as if he thought very well of them.

JOE: [*To* CHARLIE] What do you think of it, Tosh?

CHARLIE: [*Chewing*] Smashing, ain't it?

CHEWLIPS: I reckon 'e's finishing up now.

BRENDAN: So he is.

JOCK: We better scarper back. Ta for now.

JOE: Ta.

CHARLIE: Ta.

BRENDAN: We'll see you tomorrow—with the help of God. Come on, Chewlips.

[*They all go out, except* CHEWLIPS, BRENDAN *and the* WARDER]

WELSH WARDER: [*Pounces on* CHEWLIPS] Now, when were you converted?

CHEWLIPS: Eh—wot—sir?

WELSH WARDER: You're not a Roman Catholic.

CHEWLIPS: [*Gulping*] No, sir. But my gran was an R.C. and always eat fish on Friday.

WELSH WARDER: [*Menacingly*] You and your gran, eh?

CHEWLIPS: And taters. [*Trailing off*] She'd eat buckets of fish and taters . . .

WELSH WARDER: [*To* BRENDAN] And you knew he wasn't a Catholic, Behaun.

BRENDAN: It's all equal to me what he is. I don't own the Church.

WELSH WARDER: I don't want any of your old buck, Behaun. You'll behave yourself in church and not be talking and whispering and laughing. Now, off with you. [*He turns back to* CHEWLIPS. BRENDAN *leaves*] You don't come again, understand? Now come and explain yourself to the officer of the mailbag class.

[CHEWLIPS *genuflects primly once more. The* WARDER *hustles him off.* BEHAN *enters and sings as the* BOYS *bring on and set the beds for the dormitory*]

BEHAN: [*Sings*]
Now, Borstal is a lovely place,
At nighttime there they wash your face.
"Good night, my son," the screw will say,
"There ends another happy day!"
There's a screw to tuck you into bed,
And lay a pillow 'neath your head.
And as you lie there fast asleep,
'E'll plant a kiss right on your cheek!

[BEHAN *exits*]

BORSTAL BOYS: [*Sing*]

Right on your cheek.

[BRENDAN *runs in*]

CHARLIE: Hi—there 'e is now. Where've you been, Pad?

BRENDAN: Talking to the other altar boy. He's an Irishman—I.R.A. He worked me some snout.

[*They all gather around* BRENDAN]

CHEWLIPS: Cor! The I.R.A. worked the snout and chocolates in for you.

SHAGGY: Old Paddy's got snout.

HARTY: Another R.I.A. man worked it to 'im.

JOE: Tain't R.I.A. It's I.R.A., ain't it, Paddy?

CHARLIE: Wohzamarafawghwohihis, if it's I.R.A. or R.A.F., so long as 'e's got the snout.

HARTY: Dog-ends on you, Paddy.

SHAGGY: Hey, bugger off. I was dog-ends on 'im first.

CHARLIE: [*Indignantly*] Hump off, you puffs, 'is chinas come first.

SHAGGY: Don't tell me to 'ump off, you silly-born bastard, or I shall go over there and bloody pop you one.

CHARLIE: You bloody well won't, you know.

BRENDAN: For the love of Jaysus, keep easy, or none of us will get a bash. The screw will be 'round. There's enough for everybody. Here, Charlie. Here, Shaggy.

[*He distributes cigarettes and candy*]

SHAGGY: [*Offering* CRAGG *some*] Here, Cragg.

CRAGG: Hump off, you lot. I'm improving me mind.

JOCK: Say, Cragg, what are you reading?

CRAGG: *The Decline and Fall of the Roman Empire*. Not for you blokes.

JOCK: Read us a wee bit. [*The others protest*] Go on.

CRAGG: "Such was the depravity of the times that she preferred the timorous touchings of the eunuch to the ponderous ballocks of the Roman Emperor."

[*Several* BOYS *exclaim and run to look at the book*]

BRENDAN: I never knew *The Decline and Fall of the Roman Empire* had such interesting things in it.

RIVERS: Ever read this, Paddy?

BRENDAN: [*Reads the title*] The Life of Oscar Wilde by Frank Harris. [*Eagerly*] I was born only a few hundred yards from where Wilde was born.

RIVERS: Oh?

BRENDAN: I used to think Wilde was sent to the nick for being an Irish patriot. But I believe now it was over sex.

RIVERS: And you don't know what he was really in for?

BRENDAN: Well, not exactly.

RIVERS: I'll show you exactly. [*Shows him a page.* CHEWLIPS *looks, too; says,* "Cor"] Well, what do you think of your *wild* Irishman, now?

BRENDAN: I think that every cripple has his own way of dancing, and I think that if that shocks you, it's just as well ordinary people didn't hear about it. Because, bejaysus, if it shocked you, it'd turn thousands gray.

JOE: The best book I ever saw in the nick was the Bible.

CHARLIE: 'Ark at 'im. The Bible!

JOE: Smashing thin paper for rolling fags in. I must 'ave smoked my way through the Book of Genesis before I went to court.

JOCK: Ssh! Here comes the screw!

[*All dive into bed.* WARDER O'SHEA *enters with a flashlight. He shines the light on each bed in turn*]

O'SHEA: Hey you! Hey you! [*Shouts*] Hey you! [CHEWLIPS *struggles awake*] Dormitory captain! [RIVERS *gets up and comes to* O'SHEA *and stands with the* WARDER *at the foot of* CHEWLIPS' *bed*] Who is this fellow? Get 'im out of it. [RIVERS *shakes* CHEWLIPS] Come on, out of it! Throw him out of it! [CHEWLIPS *slowly and fearfully gets up and stands next to the bed*] Come on, get them off. [CHEWLIPS *starts to take off his shirt*] Your bloody socks! [*He points to* CHEWLIPS' *feet, which are still in stockings pulled up over his pajamas in the manner of a cyclist*] Nice thing, and a bloody 'ouse captain in, and I 'ave to come in and find a fellow with 'is socks on in bed.

RIVERS: I'm sorry, sir.

O'SHEA: As long as I'm officer 'ere, I'll stand no man going to bed with 'is socks on, winter or summer. I don't care 'ow cold it is. It's not a 'ealthy 'abit and I'll get the man out of bed fifty times in the night if I suspect 'e's got anything on besides 'is pajamas. [*To* CHEWLIPS] Now, you remember that.

    [*He leaves*]

RIVERS: Bad show, Chewlips!

BORSTAL BOYS: Bloody bad show!

    [CHEWLIPS *nods fearfully.* RIVERS *climbs back into bed.* CHEWLIPS *gets slowly back into bed and covers himself*]

JOCK: Hey, Chewlips, that screw is dead nuts on anyone trying to sleep with 'is socks on.

CHEWLIPS: [*Mournfully*] I wonder 'ow 'e knows I 'ad them on?

JOCK: Why, you silly-born sod, when he didn't see them with your shoes under the bed he knew, didn't he?

CHEWLIPS: I never thought of that. But if I did 'ave a pair under me bed, 'e wouldn't bother, would 'e?

    [CHEWLIPS *leaps from his bed, fetches some spare socks from under the pillow, puts them on, places the first pair in his shoes, hollers, "Foh-pance a pahnd—pehhs!" and leaps back into bed. The lights grow dim. In the darkness, voices call to* BRENDAN]

SHAGGY: Thanks, Paddy, for the snout.

BRENDAN: That's all right, kid, you're welcome.

BORSTAL BOYS: [*Together*] Thanks, Paddy.

JOE: Good night, Pad.

BRENDAN: Good night, Joe. Good night, Charlie. Good night, Harty.

CHARLIE: Good night, Joe. 'Night, Paddy.

CHEWLIPS: Good night, Paddy—and Up the Hey R. Hey, or whatever you call it.

[*They all laugh in the dark*]

BRENDAN: Good night, Chewlips; good night, all.

[*They settle down for sleep.* BEHAN *enters*]

BEHAN: Reposed and innocent they look now, every mother's son of them, including myself. [*The lights change; a bugle blows—it is morning. The* BOYS *remove the beds—but* CHEWLIPS *is still sleeping in his bed. They call to him to wake up. Finally they all gather at his bed and shout together:* "Rise and shine, the day is fine/ The sun will scorch your balls off!" *They pick up his bed with him in it, and carry it offstage as he sits up in bed and yells;* "Foh-pance a pahnd—pehhs!" TOM MEADOWS *enters during the following, carrying a ladder and paint pot and brush. He sets them down and commences to work*] Time passing is like a bank balance growing to a prisoner, and every day, week and month for pounds, shillings and pence. Though I was not thinking of discharge yet. It was a bit soon for that. But still, roll on. I got a detached job at last! No more of that goddamned navvy gang. Wondering every morning who you'll have to fight before the day is out!

[BRENDAN *enters*]

TOM: Hello, Paddy.

BRENDAN: [*Smiling*] Hello, Tom.

BEHAN: Tom Meadows was the only other painter left on the skeleton staff while the rest were out fruit pickin'. Joe said he was the right one to leave on the skeleton staff 'cause he looked like a bleedin' skelton.

TOM: Do you know, Paddy, they're a bloody rum lot here, if you ask me, a bloody rum lot. I shan't be sorry when I get out again among decent, honest folk. [*He sighs*] Whenever that may be.

BRENDAN: Very soon, I hope, Tom, please God.

TOM: I don't 'old with the I.R.A., Paddy, but it's a disgrace to put you into Borstal among a lot of scum.

BRENDAN: Ah, sure, the blokes are only working-class kids like our-selves, Tom.

TOM: [*Indignantly*] They're not. They're not working-class blokes. They're reared up to thieving and stealing and living off prostitutes the same as the boss class. And they know it. If you ever hear them talking of any heroes outside the nick, it's about the way Anthony Eden dresses, or the way the Duke of Windsor ties a knot in 'is tie. 'Aven't you noticed nearly all thieves are Tories?

BRENDAN: Maybe it's because all Tories are thieves.

TOM: And you can't talk to these other daft bastards. They're too stupid, and when they 'ave owt to say, it's about filth and muck, when it's not shagging lies about all the millions of money they 'ave stacked away for when they get out. One fellow was 'ere, 'e 'ad me near driven barmy telling me about 'is spiv suits and about running about with 'oors in taxis.

BRENDAN: [*Laughing as though he has to*] By God, Tom, you never lost it. You don't care a damn what you say, but speak it right out of your mind. And do you know what I'm going to tell you? [BRENDAN *looks at him seriously*] You're bloody well right, too.

TOM: [*Smiles deprecatingly*] Well, Pad, we're blunt folk where I come from. [BRENDAN *starts the first line of a song.* TOM *interrupts*] Know this one, Pad? [*He sings*]

. . . It looked around our infant might,
When all beside looked dark as night,
It witnessed many a deed and vow,
We will not change its color now . . .

[BRENDAN *joins in*]

BRENDAN and TOM:

Then by this banner swear we all,
To bear it onward till we fall,
Come dungeons dark or gallows grim,
This song will be our parting hymn—
Then raise the scarlet standard high,
Beneath its folds we'll live or die,

Let cowards mock or traitors sneer,
We'll keep the red flag flying here!

[JOE, JOCK, CHARLIE *and* CHEWLIPS *limp on, singing: "We are the nite shite shifters," holding their aching backs, and carrying forks. They collapse onto some benches.* TOM *keeps well away from them*]

BEHAN: The four just men, home for their tea.

JOCK: [*Looking at* TOM] Paddy and the head boy on the painters had a bleeding choir practice. Singing the whole evening, they were.

JOE: [*So that* TOM *can't hear*] Hey, Paddy, come 'ere. Don't 'ave anything to do with that bloke. 'E's been in trouble with the police.

BRENDAN: In trouble with the police? Sure haven't we all been in trouble with the police?

JOE: But 'e's the bleeding Lancashire strangler. Doing H.M.P. for croaking 'is judy—with 'er own stocking. She was going with some other bloke in 'er off-time.

CHEWLIPS: Stuff me!

BRENDAN: That accounts for his givin' out about you blokes!

JOCK: And he wasn't married to her. It was bloody savage. She was only seventeen, and all.

BRENDAN: It was a bit stern, all right.

JOCK: Maybe she was knocked up. In Scotland, the old dolls in the place would never let you forget that.

BRENDAN: And in Ireland, down the country anyway, if a girl got knocked up she might as well leave on the next boat or drown herself and have done with it. The people there are so Christian and easily shocked.

[*The* COOK *comes in, an old ex-army type, with a flagon of cider and some mugs*]

BEHAN: The cook's name, by the way, in case I didn't mention it

before, was Tucker. Humorously referred to as Tucker the—oh
well, never mind.

[*The* COOK *gives out mugs of cider*]

BRENDAN: Good old . . . Tucker!

COOK: You're the Irish bloke, ain't you?

BRENDAN: [*Nods*] That's right, and may the giving hand never
falter. [*He sips*] It's like cider.

COOK: Like Guinness, ain't it? Ah, the old scrump. Know the way
my old dad used to make it, Paddy?

BRENDAN: It's made from apples, ain't it?

COOK: 'Course. All cider is made from apples. But not everyone can
make it like everyone else, or as good.

BRENDAN: Stands to common sense, that does, like everything else.

COOK: Well, my old dad, when 'e 'ad the juice of the apples
pressed out and casked like, before 'e closed the cask 'e'd throw
into the ten-gallon cask a quart of brandy, seven pounds of the
best beef and a dead rat.

[JOE, JOCK, CHARLIE *and* CHEWLIPS *spew out the cider and
look at him in horror*]

BRENDAN: [*Calmly*] It must have been a recipe handed down.

COOK: That's what it was, Paddy, 'anded down. [*Pauses*] 'Course,
rat, he was skinned.

JOCK: [*Still spitting out cider*] Jesus!

[*He runs off, holding his mouth*]

COOK: Put them mugs up in the window sill when you've finished.
I've got to get back to me soup.

[*He goes into the kitchen*]

JOE: 'Anded down. What was 'anded down, the bloody rat?

JOCK: He's a disgusting old bastard, and no mistake.

CHEWLIPS: I wonder how many he put in the soup. Four pence a

pair—rats! [*The* BOYS *throw their cider in his face and go out*]
What have I done now?

[*He goes out, too.* TOM MEADOWS, *who has been apart from all this, collects his paints, etc., and starts to leave*]

BEHAN: [*Sings*]
I had no mother to break her heart
I had no father to take my part
I had one friend and a girl was she . . .
And he croaked her with her own silk stocking . . . At Christmas, Matron put on a Nativity play. Harty and Joe were census takers. [*They enter*] Jock and Charlie were shepherds. [*They enter*] Chewlips was a wise man. [*He enters*] Ken Jones was St. Joseph. [*He enters and* BRENDAN *enters*] And believe it or not, Shaggy was a shagging angel. [SHAGGY *enters. They are all dressed in costumes for their various parts.* SHAGGY *crosses the stage, climbs a ladder and stands in an angelic attitude*] One of the screws' wives, a young girl, was to play the Virgin Mary.

[*A stunning girl crosses the stage*]

WARDER'S WIFE: Cragg! Anyone seen Cragg?

[*She exits*]

JOE: [*Smitten*] I want to be St. Joseph. I am Joseph anyway, always have been in real life.

BRENDAN: You'd be a bit too much like real life, Joe.

JOE: Well, then, I want to be the Holy Ghost.

JOCK: You silly-born twerp, there's no Holy Ghost in this play.

BRENDAN: Nick, nick, here she comes again.

[*The "Virgin Mary" crosses back in, carrying a doll in a manger, smiles at all, and leaves*]

JOE: [*Desperately*] Well, then, I want to be the baby.

[*He runs after the girl. The boys trip him up*]

SHAGGY: Rise up, Joseph.

[*They all rush off, chased by* JOE]

BEHAN: That night we had a singsong, and they all shouted,
"Paddy, give us a song!" So this is what I sang. [*Sings, with*
BRENDAN *joining in betimes*]
I took me girl up to the zoo
To show her the lion and the kangaroo
All she wanted to see was me oul' cockatoo
Up in the zoological gardens.

Thunder and lightning, it's no lark
When Dublin City is in the dark
If you have any money go up to the park
And view the zoological gardens.

Oh, says she, it's seven o'clock
I have to go home for you've ruined me frock
And I knew she was one of the rale oul' stock
Up in the zoological gardens.

Thunder and lightning, it's no lark
When Dublin City is in the dark
If you have any money go up to the park
And view the zoological gardens.

As we went up be the old park gate
The policeman was upon his beat.
He waves his baton at me darlin' Kate
Outside the zoological gardens.

Thunder and lightning, it's no lark
When Dublin City is in the dark
If you have any money go up to the park
And view the zoological gardens.

We went up there on me honeymoon
Say she, me love, if you don't come soon
I'll have to get in with the hairy baboon
Up in the zoological gardens.

Thunder and lightning, it's no lark
When Dublin City is in the dark
If you have any money go up to the park
And view the zoological gardens.
    [*All the* BOYS *cheer offstage*]

CHEWLIPS: [*Shouting, offstage*] You're a good kid, Paddy!

BEHAN: A *vico*,* you're all good kids.

BRENDAN: We're all good kids. We're all the kids our mothers warned us against.

[JOCK, HARTY, JOE, SHAGGY, *and* CHEWLIPS *enter in civilian clothes, carrying luggage and singing*]

One more hour and we shall be,
Out of the dump of misery
Bye, bye, Borstal.

Out the door and we'll be free,
You'll see sweet feck-all of me,
Bye, bye, Borstal.

The Governor and the screws don't understand us,
All that Borstal bullshit they all hand us.

I've packed my bag and packed my grip,
We're not coming back next trip,
Borstal—bye, bye!

[*As they go off*]
Goodbye, Pad! See you, Pad! Up the Hi! Har! Hey!

CHEWLIPS: [*Sings*]
Foh-pance a pahnd—pehhs!

[CHARLIE *comes in slowly alone, in his sailor's uniform*]

BRENDAN: Begod, china, the Germans will be dead frit when they hear you're back in the crow's-nest.

CHARLIE: Oh, get stuffed, you bloody mad bomber. 'Eeere, what's that, something you nicked?

BRENDAN: If you weren't such a bloody heathen, Charlie, you'd know today's St. Patrick's Day, and this is shamrock. Here, I'll put it in your hat for luck.

CHARLIE: [*Smiling*] Pad, remember that song you used to sing in the summer, down by the beach?

*My son.

BRENDAN: [*Sings*]
The sea, oh, the sea, a ghradh gheal mo chroidhe . . .

CHARLIE: That's it! Well, listen, I've got a new way to sing it.
[*Sings*]
The sea, oh the sea, a ghradh gheal mo chroidhe,
O long may you roll between Borstal and me!
[*They both laugh*]

They were smashin' days, down there last summer, Pad.

BRENDAN: They were and all, Charlie.

CHARLIE: [*Extending his hand*] Goodbye, Pad.

BRENDAN: Goodbye, Charlie.
[*Sings*]
Is go dtéighidh tú, a mhúirnín, slán.

CHARLIE: Up the I.R.A.

[*He goes out slowly*]

BEHAN: [*After a pause*] Summer came again, and every day, there
I was, going up the road to work, grown up now like Ossian after
the Fianna. And then one October day—

[WARDER O'SHEA *comes in slowly*]

O'SHEA: Remember your china, Paddy?

BRENDAN: Which of them? Is it Charlie Millwall?

O'SHEA: [*Handing* BRENDAN *a cigarette and lighting it for him*]
Yes. I just heard today in the mess. Millwall—

BRENDAN: Charlie is dead.

O'SHEA: You knew? You'd heard already?

BRENDAN: Oh, I just fecking guessed. [*Pauses*] Where was it? At
sea, I suppose.

O'SHEA: Remember the convoy was attacked, and the *Southampton*
was sunk a couple of weeks ago?

BRENDAN: I suppose I do. I don't take that much interest in your
bloody convoys, as a rule.

O'SHEA: Well, it was in the Straits of Gibraltar.

BRENDAN: I'd have guessed it—that he'd have been croaked before the end of the war.

O'SHEA: How's that?

BRENDAN: [*He starts to answer, but changes his mind*] Thanks for telling us, Mr. O'Shea, and thanks for the bit of snout.

O'SHEA: [*Pats* BRENDAN *on the shoulder*] That's all right, Paddy boy.

[*He goes.* BRENDAN *sits down, lost in thought*]

BRENDAN: [*Sings softly*]
Walk, walk, walk, my own,
Not even God can make us one,
Now you have left me here alone,
Is go dtéighidh tú, a mhúirnín, slán.

[*He sits with his head bowed. The* WELSH WARDER *enters and calls, "Behaun! Behaun!" He has a bucket and sandpaper. He is followed by* TOM, KEN, CRAGG, *and another boy. They all have buckets and sandpaper*]

WELSH WARDER: Now, Bee-haun, you'll clean this bucket till it's like silvair.

BRENDAN: I will in my ass.

WELSH WARDER: What is that you say, Bee-haun?

BRENDAN: I never saw a silver bucket in my whole bloody life.

WELSH WARDER: I'll show you. [*He takes a piece of sandpaper and begins polishing the bucket.* BRENDAN *looks at the bucket in mock idiocy. The* WARDER *throws it down in a temper*] All right, Bee-haun, I've just 'ed enuv off yew. You're for the Governor in the morning.

BRENDAN: [*Mimicking*] I'm not, yew know.

WELSH WARDER: Yew are for 'im in the morning.

BRENDAN: I'm not for him in the morning, or any other fecking time. And sod him, and sod you, too, you stringy-looking puff.

[*The* WARDER *is agape. He blasts furiously on his whistle.*
BRENDAN *grimaces behind his back. The* BOYS *are delighted,
and laugh silently.* O'SHEA *comes on the run with another*
WARDER]

O'SHEA: What's up, Mr. Hacknell?

WELSH WARDER: It's this Irish pig—

O'SHEA: Paddy? 'Ere, what's all this?

WELSH WARDER: He said sod me and sod the Governor and called
me a stringy-looking puff!

O'SHEA: [*Looking the* WARDER *up and down*] Did you, Paddy?

BRENDAN: Yes, I did.

O'SHEA: It's chokey for him so! Come on, grab him—into the cell
with him.

[*The other two* WARDERS *throw* BRENDAN *into a cell. The
lights dim, except for a light on* BRENDAN. *The* PRIEST *is in the
shadows*]

BRENDAN: To hell with you all! Leave me alone!

BEHAN: Take it easy, son!

BRENDAN: They're not going to pull that Walton stuff on me again!

BEHAN: We won't forget Walton in a hurry, will we? Or the excommunication?

[*The* PRIEST *moves toward* BRENDAN]

BRENDAN: Keep away from me, you fat bastard! You and your excommunication. I suppose you think excommunication is something new to the I.R.A. Wasn't my own father excommunicated?
To hell with Rome! To hell with England! Up the Republic!

[*The* PRIEST *comes into the light*]

PRIEST: Up the Republic every time, Brendan.

BRENDAN: [*Dazedly*] There was a priest in Walton—

PRIEST: Walton? You've come a long way from Walton, my son.

And soon you'll be a long way from Hollesley Bay—back safe and sound in that Republic you love.

BRENDAN: What?

PRIEST: You're going out this morning, Brendan. We've known about it all week.

[*The* WARDERS, *the* GOVERNOR *and the* BOYS *are gathered around. The* BOYS *are cheering. The lights come up*]

O'SHEA: That's right, Paddy. The Governor locked you up to keep you out of trouble. The boys want to give you a big cheer in the dining hall.

[*Cheers are heard offstage*]

PRIEST: [*Smiling*] Well, my dear Brendan, what will I do now for a mass server?

BRENDAN: Get another I.R.A. man, I suppose.

PRIEST: [*Earnestly*] I wish I could hear your confession before you go out—

BRENDAN: [*Smiling*] Only sinful people have to go to confession.

BEHAN: It's only dirty people have to wash.

PRIEST: But His Lordship, the Bishop—

BRENDAN: That's all right, Father, I understand.

PRIEST: Well, my son, goodbye and good luck, and may God bless you always.

BRENDAN: [*Taking the* PRIEST's *proffered hand*] And you too, Father.

O'SHEA: Goodbye, Paddy.

GOVERNOR: Goodbye and good luck, Brendan.

BORSTAL BOYS: Good old Paddy! Hooray for Pad! Up the Hey! Ar! Hey! Good old, Pad!

[*All exit, except* BEHAN]

BEHAN: [*Sings*]
As I walk out of this lovely dump

In my throat will come a great big lump,
And I will gaze with eyes so full of tears
At the place where I spent three 'appy years.

BORSTAL BOYS: [*Offstage*] Some fecking 'opes!

[BRENDAN *emerges, all dressed up in a new suit, shouting*
"Goodbye!" The BOYS *offstage shout goodbyes*]

BEHAN: . . . and I will make my journey, if life and death but
stand/ Unto that pleasant country, that fresh and fragrant strand/
And leave your boasted braveries, your wealth and high com-
mand/For the fair hills of Holy Ireland . . . There they are, as if
you'd never left them, in their sweet and stately order 'round the
bay—the Dublin mountains and the spires and the chimneys, all
counted, present and correct, from Bray head right 'round to Kilbarrack.

BRENDAN: I can't really see Kilbarrack, but I know it's there. So
many belonging to us lie buried in Kilbarrack.

BEHAN: The healthiest graveyard in Ireland because it's so near the
sea.

[*There is the blast of a ship's whistle.* BRENDAN *searches in*
his pocket and brings out the expulsion order. An IMMIGRA-
TION MAN *comes in. The crowds, with their luggage, move*
around, talking and laughing, covering BRENDAN *up for a*
moment]

IMMIGRATION MAN: Passport, travel permit or identity document,
please. [BRENDAN *hands him the document; he reads*] Behan,
Brendan. [*Hands it back. He takes* BRENDAN's *hand*] *Cead mile*
failte abhaile romhat. A hundred thousand welcomes home to you.

BRENDAN: [*Smiling*] *Go raibh maith agat.*

IMMIGRATION MAN: [*Tenderly*] *Caithfidh go bhfuil se go h-ion-*
tach bheith saor?

BRENDAN: *Caithfidh go bhfuil.*

IMMIGRATION MAN: It must be wonderful to be free.

BRENDAN: It must.

[*He goes*]

BEHAN: It must indeed . . . [*Sings*]
. . . *Is go dtéighidh tú, a mhúirnín slán* . . .

CURTAIN

STICKS AND BONES

David Rabe

David Rabe

Within a comparatively short time, David Rabe, author of the 1972 Tony Award play, *Sticks and Bones*, has joined the ranks of America's outstanding playwrights.

It all began in 1971 when the New York Shakespeare Festival (Joseph Papp, producer) presented the first play of his Vietnam trilogy, *The Basic Training of Pavlo Hummel*. The play ran for 363 performances and won him a Drama Desk Award for "most promising playwright," an "Obie" (for Off-Broadway excellence), as well as the Elizabeth Hull–Kate Warriner Award voted by the Dramatists Guild Council as the season's best play on a controversial subject.

While *Pavlo Hummel* was still attracting capacity audiences, *Sticks and Bones* opened on November 7, 1971, at another theatre in the Off-Broadway Shakespeare Festival complex.

One of the first of the journalistic cheers came from Clive Barnes of the New York *Times*: "*Sticks and Bones* is a remarkable new play and I urge anyone interested in the modern theatre or even in contemporary America to see it . . . It is a poet's vision of the disaster of moral bankruptcy . . . written in a quite amazing style."

George Oppenheimer declared in *Newsday*: "There is a new voice in the American theatre and it speaks fiercely, bravely and eloquently. It is that of David Rabe. We heard it first in last season's *The Basic Training of Pavlo Hummel*, a black comedy-drama of the Vietnam war with rich humor and great originality. Last night we heard it again and with infinitely more power and quality in *Sticks and Bones*.

"Once again Rabe has written an anti-war play with a fury that mounts to an almost unbearable conclusion. It is a story of the return of a blind soldier to an 'American Dream' home . . . here is a trio (mother, father, younger brother) that is even blinder than David, refusing to see what is going on in the shattered world of today . . . Here, at long last, is a magnificent play by a man who may well become our most important new American playwright."

Other journalistic voices concluded that it was "A harrowing and powerful play . . . It clearly is a work of passion by a gifted writer and has a shattering impact."

Sticks and Bones played for 121 performances Off-Broadway, then was transferred to Broadway on March 1, 1972, where it ran for an additional 245 performances.

A Tony Award also went to actress Elizabeth Wilson for her portrayal of the blinded soldier's mother.

David Rabe was born on March 10, 1940, in Dubuque, Iowa. He was educated at Loras Academy and Loras College, both in Dubuque, and served in the U. S. Army for two years, the final eleven months in Vietnam.

Mr. Rabe studied writing at Villanova University where he wrote the first drafts of *The Basic Training of Pavlo Hummel* and *Sticks and Bones*—the latter was originally staged at Villanova in 1969.

In his introduction to the first publication of both plays, the author admitted: "When I returned from Vietnam, I was home for six months before I thought seriously of writing (finally there was nothing else to do with the things I was thinking). But oddly enough, it was a novel rather than a play that I wanted to work on. I had written both plays and novels earlier in my life and my writing came from something in me not dedicated to any one form. And upon return, theatre seemed lightweight, all fluff and metaphor, spangle, posture, and glitter crammed into a form as rigid as any machine geared to reproduce the shape of itself endlessly. In the way that all machines are unnatural in a natural universe, theatrical form seemed artificial beyond what was necessary.

"But then I chanced upon a grant of money, a Rockefeller grant in playwriting, enough to live on for a year and a half. I remember thinking, 'I'll dash off some plays real quick, then focus in on the novel.'

"But when I sat down to write, regardless of the form, I found it impossible to avoid the things most crowding my mind, and because these memories and ideas were of such extreme value to me, I could deal with them with nothing less than my best effort.

"What I am trying to say is simply that if things had turned out differently, I don't know if I would have written what I have in the way I have, but the grant was a playwriting grant."

After Villanova, Mr. Rabe joined the staff of the New Haven *Register*, where he won an Associated Press Award for feature writing.

Other honors that have been bestowed upon the writer are a New York Drama Critics' Circle Citation and an Outer Circle Award, both for *Sticks and Bones*, and an award from the National Institute of Arts and Letters.

With Madeline Kahn in the leading role, Mr. Rabe's *Boom Boom Room* had its première at Lincoln Center in 1973. Joseph Papp served as both producer and director.

The third and final play of Mr. Rabe's Vietnam trilogy, *Streamers*, opened at Lincoln Center in April 1976. The play was directed by Mike Nichols and once again the author was acclaimed by the press as "the most significant young playwright of this generation" and "one of the finest playwrights in America."

The play was named the best American play of the 1975–76 season by the New York Drama Critics' Circle.

Sticks and Bones was first produced professionally by Joseph Papp, on November 7, 1971, at the New York Shakespeare Festival Public Theatre. The cast was as follows:

OZZIE	*Tom Aldredge*
HARRIET	*Elizabeth Wilson*
RICK	*Cliff DeYoung*
SERGEANT MAJOR	*Hector Elias*
DAVID	*David Selby*
GIRL	*Asa Gim*
PRIEST	*Charles Siebert*

Sticks and Bones was first produced on Broadway by Joseph Papp, on March 1, 1972, at the John Golden Theatre. The cast was as follows:

OZZIE	*Tom Aldredge*
HARRIET	*Elizabeth Wilson*
PRIEST	*Charles Siebert*
RICK	*Cliff DeYoung*
SERGEANT MAJOR	*Hector Elias*
DAVID	*Drew Snyder*
GIRL	*Asa Gim*

Directed by Jeff Bleckner
Associate Producer: Bernard Gersten
Setting by Santo Loquasto
Costumes by Theoni V. Aldredge
Lighting by Ian Calderon

TIME: *Autumn.*

PLACE: *The family home.*

ACT ONE

PLACE: *The family home.*
Darkness; silence. Slides appear on both sides of the stage: the first is a black-and-white medium close-up of a young man, mood and clothing of the early 1900s; he is lean, reasonably handsome, black hair parted in the center. Voices speak. They are slow and relaxed, with an improvisational quality.

1ST CHILD'S VOICE: Who zat?

MAN'S VOICE: Grandpa Jacob's father.

[*New slide: group photo, same era, eight or ten people, all ages*]

2ND CHILD'S VOICE: Look at 'em all!

1ST CHILD'S VOICE: How come they're all so serious?

[*New slide: small boy, black hair, black knickers*]

WOMAN'S VOICE: There's Grandpa Oswald as a little boy.

1ST CHILD'S VOICE: Grandpa?

[*New slide: different boy, same pose*]

WOMAN'S VOICE: And that's his brother Thomas. He died real young.

MAN'S VOICE: Scarlet fever.

[*New slide: young girl, seventeen or eighteen*]

And that's his sister Christina.

WOMAN'S VOICE: No, that's Grandma.

MAN'S VOICE: No.

WOMAN'S VOICE: Sure.

   [*New slide:* OZZIE *and* HARRIET, *young, 1940s era*]

There's two of them.

MAN'S VOICE: Mmmmm, you're right, because that's Grandpa.

   [*New slide: two boys, five and nine years old*]

WOMAN'S VOICE: The taller one's David, right?

   [*New slide: color close-up of* DAVID *from the last moment of the play, a stricken look*]

1ST CHILD'S VOICE: What's that one?

MAN'S VOICE: Somebody sick.

1ST CHILD'S VOICE: Boy . . . !

   [*New slide: color photo of* OZZIE, HARRIET, *and* FATHER DONALD. FATHER DONALD, *wearing a gym suit, his back to the camera, stands holding a basketball in one hand.* OZZIE *and* HARRIET *face him, one on either side*]

2ND CHILD'S VOICE: Oh, look at that one!

MAN'S VOICE: That's a funny one, isn't it.

WOMAN'S VOICE: That's one—I bet somebody took it—they didn't know it was going to be taken.

   [*There is a bright flash and the stage is immediately illuminated. The set is an American home, very modern, with a quality of brightness, green walls, green rug. Stairs lead up to a bedroom—not lighted now—with a hallway leading off to the rest of the upstairs beyond. There is naturalness, yet a sense of space and, oddly, a sense also that this room, these stairs belong in the gloss of an advertisement.*
   Downstage, a TV on wheels faces upstage, glowing, murmuring. OZZIE, HARRIET, *and* FATHER DONALD—*a slightly rotund, serious man—are standing as they were in the slide last seen*]

FATHER DONALD: A feel for it is the big thing. A feel for the ball. You know, I mean, bouncing it, dribbling it. You don't even look at it.

[*Phone rings*]

OZZIE: I'll get it.

FATHER DONALD: You can do it, Harriet. Give it a try. [*He bounces the ball to* HARRIET]

OZZIE: Hello? . . .

FATHER DONALD: [*As* HARRIET *catches the ball*] That a girl.

HARRIET: Oh, Father . . .

OZZIE: [*Hanging up*] Nobody there.

FATHER DONALD: That's what I'm telling you. You gotta help kids. Keeps 'em outa trouble. We help. Organized sports activities; it does 'em a world a good. You know that. And they need you.

OZZIE: I was a track and field man. Miler. Dash man—I told you.

[*Phone rings*]

FATHER DONALD: But this is basketball season. [*He moves toward* HARRIET *and then the door, as* OZZIE *goes to the phone, says* "Hello," *then listens intently*] You listen to me, you get that husband of yours out there to help us. It'll do him good. Tell him he'd be a good little guard. A play maker.

HARRIET: Oh, Father Donald, bless me.

FATHER DONALD: Of course. [*He blesses her, holding the ball under his left arm*] Bye-bye.

HARRIET: [*As* FATHER DONALD *goes*] Good-bye, Father. [*And she turns to look for a moment at* OZZIE *on the phone*] Why aren't you talking? [*Silence: she is looking at him*] Ozzie, why aren't you talking?

OZZIE: [*Slowly lowering the phone*] They're gone. They hung up.

HARRIET: You didn't say a word. You said nothing.

OZZIE: I said my name.

HARRIET: What did they want?

OZZIE: I said hello.

HARRIET: Were they selling something—is that what they wanted?

OZZIE: No, no.

HARRIET: Well . . . who was it?

OZZIE: What?

HARRIET: What are we talking about?

OZZIE: The Government. It was . . . you know . . .

HARRIET: Ozzie! [*In fear*] No!

OZZIE: [*Some weariness in him*] No, he's all right, he's coming home!

HARRIET: Why didn't you let me speak? Who was it?

OZZIE: No, no.

HARRIET: It was David.

OZZIE: No, somebody else. Some clerk. I don't know who.

HARRIET: You're lying.

OZZIE: No. There was just all this static—it was hard to hear. But he was coming home was part of it, and they had his records and papers but I couldn't talk to him directly even though he was right there, standing right there.

HARRIET: I don't understand.

OZZIE: That's what they said . . . And he was fine and everything. And he wanted them to say hello for him. He'd lost some weight. He would be sent by truck. I could hear truck engines in the background—revving. They wanted to know my name. I told them.

HARRIET: No more?

OZZIE: They were very professional. Very brusque . . .

HARRIET: No more . . . at all? . . .

[*The front door opens and* RICK *comes in. And the door slams. He is young, seventeen. His hair is long and neat, with sideburns. His clothing is elaborate—very, very up-to-date. He carries a guitar on his shoulder*]

RICK: Hi, Mom. Hi, Dad.

HARRIET: Hi, Rick.

OZZIE: Hi, Rick.

HARRIET: Ohhh, Ricky, Ricky, your brother's on his way home. David's coming home!

OZZIE: We just got a call.

RICK: Ohhh, boy!

HARRIET: Isn't that wonderful? Isn't it? Your father talked to him. Oh, I bet you're starving. Sit, sit.

OZZIE: I talked to *somebody*, Rick.

HARRIET: There's fudge and ice cream in the fridge; would you like that?

RICK: Oh, yeah, and could I have some soda? [*She is on her way to the kitchen, nodding*] Wow, some news. I'm awful hungry.

OZZIE: Never had a doubt. A boy like that—if he leaves, he comes back.

RICK: [*As he picks up a comic book*] How about me? What if I left?

OZZIE: Absolutely. Absolutely. [*Silence.* RICK *reads the comic*] I built jeeps . . . tanks, trucks.

RICK: What?

OZZIE: In the other war, I mean. Number Two. I worked on vehicles. Vehicles were needed and I worked to build them. Sometimes I put on wheels, tightened 'em up. I never . . . served . . . is what I mean. [*Slight pause*] They got all those people—soldiers, Rick—you see what I mean? They get 'em across the ocean, they don't have any jeeps or tanks or trucks, what are they gonna do, stand around? Wait for a bus on the beachhead? Call a cab?

RICK: No public transportation in a war.

OZZIE: That's right, that's right.

[HARRIET *enters, carrying fudge and ice cream*]

HARRIET: Oh, Ozzie, Ozzie, do you remember—I just remembered that time David locked himself in that old icebox. We didn't know where he was. We looked all over. We couldn't find him. And then there was this icebox in this clearing . . . out in the middle. I'll bet you don't even remember.

OZZIE: Of course I remember.

HARRIET: And he leaped to us. So frightened.

OZZIE: He couldn't even speak—he couldn't even speak—just these noises.

HARRIET: Or that time he fell from that tree.

OZZIE: My God, he was somethin'! If he wasn't fallin', he was gettin' hit.

HARRIET: And then there was that day we went out into the woods. It was just all wind and clouds. We sailed a kite!

OZZIE: I'd nearly forgotten! . . .

RICK: Where was I?

HARRIET: You were just a baby, Rick. We had a picnic.

RICK: I'm gonna get some more soda, okay?

[HARRIET *touches him as he passes*]

OZZIE: What a day that was. I felt great that day.

HARRIET: And then Hank came along. Hank Grenweller. He came from out of the woods calling that—

OZZIE: That's right.

HARRIET: He was happy.

OZZIE: We were all happy. Except he'd come to tell us he was going away, leaving. And then we had that race. Wasn't that the day?

HARRIET: I don't remember.

OZZIE: Hank and me! Hank Grenweller. A foot race. And I beat him. I did it; got him.

HARRIET: Noooo.

OZZIE: It was only inches, but—

HARRIET: Ozzie, he took it easy. He wasn't trying.

OZZIE: He had to do his very best. Always. Never less. That was one thing you knew—no matter what he did or said, it was meant and true. All those long talks. Do you ever miss him?

HARRIET: He was a fine strong man.

OZZIE: I don't know why he left.

HARRIET: Do you remember when he showed us this house?

OZZIE: I remember when he showed me you.

HARRIET: You know that's not true. If it was close—and it was— that race you ran—[*This is not loud: there is intimacy; they are near one another*] I remember now—it was because he let it be— no other reason. We were all having fun. He didn't want to make you feel badly. He didn't want to ruin all the fun. You know that. You know you do.

RICK: [*Calling from the kitchen*] You people want some fudge?

HARRIET: No, Rick.

OZZIE: I don't know he didn't try. I don't know that. [*He stares at* HARRIET]

HARRIET: I think I'll be going up to bed; take a little nap.

RICK: Sleepy, Mom?

HARRIET: A little. [*She is crossing toward* OZZIE]

RICK: That's a good idea then.

HARRIET: Call me.

RICK: Okay.

HARRIET: Do you know, the day he left? It was a winter day. No- vember, Ozzie. [*She moves toward the stairs*]

OZZIE: I know.

HARRIET: I prayed; did you know that? Now he's home.

OZZIE: It was a winter day.

HARRIET: [*At the top of the stairs*] I know.

RICK: [*Toying with his guitar*] Night, Mom. [*She doesn't answer but disappears down the hall. He looks up and yells after her*] Night, Mom!

HARRIET: [*From off*] Turn off the TV, somebody.

[RICK *crosses to the TV. He turns it off and wheels it back under the stairs.* OZZIE *watches. Silence*]

OZZIE: I knew she was praying. She moves her lips. [RICK *does not look up. He begins, softly, to strum and tune the guitar*] And something else—yes, sir, boy, oh, boy, I tell you, huh? What a day, huh? [*Slight pause*] They got seventeen hundred million men they gotta deal with, how they gonna do that without any trucks and tanks and jeeps? But I'm some kinda jerk because I wasn't out there blastin' away, huh? I was useful. I put my time to use. I been in fights. Fat Kramer. . . . How we used to fight! [RICK *strums some notes on the guitar.* OZZIE *stares at him*] How come I'm restless? I . . . seen him do some awful, awful things, ole Dave. He was a mean . . . foul-tempered little baby. I'm only glad I was *here* when they sent him off to do his killing. That's right. [*Silence*] I feel like I swallowed ants, that's how restless I am. Outran a bowlin' ball one time. These guys bet me I couldn't do it and I did, beat it to the pins. Got a runnin' start, then the—[*A faint, strange rapping sound has stopped him, spun him around*] Did you do that?

RICK: Somebody knockin'.

OZZIE: Knockin'?

RICK: The door, Dad.

OZZIE: Oh.

RICK: You want me to get it?

OZZIE: No, no. It's just so late.

[*He moves for the door*]

RICK: That's all right.

OZZIE: Sure.

[*He opens the door just a crack, as if to stick his head around. But the door is thrust open and a man enters abruptly. He is black or of Spanish descent, and is dressed in the uniform of a sergeant major and wearing many campaign ribbons*]

SGT. MAJOR: Excuse me. Listen to me. I'd like to speak to the father here. I'd like to know who . . . is the father? Could . . . you tell me the address?

OZZIE: May I ask who it is who's asking?

SGT. MAJOR: I am. I'm asking. What's the address of this house?

OZZIE: But I mean, who is it that wants to know?

SGT. MAJOR: We called; we spoke. Is this seven-seventeen Dunbar?

OZZIE: Yes.

SGT. MAJOR: What's wrong with you?

OZZIE: Don't you worry about me.

SGT. MAJOR: I have your son.

OZZIE: What?

SGT. MAJOR: Your son.

OZZIE: No.

SGT. MAJOR: But he is. I have papers, pictures, prints. I know your blood and his. This is the right address. Please. Excuse me. [*He pivots, reaches out into the dark*] I am very busy. I have your father, David.

[*He draws* DAVID *in—a tall, thin boy, blond and, in the shadows, wearing sunglasses and a uniform of dress greens. In his right hand is a long, white, red-tipped cane. He moves, probing the air, as the sergeant major moves him past* OZZIE *toward the couch, where he will sit the boy down like a parcel*]

OZZIE: Dave? . . .

SGT. MAJOR: He's blind.

OZZIE: What?

SGT. MAJOR: Blind.

OZZIE: I don't . . . understand.

SGT. MAJOR: We're very sorry.

OZZIE: [*Realizing*] Ohhhhh. Yes. Ohhhh. I see . . . sure. I mean, we didn't know. Nobody said it. I mean, sure, Dave, sure; it's all right—don't you worry. Rick's here, too, Dave—Rick, your brother, tell him hello.

RICK: Hi, Dave.

DAVID: [*Worried*] You said . . . "father."

OZZIE: Well . . . there's two of us, Dave; two.

DAVID: Sergeant, you said "home." I don't think so.

OZZIE: Dave, sure.

DAVID: It doesn't feel right.

OZZIE: But it is, Dave—me and Rick—Dad and Rick. Harriet! [*Calling up the stairs*] Harriet!

DAVID: Let me touch their faces . . . I can't see. [*Rising, his fear increasing*] Let me put my fingers on their faces.

OZZIE: [*Hurt, startled*] What? Do what?

SGT. MAJOR: Will that be all right if he does that?

OZZIE: Sure. . . . Sure. . . . Fine.

SGT. MAJOR: [*Helping* DAVID *to* OZZIE] It will take him time.

OZZIE: That's normal and to be expected. I'm not surprised. Not at all. We figured on this. Sure, we did. Didn't we, Rick?

RICK: [*Occupied with his camera, an Instamatic*] I wanna take some pictures, okay? How are you, Dave?

DAVID: What room is this?

OZZIE: Middle room, Dave. TV room. TV's in—

HARRIET: [*On the stairs*] David! . . . Oh, David! . . . David . . .

    [*And* OZZIE, *leaving* DAVID, *hurries toward the stairs and looks up at her as she falters, stops, stares.* RICK, *moving near, snaps a picture of her*]

OZZIE: Harriet . . . don't be upset. . . . They say . . . Harriet, Harriet . . . he can't see! . . . Harriet . . . they say—he—can't . . . see. That man.

HARRIET: [*Standing very still*] Can't see? What do you mean?

SGT. MAJOR: He's blind.

HARRIET: No. Who says? No, no.

OZZIE: Look at him. He looks so old. But it's nothing, Harriet, I'm sure.

SGT. MAJOR: I hope you people understand.

OZZIE: It's probably just how he's tired from his long trip.

HARRIET: [*Moving toward him*] Oh, you're home now, David.

SGT. MAJOR: [*With a large sheet of paper waving in his hands*] Who's gonna sign this for me, Mister? It's a shipping receipt. I got to have somebody's signature to show you got him. I got to have somebody's name on the paper.

OZZIE: Let me. All right?

SGT. MAJOR: Just here and here, you see? Your name or mark three times.

   [*As they move toward a table and away from* HARRIET, *who is near* DAVID]

OZZIE: Fine, listen, would you like some refreshments?

SGT. MAJOR: No.

OZZIE: I mean while I do this. Cake and coffee. Of course, you do.

SGT. MAJOR: No.

OZZIE: Sure.

SGT. MAJOR: No. I haven't time. I've got to get going. I've got trucks out there backed up for blocks. Other boys. I got to get on to Chicago, and some of them to Denver and Cleveland, Reno, New Orleans, Boston, Trenton, Watts, Atlanta. And when I get back they'll be layin' all over the grass; layin' there in pieces all over the grass, their backs been broken, their brains jellied, their insides turned into garbage. One-legged boys and no-legged boys. I'm due in Harlem; I got to get to the Bronx and Queens, Cincinnati, Saint Louis, Reading. I don't have time for coffee. I got deliveries to make all across this country.

DAVID: [*With* HARRIET, *his hands on her face, a kind of realization*] Nooooooo. . . . Sergeant . . . nooo; there's something wrong; it all feels wrong. Where are you? Are you here? I don't know these people!

SGT. MAJOR: That's natural, Soldier; it's natural you feel that way.

DAVID: Nooooo.

HARRIET: [*Attempting to guide him back to a chair*] David, just sit, be still.

DAVID: Don't you hear me?

OZZIE: Harriet, calm him.

DAVID: The air is wrong; the smells and sounds, the wind.

HARRIET: David, please, please. What is it? Be still. Please . . .

DAVID: GODDAMN YOU, SERGEANT, I AM LONELY HERE! I AM LONELY!

SGT. MAJOR: I got to go.

[*And he pivots to leave*]

DAVID: [*Following the sound of the* SERGEANT MAJOR's *voice*] Sergeant!

SGT. MAJOR: [*Whirling, bellowing*] You shut up. You piss-ass soldier, you shut the fuck up!

OZZIE: [*Walking to the* SERGEANT MAJOR, *putting his hand on the man's shoulder*] Listen, let me walk you to the door. All right? I'd like to take a look at that truck of yours. All right?

SGT. MAJOR: There's more than one.

OZZIE: Fine.

SGT. MAJOR: It's a convoy.

OZZIE: Good.

> [*They exit, slamming the door, and* RICK, *running close behind them, pops it open, leaps out. He calls from off.*]

RICK: Sure are lots a trucks, Mom!

HARRIET: [*As he re-enters*] Are there?

RICK: Oh, yeah. Gonna rain some more, too. [*And turning, he runs up the stairs*] See you in the morning. Night, Dave.

HARRIET: It's so good to have you here again; so good to see you. You look . . . just . . . [OZZIE *has slipped back into the room behind her, he stands, looking*] fine. You look—[*She senses* OZZIE's *presence, turns, immediately, speaking*] He bewilders you, doesn't he? [*And* OZZIE, *jauntily, heads for the stairs*] Where are you going? [*He stops; he doesn't know. And she is happily sad now as she speaks—sad for poor* OZZIE *and* DAVID, *they are so whimsical, so childlike*] You thought you knew what was right, all those years, teaching him sports and fighting. Do you understand what I'm trying to say? A mother knows *things* . . . a father cannot ever know them. The measles, smallpox, cuts and bruises. Never have you come upon him in the night as he lay awake and staring . . . praying.

OZZIE: I saw him put a knife through the skin of a cat. I saw him cut the belly open.

DAVID: Noooo . . .

HARRIET: [*Moving toward him in response*] David, David. . . .

DAVID: Ricky!

> [*There is a kind of accusation in this as if he were saying* RICKY *did the killing of the cat. He says it loudly and directly into her face*]

HARRIET: He's gone to bed.

DAVID: I want to leave.

> [*There is furniture around him; he is caged. He pokes with his cane*]

HARRIET: What is it?

DAVID: Help me. [*He crashes*]

OZZIE: Settle down! Relax.

DAVID: I want to leave! I want to leave! I want to leave. I . . . [*And he smashes into the stairs, goes down, flails, pounding his cane*] want to leave.

OZZIE AND HARRIET: Dave! David! Davey!

DAVID: . . . to leave! Please.

[*He is on the floor, breathing. Long, long silence in which they look at him sadly, until* HARRIET *announces the problem's solution*]

HARRIET: Ozzie, get him some medicine. Get him some Ezy Sleep.

OZZIE: Good idea.

HARRIET: It's in the medicine cabinet; a little blue bottle, little pink pills. [*And when* OZZIE *is gone up the stairs, there is quiet. She stands over* DAVID] It'll give you the sleep you need, Dave— the sleep you remember. You're our child and you're home. Our good . . . beautiful boy.

[*And front door bursts open. There is a small* GIRL *in the doorway, an Asian girl. She wears the Vietnamese ao dai, black slacks and white tunic slit up the sides. Slowly, she enters, carrying before her a small straw hat.* HARRIET *is looking at the open door*]

HARRIET: What an awful . . . wind. [*She shuts the door*]

[*Blackout. Guitar music*]

[*A match flickers as* HARRIET *lights a candle in the night. And the* GIRL *silently moves from before the door across the floor to the stairs, where she sits, as* HARRIET *moves toward the stairs and* OZZIE, *alseep sitting up in a chair, stirs.*]

HARRIET: Oh! I didn't mean to wake you. I lit a candle so I wouldn't wake you. [*He stares at her*] I'm sorry.

OZZIE: I wasn't sleeping.

HARRIET: I thought you were.

OZZIE: Couldn't. Tried. Couldn't. Thinking. Thoughts running very fast. Trying to remember the night David . . . was made. Do you understand me? I don't know why. But the feeling in me that I had to figure something out and if only I could remember that night . . . the mood . . . I would be able. You're . . . shaking your head.

HARRIET: I don't understand.

OZZIE: No.

HARRIET: Good night. [*She turns and leaves* OZZIE *sitting there, gazing at the dark. Arriving at* DAVID's *door, she raps softly and then opens the door.* DAVID *is lying unmoving on the bed. She speaks to him*] I heard you call.

DAVID: What?

HARRIET: I heard you call.

DAVID: I didn't.

HARRIET: Would you like a glass of warm milk?

DAVID: I was sleeping.

HARRIET: [*After a slight pause*] How about that milk? Would you like some milk?

DAVID: I didn't call. I was sleeping.

HARRIET: I'll bet you're glad you didn't bring her back. Their skins are yellow, aren't they?

DAVID: What?

HARRIET: You're troubled, warm milk would help. Do you pray at all any more? If I were to pray now, would you pray with me?

DAVID: What . . . do you want?

HARRIET: They eat the flesh of dogs.

DAVID: I know. I've seen them.

HARRIET: Pray with me; pray.

DAVID: What . . . do . . . you want?

HARRIET: Just to talk, that's all. Just to know that you're home and safe again. Nothing else; only that we're all together, a family. You must be exhausted. Don't worry; sleep. [*She is backing into the hallway. In a whisper*] Good night.

[*She blows out the candle and is gone, moving down the hall. Meanwhile the* GIRL *is stirring, rising, climbing from the living room up toward* DAVID's *room, which she enters, moving through a wall, and* DAVID *sits up*]

DAVID: Who's there? [*As she drifts by, he waves the cane at the air*] Zung? [*He stands*] Chào, Cô Zung. [*He moves for the door, which he opens, and steps into the hall, leaving her behind him in the room*] Zung. Chào, Cô Zung. [*And he moves off up the hallway. She follows*] Zung! . . .

[*Blackout. Music*]

[*Lights up. It is a bright afternoon, and* OZZIE *is under the stairs with a screwdriver in his hand, poking about at the TV set*]

OZZIE: C'mon, c'mon. Ohhhh, c'mon, this one more game and ole State's Bowl-bound. C'mon, what is it? Ohhh, hey . . . ohhhhh . . .

HARRIET: [*Entering from the kitchen carrying a tray with a bowl of soup and a glass of juice*] Ozzie, take this up to David; make him eat it.

OZZIE: Harriet, the TV is broke.

HARRIET: What?

OZZIE: There's a picture but no sound. I don't—

[*Grabbing her by the arm, he pulls her toward a place before the set*]

HARRIET: Stoppit, you're spilling the soup. [*She pulls free*]

OZZIE: It's Sunday. I want to watch it. I turned it on, picture came on just like normal. I got the volume up full blast. [*Having set the tray down,* HARRIET *now shoves the TV set deeper under the stairs, deeper into the place where it is kept when not in use*] Hey! I want to watch it!

HARRIET: I want to talk about David.

OZZIE: David's all right. [*He turns, crosses toward the phone, picks up the phone book*] I'm gonna call the repairman.

HARRIET: [*Following him*] Ozzie, he won't eat. He just lays there. I offer him food, he won't eat it. No, no. The TV repairman won't help you, you silly. [*She takes the phone book from him*] He doesn't matter. There's something wrong with David. He's been home days and days and still he speaks only when spoken to; there's no light in his eye, no smile; he's not happy to be here and not once has he touched me or held me, nor has he even shaken your hand.

[*OZZIE flops down in a chair*]

OZZIE: Oh, I don't mind that. Why should I mind—

HARRIET: And now he's talking to himself! What about that? Do you mind that? He mutters in his sleep.

OZZIE: [*Exasperated*] Ohhhhhh.

HARRIET: Yes. And it's not a regular kind of talking at all. It's very strange—very spooky.

OZZIE: Spooky?

HARRIET: That's right.

OZZIE: I never heard him.

HARRIET: You sleep too deeply. I took a candle and followed. I was in his room. He lay there, speaking.

OZZIE: Speaking what?

HARRIET: I don't know. I couldn't understand.

OZZIE: Was it words?

HARRIET: All kind of funny and fast.

OZZIE: Maybe prayer; praying.

HARRIET: No. No, it was secret. Oh, Ozzie, I know praying when I hear it and it wasn't praying he was doing. We meant our sons to be so different—I don't understand—good and strong. And yet

. . . perhaps he is. But there are moments when I see him . . . hiding . . . in that bed behind those awful glasses, and I see the chalkiness that's come into—

OZZIE: [*Headed for the kitchen, looking for juice to drink*] Those glasses are simply to ease his discomfort.

HARRIET: I hate them.

OZZIE: They're tinted glass and plastic. Don't be so damn suspicious.

HARRIET: I'm not, I'm not. It's seeing I'm doing, not suspicion. Suspicion hasn't any reasons. It's you—now accusing me for no reason when I'm only worried.

OZZIE: [*Returning from the kitchen, angered*] Where's my juice?

HARRIET: I want to talk.

OZZIE: The hell with David for a minute—I want some juice.

HARRIET: Shut up. You're selfish. You're so selfish.

OZZIE: [*Walking to the tray and juice, attempting to threaten her*] I'll pour it on the floor. I'll break the glass.

[*She turns to move to get the juice*]

HARRIET: A few years ago you might have done that kind of thing.

OZZIE: I woke up this morning, I could see so clearly the lovely way you looked when you were young. Beside me this morning, you were having trouble breathing. You kept . . . trying . . . to breathe. [*She approaches him to hand him the juice*] What do you give me when you give me this?

HARRIET: I always looked pretty much as I do now. I never looked so different at all.

[*DAVID appears from off the upstairs, dressed in a red robe, and descends toward them*]

DAVID: [*Sounding happy, yet moving with urgency*] Good morning.

OZZIE: Oh, David! Ohhh, good morning. Hello. How do you feel this fine bright morning; how do you feel?

DAVID: He was a big man, wasn't he?

OZZIE: What?

DAVID: Hank. You were talking about Hank Grenweller. I thought you were.

OZZIE: Oh, yes. Hank. Very big. Big. A good fine friend, ole Hank.

DAVID: You felt when he was with you he filled the room.

OZZIE: It was the way he talked that did that. He boomed. His voice just boomed.

DAVID: He was here once and you wanted me to sit on his lap, isn't that right? It was after dinner. He was in a chair in the corner.

HARRIET: That's right.

DAVID: His hand was gone—the bone showed in the skin.

OZZIE: My God, what a memory—did you hear that, Harriet? You were only four or five. He'd just had this terrible, awful auto accident. His hand was hurt, not gone.

DAVID: No. It was congenital and none of us knew.

OZZIE: What?

DAVID: That hand. The sickness in it.

OZZIE: Congenital?

DAVID: Yes.

OZZIE: What do you mean? What do you think you mean?

DAVID: I'd like some coffee.

[*He is seated now, but not without tension*]

OZZIE: Hank's parents were good fine people, David.

DAVID: I know.

OZZIE: Well, what are you saying then?

DAVID: I'd like that coffee.

HARRIET: Of course. And what else with it?

DAVID: Nothing.

HARRIET: Oh, no, no, you've got to eat. To get back your strength. You must. Pancakes? How do pancakes sound? Or wheat cakes? Or there's eggs? And juice? Orange or prune: or waffles. I bet it's eggs you want. Over, David? Over easy? Scrambled?

DAVID: I'm only thirsty.

HARRIET: Well, all right then, coffee is what you'll have and I'll just put some eggs on the side; you used to love them so; remember?

[*And, picking up the tray, she is off toward the kitchen. There is a pause*]

OZZIE: I mean, I hate to harp on a thing, but I just think you're way off base on Hank, Dave. I just think you're dead wrong.

DAVID: He told me.

OZZIE: Who?

DAVID: Hank.

OZZIE: You . . . talked to Hank?

DAVID: In California. The day before they shipped me overseas.

OZZIE: No, no. He went to Georgia when he left here. We have all his letters postmarked Georgia.

DAVID: [*With great urgency*] It was California, I'm telling you. I was in the barracks. The C.Q. came to tell me there was someone to see me. It was Hank asking did I remember him? He'd seen my name on a list and wondered if I was Ozzie's boy. He was dying, he said. The sickness was congenital. We had a long, long talk.

OZZIE: But his parents were good fine people, David.

DAVID: Don't you understand? We spoke. Why did you make me think him perfect? It was starting in his face the way it started in his hand.

OZZIE: Oh! I didn't realize—I didn't know. You weren't blind. You could see. I didn't realize, Dave.

DAVID: What?

OZZIE: Did he wanna know about me? Did he mention me?

DAVID: [*After thinking a moment*] He asked . . . how you were.

OZZIE: Well, I'm fine. Sure. You told him.

HARRIET: [*Entering with a cup of coffee*] It must be so wonderful for you to be home. It must just be so wonderful. A little strange, maybe . . . just a little, but time will take care of all that. It always does. You get sick and you don't know how you're going to get better and then you do. You just do. You must have terrible, awful, ugly dreams, though.

[*Slight pause*]

OZZIE: She said you probably have terrible, awful, ugly dreams . . . though.

DAVID: What?

HARRIET: Don't you remember when we spoke last night?

DAVID: Who?

HARRIET: You called to me and then you claimed you hadn't.

DAVID: I didn't.

HARRIET: Ohhh, we had a lovely conversation, David. Of course you called. You called; we talked. We talked and laughed and it was very pleasant. Could I see behind your glasses?

DAVID: What? [*Moving away, crossing in flight from them*] Do . . . what?

HARRIET: See behind your glasses; see your eyes.

OZZIE: Me too, Dave; could we?

DAVID: My eyes . . . are ugly.

OZZIE: We don't mind.

HARRIET: We're your parents, David.

DAVID: I think it better if you don't.

OZZIE: And something else I've been meaning to ask you—why did you cry out against us that first night—to that stranger, I mean, that sergeant?

HARRIET: And you do dream. You do.

OZZIE: Sure. You needn't be ashamed.

HARRIET: We all do it. All of us.

OZZIE: We have things that haunt us.

HARRIET: And it would mean nothing at all—it would be of no consequence at all—if only you didn't speak.

DAVID: I don't understand.

OZZIE: She says she heard you, Dave.

HARRIET: I stood outside your door.

DAVID: No.

OZZIE: A terrible experience for her, Dave; you can see that.

HARRIET: Whatever it is, David, tell us.

OZZIE: What's wrong?

DAVID: No.

HARRIET: We'll work it out.

OZZIE: You can't know how you hurt us.

DAVID: I wasn't asleep.

OZZIE: Not until you have children of your own.

HARRIET: What? [*Silence*] Not . . . asleep? . . .

DAVID: I was awake; lying awake and speaking.

OZZIE: Now wait a minute.

DAVID: Someone was with me—there in the dark—I don't know what's wrong with me.

HARRIET: It was me. I was with you. There's nothing wrong with you.

DAVID: No. In my room. I could feel it.

HARRIET: I was there.

[*And they have him cornered in another chair*]

DAVID: No.

OZZIE: Harriet, wait!

HARRIET: What are you saying, "Wait"? I was there.

OZZIE: Oh, my God. Oh, Christ, of course. Oh, Dave, forgive us.

HARRIET: What?

OZZIE: Dave, I understand. It's buddies left behind.

DAVID: No.

OZZIE: But I do. Maybe your mother can't but I can. Men serving together in war, it's a powerful thing—and I don't mean to sound like I think I know it—all of it, I mean—I don't, I couldn't—but I respect you having had it—I almost envy you having had it, Dave. I mean . . . true comradeship.

DAVID: Dad . . .

OZZIE: I had just a taste—not that those trucks and factory were any battlefield, but there was a taste of it there—in the jokes we told and the way we saw each other first in the morning. We told dirty, filthy jokes, Dave. We shot pool, played cards, drank beer late every night, singing all these crazy songs.

DAVID: That's not right, Dad.

OZZIE: But all that's nothing, I'm sure, to what it must be in war. The things you must touch and see. Honor. You must touch honor. And then one of you is hurt, wounded . . . made blind . . .

DAVID: No. I had fear of all the kinds of dying that there are when I went from here. And then there was this girl with hands and hair like wings. [*The poetry is like a thing possessing him, a frenzy in which he does not know where he is*] There were candles above the net of gauze under which we lay. Lizards. Cannon could be heard. A girl to weigh no more than dust.

HARRIET: A nurse, right . . . David?

OZZIE: No, no, one of them foreign correspondents, English maybe or French.

[*Silence*]

HARRIET: Oh, how lovely! A Wac or Red Cross girl? . . .

DAVID: No.

OZZIE: Redhead or blonde, Dave?

DAVID: No.

[HARRIET *is shaken*]

OZZIE: I mean, what you mean is you whored around a lot. Sure. You whored around. That's what you're saying. You banged some whores . . . had some intercourse. Sure, I mean, that's my point. [DAVID, *turning away, seems about to rise*] Now Dave, take it easy. What I mean is, okay, sure, you shacked up with. I mean, hit on. Hit on, Dave. Dicked. Look at me. I mean, you pronged it, right? Right? Sure, attaboy. [*Patting* DAVID *on the shoulder*] I mean, it's like going to the bathroom. All glands and secretions. Look, Dave, what are you doing? [A *rage is building in* DAVID, *tension forcing him to stand, his cane pressing the floor*] We can talk this over. We can talk this over. [DAVID, *heading for the stairs, crashes into* OZZIE] Don't—goddamnit, don't walk away from me. [*He pushes* DAVID *backward*] What the hell do you think you're doing? It's what you did. Who the hell you think you are? You screwed it. A yellow whore. Some yellow ass. You put in your prick and humped your ass. You screwed some yellow fucking whore!

[*He has chased* DAVID *backward,* HARRIET *joining in with him*]

HARRIET: That's right, that's right. You were lonely and young and away from home for the very first time in your life, no white girls around—

DAVID: They are the color of the earth, and what is white but winter and the earth under it like a suicide? [HARRIET'S *voice is a high humming in her throat*] Why didn't you tell me what I was?

[*And* HARRIET *vomits, her hands at her mouth, her back turning. There is a silence. They stand.* OZZIE *starts toward her, falters, starts, reaches, stops*]

OZZIE: Why . . . don't . . . you ask her to cook something for you, David, will you? Make her feel better . . . okay.

DAVID: I think . . . some eggs might be good, Mom.

OZZIE: [*Wanting to help her*] Hear that, Harriet? David wants some eggs.

HARRIET: I'm *all right.*

OZZIE: Of course you are. [*Patting her tenderly, he offers his clean white handkerchief*] Here, here: wipe your mouth; you've got a little something—on the corner, left side. That's it. Whattayou say, David?

HARRIET: What's your pleasure, David?

DAVID: Scrambled.

OZZIE: There you go. Your specialty, his pleasure. [OZZIE, *between them, claps his hands; off she goes for the kitchen.* OZZIE, *looking about the room like a man in deep water looking for something to keep him afloat, sees a pack of cigarettes*] How about a cigarette? [*Running to grab them, show them*] Filter, see, I switched. Just a little after you left, and I just find them a lot smoother, actually. I wondered if you'd notice. [*And speaking now, his voice and manner take on a confidence; he demonstrates; he is self-assured*] The filter's granulated. It's an off-product of corn husks. I light up —I feel like I'm on a ship at sea. Isn't that one hell of a good tasting cigarette? Isn't that one beautiful goddamn cigarette?

[HARRIET *enters with two bowls. One has a grapefruit cut in half; the second has eggs and a spoon sticking out*]

HARRIET: Here's a little grapefruit to tide you over till I get the eggs. [*And now she stirs the eggs in preparation for scrambling them*] Won't be long, I promise—but I was just wondering, wouldn't it be nice if we could all go to church tonight. All together and we could make a little visit in thanksgiving of your coming home. [DAVID *is putting his cigarette out in his grapefruit. They see*] I wouldn't ask that it be long—just—[*He is rising now, dropping the grapefruit on the chair*] I mean, we could go to whatever saint you wanted, it wouldn't . . . matter . . . [*He has turned his back, is walking toward the stairs*] Just in . . . just out . . . [*He is climbing the stairs*] David.

OZZIE: Tired . . . Dave? [*They watch him plodding unfalteringly toward his room*] Where you going . . . bathroom?

DAVID: No.

OZZIE: Oh. [DAVID *disappears into his room and* HARRIET *whirls and heads for the telephone.* OZZIE, *startled, turns to look at her*] Harriet, what's up?

HARRIET: I'm calling Father Donald.

OZZIE: Father Donald?

HARRIET: [*Dialing*] We need help, I'm calling for help.

OZZIE: Now wait a minute. No; oh, no, we—

HARRIET: Do you still refuse to see it? He was involved with one of them. You know what the Bible says about those people. You heard him.

OZZIE: Just not Father Donald; please, please. That's all I ask—just —[*She is obstinate, he sees. She turns her back waiting for someone to answer*] Why must everything be personal vengeance?

[*The front door pops open and in comes bounding* RICK, *guitar upon his back*]

RICK: [*Happy*] Hi, Mom. Hi, Dad.

HARRIET: [*Waiting, telephone in hand—overjoyed*] Hi, Rick!

RICK: [*Happy*] Hi, Mom.

OZZIE: [*Feeling fine*] Hi, Rick.

RICK: Hi, Dad.

OZZIE: How you doin', Rick?

[*He is happy to see good ole regular* RICK]

RICK: Fine, Dad. You?

OZZIE: Fine.

RICK: Good.

HARRIET: I'll get you some fudge in just a minute, Rick!

RICK: Okay. How's Dave doin', Dad?

[*He is fiddling with his camera*]

OZZIE: Dave's doin' fine, Rick.

RICK: Boy, I'm glad to hear that. I'm really glad to hear that, because, boy, I'll sure be glad when everything's back to the regular way. Dave's too serious, Dad; don't you think so? That's what I think. Whattayou think, Dad?

[*He snaps a picture of* OZZIE, *who is posing, smiling, while* HARRIET *waves angrily at them*]

HARRIET: SHHHHHHH! *Everybody!* [*And then, more pleasantly she returns to the phone*] Yes, yes. Oh, Father, I didn't recognize your voice. No, I don't know who. Well, yes, it's about my son, Father, David. Yes. Well, I don't know if you know it or not, but he just got back from the war and he's troubled. Deeply. Yes. [*As she listens silently for a moment,* RICK, *crouching, snaps a picture of her. She tries to wave him away*] Deeply. [*He moves to another position, another angle, and snaps another picture*] Deeply, yes. Oh. So do you think you might be able to stop over some time soon to talk to him or not? Father, any time that would be convenient for you. Yes. Oh, that would be wonderful. Yes. Oh, thank you. And may God reward *you*, Father.

[*Hanging up the phone, she stands a moment, dreaming*]

OZZIE: I say to myself, what does it mean that he is my son? How the hell is it that . . . he . . . is my son? I mean, they say something of you joined to something of me and became . . . him . . . but what kinda goddamn thing is that? One mystery replacing another? Mystery doesn't explain mystery!

RICK: [*Scarcely looking up from his comic*] Mom, hey, c'mon, how about that fudge, will ya?

HARRIET: Ricky, oh, I'm sorry. I forgot.

OZZIE: They've got . . . diseases! . . .

HARRIET: [*Having been stopped by his voice*] What? . . .

OZZIE: Dirty, filthy diseases. They got 'em. Those girls. Infections. From the blood of their parents into the very fluids of their bodies. Malaria, TB. An actual rot alive in them . . . gonorrhea, syphilis. There are some who have the plague. He touched them. It's disgusting. It's—

RICK: Mom, I'm starving, honest to God; and I'm thirsty, too.

HARRIET: [*As she scurries off, clapping, for the kitchen*] Yes, of course. Oh, oh.

RICK: And bring a piece for Dad, too; Dad looks hungry.

OZZIE: No.

RICK: Sure, a big sweet chocolate piece of fudge.

OZZIE: No. Please. I don't feel well.

RICK: It'll do you good.

HARRIET: [*Entering with fudge and milk in each hand*] Ricky, here, come here.

RICK: [*Hurrying toward her*] What?

HARRIET: [*Hands him fudge and milk*] Look good?

[*And she moves toward* OZZIE]

OZZIE: And something else—maybe it could just be that he's growing away from us, like we did ourselves, only we thought it would happen in some other way, some lesser way.

HARRIET: [*Putting the fudge and milk into* OZZIE's *hands*] What are you talking about, "going away"? He's right upstairs.

OZZIE: I don't want that.

HARRIET: You said you did.

OZZIE: He said I did.

RICK: [*Having gobbled the fudge and milk*] You want me to drive you, Mom?

HARRIET: Would you, Ricky, please?

RICK: [*Running*] I'll go around and get the car.

HARRIET: [*Scolding, as* OZZIE *has put the fudge and milk down on a coffee table*] It's all cut and poured, Ozzie; it'll just be a waste.

OZZIE: I don't care.

HARRIET: You're so childish.

[*She marches off toward the front door, where she takes a light jacket from a hook, starts to slip it on*]

OZZIE: Don't you know I could throw you down onto this floor and make another child live inside you . . . now! . . .

HARRIET: I . . . doubt that . . . . Ozzie.

OZZIE: You want me to do it?

HARRIET: [*Going out the door*] Ohhh, Ozzie, Ozzie.

OZZIE: Sure. Bye-bye. Bye-bye. [*After a pause*] They think they know me and they know nothing. They don't know how I feel. . . . How I'd like to beat Ricky with my fists till his face is ugly! How I'd like to banish David to the streets. . . . How I'd like to cut her tongue from her mouth. [DAVID *moves around upstairs*] I was myself. [*And now he is clearly speaking to the audience, making them see his value. They are his friends and buddies, and he talks directly to them*] I lived in a time beyond anything they can ever know—a time beyond and separate, and I was nobody's goddamn father and nobody's goddamn husband! I was myself! And I could run. I got a scrapbook of victories, a bag of medals and ribbons. In the town in which I lived my name was spoken in the factories and in the fields all around because I was the best there was. I'd beaten the finest anybody had to offer. Summer . . . I would sit out on this old wood porch on the front of our house and my strength was in me, quiet and mine. Round the corner would come some old Model T Ford and scampering up the walk this ancient, bone-stiff, buck-toothed farmer, raw as winter and cawing at me like a crow: they had one for me. Out at the edge of town. A runner from another county. My shoes are in a brown-paper bag at my feet. I snatch 'em up. I set out into the dusk, easy as breathing. There's an old white fence and we run for the sun. . . . For a hundred yards or a thousand yards or a thousand thousand. It doesn't matter. Whatever they want. We run the race they think their specialty and I beat them. They sweat and struggle; I simply glide on, one step beyond, no matter what their effort, and the sun bleeds before me. . . . We cross rivers and deserts; we clamber over mountains. I run the races the farmers arrange and win the bets they make. And then a few days after the race, money comes to me anonymously in the mail; but it's not for the money that I run. In the fields and factories they speak my name when they sit down to their lunches. If there's a prize to be run for, it's me they send for. It's to be the-one-sent-for that I run.

[DAVID, *entering from his room, has listened to the latter part of this*]

DAVID: And . . . then . . . you left.

OZZIE: [*Whirling to look at him*] What?

DAVID: I said . . . "And . . . then you left." That town.

OZZIE: Left?

DAVID: Yes. Went away; traveled.

OZZIE: No. What do you mean?

DAVID: I mean, you're no longer there; you're here . . . now.

OZZIE: But I didn't really *leave* it. I mean, not *leave*. Not really.

DAVID: Of course you did. Where are you?

OZZIE: That's not the point, Dave. Where I am isn't the point at all.

DAVID: But it is. It's everything; all that other is gone. Where are you going?

OZZIE: Groceries. Gotta go get groceries. You want anything at the grocery store? [*He looks at his watch*] It's late. I gotta get busy.

DAVID: [*As* OZZIE *exits*] That's all right, Dad. That's fine.

[*Blackout*]

[*The lights rise to brightness, and* RICK *enters from the kitchen, carrying his guitar, plinking a note or two as* HARRIET *emerges also from the kitchen, carrying a bowl of chips and a tray of drinks, and* OZZIE *appears upstairs, coming down the hall carrying an 8-mm movie projector already loaded with film*]

HARRIET: Tune her up now, Rick.

OZZIE: What's the movie about anyway?

HARRIET: It's probably scenery, don't you think?—trees and fields and those little ponds. Everything over there's so green and lovely. Enough chips, Ricky?

[*All during this, they scurry about with their many preparations*]

RICK: We gonna have pretzels, too? 'Cause if there's both pretzels and chips then there's enough chips.

OZZIE: [*At the projector*] David shoot it or somebody else? . . . Anybody know? I tried to peek—put a couple feet up to the light . . .

HARRIET: What did you see?

OZZIE: Nothing. Couldn't.

HARRIET: Well, I'll just bet there's one of those lovely little ponds in it somewhere.

OZZIE: Harriet . . . you know when David was talking about that trouble in Hank's hand being congenital, what did you think? You think it's possible? I don't myself. I mean, we knew Hank well. I think it's just something David got mixed up about and nobody corrected him. What do you think? Is that what you think? Whatsamatter? Oh.

[*He stops, startled, as he sees she is waving at him. Looking up the stairs, which are behind him, he sees* DAVID *is there, preparing to descend.* DAVID *wears his robe and a bright-colored tie*]

HARRIET: Hello!

OZZIE: Oh. Hey, oh, let me give you a hand. Yes. Yes. You look good. Good to see you. [*And he is on the move to* DAVID *to help him down the stairs*] Yes, sir. I think, all things considered, I think we can figure we're over the hump now and it's all downhill and good from here on in. I mean, we've talked things over, Dave, what do you say? The air's been cleared, that's what I mean—the wounds acknowledged, the healing begun. It's the ones that aren't acknowledged—the ones that aren't talked over—they're the ones that do the deep damage. That's always what happens.

HARRIET: [*Moving to* DAVID] I've baked a cake, David. Happy, happy being home.

[DAVID, *on his own, finds his way to a chair and sits*]

OZZIE: And we've got pop and ice and chips, and Rick is going to sing some songs.

HARRIET: Maybe we can all sing along if we want.

RICK: Anything special you'd like to hear, Dave?

OZZIE: You just sing what you know, Rick; sing what you care for and you'll do it best.

[*And he and* HARRIET *settle down upon the couch to listen, all smiles*]

RICK: How about "Baby, When I Find You"?

HARRIET: Ohhh, that's such a good one.

RICK: Dave, you just listen to me go! I'm gonna build! [*He plays an excited lead into the song*] I'm gonna build, build, build.

[*And he sings*]
Baby, when I find you,
never gonna stand behind you,
gonna, gonna lead
softly at the start,
gently by the heart,
Sweet . . . Love! . . . .

Slipping softly to the sea
you and me both mine
wondrous as a green
growing forest vine . . .

Baby, when I find you,
never gonna stand behind you,
gonna, gonna lead you
softly at the start,
gently by the heart,
Sweet . . . Love! . . .
Baby, when I find you.

OZZIE: [*As both he and* HARRIET *clap and laugh*] Ohhh, great, Rick, great. You burn me up with envy, honest to God.

HARRIET: It was just so wonderful. Oh, thank you so much.

RICK: I just love to do it so much, you know?

OZZIE: Has he got something goin' for him, Dave? Huh? Hey! You don't even have a drink. Take this one; take mine!

[*Now they hurry back and forth from* DAVID *to the table*]

HARRIET: And here's some cake.

OZZIE: How 'bout some pretzels, Dave?

RICK: Tell me what you'd like to hear.

DAVID: I'd like to sing.

[*This stops them. They stare at* DAVID *for a beat of silence*]

RICK: What?

OZZIE: What's that?

DAVID: I have something I'd like to sing.

RICK: Dave, you don't sing.

DAVID: [*Reaching at the air*] I'd like to use the guitar, if I could.

HARRIET: What are you saying?

OZZIE: C'mon, you couldn't carry a tune in a bucket and you know it. Rick's the singer, Rick and your mom.

[*Not really listening, thinking that his father has gotten everything back to normal,* RICK *strums and strums the guitar, drifting nearer to* DAVID]

C'mon, let's go, that all we're gonna hear?

DAVID: You're so selfish, Rick. Your hair is black; it glistens. You smile. You sing. People think you are the songs you sing. They never see you. Give me the guitar.

[*And he clamps his hand closed on the guitar, stopping the music*]

RICK: Mom, what's wrong with Dave?

DAVID: Give me.

RICK: Listen, you eat your cake and drink your drink, and if you still wanna, I'll let you.

[DAVID *stands, straining to take the guitar*]

DAVID: Now!

HARRIET: Ozzie, make David behave.

OZZIE: Don't you play too roughly . . .

DAVID: Ricky! . . .

RICK: I don't think he's playing, Dad.

OZZIE: [*As* DAVID, *following* RICK, *bumps into a chair*] You watch out what you're doing . . .

[DAVID *drops his glass on the floor, grabs the guitar*]

RICK: You got cake all over your fingers, you'll get it all sticky, the strings all sticky—[*Struggling desperately to keep his guitar*] Just tell me what you want to hear, I'll do it for you!

HARRIET: What is it? What's wrong?

DAVID: GIVE ME! [*With great anger*] GIVE ME!

OZZIE: David! . . .

[*And* DAVID *wrenches the guitar from* RICK's *hands, sends* RICK *sprawling, and loops the strap of the guitar over his shoulder, smiling, smiling*]

HARRIET: Ohhhh, no, no, you're ruining everything. What's wrong with you?

OZZIE: I thought we were gonna have a nice party—

DAVID: I'm singing! We are!

OZZIE: No, no, I mean a *nice* party—one where everybody's happy!

DAVID: I'm happy. I'm singing. Don't you see them? Don't you see them?

OZZIE: Pardon, Dave?

HARRIET: What . . . are you saying?

DAVID: [*Changing, turning*] I have some movies. I thought you . . . knew.

HARRIET: Well . . . we . . . do.

OZZIE: Movies?

DAVID: Yes, I took them.

RICK: I thought you wanted to sing.

OZZIE: I mean, they're what's planned, Dave. That's what's up. The projector's all wound and ready. I don't know what you had to get so angry for.

HARRIET: Let's get everything ready.

OZZIE: Sure, sure. No need for all that yelling.

[*He moves to set up the projector*]

DAVID: I'll narrate.

OZZIE: Fine, sure. What's it about anyway?

HARRIET: Are you in it?

OZZIE: Ricky, plug it in. C'mon, c'mon.

DAVID: It's a kind of story.

RICK: What about my guitar?

DAVID: No.

OZZIE: We oughta have some popcorn, though.

HARRIET: Oh, yes, what a dumb movie house, no popcorn, huh, Rick!

[RICK *switches off the lights*]

OZZIE: Let her rip, Dave. [DAVE *turns on the projector*; OZZIE *is hurrying to a seat*] Ready when you are, C.B.

HARRIET: Shhhhhhh!

OZZIE: [*A little child playing*] Let her rip, C.B. I want a new contract, C.B.

[*The projector runs for a moment. Note: In proscenium, a screen should be used if possible, or the film may be allowed to seem projected on the fourth wall; in three-quarter or round the screen may be necessary. If the screen is used, nothing must show upon it but a flickering of green*]

HARRIET: Ohhh, what's the matter? It didn't come out, there's nothing there.

DAVID: Of course there is.

HARRIET: Noooo . . . It's all funny.

DAVID: Look.

OZZIE: It's underexposed, Dave.

DAVID: [*Moving nearer*] No. Look.

HARRIET: What?

DAVID: They hang in the trees. They hang by their wrists half-severed by the wire.

OZZIE: Pardon me, Dave?

HARRIET: I'm going to put on the lights.

DAVID: NOOOOOO! LOOK! They hang in the greenish haze afflicted by insects; a woman and a man, middle aged. They do not shout or cry. He is too small. Look—he seems all bone, shame in his eyes; his wife even here come with him, skinny also as a broom and her hair is straight and black, hanging to mask her eyes.

[*The girl,* ZUNG, *drifts into the room*]

OZZIE: I don't know what you're doing, David; there's nothing there.

DAVID: LOOK! [*And he points*] They are all bone and pain, uncontoured and ugly but for the peculiar melon-swelling in her middle which is her pregnancy, which they do not see—look! these soldiers who have found her—as they do not see that she is not dead but only dying until saliva and blood bubble at her lips. Look. . . . Yet . . . she dies. Though a doctor is called in to remove the bullet-shot baby she would have preferred . . . to keep since she was dying and it was dead. [*And* ZUNG *silently, drifting, departs*] In fact, as it turned out they would have all been better off left to hang as they had been strung on the wire—he with the back of his head blown off and she, the rifle jammed exactly and deeply up into her, with a bullet fired directly into the child living there. For they ended each buried in a separate place; the husband by chance alone was returned to their village, while the wife was dumped into an alien nearby plot of dirt, while the child, too small a piece of meat, was burned. Put into fire, as the shattered legs and arms cut off of men are burned. There's an oven. It is no ceremony. It is the disposal of garbage! . . .

[HARRIET *gets to her feet, marches to the projector, pulls the plug, begins a little lecture*]

HARRIET: It's so awful the things those yellow people do to one another. Yellow people hanging yellow people. Isn't that right? Ozzie, I told you—animals—Christ, burn them. David, don't let it hurt you. All the things you saw. People aren't themselves in war. I mean like that sticking that gun into that poor woman and then shooting that poor little baby, that's not human. That's inhuman. It's inhuman, barbaric and uncivilized and inhuman.

DAVID: I'm thirsty.

HARRIET: For what? Tell me. Water? Or would you like some milk? How about some milk?

DAVID: [*Shaking his head*] No.

HARRIET: Or would you like some orange juice? All golden and little bits of ice.

OZZIE: Just all those words and that film with no picture and these poor people hanging somewhere—so you can bring them home like this house is a meat house—

HARRIET: Oh, Ozzie, no, it's not that—no—he's just young, a young boy . . . and he's been through terrible things and now he's home, with his family he loves, just trying to speak to those he loves—just—

DAVID: Yes! That's right. Yes. What I mean is, yes, of course, that's what I am—a young . . . blind man in a room . . . in a house in the dark, raising nothing in a gesture of no meaning toward two voices who are not speaking . . . of a certain . . . incredible . . . *connection!*

[*All stare.* RICK *leaps up, running for the stairs*]

RICK: Listen, everybody, I hate to rush off like this, but I gotta. Night.

HARRIET: Good night, Rick.

OZZIE: [*Simultaneously*] Good night.

[DAVID *moves toward the stairs, looking upward*]

DAVID: Because I talk of certain things . . . don't think I did them. Murderers don't even know that murder happens.

HARRIET: What are you saying? No, no. We're a family, that's all— we've had a little trouble—David, you've got to stop—please—no more yelling. Just be happy and home like all the others—why can't you?

DAVID: You mean take some old man to a ditch of water, shove his head under, talk of cars and money till his feeble pawing stops, and then head on home to go in and out of doors and drive cars and sing sometimes. I left her like you wanted . . . where people are thin and small all their lives. [*The beginning of realization*] Or did . . . you . . . think it was a . . . place . . . like this? Sinks and kitchens all the world over? Is that what you believe? Water from faucets, light from wires? Trucks, telephones, TV. Ricky sings and sings, but if I were to cut his throat, he would no longer and you would miss him—you would miss his singing. We are hoboes! [*And it is the first time in his life he has ever thought these things*] We make signs in the dark. You know yours. I understand my own. We share . . . coffee! [*There is nearly joy in this discovery: a hint of new freedom that might be liberation. And somewhere in the thrill of it he has whirled, his cane has come near to* OZZIE, *frightening him, though* HARRIET *does not notice. Now* DAVID *turns, moving for the stairs, thinking*] I'm going up to bed . . . now. . . . I'm very . . . tired.

OZZIE: Well . . . you have a good sleep, Son . . .

DAVID: Yes, I think I'll sleep in.

OZZIE: You do as you please . . .

DAVID: Good night.

HARRIET: Good night.

OZZIE: Good night.

HARRIET: Good night. [*Slight pause*] You get a good rest. [*Silence*] Try . . . [*Silence*. DAVID *has gone into his room.* OZZIE *and* HARRIET *stand*] I'm . . . hungry . . . Ozzie. . . . Are you hungry?

OZZIE: Hungry? . . .

HARRIET: Yes.

OZZIE: No. Oh, no.

HARRIET: How do you feel? You look a little peaked. Do you feel all right?

OZZIE: I'm fine, I'm fine.

HARRIET: You look funny.

OZZIE: Really. No. How about yourself?

HARRIET: I'm never sick; you know that. Just a little sleepy.

OZZIE: Well . . . that's no wonder. It's been a long day.

HARRIET: Yes, it has.

OZZIE: No wonder.

HARRIET: Good night.

[*She is climbing the stairs toward bed*]

OZZIE: Good night.

HARRIET: Don't stay up too late now.

OZZIE: Do you know when he pointed that cane at me, I couldn't breathe. I felt . . . for an instant I . . . might never breathe . . . .

HARRIET: Ohhh . . . I'm so sleepy. So . . . sooooo sleepy. Aren't you sleepy?

OZZIE: [*To make her answer*] Harriet! I couldn't breathe.

HARRIET: WHAT DO YOU WANT? TEACHING HIM SPORTS AND FIGHTING. [*This moment—one of almost a primal rage—should be the very first shattering of her motherly self-sacrificing image*] WHAT . . . OZZIE . . . DO YOU WANT?

OZZIE: Well . . . I was . . . wondering, do we have any aspirin down here . . . or are they all upstairs?

HARRIET: I thought you said you felt well.

OZZIE: Well, I do, I do. It's just a tiny headache. Hardly worth mentioning.

HARRIET: There's aspirin in the desk.

OZZIE: [*Crossing*] Fine. Big drawer?

HARRIET: Second drawer, right-hand side.

OZZIE: Get me a glass of water, would you, please?

HARRIET: Of course.

[*She gets a glass from a nearby table, a drink left over from the party, and hands it to him*]

OZZIE: Thank you. It's not much of a headache, actually. Actually it's just a tiny headache.

[*He pops the tablets into his mouth and drinks to wash them down*]

HARRIET: Aspirin makes your stomach bleed. [*He tries to keep from swallowing the aspirin, but it is too late*] Did you know that? Nobody knows why. It's part of how it works. It just does it, makes you bleed. This extremely tiny series of hemorrhages in those delicate inner tissues. [*He is staring at her: there is vengeance in what she is doing*] It's like those thin membranes begin, in a very minor way, to sweat blood and you bleed; inside yourself you bleed.

[*She crosses away*]

OZZIE: That's not true. None of that. You made all that up. . . . Where are you going? [*With a raincoat on, she is moving out the front door*] I mean . . . are you going out? Where . . . are you off to? [*She is gone*] Goddamnit, there's something going on around here, don't you want to know what it is? [*Yelling at the shut door*] I want to know what it is. [*Turning, marching to the phone, dialing*] I want to know what's going on around here. I want to; I do. Want to—got to. Police. That's right, goddamnit— I want one of you people to get on out to seven-seventeen Dunbar and do some checking, some checking at seven-seventeen— What?— Ohhh—[*Hissing*] Christ! . . . [*And he is pulling a handkerchief from his pocket, and covering the mouthpiece*] I mean, they got a kid living there who just got back from the war and something's going on and I want to know what it . . . No, I don't wanna give my name—it's them, not me—Hey! Hey!

RICK: [*Popping in at the hallway at the top of the stairs*] Hey, Dad! How you doin'?

[*OZZIE slams down the phone*]

OZZIE: Oh, Rick! Hi!

RICK: Hi! How you doin'?

[*Guitar over his shoulder, he is heading down the stairs and toward the front door*]

OZZIE: Fine. Just fine.

RICK: Good.

OZZIE: How you doin', Rick?

RICK: Well, I'll see you later.

OZZIE: [*Running*] I WANT YOU TO TEACH ME GUITAR!

RICK: [*Faltering*] What?

OZZIE: I want you to teach me . . . guitar! . . . To play it.

RICK: [*As OZZIE pulls the guitar from his hands*] Sure. Okay.

OZZIE: I want to learn to play it. They've always been a kind of mystery to me, pianos, guitars.

RICK: Mystery?

[*And OZZIE is trying, awkwardly, desperately, to play*]

OZZIE: I mean, what do you think? Do you ever have to think what your fingers should be doing? What I mean is do you ever have to say—I don't know what—"This finger goes there and this other one does—" I mean, "It's on *this* ridge; now I chord all the strings and then switch it all." See? And do you have to tell yourself, "Now switch it all—first finger this ridge—second finger, down—third—somewhere." I mean, does that kind of thing ever happen? I mean, *How do you play it?* I keep having this notion of wanting some . . . thing . . . some material thing, and I've built it. And then there's this feeling I'm of value, that I'm on my way—I mean, moving—and I'm going to come to something eventually, some kind of achievement. All these feelings of a child . . . in me. . . . They shoot through me and then they're gone and they're not anything . . . anymore. But it's . . . a . . . wall . . . that I want . . . I think. I see myself doing it sometimes . . . all brick and stone . . . coils of steel. And then I finish . . . and the success of it is monumental and people come from far . . . to see . . . to look. They applaud. Ricky . . . teach me . . .

RICK: Ahhh . . . what, Dad?

OZZIE: Guitar, guitar.

RICK: Oh, sure. First you start with the basic C chord. You put the first finger on the second string—

OZZIE: But that's what I'm talking about. You don't do that. I know you don't.

RICK: [*Not understanding*] Oh.

OZZIE: You just pick it up and play it. I don't have time for all that you're saying. That's what I've been telling you.

RICK: [*On his way for the door*] Well, maybe some other day then. Maybe Mom'll wanna learn, too.

[*All this dialogue is rapid, overlapping*]

OZZIE: No, no.

RICK: Just me and you then.

OZZIE: Right. Me and you.

RICK: I'll see you later.

OZZIE: What?

RICK: Maybe tomorrow.

OZZIE: No.

RICK: Well, maybe the next day then.

[*And he is gone out the door*]

OZZIE: NOW! Now! [*And the door slams shut*] I grew too old too quick. I had no choice. It was just a town, I thought, and no one remained to test me. I didn't even know it was leaving I was doing. I thought I'd go away and come back. Not leave. [*And he looks up at* DAVID's *room*] YOU SONOFABITCH [*Running up to* DAVID's *room*] NOT LEAVE! [*He bursts into the room. Silence*] Restless, Dave; restless. Got a lot on my mind. Some of us can't just lay around, you know. You said I left that town like I was wrong, but I was right. A man proved himself out there, tested himself. So I went and then I ended up in the goddamn Depression, what about that? I stood in goddamn lines of people begging bread and soup. You're not the only one who's had troubles. All of us, by God, David; think about that a little. [*Stepping out the door, slamming it*] Just give somebody besides yourself some goddamn thought for a change. [*Pause. He talks to the audience again; they are his friends*] Lived in goddamn dirty fields, made tents of our coats. The whole length of this country again and again, soot in our fingers, riding the rails, a bum, a hobo, but young. I remember. And then one day . . . on one of those trains, Hank was there, the first time I ever saw him. Hank, the brakeman, and he sees me hunched down in that car and he orders me off. He stands distant, ordering that I jump! . . . I don't understand and then he stops speaking . . . and . . . when he speaks again, pain is in his eyes and voice—"You're a runner," he says. "Christ, I didn't know you were a runner." And he moves to embrace me and with both hands lifts me high above his head— holds me there trembling, then flings me far out and I fall, I roll. All in the air, then slam down breathless, raw from the cinders . . . bruised and dizzy at the outskirts of this town, and I'm here, gone from that other town. I'm here. We become friends, Hank and me, have good times even though things are rough. He likes to point young girls out on the street and tell me how good it feels to touch them. I start thinking of their bodies, having dreams of horses, breasts and crotches. I remember. And then one day the feeling is in me that I must see a train go by and I'll get on it or I won't, something will happen, but halfway down to where I was thrown off, I see how the grass in among the ties is tall, the rails rusted . . . Grass grows in abundance. No trains any longer come that way; they all go some other way . . . and far behind me Hank is calling, and I turn to see him coming, Harriet young and lovely in his hand, weaving among the weeds. I feel the wonder of her body moving toward me. She's the thing I think I'll enter to find my future. "Hank," I yell, "you sonofabitch! Bring her here. C'mon. Bring her on." Swollen with pride, screaming and yelling, I stand there, I stand: "I'm ready. I'm ready . . . I'm ready."

[*He has come down the stairs. He stands, arms spread, yelling. Blackout. Music*]

[*Lights slowly up.* OZZIE *sleeps on the couch.* RICK *sits in a chair, looking at his guitar.* ZUNG *is in* DAVID'S *room, sitting on the bed behind* DAVID, *who is slouched in a chair.* HARRIET *dressed in a blue robe, enters from the upstairs hallway and comes down the stairs*]

HARRIET: Have you seen my crossword-puzzle book?

RICK: In the bathroom, Mom.

HARRIET: Bathroom? . . . Did I leave it there?

[*Turning, she heads back up the stairs*]

RICK: Guess so, Mom.

DAVID: [*Sitting abruptly up in his chair as if at a sudden, frightening sound*] Who's there? There's someone there? [RICK *looks up;* DAVID *is standing, poking the air with his cane*] Who's there?

[*He opens the door to his room and steps into the hallway*]

RICK: Whatsamatter? It's just me and Dad, and Dad's sleeping.

DAVID: Sleeping? Is he?

RICK: On the davenport. . . . You want me to wake him?

DAVID: Nooo . . . nooo.

[*He moves swiftly to descend to the living room*]

RICK: Hey . . . could I get some pictures, Dave? Would you mind?

DAVID: Of course not. No.

RICK: [*Dashing off up the stairs, while* DAVID *gropes to find the couch*] Let me just go get some film and some flashes, okay.

DAVID: [*Standing behind the couch on which* OZZIE *sleeps and looking after* RICK] Sure . . .

OZZIE: Pardon? Par . . . don?

DAVID: [*Whispering into his father's ear*] I think you should know I've begun to hate you. I feel the wound of you, yet I don't think you can tell me any more, I . . . must tell you. If I had been an orphan with no one to count on me, I would have stayed there. Now . . . she is everywhere I look. I can see nothing to distract me. [OZZIE *stirs*] You think us good, we steal all you have.

OZZIE: Good . . . ole Hank. . . .

DAVID: No, no, he has hated us always—always sick with rot.

OZZIE: Noooo . . . nooooooo. . . .

DAVID: She would tell me you would not like her. She would touch her fingers to her eyes, and she knew how I must feel sometimes as you do.

OZZIE: Ohhh, noooo . . . sleeping . . .

DAVID: You must hear me. It is only fraud that keeps us sane, I swear it.

OZZIE: David, sleeping! . . . Oh, oh . . .

DAVID: It is not innocence I have lost. What is it I have lost?

OZZIE: Oh . . . oh . . .

[RICK *has appeared high in the hallway and hesitates there*]

DAVID: Don't you know? Do you see her in your sleep?

RICK: [*Hurrying down*] I meant to get some good shots at the party, but I never got a chance the way things turned out. You can stay right there.

DAVID: [*Moving toward the chair on which* RICK's *guitar rests*] I'll sit, all right?

[RICK *rushes to save the guitar*]

RICK: Sure. How you feelin' anyway, Dave? I mean, honest ta God, I'm hopin' you get better. Everybody is. I mean . . . [*He takes a picture*] . . . you're not gonna go talkin' anymore crazy like about that guitar and all that, are you? You know what I mean. Not to Mom and Dad anyway. It scares 'em and then I get scared and I don't like it, okay?

[*He moves on, taking more pictures*]

DAVID: Sure. That guitar business wasn't serious anyway, Rick. None of that. It was all just a little joke I felt like playing, a kind of little game. I was only trying to show you how I hate you.

RICK: Huh? [*Stunned, he stares*]

DAVID: To see you die is why I live, Rick.

RICK: Oh.

HARRIET: [*Appearing from off upstairs, the crossword-puzzle book in her hands*] Goodness gracious, Ricky, it was just where you said it would be, though I'm sure I don't know how it got there because I didn't put it there. Hello, David.

DAVID: Hello.

OZZIE: OHHHHHHHHHHHHHHH! [*Screaming, he comes awake, falling off the couch*] Oh, boy, what a dream! Oh . . . [*Trying to get to his feet, but collapsing*] Ohhhhhh! God, leg's asleep. Jesus! [*And he flops about, sits there rubbing his leg*] Ohhhh, everybody. Scared hell out of me, that dream. I hollered. Did you hear me? And my leg's asleep, too. [*He hits the leg, stomps the floor.* HARRIET *sits on the couch, working her crossword-puzzle book.* RICK, *slumped in a chair, reads a comic.* DAVID, *though, leans forward in his chair. He wants to know the effect of his whispering on his father*] Did anybody hear me holler?

HARRIET: Not me.

RICK: What did you dream about, Dad?

OZZIE: I don't remember, but it was awful. [*Stomping the foot*] Ohhhh, wake up, wake up. Hank was in it, though. And Dave. They stood over me, whispering—I could feel how they hated me.

RICK: That really happened; he really did that, Dad.

OZZIE: Who did?

RICK: What you said.

OZZIE: No. No, I was sleeping. It scared me awful in my sleep. I'm still scared, honest ta God, it was so awful.

DAVID: It's that sleeping in funny positions, Dad. It's that sleeping in some place that's not a bed.

OZZIE: Pardon?

DAVID: Makes you dream funny. What did Hank look like?

HARRIET: Ozzie, how do you spell "Apollo"?

OZZIE: What?

RICK: Jesus, Dad, Schroeder got three home runs, you hear about that? Two in the second of the first and one in the third of the second. Goddamn, if he don't make MVP in the National, I'll eat my socks. You hear about that, Dad?

OZZIE: Yes, I did. Yes.

RICK: He's somethin'.

OZZIE: A pro.

HARRIET: Ozzie, can you think of a four letter word that starts with G and ends with B?

RICK: Glub.

HARRIET: Glub?

OZZIE: [*Almost simultaneously*] Glub?

RICK: It's a cartoon word. Cartoon people say it when they're drowning. G-L-U-B.

OZZIE: [*On his feet now*] Ricky. Ricky, I was wondering . . . when I was sleeping, were my eyes open? Was I seeing?

RICK: I didn't notice, Dad.

HARRIET: *Glub* doesn't work, Rick.

RICK: Try *grub*. That's what sourdoughs call their food. It's G-R—

OZZIE: WAIT A MINUTE!

RICK: G-R—

OZZIE: ALL OF YOU WAIT A MINUTE! LISTEN! Listen. I mean, I look for explanations. I look inside myself. For an explanation, I mean, I look inside *my* self. As I would look into water . . . or the sky . . . the ocean. They're silver. Answers . . . silver and elusive . . . like fish. But if you can catch them in the sea . . . hook them as they flash by, snatch them . . . drag them down like birds from the sky . . . against all their struggle . . . when you're adrift . . . and starving . . . they . . . can help you live.

[*He falters; he stands among them, straining to go further, searching some sign of comprehension in their faces*]

RICK: Mom . . . Dad's hungry . . . I think. He wants some fish, I—

OZZIE: SHUT UP!

RICK: [*Hurt deeply*] Dad?

OZZIE: PIECE OF SHIT! SHUT UP! SHUT UP!

HARRIET: Ozzie! . . .

OZZIE: [*Roaring down at* DAVID] I don't want to hear about her. I'm not interested in her. You did what you did and I was no part of it. You understand me? I don't want to hear any more about her! Look at him. Sitting there. Listening. I'm tired of hearing you, Dave. You understand that? I'm tired of hearing you and your crybaby voice and your crybaby stories. And your crybaby slobbering and your . . . [*And his voice is possessed with astonished loathing*] LOOK . . . AT . . . HIM! YOU MAKE ME WANT TO VOMIT! HARRIET! YOU—[*He whirls on* HARRIET] YOU! Your internal organs—your internal female organs—they've got some kind of poison in them. They're backing up some kind of rot into the world. I think you ought to have them cut out of you. I MEAN, I JUST CAN'T STOP THINKING ABOUT

IT. I JUST CAN'T STOP THINKING ABOUT IT. LITTLE
BITTY CHINKY KIDS HE WANTED TO HAVE! LITTLE
BITTY CHINKY YELLOW KIDS! DIDN'T YOU! FOR OUR
GRANDCHILDREN! [*And he slaps* DAVID *with one hand*] LIT-
TLE BITTY YELLOW PUFFY—[*He breaks, groping for the
word*] . . . creatures! . . . FOR OUR GRANDCHILDREN! [*He
slaps* DAVID *again, again*] THAT'S ALL YOU CARED!

[DAVID, *a howl in his throat, has stood up*]

HARRIET: Ohhh, Ozzie, God forgive you the cruelty of your words.
All children are God's children.

[DAVID *is standing rigid. The front door blows open, and in a
fierce and sudden light* ZUNG *steps forward to the edge of*
DAVID's *room, as he looks up at her*]

DAVID: I didn't know you were here. I didn't know. I will buy you
clothing. I have lived with them all my life. I will make them not
hate you. I will buy you boots. [*And he is moving toward her,
climbing the stairs*] They will see you. The seasons will amaze
you. Texas is enormous. Ohio is sometimes green. There will be
time. We will learn to speak. And it will be as it was in that moment when we looked in the dark and our eyes were tongues that
could speak and the hurting . . . all of it . . . stopped, and there
was total understanding in you of me and in me of you . . . and
. . . [*Near her now, stepping into his room through the wall, he
reaches in a tentative way toward her*] such delight in your eyes
that I felt it; [*And she has begun to move away from him*] yet
. . . I [*She is moving away and down the stairs*] discarded you. I
discarded you. Forgive me. You moved to leave as if you were
struggling not to move, not to leave. "She's the thing most possibly of value in my life," I said. "She is garbage and filth and I
must get her back if I wish to live. Sickness. I must cherish her."
Zung, there were old voices inside me I had trusted all my life as if
they were my own. I didn't know I shouldn't hear them. So rea-
sonable and calm they seemed a source of wisdom. "She's all of everything impossible made possible, cast her down," they said. "Go
home." And I did as they told; and now I know that I am not
awake but asleep, and in my sleep . . . there is nothing . . .
[ZUNG *is now standing before the open door, facing it, about to*

leave] Nothing! . . . What do you want from me to make you stay? I'll do it. I'll do what you want!

RICK: [*In the dark before his father, camera in hand*] Lookee here, Dad. Cheer up! Cheer up!

DAVID: [*As* ZUNG *turns to look up at him*] Noooooooo . . . [*And there is a flash as* RICK *takes the picture*] NOOOOOOOOOO-OOOO! STAAAAAAAY!

[*And the door slams shut, leaving* ZUNG *still inside. A slide of* OZZIE *appears on the screen, a close-up of his pained and puzzled face. Music, a falling of notes. The lights are going to black. Perhaps "Intermission" is on the bottom of the slide. The slide blinks out*]

ACT TWO

Blackness. Slide: color close-up of a man's ruddy, smiling, round face.

1ST CHILD'S VOICE: Who zat?

WOMAN'S VOICE: I don't know.

MAN'S VOICE: Looks like a neighbor.

WOMAN'S VOICE: How can you say it's a neighbor? You don't know.

[*New slide appears: scenery, in color*]

2ND CHILD'S VOICE: Oh, that's a pretty one.

[*New slide:* FATHER DONALD *in a boxing pose, color*]

1ST CHILD'S VOICE: Oh, lookee that.

MAN'S VOICE: Father What's-his-name. You know.

[*Another slide:* FATHER DONALD, *slightly different boxing pose*]

WOMAN'S VOICE: There he is again.

2ND CHILD'S VOICE: Wow.

[*Lights up on the downstairs.* DAVID *is up in his room on his bed. Downstairs,* HARRIET *sits on the couch,* FATHER DONALD *is on a chair;* OZZIE *is in the chair beside him. We have the feeling they have been there a long, long time*]

FATHER DONALD: I deal with people and their uneasiness on a regular basis all the time, you see. Everybody I talk to is nervous . . . one way or another . . . so . . . I anticipate no real trouble in dealing with Dave. You have no idea the things people do and then tell me once that confessional door is shut. I'm looking forward actually, to speaking with him. Religion has been sloughed off a lot lately, but I think there's a relevancy much larger than the credit most give. We're growing—and our insights, when we have them, are twofold. I for one have come recently to understand how very often what seems a spiritual problem is in fact a problem of the mind rather than the spirit—not that the two can in fact be separated, though, in theory, they very often are. So what we must do is apply these theories to fact. At which point we would find that mind and spirit are one and I, a priest, am a psychiatrist, and psychiatrists are priests. I mean—I feel like I'm rambling. Am I rambling?

HARRIET: Oh, no, Father.

OZZIE: Nooo . . . noo.

HARRIET: Father, this is hard for me to say, but I . . . feel . . . his problem is he sinned against the sixth commandment with whores.

FATHER DONALD: That's very likely over there.

HARRIET: And then the threat of death each day made it so much worse.

FATHER DONALD: I got the impression from our earlier talk that he'd had a relationship of some duration.

HARRIET: A day or two, wouldn't you say, Ozzie?

OZZIE: [*Distracted, oddly preoccupied with his chair*] A three-day pass I'd say . . . though I don't know, of course.

FATHER DONALD: They're doing a lot of psychiatric studies on that phenomenon right now, did you know that?

[*The front door pops open, and in bounds* RICK]

HARRIET: Oh, Rick! . . .

RICK: Hi, Mom. Hi, Dad.

OZZIE: Hi, Rick.

FATHER DONALD: [*Rising*] Rick, hello!

RICK: Oh, Father Donald . . . hi.

[*No time for* FATHER DONALD, RICK *is speeding for the kitchen*]

OZZIE: Look at him heading for the fudge.

FATHER DONALD: Well, he's a good big strong sturdy boy.

RICK: [*As he goes out*] Hungry and thirsty.

FATHER DONALD: And don't you ever feel bad about it, either! [*He stands for an instant, a little uncertain what to do*] Dave's up in his room, I imagine, so maybe I'll just head on up and have my little chat. He is why I'm here after all.

HARRIET: Fine.

OZZIE: [*Standing, still distracted, he stares at the chair in which* FATHER DONALD *was sitting*] First door top of the stairs.

FATHER DONALD: And could I use the bathroom, please, before I see ole Dave? Got to see a man about a horse.

HARRIET: Oh, Father, certainly: it's just down the hall. Fifth door.

OZZIE: [*Stepping nearer to the chair*] What's wrong with that chair? . . .

HARRIET: It's the blue door, Father! . . .

OZZIE: I . . . don't like that chair. I think it's stupid . . . looking . . . [*As* RICK *enters from the kitchen eating fudge*] Ricky, sit. Sit in that chair.

RICK: What? . . .

OZZIE: Go on, sit, sit.

[RICK *hurries to the chair, sits, eats.* OZZIE *is fixated on the chair*]

HARRIET: Oh, Ricky, take your father's picture, he looks so silly.

OZZIE: I just don't think that chair is any good. I just don't think it's comfortable. Father Donald looked ill at ease all the while he was sitting there.

HARRIET: Well, he had to go to the bathroom, Ozzie, what do you expect?

OZZIE: [*To* RICKY] Get up. It's just not right. [RICK *gets up and* OZZIE *flops into the chair, sits, fidgets.* RICK *goes back out to the kitchen*] Noooooo. It's just not a comfortable chair at all, I don't know why. [*He rises and moves toward the couch*] I don't like it. How much did we pay?

HARRIET: What do you think you're doing?

OZZIE: And this couch isn't comfortable either.

HARRIET: It's a lovely couch.

OZZIE: [*Tests it*] But it isn't comfortable. Noooo. And I'm not really sure it's lovely, either. Did we pay two hundred dollars?

HARRIET: What? Oh, more.

OZZIE: How much?

HARRIET: I don't know, I told you.

OZZIE: You don't. I don't. It's gone anyway, isn't it?

HARRIET: Ozzie, what does it matter?

OZZIE: [*Already on the move for the stairs*] I'm going upstairs. I'll be upstairs.

HARRIET: Wait a minute. [*As he keeps moving, up the stairs*] I want to talk to you. *I think we ought to talk!* [*Emotion well beneath her voice stops him, turns him*] I mean, it's nothing to worry about or anything, but you don't know about it and it's your house, you're involved—so it's just something I mention. You're the man of the house, you ought to know. The police were here . . . earlier today.

OZZIE: What? Oh, my God.

HARRIET: The police. Two of them. Two. A big and a small . . . they—[*He is dazed; he doesn't know whether to go up or down, listen or leave. He nods*] It was just a little bit ago; not long at all.

OZZIE: Jesus Christ! [*He descends*]

HARRIET: Oh, I know, I know. Just out of the blue like that—it's how I felt, too. I did, I did.

OZZIE: *What—police?*

HARRIET: It was when you were gone for groceries. I mean, they thought they were supposed to be here. We wanted it, they thought.

OZZIE: No, no.

HARRIET: Somebody called them to come here. They thought it had been us. They were supposed to look through David's luggage, they thought.

OZZIE: They . . . were . . . what?

HARRIET: That's what I mean. That's exactly what I—

OZZIE: *Look through his luggage? There's nothing wrong with his luggage!*

HARRIET: Isn't it incredible? Somebody called them—they didn't know who—no name was given and it sounded muffled through a handkerchief, they said. I said, "Well, it wasn't us." Told them, "Don't you worry; we're all all right here." It must have been a little joke by somebody.

OZZIE: What about Dave?

HARRIET: No, no.

OZZIE: Or Ricky? Did you ask Ricky?

HARRIET: Ricky?

OZZIE: RICKY! RICKY!

RICK: [*Popping in from the kitchen, thinking he was called*] What's up, Dad?

OZZIE: I DON'T KNOW.

RICK: I thought you called.

[*He pops back out into the kitchen*]

OZZIE: [*To* HARRIET] You ask him; you ask him. I think the whole thing's preposterous—absolutely—

HARRIET: [*As* RICK *re-emerges to look and listen*] Ricky, do you know anything about anybody calling the police to come here?

OZZIE: [*Turning and moving for the stairs*] I'm going upstairs. I'll be upstairs.

RICK: The police? [*As* HARRIET *turns to look and half step after* OZZIE] Oh, no, Mom, not me. Okay if I use the car?

HARRIET: What?

FATHER DONALD: [*Encountering* OZZIE *in the upstairs hallway*] Gonna take care of old Dave right now.

OZZIE: I'm going upstairs. I'll be upstairs.

[*He exits, as* HARRIET *stands looking up at them*]

RICK: Bye, Mom.

HARRIET: What? Oh. [*Looking back as* RICK *goes out the door*] BE CAREFUL!

FATHER DONALD: [*After a slight hesitation*] Ozzie said to tell you he was going upstairs.

HARRIET: What?

FATHER DONALD: Ozzie said to tell you he was going upstairs.

HARRIET: [*Stares at him a moment*] Oh, Father, I'm so glad you're here.

[*And she exits into the kitchen, leaving* FATHER DONALD. *He nods, knocks on* DAVID's *door*]

FATHER DONALD: Dave? [*He opens the door, eases into the semi-dark of the room*] Dave? It's me . . . Dave. . . . [*Finding a light, he flicks it on*] Ohh, Dave, golly, you look just fine. Here I expected to see you all worn out and there you are looking so good. It's me, Dave, Father Donald. Let me shake your hand. [DAVID's *rising hand comes up far off from* FATHER DONALD. *The priest, his own hand extended, has to move nearly around the bed before he can shake* DAVID's *hand*] No, no, David. Here. Over here. Can't see me, can you? There you go. Yes, sir, let me tell you, I'm proud. A lot of people might tell you that, I know, but I mean it, and I'll stand behind it if there's anything I can do for you—anything at all.

DAVID: No. I'm all right.

FATHER DONALD: And that's the amazing part of it, Dave, you are. You truly are. It's plain as day. Golleee, I just don't know how to tell you how glad I am to see you in such high fine spirits. Would you like my blessing? [*He gets to his feet.*] Let me just give you my blessing and then we'll talk things over a little and—[DAVID *slashes with his cane and strikes the hand moving into the position to bless*] Ohhhhhhhhhhhhhh! [*Wincing, teeth gritted*] Oh, Dave; oh, watch out what you're doing!

DAVID: I know.

FATHER DONALD: No, no, I mean, you swung it in the air, you—hit me.

DAVID: Yes.

FATHER DONALD: No, no, you don't understand, you—

DAVID: I was trying to hit you, Father.

[FATHER DONALD *stares, taking this in*]

FATHER DONALD: What?

DAVID: I didn't send for you.

FATHER DONALD: I know, I know, your poor mother—your poor mother—

DAVID: I don't want you here, Father; get out!

FATHER DONALD: David!

DAVID: Get out, I'm sick of you. You've been in one goddamn corner or another of this room all my life making signs at me, whispering, wanting to splash me with water or mark me with oil —some goddamn hocus-pocus. I feel reverence for the air and the air is empty, Father. Now get the fuck out of here!

FATHER DONALD: No, no, no, no, David. No, no. I can't give that to you. You'll have to get that from somewhere else.

DAVID: I don't want anything from you!

FATHER DONALD: I'm supposed to react now in some foolish way—I see—some foolish, foolish way that will discredit me—isn't that right? Oh, of course it is. It's an excuse to dismiss my voice that you're seeking, an excuse for the self-destruction your anger has made you think you want, and I'm supposed to give it. I'm supposed to find all this you're doing obscene and sacrilegious instead of seeing it as the gesture of true despair that it is. You're trying to make me disappear, but it's not going to happen. No, no. No such luck, David. I understand you, you see. Everything about you.

DAVID: Do you?

FATHER DONALD: The way you're troubled.

DAVID: I didn't know that, Father.

FATHER DONALD: You say that sarcastically—"Do you? I didn't know that." As if to imply you're so complicated I couldn't ever understand you when I already have. You see, I've been looking into a few things, David, giving some things some thought. [*Producing a magazine with a colorful cover*] I have in my hand a magazine—you can't see it, I know—but it's there. A psychiatric journal in which there is an article of some interest and it deals with soldiers and some of them carried on as you did and then there's some others who didn't. It's not all just a matter of hocus-pocus any longer.

DAVID: Carried . . . on . . . Father?

FATHER DONALD: That whore. That yellow whore. You understand. You knew I was bringing the truth when I came which is why you hit me.

DAVID: I thought you didn't even know the problem. You came in here all bubbly and jolly asking how did I feel.

FATHER DONALD: That was only a little ruse, David; a little maneuver to put you off your guard. I only did that to mislead you. That's right. Your mother gave me all the basics some weeks ago and I filled in the rest from what I know. You see, if it's a fight you want, it's what you'll get. Your soul is worth some time and sweat from me. You're valued by others, David, even if you don't value yourself. [*Waving the magazine in the air*] It's all here—right here—in these pages. It was demonstrated beyond any possible doubt that people—soldiers—who are compelled for some reason not even they themselves understand to establish personal sexual relationships with whores are inferior to those who don't; they're maladjusted, embittered, non-goal-oriented misfits. The sexual acceptance of another person, David, is intimate and extreme; this kind of acceptance of an alien race is in fact the rejec-

tion of one's own race—it is in fact the rejection of one's own self
—it is sickness, David. Now I'm a religious man, a man of the
spirit, but knowledge is knowledge and I must accept what is
proven fact whether that fact come from science or philosophy or
whatever. What kind of man are you that you think you can deny
it? You're in despair, David, whether you think of it that way or
not. It's only into a valley of ruin that you are trying to lock yourself. You can only die there, David. Accept me. Let God open
your eyes; let Him. He will redeem you. Not I nor anyone, but
only Him—yet if you reject me, you reject Him. My hand is His.
His blessing. [*The hand is rising as if the very words elevate it*]
My blessing. Let me give you my blessing. [*And* DAVID's *cane hits
like a snake.* FATHER DONALD *cries out in surprise and pain. He
recovers and begs*] Let me bless you. [*His hand is again rising in
blessing*] Please! [DAVID, *striking again, stands. He hits again and
again*] David! David! [*Terrified*] Stop it! Let me bless you.

[DAVID *hits* FATHER DONALD's *arm, hits his leg*]

DAVID: I don't want you here!

FATHER DONALD: You don't know what you're saying. [*But now
the blow seems about to come straight down on his head. He yells
and covers his head with his arms. The blow hits. He picks up a
chair, holds it up for protection*] Stop it! Stop it! Goddamnit,
stop hitting me. Stop it. You are in despair. [*He slams the chair
down*] A man who hits a priest is in despair! [*Whistling, the
cane slams into his arm*] Ohhhhh, this pain—this terrible pain in
my arm—I offer it to earn you your salvation.

DAVID: Get out!

FATHER DONALD: Death! Do you understand that. Death. Death is
your choice. You are in despair.

[*He turns to leave*]

DAVID: And may God reward *you*, Father.

FATHER DONALD: [*Turning back, as* DAVID *flops down on the bed*]
Oh yes; yes of course, you're so confident now, young and strong.
Look at you—full of spunk, smiling. But all that'll change. Your
tune'll change in time. What about pain, Dave? Physical pain.
What do you do when it comes? Now you send me away, but in a

little while you'll call me back, run down by time, lying with death on your bed . . . in an empty house . . . gagging on your own spit you cannot swallow; you'll call me then, nothing left to you but fear and Christ's black judging eyes about to find and damn you; you'll call.

[*Slight pause*]

DAVID: That's not impossible, Father.

FATHER DONALD: I don't even like you; do you know that? I DON'T EVEN LIKE YOU!

DAVID: Tell them I hit you when you go down.

FATHER DONALD: [*Near the door, thinking about trying to bless from there*] No. No, they've pain enough already.

DAVID: Have they? You get the fuck out of here before I kill you.

[*As if he has read* FATHER DONALD's *mind and knows what the man is thinking,* DAVID's *cane has risen like a spear; it aims at the priest's heart*]

FATHER DONALD: [*Moving not a muscle*] THOUGH I DO NOT MOVE MY HAND, I BLESS YOU! YOU ARE BLESSED!

[*And he exits hurriedly, heading straight down the hall toward the bathroom. Lights up downstairs: it seems a lovely afternoon as* RICK *and* HARRIET *enter from the kitchen, chatting*]

HARRIET: So the thing I want to do—I just think it would be so nice if we could get Dave a date with some nice girl.

RICK: Oh, sure.

HARRIET: Do you think that would be a good idea?

[OZZIE, *descending from the attic, pauses to peek into* DAVID's *room; he finds* DAVID *asleep, and, after a moment, continues on down*]

RICK: Sure.

HARRIET: Do you know any girls you think might get along with David?

RICK: No, but I still think it's really a good idea and I'll keep it in mind for all the girls I meet and maybe I'll meet one. Here comes Dad. Hi, Dad. Bye, Mom.

HARRIET: Oh, Ozzie, did you see what they were doing?

OZZIE: Dave's sleeping, Harriet; Father Donald's gone.

HARRIET: What? He can't be gone.

OZZIE: I thought maybe he was down here. How about the kitchen?

HARRIET: No, no, I just came out of the kitchen. Where were you upstairs? Are you sure he wasn't in David's room?

OZZIE: I was in the attic.

HARRIET: Well, maybe he saw the light and came up to join you and missed each other on the way up and down. Why don't you go check?

OZZIE: I turned off all the lights, Harriet. The attic's dark now.

HARRIET: Well, yell up anyway—

OZZIE: But the attic's dark now, Harriet.

HARRIET: Just in case.

OZZIE: What are you trying to say? Father Donald's up in the attic in the dark? I mean, if he was up there and I turned off the lights, he'd have said something—"Hey, I'm here," or something. It's stupid to think he wouldn't.

[*And he sits down*]

HARRIET: No more stupid to think that than to think he'd leave without telling us what happened with David.

OZZIE: All right, all right. [*Storming to the foot of the stairs*] HEEEEEEYYYYYYYYYYYYYYY! HEEEEYYYYYYYYY! UP THEEEEERRE! ANYBODY UP THERE?

[*There is a brief silence. He turns toward* HARRIET]

DAVID: [*On his bed in his room*] WHAT'S THAT, DAD?

OZZIE: [*Falters, looks about*] What?

DAVID: WHAT'S UP, DAD?

OZZIE: OH, DAVE, NO, NOT YOU.

DAVID: WHY ARE YOU YELLING?

OZZIE: NO, NO, WE JUST THOUGHT FATHER DONALD WAS UP THERE IN THE ATTIC, DAVE. DON'T YOU WORRY ABOUT IT.

DAVID: I'M THE ONLY ONE UP HERE, DAD!

OZZIE: BUT . . . YOU'RE NOT IN THE ATTIC, SEE?

DAVID: I'M IN MY ROOM.

OZZIE: I KNOW YOU'RE IN YOUR ROOM.

DAVID: YOU WANT ME TO GO UP IN THE ATTIC?

OZZIE: NO! GODDAMNIT, JUST—

DAVID: I DON'T KNOW WHAT YOU WANT.

OZZIE: I WANT YOU TO SHUT UP, DAVE, THAT'S WHAT I WANT, JUST—

FATHER DONALD: [*Appearing from off upstairs*] What's the matter? What's all the yelling?

HARRIET: Oh, Father!

OZZIE: Father, hello, hello.

HARRIET: How did it go? Did it go all right?

FATHER DONALD: [*Coming down the steps, seeming as if nothing out of the ordinary has happened*] Fine, just fine.

HARRIET: Oh, you're perspiring so though—look at you.

FATHER DONALD: [*Maneuvering for the door*] Well, I've got a lot on my mind. It happens. Nerves. I've other appointments. Many, many.

HARRIET: You mean you're leaving? What are you saying?

FATHER DONALD: I must.

HARRIET: But we've got to talk.

FATHER DONALD: Call me.

HARRIET: Father . . . bless me! . . .

FATHER DONALD: What? . . .

HARRIET: Bless me . . .

FATHER DONALD: Of course.

> [*She bows her head, and the priest blesses her, murmuring the Latin*]

HARRIET: Ohhh, Father, thank you so much. [*Touching his hand*] Shall I walk you to your car?

FATHER DONALD: [*Backing for the door*] Fine, fine. That's all right. Sure.

OZZIE: [*Nodding*] DAVE, SAY GOOD-BYE TO FATHER DONALD, HE'S LEAVING NOW.

FATHER DONALD: GOOD-BYE, DAVE!

DAVID: GOOD-BYE, FATHER!

> [*Blackout as* HARRIET *and* FATHER DONALD *are going out the door. Music*]

> [*OZZIE is discovered in late night light, climbing the stairs to* DAVID'S *door, where, after hesitating an instant, he gently knocks*]

OZZIE: Dave, I'd like to come in . . . if I could. [*Easing in*] Awful dark; can I put on a light? [*Silence*] I mean, we don't need one—not really. I just thought we might . . . I mean, first of all, I want to apologize for the way I hit you the other day. I don't know why I did it. I'm . . . gonna sit down here on the edge of the bed. Are you awake enough to understand? I am your father, you know, and I could command . . . if I wanted. I don't; but I could. I'm going to sit. [*Slight pause*] I mean, it's so sad the way you just go on and on . . . and I'd like to have time for you, but you want so much; I have important things, too. I have plans; I'm older, you know; if I fail to fulfill them, who will do it: Not you, though you could. And Rick's too busy. Do you understand? There's no evidence in the world of me, no sign or trace, as if everything I've ever done were no more than smoke. My life has closed behind me like water. But I must not care about it. I must not. Though I have inside me a kind of grandeur I can't realize, many things and memories of a darker time when we were very different—harder—nearer to the air and we thought of nothing as a gift. But I can't make you see that. There's no way. It's what I am, but it's not what you are. Even if I had the guitar, I would only stand here telling my fingers what to do, but they would do nothing. You would not see. . . . I can't get beyond these hands, I jam in the fingers. I break on the bone. I am . . . lonely, I mean, oh, no, not exactly lonely, not really. That's a little strong, actually . . . [*Silence*] I mean . . . Dave . . . [*He pulls from his back pocket* DAVID's *overseas cap*] What's this?

DAVID: What?

OZZIE: This cap. What is it? I cut myself on it. I was rummaging in your stuff upstairs, your bags and stuff, and I grabbed it. It cut me.

DAVID: [*Reaching for the cap*] Oh . . . yes.

OZZIE: There are razors sewn into it. Why is that?

DAVID: To cut people.

[*Slowly he puts the cap on his head*]

OZZIE: Oh.

DAVID: Here . . . I'll show you. . . . [*Getting slowly to his feet*] You're on the street, see. You walk . . . and see someone who's after you. . . . You wait . . . [*He tenses. His hand rises to the tip of the cap*] As they get near .. slowly you remove the hat— they think you're going to toss it aside, see? You . . . *snap it! You snap it!* [*Seizing the front edge of the cap between thumb and finger, he snaps it down. It whistles past* OZZIE, *who jumps*] It cuts them. They hold their face. However you want them, they're yours. You can stomp them, kick them. This is on the street. I'd like to do that to somebody, wouldn't you?

OZZIE: Huh?

DAVID: It'd be fun.

OZZIE: Oh, sure. I . . .

DAVID: Hank told you to buy this house, didn't he?

OZZIE: What?

DAVID: "Get that house," he said. "Get it."

OZZIE: It's a good house. Solid. Not one of those prefabs, those—

DAVID: It's a coffin. You made it big so you wouldn't know, but that's what it is, and not all the curtains and pictures and lamps in the world can change it. He threw you off a fast free train, Ozzie.

OZZIE: I don't believe you saw him.

DAVID: He told you gold, he gave you shit.

OZZIE: I don't believe you saw him. You're a liar, David.

[ZUNG *appears*]

DAVID: Do you know, Dad, it seemed sometimes I would rise and slam with my fists into the walls of a city. Pointing at buildings, I turned them into fire. I took the fleeing people into my fingers and bent them to touch their heads to their heels, each screaming at the sight of their brain turning black. And now sometimes I miss them, all those screaming people. I wish they were here with us, you and Mom and Rick and Zung and me.

[*Pause*]

OZZIE: Mom and Rick and who and you, Dave?

DAVID: Zung.

[ZUNG *is moving nearer to them now*]

OZZIE: Zung, Dave?

DAVID: She's here. They were all just hunks of meat that had no mind to know of me until I cared for her. It was simple. We lived in a house. She didn't want to come back here, Dad; she wanted me to stay there. And in all the time I knew her, she cost me six dollars that I had to sneak into her purse. Surprised? In time I'll show you some things. You'll see them. I will be your father.

[*He tosses the cap at* OZZIE]

OZZIE: [*Shaken, struggling to catch the cap*] Pardon, Dave?

DAVID: What's wrong? You sound like something's terribly wrong?

OZZIE: No. No, no. I'm fine. Your poor mother—she's why I'm here. Your poor mother, sick with grief. She's mine to care for, you know. It's me you're after, yet you torment her. No more. No more. That's what I came up here to tell you.

DAVID: [Getting to his feet] Good.

OZZIE: You're phony, David—phony—trying to make up for the thousands you butchered, when if you were capable of love at all you would love us, your mother and me—not that we matter—instead of some poor little whore who isn't even here.

DAVID: [Exiting the room] I know.

OZZIE: I want her happy.

DAVID: [As OZZIE follows a little into the hall] I know.

[And DAVID is gone. HARRIET enters slowly from the kitchen, sees OZZIE, then the room's open door]

HARRIET: Did you have a nice talk?

OZZIE: [Heading toward her] Harriet, what would you say if I said I wanted some checking done?

HARRIET: I don't know what you mean. In what way do you mean?

OZZIE: Take a look at that. But just be careful.

HARRIET: What is it?

OZZIE: His cap. There are razor blades sewn in it; all along the edge.

HARRIET: Ozzie . . . ohhh! Goodness.

OZZIE: That's what I mean. And I was reading just yesterday—some of them bring back guns and knives. Bombs. We've got somebody living in this house who's killed people, Harriet, and that's a fact we've got to face. I mean, I think we ought to do some checking. You know that test where they check teeth against old X-rays. I think—

HARRIET: Ohhh . . . my God! . . .

OZZIE: I know, I know, it scares me, too, but what are we talking about? We're talking about bombs and guns and knives, and sometimes I don't even think it's David up there. I feel funny . . . sometimes . . . I mean, and I want his fingerprints taken. I think we should have his blood type—

HARRIET: Oh, Ozzie, Ozzie, it was you.

OZZIE: Huh?

HARRIET: You did it. You got this out of his luggage, all his baggage upstairs. You broke in and searched and called the police.

OZZIE: No. What?

HARRIET: You told them to come here, and then you lied and said you didn't.

OZZIE: What?

HARRIET: You did, and then you lied and now you're lying again.

OZZIE: Oh, no. No.

HARRIET: What's wrong with you? What's happening to you?

OZZIE: But I didn't do that. I didn't. [DAVID *appears in the upstairs hallway, moving to return to his room*] I didn't. No, no. And even if I did, what would it mean but I changed my mind, that's all. Sure. [*Looking up at* DAVID *moving in the hall toward his room*] I called and then changed my mind and said I didn't when I did, and since when is there anything wrong in that? It would mean only that I have a little problem of ambivalence. I got a minor problem of ambiguity goin' for me here, is all, and you're exaggerating everything all out of proportion. You're distorting everything! All of you! [*And he whirls to leave*] If I have to lie to live, I will!

   [*He runs*]

HARRIET: Where are you going? Come back here, Ozzie. Where are you going?

OZZIE: Kitchen. Kitchen.

   [*He gallops away and out the front door. Blackout. Music*]

[*Lights up. Bright afternoon.* HARRIET *is alone, dusting.* RICK, *carrying books, enters from the kitchen and heads for the stairs to go to his room*]

HARRIET: One day, Ricky . . . there were these two kittens and a puppy all in our back yard fighting. The kittens were little fur balls, so angry, and the little puppy, yapping and yapping. I was just a girl, but I picked them up in my arms. I held them all in my arms and they got very, very quiet.

RICK: I'm going up to my bedroom and study my history and English and trigonometry, Mom.

HARRIET: Do you know, I've called Father Donald seven times now —seven times, and haven't got an answer? Isn't that funny? He's starting to act like Jesus. You never hear from him. Isn't that funny?

RICK: I'm going up to my bedroom and study my history and English and trigonometry, Mom, okay?

HARRIET: Fine, Ricky. Look in on David, would you?

RICK: Sure.

HARRIET: Good night.

RICK: [*Calling as he passes* DAVID's *door*] Hi, Dave.

DAVID: Hi, Rick.

RICK: DAVE'S OKAY, MOM.

[*She is at the foot of the stairs.* RICK *goes from view. She turns back to her work, and the front door opens and* OZZIE *enters*]

OZZIE: [*Excited, upset*] Harriet! Can you guess what happened? You'll never guess what happened. [*She continues cleaning*] Harriet, wait. Stop.

HARRIET: Ozzie, I've got work to do.

OZZIE: But I want to tell you something.

HARRIET: All right, tell me; I can clean and listen; I can do both.

[*As she moves, he rushes toward her, stretching out the lapel of his jacket to show her a large stain on it. She must see*]

OZZIE: Lookit; look at that. What do you think that is? That spot on my coat, do you see it? That yellow?

HARRIET: [*Distressed, touching the spot*] Ohhhh, Ozzie! . . .

OZZIE: And the red mark on my neck.

HARRIET: [*Wincing*] Ohh, Ozzie, what happened? A bee sting! You got stung by a bee!

OZZIE: No, no; I was walking—thinking—trying to solve our problems. Somebody hit me with an egg. They threw it at me. I got hit with an egg. [*She stares, incredulous*] That's right. I was just walking down the street and—bang—I was hit. I almost blacked out; I almost fell down.

HARRIET: Ozzie, my God, who would do such a thing?

OZZIE: I don't know. That's the whole point. I've racked my brain to understand and I can't. I was just walking along. That's all I was doing.

HARRIET: You mean you didn't even see them?

OZZIE: [*Pacing, his excitement growing*] They were in a car. I saw the car. And I saw the hand, too. A hand. Somebody's hand. A very large hand. Incredibly large.

HARRIET: What kind of car?

OZZIE: I don't know. An old one—black—big high fenders.

HARRIET: A Buick.

OZZIE: I think so; yes. Cruising up and down, up and down.

HARRIET: Was it near here? Why don't you sit down? [*Trying to help him sit, to calm and comfort him*] Sit down. Relax.

[*He obeys, hardly aware of what he is doing, sort of squatting on the couch, his body rigid with tension, as the story obsesses him*]

OZZIE: And I heard them, too. They were hollering.

HARRIET: What did they say?

OZZIE: I don't know. It was just all noise. I couldn't understand.

HARRIET: [*As if the realization doubles the horror*] It was more than just one? My God!

OZZIE: I don't know. Two at least, at the very least. One to drive and one to throw. Maybe even three. A lookout sort of, peering up and down, and then he sees me. "There," he says; he points me out. I'm strolling along like a stupid ass, I don't even see them. The driver picks up speed. [*And now he is rising from the couch, reliving the story, cocking his arm*] The thrower cocks his arm . . .

HARRIET: Ozzie, please, can't you relax? You look awful.

OZZIE: Nooo, I can't relax, goddamnit!

[*Off he goes, pacing again*]

HARRIET: You look all flushed and sweating; please.

OZZIE: It just makes me so goddamn mad the more I think about it. It really does. GODDAMNIT! GODDAMNIT!

HARRIET: Oh, your poor thing.

OZZIE: Because it was calculated; it was calculated, Harriet, because that egg had been boiled to just the right point so it was hard enough to hurt but not so hard it wouldn't splatter. The filthy sonsabitches, but I'm gonna find 'em, I swear that to God, I'm gonna find 'em. I'm gonna kill 'em. I'm gonna cut out their hearts!

[RICK *appears at the top of the stairs*]

RICK: Hey! What's all the racket? What's—

OZZIE: Ricky, come down here! . . . Goddamn 'em. . . .

HARRIET: Ricky, somebody hit your father with an egg!

RICK: Hit him? [*Descending hurriedly, worried*] Hit Dad?

OZZIE: They just threw it! Where's Dave? Dave here? [*He is suddenly looking around, moving for the stairs*] I wanna tell Dave. DAVE!

HARRIET: Ozzie, give me your jacket!

[*She follows him part way up the stairs, tugging at the jacket*]

OZZIE: I wanna tell Dave!

[*He and* HARRIET *struggle to get the jacket off*]

HARRIET: I'll take the spot off.

OZZIE: I gotta tell ole Dave! [*And the jacket is in her arms. He races on up the stairs*] DAVE? DAVE! HEY, DAVE?

[*But* DAVID *is not in his room. While* HARRIET *descends and goes to a wall counter with drawers,* OZZIE *hurries off down the hallway. From a drawer* HARRIET *takes a spray container and begins to clean the jacket*]

RICK: [*Wandering near to her*] Boy, that's something, huh. What you got there, Mom?

HARRIET: [*As* RICK *watches*] Meyer Spot Remover, do you know it? It gives just a sprinkling . . . like snow, which brushed away, leaves the fabric clean and fresh like spring.

[OZZIE *and* DAVID *rush out from the hallway and down the stairs.* RICK *moves toward them to take a picture*]

OZZIE: But it happened—and then there's this car tearin' off up the street. "Christ Jesus," I said, "I just been hit with an egg. Jesus Christ, that's impossible." And the way I felt—the way I feel—Harriet, let's have some beer; let's have some good beer for the boys and me. [*With a sigh, she moves to obey. As* OZZIE *continues, she brings beer, she brings peanuts.* OZZIE *now is pleased with his high energy, with his being the center of attention*] It took me back to when I was a kid. Ole Fat Kramer. He lived on my street and we used to fight every day. For fun. Monday he'd win, and Tuesday, I'd beat him silly, my knees on his shoulders, blam, blam, blam. Later on, he grew up, became a merchant marine, sailed all over the world, and then he used to race sailboats up and down both coasts—he had one he lived on—anything that floated, he wanted to sail. And he wasn't fat either. We just called him that . . . and boy, oh boy, if he was around now—ohhhh, would we go get those punks threw that egg at me. We'd run 'em into the ground. We'd kill 'em like dogs . . . poor little stupid ugly dogs, we'd cut out their hearts.

RICK: [*Suddenly coughing and coughing—having gulped down*

beer—and getting to his feet] Excuse me, Dad; excuse me. Listen,
I've got to get going. You don't mind, do you? Got places to go;
you're just talking nonsense anyway.

[*He moves for the front door*]

HARRIET: Have a good time, Rick.

RICK: I'm too pretty not to, Mom!

[*And he is gone*]

OZZIE: Where is . . . he . . . going? Where does he always go?
Why does he always go and have some place to go? Always! . . .

HARRIET: Just you never mind, Ozzie. He's young and you're not.
I'm going to do the dishes, but you just go right ahead with your
little story and I'll listen from the kitchen.

[*Gathering the beer and glasses, she goes*]

OZZIE: [*Following a little after her, not knowing quite what to
do*] I . . . outran a bowling ball. . . . They bet I couldn't. [*And
he starts as if at a sound. He turns toward* DAVID] What are you
. . . looking . . . at? What do you think you're seeing?

DAVID: I'm not looking.

OZZIE: I feel watched; looked at.

DAVID: No.

OZZIE: Observed.

DAVID: I'm blind.

OZZIE: Did you do it? Had you anything to do with it?

DAVID: What?

OZZIE: That egg.

DAVID: I can't see.

OZZIE: I think you did. I feel like you did it.

DAVID: I don't have a car. I can't drive. How could I?

HARRIET: [*Hurrying in to clean up more of the party leftovers*]
Ohh, it's so good to hear men's voices in the house again, my two

favorite men in all the world—it's what I live for really. Would you like some coffee? Oh, of course you would. Let me put some on. Your humble servant at your command; I do your bidding, bid me be gone.

[*And she is gone without a pause, leaving* OZZIE *staring after her*]

OZZIE: I could run again if I wanted. I'd . . . like . . . to want to. Christ, Fat Kramer is probably dead . . . now . . . not bouncing about in the ocean in some rattletrap, tin-can joke of a ship . . . but dust . . . locked in a box . . . held in old . . . cold hands. . . . And I just stand here, don't I? and let you talk any way you want. And Ricky gets up in the middle of some sentence I'm saying and walks right out and I let him. Because I fear him as I fear her . . . and you. Because I know the time is close when I will be of no use to any of you any longer . . . and I am so frightened that if I do not seem inoffensive . . . and pleasant . . . if I am not careful to never disturb any of you unnecessarily, you will all abandon me. I can no longer compel recognition. I can no longer impose myself, make myself seen.

HARRIET: [*Entering now happily with a tray of coffee*] Here you go. One for each and tea for me. Cream for David . . . [*Setting a cup for* DAVID, *moving toward* OZZIE] and cream and sugar for—

OZZIE: Christ how you must have beguiled me!

HARRIET: Pardon?

OZZIE: Beguiled and deceived!

HARRIET: Pardon . . . Ozzie? . . .

OZZIE: And I don't even remember. I say "must" because I don't remember, I was so innocent, so childish in my strength, never seeing that it was surrendering I was doing, innocently and easily giving to you the love that was to return in time as flesh to imprison, detain, disarm and begin . . . to kill.

HARRIET: [*Examining him, scolding him*] Ozzie, how many beers have you had? You've had too many beers!

OZZIE: Get away! [*He whirls to point at* DAVID *who sits on the floor facing upstage*] Shut up! You've said enough! Detain and kill! Take and give nothing. It's what you meant, isn't it. You said it yesterday, a warning, nearly exactly this. This is your meaning!

DAVID: You're doing so well, Dad.

OZZIE: [*Not understanding*] What?

DAVID: You're doing so well.

OZZIE: No.

DAVID: You are.

OZZIE: Nooo, I'm doing awful. I'm doing terrible.

DAVID: This is the way you start, Dad. We'll be runners. Dad and Dave!

OZZIE: What's he saying?

HARRIET: My God, you're shaking; you're shaking.

OZZIE: I don't know what he's talking about. What's he talking about? [*To* HARRIET] Just let me alone. Just please let me be. I don't really mean these things I'm saying. They're not really important. They'll go away and I don't mean them; they're just coming out of me; I'm just saying them, but I don't mean them. Oh, please, please, go away.

[*And* DAVID, *behind them, pivots to go up the stairs. She whirls, drawn by his sudden movement*]

HARRIET: [*Dismayed*] David? . . .

DAVID: I'm going upstairs.

HARRIET: Oh, yes. Of course, of course.

DAVID: Just for a while.

HARRIET: Fine. Good. Of course.

DAVID: I'll see you all later.

[*And he quietly enters his room, lies down*]

OZZIE: [*Coiled on the couch, constricted with pain*] I remember . . . there was a day . . . when I wanted to leave you, all of you, and I wanted desperately to leave, and Hank was there . . . with me. We'd been playing cards. "No," he told me. "No," I couldn't, he said. "Think of the children," he said. He meant something by that. He meant something and I understood it. But now . . . I don't. I no longer have it—that understanding. It's left me. What did he mean?

HARRIET: [*Approaching, a little fearful*] You're trembling again. Look at you.

OZZIE: For a while . . . just a while, stay away. That's all I ask.

HARRIET: [*Reaching to touch him*] What?

OZZIE: Stay the hell away from me!

HARRIET: Stay away! How far away? Ozzie, how far away? I'll move over . . . [*And she scurries, frightened*] . . . here. Is this far enough away? Ozzie . . .

OZZIE: It's my hands, my feet. There's tiredness in me. I wake up each morning, it's in my fingers . . . sleep . . .

HARRIET: Ohhh, it's such a hateful thing in you the way you have no love for people different from yourself . . . even when your son has come home to tell you of them. You have no right to carry on this way. He didn't bring her back—didn't marry her—we have those two things to thank God for. You've got to stop thinking only of yourself. We don't matter, only the children. When are you going to straighten out your thinking? Promise. You've got to straighten out your thinking.

OZZIE: I do. I know.

HARRIET: We don't matter; we're nothing. You're nothing, Ozzie. Only the children.

OZZIE: I know. I promise.

HARRIET: [*Moving toward the stairs*] All right . . . just . . . rest . . . for a little; I'll be back . . .

OZZIE: I promise, Harriet.

HARRIET: [*More to herself than to him*] I'll go see how he is.

OZZIE: [*Coiled on the couch*] It's my hands; they hurt . . . I want to wrap them; my feet . . .

HARRIET: I'll tell him for you. I'll explain—how you didn't mean those terrible things you said. I'll explain.

OZZIE: It's going to be so cold; and I hurt . . . already . . . So cold; my ankles! . . .

HARRIET: [*Hesitating on the stairway*] Oh, Ozzie, Ozzie, we're all so worried, but I just think we must hope for the fine bright day coming when we'll be a family again, as long as we try for what is good, truly for one another, please.

[*And she goes upstairs. The front door pops open*]

RICK: Hi, Mom. Hi, Dad.

OZZIE: Hi, Rick. Your mom's upstairs. You have a nice time? I bet you did.

RICK: Fine; sure. How about you?

OZZIE: Fine; sure.

RICK: Whata you doin', restin'?

OZZIE: Workin'. Measurin'. Not everybody can play the guitar, *you know*. I'm going to build a wall . . . I think—a wall. Pretty soon . . . or . . . six walls. Thinkin' through the blueprints, lookin' over the plans.

RICK: [*Moving for the kitchen*] I'm gonna get some fudge, Dad; you want some?

OZZIE: No. Too busy.

RICK: I had the greatest piece a tail tonight, Dad; I really did. What a beautiful piece a ass.

OZZIE: Did you, Rick?

RICK: She was bee-uuuuu-ti-ful.

OZZIE: Who was it?

RICK: Nobody you'd know, Dad.

OZZIE: Oh. Where'd you do it—I mean, get it.

RICK: In her car.

OZZIE: You were careful, I hope.

RICK: [*Laughing a little*] C'mon, Dad.

OZZIE: I mean, it wasn't any decent girl.

RICK: Hell, no . . .

[*He is still laughing, as* OZZIE *gets to his feet*]

OZZIE: [*Starting for the door*] Had a dream of the guitar last night, Rick. It was huge as a building—all flecked with ice. You swung it in the air and I exploded.

RICK: I did?

OZZIE: Yes. I was gone.

RICK: Fantastic.

OZZIE: [*Exaggeratedly happy, almost singing*] Good night.

[OZZIE *is gone out the door. Blackout. Music*]

[*Late night.* HARRIET *comes down the hall toward* DAVID's *room. She is wearing a bathrobe and carries a towel, soap, a basin of water. Giving just the lightest tap on the door, she enters, smiling*]

HARRIET: A little bath . . . David? A little sponge bath, all right? You must be all hot and sticky always in that bed. And we can talk. Why don't you take your shirt off? We've an awful lot to talk about. Take your shirt off, David. Your poor father . . . he has no patience, no strength. Something has to be done . . . A little sponge bath would be so nice. Have you talked to him lately? I think he thinks you're angry, for instance, with . . . us . . . for some reason . . . I don't know. [*Tugging at his shirt a little*] Take your shirt off, David. You'll feel cool. That's all we've ever wanted, your father and me—good sweet things for you and Rick —ease and lovely children, a car, a wife, a good job. Time to relax and go to church on Sundays . . . and on holidays all the children and grandchildren come together, mingling. It would be so wonderful—everyone so happy—turkey. Twinkling lights! [*She is puzzled, a little worried*] David, are you going to take your shirt off for me?

DAVID: They hit their children, did you know that? They hit them with sticks.

HARRIET: What?

DAVID: The yellow people. They punish the disobedience of their children with sticks. And then they sleep together, one family in a bed, limbs all entwined like puppies. They work. I've seen them . . . laugh. They go on picnics. They murder—out of petty jealousy. Young girls wet their cunts with spit when they are dry from wear and yet another GI stands in line. They spit on their hands and rub themselves, smiling, opening their arms.

HARRIET: That's not true.

DAVID: I saw—

HARRIET: [*Smilingly scolding him*] None of what you say. No. No. All you did was something normal and regular, can't you see? And hundreds of boys have done it before you. Thousands and thousands. Even now. Now. Now. Why do you have to be so sick and morbid about something so ordinary?

DAVID: She wasn't always a whore. Not always. Not—

HARRIET: If she is now, she was then, only you didn't know. You didn't know. [*She is reaching for him. He eludes her, stands above her, as she is left sitting on the bed, looking up*] Oh, David, David, I'm sure she was a lovely little girl, but I would be insane if I didn't want you to marry someone of your own with whom you could be happy, if I didn't want grandchildren who could be free and welcome in their world. I couldn't want anything else and still think I loved you. David, think of their faces, their poor funny little faces. . . .

[*And the cane is moving, slowly moving along the floor; it grazes her ankle*]

DAVID: I know . . . I know . . .

[*The cane moves now along her inner calf, rising under the hem of her robe, lifting. She tries to ignore it*]

HARRIET: The human face was not meant to be that way. A nose is a thinness—you know that. And lips that are not thin are ugly, and it is we who disappear, David. They don't change, and we are gone. It is our triumph, our whiteness. We disappear. What are you doing? [*The cane has driven her back along the bed; no longer can it be ignored. It has pressed against her*] They take us back and down if our children are theirs—it is not a mingling of blood, it is theft. [*And she hits the cane away. In revulsion she stands, wanting only to flee*] Oh, you don't mean these awful things you do. Your room stinks—odors come from under the door. You don't clean yourself. David, David, you've lost someone you love and it's pain for you, don't you see? I know, I know. But we will be the same, lost from you—you from us—and what will that gain for anyone? What?

[*Now the cane begins to scrape along the floor. It begins to lift toward her, and, shuddering, she flees down the hall.* DAVID *opens the door, listens. Stepping into the hall, he carefully shuts the door before moving down the stairs. In the living room, he moves to plant himself before the front door.* HARRIET, *wearing a raincoat over her robe and a scarf on her head, comes down the stairs, when she turns toward the door and she sees* DAVID, *she stops, nods hello, and stands as he begins to advance upon her*]

DAVID: Do you remember? It was a Sunday when we had all gone to church and there was a young man there with his yellow wife and child. You spoke to us . . . Dad and Rick and me, as if we were conspirators. "I feel so sorry for that poor man—the baby looks like *her*," you said, and your mouth twisted as if you had been forced to swallow someone else's spit.

HARRIET: No, no. You want only to hurt us, don't you? Isn't that right? That's all you want. Only to give us unhappiness. You cheat her, David. That lovely, lovely little girl you spoke of. She merits more to be done in her memory than cruelty.

[*She has seated herself on the couch, clinging to some kind of normalcy, an odd and eerie calmness on both of them now*]

DAVID: And I felt that I must go to her if I was to ever live, and I felt that to touch truly her secret stranger's tongue and mind would kill me. Now she will not forgive the way I was.

HARRIET: [*Standing up*] No. No, no. No, you don't know how badly I feel. I've got a fever, the start of a cold or flu. Let me be. I can't hardly . . . [*And she is moving away from him, back toward the stairs*] move . . . or stand up. I just want to flop somewhere and not have to move. I'm so weak . . . don't hurt me anymore. Don't hurt me—no more—I've got fever; please, fever; don't hurt me.

[*She is on the stairs*]

DAVID: But I have so much to show you.

HARRIET: [*Stops to stare helplessly down at him*] Who are you? I don't know who you are.

DAVID: David.

HARRIET: Noooooo.

DAVID: But I am.

HARRIET: No, no. Oh, no.

[*Moving now as in a trance, she walks up the stairs and down the hallway, all slowly, while* ZUNG *comes forward in* DAVID'S *room, and* DAVID, *in the living room, calls after his mother*]

DAVID: But it's what you want, don't you see? You can see it. Her wrists are bound in coils of flowers. Flowers are strung in her hair. She hangs from the wind and men strike and kick her. They are blind so that they may not see her, yet they howl, wanting not to hurt her but only as I do, to touch and hold her . . . and they howl. I'm home. Little David . . . Home. [*And he is turning now to take possession of the house. As he speaks, he moves to take the space. A conquerer, he parades in the streets he has taken; among the chairs, around the lamp*] Little Davey . . . of all the toys and tops and sailor suits, the plastic cars and Tinkertoys. Drum-player, bed-wetter, home-run-hitter, I'm home . . . now . . . and I want to drink from the toilet, wash there. [*As he climbs the stairs, he passes by* ZUNG, *who stands in his room looking at him. He walks on down the hall in the direction* HARRIET *fled*] And you will join me. You . . . will . . . join me!

[*When he has gone,* ZUNG *sits to gaze down upon the living room, as the front door opens.* OZZIE, *dressed in a suit or perhaps even a tuxedo, enters from the outside. Under his arm he carries a packet of several hundred sheets of paper. He moves*

now with an absolute confidence, almost smugness, as he care-
fully sets down the papers and proceeds to arrange three items
of furniture—perhaps two chairs and a footstool—in such a
way that they face him. He is cocky. Now he addresses them]

OZZIE: [*To the large chair*] Harriet. . . . [*Nodding to the sec-*
ond chair] David . . . [*Patting the footstool*] Ricky. [*He looks*
them over, the three empty chairs, and then speaks in the manner
of a chairman of the board addressing the members of his board,
explaining his position and plan of action for total solution. This
is a kind of commercial on the value of OZZIE] I'm glad we've gotten finally together here, because the thing I've decided to do—
and you all, hopefully, will understand my reasoning—is to *com-*
bat the weariness beginning in me. It's like stepping into a hole,
the way I feel each morning when I awaken, I see the day and the
sun and I'm looking upward into the sky with a sense of looking
down. A sense of hovering over a great pit into which I am about
to fall. The sky. Foolishness and deceit, you say, and I know you're
right—a trick of feeling inside me being played against me, seeking to diminish me and increase itself until it is larger than me
filling me and who will I be then? It. That feeling of being nothing. At first . . . at first . . . I thought the thing to do would be to
learn the guitar. . . . But *that* I realized in just the nick of time
was a folly that would have taken me into the very agony of frustration I was seeking to avoid. The skill to play like Ricky does is a
great gift and only Ricky has it. He has no acid rotting his heart.
He is all lies and music, his brain small and scaly, the brain of a
snake forever innocent of the fact that it crawls. Lucky Ricky. But
there are other things that people can do. And I've come at last to
see the one that I must try if I am to become strong again in my
opinion of myself. [*Holding up, with great confidence, one of the*
many packets of paper] What I have here is an inventory of everything I own. Everything. Every stick of furniture, pot and pan,
every sock, T-shirt, pen or pencil. And opposite is its price. For instance—here—that davenport—five hundred an' twelve dollars an'
ninety-eight cents. That chair—a hundred twenty ninety-nine.
That table . . . [*He hurries to the table*] . . . this table—thirty-
two twenty-nine. Et cetera. Et cetera. Now the idea is that you
each carry a number of these at all times. [*He is distributing*
more papers to the chairs, his control, however, diminishing, so

that the papers are thrown about] Two or three copies at all
times, and you are to pass them out at the slightest provocation.
Let people know who I am, what I've done. Someone says to you,
"Who are you?" You say, "I'm Ozzie's son." "I'm Ozzie's wife."
"Who?" they'll say. "Take a look at that!" you tell 'em. Spit it
out, give 'em a copy, turn on your heel and walk right out. That's
the way I want it; from all of you from here on out, that's the
WAY I WANT IT! [*And the room goes suddenly into eerie
light.* ZUNG, *high behind him in* DAVID's *room, is hit with a sudden
light that makes* OZZIE *go rigid, as if some current from her has entered into him, and he turns slowly to look up at her*] Let him
alone. Let David alone.

> [HARRIET *is in the hallway*]

HARRIET: Is there any aspirin down there? I don't feel well . . .
Ozzie. I don't feel well at all. David poked me with his cane and I
don't like . . . what's . . . going on. [OZZIE *is only staring at*
ZUNG] I don't want what's happening to happen. [*She has halted
on the stairway*] It must be some awful flu, I'm so weak, or some
awful cold. There's an odor . . .

OZZIE: I'll go to the drugstore. My eyes hurt; funny . . .

HARRIET: Oh, Ozzie . . . oh my God. It was awful. I can't help it.
He's crazy—he—

OZZIE: I don't want to hear about him. I don't want to hear. Oh,
no, oh, no. I can't. No more, no more. Let him do what he wants.
No more of him, no more. Just you—you're all that I can see. All
that I care for or want.

> [*He has moved to her as she moved down, and they
> embrace*]

HARRIET: David's crazy! . . .

OZZIE: You're everything.

HARRIET: Please . . .

OZZIE: Listen; we must hide; please.

HARRIET: [*Moving to kneel and he, while helping her, kneels
also*] Pray with me.

OZZIE: We won't move. We'll hide by not moving.

HARRIET: We must beg God to not turn against him; convince him. Ozzie, pray . . .

OZZIE: Yes! . . .

HARRIET: Now! . . .

[*They pray: kneeling, murmuring, and it goes on and on. The front door opens*]

RICK: Hi, Mom. Hi, Dad. [*They continue. He stops*] Hi . . . Mom. Hi, Dad . . . [*Very puzzled*] Hi . . . Mom . . . Hi . . . Dad. . . . [*He thinks and thinks*] DAVID! [*He screams at* DAVID. *He goes running up to look in* DAVID's *room, but the room is empty.* DAVID, *in ragged combat fatigues, appears on the top of the stairs.* RICK, *frightened, backs away*] Dave . . . what have you got to say for yourself? What can you? Honest ta God, I've had it. I really have. I can't help it, even if you are sick, and I hate to complain, but you're getting them so mixed up they're not themselves anymore. Just a minute ago—one minute—they were on their knees, do you know that? Just a minute ago—right here on the living room floor. Now what's the point of that? They're my mom and dad, too.

DAVID: He doesn't know, does he, Dad? Did you hear him?

RICK: [*As* OZZIE *and* HARRIET *are getting from their knees and struggling to sit on the couch*] Let Dad alone.

DAVID: [*On the landing, looking down on them*] He doesn't know how when you finally see yourself, there's nothing really there to see . . . isn't that right? Mom?

RICK: Dave, honest to God, I'm warning you, let them alone.

[DAVID *descends with* ZUNG *behind him. Calmly he speaks, growing slowly happy*]

DAVID: Do you know how north of here, on farms, gentle loving dogs are raised, while in the forests, other dogs run wild? And upon occasion, one of those that's wild is captured and put in among the others that are tame, bringing with it the memory of when they had all been wild—the dark and terror—that had made them wolves. Don't you hear them?

[*And there is a rumbling*]

RICK: What? Hear what?

[*It is windlike, the rumbling of many trucks*]

DAVID: Don't you hear the trucks? They're all over town, lined up from the center of town into the country. Don't you hear? They've stopped bringing back the blind. They're bringing back the dead now. The convoy's broken up. There's no control . . . they're walking from house to house, through the shrubbery, under the trees, carrying one of the dead in a bright blue rubber bag for which they have no papers, no name or number. No one knows whose it is. They're at the Jensens' now. Now Al Jensen's at the door, all his kids behind him trying to peek. Al looks for a long, long time into the open bag before he shakes his head. They zipper shut the bag and turn away. They've been to the Mayers', the Kellys', the Irwins' and Kresses'. They'll be here soon.

OZZIE: Nooo.

DAVID: And Dad's going to let them in. We're going to let them in.

HARRIET: What's he saying?

DAVID: He's going to knock.

OZZIE: I DON'T KNOW.

DAVID: Yes. Yes.

[*A knocking sound. Is it* DAVID *knocking with his fist against the door or table?*]

OZZIE: Nooooo.

RICK: Mom, he's driving Dad crazy.

[*Knocking loud: it seems to be at the front door*]

OZZIE: David, will I die?

[*He moves toward the door*]

HARRIET: Who do you suppose it could be so late?

RICK: [*Intercepting* OZZIE, *blocking the way to the door*] I don't think you should just go opening the door to anybody this time of the night, there's no telling who it might be.

DAVID: We know who it is.

OZZIE: Oh, David, why can't you wait? Why can't you rest?

[*But* DAVID *is the father now, and he will explain. He loves them all*]

DAVID: Look at her. See her, Dad. Tell her to go to the door. Tell her yes, it's your house, you want her to open the door and let them in. Tell her yes, the one with no name is ours. We'll put it in that chair. We can bring them all here. I want them all here, all the trucks and bodies. There's room. [*Handing* RICK *the guitar*] Ricky can sing. We'll stack them along the walls . . .

OZZIE: Nooo . . .

DAVID: Pile them over the floor . . .

OZZIE: No, no . . .

DAVID: They will become the floor and they will become the walls, the chairs. We'll sit in them; sleep. We will call them "home." We will give them as gifts—call them "ring" and "pot" and "cup." No, no; it's not a thing to fear . . . We will notice them no more than all the others.

[*He is gentle, happy, consoling to them*]

OZZIE: What others? There are no others. Oh . . . please die. Oh, wait . . . [*And he scurries to the TV where it sits beneath the stairs*] I'll get it fixed. I'll fix it. Who needs to hear it? We'll watch it. [*Wildly turning TV channels*] I flick my rotten life. Oh, there's a good one. Look at that one. Ohhh, isn't that a good one? That's the best one. That's the best one.

DAVID: They will call it madness. We will call it seeing.

[*Calmly he lifts* OZZIE]

OZZIE: I don't want to disappear.

DAVID: Let her take you to the door. We will be runners. You will have eyes.

OZZIE: I will be blind. I will disappear.

[*Knocking is heard again. Again*]

DAVID: You stand and she stands. "Let her go," you say; "she is garbage and filth and you must get her back if you wish to live. She is sickness, I must cherish her." Old voices you have trusted all your life as if they were your own, speaking always friendly. "She's all of everything impossible made possible!"

OZZIE: Ricky . . . nooo! . . .

DAVID: Don't call to Ricky. You love her. You will embrace her, see her and—

OZZIE: He has no right to do this to me.

DAVID: Don't call to Ricky!

OZZIE: [*Suddenly raging, rushing at* DAVID, *pushing him*] You have no right to do this.

RICK: Nooooo! [*Savagely he smashes his guitar down upon* DAVID, *who crumples*] Let Dad alone. Let him alone. He's sick of you. What the hell's the matter with you? He doesn't wanna talk anymore about all the stupid stuff you talk. He wants to talk about cake and cookies and cars and coffee. He's sick a you and he wants you to shut up. We hate you, goddamn you!

[*Silence:* DAVID *lies still*]

ZUNG: Chào ông! [OZZIE *pivots, looks at her*] Chào ông! Hôm nay ông mạnh không?

OZZIE: Oh, what is it that you want? I'm tired. I mean it. Forgive me. I'm sick of the sight of you, squatting all the time. In filth like animals, talking gibberish, your breath sick with rot . . . And yet you look at me with those sad pleading eyes as if there is some real thing that can come between us when you're not even here. You are deceit. [*His hands, rising, have driven to her throat. The fingers close*] I'm not David. I'm not silly and soft . . . little David. The sight of you sickens me. YOU HEAR ME, DAVID? Believe me. I am speaking my honest true feelings. I spit on you, the both of you; I piss on you and your eyes and pain. Flesh is lies.

You are garbage and filth. You are darkness. I cast you down. Deceit. Animal. Dirty animal.

[*And he is over her. They are sprawled on the ground. Silence as no one moves. She lies like a rag beneath him*]

RICK: I saw this really funny movie last night. This really . . . funny, funny movie about this young couple and they were going to get a divorce but they didn't. It was really funny.

[OZZIE *is hiding the girl. In a proscenium production, he can drag her behind the couch; in three-quarter, he covers her with a blanket brought to him by* HARRIET *which matches the rug*]

HARRIET: What's that? What's that?

RICK: This movie I saw.

HARRIET: Anybody want to go for groceries? We need Kleenex, sugar, and milk.

RICK: What a really funny movie.

OZZIE: I'll go; I'll go.

HARRIET: Good. Good.

OZZIE: I think I saw it on TV.

[*They are cleaning up the house now, putting the chairs back in order, dumping all of* OZZIE's *leaflets in the waste can*]

HARRIET: Did you enjoy it, Rick?

RICK: Oh, yeh. I loved it.

OZZIE: I laughed so much I almost got sick. It was really good. I laughed.

RICK: I bet it was; I bet you did.

OZZIE: Oh, I did.

[*Even* DAVID *helps with the cleaning: he gets himself off the floor and seated in a chair*]

HARRIET: How are you feeling, Ricky?

RICK: Fine.

HARRIET: Good.

RICK: How do you feel?

HARRIET: Oh, I'm all right. I feel fine.

OZZIE: Me, too. I feel fine, too. What day is it anyway? Monday?

HARRIET: Wednesday.

RICK: Tuesday, Mom.

[*Now all three are seated on the couch*]

OZZIE: I thought it was Monday.

RICK: Oh, no.

HARRIET: No, no. You're home now, David . . .

RICK: [*Moving to* DAVID, *who sits alone in a chair*] Hey, Dave, listen, will you. I mean I know it's not my place to speak out and
give advice and everything because I'm the youngest, but I just
gotta say my honest true feelings and I'd kill myself if I were you,
Dave. You're in too much misery. I'd cut my wrists. Honestly
speaking, brother to brother, you should have done it long ago.
[DAVID *is looking about*] You looking for her, Dave? You looking
for her? She's not here.

DAVID: What?

RICK: Nooo. She's never been here. You just thought so. You decided not to bring her, Dave, remember? You decided, all things
considered that you preferred to come back without her. Too
much risk and inconvenience . . . you decided. Isn't that right?
Sure. You know it is. You've always known. [*Silence.* HARRIET
moves to look out the front door] Do you want to use my razor,
Dave? [*Pulling a straight razor from his pocket*] I have one right
here and you can use it if you want. [DAVID *seems to be looking at
the razor*] Just take it if you want it, Dave.

HARRIET: Go ahead, David. The front yard's empty. You don't
have to be afraid. The streets, too . . . still and empty.

RICK: It doesn't hurt like you think it will. Go ahead; just take it,
Dave.

OZZIE: You might as well.

RICK: That's right.

OZZIE: You'll feel better.

RICK: I'll help you now, Dave, okay?

HARRIET: I'll go get some pans and towels.

RICK: [*Moving about* DAVID, *patting him, buddying him*] Oh, you're so confused, you don't know what to do. It's just a good thing I got this razor, Boy, that's all I gotta say. You're so confused. You see, Dave, where you're wrong is your point of view, it's silly. It's just really comical because you think people are valuable or something and, given a chance like you were to mess with 'em, to take a young girl like that and turn her into a whore, you shouldn't, when of course you should or at least might . . . on whim . . . you see? I mean, you're all backwards, Dave—you're upside down. You don't know how to go easy and play—I bet you didn't have any fun the whole time you were over there—no fun at all—and it was there. I got this buddy Gerry, he was there, and he used to throw bags of cement at 'em from off the back a his truck. They'd go whizzin' through those villages, throwin' off these bags a cement. You could kill people, he says, you hit 'em right. Especially the kids. There was this once they knocked this ole man off his bicycle—fifty pounds a dry cement—and then the back a the truck got his legs. It was hysterical—can't you just see that, Dave? Him layin' there howlin', all the guys in the truck bowin' and wavin' and tippin' their hats. What a goddamn funny story, huh?

[HARRIET *has brought silver pans and towels with roosters on them. The towels cover the arms of the chair and* DAVID's *lap. The pans will catch the blood. All has been neatly placed.* DAVID, *with* RICKY's *help, cuts one wrist, then the other, as they talk*]

DAVID: I wanted . . . to kill you . . . all of you.

RICK: I know, I know; but you're hurt; too weak.

DAVID: I wanted for you to need what I had and I wouldn't give it.

HARRIET: That's not possible.

OZZIE: Nooooo.

DAVID: I wanted to get you. Like poor bug-eyed fish flung up from the brief water to the lasting dirt, I would gut you.

HARRIET: David, no, no, you didn't want that.

OZZIE: No, no.

RICK: I don't even know why you'd think you did.

OZZIE: We kill you is what happens.

RICK: That's right.

OZZIE: And then, of course, we die, too . . . Later on, I mean. And nothing stops it. Not words . . . or walls . . . or even guitars.

RICK: Sure.

OZZIE: That's what happens.

HARRIET: It isn't too bad, is it?

RICK: How bad is it?

OZZIE: He's getting weaker.

HARRIET: And in a little, it'll all be over. You'll feel so grand. No more funny talk.

RICK: You can shower; put on clean clothes. I've got deodorant you can borrow. After Roses, Dave. The scent of a thousand roses.

[*He is preparing to take a picture—crouching, aiming*]

HARRIET: Take off your glasses, David.

OZZIE: Do as you're told.

RICK: [*As* DAVID'S *hands are rising toward the glasses to remove them*] I bet when you were away there was only plain water to wash in, huh? You prob'ly hadda wash in the rain. [*He takes the picture; there is a flash. A slide appears on the screen: a close-up of* DAVID, *nothing visible but his face. It is the slide that, appearing at the start of the play, was referred to as "somebody sick." Now it hovers, stricken, sightless, revealed*] Mom, I like David like this.

HARRIET: He's happier.

OZZIE: We're all happier.

RICK: Too bad he's gonna die.

OZZIE: No, no, he's not gonna die, Rick. He's only gonna nearly die. Only nearly.

RICK: Ohhhhhhhhhh.

HARRIET: Mmmmmmmmmmmm.

[And RICK, *sitting, begins to play his guitar for* DAVID. *The music is alive and fast. It has a rhythm, a drive of happiness that is contagious. The lights slowly fade*]

THE RIVER NIGER

Joseph A. Walker

Joseph A. Walker

The River Niger, the 1974 Tony Award play, originally opened at the Off-Broadway St. Marks Playhouse on December 5, 1972, where it played 120 performances. Such was its success and acclaim that the Negro Ensemble Company transferred the production to Broadway and the much larger capacity Brooks Atkinson Theatre on March 27, 1973, for an additional 280 performances.

Both in its initial, and subsequent Broadway coverage, it was lauded by most of the press corps. Mel Gussow described it in the New York *Times* as "a powerful and compassionate new play . . . This is a family play, with a universality that should make it relevant to white and black audiences, but it is firmly rooted in the contemporary black experience. The playwright knows his people and we grow to know them, too, to understand their fears, appetites, frustrations and vulnerabilities . . . The play is rich with character, atmosphere and nuance."

Lawrence Wunderlich reported in *Cue* magazine: "Joseph A. Walker's play is a remarkable, close to magnificent achievement—a work in the true Chekhovian comedy-drama genre—about a whole class of society in frightening transition . . . The Negro Ensemble Company has brought us a cameo view of a class half dying, half fighting to be re-born, and it is a stunning new American play."

Edith Oliver conveyed to readers of *The New Yorker* that "The play is so generous—so rich in character, detail, incident, emotion, and humor—that it more than fulfills the promise of Mr. Walker's *The Harangues* of a few years ago."

Others found it "the work of a forceful and talented writer" that overflows with "affection, humor and extraordinary moments of strength."

"The title refers to a poem written by the leading character, a house painter by trade. The piece is an expression of racial determination and faith, using the name of the river as a symbol of the Negro genesis, power and endurance."

Its transferral to Broadway perhaps was best summed up by Clive Barnes in the New York *Times: "The River Niger* flowed into Broadway last night, and *The River Niger* is big, wide and deep. It is one of the best black plays to be seen hereabouts, and should be at the Brooks Atkinson Theatre for a long, long time . . . This play by Joseph A. Walker is not simply a black play, although black it is . . . But this strong family drama eludes simple labels such as black. Mr. Walker is writing about people in the black fashion that is his own. Yet Broadway audiences, whether they be black, white or sky-blue pink will assuredly react to the strength of its melodrama and the pulse of its language . . . Broadway has gotten itself a most remarkable black play. Its blackness is beautiful, but its common humanity is everything."

The drama, which Mr. Walker has dedicated "to my mother and father and to highly underrated black daddies everywhere," also was named as one of the ten best plays of the 1973–74 season. Additionally, it brought the author the Elizabeth Hull–Kate Warriner Award—presented to the playwright whose work produced within each year dealt with controversial subjects involving the fields of political, religious or social mores of the time, selected by the Dramatists Guild Council. Other honors include an "Obie" (for Off-Broadway excellence) and a Drama Desk citation for "most promising playwright."

A film version of the play was released in 1976 with Cicely Tyson, James Earl Jones and Lou Gossett in three of the principal roles.

For the original publication of *The River Niger*, the author provided the following autobiographical note:

"Born 6:44 P.M. on February 24, 1935, under the sun sign of Pisces, moon in Scorpio, rising—Leo—Virgo via a Cancer mother and an I-don't-remember-what-sign daddy, who was a bad-loud-talking dude of five feet eight inches tall, whom I once saw beat up a man six foot five because he insulted my seven-year-old dignity by beating the daylights out of me on account of I and my buddies were on a hate-little-girls campaign, throwing bottle tops at the cutest little brown-oak girl with skinny legs and a yellow ribbon on her greased ponytail, whom I don't think I hated in retrospect because of her almond-shaped eyes—anyway, my pop was some dude—used to sleep out on the back porch in the dead of winter because he didn't want Ma to know he was drunk, because my ma, man, was a scornful bittersweet lovable crazy lady who was not quite as sweet as

Mattie in *The River Niger* but who was pretty goddamn sweet and *giving* anyway, who once hit me over my head with the heel of her shoe, chasing me all the way from the dining room to my bedroom on account of I said Grandma was not the nicest person in the world —Ma didn't allow nobody to talk about her mama; no, man, and I can dig it. I started to become a professional philosopher, whatever that means, changed my mind on account of I got what you may stuffily call an artistic temperament and I like to do my thinking through plays and things—who am I, who am I, why, I'm Joe Walker—here today, gone tomorrow, yet somehow eternal—If you can see your way clear to call yourself God, I will allow you to call me the same—otherwise, the universe is doing its thing—leave the mother alone. I love lions 'cause they is so, so motherf—so motherfu —so goddamn motherfucking sweet!"

Although now recognized as a prominent and forceful playwright of enormous individuality and mettlesome dramatic spirit, Mr. Walker, admittedly, is no newcomer to the theatre. As an actor, he has appeared in many stage productions and has been seen on television and in films. He also has directed plays, written lyrics, choreographed, designed sets and, upon occasion, taken a turn at the backstage lighting control board.

In 1968, he collaborated on the book and lyrics for the musical, *The Believers*, that ran for 295 performances at the Off-Broadway Garrick Theatre. (He also appeared in the production.) In January 1970, the Negro Ensemble Company presented his four-part play, *The Harangues*, which Clive Barnes termed "a remarkable series of white-black vignettes in an evening that makes a plea for less racial racism and more racial understanding." The presentation ran for 56 performances. Later in the same year, the Negro Ensemble Company presented another work by Mr. Walker, a musical entitled *Ododo*, which he also staged and choreographed.

A native of Washington, D.C., the author received his B.A. in philosophy from Howard University and his M.A. in drama from Catholic University. In addition to his diverse activities in the theatre, Mr. Walker also has taught in various schools both in Washington, D.C., and New York City, and has served as playwright-in-residence at the Yale School of Drama.

The River Niger was first presented by the Negro Ensemble Company, Inc. on December 5, 1972, at the St. Marks Playhouse, New York. On March 27, 1973, it moved to the Brooks Atkinson Theatre, New York. The cast for both presentations was as follows:

JOHN WILLIAMS	*Douglas Turner Ward*
MATTIE WILLIAMS	*Roxie Roker*
GRANDMA WILHEMINA BROWN	*Frances Foster*
DR. DUDLEY STANTON	*Graham Brown*
JEFF WILLIAMS	*Les Roberts*
ANN VANDERGUILD	*Grenna Whitaker*
MO	*Neville Richen*
GAIL	*Saundra McClain*
CHIPS	*Lennal Wainwright*
AL	*Dean Irby*
SKEETER	*Charles Weldon*
VOICE OF LT. STAPLES	*Wyatt Davis*
BASS PLAYER	*Jothan Callins*

Directed by Douglas Turner Ward
Scenery by Gary James Wheeler
Costumes by Edna Watson
Lighting by Shirley Prendergast
Scenery and Costumes Supervised by Edward Burbridge
Incidental Music by Dorothy Dinroe

CHARACTERS

JOHN WILLIAMS, *in his fifties, an alive poet.*

MATTIE WILLIAMS, *in her fifties, an embittered but happy woman.*

GRANDMA WILHEMINA BROWN, *eighty-two, very alive, Mattie's mother.*

DR. DUDLEY STANTON, *in his fifties, cynical, classic Jamaican, lover of poetry.*

JEFF WILLIAMS, *twenty-five, John's son, thoughtful, wild, a credit to his father.*

ANN VANDERGUILD, *twenty-two, strong black South African girl, lover of quality.*

MO, *twenty-four, young black leader of underlying beauty and integrity.*

GAIL, *twenty-one, very much in love with Mo.*

MO'S MEN:

CHIPS, *sexually perverted, a young fool.*

AL, *the closet homosexual, capable, determined, very young.*

SKEETER, *basically good, but hung on dope.*

LIEUTENANT STAPLES, *police officer (voice only).*

BASS PLAYER, *highly skillful at creating a mood (not seen), provides musical poetry for the play.*

ACT ONE

TIME: *February 1, the Present: 4:30 P.M.*
PLACE: *New York City—Harlem.*
SETTING: *Brownstone on 133rd between Lenox and Seventh.
Living room and kitchen cross section. Living room a subdued green. Modest living room suite consisting of coffee
table, two easy chairs, and a sofa. The chairs and sofa are
covered with transparent plastic slipcovers. There is a television set with its back to the audience.
The kitchen is almost as large as the living room. There are a
large kitchen table and four chairs. Stage right is an entrance
from the back porch to the kitchen. Stage left is an entrance
that leads from a small vestibule to a hallway—to the living
room. In the hallway is a stairway that leads upstairs.
The house is not luxuriously decorated, of course, but it is not
garish either. The "attempt" is to be cozy. Even though the
place is very clean, there are many magazines and old newspapers around—giving the general appearance of casual "clut-
ter."*

At rise, a bass counterpoint creeps in, and GRANDMA WILHEMINA
BROWN, *a stately, fair-skinned black woman in her middle eight-
ies is in the kitchen. She is humming "Rock of Ages" and
pouring herself an oversized cup of coffee. She drops in two
teaspoons of sugar and a fraction of cream, which she returns
to the refrigerator. For a moment she stops humming and looks
around stealthily. She goes to the kitchen window and peeps
out into the backyard. Satisfied that she is alone, she opens the
cabinet under the sink. With one final furtive glance around,
she reaches under the cabinet and feels about till she finds
what she's been looking for—a bottle of Old Grand-dad. Apparently, she unhooks it from under the top of the cabinet,
glances around once more, then pours an extremely generous
portion into her coffee. There is a sound from the backyard—*

as if someone or something has brushed by a trash can. She freezes for a second. With unbelievable speed she "hooks" the bottle back into her secret hiding place, snatches her coffee, and hurries out of the kitchen. GRANDMA *pauses on the stairs. In the next moment we hear a key in the back door.* GRANDMA *hurries out of view. The back door opens cautiously. It is* JOHN WILLIAMS, *a thin, medium-sized brown man in his middle fifties. His hair is gray at the temples and slicked down. He has a salt-and-pepper mustache. He wears a brown topcoat, combat boots, corduroy pants—on his head a heavily crusted painter's cap. He is obviously intoxicated but very much in control. From his topcoat pocket he removes a bottle of Johnnie Walker Red Label, which he opens, and takes a long swallow, grimacing as he does so. He then stuffs the bottle into his "hiding place," behind the refrigerator. He pushes the refrigerator back in place and removes his topcoat. Pulling out his wallet, he begins counting its contents. Extremely dissatisfied with the count, he sits heavily and ponders his plight. A second later he takes out a piece of paper.*

JOHN: [*Reading aloud to himself as bass line comes back in*]
I am the River Niger—hear my waters.
I wriggle and stream and run.
I am totally flexible—
Damn!

[*He crumples the paper and stuffs it into his pants pocket. In the very next instant, he remembers something—goes out the back door and returns with a small cedar jewelry box which he places on the table with great pride. There is a rapping at the back door. Bass fades out.* JOHN *is startled. He begins sneaking out of the room when he hears . . .*]

VOICE: [*Softly but intensely*] Johnny Williams! Open the damn door. [*Raps again*] It's me, Dudley. Open up! [JOHN *goes to the door*] It's Dudley Stanton, fool.

[JOHN *opens the door.* DUDLEY STANTON, *a thin, wiry, very dark black man—in his late fifties—graying. He is impeccably but conservatively dressed. The two men stare at each other. Much love flows between them*]

JOHN: Well, I'll be a son-of-a-bitch.

DUDLEY: [*In a thick and beautiful Jamaican accent*] Yeah, man, that's what you are, a son-of-a-bitch. Now, will a son-of-a-bitch let a son-of-a-whore in? It's very cold out here, man! Did I ever tell you my ma was a whore?

JOHN: Only a thousand times. Come on in, ya monkey chaser.

DUDLEY: [*Coming in*] Now, you know I can't stand that expression. Why do you want to burden our friendship with that expression?

JOHN: Where in the hell you been?

DUDLEY: Can I take off my coat first?

JOHN: Take off your jockstrap for all I care. Where in the hell you been?

DUDLEY: To Mexico on vacation—fishing, man. And oh, what fishing. Man, I tell you.

JOHN: Did it ever occur to you that your old buddy might like to go fishing, too? Did that ever cross your mind?

DUDLEY: You ain't never got no vacation time coming. You use it up faster than you earn it.

JOHN: Well, at least you could have let a buddy know you were going. [*Sees the bottle under* DUDLEY's *arm*] Give me a drink?

DUDLEY: Sure thing.

[*Hands* JOHN *the bottle*]

JOHN: Vodka! I be damned! You know I can't stand vodka.

DUDLEY: You don't want my vodka, go on behind the refrig and get your Scotch. I saw you hide it there.

JOHN: You been spying on me with that damn telescope again.

DUDLEY: *Yeah.* I saw you coming in. Closed my office.

JOHN: You old monkey chaser.

DUDLEY: One day, I'm going to brain you for that expression.

JOHN: Goddamn black Jew doctor. You make all the money in the world and you can't even buy your buddy a bottle of Scotch.

DUDLEY: Hell, I shouldn't even drink with you. [*Pause*] If you don't stop boozing the way you do, you'll be dead in five years. You're killing yourself bit by bit, Johnny.

JOHN: Well, that's a helluva sight better than doing it all at once. Besides, I can stop any time I want to.

DUDLEY: Then why don't you?

JOHN: I don't want to. [*Changing the subject purposely*] Dudley, my son's due home tomorrow.

DUDLEY: Jeff coming home? No lie! That's wonderful! Old Jeff. Let's take a run up to the Big Apple and celebrate!

JOHN: That's where I'm coming from. I left work early today—I got so damned worked up, you know. I mean, all I could see was my boy—big-time first lieutenant in the United States of America Air Force—Strategic Air Command—navigator—walking through the front door with them bars—them shining silver bars on his goddamn shoulders. [*He begins saluting an imaginary Jeff*] Yes, sir. Whatever you say, sir. Right away, Lieutenant Williams. Lieutenant Jeff Williams.

DUDLEY: Johnny Williams, you are the biggest fool in God's creation. How in the name of your grandma's twat could you get so worked up over the white man's air force? I've always said, "That's what's wrong with these American niggers. They believe anything that has a little tinsel sprinkled on it." "Shining silver bars." Fantasy, man!

JOHN: He's my son, Dudley, and I'm proud of him.

DUDLEY: You're supposed to be, but because he managed to survive this syphilitic asshole called Harlem, not because he's a powerless nub in a silly military grist mill. What you use for brains, man?

JOHN: I'm a fighter, Dudley. I don't like white folks either, but I sure do love their war machines. I'm a fighter who ain't got no battlefield. I woke up one day, looked around, and said to myself, "There's a war going on, but where's the battlefield?" I'm gonna find it one day—you watch.

DUDLEY: In other words, you'd gladly give your life for your poor downtrodden black brothers and sisters if you only knew where to give it?

JOHN: Right! For my people!

DUDLEY: I wonder how many niggers have said those words: "For my people!"

JOHN: Give me the right time and I'd throw this rubbish on the rubbish heap in a minute.

DUDLEY: Cop-out! That's all that is!

JOHN: Ya goddamn monkey chaser—you're the cop-out!

DUDLEY: Cop-out! The battlefield's everywhere. That's what's wrong with niggers in America—everybody's waiting for *the* time. I don't delude myself, nigger. I know that there's no heroism in death—just death, dirty nasty death. [*Pours another drink*] The rest is jive, man! Back people are jive. The most unrealistic, unphilosophical people in the world.

JOHN: Philosophy be damned. Give me a program—a program!

DUDLEY: A program!?! We're just fools, Johnny, white and black retarded children, playing with matches. We don't have the slightest idea what we're doing. Do you know, I no longer believe in medicine. Of all man's presumptions medicine is the most arrogantly presumptuous. People are supposed to die! It's natural to die. If I find that a patient has a serious disease, I send him to one of my idealistic colleagues. I ain't saving no lives, man. I treat the hypochondriacs. I treat colds, hemorrhoids, sore throats. I distribute sugar pills and run my fingers up the itching vaginas of sex-starved old bitches. Women who're all dried up, past menopause —but groping for life. They pretend to be unmoved, but I feel their wrigglings on my fingers. I see 'em swoon with ecstasy the deeper I probe. Liars—every one of them who would never admit their lives are up—what they really want is a good dose of M and M.

JOHN: M and M?

DUDLEY: Male meat! Old biddies clinging to life like tenants in condemned houses, and medicine keeps on finding cures. Ridiculous! Nature has a course. Let her take it!

JOHN: But what I do is part of nature's course, ya idiot!

DUDLEY: Go on, Johnny, be a hero and a black leader, and die with a Molotov cocktail in your hand, screaming, "Power to the People." The only value your death will have is to dent the population explosion. You can't change your shitting habits, let alone the world.

JOHN: You know what your trouble is, Dudley? You're just floating, man, floating downwind like a silly daisy.

DUDLEY: Come on! What the hell are you rooted to?

JOHN: To the battlefield. To my people, man!

DUDLEY: You ain't got no people, nigger. Just a bunch of black crabs in a barrel, lying to each other, always lying and pulling each other back down.

JOHN: Who do you suppose made us that way?

DUDLEY: You want me to say *whitey*, don't you?

JOHN: Who else?

DUDLEY: You goddamn idealists kill me. You really do, you know. No matter what the *cause* is, the fact remains that we *are* crabs in a barrel. Now deal with that, nigger!

JOHN: Aw, go screw yourself.

DUDLEY: There you go. Hate the truth, don't you? The truth is, you're a dying wino nigger who's trying to find some reason for living. And now you're going to put that burden on your son. Poor Jeff! Doesn't know what he's in for.

JOHN: [*Pause*] The fact remains, monkey-chasing son-of-a-bitch, the fact remains that I got a son coming home from the air force tomorrow and you ain't got nobody— [*A loving afterthought*] but me—

DUDLEY: You are a big fool! Jessie wanted children. Every time she missed her period, I'd give her something to start it over again. Poor lovable bitch, till the day she died she never knew. But I knew—I knew it was a heinous crime to bring any more children into this pile of horse shit.

JOHN: You're sick, you know that, monkey chaser—sick. To satisfy your own perverted outlook, you'd destroy your wife's right to motherhood. Sick!

DUDLEY: . . . The day Jessie died she made me promise I'd marry again and have children, and I lied to her—told her I would—Didn't make her dying any easier, though. She still died twitching and convulsing, saliva running from the corners of her mouth—death phlegm rattling in her throat. She still died gruesomely. That's the way it is. That's life! I'm the last of my line—thank God. No more suffering for the Stantons. Thank God—that cruel son-of-a-bitch.

JOHN: You depress the shit out of me, you know that, monkey chaser—but you can still be my friend, even if you're just a chicken-hearted rabbit, afraid to make a motion.

DUDLEY: [*Genuinely angry*] Look, nigger—any motion you make is on a treadmill.

JOHN: Aw, drink ya drink. What's the matter with you? It don't take no genius to figure out that none of this shit's gonna matter a hundred years from now—that the whole thing's a game of musical chairs—so what? What's your favorite word—presumptuous? Well, man, it is presumptuous as hell of you to even think you can figure this shit out.

DUDLEY: Ain't that what we're here for, stupid? What we've got brains for? To figure it out?

JOHN: Hell no! To play a better game, fool. Just play the motherfucker, that's all. And right now the game is Free My People. Ya get that! And if you don't play it, nigger, you know what you're gonna become—what you *are*—you know what you are, Dr. Dudley Stanton? You're a goddamn spiritual vegetable. Thinking's for idiots—wise men act; thinking is all dribble anyhow, and idiots can do a helluva damn better job at it than you can. My advice to you, Mr. Monkey Chaser, is fart, piss, screw, eat, fight, run, beat your meat, sympathize, and criticize, but for God's sake, stop thinking. It's the white folks' sickness.

DUDLEY: I'm talking to a bloody amoeba.

JOHN: Amoebas are the foundation, man, and they ain't got no blood. Now loan me one hundred and ninety dollars.

DUDLEY: What?

JOHN: A hundred and ninety dollars—shit. Don't I speak clearly? I had two years of college, you know.

DUDLEY: You drank all your money away?

JOHN: Hell yes.

DUDLEY: At the Apple?

JOHN: Right!

DUDLEY: Setting up everybody and his ma?

JOHN: Uh huh!

DUDLEY: Bragging like a nigger about how your first lieutenant, Air Force, Strategic Air Command son is due home tomorrow?

JOHN: Right!

DUDLEY: And they all smiled, patted you on your back, and ordered two more rounds of three-for-one bar slop?

JOHN: Right, nigger. Now, do I get the bread or not— Shit, I ain't required to give you my life story for a measly handout—

DUDLEY: Of a hundred and ninety dollars—

JOHN: Shit! Right!

DUDLEY: You already owe me three hundred and forty.

JOHN: That much?

DUDLEY: [*Takes out a small notebook*] See for yourself—

JOHN: Well, a hundred and ninety more won't break you. Do I get it or not? [*There is a knock on the front door*] Come on, man, that's Mattie.

DUDLEY: Well, well, well, look at the great warrior now—about to get his ass kicked!

JOHN: Come on! Yes or no?

DUDLEY: But here's your battlefield, man. Start fighting! I tell you one thing though, I'm putting my money on Mattie, man.

[*Again there is a knock on the front door*]

JOHN: See ya later.

[*Starts for the back door*]

DUDLEY: Wait a minute! If it were Mattie, she'd use her key, right?

JOHN: [*Comes back*] Hey, yeah, that's right. Didn't think of that!

DUDLEY: You don't believe in thinking.

[JOHN *goes to door and sneaks a look through the pane*]

JOHN: [*Comes back*] Hey, it's a young chick. Good legs—like she might have a halfway decent turd cutter on her.

DUDLEY: Let her in, man, let her in!

JOHN: Look—am I going to get the money?

DUDLEY: [*Interrupting him*] We'll talk about it. I ain't saying yes and I ain't saying no.

JOHN: Sadistic bastard!

[*A more insistent knock*]

DUDLEY: Open the goddamn door, nigger!

[JOHN *opens the door.* ANN VANDERGUILD—*a very attractive black woman in her early twenties—enters. She sparkles on top of a deep brooding inner core. A bass line of beautiful melancholy comes in*]

JOHN: Yes, ma'am.

ANN: I'm Ann—

JOHN: Uh huh.

ANN: I'm a friend of Jeff Williams's. This, uh, is his, where he lives, isn't it?

JOHN: When he's home, yes. He won't be here until noon tomorrow.

ANN: Yes, I know—may I come in?

JOHN: Oh, I'm sorry. Come in.

ANN: Would you help me with my suitcases? They're in the cab.

JOHN: Suitcases!

ANN: Yes, I'd like to spend the night—if I may.

JOHN: Spend the night—

DUDLEY: [*Coming in from the kitchen*] Go get the young lady's suitcases, man. And close the damn door. It's colder than a virgin's—

    [*Catches himself*]

JOHN: Suitcases!

    [JOHN *exits.* DUDLEY *and* ANN *size each other up*]

DUDLEY: Come on in. Let me have your coat.

ANN: Thank you.

DUDLEY: So you're Jeff's intended?

ANN: Well, not exactly, sir. We're very good friends, though.

DUDLEY: But you intend to make yourself Jeff's intended. Am I right? [ANN *smiles*] What a nice smile! Then I am right. Have a seat—

    [JOHN *staggers into the room with an armful of suitcases, plops them down, stares at* ANN *for a second. Bass fades*]

JOHN: There's more.

    [*Exits*]

DUDLEY: Planning a long stay?

ANN: I'll go to a hotel tomorrow.

DUDLEY: I wasn't saying that for that. I'm merely intrigued with your determination. Young women—strong-willed young women —always fascinate me.

    [JOHN *enters with a small trunk on his back which he unloads heavily*]

JOHN: That'll be three dollars and fifty cents, young lady.

DUDLEY: I've got it, Miss— What's your last name?

ANN: Vanderguild.

DUDLEY: Miss Vanderguild.

ANN: I wouldn't think of it.

DUDLEY: [*Hurriedly pays* JOHN, *who is somewhat bewildered*] I told you about my weakness for strong women. My mother was strong. Lord, how strong. Could work all day and half the night.

JOHN : Flat on her back! Anybody can do that.

DUDLEY: Only a strong woman, man. Besides who says she was always on her back? I'm certain she was versatile. Sorry, dear. We're two very dirty old men. Stick out your tongue!

ANN: What is this—

DUDLEY: [*Grabs her wrist, examining her pulse*] Stick out your tongue, young lady! [*She obeys like a child*] Had a rather severe cold recently, girl?

ANN: Why yes, but . . .

DUDLEY: You're all right now. Can tell a lot from tongues.

JOHN: There you go, getting vulgar again. You can take a man out of his mother, but you can't take the mother out of the man.

DUDLEY: That's just his way of getting back at me. Actually, I loved my mother very much. She worked my way through college and medical school, though I didn't find out how until the day I graduated.

JOHN: Stop putting your business in the street!

DUDLEY: I'm not. It's all in the family. Miss Ann Vanderguild here's a part of the family, or almost. Ann, here, is your prospective daughter-in-law, and she'll make a good one too, Johnny. I stamp her certified.

JOHN: [*To* ANN] Jeff never wrote us about you.

ANN: Well, he doesn't exactly know I'm here, sir. I mean we never discussed it or anything.

JOHN: Where you from, little lady?

ANN: Canada, sir—I mean, originally I'm from South Africa, sir.

JOHN: This gentleman here is Dudley. Dr. Dudley Stanton.

ANN: [*To* DUDLEY] My EKG is excellent too, sir.

DUDLEY: Excellent?

ANN: I mean it's within normal limits, sir. I guess my pulse is very slow, because I used to run track—the fifty-yard dash. I'm a nurse. Perhaps you can help me find a job, sir?

DUDLEY: Oh, these strong black women!

ANN: I'm only strong if my man needs me to be, sir.

JOHN: [*Genuinely elated*] You hear that, Dudley, a warrior's woman! A fighter—

DUDLEY: Women always were the real fighters, man, don't you know that? Men are the artists, philosophers—creating systems, worlds. Silly dreams and fictions!

JOHN: Fiction is more real, stupid.

DUDLEY: You see, young lady, your prospective father-in-law here is a philosopher-poet!

JOHN: A poet!

DUDLEY: Philosopher-poet!

JOHN: I'm a poet! A house painter and a poet!

DUDLEY: Then read us one of your masterpieces.

JOHN: Do I have to, Dudley?

DUDLEY: A hundred and ninety bucks' worth—hell yes! You don't think I come over here to hear your bull, do you? Your poems, man, by far the better part of you—now read us one—then give it to me. [*To* ANN] You see, I'm collecting them for him, since he doesn't have enough sense to do it for himself— One day I'm gonna publish them—

JOHN: Probably under your own name, you goddamn Jew.

DUDLEY: Read us your poem!

JOHN: [*Fumbles through his pants pockets and comes up with several scraps of paper, which he examines for selection. He smooths out one piece of paper and begins reading*] I am the River Niger—hear my waters— No, that one ain't right yet.

ANN: Please go on!

JOHN: No, it ain't complete yet. Let's see, yeah, this one's finished. [*Begins reading from another scrap of paper as lights fade to a soft amber. A bass jazz theme creeps in. JOHN is spotlighted*]
"Lord, I don't feel noways tired."
And my soul seeks not to be flabby.
Peace is a muscleless word,
A vacuum, a hole in space,
An assless anesthesia,
A shadowy phantom,
Never settling anyway— Even in sleep.
In my dreams I struggle; slash and crash and cry,
"Damn you, you wilderness! I will cut my way through!"
And the wilderness shouts back!
"Go around me!"
And I answer,
"Hell, no! The joke's on both of us
And I will have the last laugh."
The wilderness sighs and grows stronger
As I too round out my biceps in this ageless, endless duel.
Hallelujah! Hallelujah! Hallelujah!
I want a muscle-bound spirit,
I say, I want a muscle-bound soul—'cause,
Lord, I don't feel noways tired.
I feel like dancing through the valley of the shadow of death!
Lord, I don't feel noways tired.

ANN: Beautiful!

[*Bass fades*]

DUDLEY: [*Takes sheet of paper*] This is a blank sheet of paper!

JOHN: I made it up as I went along. Hell, I'll write it down for you. [*Holds out his hand insistently for the money. DUDLEY counts it out. The doorbell rings suddenly and MATTIE's voice is heard— "Mama—John." JOHN takes the money eagerly, stuffs it in his pocket, then starts for the door. En route he stops suddenly, looks at* ANN *as if in a dilemma, thinks quickly, then crosses to* ANN *and whispers urgently*] Look, Ann, if my wife thinks for one minute that you're trying to get Jeff hooked, she and her crazy mama'll reduce the whole thing to ashes. Tell 'em you're just passing through —you and Jeff were friends up there in Canada—just friends, see—

DUDLEY: Gradually—you've got to ease in gradually. They think Jeff fell off a Christmas tree or something. No one's good enough for Jeff— Not even Jeff.

JOHN: Act like a good-natured sleep-in—

ANN: Sleep-in?

DUDLEY: A maid!

MATTIE: Will someone please open the door! I can't get to my key.

GRANDMA: [*At the top of the stairs; she is slightly intoxicated*] I'm coming, daughter. I'm coming—

[*Starts humming "Rock of Ages" as she descends the stairs*]

JOHN: [*To* ANN] Now remember. [*Opens door*] Hello, Mattie!

MATTIE: The groceries—help me with the groceries.

ANN: Let me give you a hand, Mrs. Williams.

[DUDLEY *gestures to* ANN *approvingly.* MATTIE *takes off her coat, kicks off her shoes, and settles in an easy chair while* ANN *and* JOHN *take the groceries to the kitchen*]

MATTIE: Who's that young lady?

DUDLEY: A friend of the family.

GRANDMA: How you feeling, daughter? Look a bit peaked to me.

MATTIE: Not too well, Mama; almost fainted on the subway. Was all I could do to get the groceries.

JOHN: [*Coming back*] Just need a little soda and water, that's all.

MATTIE: That's what you always say. Something is wrong with me, John. I don't know what, but something's wrong.

DUDLEY: Tomorrow's Saturday. Why don't you come into my office
around eleven, let me take a look at you?

MATTIE: No thanks, Dudley. You always manage to scare a person
half to death. Have you ever heard of a doctor who ain't got no
bedside manner at all, Mama?

[*Laughs*]

DUDLEY: Well, what do you want—the truth or somebody to hold
your hand?

GRANDMA: Both, fool.

MATTIE: Mama!

GRANDMA: Well, he is a fool.

DUDLEY: Well, I guess that's my cue to go home!

JOHN: I'll be damned! Mrs. Wilhemina Brown is going to apologize—

GRANDMA: Over my dead husband's grave—

MATTIE: Mama. You must not feel well yourself.

GRANDMA: I don't, child, I don't. Planned to have your dinner
ready, but I been feeling kinda poorly here lately.

JOHN: That's what she always says.

MATTIE: Come to think of it, Mama, your eyes—

GRANDMA: [*Defensively*] What about my eyes?

MATTIE: Well, they look kinda glassy—

JOHN: [*Knowingly*] I wonder why?

GRANDMA: [*On her feet*] And what in the Lord's name is that
supposed to mean?

MATTIE: [*Raising her voice*] Will you stop it—all of you.

GRANDMA: [*To* MATTIE] Are you talking to me? You screaming at
your mama?

MATTIE: At everybody, Mama.

GRANDMA: My own daughter, my own flesh and blood, taking a no-good drunk's part against her own mother.

MATTIE: I'm not taking anybody's part. I just want some peace and quiet when I come home. Now I think you owe Dr. Stanton an apology.

GRANDMA: I'll do no such thing.

[*Starts humming "Rock of Ages"*]

MATTIE: I apologize for my mother, Dudley.

DUDLEY: That's okay, Mattie, I wasn't going anywhere anyway.

GRANDMA: I got two more daughters and two manly sons. They'd just love to have me. Maybe I should go live with Flora.

JOHN: Good idea! Plenty of opportunity to get glassy-eyed over at Flora's. Yes, indeed.

MATTIE: John, what are you agitating her for?

DUDLEY: . . . Are you afraid, Mattie? To have a checkup, I mean?

MATTIE: [*Pause*] Stay for dinner, Dudley.

DUDLEY: Thanks, I will.

ANN: [*At the door*] Would you like for me to fix dinner, Mrs. Williams?

[*Pause*]

MATTIE: Who is this child?

JOHN: Ann Vanderguild. She's from South Africa. She's a friend of Jeff's—just passing through. I asked her to spend the night.

GRANDMA: Where's she going to spend it—the bathroom?

MATTIE: Mama, what's wrong with you tonight?

JOHN: She had a little too much, that's all.

MATTIE: [*To* ANN] You're welcome, dear. You can stay in Jeff's room tonight. I got it all cleaned up for him. He'll be here tomorrow, you know? Thank the Lord.

ANN: Yes, ma'am! It certainly will be pleasant to see him again. [MATTIE *looks at* ANN *curiously*] I make a very good meat loaf, ma'am. I noticed you've got all the ingredients as I was putting the food away.

MATTIE: You put the food away?

ANN: You seem so bushed.

MATTIE: What a nice thing for you to do. And you read my mind, too. Meat loaf is exactly what I was planning to fix. Yes, indeed. Such a pretty girl, too.

JOHN: [*To* DUDLEY] Why don't we make a little run and leave these black beauties to themselves. To get acquainted—

GRANDMA: Don't be calling me no black nothing. I ain't black! I'm half-full-blooded Cherokee Indian myself. Black folks is "hewers of wood and drawers of water" for their masters. Says so in the Scriptures. I ain't no hewer of no wood myself. I'm a Cherokee aristocrat myself.

JOHN: Go on, Grandma, show us your true Cherokee colors, yes, indeed.

GRANDMA: [*She is obviously inebriated—sings at the top of her voice*]
Onward, Christian soldiers,
Marching on to war,
With the cross of Jesus
Going on before!
[*Begins shouting as if in church*] I'm a soldier myself. I ain't no nigger. A soldier of the Lord. I ain't no common nigger. So don't you be calling me no black nothing. Bless my Jesus. Don't know what these young folks is coming to, calling everybody black!
I'm going home to see my Jesus.
This little light of mine,
Let it shine, let it shine, oh, let it shine. Do Jesus!
      [*Shouting gestures*]

DUDLEY: What I tell you, Johnny. Crabs in a barrel, waiting for a hand from Canaan land to lift 'em out. Each one shoving and pushing, trying to be first to go. And if Jesus was to put his hand down there, they'd probably think it belonged to just another nigger crab and pinch it off.

JOHN: Ain't that poetic. I can just read the headlines: "Jesus extends his hand to bless his chosen"—'cause we are the chosen, Dudley—"and a hustling dope addict takes out his blade and cuts it off at the wrist."

DUDLEY: For the ring on his little finger. Rub-a-dub-dub, niggers in a tub. Christ extends a helping hand and [JOHN *joins in and they deliver the end of the line in unison*] draws back a nub.

MATTIE: WILL YOU TWO PLEASE STOP IT! [GRANDMA's *still singing*] Mama, why don't you go upstairs and take a rest. Ya'll 'bout to drive me crazy.

GRANDMA: My own daughter treats me like a child. Sending me upstairs. Punishing me 'cause I got the spirit. [*Starting for the stair. Starts singing once again, but in a more subdued and soulful manner*]
I know his blood will make me whole.
I know his blood will make me whole.
If I just touch the hem of his garment
I know his blood will make me whole.
    [JOHN *tries to help her up the stairs*]

Don't need no help from nobody but Jesus. [*Starts up steps*] I got Minerva and Flora, and Jacob and Jordan—fine children. Any one of 'em be tickled pink to have me—tickled pink! I don't have to stay here.

MATTIE: Mama, go lie down for a while.

GRANDMA: And ain't none of 'em black either. Christian soldiers every last one of 'em. Mattie's the only black child I ever spawned —my first and last, thank Jesus. [GRANDMA *starts up the steps— on the verge of tears*] I don't have to stay here—

    [*Sings*]
I ain't got long,
I ain't got long
To stay here.
Ben Brown was black though. Looked like an eclipse—sho' nuff.

Lord, my God, hallelujah and do Jesus—he was the ace of spades. And a man, afore God, he was a man—you hear me, Johnny Williams? My man was a man.

[*Exits, humming "Steal Away"*]

MATTIE: [*To* ANN] She gets like that every now and then.

JOHN: More like every other night.

MATTIE: We have a guest, John.

JOHN: Come on, Dudley, let's make that run!

MATTIE: Hold on, Johnny Williams. Where is it?

JOHN: Where's what?

MATTIE: Don't play games, John. This is rent week—remember. Now give it to me.

DUDLEY: All right, great African warrior, do your stuff.

JOHN: Mind your business—

MATTIE: John, I don't feel well. Now, do we have to play your games tonight— Now give it to me. [JOHN *counts out the money and gives it to her. She counts it rapidly*] It's ten dollars short, John.

JOHN: Come on, Mattie. I got to have train fare and cigarettes for the next two weeks.

MATTIE: Stop playing, Johnny. You know if I don't keep it for you, you'll drink it up all at once. Come on, now.

[*He gives her the ten*]

JOHN: Look, let me have five at least. There's more than enough for the rent. [*Pause*] Good God, woman. Jeff'll be here tomorrow. Dudley and I just want to do a little celebrating. Five, woman, hell.

MATTIE: Promise you won't be out late. We got a lot of gettin' ready to do tomorrow morning.

JOHN: I got this chick, see, sixteen years old, and she is as warm as gingerbread in the winter time, and we gon' lay up all night—

MATTIE: We have a young lady here, Johnny.

JOHN: Jeff'll be here by noon. Now, let's see! My little mama just might let me out of the saddle by noon. Yes, indeed—she just might!

MATTIE: John!

JOHN: But if I'm not back in time, Jeff'll understand—ain't too often a man my age gets himself into some young and tender, oven-ready, sixteen-year-old stuff what can shake her some tail feathers like the leaves in March.

   [*She hands him the five*]

MATTIE: Get out of here, Johnny Williams.

DUDLEY: Whew! What a warrior—have mercy! You sure do win your battles, man!

JOHN: Oh, shut up! Why fight when you know you're wrong. Let's go!

MATTIE: Dudley—don't let him overdo it. Tomorrow's gonna be a long day.

   [JOHN *gets their coats from the hallway*]

DUDLEY: I'll do my best, Mattie . . .

JOHN: [*Coming back*] Don't worry—this black-ass Jew ain't gon' spend enough to even get a buzz—he'll watch over me—just like an old mongrel hound dog I used to own. Damn dog stayed sober all the time—wouldn't even drink beer. He was the squarest, most unhip dog in the world! Come on, monkey chaser, let me tell you 'bout that dog. Named him Shylock!

DUDLEY: Niggers invented name-calling. Mouth, that's all they are, mouth. Good night, ladies. Ann, see you tomorrow.

JOHN: Come on, sickle head. See ya, Ann!

DUDLEY: I'm coming, O great African warrior!

   [*They exit*]

MATTIE: Well, Ann, now you've met the whole family. I hope Johnny's cussing don't bother you too much.

ANN: No, ma'am I think he's delightful—he and Dr. Stanton. My father had a friend like him—always attacking each other something terrible.

MATTIE: Sometimes they get to going at each other so hard you think they're gonna come to blows.

ANN: But when they put my father in prison—

MATTIE: In prison—for what?

ANN: They accused him of printing these pamphlets which criticized the government—

MATTIE: Lord, you can't criticize the government over there?

ANN: No, ma'am. Anyway, just after my father was jailed, his friend just pined away. God—those two men loved each other.

MATTIE: Men can really love each other, and the funny thing about it is, don't nobody really know it but them.

ANN: Women don't seem to be able to get along with each other that way—I mean that deep-loving way. You know what I mean, Mrs. Williams?

MATTIE: Of course I do. It's all 'cause women don't trust one another. Your father? Is he still in prison?

ANN: Yes, ma'am. This is going on his ninth year.

MATTIE: Nine years in prison, my God! How does your mother take it?

ANN: [Bass melancholy enters] Quietly. Ma takes everything quietly. Dad turned himself in to protect my two brothers. They were the ones operating the press. Dad was just as surprised as the rest of us when the police found the setup in an old chest of drawers in the attic. Before anyone could say a word, Dad was confessing to everything. This dirty old sergeant got mad and hit him in the stomach with his billy club. Dad had a violent temper, but when he got back on his feet, I could see it in his eyes, the decision, I mean. He turned and said, "Boss, if I said something offensive, please forgive an old black fool." And you know what that sergeant did? He hit him again. He hit him again, Mrs. Williams!

[*Overcome with rekindled grief*]

MATTIE: Oh, I'm sorry, Ann. I must write your mother.

ANN: She'd like that. [*Pause. She collects herself*] My brothers escaped though—stole their way across the border. At first they didn't want to go, they wanted to turn themselves in for Dad, but Ma made 'em go. They live in England now and have families of their own. It wasn't long before the authorities found out that Dad was really innocent, but just because my brothers got away and are free, and just to be plain mean, they kept him in prison anyway. Nine years—nine long years. Those bastards! I despise white people, Mrs. Williams.

MATTIE: Let's talk about something nicer. Tell me about Jeff—

[*Bass fades*]

ANN: Yes, ma'am.

MATTIE: And you—

ANN: Ma'am?

MATTIE: About Jeff and you . . . or you and Jeff.

ANN: I was nursing in Quebec when they brought him into the hospital. He had fractured his ankle skiing. Every time it started paining him, he'd laugh—

MATTIE: He's such a fool.

ANN: Said his dad had taught him to do that. The second night there were some minor complications and he was in so much pain until the doctor ordered me to give him a shot of morphine. Then he got to talking. Very dreamily at first, like he was drifting in a beautiful haze. He told me all about you and Mr. Williams and Grandma Wilhemina Brown and Dr. Stanton. I almost lost my job—I kept hanging around his room so much, listening to one episode after another.

MATTIE: And that's when you started loving him half to death.

ANN: [*Pause*] Yes, ma'am.

MATTIE: That boy sure can talk up a storm. He'll make a fine lawyer. Don't you think so?

ANN: [*Pause*] I won't get in his way, Mrs. Williams.

MATTIE: [*After a long pause*] No, I don't think you will. [*Pause*] Well, let's see if we can trust each other good enough to make that meat loaf. Why don't you chop the onions while I do the celery?

[*Starts to rise*]

ANN: [*Stopping her*] Oh, no, ma'am, this one's on me.

MATTIE: [*Laughing*] I'm very particular, you know.

ANN: I know you are. Jeff's told me a lot about how good your cooking is.

MATTIE: [*Happy to hear it*] That boy sure can eat—Lord today. Well, all right, Ann. Let me go on up and get myself comfortable. I'll be right back. [*She sees the jewelry box on the table—opens it up—takes out a card*] What's this? [*Reads card*] "Big-legged woman, keep your dress tail down. Big-legged woman, keep your dress tail down, 'cause you got something under—"

ANN: Go on, Mrs. Williams.

MATTIE: Lord, child, that man of mine.

ANN: Read it, please, ma'am.

MATTIE: "Big-legged woman, keep your dress tail down, 'cause you got something under there to make a bulldog hug a hound." [*They laugh*] Tomorrow's our anniversary, you know.

ANN: Congratulations!

MATTIE: He made this. Can do anything with his hands, or with his head for that matter, when he ain't all filled up on rotgut. [*Pause*] He's killing himself drinking. I guess I'm to blame though.

ANN: Oh, you don't mean that, Mrs. Williams.

MATTIE: It's true.

ANN: But he seems so full of life.

MATTIE:　Is it "life" he's full of—or something else?

[MATTIE *exits up the steps.* ANN *busies herself about the kitchen. There is a knock on the front door*]

MATTIE'S VOICE:　Will you get that, please, Ann.

ANN:　Yes, ma'am.

[*She crosses and opens the door. A tall, rangy young man in his early twenties rudely pushes his way in. He looks around boldly. He has an air of "I'm a bad nigger" about him*]

CHIPS:　Jeff here?

ANN:　[*Sarcastically*] Come in!

CHIPS:　I'm already in. Is Jeff home yet?

ANN:　Are you a friend of Jeff's?

CHIPS:　Could be. You a friend of Jeff's?

ANN:　Yes.

CHIPS:　[*Looking her over lewdly*] Not bad! As a matter of fact, you look pretty stacked up there.

ANN:　Jeff's not home.

CHIPS:　Hey, what kinda accent is that? You puttin' on airs or something—[*She opens the door*] Yeah, yeah, I'm going. Tell him Chips came by. Big Mo wants to see him at headquarters as soon as possible. Like it's urgent, ya dig it?

ANN:　He won't be here until noon tomorrow.

CHIPS:　That's what he wrote the family. He wrote Mo—

ANN:　Who's Mo?

CHIPS:　[*Laughs*] Who's Mo? Mo's the leader.

ANN:　The leader of what?

CHIPS:　The leader! Wrote Mo he'd be here tonight. Tell him we'll be back around midnight. [*Leers at* ANN] Yes, sir—just like a brick shithouse. [*Slaps her on the rear.* ANN *instictively picks up a heavy ashtray*] Now, don't get rambunctious! If there's anything I can't stand it's a rambunctious black bitch.

ANN: You get the hell out of here!

CHIPS: [*Takes out a switchblade*] Now, what's that ashtray gonna do? If I wanted to, I could cut your drawers off without touching your petticoat and take what I want. Now, dig on that?

ANN: Over my dead body.

CHIPS: I made it with a corpse once. Knew a guy that worked in a funeral home. Pretty chick too—looked something like you. Wasn't half bad either—once I got into it.

ANN: You damn dog—get out of here!

CHIPS: [*Laughing*] Yeah, little fox. I'm going, but I'll be back to-night with Big Mo.

[*Exits.*]

[ANN *slams the door. She is obviously shaken.* MATTIE *comes down the steps wearing a robe and house slippers*]

MATTIE: Who was that, honey? [*Sees* ANN's *fear*] What happened?

ANN: Some fellow to see Jeff. Called himself Chips.

MATTIE: Chips! That bum! If he or any of them other bums show up around here again, you call somebody. They're vicious! Come on, sit down. Catch your breath.

ANN: I'm fine.

MATTIE: Do as I say now! [ANN *sits*] . . . I wonder what they want with Jeff. Jeff used to be the gang leader around here when he was a teenager. By the time he got to college, Jeff and his friend Mo had made the gang decent—you know, doing good things to help the neighborhood. But I heard lately, the bums gone back to their old ways. I wonder what they want with Jeff now . . . Well, let's get this thing ready, and into the oven so we can eat and you can get a good night's rest. You must be exhausted. Bought a new bed for Jeff. You'll sleep like a log.

ANN: Doesn't the couch in the living room let out into a bed, ma'am?

MATTIE: Why, yes.

ANN: Then I'll sleep on the couch. If it's all right with you.

MATTIE: Jeff wouldn't mind a bit you sleeping in his new bed, child! He'll probably say something vulgar about it. Chip off the old block, you know.

ANN: Let it be fresh for him, ma'am, let him christen it with that pretty long frame of his.

MATTIE: [*Laughs*] Is he skinny, Ann?

ANN: As a rail.

MATTIE: You're welcome to stay as long as you want. But no tom-foolery between you two, ya understand?

ANN: Oh, no, ma'am.

MATTIE: And another thing. Between you and me and the lamp-post, don't let on to my mother how you feel about Jeff. She don't think nobody's good enough for Jeff. Says he's the spittin' image of my father. Lord, child, she sure loved my father. I'm very lucky in a way, Ann. I come from very loving parents—in their fashion.

ANN: Yes, ma'am, I can see that!

MATTIE: I've often wondered why my sisters turned out to be such hogs.

[*They start on food preparations as lights fade out*]

[*When the lights come up once more, the house is in darkness.* ANN *is asleep on the living room couch. It is 2 A.M. There is a low rapping at the front door.* ANN *bolts upright. The knocking becomes insistent. Sleepily she answers the door*]

ANN: Is that you, Mr. Williams? [*No response*] Mr. Williams?

[*No answer. She opens the door.* MO, *an athletic-looking young man in his mid-twenties; his girl friend,* GAIL, *sincere and very much in love with* MO; SKEETER, *who seems constantly out of it and desperate;* AL, *who appears to be intensely observant; and* CHIPS—*all force their way in*]

CHIPS: Ann—Big Mo. Big Mo—Ann.

MO: Hello, Ann.

CHIPS: Ain't she fine, Mo?

GAIL: Why don't you hush your lips! Simpleton!

MO: [*To* GAIL] Cool it! [*To* CHIPS] Get yourself together, Chips!

AL: Yeah! Get yourself together, nigger. It's past the witching hour.

MO: [*Ferociously to everybody*] Ease off! Ease off me! [*Silent respect*] Is Jeff home?

ANN: No!

MO: No! How ya mean—no?

ANN: Just what I said—no!

CHIPS: She's a smarty, Mo.

MO: . . . Okay. You sound like you're for real!

CHIPS: She is, Mo, baby—she is! Let me squeeze up on her a bit.

MO: [*Intensely*] Shut the fuck up! Excuse me, Ann. [*To* CHIPS] And sit down somewhere. [*To* SKEETER, *falling alseep in the chair*] You fall asleep—I'm gonna crack your skull, nigger!

SKEETER: Just meditating, chief—just meditating.

MO: [*To* ANN] Pardon that dumb shit, baby, but, er, we gonna wait right here till your man shows—all right?

ANN: Look! It is 2 A.M. in the morning. Jeff won't be here until noon. Now what is it that can't wait till noon?

MO: I can't wait. [*Pause*] Besides—said he'd be here tonight!

ANN: You know what I think? I think you're being very rude—a bunch of very rude bastards! That's what I think.

CHIPS: Let me squeeze up on her a bit, Big Mo!

[*The conversation is interrupted by the somewhat noisy entrance of* JOHN *and* DUDLEY *through the back door*]

DUDLEY: That's all you ever do! Blow off at the mouth! Blow off! Blow off! Pardon me, but kiss my brown eye!

JOHN: Looks too much like your face.

DUDLEY: You gimme a royal pain. Give me one for the road, and let me go home.

JOHN: One for the road! Why didn't you buy one for the road before we hit the road. Shylock stingy bastard.

ANN: Mr. Williams! Mr. Williams!

JOHN: [*Coming into the living room—closely followed by* DUDLEY] Yes, Ann—sweet Ann? [*Sees the crowd*] Company, I see.

ANN: Unwanted company, sir.

MO: We're gonna wait for Jeff, Mr. Williams—that's all.

JOHN: Is that Mo—Mo Hayes?

MO: Yes, it is.

JOHN: Well, well, well—I ain't seen you since Skippy was a punk.

MO: I've been around, Mr. Williams.

JOHN: Nice to see you again, son. Who're your friends?

MO: [*Introducing them*] Well, sir, this is Gail—my girl. Chips and Skeeter, remember? And Al.

JOHN: Nice to meet you. [*They exchange greetings*] Now go home, gentlemen. It's the wee hours of the morning.

MO: We're gonna wait for Jeff.

GAIL: Let's go, Mo, we can come back later.

JOHN: What'd you say, Li'l Mo? Ain't that your nickname? Li'l Mo? Ain't that what we used to call you?

MO: I said, "We're gonna wait for Jeff."

JOHN: We're planning a celebration for Jeff noon tomorrow, and you're welcome to come—all of you. But that's noon tomorrow.

MO: Can't leave until I see Jeff. Sorry.

JOHN: You're "sorry." You wait until you see how sorry I am when I get back—okay.

[*Exits*]

GAIL: Mo, baby, let's go. Jeff ain't gon' run nowhere. I mean, what's the hurry?

CHIPS: [*Eyeing* ANN] Yeah, what's the hurry?

GAIL: [*Turning on him*] You should be in the biggest hurry, nigger, 'cause when Jeff finds out how you been insulting his woman, you're gonna be in a world of trouble.

DUDLEY: Gentlemen, I'd advise you all to leave. Before something presumptuous happens. Can never tell about these black African warrior niggers.

AL: [*Pushing* DUDLEY *into a chair*] Shut up!

DUDLEY: [*Blessing himself*] Father, forgive them, for they know not what they do.

[JOHN *comes back with an M-1 and a World War II hand grenade*]

JOHN: [*Highly intoxicated but even more deadly serious because of it*] Yeah—well, Father may forgive 'em, but I don't, not worth a damn.

CHIPS: You ain't the only one in here with a smoking machine, man.

[*Opens his coat to reveal a shoulder holster and a revolver*]

MO: Close your jacket, stupid.

JOHN: Come over here, Ann. Dudley, get your drunk self outta that chair and make it on over here. [*They follow his instructions. To them*] I don't know if this old grenade'll work or not, but when I pull the pin and throw it at them niggers, we duck into the kitchen—all right.

AL: This old stud's crazy as shit.

MO: Shut up!

CHIPS: I bet he's faking.

[*Reaches for his revolver.* JOHN *instantly throws the bolt on the M-1. They all freeze for a long moment; finally . . .*]

MO: [*Laughing*] You win. You win, Mr. Williams. Dig it? We'll see ya 'round noon. Let's go. [*They file out.* MO *stops at the door, still laughing*] Ya got some real stuff going for you, Mr. Williams.

DUDLEY: Impressive. Presumptuous as hell, but impressive.

[*At this moment* GRANDMA *comes down the steps. She pretends to be sleepwalking. She hums "Rock of Ages" under her breath*]

JOHN: Shh. The old bag's dreaming.

DUDLEY: What?

JOHN: I've been waiting for this a solid week, Dudley.

DUDLEY: What?

JOHN: Shh. You said you wanted one for the road, didn't you? Then be patient, nigger, be patient.

[GRANDMA *makes her way into the kitchen—seeing nobody. Bass line enters*]

GRANDMA: Possum ain't nothing but a big rat. I used to say so to Big Ben Brown. "Call it what you want, wife." Always called me wife, you know. "Possum sure got a powerful wild taste to it." [*She finds her hiding place, pours herself a huge glass of whiskey —talking all the time*] That big old black man of mine. Sure could hunt him some possum. Always knew exactly where to find 'em. I sure hated picking out the buckshot though. Sometimes I'd miss one or two, and I'd jes' be eating and all a sudden I chomp down on one. Lordy, that was a hurting thing. Felt like my tooth was gonna split wide open. Sassafras root—and burning pine cones. Do Jesus! Possum's got a wild taste.

[*Bass line fades out.* JOHN *throws his keys into the hall. Startled,* GRANDMA *caps the bottle, hides it, and mumbles her way back up the steps, intermittently humming "Rock of Ages." When she's out of sight,* JOHN *lets out a yelp, gets* GRANDMA's *bottle, and pours each of them a drink*]

JOHN: Here's to Grandmammy. [*They drink as* JEFF *enters silently, loaded down with duffel bags and luggage. He sees them, sneaks into hallway without being seen, and hides*] Here's to us.

[*Again*] Here's to Jeff. [*Again*] Here's to his daddy. [*Again*] Here's to his sweet old mama. Here's to Jesus Christ—one of the baddest cats to ever drop.

> [*They exchange "good nights."* DUDLEY *exits front door.* JOHN *goes upstairs.* ANN *goes back to sofa—switches off light. Lights fade to night. Music covers.* JEFF *enters, sees* ANN *on sofa, and is very pleased. He is a lanky young man in his middle twenties. There is a heavy seriousness about him, frosted over with the wildness he has inherited from his father. His presence is strong and commanding. He is dressed casually in a turtleneck, bell-bottom slacks, boots, and long-styled topcoat. Magazines protrude from his overcoat pocket. His hair is a modified or shortened afro. His face is clean. He takes off his coat, sits directly opposite* ANN, *fumbles in his pockets, comes up with a plastic bag of marijuana, rolls a joint, and lights up. After a couple of puffs, he leans over and kisses* ANN *on the lips. She groans; he then takes a heavy drag on the joint and blows it full in her face. She awakens with a soft sputter. She is overwhelmed at seeing him. Without saying a word, he extends the joint to her. She sits upright and drags on it. He grabs her foot and gently kisses the arch*]

JEFF: Three whole days—um, um—and I sho' have missed them big old feet of yours.

ANN: [*Hands him the joint*] Are my feet big?

JEFF: Why do you think I always walk behind you in the snow? You got natural snowshoes, baby.

> [*He grabs her roughly but lovingly and kisses her*]

ANN: I had to come, Jeff.

JEFF: I know. Now, let's get down to the nitty-gritty. How 'bout some loving, mama?

ANN: Oh, Jeff—I promised your mother.

JEFF: She won't know. And whatcha don't know— [*Starts taking off his clothes, talking as he does*] My dad taught me that where there's a will, there's a way.

ANN: Your dad taught you a lot of things.

JEFF:　Yeah. Now we're banging away, right. Oo, ahh, oo, ahh. And it's sweet—like summer time in December, right? And just when it really gets good, right? And we're about to reach the top of the mountain, down the steps comes Grandma—on one of her frequent sleepwalking things. And what do I do? I roll over to the wall and drop down to the other side. Like this—[*Demonstrates*] And nobody knows but us. [*She kisses him*] Daddy Johnny says before a man settles down—which shouldn't oughta be until he's damn near thirty or more—[*She kissses him*] a young man's mission is the world.

ANN:　Well, isn't that what you've been trying to do?

　　　[*She kisses him*]

JEFF:　You keep taking up my time.

ANN:　Uh huh. [*Kisses him as the lights begin to dim. Bass line plays under*] You like my feet?

JEFF:　Is the Pope Catholic? Can a fish swim? Do black folks have rhythm? Do hound dogs chase rabbits? Your feet got more beauty than sunshine, mama.

　　　[*They kiss as the lights fade to black. Bass line fades*]

ACT TWO

It is 10:45 the next morning. JOHN, *wearing coveralls made rough with dry paint and a painter's cap, is sweating heavily as he sits pondering his poem. It is obvious that he has suspended the activity of mopping the kitchen floor.*

JOHN: [*Bass enters*]
I am the River Niger—hear my waters!
I wriggle and stream and run.
I am totally flexible.
I am the River Niger—hear my waters!
My waters are the first sperm of the world—
When the earth was but a faceless whistling embryo
Life burst from my liquid kernels like popcorn.
Hear my waters—rushing and popping in muffled finger-drum staccato.
It is life you hear stretching its limbs in my waters—
[*To himself*] *Yeah.*

> [*Quietly he gathers his multiple scraps of paper, folds them neatly, stuffs them into his pocket. Bass fades. He rises to continue mopping the still-half-wet floor. Abruptly he decides to quit and starts for the closet to get his overcoat. He stops as a knock is heard at the kitchen door. He answers it. It is* DUDLEY]

JOHN: Man, you just in time.

DUDLEY: For what?

JOHN: To make it with me to the Big Apple. The labor's too deep around here for me. Mattie's gon' off her head. Do you know that, I—me—Lightnin' John Williams—more powerful than a speeding locomotive—do you realize that I have mopped this entire house by myself? And now I am making it.

DUDLEY: Without telling the captain?

JOHN: What's that suppose to mean?

DUDLEY: It means that the African warrior is always sneaking around like Brer Rabbit instead of walking up to the captain and saying, "Captain Mattie, I's worked hard 'nuff—I's taking a rest and a mint julep at the Apple!" I mean, I want to see some evidence of your spear-throwing, baby—not just words. Words are outta style.

JOHN: [*Goes to closet in living room. Gets overcoat, comes back, stepping lightly on wet floor*] Look, my West Indian corn roaster, I accept the fact that you're a gutless black aristocrat, going thumbs up or thumbs down while your brothers and sisters are being fed to the Lion's Club—So beat your meat while Rome burns—I don't give a piss. Just allow me to paint my own self-portraits—okay, ugly?

DUDLEY: It's pretty chilly out there, man, you better put on a sweater or something, you know.

JOHN: You mean it's pretty chilly for you—that's what I'm trying to tell you. That's you, man, not me!

DUDLEY: Johnny—

JOHN: And don't step on my floor—

DUDLEY: Mattie came over this morning—early. I examined her—and, well, I felt a lot of—irregularities— Anyway—

JOHN: [*Sardonically*] Well, what're you quacks gonna do now—remove her other tit?

DUDLEY: Johnny. [*Pause*] Maybe even worse. I don't want to alarm her until I'm sure. I made an appointment for her at Harlem—they'll do a biopsy—anyway, I'll know as soon as the lab gets done with it.

[*Pause*]

JOHN: [*Stricken but defensive*] Why you telling me all this if you don't know for sure?

[*Pause*]

DUDLEY: She came over while you were still asleep—she doesn't want you to know. I promised I wouldn't tell you.

JOHN: Does she suspect?

DUDLEY: I was very honest with her.

JOHN: That figures! Honesty sticks to some people's mouths like peanut butter.

DUDLEY: Like you just said, man, I have to deal with things the way I think best.

MATTIE'S VOICE: [From upstairs] Johnny—Johnny—have you finished the kitchen?

JOHN: She just keeps going, Dudley. I don't know how in hell, but she keeps on keeping on. [Pause] When'll you know for sure?

DUDLEY: By Friday evening.

MATTIE'S VOICE: If you've finished the kitchen, John, how about taking out those bags of trash.

JOHN: Just keeps on keeping on!

[Pause]

MATTIE'S VOICE: John! Johnny!

JOHN: [Quietly] Johnny's gone to the Apple, you amazing bitch, to celebrate an amazing bitch.

[He and DUDLEY exit just as MATTIE and ANN come down the steps]

MATTIE: [On the landing, followed by ANN] Ann, I do believe that man's gone! Sneaked out!

ANN: I'll finish, Mrs. Williams.

MATTIE: Ann, thank you so much for your help. I don't think we coulda finished without you, and that's a fact. [Pause] Mama, will you please hurry! [To ANN] The store will be jam-packed when we get there.

GRANDMA'S VOICE: [From upstairs] If you can't wait for your mother, then go on without me!

MATTIE: Please, Mama!

GRANDMA: Just go on without me, just go on!

MATTIE: [*To* ANN] There's too much drinking in this house. That's the problem. She's probably hungover.

ANN: Pardon me, Mrs. Williams, but you know about your mother's drinking?

MATTIE: Of course! It's all in her eyes.

ANN: But last night I thought—well—

MATTIE: Child, you got to swallow a lot of truth 'round here to give folks dignity. If Mama knew I knew—I mean really knew I knew—she'd be so embarrassed. Don't you know, I even pretend that John ain't the alcoholic he really is?

ANN: But you're not helping them that way.

MATTIE: Helping them! Who says I ain't? Johnny soon be pushing sixty. He ain't got but a few more years left. If he wants to spend 'em swimming in a fifth a day, who am I to tell him he can't? And Mama, she'll be eighty-three this September. I'm supposed—as the youngsters on my job say—"to blow their cool"? Honey, all we're doing in this life is playing what we ain't. And well, I play anything my folks need me to play.

ANN: I guess that makes sense.

MATTIE: [*Bass enters*] That man had two years of college, Ann. Wanted to be a lawyer like Jeff wants to be, you know. He had to stop school because my mother and my two sisters—Flora and Minerva—came up from the South to live with us—for a short time, so they said. Ignorant country girls—they weren't trained to do nothing. I got a job, and together Johnny and I fed 'em, clothed 'em. In a couple of years, John was ready to go back to school, raring to go, don't you know. Then Flora's boy friend came up from good old South Carolina and didn't have a pot to piss in or a window to throw it out of. He and Flora got married, and where do you think they stayed? [*Yells upstairs*] MAMA! [*Back to* ANN] On top of it all, Minerva got herself pregnant by some silly, buck-toothed nineteen-year-old who just vanished. So here comes another mouth to feed— Child, Johnny was painting houses all morning, working the graveyard shift at the Post Office, and driving a cab on his days off. [*Again yells*] MAMA PLEASE! [*Back to* ANN] He kept on reading though. And I mean heavy reading. Smart, Lord knows that man is smart. Student friends of his were always coming 'round here getting his help in stuff like trigonometry, organic chemistry, philosophy—stuff like that—heavy stuff, you know. They used to call him Solomon. Some of his bummified wino friends still call him that at the Apple. Solomon!

ANN: Every other word out of Jeff's mouth is "Daddy Johnny says—"

MATTIE: That's what he did. He poured himself into Jeff. Lord, had that boy reading Plato and Shakespeare when he was thirteen years old. [*Yelling upstairs*] I gonna leave without you, Mama.

GRANDMA'S VOICE: I'm a child to be told when to come and go!

MATTIE: You can be too good, Ann. I was actually proud of the way John worked himself. I read somewhere—in one of John's psychology magazines—where it's called a Christ fixation, or something like that.

ANN: But that's kinda nice, isn't it?

MATTIE: Honey, the meek ain't never inherited nothing. No, Ann, if I had to do all over again, I'd do it a whole lot different, believe me. What did we get for it? A chest full of bitterness, that's all. These past few years I've had nothing but bile in my mouth. No, Ann, we got nothing, honey. I mean you'd think they'd call every once in a while.

ANN: My mother used to say, "The giver receives all."

MATTIE: Not in this world, child.

ANN: Somewhere! It must be somewhere—some place—

MATTIE: [*Growing heated*] In heaven, honey?

ANN: In a manner of speaking. Treasures—

MATTIE: [*Brooding with anger*] In heaven! Treasures in heaven! My man is an alcoholic, the city's trying to condemn this firetrap we ain't even finished paying for yet, and Flora's got a fancy house and a fancy lawnmower upstate. There were times, Ann, times when I wanted John to get mad—really mad—get a bull whip and whip 'em out—just whip 'em right on out. Johnny woulda done it, ya know. Started to several times, but I'd always managed to cool him down. I got nobody to blame but myself. [*Pause*] Treasures in heaven—shit. A good man is a treasure. White folks proclaim that our men are no good and we go 'round like fools trying to prove them wrong. And I fell right into the same old dumb trap myself. That's why I can't get angry with that man no more. Oh, I pretend to be, but I'm not. Johnny ran a powerful race with a jockey on his back who weighed a ton. So now he's tired. Do you hear me? Tired—and he's put himself out to pasture—with his fifth a day; and I say good for Johnny. I knew he was a smart man. Good for Johnny. [*On the verge of tears*] If our men are no good, then why are all these little white girls trying to gobble 'em up faster than they can pee straight? I rejoice in you young people, Ann. You're the spring rains we need, 'cause we as a people got a lot of growing to do. Bless our young folk.

GRANDMA: [*Down the steps*] Well, I ain't young like them people you blessing. Them steps is mighty steep.

[*Bass line fades*]

ANN: Morning, Mrs. Brown.

GRANDMA: You still here?

MATTIE: Mama, she's here on my invitation. Let's go.

GRANDMA: The gall of a young girl, planting herself right on the boy's doorstep.

[*Crosses to the kitchen*]

ANN: I'm leaving as soon as Jeff's party's over—

MATTIE: You'll do no such thing. Mama, hush! [*Embarrassed*] Ann, would you kinda give Jeff's room a onceover? I started to do it myself, but for some strange reason the door was locked. Been searching for the key half the morning.

[*Hands* ANN *the key from her apron pocket*]

ANN: [*Exiting up the stairs*] Yes, ma'am.

MATTIE: [*Going to the hall closet, which gives* GRANDMA *a chance to check her bottle in the kitchen.* MATTIE *gets their coats, plus an old creaky shopping cart*] Mama, will you stop insulting that child!

GRANDMA: [*Astonished to see empty bottle*] That boy needs some time to grow up.

MATTIE: Who's stopping him?

GRANDMA: That audacious girl! That's who.

MATTIE: Mama, she's a nice girl. Besides, Jeff has a mind of his own.

GRANDMA: Ain't no such thing. Not when it comes to a pretty face. And I got a feeling she's animal-natured.

MATTIE: Then you admit she's pretty?

GRANDMA: Well, she's halfway light skin—got good hair. You know what that does to a colored man's mind!

MATTIE: Not today, Mama. [*Yelling upstairs*] Ann, Ann, would you come here a minute.

GRANDMA: Young niggers—old niggers—they all the same! High yellows is still what they want! Young girls these days just like vipers! Anyhow, why you rushing the boy?

MATTIE: I'm not doing a thing, Mama. It's all in your mind. [ANN *appears at the top of the stairs. She looks like a cyclone has hit her*] My God, child, what on earth—is the room that dirty?

ANN: It's a very strong room, ma'am, I can tell you that.

MATTIE: Listen, honey, I got a roast in the oven. Take it out in twenty-five minutes exactly.

ANN: Yes, ma'am.

MATTIE: Come on, Mama.

GRANDMA: [*Icy wind hits her full in the face as* MATTIE *opens the door*] Do Jesus!

[MATTIE *and* GRANDMA *exit.* JEFF *appears at the top of the stairs*]

JEFF: How your feets feeling this morning, mama?

ANN: You're insane, you know that—trying to pull my clothes off with your mother right downstairs.

JEFF: Hey, ain't I got a groovy mama?

ANN: She's wonderful.

JEFF: You ever look at her feet? She's got some boss dogs—

ANN: Jeff, I'm moving into a hotel this evening—your grandma's a little too much—even for me.

JEFF: Look, today's my homecoming and tomorrow's Sunday—a day of rest. Monday we'll find you a place—okay? Now, why don't you cool your heels and let's get a quickie before the inmates return—[*Pause*] Don't worry! Dad won't be back for at least an hour and Mama always gets carried away shopping—[*Knock on the front door*] And you will not be saved by the bell. See who it is.

[*She goes to peephole in door*]

ANN: It's Mo's friend—Skeeter, and I believe the other one's called Al.

JEFF: Skeeter! Send them away! No! That wouldn't be cool. That means Mo's not far behind. Let them in! Tell them to make themselves comfortable, that you've got some last-minute cleaning to do upstairs, and come on up. For all they know, I'm not here yet.

ANN: As simple as that, huh?

JEFF: Right!

[*Another knock*]

ANN: You're crazy.

JEFF: [*Starts upstairs*] Can I help it if I'm in heat for your feet?

[*Exits.* ANN *answers the door*]

SKEETER: Hey, we come for the party. Mo wanted us to break in early so's we could rap a taste before Jeff's folks gits into him, ya dig.

ANN: Come on in. Skeeter, isn't it?

SKEETER: Ain't it.

ANN: And Al? [AL *nods. They enter.* SKEETER *is jittery. It is obvious he is in heavy need of a fix, but he's clever enough to hide the chilling cold running through him*] Can I take your coat? [AL *gives her his coat*] What about you?

SKEETER: That's okay—I mean, I'm cool.

ANN: Can I get you a beer or something?

AL: Not right now, thanks.

ANN: Skeeter?

SKEETER: I'm cool, sister, I'm cool. Is Jeff here?

ANN: Not yet.

   [*There is a pounding from upstairs*]

SKEETER: What's that?

ANN: Please make yourselves comfortable. Jeff's due shortly, and I've got to get his room cleaned up a bit. [*Starts up the stairs*] There's beer and stuff in the refrig. Just call if you need me.

SKEETER: Yeah. Everything's everything. [ANN *exits*] I hate smart-ass black bitches.

   [*Lights a cigarette*]

AL: So do I, sweet baby.

SKEETER: Stop being so obvious. If Mo ever finds out about your sweet shit—

AL: He won't, sweet baby.

SKEETER: Don't give me that sweet-baby jive. Have you got it?

AL: Well, fuck you. I hate smart-ass dope fiends.

SKEETER: Aw, come on, Al, don't catch an attitude.

AL: I'll catch a 'tude if I so desire. I got the shit and you want it, so walk soft or go to Phoenix House, nigger man.

SKEETER: [*Shivering*] Come on, man. I'm sorry.

AL: You sure is. You the sorriest motherfucker I ever run across.

SKEETER: Come on, man. Mo'll be here in a minute.

AL: Finish telling me 'bout Buckley.

SKEETER: Gimme the stuff first.

AL: I want to know 'bout Buckley.

SKEETER: [*Shivering*] I'm cold, man—cold.

AL: Then talk to me, sugar baby.

SKEETER: What you want to know?

AL: Who ripped him off?

SKEETER: Why you so anxious to know?

AL: Those motherfuckers in Queens claim they did it. They always claiming credit for what we do.

SKEETER: We? You weren't even heard of when it happened.

AL: Well, it's we now, ain't it? Had to be you, Chips, or Mo!

SKEETER: Why's that?

AL: Well, I know you cats wouldn't trust none of the young bloods in the organization to do an important job like that.

SKEETER: Why you want to know 'bout Buckley? You sure you from the home office, nigger? Ever since they sent you here, you been bugging me 'bout Buckley!

AL: Look, I fight for niggers, 'cause I hate the devil pig—but I don't trust niggers as far as I can spit. If there's a finger man on the team, I want to know who it is. Somebody might make a mistake and put him on my ass. You sure get heated up 'bout simple party gossip. So heated up, sugar baby, you clean forget all 'bout that deep-freeze chill slipping and sliding through your bones. You even bite the hand that lights your fire, don't you, sugar baby? [*In furious desperation,* SKEETER *suddenly reaches inside his coat, but* AL *is too quick. At about the same time they both produce their revolvers*] Don't make the mistake of thinking a sissy can't play that Gary Cooper shit if he want to, nigger man.

[*They face each other*]

SKEETER: [*Seething*] I hate your guts.

AL: All that's cool. But I got what it takes to get your guts together, and don't you forget it. I can draw a gun like Sammy Davis, and I was a Golden Gloves champion two years in a row. I got all the hole cards, baby. I could even pull the trigger faster than you right now, 'cause I stays in shape, baby, and you is a dope fiend.

[SKEETER *puts his gun away.* AL *follows suit.* SKEETER *paces about the room, clutching his stomach as* AL *watches, underneath enjoying* SKEETER's *pain. Finally* SKEETER *turns to* AL, *pleading in anguish*]

SKEETER: Give me the shit, Al.

AL: I had it for you all the time. You just been running backward and now you're facing the right way, that's all, sugar baby. Just answer me one teeny-tiny little question. Was it you?

SKEETER: No.

AL: Chips?

SKEETER: [*Almost screaming*] It was an outside dude.

AL: Who?

SKEETER: [*He clutches his stomach*] He wouldn't give his name. He just did it and split. Last I heard he was in Frisco.

[*Satisfied,* AL *searches his pockets. Unknown to* AL, SKEETER *suppresses a chuckle*]

AL: [*Handing him a package of wrapped tin foil*] Here, snort on this. It oughta hold you till after the meeting. It's strong as a horse's ass. [*Using the tip of his little finger,* SKEETER *snorts greedily—first one nostril, then the next*] Later on we can really take care of business. [*Watches* SKEETER *awhile*] Why'd ya'll hate Buckley so?

SKEETER: [*Calming down rapidly*] He was on the narco squad. Useta raid and steal scag and push it to the school kids. Always little girls. He'd get 'em hooked, strung out, then make 'em do freakish shit for a fix. Any one of us woulda blown him away. [*Pause*] Hey, I seen you trying to feel up on Chips's little brother.

AL: [*Excitedly*] You lie, nigger.

SKEETER: If you'd make it with Chips, you'd make it with anybody. Don't give me that funny look, nigger.

AL: You lie!

SKEETER: If I tell Mo 'bout it, he'll bust both of you mothers. Ain't that some shit. And you mean to tell me you don't know 'bout Chips? He stuck his joint in an embalmed cunt. And he brags about it! You know what Mo calls him when he really gets mad at him? Femaldehyde Dick.

   [*Laughs*]

AL: That shit you just snorted ain't gon' last forever, you know.

SKEETER: Oughta call you Femaldehyde Brown Eye.

AL: Ya never miss the water till the well runs dry.

SKEETER: Don't give me that shit. We got a working relationship— the three of us.

AL: What three?

SKEETER: You, me, and Chips. You give me scag 'cause you know I know where you at— I don't tell Mo where you at 'cause I need the scag. Chips don't tell him 'cause he digs fags. That's where he's at! Now, you keep your eye—your brown eye—on that relationship 'cause all three of us is walking on the same razor blade, sugar baby, and don't you forget it, 'cause our asses could get cut in half!

   [*Laughs uproariously. There is a knock on the door*]

AL: Answer the door, dope fiend!

   [SKEETER *goes to the door, peeks through*]

SKEETER: It's Femaldehyde himself.

AL: Flake off, nigger—I'm warning you!

SKEETER: You want to know something else, Alfreida? That shit about an outside man ripping off Buckley—I made that up.

AL: Your ass is gon' be mine. Wait and see!

SKEETER: [*Laughing*] You wanta know something else? I'm supposed to pick up some good stuff as soon as we finish rapping with Jeff. I don't really need your shit.

[*Laughs and opens the door*]

CHIPS: [*To* AL] What's this clown laughing about?

SKEETER: [*Holding his sides*] Gary Cooper here just got some lemon in his sucker—

[*Laughs. The front door is left slightly ajar*]

CHIPS: Dig these happenings. A young dude who said he was from the *Times* was hanging around headquarters all morning, asking questions about you know who.

SKEETER: Buckley!

CHIPS: Dig it!

SKEETER: [*Eyeing* AL] Ain't that interesting!

[*Laughs*]

CHIPS: The pigs is restless. So you cats be careful. [ANN *appears at top of stairs*] Well, bless my soul—if it ain't foxy mama. How 'bout a hug and a squeeze, foxy mama? [*To* SKEETER] Who else is here?

SKEETER: Just us chickens.

CHIPS: You mean foxy mama is by her little old self—in this big house?

ANN: [*Trying to ignore him*] Jeff'll be here in a minute, everybody.

CHIPS: Then we got to git it before he gets here, right, mama? All I want you to do is show me the upstairs.

[CHIPS *starts up the steps after her*]

ANN: What are you trying to prove?

AL: Chips—

SKEETER: Man, can't you act civilized?

CHIPS: Mind ya business.

SKEETER: Chips—come on, man.

ANN: It's all right—he wants to see upstairs—I'll show him.

CHIPS: [*Swats her on her rear*] Now you talking, foxy mama. All I wants is a hug and a squeeze. You dudes take it easy now. And call me when you see Mo coming. [ANN *hesitates, and he shoves her ahead of him*] He who hesitates is lost, mama.

[*They exit upstairs*]

AL: Some niggers ain't got no couth—

SKEETER: There goes Femaldehyde! [*In the next moment we hear a loud yell from* JEFF *and much commotion. A second later* JEFF *comes down the stairs with* CHIPS's *revolver pressed against* CHIPS's *head.* ANN *brings up the rear*] Here comes Femaldehyde!

CHIPS: Come on, Jeff, man, I was only fooling, man. I mean, you know me, Jeff. I didn't know she was your woman, man. Honest!

[JEFF *smacks him brutally across the face*]

SKEETER: Lighten up, Jeff.

AL: Yeah, like you made your point, man.

[JEFF *turns and looks at them, saying nothing. The ferocity of his stare silences them*]

ANN: Jeff—it's okay.

[JEFF *wallops* CHIPS *in the pit of his stomach.* CHIPS's *knees buckle to the floor*]

CHIPS: It's your world, baby! It's your world!

ANN: He's not worth it, Jeff. Please, baby, for me—okay?

[MO *and* GAIL *enter, almost unseen*]

CHIPS: I was only fooling, Jeff. Honest.

JEFF: Fooling with a gun at my woman's head?

CHIPS: I wouldn't hurt ya woman, man. It ain't even loaded.

JEFF: [*Places gun against* CHIPS's *temple*] So if I pull the trigger, it won't matter. [*Cocks hammer*]

CHIPS: [*Hysterical*] Oh shit—oh shit— Don't do that, Jeff. Please don't do that.

JEFF: The next time I catch you looking cross-eyed at my woman, I'm gonna rid the world of one more jive-ass nigger. Now, get out of here.

MO: Let him stay, Jeff. As a favor to me.

JEFF: [*Turns to see* MO] I despise irresponsible niggers, Mo.

MO: I'll be responsible for him.

JEFF: Then he'd better become shy, quiet, and unassuming. 'Cause that's the only kind of nigger I tolerate in my house.

MO: Well, you sound like the Jeff I used to know back when.

GAIL: [*To* CHIPS] You act more like a pig than the pigs.

MO: Old Femaldehyde!

SKEETER: [*Laughing*] Rides again.

MO: [*Referring to the revolver*] Is that your steel, man?

SKEETER: It's Chips's.

[*Laughs*]

MO: [*Collaring* CHIPS *angrily*] What! Not only do you insult a personal friend of mine—but you let him take your steel! That's unforgivable, cluck. You better get it back or another one just like it—posthaste—you dig me. Loss of a weapon is a crime against the organization. Do you dig them apples, Femaldehyde? [SKEETER *holds his sides laughing.* To SKEETER] Shut up!

GAIL: [*Extends her hand to a still angry* JEFF] I'm Gail.

JEFF: Hi!

MO: This is my woman, Jeff. And of course you know Skeeter—

JEFF: Hey, Skeets.

SKEETER: [*Shaking* JEFF's *hand*] What's happening, big Jeff?

MO: And Al here I wrote you 'bout. [*They shake hands*] Now, can we all settle down awhile and rap?

[*Everybody finds a comfortable spot, and there is an uneasy silence*]

ANN: Who wants a beer?

[*Everybody nods*]

MO: Why don't you help her, Gail?

GAIL: Sure.

[ANN *and* GAIL *cross the room to the kitchen*]

MO: Now, dig this, Brother Jeff. What I'm about to run down to you is only to make a point, and stop being so pissed. Everybody's edgy.

JEFF: I'm not edgy, baby, I'm about to draw blood.

CHIPS: Look, man, I'm sorry—okay.

JEFF: Negative, baby—not okay, not okay worth a damn.

MO: Jeff—Jeff—why do you think Chips had the nerve to shoot on your woman like he did? I think it's because of your letters, man!

JEFF: You showed *them* my personal letters to you?!

MO: Yeah! And you know why? 'Cause they sounded like you were turning, man, dig it—turning into a weak, halfway-in-between, neither here nor there Oreo cookie. I mean, the last thing we expected was Big Brother, bad-ass Jeff, our main man who we been waiting to welcome back to the trenches suddenly deciding to go trip off to law school, rapping 'bout the Constitution and a whole lot of the upside of the wall shit . . . Jeff, remember the time I had to fight Billy Richardson? Remember how his brothers kept clipping me and pushing on me every time it looked like I was winning? Remember that shit?

JEFF: What's the point?

MO: It was supposed to be a fair fight to see who was to gain control over St. Nicholas Avenue, right? I mean we parlayed and parlayed, and it was agreed upon—we had a verbal contract. And what they do? Billy's older brothers held you against the fence while he and the younger punks in his gang went to work on me. I was ready to give up, man, I mean all the wind was outta my sail, baby. And I looked up, and there you were, crying, baby, crying—trying to break loose from cats twice your size, can you dig it? Trying to break loose to help your main man, your brother, and crying, and somehow your shit got into me, and I beat Billy until he was screaming for mercy—his own boys let up when they dug what was happening!

Well, a dumb-ass nigger and a pig are one and the same! They don't understand agreements and contracts, they're beasts—the only thing a beast understands is guts and determination. We ran the whole goddamn neighborhood after that, and we had one motto, "Keep on keeping on!" And anybody who gave up in a fight got his ass kicked when he got back to the club.

All that shit about legal pressure, the democratic process bullshit. I tell you, man, the law ain't never helped the black man do nothing. The law is the will of the prevailing force, which is the pig in this country—and you want to be a lawyer? That Constitution ain't nothing but bullshit, don't you know that yet, man?

JEFF: Make it work and you've got a formidable weapon.

MO: I say, burn the motherfucker! Look, man, we've gone all those routes. We've petitioned, we've sat in, shitted in, demonstrated until we got fallen arches, etc., etc., etc., and where did it get us, huh? Things are worse! Contracts!? I'm talking 'bout revolution, man.

JEFF: That word's been talked to death. The revolution ain't nothing but talk, talk, talk, and I ain't gonna waste my life on talk. Niggers are jiving, man, can't you see it? That's all I heard from the black troops in the air force—revolution. Where's the gun factory, the bomb-assembly plant? We're shucking and jiving, man—

that's all. Law is something concrete, something I can *do*, not talk about.

MO: To a certain extent, you're right, Brother Jeff. Black people have been shucking and jivin', passing the buck. Well, we are the buck-ending committee. We ain't just talking, baby. We proving it. And in a few days we gonna serve notice on whitey that the shit has only begun to hit the fan. We want you with us, man.

JEFF: You've got it all figured out, Mo. You don't need me.

MO: We don't need nothing, baby, we just *want* you with us.

JEFF: Maybe I'm out of it, Mo. Maybe I don't know what's really happening any more. Yes, I'm still for whatever advances the cause of black folks, but I reserve the right to choose my own weapons. I don't have to fight with yours, Mo, and I respect your right not to have to fight with mine . . . All I know is that right now my convictions rest elsewhere . . . Now, gentlemen, my folks will be making it back pretty soon and I'd like the atmosphere to change into something a little bit more groovy, ya dig?

MO: Yes, sir, Lieutenant Williams, sir.

JEFF: Or *leave.*

MO: Is that an order, sir?

JEFF: You're in my house, nigger.

MO: I don't play that word, man. You throw it 'round a little too much.

JEFF: Oh yeah, well, you pat your foot while I play it, nigger.

MO: You either gon' be with us or against us, Brother Jeff. Nobody stays uncommitted in this neighborhood. Besides, we can make you do anything we want you to do.

JEFF: How you gonna do that, brother?

MO: Every time you poke your head out your door, you can be greeted with rocks, broken glass, garbage bags, or doo-do. And if that don't work . . . [ANN *and* GAIL *return from kitchen*] And if that don't work . . .

JEFF: [*Furious*] If that don't work, what?

MO: We can work on your moms and pops. They might come home and find the whole house empty, no furniture or nothing, motherfucker.

JEFF: Oh no, baby, you're the motherfucker. You really are the motherfucker! [*Controlling his fury at* MO] You jive-ass nigger. Mr. Zero trying to be Malcolm X. List' old world, list' to *the* revolutionary. See him standing there with his Captain America uniform on. Look at his generals. Skeeter the dope head and Chips the sex pervert. Mo the magnificent, playing cops and robbers in his middle twenties, trying to be somebody and don't know how. The one advantage I have over you, Mo, is my daddy taught me to see through my own bullshit, to believe that I don't need bullshit to be somebody. Go back to school, Mo, you're smart enough.

GAIL: Don't talk to him like that!

MO: You been thinking this shit for a long time, ain't you, nigger?

JEFF: Affirmative. And if you try any shit on my folks, your ass is mine, nigger. Or have you forgotten what a mean, evil, black bastard I can be, how you could whip everybody in the neighborhood and how I could whip the piss out of you, how I got more determination in my little toenail than you got in your whole soul, nigger!

MO: At least you still talk bad.

JEFF: I ain't bad. I'm crazy, motherfucker. Now you, your dope fiend, and Marquis de Sade, get the fuck outta here, and don't call me—I'll call you.

MO: [*Not too frightened but impressed*] Let's go. This ain't the end, Jeff. I suggest you think about what I said and think hard.

JEFF: Just make it, man. And remember [*Places gun to* CHIPS's *temple*] I'm fully armed, thanks to General Chips here.

MO: Don't make fun of me, Jeff.

JEFF: Why should I do that, you're a self-made comedian.

CHIPS: I think we should—

MO: You ain't had a thought in your life, cluck.

[*They all exit*]

JEFF: [*Walking around the room*] Goddamn, goddamn! . . . Where's the hootch? I know Pop got some somewhere. [*Looks around frantically*] I know the refrig used to be one of his favorite places. [*Finds it*] Damn! Almost half full! Lawd hep me! 'Cause these niggers don' gon' crazy. [*Takes a drink*] Hep me, Lawd. Hep me, hep me, Lawd. [*Takes another drink and sings the words . . .*] " 'Cause the niggers don' gon' crazy!"

ANN: That's enough.

JEFF: Ann, my love, the most glorious bitch I ever don' run across —let's get married. Let's get married and screw right at the ceremony. Monday we'll get the license. There's a three-day wait— Tuesday, Wednesday, and Thursday—Friday we'll get high off this bad-ass smoke I been saving and fly on to the preacher.

ANN: Are you serious?

JEFF: Indubitably.

ANN: Oh, Jeff, why so sudden?

JEFF: Honey, with the way these niggers is acting up 'round here, I figure I better get me some hep.

ANN: Jeff, I—

JEFF: I know you love me to pieces, and I don't blame you one bit.

ANN: You conceited—

JEFF: The problem is, I don't really love you. [*Pause*] I glory for you, baby. Besides, you got the bossest dogs I ever seen.

[*They kiss and embrace. There's a knock at the door. It's* GAIL]

GAIL: Can I come in?

ANN: Of course.

[ANN *brings her into the kitchen*]

GAIL: Mo thinks I stopped at the store to get cigarettes.

ANN: Would you like a drink?

GAIL: No, I don't drink.

ANN: Relax, Gail.

GAIL: Jeff, when I was a little girl, all I used to do was watch you and Mo running everything, the whole neighborhood together, always cool—no strain, ya know what I mean? You two cats were so beautiful together . . . Maybe it was wrong for Mo to come down on you so hard today, Jeff, after three years—but you the only person he trusts, Jeff. Writing to you the years you were away was his way of forgetting you had ever left. Now he needs you more than ever, Jeff. The organization has gotten to be a real hassle.

JEFF: How could it be anything else with those nothings he's got at his back? I mean, it's hard to be out front when you got shit at your back.

GAIL: That's why he needs you bad, Jeff. Mo only looks at the good in people. Skeeter and Chips been with you cats ever since you started gang-bopping. Mo's not dumb, he knows their hang-ups. But they swore to him they'd stay clean. Anyway, when you trying to build an army outta people who been buried in garbage all their lives, you can't expect they gon' all of a sudden start smelling like roses. In time, Mo believes, the movement will straighten 'em out for good.

JEFF: Mo's a saint. I'm a realist.

GAIL: Then help him, Jeff, help him.

JEFF: It's not just those okeydoke creeps 'round him, Gail. We don't see eye to eye. Mo thinks he's still back in the old days, leading a gang. Times have changed.

GAIL: You could influence him, Jeff.

JEFF: He doesn't need me, Gail. He's sure about where he's going and confident about how to get there—

GAIL: That's not true, Jeff.

JEFF: And all that bull about threatening me and my folks—I'd jump in an elephant's chest behind that jive.

GAIL: He was only saying that for them—

JEFF: Why crucify me for a bunch of nothings, baby?

GAIL: Do you know Mo, Jeff?

JEFF: I thought I did.

GAIL: If you really know him, Jeff, then you know he didn't mean what he said. He's desperate, Jeff. Things are all mixed up. A few years ago, everything was straight up and down—simple—*right on for the people*. Now everything's falling apart, splitting up, people going every which way. And Mo's gotten into some heavy, scary things, Jeff. Right now the heat's on 'cause a pig cop was wasted a few months ago. And this Friday Mo plans to destroy a new state office building going up, or else mess with one of the police stations.

You think he's so cocksure? Well, he ain't. He don't even know if what he's doing is right any more. I know—'cause I see him get up in the middle of the night and stare out the window and talk to himself—talk to his demons. Don't let his tough act fool you, Jeff. Behind his real together front, he's about to snap. You hear me, Jeff, he's gonna snap. I know it. Lord God, help him, Jeff Williams. Even if you don't see eye to eye with him, find a way to help him. The hell with the movement, help HIM! Help him, please, before he breaks apart. Help him, Jeff.

[*She sobs uncontrollably.* ANN *comforts her*]

ANN: He will, Gail, he will—I know he will. [*To* JEFF] I like him, Jeff. His approach may be all wrong, but he's fighting. He's honest and he's fighting. He's a determined black man, just like you, Jeff.

JEFF: All right. I'll try, Gail, I'll try. I promise you.

[*The front door swings open. It's* MATTIE *and* GRANDMA, GRANDMA *pushing a shopping cart,* MATTIE *loaded down with grocery bags. Bass line enters*]

MATTIE: Lawdamercy. The door's wide open!

GRANDMA: That hussy girl's doings!

[MATTIE *sees* JEFF]

MATTIE: Lawdamercy! Lawdamercy! Jeff! [*She rushes to embrace him*] You big old good-for-nothing thing.

[GRANDMA *starts for him*]

GRANDMA: Ben Brown! The spitting image of Ben Brown. Ben Brown all over again. [*She embraces him*] Ain't black like Ben Brown, but he sho' do carve himself out a fine figure, don't he, Mattie?

JEFF: [*Eyeing her lewdly*] You don't do so bad yourself, sweet meat!

GRANDMA: You ought to be ashamed of yourself.

[*Hugs him once more*]

MATTIE: You weren't supposed to be here till noon.

JEFF: I'll go back and come at noon.

MATTIE: Go on, boy, stop acting so simple.

JEFF: Can't help it, Mama. I got my two foxes back again— Cleopatra—[*Referring to* GRANDMA] and her sidekick.

[*Referring to his mother*]

MATTIE: I'll sidekick you.

JEFF: [*Hugging them both at the same time*] Got my two womens back again.

MATTIE: Stop being so rough with your simple self. What they been feeding you—bread and water? You too thin to say grace over.

JEFF: Know what I wants for dinner? Some corn bread, yeah. And some of Grandma's mustard greens, Mama.

GRANDMA: [*Salutes him*] Yes, sir.

JEFF: And black-eyed peas. And some of your candied sweets, Grandma, with lemon and raisins all over 'em, yeah!

GRANDMA: And roast beef!

JEFF: Do Jesus, and bless my soul, Grandma Brown! And don't forget the lemonade.

GRANDMA:　A gallon of it. Made it myself.

JEFF:　And some sassafras tea.

GRANDMA:　Got it fresh from that new health-food store.

[*Pause*]

JEFF:　Ma, do you realize that I'm home for good—

MATTIE:　Thank God!

JEFF:　No more okeydoke. No more time outta my race against time. No more stuff, messing with my mind. I'm me—Jeff Williams, because Daddy Johnny named me—before ya'll claimed me on your income tax! And ya'll sho' is looking gooooooood—good God, good!

MATTIE:　Go on, boy!

JEFF:　Mama, this is Gail. Mo Hayes's girl friend.

MATTIE:　Nice to know you, Gail.

GAIL:　[*Extending her hand*] Heard a lot about you, Mrs. Williams.

JEFF:　And this is my grandma, Gail. Grandma Wilhemina Geneva Brown.

GRANDMA:　There you go, acting the fool, Jeff Williams. You know I can't stand "Geneva."

GAIL:　My pleasure, Mrs. Brown.

GRANDMA:　What? Oh, yes. How do, child.

JEFF:　And this is Ann!

GRANDMA:　[*Disapprovingly*] We've met.

MATTIE:　The best—of—friends!

[GRANDMA *grunts*]

JEFF:　[*Ignoring* GRANDMA] Well, I'm glad 'cause this foxy mama here and your son—me—the baddest dude to catch an attitude—God's gift to the female race—"for God so loved the world that he gave—"

MATTIE:　I'll take off my shoe and knock holes in your head, boy!

JEFF: Mama, what I'm trying to tell you—

GRANDMA: You gon' marry this here brazen gal?

[Bass fades]

MATTIE: Mama!

JEFF: Indubitably!

GAIL: That's beautiful! Just beautiful!

GRANDMA: Do Jesus, Uncle Sam don' took my child—

MATTIE: Your child—

GRANDMA: And turned him into a cockeyed ignoramus.

MATTIE: Don't pay any attention to her, Ann.

ANN: Jeff, I think I'll walk to the corner with Gail.

JEFF: You will not!

GRANDMA: You too young to fart good—talking 'bout getting married.

JEFF: I'm twenty-five!

GRANDMA: Stop lying! You ain't outta your teens.

JEFF: I was twenty-two when I left, Grandma.

GRANDMA: [To MATTIE] Lawd, Mattie, is my child don' got that old on me?

MATTIE: Your *grandson* is that old, Mama.

GRANDMA: Do Jesus! Time sho' do fly, don't it? 'Tweren't yesterday I was getting myself all sprayed up changing your diapers.

JEFF: [Slowly, deliberately] That was twenty-five years ago, Grandma.

GRANDMA: [Coming out of her reveries] Don't make no difference. You're too young to get yourself saddled with a wife. Next thing you know, here comes one crumbsnatcher—then two—

JEFF: Then three—then four. It's pretty lonely not having any brothers and sisters, I can tell you.

GRANDMA: A lodestone! A lodestone 'round your neck, a-dragging you down.

MATTIE: What about law school, Jeff?

JEFF: Oh, we gon' do that, too. I mean them crumbsnatchers ain't coming until we are ready for 'em. Ann's gonna use the loop, birth-control pills, the rhythm method, and the diaphragm, and Emko!

GRANDMA: There sure is a whole lot Emko babies walking 'round here.

MATTIE: [*To* JEFF] Well, you certainly seem to know an awful lot 'bout it.

JEFF: Like I said before, I'm *twenty-five*. Be twenty-six the twenty-fourth of this month, Mama.

MATTIE: You still don't have to know so much in front of your mother.

JEFF: I apologize.

GRANDMA: [*Blurting out a long-pent-up reality*] Look at your father. He wanted to be a lawyer, didn't he? Then I jumped on his back, then them two no good daughters of mine, then their two empty-headed husbands—then you. The load was so heavy till he couldn't move no more. He just had to stand there, holding it up.

MATTIE: [*Very serious*] Then you know about it?

GRANDMA: What do you think I am? A sickle-headed, lopsided, cockeyed ignoramus like your son here?

MATTIE: Oh, so you admit he's my son?

GRANDMA: He's your son, but he's my child.

MATTIE: [*Turning to* ANN] Have ya'll given it serious thought, Ann?

ANN: He just asked me, Mrs. Williams.

GRANDMA: Is that all you gon' do? Talk? You gon' let this brazen hussy just take my child away?

MATTIE: Mama, why don't you go to your room and cool off a bit.

GRANDMA: She is brazen. Camping right on his doorstep. I call that bold, brash, and brazen! And conniving, too! A pretty face'll sho' kill a man—even a good man. [*To* ANN] And not even mean to! You gon' take that on your shoulders, child, you gon' kill your man before he can stand up good yet? Is that what you gon' do? I did it. Mattie did it. She let me help her do it.

MATTIE: Mama!

GRANDMA: Don't mama me. Where's my medicine? I don't want to be here and watch my child leap into deep water. Lawdamercy, no! Where is my medicine? Where's my pocketbook?

JEFF: [*To* MATTIE] Is Grandma sick, Ma?

MATTIE: In a manner of speaking.

[GRANDMA *finds her purse. There is a large bulge in it. She seems satisfied. She starts up the stairs, singing "Rock of Ages"*]

GRANDMA: Hep him, Lawd! Hep my child!

[*She exits, singing*]

JEFF: [*To* ANN] Is this what you've been putting up with?

MATTIE: Ann's a fine girl, Jeff. You know I believe that, don't you, Ann?

ANN: Thank you, Mrs. Williams.

MATTIE: And you know women get silly over their sons and, well, grandsons.

ANN: Yes, ma'am.

MATTIE: My personal opinion—if ya'll are interested—is that you should wait awhile—at least until Jeff's finished law school.

JEFF: Ever since I got home, people been telling me what to do and what not to do. You talking about a lodestone—that's the heaviest lodestone in the world . . . I want to marry Ann 'cause she is a fine girl, Mama. Something rare—came home and found my sweet baby here—it was like God was saying, "This is your woman, son. I can't let you do nothing that dumb. I can't let you leave her. I made her for you!" And goddamn it—

MATTIE: Jeff!

JEFF: I'm following what I hear inside my soul!

MATTIE: [*Pauses for a long moment, finally embracing him strongly, on the verge of tears*] Then you do that, baby. You follow the Lord. As mad as He makes me sometimes, I don't think He's ever really told me wrong. [*Hugs* ANN *lovingly*] Come on in here and help me fix this food, girl. You're one of the family now. I guess I knew you were the moment I laid eyes on you. [*To* JEFF] Why do you like to shock people so? You know how your grandmother dotes on you.

[*She exits into the kitchen*]

GAIL: A beautiful black brother and sister, doing a beautiful thing.

[*She embraces* ANN]

JEFF: Gail, I'll try to talk to Mo. I'm not certain it will do any good, but I'll try to talk to him—when he's alone— Just him and me. Okay?

GAIL: I appreciate it, Jeff.

[*She exits as* JOHN, *very intoxicated, and* DUDLEY, *still in control of himself, enter. They are arguing some philosophical point.* JOHN *sees* JEFF]

JOHN: Jeff! Well, I'll be goddamned. Jeff!

[*He ruffles* JEFF's *hair*]

JEFF: How you been, Pop?

JOHN: Where's your uniform?

JEFF: Dr. Stanton.

DUDLEY: You're looking fine, boy! Just fine. Skinny, but fine.

JOHN: Where's your uniform?

MATTIE: [*Coming back in, followed by* ANN, *with a cake*] John, you're drunk.

JOHN: Yes, my love.

[GRANDMA *comes down the stairs. She too is loaded. She's singing "Onward, Christian Soldiers"*]

JEFF: Why don't you take the load off your feet, Pop.

JOHN: Where's your uniform, Jeff? Go put it on.

JEFF: If it's all the same to you, Pop—

JOHN: I've got a theory, Dudley—Dr. Dudley Stanton—

MATTIE: Why don't you go sleep it off—

JOHN: My theory is that if you as a doctor don't try to keep the living from dying, then you're dead yourself. You're a dead doctor. [GRANDMA *crosses to* JOHN *and sings directly into his ear*] Mrs. Brown, I have never hit an old lady in my life—

GRANDMA: Ya hit this old lady—

JOHN: And what?

GRANDMA: She's gon' jump down your throat—

JOHN: And what?

GRANDMA: Straddle your gizzard—

JOHN: And what?

GRANDMA: And gallop your brains out!

[*He picks her up and whirls her around the room, laughing*]

JOHN: Grandma, you are the biggest fool in the world, but I sure do love me some Grandma Wilhemina Geneva Brown.

GRANDMA: Stinking old wino.

JOHN: I love you too, Dudley—Dr. Dudley Stanton—even if you do walk through life with a broomstick up your ass. [*To* ANN] And even though we just met, I loves me some Ann—sweet fighting lady that you are. Jeff, ya got yourself a mama—a mama who's gonna protect your flanks—a sweet fighting lady.

JEFF: I know, Pop.

[GRANDMA *grunts disapprovingly*]

JOHN: And my son I loves better than I love myself. My big old big-time United States Air Force lieutenant son. He's coming home today—

JEFF: I'm here, Pop.

JOHN: [*Really annoyed*] No, you ain't—you ain't here. 'Cause if you were, you'd have on your uniform—

JEFF: I don't like to wear it, Daddy Johnny.

JOHN: Why not?

JEFF: Well, I guess—

JOHN: Spit it out.

JEFF: I feel ashamed of it. I feel that it's a kinda cop-out, Pop—it makes me feel like a buffoon every time I put it on. I should have burned my commission, not shown up, made it to Canada or something. I really don't believe in this country any more.

DUDLEY: Boy, you don't believe in the United States of America— land of the free, home of the brave, this democratic, constitutional, industrial giant?

JEFF: I don't believe in lies any more, Dr. Stanton.

DUDLEY: [*Jokingly but meaning it*] Welcome home, Jeff. Welcome home, Brother Jeff.

[*Pats him on the back*]

JOHN: Have I been waiting around here, waiting to see you in that goddamn uniform—for you to— Go put it on!

JEFF: I made a vow with myself, Daddy Johnny.

JOHN: [*Getting angry*] It's an accomplishment, fool. How many of us ever get there—to be an officer? God knows, this country needs to be torn down, but don't we want it torn down for the right to be an officer if you're able? It's an accomplishment. And I'm proud of your accomplishment.

DUDLEY: A dubious accomplishment.

JOHN: Laugh and ridicule the damn thing all you want, goddamn it, but recognize that it's another fist jammed through the wall.

DUDLEY: Man, he became the protector of a system he believes should be destroyed.

JOHN: So we're contradictions—so what else is new? That could apply to every black man, woman, and child who ever lived in this country. Especially the taxpayers. They been financing the system for a long time. Besides, who ever said we wanted total destruction anyway? If you get right on down to the real nitty-gritty, I don't want to totally destroy what, by rights, belongs to me anyway. I just want to weed out the bullshit. Change the value system so that the Waldorf has as many welfare tenants as Rockafellows.

JEFF: The Rockafellows will never allow it.

JOHN: They will if you put *them* on welfare.

DUDLEY: How in the hell you gonna do that, fool?

JOHN: By finding the battlefield—like I told you—like I been telling you—each and every motherfucker—

MATTIE: John!

JOHN: Whoever dropped from a pretty black poontang has got to find his own battlefield and go to war. In his own way—his own private war.

DUDLEY: All hail to the philosopher-poet.

JOHN: [*Grabbing* DUDLEY *roughly in the collar and screaming as bass line enters*] I'm a poet, ya hear me, a poet! When this country—when this world, learns the meaning of poetry—
    Don't you see, Jeff, poetry is what the revolution's all about—never lose sight of the true purpose of the revolution, all revolutions—to restore poetry to the godhead!
    Poetry is religion, the alpha and the omega, the cement of the universe. The supereye under which every other eye is scrutinized, and it stretches from one to infinity, from bullshit to the beatific, the rocking horse of the human spirit—God himself. God himself is pure distilled poetry.

DUDLEY: Bravissimo!

JOHN: Preserve the Empire State Building—if you can. It was built from over three hundred years of black poetry, 'cause sweat is poetry too, son. Kick out the money changers and reclaim it. Ain't none of us gonna be free until poetry rides a mercury-smooth silver stallion. [*Pause*] Seeing you in your uniform with bars on your shoulders and them navigator wings on your chest is a kinda—

[*Bass fades*]

DUDLEY: [*Undaunted*] Heresy!

JOHN: Poetry, Jeff. Black poetry.

JEFF: Pop, I didn't make it through navigator school—I washed out—flunked out—whatever.

JOHN: [*Furious*] My son flunked out— You lie— Go get that uniform!

JEFF: No, Daddy Johnny, no!

MATTIE: Leave him alone, Johnny.

JOHN: I'm the head of this house.

MATTIE: Ain't nobody disputing that.

JOHN: And when I ask my son—who I ain't seen but three or four times in three years—to do me one simple favor—

ANN: But if it's against his principles, Mr. Williams—

JOHN: There goes the little fighting lady, protecting your flanks.

JEFF: I don't need nobody to protect my flanks.

ANN: I know you don't, baby.

GRANDMA: [*Half high*] "I know you don't, baby!" Brazen hussy.

JEFF: Don't call her that again, Grandma!

GRANDMA: I calls 'em as I sees 'em. My Ben Brown told me—

MATTIE: Hush, Ma!

JEFF: I'll leave, Pop. I'll leave now—tonight—ya dig that? 'Cause I've had me enough homecoming for a lifetime.

JOHN: Ain't nobody asking you to leave—

JEFF: Ya telling me what to do like I was sweet sixteen or something. Everybody 'round here wants to tell me what to do.

MATTIE: You didn't write to us about flunking out, Jeff.

JEFF: Ya want to know why I didn't write home about it, Mama? 'Cause every single letter I got from you or Pop was telling me how proud you were of your navigator son.

JOHN: We thought you were doing all right.

JEFF: You thought that because that's what you wanted to think!

JOHN: What else could we think?

JEFF: About me, Daddy Johnny, about Jeff—damn your pride! You coulda thought about me. [*Strained pause*] I hated navigation! You know how I hate figures, Pop.

JOHN: You never worked hard enough!

JEFF: So you say, Daddy Johnny—'cause that's what you want to believe. "Jeff Williams is my son, everybody! Just like me. Anything I can do he can do."

JOHN: You can! It's all in how you think of yourself—

JEFF: Right, Pop, right. As a matter of fact, I may be able to do a few things you can't do. But not math, Pop. That's you, not me. Don't you dig that?

JOHN: Say what you got to say.

JEFF: Haven't I said it already? You said it yourself! We got to find our own battlefields. Don't you dig how that statement relates to what I'm saying?

JOHN: No! Hell, no, I don't. You flunked out. My boy, my boy failed. That's all I can see.

JEFF: Ya'll had a piece of my big toe, Pop. *Everybody* had a piece of my toe. Not just those white-pig instructors who kept checking and rechecking my work, 'cause I was what they called a belligerent nigger. There were only eight black officers out of three hundred in that school, and they kept telling me, "Man, you got to make it. You got to be a credit to your race."

JOHN: What's wrong with that?

JEFF: Then there was this girl I was shacking up with.

MATTIE: Shacking up!

JEFF: Shacking up, Mama!

GRANDMA: Another brazen hussy!

JEFF: She was the fox to end all foxes, Pop. An afro so soft and spongy, until my hands felt like they were moving through water. And she kept telling me, "Honey, we needs that extra hundred and thirty a month flight pay to keep me in the style to which you have made me accustomed."

JOHN: Come to the point!

JEFF: Don't you see the point, Pop? Everybody had a piece of my nigger toe—my fine fox, my fellow black brother officers, the pig instructors, you and Mama, Pop—everybody had a piece—but me —Jeff Williams!

JOHN: Jeff Williams is Johnny Williams's son, goddamn it!

JEFF: You mean none of me belongs to me, Pop?

JOHN: I want to see you in your uniform! Now, what is all this talk about?

JEFF: It's about you and me and the battlefields. About who is Jeff Williams, Pop.

JOHN: Then tell me who in the hell is he!

JEFF: A dude who hated navigation to the point where he got migraines. Who wanted to throw up on every flight—motion-sickness pills notwithstanding. Whose ears pained him from takeoff to landing. Do you know what it feels like when your ears don't clear?

MATTIE: My baby!

JEFF: [Bass enters] Don't baby me, Mama. I still think I'm the baddest, but I ain't—nor do I want to be a supernigger, 'cause that's all a supernigger is, a *super*nigger. Someone who spends his life trying to prove he's as good as the Man. On my last flight exam—a night celestial—I wound up eighty miles into Mexico, according to my computations, while everybody else's figures put us at Harlingen Air Force Base, Texas. We were circling the field. The sun was coming up, soft and pastel like someone had sprinkled red pepper all over the clouds. I tore off a piece of my flight log and began writing a poem. You see, Pop, I do believe in poetry. It was a simple poem—all about the awe of creation. Anyway —along came this Lieutenant Forthright—a Texas cracker whose one joke, repeated over and over again, was "Hee, haw, students, never worry about being lost. At least you knows ya'll is in the airplane. Yuk, yuk." This creep caught sight of my poem, and this big Howdy Doody grin spread all over his face, and he started laughing. This Howdy Doody pig started laughing. This subhuman, caveman, orangutan was laughing at something he couldn't even understand. Then he showed the poem to the other instructor orangutans, and they started laughing. And that did it, Pop. I said to myself, "This ain't my stick. What am I doing this for? What am I doing this shit for? This navigator jive ain't for me." They sent me before a board of senior officers. You see, this was the second time I'd failed my night celestial flying exam, and they gave me a flat-ass white all-American lieutenant for counsel, and you know what he told me? He told me to cop a plea, to cop a plea, Pop, to express my love of country and dedication to the air force! To lick ass! That way, he said, they'd only wash me back a few months and I could still come through. But I told that board, "Let go my toe!" and they replied, "What?" You know, the way white people do when they don't believe their ears. So I screamed at the top of my voice, "Let go my nigger toe so I can stand up and be a man." . . . I guess they thought I was insane. They hemmed and hawed and cleared their throats, but they let go my toe, Mama. I had cut loose the man. Then I went right home and I cut loose my fine fox, and I cut loose my so-called black brother officers, and I felt like there was no more glue holding my shoes to the track; I felt I could almost fly, Pop, 'cause I was a supernigger no more . . . So I ain't proving nothing to nobody—white, black, blue or polka dot—to nobody! Not even to you, Daddy Johnny . . . Mama, you give that thing—that uniform thing to the Salvation Army or to the Goodwill or whatever, 'cause it will never have the good fortune to get on my back again.

DUDLEY: Bravo! Bravissimo!

[*Bass fades.* GRANDMA *sings "Onward, Christian Soldiers," and for some time no one says anything*]

JEFF: [*Quietly*] It's all about battlefields—just like you said, Pop.

[JOHN *pauses for an infinite time, looking at* JEFF, *then at* MATTIE *and the others. With great deliberation he then collects his coat and starts walking out slowly*]

MATTIE: [*Trying to stop him*] John! It's Jeff's coming-home party!

[*He doesn't stop, exiting through the front door—leaving everyone suspended in a state of sad frustration. Lights fade as they all avoid looking at each other*]

ACT THREE

It is Friday evening. DUDLEY, MATTIE, GRANDMA, *and* JEFF *are
seated in the living room.* ANN *is in the kitchen busily putting
away dishes. The air is very heavy. After a long pause,* JEFF
rises, moves toward the window.

JEFF: I noticed the kids tore down the baskets on the basketball
court, Ma.

MATTIE: Yeah, well, they weren't made to be swung on, that's for
sure.

JEFF: Why are we so damn destructive, Ma?

MATTIE: I guess 'cause we're so mad . . . Lord, where could he be?

GRANDMA: [*Intoxicated*] Ain't nothing strange about a man staying away from home. Does 'em good.

MATTIE: Mama, it's Friday. He's been gone since Saturday.

DUDLEY: Oh, he'll be all right, Mattie.

MATTIE: It's like he just disappeared—

JEFF: Mama, have you checked the police station today?

MATTIE: Five times!

DUDLEY: Well, won't do any good to worry. He's a strong, capable
man with a whole lot of sense. He's probably in some hotel writing.

GRANDMA: You mean *drinking!*

DUDLEY: Well—both then.

MATTIE: [*On the verge of tears*] Anything could happen to him.
All these dope fiends running 'round Harlem, banging people in

the head for a quarter. He could be laying in some vacant lot—hurt—or, or—

JEFF: No, Mama—he's all right!

MATTIE: Six days!

DUDLEY: I'm gonna have to give you a sedative if you don't calm down, Mattie.

GRANDMA: I like sedatives myself.

DUDLEY: You starting on your medicine a little early, aren't you, Grandma?

GRANDMA: I takes my medicine whenever I need it. It opens up my chest and cuts the phlegm.

MATTIE: Poor thing—he could be seriously injured—

GRANDMA: [*Bass enters*] Now, that's exactly what happened to my Ben Brown. He was wild as a pine cone and as savage as a grizzly, and black! Black as a night what ain't got no moon. He'd stay out in the woods for days at a time—always come back with a mess of fish or a sack of rabbits, and possums—that man could tree a possum like he was a hound dog. I guess he was so black till they musta thought he was a shadow, creeping up on 'em. [*Pause*] One day he just didn't come back.

MATTIE: Mama, do we have to hear *it* again?

GRANDMA: A load of buckshot ripped his guts right out—right out on the ground!

MATTIE: Mama!

GRANDMA: It was an old redneck cracker named Isaiah what been poaching on our land. Ben said he'd kill any white man he caught hunting on our land. So there they were—both dead—Ben musta been strangling him. I guess Isaiah figured a load of buckshot would put a stop to him. But there was Ben, still holding on to that cracker's throat when we found 'em. Couldn't nothing stop my husband from doing what he had a mind to do. They had to pry his hands loose. Folks come from miles around to attend his funeral. White folks, too. Yes, they did. He was a king in his own right, and they knew it. Gawdamercy, my man was a king. And I know he's in *Glory!* Just awaiting for his Wilhemina. I knows it.

[*Starts humming "Rock of Ages." Bass fades*]

DUDLEY: The reason I asked to see you all tonight—well—well—because Mattie and I have something very serious to discuss with you.

MATTIE: Do they have to know, Dudley?

DUDLEY: It's only fair that they should know, Mattie. Mattie is going to have to be hospitalized. I guess that's why Johnny hasn't been home—I guess he's off somewhere—brooding.

MATTIE: Dudley! You promised me you wouldn't tell him—

DUDLEY: I made a decision, Mattie. It was either keep my promise to you or prepare Johnny ahead of time for what might kill him—if he heard it too sudden-like . . .

MATTIE: Then you're responsible— If anything's happened to him—you're responsible.

DUDLEY: I made a judgment—

JEFF: Will somebody please tell me what's going on?

DUDLEY: Jeff, we got the report today. Mattie's got, well, several growths—malignant growths. Mattie's got cancer.

MATTIE: There you go again—about as gentle as a sledgehammer.

JEFF: How serious?

DUDLEY: Very serious, but not hopeless—the location prevents removal, but radium treatments might arrest the—

MATTIE: Jeff, you don't see me upset, do you, son?

JEFF: [*Cupping her face in his hands lovingly*] Mama!

MATTIE: I'm gonna die—that's all there is to it.

GRANDMA: No such thing! You know Dudley here's a cockeyed quack—

MATTIE: Mama, the only thing I'm worried about is the whereabouts of my man.

JEFF: But you can't think negative like that—

[GRANDMA *sings loudly*, "For His eye is on the sparrow, and I know He watches me"]

MATTIE: Hush, Mama. [ANN *comes to the door. Bass enters*] Now, what old negative? Look at me! I've had a full life with an extraordinary man who fell upon me and fed my soul like manna from heaven—bless him, God bless him wherever he is— And you —where could I get a finer-looking, stronger-looking, more loving son than my Jeff? And I'll be around to see you marry Ann—a gift to you, Jeff, and don't you abuse her. I got my mother beside me, still alive and kicking. And Dudley Stanton—a mainstay—your father's and my spiritual brother—

DUDLEY: Thank you, sweetheart—

MATTIE: No, Dudley! Thank you. Now, what old negative thinking? If Johnny were to come through that door right now, I'd be the happiest woman in God's creation—and like my Johnny says, "Lord, I don't feel noways tired—I could go on for another century."

JEFF: [*Very upset*] You will. Mama. You will.

MATTIE: But it's my time, baby. I guess maybe I've done whatever He put me here to do.

[*There is a knock on the front door.* ANN *answers it. It is* MO *and* GAIL. ANN *shows them into the living room*]

MO: Dr. Stanton! Mrs. Williams— Grandma—

MATTIE: How've you been, Li'l Mo? Lord, you sure have grown.

GAIL: Mrs. Williams—everybody—

[GRANDMA *grunts*]

MO: I got to see you, Jeff.

JEFF: Is it important?

MO: I need your help, Jeff.

JEFF: Let's go into the kitchen. I'll be right back, Mama.

[JEFF, MO, GAIL, *and* ANN *move toward kitchen. Living room conversation continues*]

MATTIE: Looks like rain.

GRANDMA: I sure hate this dirty city when it rains—looks like a cess-pool.

DUDLEY: One thing good about rain in February—it means an early spring.

JEFF: [*From the kitchen*] Look, man, I know I promised Gail—but that's gonna have to wait. My folks are in heavy trouble.

MO: Yeah, I heard about your father.

ANN: We just found out Mrs. Williams has cancer.

GAIL: Oh, Jeff, I'm so sorry.

MO: Wow, me too, man—I see what you mean. Wow!

MATTIE: [*From the living room*] Don't you think—well—we could go on without Jeff, Dudley? He's just a child.

DUDLEY: He's a man now, Mattie, and with Grandma getting up there and Johnny—taking it so hard—

GRANDMA: Who's getting up where? A body ain't no older than their toes, and mine twinkle a damn sight better than yours—

DUDLEY: When you've had your medicine.

GAIL: [*From the kitchen*] How serious is it, Jeff?

ANN: It's inoperable. The only hope is radium treatment.

MO: I'm sorry, man. I really am.

JEFF: Thanks.

MATTIE: [*From the living room*] Mama, sing that song for me.

GRANDMA: Which song, daughter?

MATTIE: "Rock of Ages."

[GRANDMA *begins singing soothingly.* MATTIE *joins her from time to time*]

MO: [*From kitchen*] All them years we was running together, Mrs. Williams was like a mother to me too, remember, Jeff?

JEFF: Yeah.

MO: I guess that changes things 'round. I wouldn't want to put more weight on you now, especially behind news like that.

ANN: What is the problem, Gail?

GAIL: There's a stool pigeon in the organization. It's gotta be either Chips, Skeeter, or Al.

ANN: Oh, no.

GAIL: If we don't find him out quick, everything's liable to blow up in our faces. Remember what I told y'all 'bout that cop Buckley?

ANN: What can Jeff do?

GAIL: Mo's laying a trap tonight where the stoolie's gonna hafta phone his boss. He'll hafta do it from either the pool-hall phone next to headquarters, or the bar phone down the street. Mo's got both phones bugged, ready to be monitored. I'll be listening in the pool-hall basement, and we wanted Jeff to cover the phone in the bar. Jeff's the only person we can trust.

MO: What about it, Jeff?

JEFF: [Angrily] I got no time for this cloak-and-dagger shit—my folks are hurting, man, didn't you hear?

MO: Okay, man. Okay, I dig.

ANN: What about me?

JEFF: [Adamantly] Hell, no. I won't let you or my family get implicated in this shit—

ANN: Jeff, I don't intend to get implicated—but what Gail and Mo are asking doesn't seem unreasonable. Remember?—my brothers were betrayed once, Jeff. My father is still in prison as a result. Nine years with still no release in sight. No matter what you and I might think about Mo's activities, he certainly does not deserve betrayal. I could not live with myself knowing that I had an opportunity to help and didn't.

MO: Thanks for the offer, baby. But I'm afraid it's no good. What has to be done and where it's gotta happen, a woman would only draw suspicion.

JEFF: How long would it take, Mo?

MO: No more than an hour's time, Jeff. All together, you should be back here three hours from right now. I promise you, Jeff, it'll be no sweat. I just need to know, you dig?

JEFF: Why you sure he'll make contact?

MO: He's gotta. Tonight is the night of our big thing, Jeff. I'm ordering a change of plan at the last minute that's gonna make the rat hafta contact the pigs. Meanwhile, nobody but me knows that I'm crossing everybody up by following through with my original plan. Nobody's gonna get hurt, Jeff, just some property damaged. While everybody is on their way to the police station, I'll be headed—

JEFF: I don't want to know, Mo. I'll monitor the phone for you, but I don't want to know nothing. Don't crowd me, Mo, you understand?

MO: That's cool, Jeff.

JEFF: This is as far as I go, Mo.

MO: I gotcha, Brother Jeff. I dig.

ANN: And I will sit with Gail at the pool hall.

JEFF: No!

ANN: She shouldn't be alone, Jeff.

JEFF: I SAID NO!

MO: It's safe, Jeff. I swear. You know I wouldn't have my woman doing anything that would put her in a trick. No jeopardy, man, I promise.

MATTIE: [*From living room*] What time you got, Dudley?

DUDLEY: Five after seven.

MATTIE: You think he's had his dinner?

DUDLEY: Sure, sweetheart. Keep singing, Grandma.

JEFF: [*From the kitchen*] All right, Ann.

MO: Groovy. Make it to the bar about 8:45, Jeff. Take a cab so you'll be seen as little as possible. The bartender, a buddy of mine, will take you to the setup. About the same time Jeff leaves here,

Gail will pick you up outside, Ann. Okay, we'll split now—by the back door. So we won't disturb— Like I said, Jeff, I really am sorry about Mrs. Williams. I really mean it.

JEFF: Yeah, later, Mo.

MO: Okay.

[MO *and* GAIL *exit out the kitchen door.* JEFF *and* ANN *return to the living room*]

MATTIE: What happened to Mo and his girl?

JEFF: They went out the back, Mama.

[*There is an awkward silence*]

DUDLEY: Jeff, Mattie will be admitted to the hospital on Monday.

MATTIE: Couldn't I be treated at home, Dudley? Ann's a nurse. She could—

ANN: You need special equipment, Mrs. Williams, but of course I'll be your nurse.

MATTIE: Would you, Ann? I hate those nurses at Harlem. They're so indifferent and snooty.

JEFF: Goddamn!

GRANDMA: Watch your mouth! Can't even pee straight and using that kind of language.

[*There's a second sound at the back door.* JOHN: "*I'm all right! I can make it!*" JEFF *and* ANN *rush to open the door, exiting. We hear voices outside—*MO *and* GAIL *explaining.* JOHN *enters, assisted by* JEFF *and* ANN. *He has a week's growth of beard. His eyes have the deep-socket look of an alcoholic who's been on a substantial bender. His overall appearance is gaunt and shoddy. His clothes are filthy and wrinkled. He obviously smells. His hands have a slight tremor. There is a deep gash above his left eye. Bass enters.* JOHN *is helped into a chair,* MATTIE *embracing him*]

MATTIE: Johnny, sweet Johnny! We've been so worried about you.

JOHN: Don't, Mattie! I smell something awful.

DUDLEY: Move, Mattie. Let me take a look at that cut. [*Moves* MATTIE *aside*] Jeff, bring my bag. It's in the hallway there. [JEFF *exits to hallway*] Hand me a towel, Grandma.

GRANDMA: Old wino, nigger.

DUDLEY: Wet it with cold water. Maybe we can stop the bleeding.

ANN: I'll hold it, Dr. Stanton.

DUDLEY: Good girl.

[*She presses the folded paper towel to* JOHNNY's *cut*]

JOHN: Fighting lady Ann. I sure needed me a fighting lady out there. You shoulda seen me, Mattie, when them young hoods jumped me.

MATTIE: I saw you, baby. Every second.

JOHN: I was like a cornered wildcat. I was battlin' 'em to a draw. Then Li'l Mo and his fighting lady came up.

DUDLEY: It's a bird, it's a plane, it's a Supercullud Guy!

JOHN: Super Black Man, sickle head. I ain't been hanging out with them militant winos for nothing.

DUDLEY: Folks, take a look at an aging African warrior, trying to make a comeback.

JOHN: [*Singing to a made-up tune*]
When I get home to Africa
I'll buy myself a mango.
Grab myself a monkey gal
And do the monkey tango.

DUDLEY: When'd you eat last?

JOHN: Can you imagine. The great Marcus Garvey.

DUDLEY: Niggers used to sing that to make fun of Marcus Garvey. Can you imagine. The great Marcus Garvey.

DUDLEY: Answer my question! When was the last time you had a decent meal?

JOHN: Wednesday. Or was it Tuesday?

DUDLEY: What are you trying to do, Johnny?

[JEFF *returns with the bag*]

ANN: I'll do it.

[*She swabs the wound and bandages it*]

MATTIE: Where've you been, baby?

JOHN: In the desert, Mattie. Out in the desert, like Christ, talking to myself.

GRANDMA: Christ was talking to the devil, ya old wino.

JOHN: Same difference. But I took care of the old bastard. I said, Get thee behind me, Prince of Darkness! Then I got thirsty and came home. I wanted to see me some angels.

JEFF: Pop, you okay now? I mean, for real?

JOHN: Yeah, Jeff. Welcome home, son. My son is really home. And I'm happy he's found his battlefield.

MATTIE: You won't do it again, will you, Johnny? If something's troubling you, let's talk about it. Okay? Now promise!

JOHN: I was all right, Mattie—really. Dulcey gave me a room over her store. I told her I wanted to think—to write some poetry. I wanted to write a love poem—to you, Mattie. Words are like precious jewels, did you know that? But I couldn't find any jewels precious enough to match you, Mattie. So I took to drinking, and before I knew it, I was drunk all the time. I couldn't stop. Then yesterday these little men came to visit me—about one foot tall. They both had a T-shirt on with a zero on the chest. And they carried two little satchels. I asked 'em what they were carrying in 'em, and they opened up the satchels, and they were empty. I asked them their names, and they said, "The Nothing Brothers." That's when I figured it was time to go home.

DUDLEY: Delirium tremens—D.T.'s from not eating.

JOHN: Whatever. I knew it was time to come home. I knew it was Friday, too. Dudley told me he'd have some information for me on Friday.

[*Tense silence*]

DUDLEY: [*Avoiding it*] What kind of information?

JEFF: We all know, Pop.

JOHN: You all know? Then—

DUDLEY: Mattie will be admitted Monday morning.

> [*At this point,* JOHN *goes berserk. Screams at the top of his voice. Racing around the room, whipping with an imaginary whip, and screaming,* "Get out, get out, you motherfuckers. Get out of my father's house!" *He falls to the floor—somewhat exhausted, looks up as if to heaven. Bass counterpoint increases*]

JOHN: You son-of-a-bitch, why do you keep fucking with me? What do you want from me, you bastard?

MATTIE: Johnny, don't talk like that. That's blasphemy.

JOHN: He keeps fucking with me, Mattie. When I was a kid, the bigger kids used to always pick on me. I had to fight every day. They said it was because I was a smart aleck. [*To the heavens*] Is that why, you bastard, 'cause I'm a smart aleck?

MATTIE: You can't talk to Him like that. He'll turn His back on you.

JOHN: You know what I'm gonna do on Judgment Day? I'm gonna grab that motherfucker by the throat and squeeze and squeeze and squeeze until I get an answer.

MATTIE: He doesn't have to give you an answer. I thought you said, "Get thee behind me—" I thought you took care a Satan!

JOHN: [*Breaks into tears*] I tried, Mattie. I tried—you don't know how fucking hard I tried.

MATTIE: [*Embraces him*] I know, baby. I see you every second.

JOHN: You shoulda let me whip 'em out, Mattie. You shoulda let me whip out the bullshit.

MATTIE: We weren't made that way, baby.

JOHN: You shoulda let me whip out the money changers. You deserve so much more than this nothing. I wanted to do so much for you, Mattie.

MATTIE: I got *you*, baby. I got the kindest, sweetest man in the world. I got the Rolls-Royce, baby.

JOHN: I coulda done it, Mattie. God knows, I coulda done it!

MATTIE: I know, baby. I put it on you. I stopped you and I'm sorry. I'm sorry. Will you forgive me, sweet baby? Please forgive me! I was selfish, Johnny. I've been so goddam happy! All I ever cared about was seeing you walk, stumble, or stagger through that door. I only complained because I felt I should say something—but I never meant it, Johnny, I never meant a word. You couldn't have given me nothing more, baby. I'da just keeled over and died from too much happiness. Just keeled over and died.

[*Lights begin to dim as bass rises. Music remains as long as it takes actors to exit and get into place for next scene. When lights finally rise again,* MATTIE *and* DUDLEY *are sitting in living room,* MATTIE *under heavy sedation, intermittently knitting, nodding from time to time.* DUDLEY *is watching TV, smoking a cigar. Silence ensues for a long time. Finally* MATTIE *addresses* DUDLEY]

MATTIE: What'd you give me, Dudley? Sure is strong. Can hardly keep my head up.

DUDLEY: Do you feel any pain?

MATTIE: Not now.

DUDLEY: Then it's doing its job. You'll rest good when you go to bed.

MATTIE: Which can't be too long from now. The way I'm feeling.

[JOHN *appears at the top of the stairs; descends slowly, as he is absorbed in reading some pages. He enters the living room and announces quietly . . .*]

JOHN: I finished it.

MATTIE: What?

JOHN: A poem I been working on, Mattie. It's your poem, Mattie. "The River Niger." It ain't a love poem, but it's for you, sugar, dedicated to my superbitch, Mattie Jean Williams.

DUDLEY: Read it to us, nigger.

> [ANN *and* GAIL *are seen entering the back door.* JEFF, *too.*
> JOHN *begins to read, and bass begins low with African motif
> and gradually rises.* JEFF *and girls begin to engage in conver-
> sation, but desist when they hear* JOHN. *They drift to living
> room*]

JOHN:

I am the River Niger—hear my waters!
I am totally flexible.
I am the River Niger—hear my waters!
My waters are the first sperm of the world.
When the earth was but a faceless whistling embryo,
Life burst from my liquid kernels like popcorn.
*Hear my waters—rushing and popping in muffled finger-drum
   staccato.*
It is life you hear, stretching its limbs in my waters—
I am the River Niger! Hear my waters!
When the Earth Mother cracked into continents,
I was vomited from the cold belly of the Atlantic
To slip slyly into Africa
From the underside of her brow.
I see no—
Hear no—
Speak no evil,
But I know.
I gossip with the crocodile
And rub elbows with the river horse.
I have swapped morbid jokes with the hyena
And heard his dry cackle at twilight.
I see no—
Hear no—
Speak no evil,
But I know.

I am the River Niger—hear my waters!
Hear, I say, hear my waters, man!
They is Mammy-tammys, baby.
I have lapped at the pugnacious hips of brown mamas.
Have tapped on the doors of their honeydews, yeah!

I have shimmered like sequins
As they sucked me over their blueberry tongues,
As they sung me to sleep in the glittering afternoon, yeah!
I have washed the red wounds of clay-decorated warriors—
Bad, bad dudes who smirked at the leopard.
I have cast witches from gabbling babies, yeah!
Have known the warm piss from newly circumcised boy.
Have purified the saliva from sun-drenched lions—
Do you hear me talking?

I am the River Niger!
I came to the cloudy Mississippi
Over keels of incomprehensible woe.
I ran 'way to the Henry Hudson
Under the sails of ragged hope.
I am the River Niger,
Transplanted to Harlem
From the Harlem River Drive.
Hear me, my children—hear my waters!
I sleep in your veins.
I see no—
Hear no—
Speak no evil,
But I know, and I know that you know.
I flow to the ends of your spirit.
Hold hands, my children, and I will flow to the ends of the earth,
And the whole world will hear my waters.
I am the River Niger! Don't deny me!
Do you hear me? Don't deny me!

[*Pause. Bass fades*]

MATTIE:　That's very beautiful, Johnny.

JEFF:　Yeah, Pop, that's pretty nice.

DUDLEY:　[*Sarcastically*] Interesting!

JOHN:　Ya monkey chaser.

JEFF:　How you feeling, Mama?

MATTIE:　Okay, I guess. A little woozy, but I'm going to bed now, and I couldn't think of a better time than after Johnny's poem. Thank you, dear.

JOHN: Be up soon, Mattie.

MATTIE: Take your time.

DUDLEY: Yeah, I'd better get home, too.

JEFF: Good night, Mama.

ANN and GAIL: Good night, Mrs. Williams.

MATTIE: Good night. [*She exits.* GRANDMA *enters, humming "Rock of Ages." They pass each other on the stairs*] Good night, Mama.

GRANDMA: Sleep tight! Don't let the bedbugs bite.

[MATTIE *exits, shaking her head.* GRANDMA *hums throughout this scene. She comes into the living room*]

JEFF: How ya feel, Pop?

JOHN: Fine! Fine, still a little shaky, but all right.

JEFF: Ya got any booze, Pop?

JOHN: No, I'm drying out. Doctor's orders.

GRANDMA: Where's the *TV Guide?*

[*She searches for it*]

DUDLEY: [*Finding it underneath him*] Oh, here it is, Mrs. Brown. I was sitting on it.

GRANDMA: It was under you all this time?

DUDLEY: I guess so.

GRANDMA: Then let it cool off a little bit before you give it to me.

JEFF: [*To* ANN *and* GAIL] Let's make it into the kitchen.

ANN: I'm still cold from outside.

DUDLEY: [*To* JEFF] Has it started raining yet?

JEFF: It's raining and snowing at the same time.

[*They move to kitchen*]

JOHN: See, Dudley, life's full of contradictions.

DUDLEY: Ain't nothing contradictory about nature, man. Nature is everything. It's human beings who are contradictions.

JOHN: Well, ain't human beings a part of nature?

DUDLEY: [*Seriously*] Guess so, now that you mention it.

JOHN: That's why we're so messed up. We forget that we're just a part of nature. [*Pause*] Put on the TV, Dudley.

DUDLEY: I should be going home.

JOHN: Relax, man.

[DUDLEY *switches on the TV*]

JEFF: [*From the kitchen*] What'd *you* hear, Gail?

GAIL: Nothing but Skeeter, making a horse connection.

ANN: We thought it might be a code, but it sounded innocent enough.

GAIL: What about you?

JEFF: I heard something all right. But I couldn't identify the voice. The bartender was no help; he was somewhere else when the call was made.

GAIL: What did the caller say?

JEFF: Plan B.

GAIL: That's all—"Plan B"?

JEFF: Right. And the voice on the other end said, "You sure?" The caller said, "Yes—Plan B."

GAIL: You couldn't recognize the voice?

JEFF: No, but I might if I heard it again.

GAIL: I shouldn't have let you talk me into coming here. Mo might need me.

JEFF: Calm down, baby. We'll hear soon.

GAIL: But something might have happened.

ANN: He wanted you to come with us.

JEFF: Stop worrying, Mo's all right.

GAIL: I can't help it . . . [*She attempts to calm herself, crossing to the back door and looking out*] It sure is beginning to come down. Beginning to stick.

ANN: I've been away from South Africa for a long time, but I still can't get used to snow.

GAIL: Snow makes everything so quiet. It's spooky.

GRANDMA: [*Entering the kitchen*] Ya wants some spirits?

JEFF: We sure do, Grandma.

GRANDMA: Turn your backs. [*She produces a bottle of Old Grand-dad from her new hiding place on top of the cabinet—pours each of them a drink*] The way things been happening 'round here today, a body needs some spirits. Here! Besides, this child's so fidgety—[*Referring to* GAIL]—done got phlegm acting up again.

[GRANDMA *downs hers. For a second they watch in amazement—then down theirs. There is a noise at the back door.* JEFF *goes to the door*]

JEFF: It's Mo and Skeets.

[*Opens door.* MO *drags* SKEETER *in. It's obvious he's been hurt*]

MO: Pigs are swarming all over headquarters!

[DUDLEY *enters, followed closely by* JOHN. DUDLEY *examines* SKEETER]

DUDLEY: Gunshot wound. What's going on 'round here? Bring me my bag, Ann. You're very lucky, young man—no bones broken. Put a tourniquet on that arm, Ann, while I clean it out.

[ANN *and* DUDLEY *work on* SKEETER. JEFF *pulls* MO *into the living room*]

JEFF: Why in the hell did you bring him here?

MO: I figured Dr. Stanton would be here—

JEFF: I told you I don't want my family implicated in this shit— Why didn't you take him to your place?

MO: [JOHN *comes to the door*] I live over headquarters! The pigs—

JEFF: Oh, shit—shit—what happened?

MO: It's stupid—stupid. I mean, we had just crossed the street. I mean, we were just walking 'round the fence when this pig started blowing his whistle and yelling at us.

JEFF: They musta been alerted.

MO: Fucking Skeeter panicked—started running—what the hell am I supposed to do? I'm carry a tote bag with four sticks of dynamite. So I start running, too. Next thing I know, there're four pigs chasing us. One fires and spins Skeets clean 'round. Skeets is screaming and shit, and they're gaining, so I blast off a couple and knock trigger-happy on his ass.

JEFF: What—you crazy motherfucker, coming here after that?

JOHN: You mean, they just started shooting? You didn't shoot first?

MO: Why would we do that?

JOHN: You sure?

MO: I don't want to hurt nobody if I can help it, Mr. Williams.

JOHN: You think he's dead?

MO: I don't know. He hit the ground so hard I could almost feel it.

JOHN: I sure hope you killed the bastard. But if you call yourself a revolutionary, then you supposed to know where you gonna take your wounded. Takes more'n wearing a goddamn beret.

DUDLEY: [*From the kitchen*] Yeah! Why don't I set up another office over here?

[*There is a wild banging on the front door.* JEFF *answers the door.* AL *enters, followed closely by* CHIPS]

JEFF: [*Angrily*] What's going on?

AL: There are wall-to-wall pigs at headquarters. And Mo said—

JEFF: [*To* MO] And you told them to come here if that happened —[*Silence*] Didn't you? Didn't you? Didn't I tell you not to crowd me, ya stupid bastard?

MO: I was wrong, Jeff. I'm sorry.

JEFF: You're sorry. [JEFF *leaps on* MO *and is separated by* JOHN] I'll kill him, Pop, so help me. I'll kill him!

JOHN: You'll wake up your mother.

[*In the next second, a confusion of sirens and police whistles —lights shining through the front windows and the back door, and a policeman on a bullhorn*]

LIEUTENANT STAPLES'S VOICE: [*From outside*] This is Lieutenant Staples from the Thirty-second Police Precinct. We know you are in there and who's in there. We gotcha front and back, plus men on the roof. You got five minutes to throw out your weapons and come out of there. And let me remind whoever else is in there not to harbor criminals from the law. You got five minutes. If there're innocent people in there, their blood will be on your hands.

JOHN: Give me those goddamn guns. [*Pause*] Come on, come on! They can't prove a thing—except those guns. Dudley, get Skeeter's. Come on, Mo, give it to me.

[MO *hesitates, but gives it to him*]

CHIPS: Al's the one, Mo. A fucking Judas faggot.

AL: You lie!

CHIPS: There were cops everywhere. You said not to do nothing when we got to the police station until you and Skeeter showed, right? Well, when you didn't show, he ran across the street and deliberately bumped into one of 'em—

AL: He's lying.

CHIPS: And whispered something in his ear. Next thing I know, every pig and his mother is jumping into a car—that's when it hit me you was pulling a trick, and the state office building plan was still on.

AL: I didn't have a damn thing to do with that.

CHIPS: You shoulda heard the squawk boxes, "State office building —emergency—emergency." The block was vacant inside of a minute.

AL: You're not believing this shit?

CHIPS: Then he tried to shake me, Mo. Caught a cab, and you know what he told him? Told him to go to the state office building.

AL: I gave him the address of headquarters.

CHIPS: You lie, nigger. I overheard you.

SKEETER: [*Coming out of the kitchen*] And the way you keep questioning me about Buckley—

MO: Why didn't you tell me about that?

AL: He's your informer, Mo. He'd do anything for horse. [*Pause*] He told them pigs to go to the state office building. He's the one.

MO: He was with me.

JEFF: [*To* AL] It was you. I heard you.

AL: Heard me what?

JEFF: The phone—you phoned. It was your voice. You said, "B." The voice at the other end said, "Are you sure?" and you repeated, "B!"

AL: That don't prove nothing— Skeeter left, too—we both went to the phone.

JEFF: Okay, if it wasn't you then, suppose I were to tell you I killed Buckley?

AL: What do you know about Buckley?

JEFF: I did it. I killed him.

AL: How'd he die?

JEFF: Two slugs in the chest.

AL: What caliber?

JEFF: Forty-five. I stole it from the air force.

AL: Don't shit me. Buckley was killed almost a month ago. Ya only been here a week.

JEFF: What makes you so sure?

MO: What are you doing, Jeff?

JEFF: I was released from active duty exactly one month from last Friday.

AL: Bullshit!

JEFF: Wanta see my release papers?

ANN: Jeff!

JEFF: Stay out of it, Ann!

[*Fumbles through wallet and gives* AL *his release papers.* AL *reads them*]

AL: [*Pulling out his revolver*] All right, stand still, all of you! I took this assignment for one reason and one reason only, to find out who killed Buckley. And now I know. [*To* JEFF] You killed Buckley. He was worth ten of you Brillo heads. Now his friends out there are gonna take this place apart, and all of you are in trouble, you hear. You motherfuckers, fucking up the country with your slogans and your jive-ass threats. Militants, ain't that a bitch. Black cripples, trying to scale a mountain. I hate the smell of you assholes.

MO: Jeff's lying, can't you see that? I killed Buckley.

SKEETER: I did it.

CHIPS: I did it.

AL: No, no, it fits. It fits. I know where each of you mothers were when Buckley was killed. None of you coulda done it. He did it. Why didn't I think of good old Jeff? All I heard about was good old Jeff. Jeff this—Jeff that—till you bastards staged your phony scene to throw me off the track when he got here.

MO: Don't be stupid. It was an outside job.

AL: [*To* JEFF] Yeah—him.

ANN: What are you doing, Jeff? You know you were with me that whole month in Canada!

[*This causes* AL *to pause for a moment in frozen doubt.*

[JOHN *seizes the opportunity to raise the gun still in his hand, pointing it at* AL]

JOHN: Drop it, son.

[AL *whirls and shoots. There is an exchange of gun play between the two men.* AL *goes down, killed instantly.* JOHN *also goes down, mortally wounded*]

JEFF: [*Rushing to his father's side, followed closely by* DUDLEY] POP!

JOHN: The guns, Jeff—put 'em in the drain in the basement. Al's still holding his? Good.

JEFF: Pop!

JOHN: Hurry, you don't want Daddy Johnny to die for nothing, do you? [JEFF *grabs* SKEETER's *and* CHIPS's, *tries to take* MO's] No! We need Mo's—this is yours, ain't it, Mo?

MO: Yes, sir.

JOHN: Go on, son. [JEFF *exits. To* DUDLEY, *who's been trying to get at* JOHN's *wound*] Don't worry about that, ya monkey chaser. They'll be in here in a second.

DUDLEY: You're hurt, man. Ann—my bag—

[ANN *starts off*]

JOHN: Fuck your bag, Dudley. Go to the door—tell that Lieutenant Staples—tell him—to give us five more minutes—just five more—then he can make his arrests—

DUDLEY: You'll die if I don't—

JOHN: I'll die anyway. Do as I say! Before they shoot up Mattie's house.

[ANN *comes back with bag, starts preparing dressings.* JEFF *returns.* MATTIE *appears at the top of the stairs*]

MATTIE: [*Extremely drowsy.* JEFF *and* GAIL *run to her, the rest are stupefied*] I had a dream, and I heard this noise in the middle of it.

DUDLEY: [*Waving a handkerchief out the front door and shouting*] Lieutenant Staples—Lieutenant Staples.

STAPLES'S VOICE: This is Lieutenant Staples—what's going on in there?

DUDLEY: I'm Dr. Dudley Stanton—next-door neighbor. A man's been seriously wounded in here. Call an ambulance.

STAPLES'S VOICE: Throw out your guns.

DUDLEY: I think it would be best for you to see the situation for yourself.

JOHN: Good boy, Dudley. They don't care nothing 'bout niggers killing themselves nohow.

DUDLEY: [To STAPLES] Both weapons are secured. I have them. Give us five minutes, then come in.

STAPLES'S VOICE: If anyone tries to escape, my men have orders to shoot—

MATTIE: What on earth's going on?

DUDLEY: No one will. I give my word. Five minutes.

[Closes the door]

CHIPS: We got to get outta here!

MO: Shut up, and stay tight!

JEFF: [To MO] Do you see what you brought in here tonight?

[Leaps for MO once again]

JOHN: Jeff, stop it. Don't make a mockery out of my death. Sit down, all of you, and listen to me.

MATTIE: [For the first time realizing JOHN's hurt] Johnny! Johnny!

JOHN: Keep Mattie away, Dudley—keep her away—

DUDLEY: [Restraining her] Try and be calm, Mattie.

JOHN: Wipe off the handle on Mo's gun, Jeff. [JEFF does it] Okay, now give it to me. [He grips the gun firmly several times] I don't want nobody's fingerprints on it but mine.

MATTIE: Johnny, you're bleeding—

JOHN: [*With savage power*] Mattie, I love ya, Mattie. I ain't got much life left.

MATTIE: Johnny, no!

JOHN: I got to get our children straight before I go—now be my superbitch and shut the fuck up. [MATTIE *understands and obeys*] Now you youngbloods listen to me. Here's the story: I am the real leader of the organization—ya got me. I was with Skeeter when he got shot. I fired the shot which hit the cop at the office building. I made it back here—found out that Al here is a Judas, and we had a shoot-out. The rest of you have never owned a gun —only your leader—me! Ya got that?

GRANDMA: [*Drunk, and in a state of shock, comes strangely alive. She thinks* JOHN *is her Ben. She rushes up and falls at* JOHN's *knees*] BEN—BEN BROWN! [*Reaches for* JOHN's *gun*] Gimme that shotgun.

[MATTIE *blocks her*]

MATTIE: [*Very calm and solemn, almost eerie*] No, Mama.

GRANDMA: I'll just shoot right into the crowd, daughter. See 'em, look at their faces! They's glad to see my Ben dead. Lawdamercy! He's dead! [*Crying from an ancient wound*] Gimme that shotgun, child. Ten for one, ten for one—my man is a king—you crackers—ya dirty old redneck crackers.

[*Breaks into* "Rock of Ages." *Bass counterpoint seeps in*]

JOHN: Hear that, Mattie. The old battle-ax finally gave me a compliment. Where's my Mattie? Let me see my Mattie.

[MATTIE's *let through. They embrace*]

MATTIE: I'm with you every second, baby.

JOHN: I knew she'd slip one day. I'm sorry, Mattie.

MATTIE: What for, baby?

JOHN: I'm cheating ya, honey—going first this way.

MATTIE: Hush now!

JOHN: Don't suffer long, honey. Just give up and take my hand.

The children—the children will be all right now. [*Pause*] Look at Dr. Dudley Stanton down there. Trying to save my life. Ain't that a bitch! See what a big old fake you've been all along. Don't worry, Dudley—fighting lady Ann—Jeff—ya got a fighting lady to protect your flanks, son—don't worry, I don't feel nothing now. Just sweetness—a sweet sweetness.

DUDLEY: Your poems—I'll get 'em published.

JOHN: Fuck them poems—this is poetry, man—what I feel right here and now. This sweetness. Sing on, Grandma. [*Pause. He shivers*] I found it, Dudley—I found it.

DUDLEY: What, Johnny?

JOHN: My battlefield—my battlefield, man! I was a bitch too, ya monkey chaser. See my shit! I got two for the price of one.

DUDLEY: Yeah, chief.

[JOHN *dies. Pause*]

CHIP: [*Whimpering*] Oh God, oh my God!

MATTIE: Shut up! And tell it like Johnny told ya. He ain't gonna die for nothing, 'cause you ain't gonna let him! Jeff—open the door, son! Tell 'em to come on in here! [JEFF *crosses to the door*] And you better not fuck up!